ANTHROPOLOGY

ANTHROPOLOGY

Carol R. Ember · **Melvin Ember**
Hunter College of the City University of New York

ACC

APPLETON-CENTURY-CROFTS, NEW YORK
Educational Division, Meredith Corporation

To Hy and Elsie and Matthew and Rachel
with love and appreciation

73 74 75 76 77 / 10 9 8 7 6 5 4 3 2

Library of Congress Card Number: 72-90950

PRINTED IN THE UNITED STATES OF AMERICA

Designer: Arthur D. Ritter   Cover designer: Ladislav Svatos

Illustrations: Danmark and Michaels

Photo research: Ann Novotny

Text set in 10/12 Vladimir

390-29000-9

This book was printed on recycled paper.

Pages i, ii. "The Bushman's Dance," Bushman painting on rock shelter, South Africa. (Courtesy of the Bettmann Archive.)

Pages xii–1. Front of Sepik spirit house, bark painting on sago palm, New Guinea. (Reproduced by permission of Charles Scribner's Sons from HUMAN AVIARY: A PICTORIAL DISCUSSION OF NEW GUINEA by Kenneth E. Read. Photographs by George Holton. Text copyright © 1971 Kenneth E. Read. Photographs copyright © 1971 George Holton.)

Pages 36–37. Scenes of everyday life, ancient Egypt. From the tomb of Menna (scribe of Thutmose IV), Luxor. (Erich Lessing, Magnum Photos.)

Pages 196–197. Ceremonial Chilkat blanket, Northwest Coast Indians, Alaska. (Courtesy of the American Museum of Natural History.)

Pages 486–487. Textile design, Peru. (Courtesy of the American Museum of Natural History.)

Contents

Part 1
INTRODUCTION TO ANTHROPOLOGY

Part 2
THE EVOLUTION OF MAN AND HIS CULTURE

Part 3
CULTURAL VARIATION

Part 4
CULTURE AND ANTHROPOLOGY IN THE MODERN WORLD

PORTFOLIOS

Preface

This text is designed for general introductory anthropology courses, as well as for introductory courses in cultural anthropology, at the college level. It covers all four subdisciplines of anthropology—physical anthropology, prehistoric archaeology, anthropological linguistics, and ethnology. The book also functions as an introduction to the major topical areas within each anthropological subdiscipline, which are often treated in separate advanced courses.

Orientation of the Book

In the preparation of this text, and in each individual chapter, we have tried to integrate the materials so that the sequence of presentation is ordered, rather than encyclopedic. We feel that this style of organization makes the book both more readable and more comprehensible. At the same time we have tried to cover many of the major problems and achievements of research in the specialized field of study to which each chapter is devoted.

Our aim in this text is to arouse the curiosity of students about how and why human populations have come to be different or similar. We have discussed theories and the arguments and evidence pertaining to them, even if there is no agreement in the field on a particular explanation. We believe it is important to convey not only what is known but also what is not known or only dimly suspected, so that students may acquire a feel for what anthropology is and what it could be. We think that this way of writing a textbook may succeed in arousing the interest and involvement of the student, because it conveys some of the excitement and problems and disappointments of researchers who are working on the frontiers of our discipline.

Plan of the Book

In Part 1, *Introduction to Anthropology,* we discuss what is special and distinctive about anthropology as a whole, about each of the subfields in particular, and how each of the subfields is related to other disciplines. Chapter 2 discusses the core concept of culture: its defining features, how anthropologists study it, and some assumptions about it.

Part 2, *The Evolution of Man and His Culture,* begins with a discussion of evolutionary theory as it applies to all forms of life, including man. Then we discuss our living primate relatives as well as the reasons for studying them. Chapters 5 through 8 focus on what paleontologists and archaeologists have learned about the evolution of the primates, the emergence of man, and his subsequent biological and cultural evolution. Chapter 8 deals specifically with the origin of domestication and the rise of civilization. The final chapter in this section, Chapter 9, discusses biological variation in living human populations.

In Part 3, *Cultural Variation,* we begin with an overview of theories and methods in cultural anthropology. We then go on to discuss how recent populations vary culturally—in language; food getting; systems of economic distribution and exchange; social stratification; sex, marriage, and the family; marital residence and kinship; associations and interest groups; political systems; religion; the arts; and in personality.

Finally, Part 4, *Culture and Anthropology in the Modern World,* covers such topics as contemporary culture change, applied anthropology, and the relationship of anthropology to the modern world.

Features of the Book

Readability. The only good textbook is one that students can and will read. So a first step in producing this book was to define readability in the context of the teaching situation and to determine how it might be achieved. After much discussion and analysis, and with the help of professionals, it was decided that readability depends on organization, language, and relevance.

Clear and familiar language makes a book readable. A student should not have to learn a whole new vocabulary before he can understand his text. It is often possible to introduce even the most complicated concepts in simple language. This book uses only the amount of technical terminology that a student must know in order to understand the concepts or to be prepared for a more advanced course. When new terms are introduced here, they are set off in italics and clearly defined. A glossary at the back of the book serves as a convenient reference and study aid.

Relevance makes a book readable, because it provides motivation to read. Therefore, in this book, theories and concepts are illustrated not only with the results of published studies but also with examples drawn from the students' own personal or social experiences—the daily behavior of friends, parents, classmates, and neighbors. Each example was chosen because of its significance to the subject of the chapter in which it appears and its interest to introductory students.

Illustrations. Our concern was to select illustrations primarily for their functional value, to clarify points which are difficult to make verbally. The text also includes color portfolios on evolution, food getting, the arts, and culture change that are both visually appealing and instructive.

Summaries and Suggested Readings. A summary of important concepts included at the end of each chapter should provide a convenient review for students. Each chapter also contains a list of books students might consult for additional information. Books are annotated to describe their subject matter, approach, and readability.

Supplements. Accompanying the text are an Instructor's Manual and Study Guide and ACCESS® Workbook. The workbook is designed to help students interrelate concepts from various sections and chapters and to review the important points of the text. For each chapter of the text, the workbook includes a review outline and a self-test review, using short-answer application questions. (The self-test utilizes

ACCESS®, a process in which an answer printed in invisible ink is revealed by rubbing it with the ACCESS® activator. The student thus receives immediate verification of his self-test responses.)

The Instructor's Manual includes suggested lecture topics and questions for class discussions for many of the major points of the text. For each chapter, there are suggestions for research papers and projects and for essays or essay-type exam questions. A test item file of additional questions is also available.

Acknowledgments

To make the book as readable as possible, and to increase the likelihood that it will be useful to instructors and students, a team of specialists who know and understand the interests and needs of the beginning student in anthropology have helped us prepare it. They included marketing, production, and editorial specialists, research assistants, designers, and photo researchers. We want to take this opportunity, particularly, to thank our editors, Mary Schieck, Roberta Bauer, and Sandra Stein. We would also like to thank two colleagues who read and commented on the portions of the manuscript dealing with physical anthropology and archaeology, Frederick Szalay and John Speth, respectively. To all of the above we are grateful for their contributions to whatever completeness of coverage, clarity of expression, and felicity of style we may have achieved.

C. R. E. and M. E.

New York, New York

Part 1
INTRODUCTION TO ANTHROPOLOGY

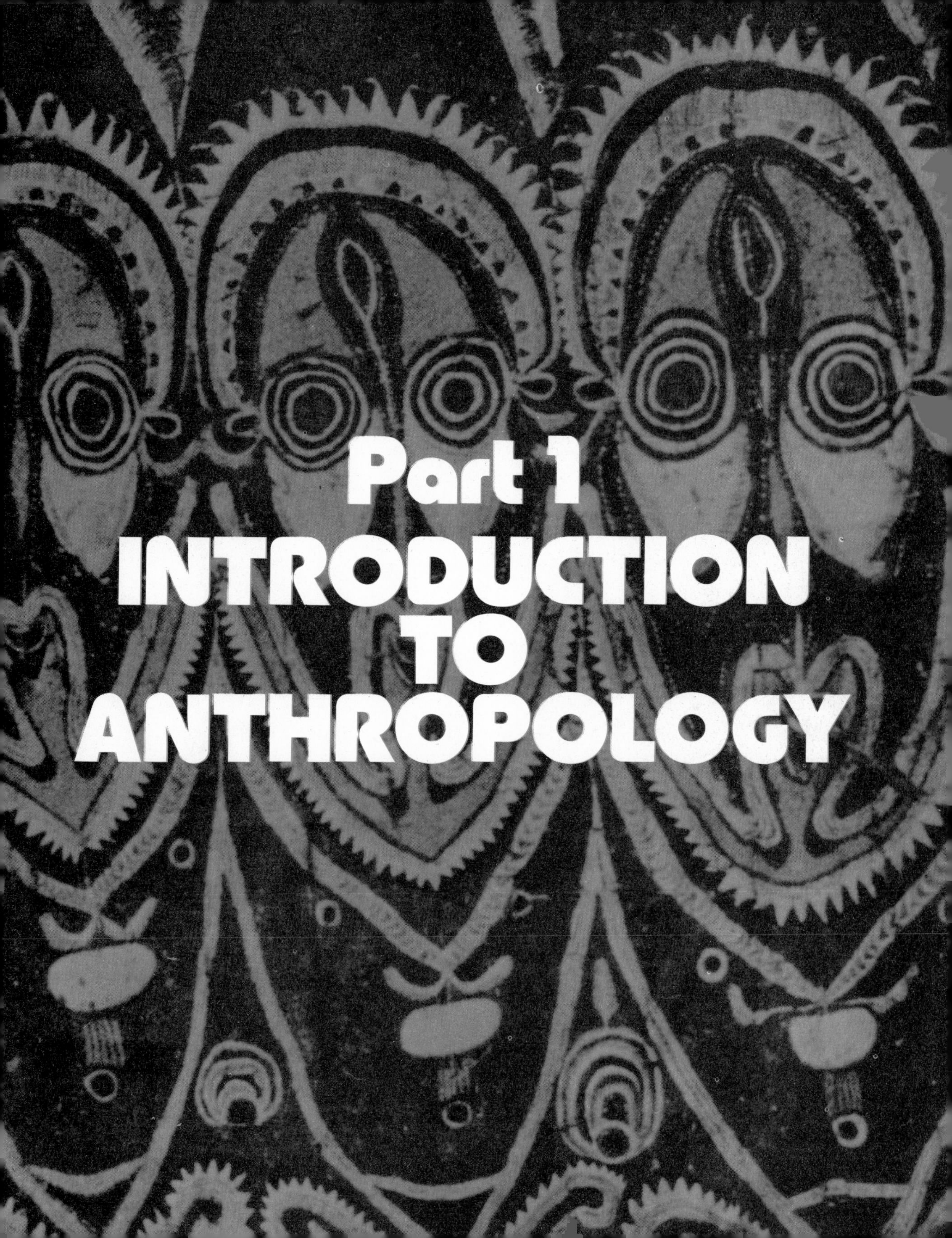

1

What Is Anthropology?

An American anthropologist once remarked that "the subject matter of anthropology is limited only by man." In this simple statement, Alfred Kroeber had paid tribute to the vast expanse of knowledge covered by anthropology. The species of animal called *Homo sapiens* is indeed a very large subject, encompassing man as a physical being, man in his prehistoric setting, and man in the context of his culture, heir to a complex system of customs, attitudes, and behaviors. In its very name—from the Greek *anthropos* for "man," and *logos* for "study"—anthropology defines itself as a discipline of infinite curiosity about mankind.

To define anthropology in terms of its interest in man is admittedly to be less than explicit, for according to this definition anthropology would appear to encompass a whole catalogue of disciplines: sociology, psychology, political science, economics, history, human biology, and perhaps even the humanistic disciplines of philosophy and literature. Needless to say, the many other disciplines concerned with man would not be very happy to be relegated to subbranches of anthropology. (After all, most of them have been separate disciplines longer than anthropology, and they consider their jurisdictions to be somewhat distinctive.) There must, then, be something unique about anthropology—a reason for its having developed as a separate discipline, and for having retained a separate identity over the hundred or so years since its inception. What is special about the anthropologist, and what is his distinctive contribution to man's understanding of himself?

THE SCOPE OF ANTHROPOLOGY

One typically envisions anthropologists as traveling to unknown corners of the world to study exotic peoples, or digging far into the earth to uncover the fossil remains or the tools and pots of men who lived so long ago that it troubles the imagination. These views, though clearly stereotyped, do indicate one way in which anthropology differs from other disciplines concerned with man: anthropology is broader in scope. It is explicitly and directly concerned with all varieties of man (not simply those closest to home), and it considers men of all periods, beginning with the emergence of man over a million years ago and tracing his development until the present. Thus, anthropologists attempt to broaden the study of man by being both comparative and historical on a world-wide basis. Every part of the world that has ever had a human population is of interest to anthropologists.

True, anthropologists have not always been as broad and comprehensive in their concerns as they are today; traditionally, they have left the study of Western civilization and similarly complex societies, and their recorded histories, to other disciplines. In recent years, however, this general division of labor among the disciplines has begun to disappear. Now, anthropologists can be found at work in primitive villages as well as in cities of the industrial world.

One might wonder what induces the anthropologist to choose so broad a subject for study. In part, he is motivated by the feeling that any generalization we entertain about man (and consequently about ourselves) should be shown to be applicable to many times and places of human existence. In this way, we can avoid believing things about man that are applicable only in a particular setting. For example, before Margaret Mead embarked on her famous field study of Samoa (which was later reported in her *Coming of Age in Samoa,* 1928) many Americans believed that adolescence was necessarily a period of "storm and stress" due to physiological changes that occur at puberty. However, on the basis of her observations of Samoan adolescents, who did not seem to show signs of emotional upheaval, Mead concluded that the Western belief about adolescence was not universally applicable and was therefore subject to question. The clear implication of her work was that emotional stress in adolescence was to some extent a function of the way that growing up is managed in Western societies. Anthropologists, then, are often in a position to illuminate beliefs and practices generally accepted by their contemporaries, for they are acquainted with human life in an unusual variety of geographical and historical settings.

Not only are anthropologists concerned with testing the universality of human beliefs and customs; they are also interested in exploring the possible universality of biological traits. In our own society, for example, children are constantly told to drink their milk because it will make them strong and healthy. Yet anthropologists have known for years that in many parts of the world where cows and goats are kept, people do not drink fresh milk. Why this is so has only recently been discovered. Physicians and physiologists have found that many human populations generally lack an enzyme that facilitates the digestion of fresh milk. For such people, drinking fresh milk would usually cause sickness. So, in some places, people sour their milk to make it digestible; or else they do not drink milk at all. Human populations, then, vary in their biological characteristics; what is healthy for some is not necessarily healthy for all.

THE HOLISTIC APPROACH

Another distinguishing feature of anthropology is its holistic approach to man: not only do anthropologists study all varieties of man, they also study all aspects of man's experience. For example, in writing a description of a group of people, an anthropologist might include a section on the history of the area, the environment, organization of family life, settlement pattern, political and economic systems, religion, styles of art and dress, general features of language, and so on.

In the past the holistic approach was exhibited by most individual anthropologists. Today, as in many other disciplines, there is a tendency toward specialization in investigations as a function of increasing knowledge. Thus, one anthropologist studies the physical characteristics of man's prehistoric ancestors, another the biological effect of the environment on a human population over time, and still another the interrelationships of cultural factors. Even though particular anthropologists may choose to specialize in a branch or subbranch of the field, the discipline of anthropology retains its holistic orientation in that its speciality areas, taken together, describe many aspects of human existence, past and present, on all levels of complexity.

THE ANTHROPOLOGICAL CURIOSITY

If anthropology differs in scope and approach from the other disciplines concerned with man, it also differs somewhat in interests. Anthropologists are concerned with many types of questions: Where, when, and why did people first begin living in cities? Why do some peoples have darker skin than others? Why do some languages have more color terms than other languages? Why in some societies are men allowed to be married to more than one wife simultaneously? Although these questions seem to deal with very different aspects of human existence, they do have at least one thing in common. They all deal with a *typical characteristic* that is shared by some particular human population. The typical characteristic might be relatively dark skin, or a language having many color terms, or the practice of marrying several wives; in fact, it could be almost any human trait or custom. The population studied is most often a single society—that is, a population occupying a particular territory and speaking a common language. At times, however, the population studied by anthropologists may be larger or smaller than a single society. For example, if an investigator is interested in differences in skin color, he may compare samples of people from Africa and Europe, each sample including people from several different societies. Or, if the investigator is interested in marriage customs, he may compare marriage arrangements in two or more parts of the same society to understand why they might be different. In short, the anthropologist is usually concerned with describing how and explaining why human populations are different or similar with respect to certain distinctive characteristics.

THE SUBFIELDS OF ANTHROPOLOGY

To understand the scope and promise of anthropology, one must experience its subdisciplines, noting how they relate to each other. Anthropology includes two broad classifications of subject matter: *physical anthropology* and *cultural anthropology.* We shall present archaeology and linguistics as subdisciplines of cultural anthropology, even though they are academic disciplines in their own right. A third subdiscipline, ethnology, encompasses so much that it is often referred to by the parent name, cultural anthropology.

Physical Anthropology

Physical anthropology studies man as an evolving physical organism and determines how and why human populations differ physically. The distinctive questions of physical anthropology are: first, questions about the emergence of man and his later evolution (an area of physical anthropology called *human paleontology*); and second, questions about how and why contemporary man varies biologically (an area referred to as *human variation*).

In order to reconstruct the emergence and evolution of man, human paleontologists search for and study fossils, the buried, hardened remains of humans and prehumans. Paleontologists working in East Africa, for example, have excavated the fossil remains of man-like creatures who lived more than 2 million years ago; their findings there have helped physical anthropology to approximate when prehistoric man acquired upright posture, flexible hands, and a larger brain.

To understand the evolutionary sequence, the human paleontologist may make use not only of the fossil record, but of geological information on the succession of climates, environments, and plant and animal populations. Moreover, the reconstruction of man's past is accompanied by an interest in the behavior and evolution of man's closest relatives among the mammals, the apes and monkeys who, like himself, are members of the order of Primates. Species of primates are observed in the field and the laboratory; especially popular is the chimpanzee, who bears a close resemblance to humans in behavior and physical appearance, has similar blood types, and is susceptible to many of the same diseases. From primate studies, the physical anthropologist seeks to distinguish those characteristics that are distinctly human from those that might be part of a generalized primate heritage. In this way we might be able to guess what the prehistoric ancestors of man were like, for if all living primates (including man) share a certain characteristic, that characteristic was probably found in the first prehuman forms from which modern man evolved. The inferences from such studies are checked against the fossil record. Thus, the evidence from the earth, collected in bits and pieces, is correlated with scientific observations of our closest living relatives.

Paleontologist Louis Leakey, at Olduvai Gorge in East Africa, closely examines remains that may yield further information about the emergence and evolution of man. (Photograph by Ian Berry, Magnum Photos, Inc.)

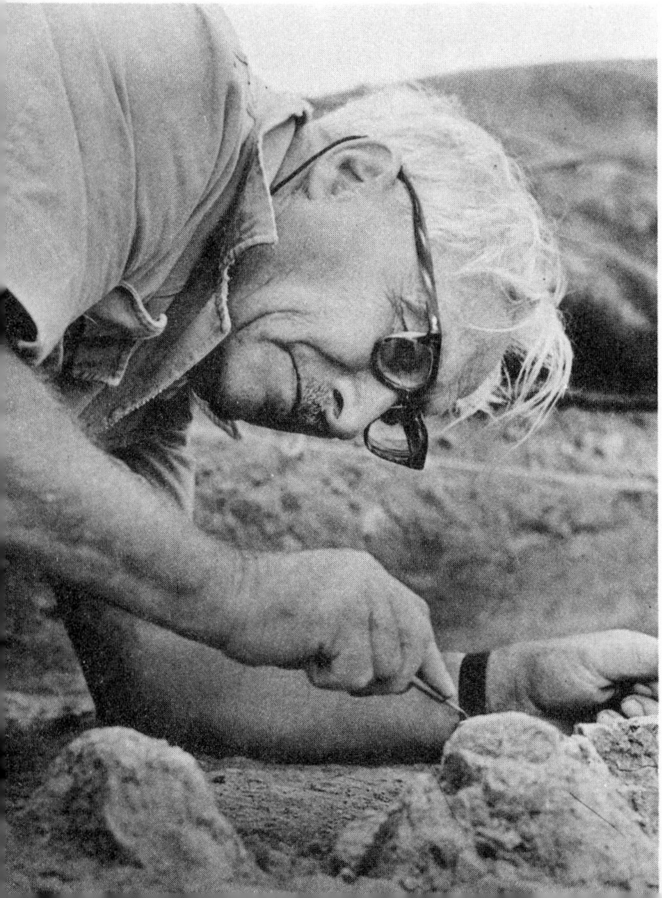

In short, physical anthropologists who are interested in the evolution of man are like detectives in that they piece together bits of information from a number of different sources, construct theories accounting for the changes observed in the fossil record, and attempt to evaluate these theories by cross-checking one kind of evidence against another. Human paleontology thus overlaps a great deal with other disciplines such as geology, general vertebrate (and particularly primate) paleontology, comparative anatomy, and the study of comparative primate behavior.

The second major area of physical anthropology—the study of human variation—discusses how and why contemporary human populations differ in physical or biological characteristics. All living peoples belong to one species, *Homo sapiens,* for all can successfully interbreed. Yet there is much that varies among human populations. The investigators of human variation ask such questions as: Why are some peoples taller than others? Why do some peoples have more body hair than others? and so on.

In order to understand the kinds of biological

variation observable in contemporary human populations, physical anthropologists employ principles, concepts, and techniques of human genetics (the study of how traits are inherited in man), population biology (the study of environmental effects on and interaction with population characteristics), and epidemiology (the study of how and why diseases differentially affect different populations). Research in human variation, therefore, overlaps with research in the other fields. Those who consider themselves physical anthropologists, however, are most centrally concerned with human populations and how they vary biologically.

Another kind of question, always of interest to physical anthropologists and now of growing general concern, asks how human populations have adapted physically to their environmental conditions. Are Eskimos better equipped than other men to endure cold? Does darker skin pigmentation offer special protection against the tropical sun? Does the capacity of the lung or blood to carry oxygen increase among populations that live at high altitudes? Speculation has led anthropologists to diverse areas of the earth. They have found answers that allow us to hope that human beings may adjust, in time, even to industrial pollution and the other noxious wastes that are continually altering our environment; for anthropologists have shown us that the bodies of men in other times and other places have often adapted to environmental conditions that threatened human life.

Because of their similarities to humans, chimpanzees are among the most closely observed nonhuman primates. Here Jane Goodall, a primatologist, observes chimps in their natural habitat, hoping to shed some light on our understanding of what our prehistoric ancestors were like. (Photo by Baron Hugo van Lawick © National Geographic Society.)

Cultural Anthropology

To an anthropologist, the term "culture" generally refers to the customary ways of thinking and behaving that are characteristic of a particular population or society. Culture, therefore, is composed of such things as language, knowledge, laws, religious beliefs, food preferences, music, work habits, taboos, and so forth.

Archaeology, linguistics, and ethnology, the subdisciplines we shall consider next, are all directly concerned with human culture and so can be grouped under the broad subheading of cultural anthropology. The concept of culture is so central to the study of anthropology that we shall spend all of the next chapter defining and discussing it. At this juncture we shall confine ourselves to descriptions of these three major subdisciplines.

Archaeology. The archaeologist seeks not only to reconstruct the daily life and customs of prehistoric peoples, but also to trace cultural changes and offer possible explanations as to why those changes occurred. His concern is similar to the historian's, but he reaches much farther back in time. The historian deals only with cultures possessing written records, limiting himself, therefore, to the last 5,000 years of human history. For all past cultures lacking a written record, and this includes many cultures within the past 5,000 years which did not develop writing, the archaeologist serves as historian. Lacking written records for study, he is compelled to reconstruct history from the remains of human cultures he finds—some of them as grandiose as the Mayan temples discovered at Chichen Itza in Yucatan, Mexico, but more often as ordinary as bits of broken pottery, stone tools, and even garbage heaps. Remains such as these enable the archaeologist to recreate a history for human societies that left no other records behind them.

Archaeologist Frank Willett, at an excavation in Ife, Nigeria, supervises and notes the precise calculations and measurements of his assistants in an attempt to ascertain the daily life and customs of prehistoric peoples. (Copyright by Dr. Georg Gerster, Rapho Guillumette Pictures.)

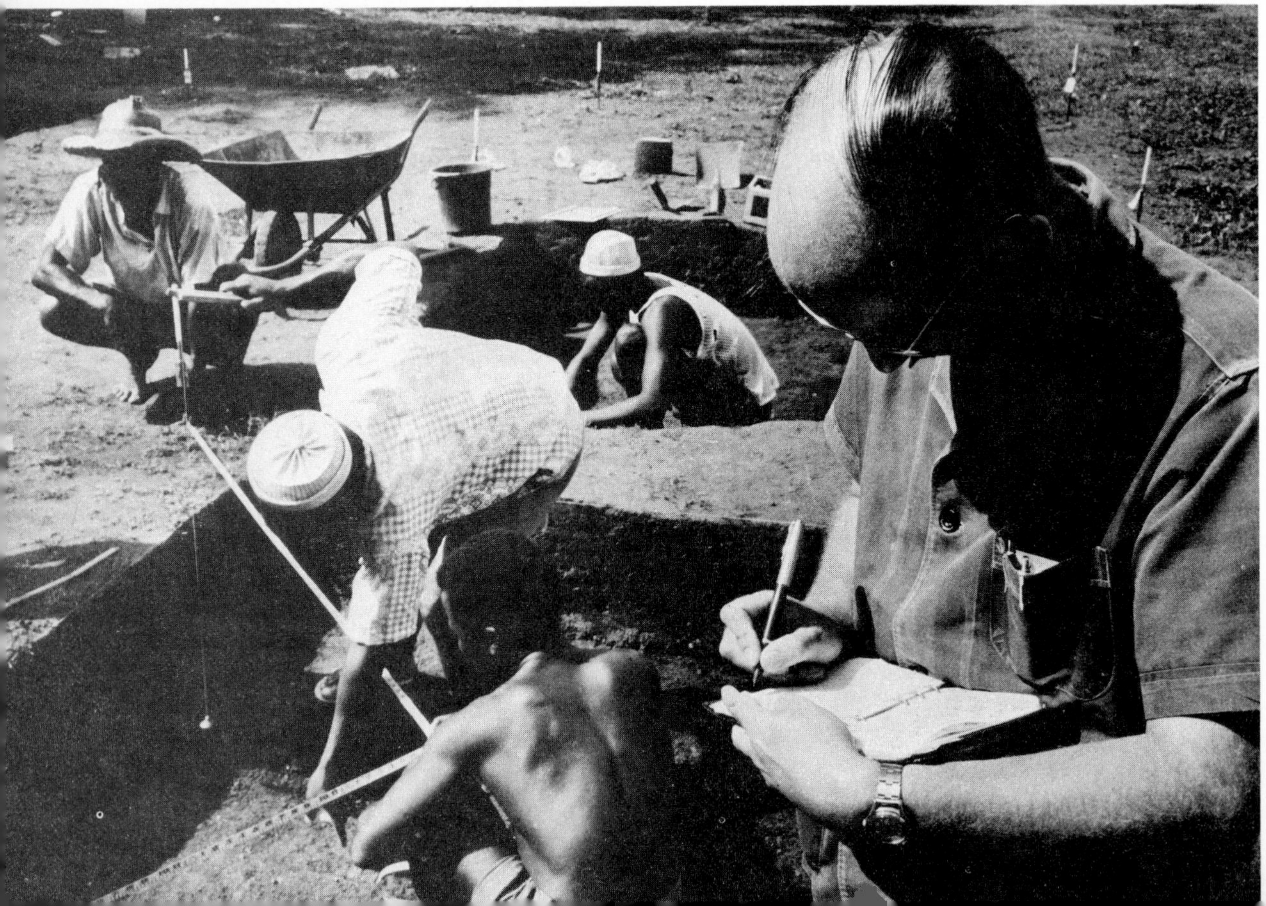

The archaeologist works in diverse areas of the world, for remains of past cultures have been discovered on all continents. One fruitful location for prehistoric data has been France, where Neandertal cultures left extraordinary records on the walls of caves and in the soil. Diggings near Les Eyzies have provided a record of a people who lived 17,000 to 12,000 years ago, the Magdalenians. From cave paintings and from the number and variety of tools found at diggings around the caves, archaeologists conclude that the Magdalenians were originally a stable and prosperous people. Later artifacts found in the surrounding area indicate a sharp cultural decline; their scarcity and character tell of the disintegration and disappearance of the Magdalenian tradition. Thus, with the discovery and study of artifacts, the archaeologist can begin to construct a reasonable account of the people who used them. His field research involves painstaking excavation, and once artifacts are collected, he will make use of the research findings in other disciplines. For example, plant and animal remains are studied for the information they yield about the climate, environmental conditions, and diet.

Archaeology has two major concerns. One is to establish the sequences of cultural development (how ways of life have changed) in different parts of the world. Thus, the archaeologist may ask such questions as: When and where did agriculture first develop? When and where did cities first emerge? and other questions relating to the details of prehistory. The second major concern of archaeology is to understand why certain changes took place when and where they did. In this regard, the archaeologist may try to understand why the hilly areas of the Near East showed the first signs of plant and animal domestication, and why cities in the Near East first appeared in the semiarid river valleys of what is now Iraq. In short, archaeologists must reconstruct what happened in prehistory before they can attempt to understand why those changes occurred.

Anthropological Linguistics. A second branch of cultural anthropology is linguistics, the study of languages. As a science, the study of language is somewhat older than anthropology. The two disciplines became closely associated in the early days of anthropological fieldwork, when anthropologists enlisted the help of linguists to learn primitive languages. When it became increasingly evident that language plays a basic role in the development of human culture—language, after all, is the primary means by which customs are transmitted from generation to generation—anthropology became more reliant on linguistics. In contrast to other linguists, however, anthropological linguists are most interested in the history and structure of *unwritten* languages. This focus requires a more extensive array of techniques of analysis and investigation than those used by earlier linguists.

Like the physical anthropologist, the linguist is interested in changes that have taken place over time, as well as in contemporary variation. Thus, anthropological linguists are concerned with the emergence of language and how languages diverge over centuries; this aspect of linguistics is known as *comparative* or *historical linguistics.* They are also interested in how contemporary languages differ, especially in regard to how they are constructed and used. This area of linguistics is generally called *descriptive linguistics.* More specifically, the study of how languages are constructed is called *structural linguistics,* while the study of how language is used in actual speech is called *sociolinguistics* or *ethnolinguistics.*

In contrast to the human paleontologist and archaeologist, who have physical remains to help them reconstruct change over time, the historical linguist is dealing only with languages—and usually unwritten ones at that. Because an unwritten language must be heard in order to be studied, it does not leave any traces once its speakers have died off. The linguist interested in reconstructing the

Robert Russell, a linguist from the Summer Institute of Linguistics, uses a tape recorder to arrive at a permanent record of the unwritten language of the Amahuaca Indians of Peru. (Photograph by Cornell Capa, Magnum Photos, Inc.)

history of unwritten languages must therefore work backwards in time, starting in the present with a comparison of contemporary languages. On the basis of such comparisons, he may arrive at inferences about the kinds of change which may have occurred in the past and which may account for similarities and differences observed in the present. The historical linguist typically asks such questions as: Are two or more particular contemporary languages related in the sense that they diverged from a common ancestral language? If they are so related, how far back in time did they begin to become different? For example, on the basis of linguistic research, the historical linguist may hypothesize that English, Russian, Hindi (the major language of contemporary India), and a number of other languages diverged from a common ancestral language, called Proto-Indo-European, starting about 5,000 years ago.

Unlike the historical linguist, the descriptive (or structural) linguist is typically concerned with discovering and recording the rules which determine how sounds and words are put together in speech. For example, a structural description of a particular language might tell us that the sounds *t* and *k* are interchangeable in a word without making a difference in meaning. In the islands of American Samoa, one could say *Tutuila* or *Kukuila* as the name of the largest island and everyone, except perhaps the visiting anthropologist, would understand that the same island is being mentioned.

Like the structural linguist, the sociolinguist is interested in describing how contemporary languages differ. Sociolinguistics is an area of study that has developed quite recently. It is particularly concerned with how people use their language in different ways depending upon the social context. In English, for example, we do not address everyone we meet in the same way. "Hi, Joe" may be the customary way that a person greets his friend, but the same person would probably feel uncomfortable addressing a doctor by his first name; instead he would probably say "Good morning, Dr. Smith." The fact that these differences in the way language is used depend upon the relative status of the two speakers is of interest to the sociolinguist.

Ethnology. The ethnologist attempts to understand how and why peoples today, and in the recent past, differ in their customary ways of thinking and acting. In other words, ethnology is concerned with patterns of behavior—such as marriage customs, kinship organization, political and economic systems, religion, folklore, arts, and music—and how these differ in contemporary societies. The ethnologist also studies the dynamics of culture—how cultures develop and change and how they interact with other cultures—as well as the interaction of diverse beliefs and practices within a culture and their effect on individual personality. Thus, the aim of the ethnologist is largely the same as that of the archaeologist. However, the ethnologist uses data which are collected first-hand by fieldworkers, whereas the archaeologist must work with fragmentary remains of past cultures, on the basis of which he can only make educated guesses about the actual customs of prehistoric peoples.

One type of ethnologist, the *ethnographer,* usually spends a year or so living with, talking to, and observing the people whose customs he is interested in. His work in the field often results in a detailed description (an *ethnography*) of many aspects of customary behavior and thought of those people. The ethnographer not only describes general patterns of life but also may ask such questions as: How are economic and political behavior related? How may the customs of people be adapted to environmental conditions? Is there any relationship between beliefs about the supernatural and beliefs or practices in the natural world? In other words, the ethnographer describes the ways of life of a particular group of people and may also suggest explanations for some of the customs he has observed.

From its beginning, ethnography has been involved in a race against time. Until about 600 to 700 years ago, the total number of human cultures continued to increase; since then, the number and diversity of world cultures have been dwindling rapidly, as the spread of advanced technological societies has brought one culture after another to swift extinction. The culture the ethnologist fails to observe today may disappear without a trace tomorrow.

Because so many cultures in the recent past have undergone extensive change, it is fortunate indeed that another type of ethnologist, the *ethnohistorian,* is prepared to study how the ways of life of a particular group of people have changed over time. The ethnohistorian investigates written documents (which may or may not have been produced by anthropologists). He may spend many years going through documents such as missionary accounts, reports by traders and explorers, and official government records to establish a sequence of the cultural changes that have occurred. Unlike the ethnographer who relies mostly on his own observations, the ethnohistorian must rely on the reports of others, often attempting to piece together and make sense of widely scattered and even apparently contradictory information. Thus, the ethnohistorian's research is very much like that of the historian, except that the ethnohistorian is usually concerned with the history of a people who did not themselves leave written records. The ethnohistorian tries to reconstruct the recent history of a people and may also suggest explanations for why certain changes took place.

With data collected and analyzed by the ethnographer and ethnohistorian, the work of a third type of ethnologist, the *comparative* or *cross-cultural researcher,* can be done. Obviously, to understand how customs may be distributed and associated, we need to know what customs are characteristic of many peoples, both in the present and in the past. The comparative or cross-cultural researcher may ask such questions as: How often and in what places do we find such customs as plural marriages (one spouse of one sex and two or more

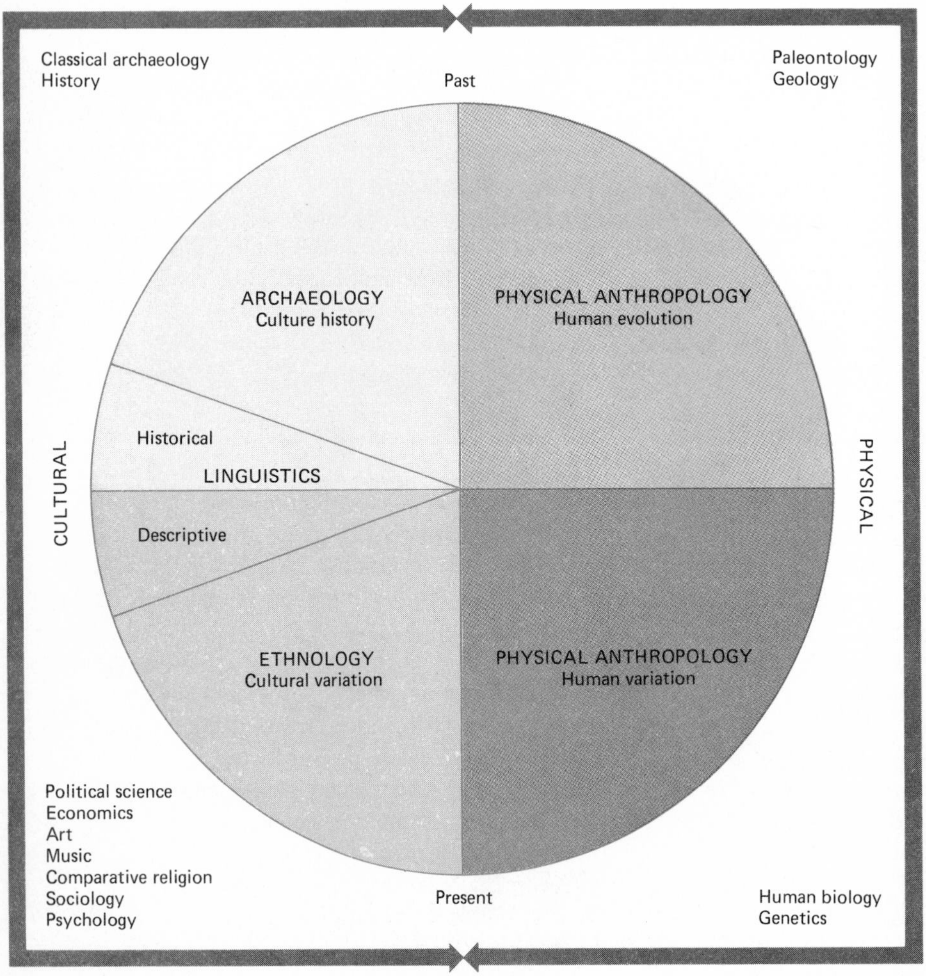

Figure 1
The subfields of anthropology and related disciplines may be classified according to subject matter (cultural or physical) and according to the time period with which they are concerned (past or present).

Ethnologist Irven DeVore is shown here asking !Kung Bushmen of Africa's Kalahari Desert about the local uses of a particular plant. His field research will contribute to anthropological knowledge about the customs of primitive peoples. (Courtesy of Stanley Washburn.)

spouses of the other sex), circumcision of adolescent boys, or the belief in a high god or supreme being? The cross-cultural researcher may also ask why a particular type of custom—witchcraft, for example—is found in some places but not in others. In this way, cross-cultural research attempts to discover which of the explanations suggested to account for particular cases may be more generally applicable.

Cultural anthropologists of whatever variety may be interested in many aspects of customary behavior and thought, ranging from economic behavior, to political behavior, to styles of art, music, and religion. Thus, cultural anthropology overlaps with other disciplines that concentrate on some particular aspect of human existence, such as sociology, psychology, economics, political science, art, musicology, and comparative religion. The distinctive feature of cultural anthropology is that it is interested in how all these aspects of human existence vary from society to society, in all historical periods and in all parts of the world.

SUMMARY

1. Anthropology has often been called the "study of man." In using such a broad definition, however, anthropology would appear to encompass many other disciplines, including sociology, psychology, political science, economics, history, human biology, and so on.

2. One way that anthropology differs from other disciplines concerned with man is that it is broader in scope. Anthropology is concerned with man in all places of the world (not simply those places closest to home), and it considers men of all historical periods, beginning with the emergence of man over a million years ago and tracing his development up to the present day.

3. Another distinguishing feature of anthropology is its holistic approach to man. Not only do anthropologists study all varieties of man, they also study all aspects of man's experience.

4. Anthropology also differs from other disciplines concerned with man in the nature of its interests. Anthropologists are concerned with identifying typical characteristics that are shared by some particular human population. The typical characteristic might be any human trait or custom; the population studied is most often a single society.

5. Physical anthropology is one of the broad classifications of subject matter included in the discipline. Physical anthropology studies the emergence of man and his later physical evolution (an area called human paleontology; it also studies how and why contemporary man varies biologically (an area referred to as human variation).

6. The second broad area of concern to anthropology is cultural anthropology. The three subdisciplines of archaeology, linguistics, and ethnology all deal with aspects of man's culture—that is, the customary ways of thinking and behaving that are characteristic of a particular society.

7. The archaeologist seeks not only to reconstruct the daily life and customs of prehistoric peoples, but also to trace cultural changes and offer possible explanations as to why those changes occurred. The archaeologist is concerned with all past cultures lacking written records; therefore, he must reconstruct history from the fragmentary remains of human cultures he finds.

8. Anthropological linguists are mainly concerned with the history and structure of unwritten languages. More specifically, they are concerned with the emergence of language and how languages diverge over time (an area known as comparative or historical linguistics, as well as with the study of how contemporary languages differ, especially how they are constructed (structural linguistics) and how they are used in actual speech (sociolinguistics or ethnolinguistics).

9. The ethnologist attempts to understand how and why peoples today, and in the recent past, differ with respect to their customary ways of thinking and acting. One type of ethnologist, the ethnographer, usually spends a year or so living with, talking to, and observing the customs of a particular population; later, he may report on his findings in a detailed account called an ethnography. Another type of ethnologist, the ethnohistorian, investigates written documents in order to establish how the ways of life of a particular group of people have changed over

time. A third type of ethnologist, the comparative or cross-cultural researcher, uses the data collected by ethnographers and ethnohistorians for a large number of societies and attempts to discover which of the explanations suggested to account for particular cases may be more generally applicable.

SUGGESTED READINGS

Birdsell, J.: *Human Evolution* (New York: Macmillan, 1972).
A good, up-to-date introductory text, covering many aspects of the subdiscipline of physical anthropology.

Burling, R.: *Man's Many Voices* (New York: Holt, Rinehart and Winston, 1970).
A readable introduction to the subject of anthropological linguistics, focusing on how language is used within its cultural context.

Gillin, J. P.: *For a Science of Social Man* (New York: Macmillan, 1954).
A group of seven prominent American social scientists discuss the ways in which their respective disciplines interrelate.

Hole, F., and R. F. Heizer: *An Introduction to Prehistoric Archaeology,* 2nd ed. (New York: Holt, Rinehart and Winston, 1969), Ch. 1.
An overview of the field of prehistoric archaeology, emphasizing the methods of interference employed in archaeological research.

Murdock, G. P.: "The Science of Culture" (*American Anthropologist,* Vol. 34 [1932]), pp. 200-215.
An early article on the use of scientific method in the study of culture.

Sturtevant, W. C.: "The Fields of Anthropology." In M. H. Fried (Ed.), *Readings in Anthropology* (New York: Thomas Y. Crowell, 1968).
The original title, "Anthropology as a Career," indicates that the focus is on what anthropology is in practice for the working scholar. The interrelatedness of the subfields is emphasized as well as the range of possible subjects of study.

Wolf, E. R.: *Anthropology* (Englewood Cliffs, N.J.: Prentice-Hall, 1964).
By giving short summaries of significant theoretical contributions of anthropologists in a chronological order, the author gives a sense of anthropology as a body of developing knowledge. An overview of the literature is provided by frequent mention of relevant books and articles.

2

The Concept of Culture

Each of us considers himself an individual, with a unique set of personal opinions, preferences, and quirks; often we pride ourselves on the fact that, in some way, each of us is different from all other persons. Yet we are unexpectedly unanimous in our response to certain phenomena. Especially, we are in agreement in our reactions to behaviors or beliefs that differ markedly from those we are accustomed to. Despite very strong individual differences, we encounter in other societies a surprising number of behavior patterns that strike each of us in a remarkably similar way.

For example, the Yanomamö Indians of the Venezuelan-Brazilian border have a custom which would probably seem undesirable to most Americans, simply because it does not conform to our own ideas of how children should behave. Yanomamö boys are encouraged to express anger felt toward their parents by striking them. Instead of being punished for beating his father on the face and head, a young boy is praised for his ferocity. By the age of four, most boys have learned that the expected, and approved, way to show anger in their society is by striking someone.[1]

[1] Napoleon Chagnon, *The Yanomamö: The Fierce People* (New York: Holt, Rinehart and Winston, 1968), p. 84.

Since our society, and our laws, attempts to discourage the use of physical force in daily interpersonal relationships, this practice would not find favor among most Americans. It violates the system of attitudes, values, and behaviors which we as a society share and which constitute our *culture.* Despite individual differences—some Americans are, after all, ready to air quite permissive philosophies concerning child rearing—we are not easily persuaded that a young boy should be encouraged to beat his parents. The fact that we have a culture explains both the type of attitude we take toward such a phenomenon, and the near unanimity of that attitude.

CULTURAL RELATIVITY

It is a common tendency to condemn as backward or uncivilized viewpoints which we, as a society, generally oppose. Yet, in the case of the Yanomamö, it is pointless for us to make judgments as to whether their customs are as "good" as our own. Yanomamö customs pertain to Yanomamö culture—not to ours. Moreover, a society's conception of "correct" behavior is itself relative and may change with time. Nineteenth-century Americans, having stricter codes concerning the proper behavior of children, might have disapproved of the Yanomamö custom even more emphatically than we do today. Customs, then, can be intelligently viewed only within their proper context, which in this case is that of a society in which intergroup hostility is so widespread that a fierce nature is a highly valuable trait.

The same tolerance, of course, should be accorded to our own customs and ideas, for many of them would otherwise appear bizarre or barbaric to an observer from another culture. A Hindu, for example, would consider our custom of eating meat both primitive and disgusting because, in his culture, the cow is a sacred animal, and slaughtering one is taboo. Even our most mundane customs—the daily rituals we take for granted—might seem thoroughly absurd when viewed from the perspective of a foreign culture. A visitor to our society might justifiably take strange notes on certain behaviors which are quite meaningful to us:

> The daily body ritual performed by everyone includes a mouth-rite. Despite the fact that these people are so punctilious about care of the mouth, this rite involves a practice which strikes the uninitiated stranger as revolting. It was reported to me that the ritual consists of inserting a small bundle of hog hairs into the mouth, along with certain magical powders, and then moving the bundle in a highly formalized series of gestures.
>
> In addition to the private mouth-rite, the people seek out a holy-mouth man once or twice a year. These practitioners have an impressive set of paraphernalia, consisting of a variety of augers, awls, probes, and prods. The use of these objects in the exorcism of the evils of the mouth involves almost unbelievable ritual torture of the client. The holy-mouth man opens the client's mouth and, using the above mentioned tools, enlarges any holes which decay may have created in the teeth. Magical materials are put into these holes. If there are no naturally occurring holes in the teeth, large sections of one or more teeth are gouged out so that the supernatural substance can be applied. In the client's view, the purpose of these ministrations is to arrest decay and to draw friends. The extremely sacred and traditional character of the rite is evident in the fact that the natives return to the holy-mouth man year after year, despite the fact that their teeth continue to decay.[2]

We are likely to protest that in order to obtain an understanding and appreciation of the behaviors of a particular society—in this case our own—it is necessary to understand that society's culture and the reasons for its customs. The observer must know, for example, that periodic visits to the "holy-mouth man" are for medical, not magical, purposes. Because strong, healthy teeth are highly valued in our society, we are willing to spend much time and money on dental care. Similarly, the Hindu, before he decides that all Americans are sacrilegious carnivores, must take into account the fact that most of us have no religious taboo against eating meat.

The anthropological attitude that a society's customs and ideas should be viewed in the context of that society's culture is called *cultural relativity.* Because it fosters empathy and understanding, it is a *humanistic* attitude; because it requires impartial observation and involves an attempt to explain customs, it is a *scientific* attitude.

In general, cultural relativity is impeded by two different, but commonly held attitudes: the first is the tendency toward negative evaluation, which usually results from ethnocentrism; the second is the tendency toward positive evaluation, which often takes the form of a naïve yearning for the simple life or an envy of the "noble savage."

Ethnocentrism

The person whose vision is strictly limited to his own needs and desires is generally ineffec-

[2] Horace Miner, "Body Rituals among the Nacirema," *American Anthropologist,* Vol. 58 (1956), pp. 504–505.

tive in dealing with others. We call him egocentric, and we would be sorry to have him for a psychiatrist. The person who judges other cultures solely in terms of his own is *ethnocentric.* Not only is he ill equipped to do anthropological work, but he may be unable to recognize and solve social problems in his own culture.

For example, an ethnocentric American would view as barbaric the ceremonies that initiate adolescent boys into manhood in many societies. Such ceremonies often involve hazing, difficult tests of courage and endurance, and painful circumcision. The ethnocentric American would be unable to understand why anyone would be willing to endure these hardships, merely to be publicly accepted as an adult—why participating in such a ceremony might in fact be considered an honor. This same ethnocentric thinking would make it difficult for such a person to question American customs—such as the confinement of the aged in institutions, a practice that observers from another culture might find indefensible. Ethnocentrism, then, prevents understanding of the customs of other peoples, as well as creative insight into our own customs.

The "Noble Savage"

Whenever men's hearts are overfull of the complexities of civilization there is a fashionable longing for societies that are "closer to nature" or "simpler" than their own. The tendency is to feel that less complicated social and economic relationships are somehow better. The American whose father holds two or three jobs in order to provide his family with bare necessities may thus be attracted to the life style of the !Kung[3] Bushmen of the Kalahari Desert, who share their food and who are free to engage in leisure activities during the greater part of the day. The Bushmen obtain all of their food by hunting animals and gathering wild plants. Since they have no facilities for refrigeration, sharing a fresh animal is clearly more desirable than hoarding rotten meat. Moreover, the Bushmen move from camp to camp and could not afford to be bogged down carrying stores of food even if they were able to preserve it. Sharing, as it turns out, provides a kind of social security system for the Bushmen—a hunter, even on the days on which he is unsuccessful, can obtain food for himself and his family from someone else. Similarly, at some later date, the game he catches will provide food for the family of some other unsuccessful hunter. This system of sharing also insures that persons too young or too old to help with food collecting will be fed. Thus, not only is hoarding impossible for the Bushmen due to practical problems, but sharing has certain concrete advantages.

However, the food-sharing system of the !Kung Bushmen is a solution to the problems posed by their special environment and is not necessarily applicable to our own society. Moreover, there are other aspects of Bushman life that would not appeal to most Americans. For example, when the nomadic Bushmen decide to move their camps, the women must carry all the family possessions, substantial amounts of food and water, as well as young children up to the age of four or five. This is a sizeable burden to carry for any distance. And since the Bushmen travel a total of about 1,500 miles in a single year,[4] it is unlikely that most Americans would find the Bushman way of life enviable.

[3] The exclamation point in the word "!Kung" signifies a clicking sound that is made with the tongue. This sound is a characteristic feature of the Bushman languages.

[4] Richard B. Lee, "Population Growth and the Beginnings of Sedentary Life among the !Kung Bushmen," in Brian Spooner, ed., *Population Growth: Anthropological Implications* (Cambridge, Mass.: MIT Press, 1972).

Because we are all innately ethnocentric about many things, it is often difficult to criticize our own customs—some of which might be shocking to a member of another society. Here an aged Chinese woman, very much the center of her large family, presents a sharp contrast to an elderly American couple who seem isolated and abandoned. (Photograph of Chinese family by Henri Cartier-Bresson and Magnum Photos; Photograph of American couple by Jim Jowers from Nancy Palmer Photo Agency.)

The point is not that we should avoid comparing our culture with other, more primitive ones, but that we should not romanticize about the simplicities of primitive peoples. In general, their behaviors are appropriate to their environment in the same sense that our behaviors are appropriate to ours. Cultural relativity demands that all behaviors and customs of a society be viewed in terms of that society rather than in terms of our own seeming perfections or imperfections.

TOWARDS A DEFINITION OF CULTURE

In everyday usage the word "culture" refers to a desirable quality that we can acquire by attending a sufficient number of plays and dance concerts and trudging through several miles of art galleries. The anthropologist, however, has a different definition. In the following extract, Ralph Linton makes clear how the layman's definition of "culture" differs from that of the anthropologist.

> It [culture] refers to the total way of life of any society, not simply to those parts of this way which the society regards as higher or more desirable. Thus culture, when applied to our own way of life, has nothing to do with playing the piano or reading Browning. For the social scientist such activities are simply elements within the totality of our culture. This totality also includes such mundane activities as washing dishes or driving an automobile, and for the purposes of cultural studies these stand quite on a par with "the finer things of life." It follows that for the social scientist there are no uncultured societies or even individuals. Every society has a culture, no matter how simple this culture may be, and every human being is cultured, in the sense of participating in some culture or other.[5]

[5] Ralph Linton, *The Cultural Background of Personality* (New York: Appleton-Century-Crofts, 1945), p. 30.

Culture, then, refers to innumerable aspects of life; it encompasses the behavior, beliefs, and attitudes, as well as the products of human activity, that are characteristic of a particular society or population. The Shinto and Buddhist religions and a strong sense of respect for the elderly are as much a part of Japanese culture as chopsticks and Kabuki theater. Each of us is born into a complex culture which will strongly influence how we will live and behave for the remainder of our lives.

Culture Is Learned

Culture is learned behavior; it does not rely on biological transmission or genetic inheritance. It is necessary to make this point in order to differentiate the cultural behaviors of man and the other primates from behavior which is almost purely instinctual in origin.

All human beings are born with instinctual behaviors and drives which, although they are not considered parts of culture, do influence culture. For example, the need for nourishment is a basic need that is not cultural. But *how* that need is satisfied—what and how we eat—is part of our culture. Thus, all people eat, but different cultures approach this basic activity in vastly different ways. In the time of Richard the Lion-Hearted (1157–1199), for example, eating utensils did not grace the English table. When people gathered together at mealtime, food was simply placed in large bowls in the center of the table, and everyone took what he wanted, eating with his fingers. As time went on, Englishmen began to eat with wooden or metal utensils. We eat because we must; but the use of eating utensils is a learned habit and thus part of our culture.

Instinctive behaviors, on the other hand, are not learned. A bear would hibernate in winter even if it were isolated from others of its species and could not imitate (that is, learn) the behavior of its forebears. An inherited pattern of behavior would make it physiologically necessary for it to do so. Because hibernation is not learned behavior, it cannot be considered a cultural trait held in common by a community of bears. Similarly, the sociable ants, for all their organized behavior, cannot be said to share a culture. They divide their labor, construct their nests, and form their raiding columns, all without having been taught to do so and without imitating the behavior of other ants.

Monkeys, however, learn a great deal from their parents and peers. For example, in 1953, a group of scientists at the Japan Monkey Center were able to observe how a particular behavioral innovation spread from monkey to monkey, eventually becoming a part of the group's culture, independent of genetic factors. The scientists left some sweet potatoes out on the beach, near the place where a group of Japanese monkeys lived. Attracted by the food, a young female began to wash the sand off the potatoes by plunging them into a nearby brook. Previously the monkeys had rubbed their food clean, but this washing behavior spread throughout the group and eventually replaced their former habit. After a number of years, 80 to 90 percent of the monkeys were washing their sweet potatoes. Thos learned habit had become a part of the monkeys' culture.[6]

Experimenters have shown that apes and monkeys learn a wide variety of behaviors—some as basic as those involved in maternal care, and some as frivolous as the taste for candy. In fact, monkeys have relatively long childhoods as compared with other animals, and they must learn much before they can function as adults. Learning accounts for a relatively higher proportion of their behavior than is the case with many other animals. Man has the longest childhood of any animal. He is unique in the number and complexity of the learned behavior patterns that he transmits to his young. And he has a unique way of transmitting his culture: through language.

Language. It is a remarkable fact that all men ever discovered, living in societies of any form, have had a highly complex system of language. "Between the clearest animal call of love or warning or anger, and a man's least, trivial *word,* there lies . . . a whole chapter of evolution."[7] Language differs from all other systems of animal communication in that it is *symbolic;* that is, a word can represent whatever it stands for whether or not that thing is present.

This has tremendous implications for the transmission of culture. It means that a human parent can tell his child, once the youngster has reached an age where he is capable of understanding simple speech, that a snake, for example, is dangerous and should be avoided. The parent can then describe the snake in great detail—giving particulars of its length, diameter, color, texture, shape, and means of locomotion. He can predict the kinds of places where his child is likely to encounter snakes and tell him how to avoid confrontations. Thus, without ever having seen a snake, the child can store the verbal information in his memory. Should he encounter a snake, he will probably recall the symbolic word for the animal, as well as the related information, and so avoid danger.

If we did not have a symbolic language, the human parent would have to wait until his baby actually saw a snake and then show him, through example, that such a creature was to be avoided. Without language we could not transmit or receive information symbolically and thus would not be heir to so rich and varied a culture.

[6] Jun'ichiro Itani, "The Society of Japanese Monkeys," *Japan Quarterly,* Vol. 8 (1961), pp. 421–430.

[7] Susanne Langer, *Philosophy in a New Key* (New York: New American Library, Mentor Books, 1942), p. 94.

At a very early age, children learn the customs of their society. Here a young boy imitates the limbering-up exercises of a soccer team, illustrating that even play involves learned behavior. (Photograph by Elliott Erwitt, © 1969 by Magnum Photos.)

Culture Is Shared

If only one person thinks or does a certain thing, that represents a personal habit, not a pattern of culture. To be worthy of its name, culture must be shared by some population or group of individuals. Thus, anthropologists speak of a population as having a "culture" only when the members of that population share a number of learned patterns of thinking and behaving.

The size and type of the group with whom these characteristics are shared can vary greatly. For example, we share certain values, beliefs, and behaviors with our families and friends (although anthropologists are not particularly concerned with this type of cultural population). We share cultural characteristics with segments of our population whose ethnic or regional origins, religious affiliations, and occupations are the same as our own. We have certain things in common with all Americans. And we even share certain characteristics with people beyond our national borders who have similar interests (such as the members of the International Union of Anthropological and Ethnological Sciences) and with the inhabitants of other societies that share so-called Western culture.

When we talk about the shared customs of a society, which is the central concern of cultural anthropology, we are referring to a *culture*. When we talk about the shared customs of a subgroup within a society, which is a central concern of sociology, we are referring to a *subculture*. And when we study the shared customs of some group that transcends national boundaries, we are talking about a phenomenon for which we do not even have a name—a fact that reflects how relatively infrequent and recent this kind of sharing is. At the moment, we must refer to such a phenomenon by labelling it geographically—for example, we speak of "Eastern European culture."

Quite possibly, newer studies will suggest other ways of considering international cultures. For example, some research has suggested that cultures may be shared by economic classes in a general and international sense. In his introductory essay to *La Vida,* Oscar Lewis suggests that many people living in poverty share a *culture* of poverty: their young people have short, insecure childhoods; they tend to feel helpless and despairing as individuals; they generally live in overcrowded slums where housing conditions are poor; there is little organization in the community beyond the level of the family; and there is little integration of the poor into the larger society. Though Lewis's thoughts are original, he is using a familiar anthropological method: he is perceiving a culture by noting the incidence of shared characteristics.

A culture may be defined as the set of learned beliefs, values, and behaviors (that is, customs) generally shared by the members of a society; by "society," the anthropologist means a group of people who occupy a particular territory and speak a common language which is not generally intelligible to neighboring peoples.[8] While it is useful to have arrived at this definition, it does not really tell us how an anthropologist, faced with the realities of field research, proceeds to investigate the culture of a particular population. To understand how one "does" anthropology, we must know how the anthropologist identifies which patterns of behavior, values, and ideas are actually part of the culture of the population under study.

DESCRIBING A CULTURE

Individual Variation

Describing a particular culture might at first seem relatively uncomplicated: one simply observes what the people in that society do and then records their behavior. But consider the very real difficulties one might encounter in doing this. How would you decide which people to observe? And what would you conclude if, out of the first dozen natives you met and studied, all twelve behaved quite differently in the same situation? Admittedly, you would be unlikely to encounter such extreme divergence of behaviors; but there would tend to be significant individual variations in the actual behavior patterns of your subjects, even when they were responding to the same generalized situation and conforming to cultural expectations.

Of course, we find this to be true of the members of our society as well as those of another

[8] It is somewhat a matter of convention where we say a particular society leaves off and another begins, since societies are not always clearly separate with respect to language. Thus, for example, some might say that Canadians and Americans form a single society because both groups speak English and also share many common beliefs, values, and practices. But because there are two political entities (nations) involved, others might prefer to speak of separate Canadian and American cultures. This kind of situation is found commonly in the world, since political boundaries do not always correspond to linguistic boundaries.

society. In order to determine how an anthropologist might make sense out of diverse behaviors, it is useful to look at this diversity as it exists in a situation with which we are all familiar—the American football game.

When Americans attend a football game and the singer performs the "Star-Spangled Banner," it is certainly true that various members of the crowd behave differently. As they stand and listen, some men remove their hats; a child munches popcorn; a former soldier stands at attention; a cheerleader searches the lines of players for her favorite athlete; and the two team coaches take a final opportunity to intone secret chants and spells designed to sap the strength of the opposing team. Yet despite these individual variations, most of the people at the game respond in a basically similar manner: nearly everyone stands silently, facing the flag. Moreover, if you go to a number of football games you will observe that many aspects of the event are notably similar: although the plays used will vary from game to game, the rules of the game are never different; and although the colors of the uniforms change depending on the team, the players never appear on the field dressed in track suits.

Although the variations in individual reactions to a given stimulus are theoretically limitless, in fact they tend to fall within easily recognizable limits. The child listening to the anthem may continue to eat his popcorn, but he probably will not do a rain dance; similarly, it is unlikely that the coaches will react to that same stimulus by running onto the field and embracing the singer. Variations in behavior, then, are confined within socially acceptable limits, and it is part of the anthropologist's goal to find out what these limits are. He may note, for example, that some limitations on behavior have a practical purpose; a spectator who disrupts the game by wandering onto the field would be required to leave. Other limitations are purely traditional. It is considered proper in our society for a man to remove his overcoat if he becomes overheated, but other spectators would undoubtedly frown upon his removing his trousers even if the weather is quite warm. Based on such observations, the anthropologist attempts to discover the customs and ranges of acceptable behavior that are part of the society under study. Focusing on customary behavior, rather than on individual variation, the anthropologist comes to describe the culture of the group.

For example, an anthropologist interested in describing courtship procedures in the United States would initially encounter a variety of behaviors. His first step would be to determine what is conventionally considered the appropriate sequence of events. He would note that, generally, the male initiates contact with the female of his choice. First, he talks to her; then he invites her out. As they get to know each other better, dates tend to become more frequent and less formal. Eventually, the couple spends weekends together and visits their respective families. They may decide to declare themselves officially "engaged" and later, after even more complicated rituals and ceremonies, the two people are considered "married."

After having identified this general pattern, the anthropologist will attempt to discover the kinds of variations that exist which are still considered acceptable. He may note that one couple prefers to go to a concert on a first date while another couple prefers to go bowling; that some couples have very long engagements and others never become engaged at all; that some couples emphasize the religious rituals in the marriage ceremony while others are married by civil authorities, and so on.

If, however, our customary pattern of courtship is completely disregarded, the desired end may never be gained. For example, if a man saw a woman on the street and decided that he wanted to marry her, he might choose a quicker and more direct form of action than our usual forms of courtship. He could get on a horse, ride to the woman's home, snatch her up in his

Although the life styles of these three American couples appear very different, their courtship patterns all have certain aspects in common. Romantic love, for example, seems to be an attitude shared by all of them. (Right: Wayne Miller, © 1970 Magnum Photos; Top: Burk Uzzle, © 1970 Magnum Photos; Bottom: Dennis Stock, © 1967 Magnum Photos.)

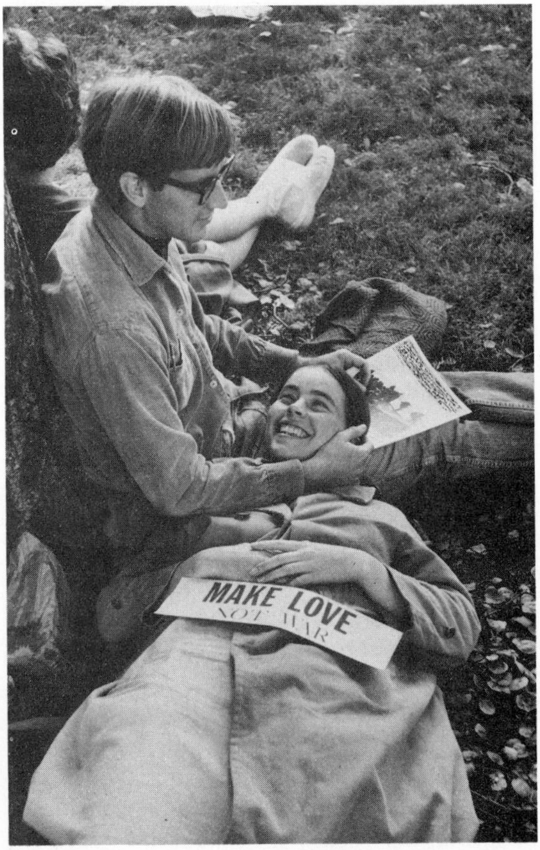

arms, and gallop away with her. In Sicily, until recently, such a couple would have been considered legally "married" even if the woman had never met the man before or had no intention of marrying. But in the United States, any man who acted in such a fashion would be arrested and jailed for kidnapping and would probably have his sanity seriously challenged. Such behavior would not be acceptable in our society; therefore it could not be considered cultural.

It is clear, then, that an anthropologist confronted with a number of individuals, all of whom behave in different ways, will attempt to discover the general patterns of behavior in the society he observes. He will determine which variations fall within these patterns and which are clearly unacceptable. He will not simply draw up a lengthy description of individuals and their behavior but will generalize from the individual behaviors to the cultural pattern.

Generalizing about Cultural Patterns

There are two basic ways in which an anthropologist can generalize about cultural patterns. When he is dealing with those customs which are overt or highly visible within a society—for example, our custom of having a nationally elected public official called the President—the investigator can determine and study such customs with the aid of a few knowledgeable persons. On the other hand, when he is dealing with a particular sphere of behavior which encompasses many individual variations, or when the people he studies are not aware of their own patterns of behavior, the anthropologist must collect his information from a sample of individuals and derive the *modal* response.

The mode is a statistical device that refers to the most frequently encountered response in a given series of responses; it is thus another way of expressing a general cultural pattern. Suppose that an anthropologist wanted to describe the time of day when the members of a society eat dinner. If his records of the behavior of 50 people show that some have dinner at 5:45 P.M., others at 6:00, still others at 6:30 or 7:00, but that most people eat dinner at 6:30, he would simply say that the members of that society generally eat dinner at 6:30 P.M., for this would represent the modal behavior of those people.

The mode is determined by measuring the variability of a given behavior pattern. When an anthropologist wants to describe a behavior in which there are many variations, he first records the behavior patterns of each of his subjects. Next, the investigator tabulates the number of times each class of behavior (for example, each dinner hour) occurs; this shows the *frequency distribution.* To obtain a frequency distribution curve, the figures are transferred to a graph which measures the range of distribution along the horizontal axis and the frequency along the vertical axis. Usually, such a curve slopes upward to a high point and then downward; the highest point represents the mode. Because of its shape, this kind of curve is called a *bell curve* (see Figure 1).

Frequency distributions may be calculated on the basis of responses given by all the members of a particular population. Obviously, however, the task of collecting such a large quantity of information would be extremely time consuming. Instead, the anthropologist usually gets his data from a representative sample of persons. Ideally, the members of this sample should be selected randomly from the society or community—that is, all kinds of individuals should have an equal chance to be chosen. If a sample is "random," it will probably include examples of all frequent variations of behavior exhibited within the society or community in roughly the proportions in which they occur. In theory, the random sample is a useful device; in fact, it has not yet been used extensively in anthropological fieldwork. Since it is relatively easy to make generalizations about *overt* or conscious aspects of a culture, such as dinner hours and courtship procedures, random sampling is often not necessary. But in dealing with *covert* or unconscious aspects of culture, such as a society's ideas about how far people should stand from one another when talking, random sampling may be necessary in order to generalize correctly about cultural patterns. This is because most people by definition are not aware of their covert or unconscious cultural patterns. Furthermore, in identifying covert aspects of culture, more subjective judgment is involved and misinterpretation is more likely to occur in the absence of random sampling.

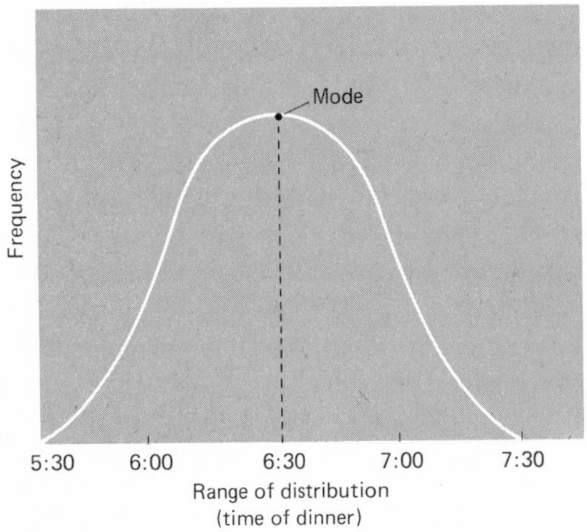

Figure 1
Frequency distribution curve.

Faced with the difficulties involved in identifying the mode of covert behavior patterns, it is fortunate for the anthropologist that the range of behavioral variation around the cultural mode is seldom wide.

Cultural Constraints

A primary factor limiting the range of individual behavior variations is the culture itself. The noted French sociologist, Emile Durkheim, stressed the fact that culture is something outside of us, external to the individual, on whom it exerts a strong coercive power. We do not always feel the constraints of our culture because we generally conform to the types of conduct and thought which it requires. Yet when we do try to brook the cultural constraints, their strength becomes apparent.

Cultural constraints are of two basic types, direct and indirect. Naturally, the direct constraints are most obvious. For example, if you wear clothing which is atypical of your culture, you will probably be subject to ridicule and a certain amount of social isolation. But if you choose to wear only a scanty loin cloth, you will receive a stronger, more direct cultural constraint—arrest for indecent exposure.

Although indirect forms of cultural constraint are less obvious than direct ones, they are not less effective. Durkheim wrote: "I am not obliged to speak French with my fellow-countrymen, nor to use the legal currency, but I cannot possibly do otherwise. If I tried to escape this necessity, my attempt would fail miserably."[9] In other words, if Durkheim had decided he would rather speak Serbo-Croatian instead of French, nobody would have tried to stop him. But no one would have understood him either. And, although he would not have been put into prison for trying to buy groceries with Icelandic money, he would have had a lot of difficulty convincing the local merchants to sell him food.

In a series of experiments on conformity, Solomon Asch revealed how strong social constraints can be. Asch coached the majority of

[9] Emile Durkheim, *The Rules of Sociological Method*, 8th ed., trans. Sarah A. Solovay and John H. Mueller, ed. George E. E. Catlin (New York: Free Press, 1936), p. 3.

a group of college students to give deliberately incorrect answers to questions involving visual stimuli. A "critical subject," the one student in the room who was not so coached, had no idea that other participants would purposely misinterpret the evidence presented to them. Asch found that in one-third of the experiments, the critical subject *consistently* allowed his own correct perceptions to be distorted by the obviously incorrect statements of the others. And in another 40 percent of the experiments, the critical subjects yielded to the opinion of the group some of the time.[10]

The existence of social or cultural constraints, however, is not necessarily incompatible with individuality. Simply because social pressure frequently prevents us from doing certain things we might otherwise do, this does not mean that our unique personalities are always subservient to the whims of the majority. In fact, in the Asch experiments, it was discovered that while many individuals could be significantly influenced by the publicly stated, unanimous opinion of a group of other people, the naturally independent individuals (about one-fourth of the critical subjects) consistently retained their independent opinions, even in the face of complete disagreement with the majority. It is unlikely, then, that cultural constraints can completely undermine individuality.

Ideal versus Actual Cultural Patterns

Every society develops a series of *ideal cultural patterns* which tend to be reinforced through cultural constraints. The ideal cultural patterns are what most members of the society say they ought to do in particular situations. Such ideal patterns are often called *norms*. We all know, however, that people do not always behave according to the standards that they express. If they did, there would be no need for direct or indirect constraints. Some of our ideal patterns differ from actual behavior because the ideal is outmoded, based on the way that society used to be. Other ideal patterns may never have been actual patterns and may therefore represent merely what people would like to see.

For example, an idealized belief, long cherished in America, is that all doctors are selfless, friendly people who chose medicine as their profession because they felt themselves "called" to serve humanity, and who have little interest in either the money or the prestige of their position. Of course, many physicians do not measure up to this ideal. Nevertheless, the continued success of television programs that portray the average American M.D. as a paragon of virtue indicates how deeply rooted in our collective psyche the ideal of the noble physician is.

The gap between ideal and actual patterns of behavior is not peculiar to our own culture. For example, among certain tribes in New Guinea the actual pattern of male-female relationships may be quite different from the cultural ideal. The Mae Enga, in the Western Highlands, express a belief in maintaining almost total separation of the sexes. They believe that, as soon as a woman reaches adolescence, she becomes unclean, possessing supernatural, evil qualities that will pollute any man who comes in contact with her. Not surprisingly, sexual intercourse is considered an unfortunate event which saps a man's masculinity. The Mae Enga's ideal behavioral pattern, then, would be for all men to shun women virtually all the time. But to allow for the birth of children, the Mae Enga have to make certain compromises with their ideal. Most of the men do marry eventually, although they continue to live apart from their wives.

[10] Solomon E. Asch, "Studies of Independence and Conformity: A Minority of One against a Unanimous Majority," *Psychological Monographs*, Vol. 70 (1956), pp. 1–70.

Sexual intercourse, though infrequent, does occur. Among the Kamanao of the Eastern Highlands, however, the gap between ideal and actual patterns of behavior is even more pronounced. The Kamanao, like the Mae Enga, have strict "rules" which prohibit sexual intercourse; but in actual practice, Kamanao men indulge in intercourse quite often, and they feel that sexual activities enhance their strength and masculinity.[11]

SOME BASIC ASSUMPTIONS ABOUT CULTURE

Culture Is Adaptive

The fact that so many cultures survive, indeed flourish, suggests that the customs a society develops tend to be suited to the particular demands of its environment. This is not surprising, for if cultural traits were ill suited to a given set of circumstances, the society's chances for survival would diminish. Any custom that enhances the survival of a society in a certain environment is an *adaptive* custom. In general, culture is said to be adaptive because it often provides people with a means of adjusting to the physiological needs of their own bodies, to their physical-geographical environment, and to their social environment as well.

Many cultural behaviors that would otherwise appear incomprehensible to us may be understandable in terms of a society's relationship with its environment. For example, we might express surprise at the postpartum sex taboos in certain societies that prohibit women from engaging in sexual intercourse until their two-year-olds are ready to be weaned. But in the tropical areas where such taboos exist, they may represent a people's means of adjusting to their physical environment. If there were no such taboo and the mother quickly became pregnant again, she could no longer continue nursing her infant. Without its mother's milk, the child might succumb to *kwashiorkor,* a severe protein deficiency disease that is common in these tropical areas. The taboo, then, may serve to give the infant a better chance for survival.[12]

Just as culture represents an adjustment to the physical environment and biological demands, so may it represent an adjustment to the social environment—that is, to neighboring peoples. For example, we do not know for sure why the Hopi Indians began building their settlements on the tops of mesas; they must have had strong reasons for doing so, for there are many practical difficulties entailed in choosing such a site—the problem of hauling water the long distance to the settlement, for example. It is possible that the Hopi chose to locate their villages on mesa tops for defensive reasons when the Athapaskan-speaking groups of Indians (the Navajo and Apache hunting tribes) moved into the Hopi area. In other words, the Hopi may have adjusted their living habits in accordance with social pressures.

A given custom represents one society's adaptation to its environment; it does not represent all possible adaptations. Different societies may choose different means of adjusting to the same situation. Thus, in low-protein areas of South America there is no long postpartum sex taboo, but induced abortion is a common practice. This may serve the same function of spacing out live births and thereby preventing too-early weaning. Similarly, the Hopi Indians, when suddenly confronted by the hostile, expansionist Navajo and Apache hunting tribes,

[11] M. J. Meggitt, "Male-Female Relations in the Highlands of Australian New Guinea," *American Anthropologist* (Special Issue, 1964), pp. 204–224.

[12] John W. M. Whiting, "Effects of Climate on Certain Cultural Practices," in Ward Goodenough, ed., *Explorations in Cultural Anthropology* (New York: McGraw-Hill, 1964), pp. 511–544.

A child by our standards too old for breast-feeding continues to be nourished by his mother. In some societies, prolonged breast-feeding is an adaptation which serves to protect the infant from diseases related to a protein-deficient diet. (Photo by George Rodger—Magnum.)

clearly had to take some action in order to protect themselves. But, instead of deciding to build their settlements on easily defended mesa tops (as we suggested), they might have developed some complex of military customs for defense. Why a society develops a particular response to a problem, rather than some other possible response, always requires explanation.

We must remember, however, that a society is not forced to adapt to its particular circumstances. Although people may generally alter their behavior according to what they perceive will be helpful to them, such is not necessarily the case. Moreover, what people perceive as being helpful does not always prove to be adaptive. Some societies may actually develop maladaptive traits—that is, customs which are detrimental to the survival of the society that adopts or retains them. We have already mentioned certain primitive tribes in New Guinea that view women as essentially unclean and dangerous individuals, with whom physical contact should be as limited as possible. Suppose one such tribe decided to adopt homosexuality as the customary sexual pattern. Clearly, we would not expect such a society to survive for long. Yet there is evidence to suggest that some societies in the past became extinct because they adopted maladaptive customs.

Still other cultural traits—such as clothing styles and rules of etiquette—may be "neutral" in terms of adaptation. That is, they may never have had any direct relationship to biological needs or environmental conditions. Other traits may be relics; they may have had an adaptive value in the past, but that value no longer obtains. For example, the buttons and incompletely closed seam at the end of men's suit jacket sleeves once had a specific purpose—to close the sleeves more tightly about the wrist. Yet, despite the fact that current fashion dictates that men's jacket sleeves should fit loosely around their wrists, the buttons and open seam have been retained.

Culture Is Integrated

Upon hearing of an unfamiliar cultural pattern, a natural response is to try to imagine how that pattern would work in our own society. We might wonder, for example, what would happen if American women adopted a long postpartum sex taboo—say, three years of abstinence after the birth of a baby. Such questions are purely whimsical, for one cannot easily graft the customs of one culture onto another culture. In the present case, a long postpartum sex taboo presupposes a lack of effective birth control methods, but our society already has many such methods. Moreover, a long postpartum sex taboo could conceivably affect a number of important aspects of our culture, ranging from the tradition that marriage is romantic to the allowable number of wives per man. The point is that with such a taboo imposed on it our culture would no longer be our culture: too many other aspects of it would need to be changed in order to accommodate the one new behavior. This is so because our culture is integrated.

In saying that a culture is *integrated,* we are saying that the elements or traits which make up that culture are not simply a random assortment of customs. One reason anthropologists assume that culture is integrated is because integration seems to follow from the assumption that culture is generally adaptive. If certain customs are more adaptive in particular settings, then those "bundles" of traits will generally be found associated under similar conditions. For example, the !Kung Bushmen subsist by hunting wild animals and gathering wild plants. They also are nomadic, have very small communities, low population densities, share food with others, and have few material possessions. These cultural traits generally occur together among peoples who depend on hunting and gathering for their food. Such associations imply that cultures tend to be integrated.

A second reason culture is assumed to be integrated is because mutually inconsistent customs would be difficult, if not impossible, to maintain simultaneously. In our own society, for example, it is customary for a motorist to stop at a red light and proceed on a green light. It would be impossible for our culture to also have a rule saying that the first car entering an intersection with a traffic light has the right of way. The two rules are mutually contradictory. Thus, cultures tend to be composed of elements that are compatible with one another.

Because culture is integrated, a change in one element often has tremendous repercussions—sometimes in areas not totally expected. Suppose that an officer from an organization for economic development decided that many people in India are poor, overcrowded, and malnourished largely because their religion does not permit them to kill and eat the cows that roam the streets. He might instigate a wholesale slaughter of cows only to find that the results of changing this one simple custom would be profoundly undesirable. The number of plow animals available to Indian farmers would be substantially reduced. Indians would no longer be provided with cow dung, which serves as a main source of cooking fuel and fertilizer. Cow skin, horns, and hoofs could no longer be used to construct clothing and other needed articles. It seems likely, then, that if Hindus were no longer forbidden to kill cattle, other problems might develop simply because India is not currently capable of supporting a large beef-producing industry.[13]

This example clearly demonstrates that a culture is more than a random collection of customs or norms. It is a highly organized structure in which a particular component may bear an intimate and necessary relationship to many other components.

Culture Is Always Changing

While it is true that one society's cultural traits cannot be introduced into the culture of another group of people without forcing a number of changes in that culture, we should remember that culture is not static—it is always changing. Even without the disruption caused by the intrusion of a foreign trait, a given society's culture is bound to change over time. There is always a certain amount of individual freedom in a culture, and individual freedom allows for behavioral variations that may eventually become shared, and so part of the culture, in the future. Or, perhaps some aspect of the environment will change, requiring new cultural adaptations.

The fact that culture is always changing is apparent when one considers many of our own customs. Clothing styles, for example, change rapidly from season to season. And even an aspect of culture which is generally considered long-enduring—such as courtship behavior—can also be seen to change with time. Thus, young people today may consider it "old-fashioned" to become formally engaged. And some couples may even live together before marriage—a custom which would have been completely unacceptable to their parents' generation.

It is apparent, then, that human culture is not a single, or a simple, thing. Each society has a culture that is distinct from that of every other society and which represents an integrated complex of shared behaviors uniquely suited to its particular environment. This raises a central question: How did man come to create culture? How did man develop, from his earliest forms, into the highly sophisticated creature that he is today, capable of establishing and sustaining such a wide variety of cultures? These are questions we will attempt to answer in Part 2. In Chapter 3 we introduce the topic of human evolution, paying particular attention to the ways in which man's physical development affected his capacity for culture.

[13] Marvin Harris, "The Cultural Ecology of India's Sacred Cattle," *Current Anthropology*, Vol. 7 (February 1966), pp. 51–66.

SUMMARY

1. In spite of very strong individual differences, the members of a particular society are in close agreement in their responses to certain phenomena. This is because they all share common attitudes, values, and behaviors which constitute their *culture.*

2. The anthropological attitude that a society's customs and ideas should be viewed within the context of that society's culture is called *cultural relativity.* In general, cultural relativity is impeded by two different commonly held attitudes: the first is the tendency toward negative evaluation, or *ethnocentrism;* the second is the tendency toward positive evaluation, which often takes the form of a naïve yearning for the simple life or an envy of the "noble savage."

3. A culture may be defined as the set of learned beliefs, values, and behaviors generally shared by the members of a society; by *society* the anthropologist means a group of people who occupy a particular territory and speak a common language which is not generally intelligible to neighboring peoples.

4. One defining feature of culture is that it is *learned;* that is, it does not rely on biological transmission or genetic inheritance. Man is unique in the number and complexity of the learned behavior patterns that he transmits to his young. And he has a unique way of transmitting his culture: through language.

5. The second defining feature of culture is that it is *shared* by the members of a particular population. The size of the group with whom cultural traits are shared can vary from a particular society (a culture) to segments of that society (a subculture) to a group that transcends national boundaries.

6. The anthropologist attempts to discover the customs and ranges of acceptable behavior that comprise the culture of the society under study. In doing so, he focuses on general or shared patterns of behavior rather than on individual variation. One way of generalizing about cultural patterns is to collect information from a sample of individuals and derive the *modal,* or most frequent, response.

7. In studying any cultural trait, the anthropologist does not have too much difficulty identifying the modal behavior because the range of variation is seldom wide. One important factor that limits the range of individual variation is the culture itself, which acts directly or indirectly as a constraint on behavior. The existence of cultural constraints, however, is not necessarily incompatible with individuality.

8. Every society develops a series of ideal cultural patterns which represent what most members of the society say they ought to do in particular situations. Such ideal patterns are often called *norms.* A society's norms, however, do not always agree with actual behavior.

9. Several assumptions are frequently made about culture. First, cultures are generally adaptive to the physiological needs of their carriers, to their physical-geographical environment, and to their social environment. Not all cultural traits, however, are specifically adaptive at the moment. Some may be neutral in terms of adaptation, some may merely have been adaptive in the past, and still others may be maladaptive.

SUGGESTED READINGS

Kroeber, A. L.: *The Nature of Culture* (Chicago: University of Chicago Press, 1952).
A collection of papers on the nature of culture by a distinguished pioneer in American anthropology.

Spindler, G. D. (Ed.): *Being an Anthropologist: Fieldwork in Eleven Cultures* (New York: Holt, Rinehart and Winston, 1970).
An engrossing description of the anthropologist's methods and how he feels about his work.

White, L. A.: *The Science of Culture: A Study of Man and Civilization* (Garden City, N.Y.: Doubleday, 1969; originally published in 1949).
A collection of papers on culture and its study, emphasizing the symbolic and evolutionary nature of culture.

Whiting, J. W. M., and I. L. Child: *Child Training and Personality* (New Haven: Yale University Press, 1953).
Chapter 2 treats the relationship between individual and cultural behavior.

Williams, T. R.: *Field Methods in the Study of Culture* (New York: Holt, Rinehart and Winston, 1967).
An interesting treatment of the way in which anthropologists study and describe cultures.

Part 2

THE EVOLUTION OF MAN AND HIS CULTURE

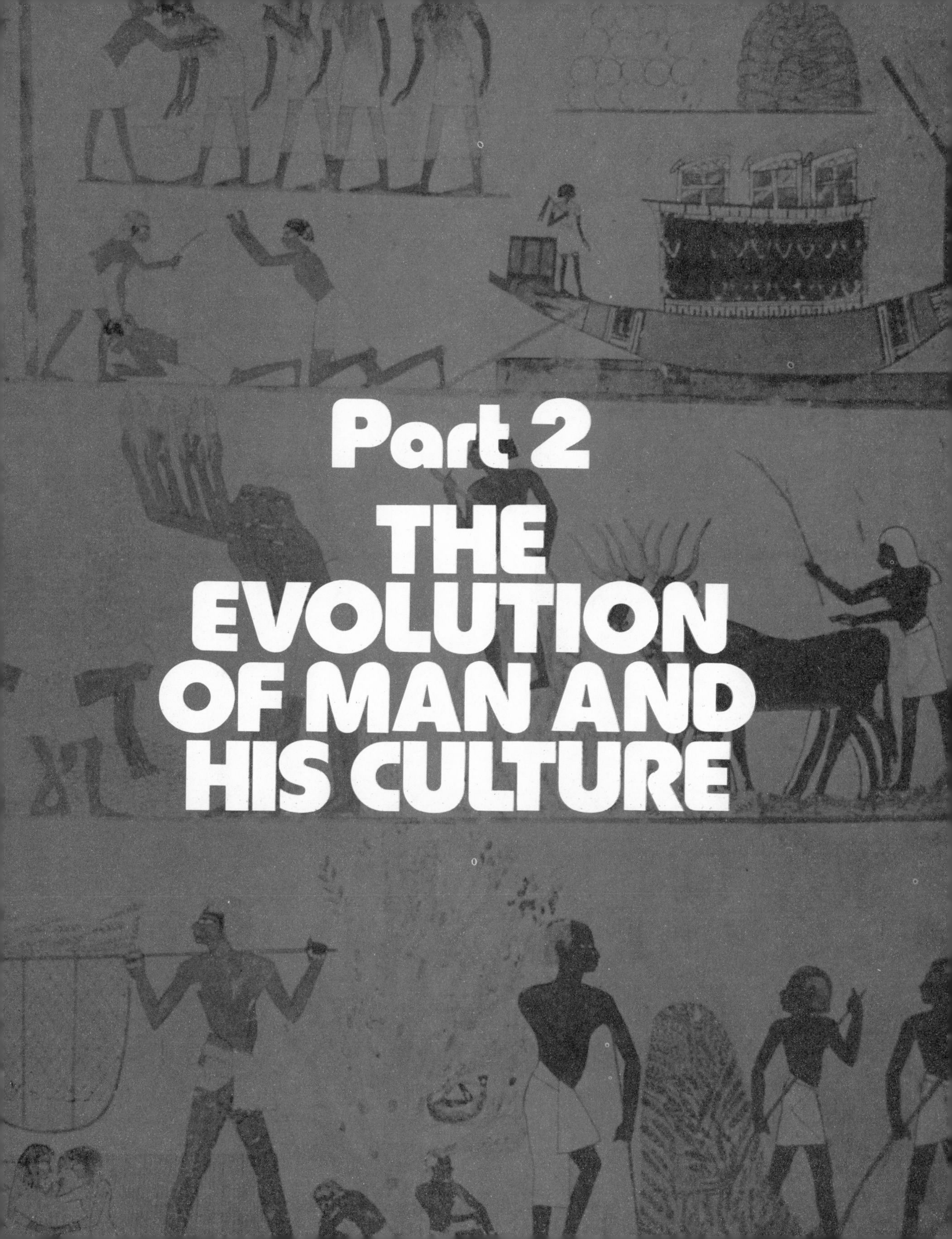

3
Evolution

THE HUMAN PAST

In the nineteenth century, Charles Darwin shocked the world by stating that men are descended from ape-like creatures. Since then we are less easily shocked: the contemporary scientist raises few tempers when he tells us we are cousins to apes and monkeys, each from different branches of the family tree.

The Darwinian theory that humans evolved from ape-like creatures explains only a fragment of man's past. Monkeys, apes, and man are believed to have common ancestors among the primitive primates which evolved following the great age of reptiles.[1] The shrew-like insectivores were the forerunners of the prosimians, the modern tarsiers and lemurs, who evolved about 54 million years ago. Our earliest estimation of monkey and ape origins extends back to 35 million years ago. The direct ancestors of man, the hominids, diverged from their ape-like ancestors about 25 million years ago. Modern man, relatively a newcomer, emerged about 50,000 years ago.

The etchings of Edward Topsell, published in 1658, illustrate a conception of early man based more on imagination than science. (Courtesy, Rare Book Division, The New York Public Library, Astor, Lenox, and Tilden Foundations.)

How do we know these changes actually occurred? Why did they happen? Archaeologists and paleontologists have helped piece together the fossil clues to the mystery of human evolution. As to the question, "Why?" we must see human evolution in the total context of natural change over eons, within the framework of an evolutionary theory that applies to all forms of life. It is a theory that has run counter to the literal Western religious interpretation of creation.

[1] The age of reptiles spanned the Mesozoic era, from 225 to 65 million years ago.

THE EVOLUTION OF EVOLUTION

In the Judaeo-Christian view of creation the world was only a few thousand years old. An eminent calculator of biblical events, Archbishop Ussher, even set the date at precisely 4004 B.C. That was the year God is said to have created Adam and, from Adam's rib, Eve. Created in God's image, man and woman and their descendants were elevated above the rest of the animal world. Evolution—the theory that the different species developed, one from another, over very long periods of time—was impossible to accept in a relatively young world dominated by creatures "little lower than the angels."

The dominant Western view of the time also held that God and all of his creations were locked into a natural hierarchy. This hierarchy was defined and perpetuated by the theological doctrine of the *Scala Naturae,* the Scale of Nature, also called the Chain of Being. It placed man above rocks, plants, and animals and below spiritual beings. Although the Scale of Nature placed man close to the apes, society was not shocked, for each creature in the Chain of Being was said to be created separately by God's Divine art. The physical resemblances between man and ape were thus the product of separate acts of Divine creation.

Belief in the Scale of Nature was accompanied by the conviction that an animal species could not become extinct. The notion of extinction threatened man's trust in God: a whole group of God's creations could not simply disappear. The irony of history is that, although the Scale of Nature rejected and delayed an evolutionary theory, its concept of a chain of stages in nature contained the roots of the theory of evolution developed by Charles Darwin and others.

Darwin's theory of evolution was not reached in isolation, nor was Darwin the first to consider the problem of organic change; the question had intrigued serious thinkers for centuries. Darwin carefully studied the writings of the pre-evolutionary naturalists, and many of their observations greatly influenced his thinking. Some of them were pointed in the right direction and others were grossly incorrect, but their total effect was to stimulate thinking, and in different ways, they prepared the scientific community for Darwin's arrival.

Early in the eighteenth century, one of the era's most influential scientists, Carl Linnaeus (1707–1778), classified plants and animals in a *Systema Naturae* which placed man in the same order as apes and monkeys. Linnaeus did not suggest a blood relationship between man and ape; he only classified both as primates, a category in a system of nature that included all things created by God. In essence, what he said was that man and ape can share the same room in a house without having the same parents. Linnaeus, fortunately, was not dogmatic, and as his research progressed, his belief changed from a notion that all living species were direct descendants of Eden's original animals to a less certain, more open-minded view of life. He recognized the possibility that new species might arise.

The Comte de Buffon (1707–1788), a contemporary of Linnaeus, was more certain that species do not remain the same. He stopped short of a truly evolutionary view, however, since he recognized that species may change, but not that one species may evolve into another.

While the Comte de Buffon could only say that change took place within species, Jean Baptiste Lamarck (1744–1829) offered an explanation for such change. If you cut off the tails of dogs and interbred them for generations, continuing to sever the tails, would a tailless dog eventually be born? Lamarck thought so. He maintained that acquired characteristics can be transmitted to offspring. The necks and legs of giraffes might thus be explained as results of successive generations of giraffes straining to reach the high leaves of trees, so that ultimately, all offspring were born with extended necks and legs.

Erasmus Darwin (1731–1802), the grandfather of the celebrated Charles, was a scientist who shared Lamarck's views about evolution, but he served history more by his influence on his grandson than by his scientific contributions. Erasmus's passion for odd facts of natural history, expressed in *Zoonomia* (1794), was eventually shared by Charles. Although Erasmus Darwin died several years before the birth of his grandson, the boy's early exposure to his grandfather's theories of evolution served to make him more open-minded than most people of the time, who were frightened by the implications of heresy in such ideas.

Charles Darwin understood, as Goethe put it, that "mysteries are not necessarily miracles," but many years were to pass before any great number of people were ready to relinquish the idea that only miracles could explain the mystery of creation. For one thing, people refused to believe Darwin because, according to the Christian calendar, the world was less than 6,000 years old. In such a relatively short time, evolution on the scale conceived by Charles Dar-

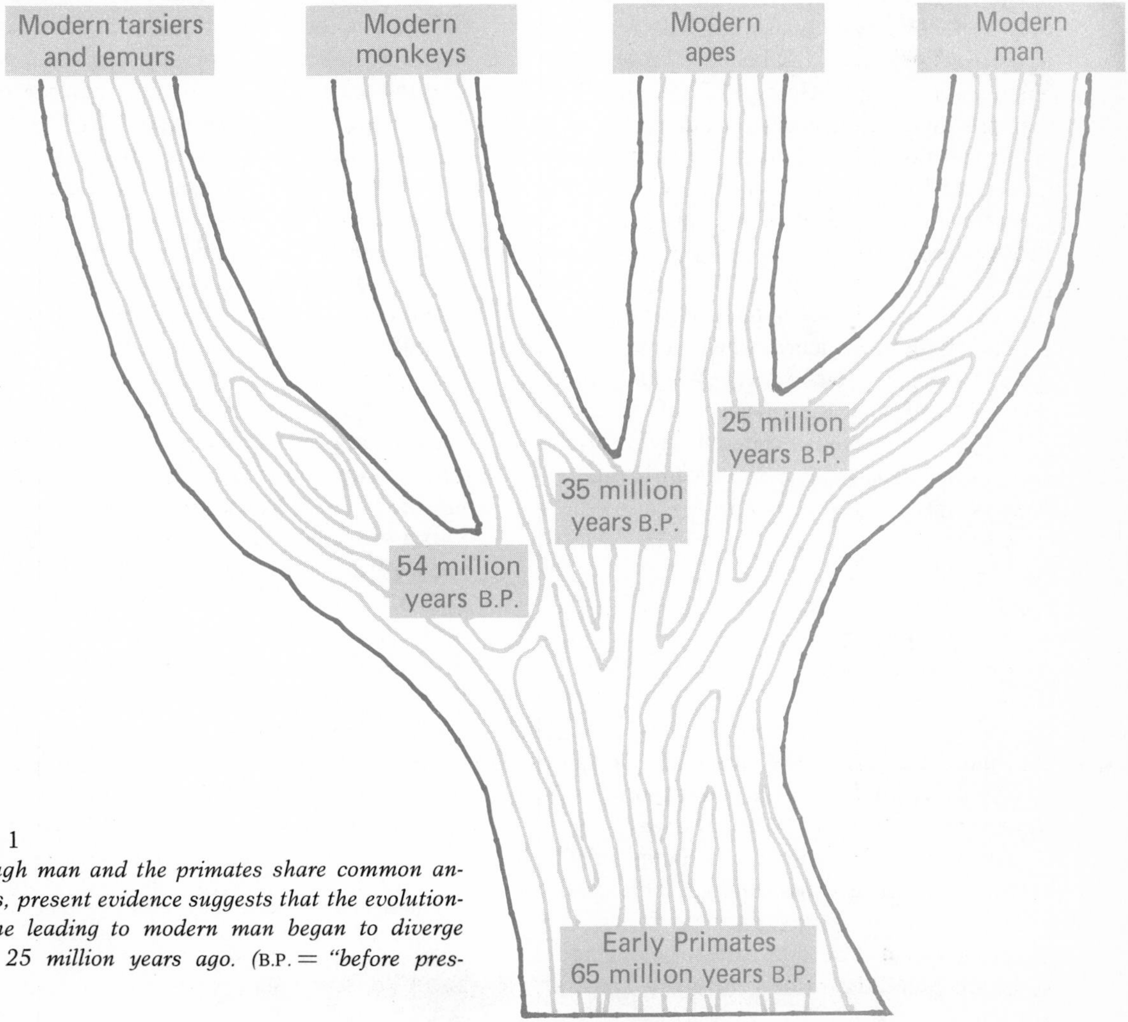

Figure 1
Although man and the primates share common ancestors, present evidence suggests that the evolutionary line leading to modern man began to diverge about 25 million years ago. (B.P. = *"before present."*)

win was unimaginable. Not everyone, however, accepted this universal birthday. One who did not was a maverick scientist, Sir Charles Lyell (1797–1875). In *Principles of Geology* (1834), Lyell presented a theory of *uniformitarianism,* which rejected the view of an unchanging earth and held that the earth was constantly being shaped and reshaped by forces that had been operating since the beginning of time—for longer than had been supposed. Fossil evidence supported Lyell's thesis. The dogma of the time was weakening; leading thinkers began to speculate seriously about evolution.

Lyell's progressive views were opposed not only by theologians, but by his fellow naturalists and scientists. A rival belief, *catastrophism,* chiefly expounded by Georges Cuvier, proposed that previous cataclysms and upheavals, such as Noah's flood, killed off all living creatures, and that new ones came to replace them. The fossils being discovered were taken, not as evidence of evolution, but as proof that catastrophes had destroyed all living things, which were then replaced by new Divine creations. The weight of fossil evidence, however, was great enough to discredit *catastrophism;* only evolution could explain the presence of specimens which were preserved in different layers of rock but obviously related and significantly different in appearance.

CHARLES DARWIN AND THE THEORY OF NATURAL SELECTION

It remained for Charles Darwin to contradict the orthodox interpretation of creation. In *On the Origin of Species* (1859), Darwin rejected the notion that each species was independently created; species evolved through change. He wrote, "I am fully convinced that species are not immutable; but that those belonging to what are called the same genera are lineal descendants of some other and generally extinct species, in the same manner as the acknowledged varieties of any one species." His revolutionary conclusions outraged those who believed, literally, the biblical account of creation. Evolutionary evidence was sufficiently convincing to make some people interpret the Bible metaphorically or figuratively, but the fundamentalists who worshipped the literal word of "The Book" would not compromise their beliefs. Years of bitter controversy ensued.

Until 1871 (when *The Descent of Man* was published), Darwin avoided stating categorically that man was descended from subhuman forms, but the implications were clear. People began to take sides for and against Darwin. In June, 1860, at the annual meeting of the British Association for the Advancement of Science, Bishop Wilberforce saw an opportunity to attack the Darwinists. Concluding his speech, he faced Thomas Huxley, one of their chief advocates, and inquired, "Was it through his grandfather or his grandmother that he claimed descent from a monkey?" Huxley responded, "If . . . the question is put to me would I rather have a miserable ape for a grandfather than a man highly endowed by nature and possessing great means and influence and yet who employs those faculties and that influence for the mere purpose of introducing ridicule into a grave scientific discussion—I unhesitatingly affirm my preference for the ape."[2]

The most famous confrontation between fundamentalists and evolutionists occurred in the 1925 Scopes Monkey Trial. In Tennessee, John Scopes, defended by the renowned Clarence Darrow, was convicted of teaching evolution. Scopes's opponents won the court decision, but the real victors were the proponents of Darwin's theory. The wide publicity given to the

[2] From Ashley Montagu, Introduction to *Man's Place in Nature* by Thomas H. Huxley, in Louise B. Young, ed., *Evolution of Man* (New York: Oxford University Press, 1970), pp. 183–184.

IF I AM DARWIN'S GRANDPAPA.
IT FOLLOWS DON'T YOU SEE,
THAT WHAT IS GOOD FOR MAN AND BEAST,
IS DOUBLY GOOD FOR ME.

trial and the discussion it generated greatly increased the public's awareness and understanding of evolution—if not its total acceptance. As late as 1968, a petition to the city of Wheeling, Illinois, protested the teaching of evolution as fact, rather than theory.

Natural Selection

Darwin was not the first to view creation as evolutionary, but he was the first to provide a rational, well-documented explanation for the way evolution had occurred. He pointed out that each species is composed of a great variety of individuals, some better-adapted to their environment than others. The better-suited ones generally live longer, producing more numerous offspring. Very gradually, the proportion of individuals with advantageous traits increases. This process of ***natural selection,*** continued for an appreciable time, brings about the evolution of better-adapted forms. For example, in *The Descent of Man,* Darwin suggested that men "descended from a hairy, tailed quadruped, probably arboreal in its habits." Between 25 and 13 million years ago, climate changes gradually reduced the lush forests; over millions of years our ancestors adapted to life on the ground and ultimately walked erect.

Since evolution has occurred over millions of years, in small, nearly imperceptible gradations, no one can point to a modern horse and say "I remember when you were the ancient *Eohippus.*" Although the short span of human life makes the observation of evolutionary changes difficult, it is nevertheless possible to observe some instances of natural selection in a relatively short time period.

Within the last 100 years, in England, for example, scientists have been able to observe natural selection in action. When certain areas became heavily industrialized, the pale bark of trees in these regions became coated with black soot. Light colored moths, formerly well adapted to blend with the environment, became clearly visible against the sooty background and were easy prey for birds. Darker moths, previously at a disadvantage against the light bark, were now better adapted for survival. Their color became an advantage in industrial regions and subsequently they became the predominant variety.

Behavioral adaptations, too, often result from environmental changes and pressures. Most baboons live in a relatively open, grassland environment. Baboons who join in groups are less easily victimized by predators than those who forage or travel alone. Grouping together is also a more efficient way of competing against other animals for food. Group membership contributes to survival, and each generation of baboons born into groups becomes conditioned to a social structure that grows increasingly complex. The baboon troop's rigid hierarchy of

To protect themselves from predators like the lion, monkeys take to the trees, positioning themselves on the outer branches. Pads of roughened skin enable them to sit comfortably for hours. (Courtesy of Irven DeVore.)

leadership and its well-defined sex and age roles represent complex, orderly adaptations to life in a challenging environment.

Even a callus can serve an adaptive function. Underneath their tails, on their sitting apparatus, Old World monkeys have callus pads. To avoid sneak attacks by predators, monkeys sleep in trees on slender branches distant from the trunk. "But sleeping on a narrow branch presents its own problem: if a monkey just stretches out, like a man in bed, it is likely to fall. To assure their balance, monkeys therefore sleep sitting on their rumps with their legs thrust upward at a sharp angle, clinging to another branch for additional support. Because the pads of toughened skin are attached directly to the haunch bones, replacing soft sensitive tissue between bone and skin, their owners sit comfortably for hours."[3] Through this combination of physical and behavioral adaptations to their environment, the Old World monkeys can sleep without moving around to stimulate circulation, thus decreasing the hazard of falling while asleep.

The theory of natural selection answered many questions, but it also raised at least one whose answer eluded even Darwin. The appearance of a beneficial trait might assist the survival of an organism, but what happens

[3] Sarel Eimerl and Irven DeVore, *The Primates* (New York: Time Incorporated, 1965), p. 39.

when the organism reproduces by mating with other members who do not possess this new variation? Would not the new adaptive trait disappear eventually if subsequent generations mated with individuals who lacked this trait? Darwin knew variations were transmitted through heredity, but he could not explain the source of new variations and the mode of inheritance. Gregor Mendel's pioneering studies in the science of genetics provided the foundations for the answers, but his discoveries remained obscure until 1900.

HEREDITY

Gregor Mendel's Experiments

Mendel, an Austrian monk and amateur botanist, bred several varieties of pea plants and noted detailed observations of their progeny. Mendel chose as breeding partners plants that differed by only one observable trait: tall plants were crossed with short ones and yellow with green, for example.

When the pollen from a yellow pea plant was transferred to a green pea plant, Mendel observed a curious phenomenon: all of the first generation offspring were yellow peas. It seemed that the green trait had disappeared. But when seeds from this first generation were crossed, both yellow and green peas resulted in a ratio of 3 to 1. Apparently, Mendel reasoned, the green factor had not been lost or altered; the yellow trait was simply *dominant* and the green factor was *recessive.* Mendel observed similar results with other traits. Tallness dominated shortness, and the factor for smooth-skinned peas dominated the factor for wrinkled ones. In each cross, the 3 to 1 ratio appeared in the second generation. Self-fertilization, however, produced different results. Pure yellow peas always yielded yellow peas, and pure short plants produced short plants.

From his numerical results, Mendel concluded that some yellow peas were pure for that trait, whereas others also possessed a green factor. That is, although two plants might both appear yellow, one of them might produce some green peas. In such cases, the full complement of inherited traits, the *genotype,* differs from the observable appearance, or *phenotype.* Clearly, genotype *determined* phenotype. But the determinants of genotype remained relatively mysterious until the twentieth century.

Figure 2
When Mendel crossed a plant with two genes for yellow (YY) with a plant with two genes for green (yy), each offspring was yellow but carried one gene for yellow and one gene for green (Yy). The plants were yellow because the gene for yellow is dominant over the recessive gene for green. Crossing the first generation yielded three yellow plants and one green plant.

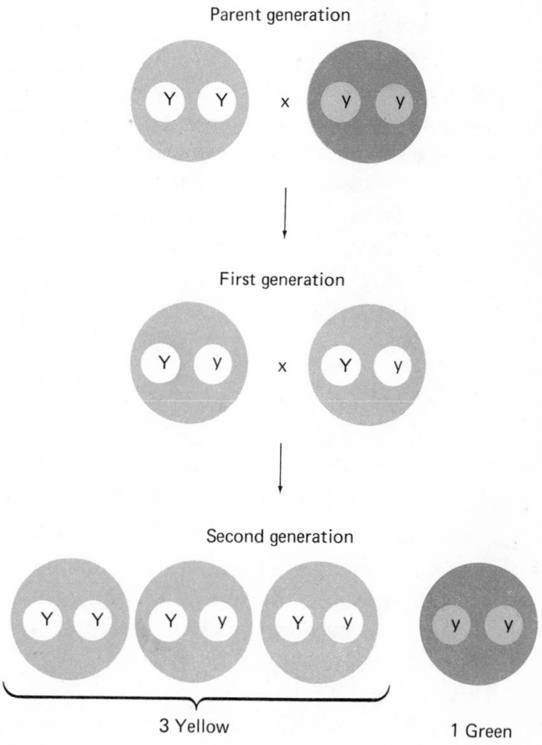

Genes: The Conveyors of Inherited Traits

Mendel's units of heredity are what we now call *genes.* He concluded that these units occurred in pairs for each trait, and that offspring inherited one unit of the pair from each parent. (Today we call each member of a gene pair or group an *allele.*) If the two genes, or *alleles,* for a trait are the same, the organism is *homozygous* for that trait; if the two genes for a characteristic differ, the organism is *heterozygous* for that trait. A pea plant that contains a pair of genes for yellow is homozygous for the trait. A yellow plant with a dominant gene for yellow and a recessive gene for green, although phenotypically yellow, has a heterozygous genotype. As Mendel demonstrated, the recessive green gene can reappear in subsequent generations. But Mendel knew nothing of the composition of genes, or the processes which transmit them from parent to offspring. Many years of scientific research have yielded much of the missing information.

The genes of an organism are located on rod-shaped bodies, called *chromosomes,* within the nucleus of every body cell. Chromosomes, like genes, occur in pairs. Each allele for a given trait is carried on the identical position of corresponding chromosomes. The two genes that determined the color of Mendel's peas, for example, were opposite each other on a pair of chromosomes.

Mitosis and Meiosis. The body cells of every plant and animal carry chromosome pairs in a number appropriate for its species. Humans have 23 pairs, a total of 46 chromosomes, each carrying many times that number of genes. Each new body cell receives this number of chromosomes during cellular reproduction, or *mitosis,* as each pair of chromosomes duplicates itself.

This naturally raises the question of what happens when a sperm cell and an egg cell unite to form a new organism? What prevents the human baby from receiving twice the number of chromosomes characteristic of its species—23 pairs from the sperm and 23 pairs from the egg? The process by which the reproductive cells are formed, *meiosis,* insures that this will not happen. Each reproductive cell contains *half* the number of chromosomes appropriate for the species. Only one member of each chromosome pair is carried in every egg or sperm. At fertilization, the human embryo normally receives 23 separate chromosomes from its mother and the same number from its father, adding up to the 23 pairs.

Genetic Recombination. The distribution of traits from the parents varies from one offspring to another. Brothers and sisters, after all, do not look exactly alike, nor does each child resemble 50 percent of his mother and 50 percent of his father. This is so because when a sperm cell or an egg cell is formed, the single member of each chromosome pair it receives is a matter of chance. Each reproductive cell, then, carries a *random assortment* of chromosomes and their respective genes. At fertilization, the egg and sperm that unite are different from every other egg carried by the mother and every other sperm carried by the father. A unique offspring is thus engendered.

The traits displayed by each organism are not simply the result of combinations of dominant and recessive genes, as Mendel had hypothesized. In humans, most traits are influenced by the activity of many genes. Skin color, for example, is the result of several inherited characteristics. A brownish shade results from the presence of a pigment, melanin; the degree of darkness in the hue depends largely on the amount of melanin present and how it is distributed in the layers of skin. Another factor that contributes to the color of all human skin is the blood that flows in blood vessels located in the superficial layers of the skin. Thus, skin color is determined by genes which bear various instructions. Humans carry at least five different genes for the manufacture of melanin, and many others for the other components of skin hue. Inheritance of ABO and Rh blood groups similarly involves several genes. In fact, almost all physical characteristics in humans are the result of the concerted action of many genes. Some traits are sex-linked. The so-called X chromosome, which, together with the presence or absence of a Y chromosome, determines sex, may also carry the gene for hemophilia or color blindness; the expression of these characteristics depends on the sex of the organism.

Such processes of genetic recombination ensure that variety is achieved and genetic variation within a species is essential for the operation of natural selection. Evolution and genetic variation, then, are inseparable.

DNA

But what about the genes themselves? What are they made of and how do they convey inherited characteristics? Genes are contained in the chromosomes, rod-like structures reproduced in the nucleus of every body cell. Each gene carries a set of instructions, encoded in the peculiar chemical structure of the gene,

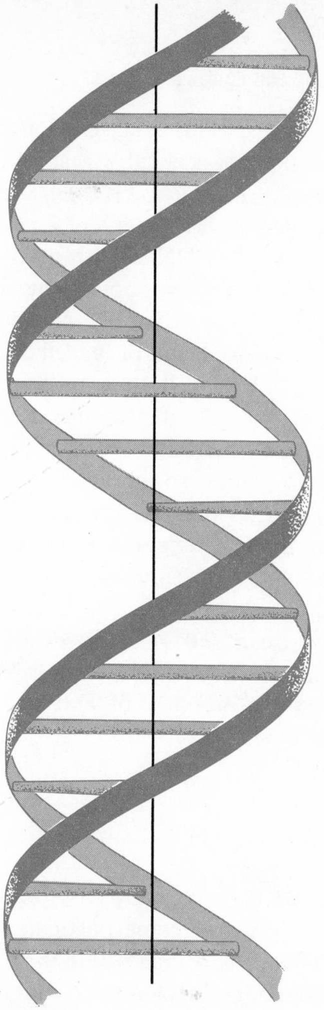

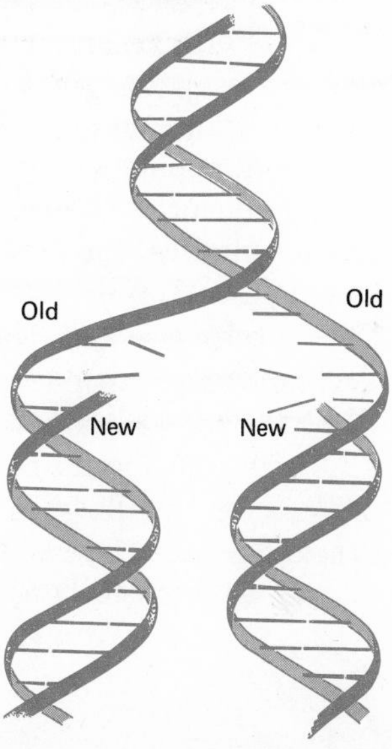

Figure 3
The DNA molecule consists of two spiral sugar-phosphate strands. The strands are linked by the nitrogenous bases, adenine, guanine, thymine, and cytosine (above). *When the DNA molecule reproduces, the bases separate and the spiral strands unwind. Each original strand serves as a mold along which a new complementary chain is formed. By this process, which is not yet fully understood, the hereditary code is duplicated* (left).

from which a cell makes all of the rest of its structural parts and chemical machinery. It follows that the appearance and functional traits of every living organism develop from the inherited make-up of all its cells. In every living organism, heredity is controlled by the same chemical substance, *DNA.*

DNA (deoxyribonucleic acid) is a very long, two-stranded molecule in a helical, or spiral, form, which holds the chemical code of the gene. Each chromosome in the nucleus of a cell is composed of a molecule of DNA (with many coded genes, or instructions), supported by a backbone composed of protein. The DNA code is transmitted to the cytoplasm of a cell by *RNA* (ribonucleic acid). Each cell, then, receives specific instructions for all of its chemical operations. A cell that manufactures brown pigment, for example, does so under orders received from genes in its nucleus. Thus, this cell, combined with many cells similarly coded to make brown pigment, gives some part of the organism a brown coloration.

The coded structure of DNA is heritable; that is, it may be passed from generation to generation, ensuring the stability of and continuity of the characteristics of a species.

Mutation

The duplication of genes, directed by DNA and RNA, on occasion may fail in some particular. The result is a *mutation,* a change in the molecular structure, or DNA code, of a gene. Such a change produces a new gene. Mutations occur randomly and generally are harmful to a species. Any change in the intricate structure of a gene is likely to impair the delicate balance within an organism, and between an organism and its environment.

Most mutations are, in fact, lethal. Tay-Sachs disease, for example, is caused by two recessive mutant genes. Its effects are blindness, severe retardation, and death by the age of three or four. The evolutionary effect of lethal mutations is usually inconsequential, since the organism with both recessive mutant genes for a given trait will probably die before it can reproduce—and often before it is born. But the trait can be passed on by individuals who are heterozygous for the recessive gene.

Dobzhansky points out that we can discuss the relative merits or disadvantages of a mutant gene *only* in terms of the physical, cultural, and genetic *environment* of that gene.[4] Galactosemia, for example, is caused by a recessive mutant gene and usually results in mental retardation and blindness. It can be prevented, however, by dietary restrictions begun at an early age. The intervention of human culture in this case counteracts the mutant gene and allows afflicted individuals to lead normal lives. The same cultural factors, however, can also modify the effect of natural selection by helping to perpetuate the mutant gene. People with the galactosemia trait, enabled to function normally, reproduce, passing on one of the recessive genes to their children. Without cultural interference, natural selection would prevent such reproduction. In most cases, natural selection works to retain only those mutations which aid survival.

The Gene Pool

Genetic inheritance provides for the stable transmission of traits and some measure of variation among individual members of a species, while evolution involves gradual changes in the genetic composition of whole populations.

The total variety of genes possessed by the members of a given population constitute that population's *gene pool.* Genes, and their corresponding traits, occur with varying frequencies within a population. Evolution proceeds as these frequencies change over the years. In the case of giraffes, for example, through natural selection, the ratio of genes for long necks to short necks gradually increased in the gene pool until the adaptive long-necked trait became characteristic of all giraffes.

[4] Theodosius Dobzhansky, *Mankind Evolving* (New Haven: Yale University Press, 1962), pp. 138–140.

Isolation and Speciation

One of the most controversial aspects of Darwin's theory was that one species could, over time, evolve into another species. *Speciation,* or the development of a new species, does not happen suddenly. Nor is it the result of one or two mutations in the history of a single family.

Speciation may occur if one group of a species's population finds itself in a radically different environment. In the group's adaptation to the new environment, enough genetic changes may occur to result in new races. Races, however, are not separate species. They are simply slight variants of a single species that can interbreed. "Perhaps there is no recorded instance of intermarriage between some races, say of Eskimos with Papuans, but Eskimos as well as Papuans do interbreed with other races; channels, however tortuous, for gene exchange exist between all human races."[5]

But a species cannot breed successfully with a different species. Generally, the genetic makeup of separate species is so different that reproduction is impossible. If members of different species did mate, it is unlikely that the egg would be fertilized, or if it were, that the embryo would survive. If birth did occur, the offspring would either die or be infertile. What is the explanation for this differentiation? How does one group of organisms become so unlike another group with the same ancestry that it forms a totally new species?

Speciation may occur if the populations become so separated from each other geographically that gene exchanges are no longer possible. In adapting to their separate environments, enough genetic changes may occur to prevent the two populations from interbreeding. Numerous factors can prevent the exchange of genes. Two species living in the same area may each breed at different times of the year; their behavior during breeding, e.g., courtship rituals, may be distinct. Or the difference in body structure of closely related species may in itself bar interbreeding. Geographic barriers may also prevent interbreeding.

Once species differentiation does occur, the evolutionary process cannot be reversed—the new species can no longer mate with other species related to its parent population. Man and the gorilla, for example, had the same distant ancestors, but their evolutionary paths have irreversibly diverged.

EVIDENCE FOR HUMAN EVOLUTION

Wheeling, Illinois, notwithstanding, most people today accept that man's ancestry is not altogether human. But what real evidence do we have that man has descended from nonhuman ancestors? And what proof is there that man is part of the whole evolutionary scheme? For answers to these questions we must examine what we know of man in relation to other species.

Anatomical Comparisons

The study of comparative anatomy has partially substantiated human evolution. Man's anatomy is similar to that of vertebrates, mammals, primates, and apes in that order of increasing similarity. In fact, "every bone of the human skeleton is represented by a corresponding bone in the skeleton of apes and monkeys."[6] Comparative anatomy does not reveal many qualitative differences between man and the apes. Most of the differences are of degree, rather than kind.

In Chapter 4, we will consider the anatomy of the living primates, man's closest relatives. A study of vertebrate and particularly mam-

[5] Dobzhansky, *Mankind Evolving,* p. 193.
[6] Dobzhansky, *Mankind Evolving,* p. 163.

malian anatomy provides further evidence for evolution. Vertebrates include all those organisms with skull-encased brains and a segmented spinal column which allows for flexibility. They have a heart, liver, urinary system, and a rather well-developed nervous system. Reptiles, birds, fishes, amphibians, and mammals are vertebrates.

Because mammals are warm-blooded animals, capable of maintaining a relatively constant body temperature, they are less affected by temperature extremes than are cold-blooded reptiles and amphibians. Body hair or fur and sweat glands aid in the regulation of body temperature. Mammals live in every climate on earth; one species, man, has adapted to extremes from the tropics to the tundra.

The ability to survive in a variety of environments has also been aided by the process of reproduction in mammals. The fertilized egg develops inside the mother's body, protected from potential predators. (The duckbill platypus and the spiny anteater are exceptions.) Following birth, the offspring is nourished by milk from the mother's mammary glands. With mother as its food-processing plant, a baby mammal need never starve as long as the mother herself has enough food to produce milk.

But animals need more than food to survive. A well-nourished baby baboon will not live long if it attempts to get acquainted with a leopard. Among mammals, imitation through close association with parents and a highly developed brain enable the young to identify natural enemies and cope with other environmental conditions. Mammals are particularly adapted to learning about their environment. Campbell writes:

> While in most animals activity and learning result from the need to satisfy the primary drives of hunger, sex, and self-preservation, a new determinant of behavior is found among mammals that does not satisfy these immediate needs. This new factor is *a drive to investigate and explore the environment without the immediate object of satisfying one of the three prime biological needs.*[7]

Mammalian curiosity would be less effective if each generation had to solve every environmental problem anew. Biology, as well as culture, is involved in the human learning process. The human infant is utterly dependent upon its mother for survival, and their prolonged, close relationship enables the growing child, like the aforementioned baboon, to learn a great deal by imitation. Through language, knowledge gained by previous generations is passed on, so that while the ape and monkey cultures have remained at a standstill, man's culture has grown increasingly complex.

Vestiges

Additional evidence for evolution is provided by *vestiges,* seemingly useless organs or structures in the anatomy of living organisms. Vestiges imply a connection with primitive ancestors for whom these organs and structures once served a useful purpose. For example, at the end of the human spinal column are small round masses of bone which seem to be the vestigial remains of tail bones. This suggests that somewhere along the line man had ancestors with tails.

Embryology

Embryology supplies another source of evidence for evolutionary development. Very young embryos of different animals resemble each other and become more distinct as they mature, a phenomenon described in Baer's law. Ernest von Haekel interpreted this to mean that the *ontogeny,* or individual development of a given embryo, is patterned after its *phylogeny,* the evolutionary development of the species to which the embryo belongs. For

[7] Bernard G. Campbell, *Human Evolution: An Introduction to Man's Adaptations* (Chicago: Aldine, 1966), p. 49. (Italics added.)

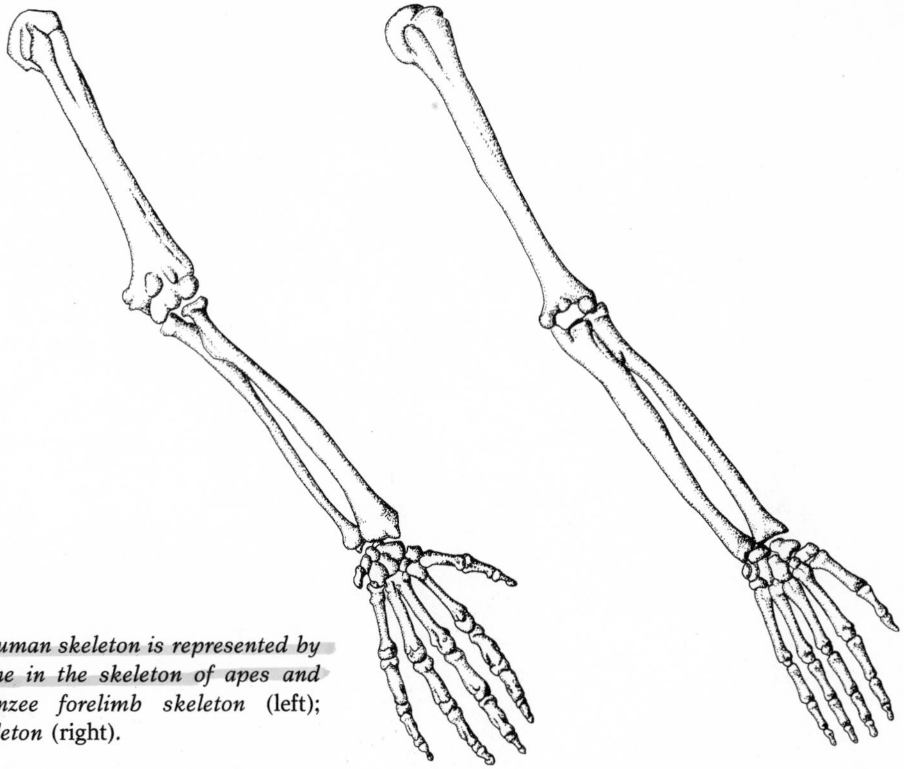

Figure 4
"Every bone of the human skeleton is represented by a corresponding bone in the skeleton of apes and monkeys." Chimpanzee forelimb skeleton (left); *human forelimb skeleton* (right).

example, the embryo of a fish develops gill arches that eventually support functioning gills through which the fish breathes. The human embryo forms similar arches at an early stage in its development, though they eventually change into features more useful to a human being. The human embryo simply repeats an ancestral form of life when it develops the gill arches; that is, a very distant ancestor of man had gills.

Physiology, Serology, and Genetics

Studies in comparative anatomy which link man with other species are reinforced by studies in *physiology, serology* (the study of blood chemistry), and *genetics*. Man and many other animals have similar body functions, such as respiration, reproduction, and digestion, and perform them in similar ways. There are measurable degrees of similarity between man and other species. This is shown, for example, by a test in which an antiserum is mixed with the blood serum of a man as well as with the blood serum of an ape. The reaction in both cases is similar. When the same test is made with monkey blood, the results are less alike. This suggests that man is more closely related to apes than to monkeys.

Fossil Evidence

Perhaps the most reliable evidence for the evolution of a given species comes from *paleontology,* the study of fossils. Fossils are the remains of plants and animals that lived in previous geological ages. (Man's ancestral remains and the methods used to interpret fossils will be discussed in more detail in Chapters 5, 6, and 7.)

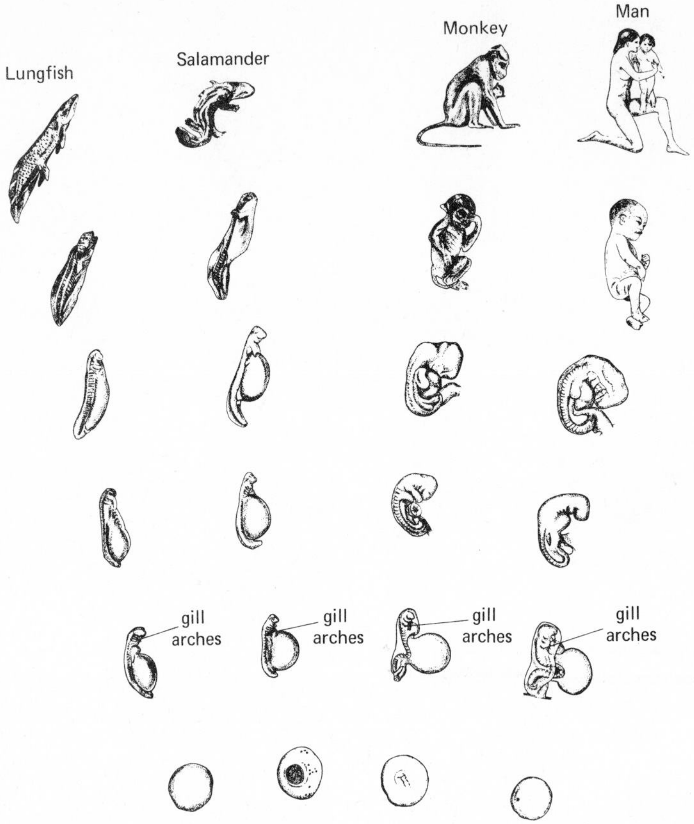

Figure 5
The early embryonic stages of a fish, salamander, monkey, and man all develop gill arches. (Courtesy of the American Museum of Natural History.)

BIOLOGICAL AND CULTURAL INTERACTION IN HUMAN EVOLUTION

Consider again the pale English moth, annihilated, in effect, by soot. Unable to adapt to a rapidly changing environment, it was replaced by darker members of the species who were better adapted for survival. The pale moth, like all creatures but man, is powerless against change. As Dobzhansky writes:

> Man, and he alone, has it within his potentialities to refuse to accept the evolutionary direction of blind forces of nature. He may be able to understand, to control, and to guide his evolution. The first basic, fundamental fact about human evolution is that mankind is simultaneously engaged in two kinds of evolutionary developments—the biological and the cultural. Human evolution can be understood only as a product of interaction of these two developments.[8]

But how does this interaction operate? Recall the child who inherits galactosemia. Without the intervention of human culture, in this case scientific knowledge, the child would die. Simi-

[8] Theodosius Dobzhansky, "Evolution—Organic and Superorganic," *The Rockefeller Institute Review,* Vol. 1, No. 2 (1963), pp. 1–2.

larly, diabetics can now live normally with the help of insulin and dietary controls, and organ transplants are increasing the life spans and reproductive potential of many persons. In all these cases, human culture has forestalled death, mitigating the effects of natural selection. But man's influence on his environment does not always work to his immediate biological advantage. Radiation has increased the mutation rate, and the effects of many drugs on genes are still debatable.

On balance, however, man's control of the environment has enabled him to flourish. Ironically, man has manipulated his environment so successfully that he has overbred his species and endangered the future by his affluence. Man, the most adaptive of creatures, now faces environmental challenges of his own making.

Only man, through cultural influence, can modify his evolution. In the modern hospital, infants who might once have died are enabled to live. (Eve Arnold, Magnum Photos.)

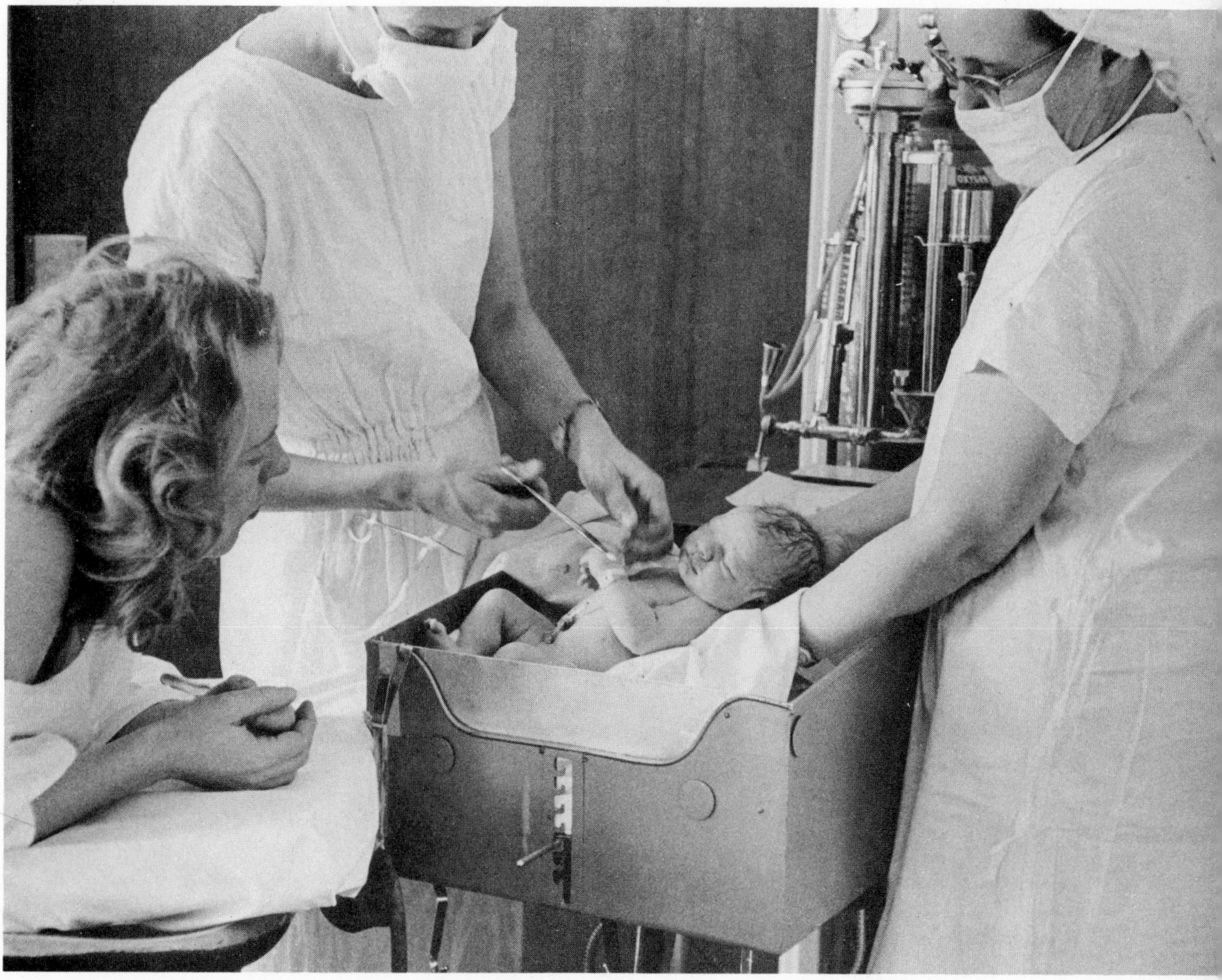

SUMMARY

1. Darwin was not the first to consider the relationships between man and other animals or to note the resemblances between man and the apes.
2. Pre-Darwinists however worked within the framework of the biblical version of creation and assumed therefore that, while there may have been some slight changes within species, the world and all its creatures continued to exist nearly as God had made them.
3. Darwin theorized that species evolved gradually, over long periods of time, through natural selection. Those organisms which were best adapted to a particular environment lived longer and produced more offspring.
4. Genetics provides an understanding of how natural selection influences the evolution of a species by describing the mechanisms by which adaptive traits may be passed from one generation to the next.
5. Support for Darwin's theory comes from comparing modern man to other species. Comparative anatomy, physiology, embryology, as well as the presence in man of certain vestigial organs that are still functional in other mammals, help us determine man's place in the history of evolutionary change, as well as providing a basis for the interpretation of fossil evidence.
6. To Darwin, man evolved from more primitive species by natural selection, in the same way other contemporary species did. But human evolution is indeed unique. Man is the only creature with the potential to consciously influence his own evolution through his ability to manipulate his environment. Man is a product of the interaction of biological and cultural evolution.

SUGGESTED READINGS

Alland, A., Jr.: *Evolution and Human Behavior* (Garden City, N.Y.: Natural History Press, 1967).
An introduction to evolutionary theory and genetics.

Dobzhansky, T.: *Genetics and Evolutionary Process* (New York: Columbia University Press, 1971).
Dobzhansky's newest and perhaps most complete book, with an excellent bibliography.

Dobzhansky, T.: *Mankind Evolving: The Evolution of the Human Species* (New Haven: Yale University Press, 1962).
Demonstrates that the mechanisms of evolution, primarily natural selection, are still active.

Eiseley, L. C.: *Darwin's Century: Evolution and the Men Who Discovered It* (Garden City, N.Y.: Doubleday, 1958).
A historical treatment of evolutionary theory.

Eiseley, L. C.: *The Firmament of Time* (New York: Atheneum, 1965).
Speculates about the acceptance of ideas of evolution in Western society and about the circumstances in which ideas associated with evolution were produced. Colorful descriptions of animals are combined with personal anecdotes.

Irvine, W.: *Apes, Angels and Victorians! Darwin, Huxley and Evolution* (New York: Meridian Books, 1971).
The personalities and domestic lives and friends of Darwin and Huxley are presented through a description of gossipy details, including letters. All of this is closely related to the scientific pursuits of both great men, whose friendship forms the core of the book.

Mayr, E.: *Animal Species and Evolution* (Cambridge, Mass.: Harvard University Press, 1963).
A definitive work on systematics, taxonomy, and evolutionary theory.

Mayr, E.: *Systematics and the Origin of Species: From the Viewpoint of a Zoologist* (New York: Dover, 1964).
This book is specialized but readable with a little effort by a beginning student. It deals with a crucial subject for evolution, bringing together genetics and ecology for an understanding of the past and continuing formation of species; the relationship between races and species and other problems are dealt with in detail.

Medawar, P. B.: *The Future of Man: The BBC Reith Lectures* (New York: Basic Books, 1960).
Delightful little book, discussing human biology and the futuristic (or perhaps not so futuristic) potential of man to control his evolution through eugenics.

Simpson, G. G.: *The Meaning of Evolution: A Study of the History of Life and of Its Significance for Man* (New Haven: Yale University Press, 1967, originally published in 1949).
A nontechnical book intended for the general public, it has now become a classic. The three parts of the book take up the following questions: What has happened during the course of evolution? How has this been brought about? What significance has all this for conclusions about human nature, humanity's future, and ethical standards? The material presented is the fossil record and the mechanisms of evolution.

4

Man and the Primates

WHY STUDY PRIMATES?

In the days when newsreels were part of every movie showing, the comic antics of trained chimpanzees used to be reported as an antidote to the news of human disasters. Since then, the news has grown no less sobering but monkey and ape watching has come a long way. Serious observers have learned to go far beyond the zoo and the laboratory to the wilderness which is the natural environment of nonhuman primates, to learn what these animals are really like and what they mean to our ancestry.

Once more it must be stressed, however, that although the chimpanzee is a close kin and sometimes appears to be very human, neither it nor any other ape is regarded as our ancestor. Monkeys and apes are related to us in that we share certain traits believed to have been passed on by some common ancestor in the far reaches of prehistory.

In attempting to understand the physical and social traits of those extinct primates which evolved into man, anthropologists study the physical and social traits of living primates, as well as fossil remains. (The fossil record will be discussed in detail in Chapters 5, 6, and 7.) To further our understanding of human development, paleontologists study the evolution of other animals and plants, and primatologists make comparative studies of the anatomy and behavior of monkeys, apes, and man.

Studies of living primates also enable us to separate characteristics of man that are distinctively human from those that are part of the generalized primate heritage. It is assumed that if all living primates, including man, possess a certain characteristic, it probably existed in our earliest primate ancestors. Furthermore, in determining the conditions under which man's differences began to evolve, we may find explanations for the emergence of culture in the line of primate evolution that ultimately produced man.

THE LIVING PRIMATES

The Primate order is divided into two suborders —the prosimians (premonkeys) and the anthropoids. The former includes tarsiers, lemurs, and tree shrews; and the latter, man, apes (the gorilla, chimpanzee, orangutan, gibbon, and siamang), and monkeys. The anthropoid suborder most resembles man in external physical features and even more remarkably in the physiology of the brain, reproductive functions, and the microscopic structure and function of most organs. In addition there are similarities in blood chemistry and chromosomal structure.

Man's close resemblance to the primates, and particularly to the apes, was suggested by Thomas Huxley over 100 years ago: "Whatever part of the animal fabric—whatever series of muscles, whatever viscera might be selected for comparison—the result would be the same—the [monkeys,] Apes and the Gorilla would differ more than the Gorilla and Man."[1] Subsequent evidence and scientific advances have borne out Huxley's prophetic assertion: our knowledge of man and his origins has been vastly broadened by study of the behavioral as well as physical characteristics of monkeys and apes.

Comparing the chemistry of proteins in human blood with that of other living primates provides further evidence for the evolutionary relationship between man and the apes. When the proteins in the blood of two species react to certain antiserums in about the same degree, the species are said to be biochemically similar, and an evolutionary relationship is assumed. Such tests have indicated that man is not only more closely related to apes than to monkeys, but that he is more like the chimpanzee and gorilla than the orangutan and gibbon. Extensive studies of primate blood chemistry involving protein research have affirmed that chimpanzees and gorillas are even closer to humans than they are to other apes.[2] Furthermore, chromosomes of the chimpanzee and the gorilla are more similar to human chromosomes than they are to the orangutan's or the gibbon's. This provides additional evidence for man's kinship to the apes. In this chapter we will consider the physical and behavioral traits that unite the Primate order, as well as those characteristics which are uniquely human.

[1] Thomas H. Huxley, *Man's Place in Nature* (1863, reprinted by University of Michigan Press, Ann Arbor, 1959).

Primate Traits

Among the over 200 living species of primates are animals ranging from the insect-eating tree shrew to the highly complex human being. No single characteristic defines the whole group. Rather, we find certain common tendencies—particularly those that facilitated living in trees. All primates, except for the anomalistic tree shrew, are able to climb by grasping. This characteristic set primates apart from most other arboreal animals who had to claw their way up, while the handy primates were able to move about with ease.

Among the higher primates, an adaptation of great importance was the conception of one offspring at a time. This favored the development of a healthy fetus by eliminating the strong competition of other fetuses for nourishment and space within the mother's body. The single fetus also has an evolutionary advantage over multiple fetuses in its slower maturation.[3] Furthermore, and perhaps most important, a single offspring would be easier for the mother to pick up and carry away in times of danger.

The common primate adaptations of grasping hands with opposable digits, stereoscopic or depth vision, ability to keep the torso erect, and small litter size—all related to the primates' arboreal background—may have been preconditions for the evolution of human culture. A grasping hand is a prerequisite for tree swinging as well as tool making. Similarly, depth perception is necessary for safe locomotion in the trees, as well as for effective hunting and tool use. An erect torso, necessary for reaching for fruit on high branches, is also essential for

[2] Morris Goodman, "Immunochemistry of the Primates and Primate Evolution," *Annals of the New York Academy of Sciences* (December 28, 1962), pp. 219–234.

[3] Bernard G. Campbell, *Human Evolution: An Introduction to Man's Adaptations* (Chicago: Aldine, 1966), p. 250.

efficient hunting and tool making. Since these traits are found, in differing degrees, and with rare exceptions, in all living primates, we can infer that they figured prominently in the life of the ancestors of man and played a crucial role in the emergence of human culture. Primates, including man, also share certain behavioral traits, discussed later in this chapter.

We must emphasize that man has never passed through an evolutionary stage in which he displayed all the traits we now observe in monkeys and apes. From a genealogical view, man and the living nonhuman primates are related in that they share a single ancestor in their evolutionary past.

The Lower Primates: Prosimians

Among the prosimians, the oldest living primates, we can see the origins of several traits shared by the entire order, including grasping hands and stereoscopic vision. Once abundant, only a few species of these tree-dwelling primates remain.

Tree Shrews. It is debatable whether the squirrel-like tree shrews of southern and southeastern Asia are primates or insectivores. These arboreal, clawed creatures possess good vision, essential for survival in the tree world. In general structure, the insect-eating tree shrews probably approximate the animals in the earliest phases of primate evolution, when mammalian ancestors began to evolve into primates.

Lemurs. The lemurs, undisputable primates, are now found only on the island of Madagascar but were once widespread throughout the New and Old Worlds. These mouse-to-cat-sized animals are well adapted to nocturnal tree life, having stereoscopic vision and unusually large eyes. Lemurs produce single offspring, to which the mothers devote great attention.

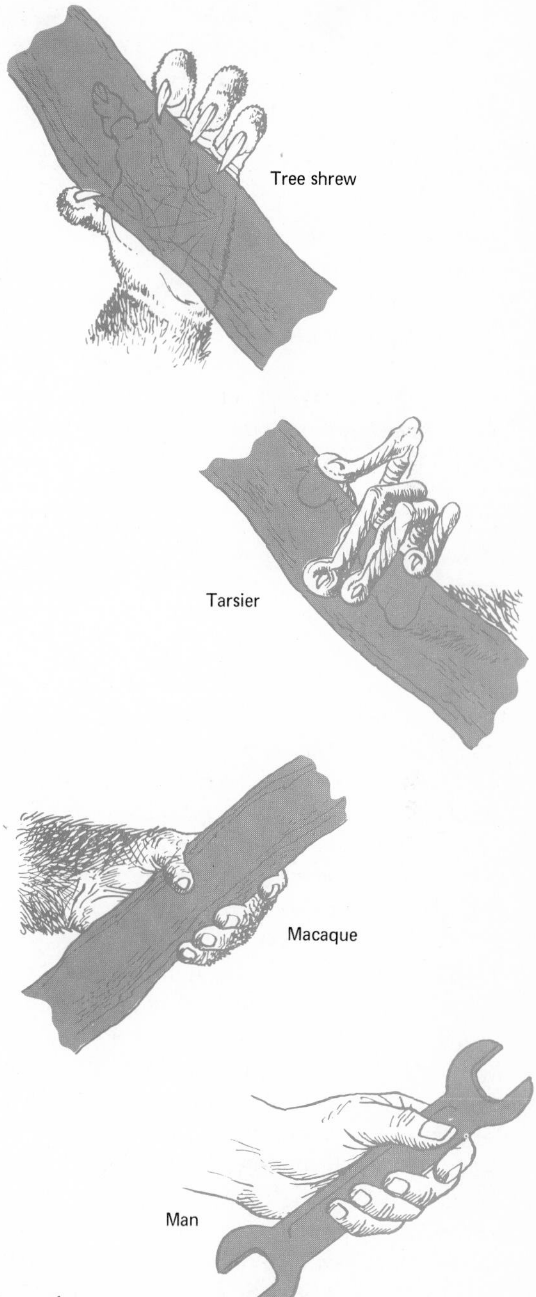

Figure 1
Comparison of primate grasps. The greater precision of the grip of the macaque (an Old World monkey) and man is due to the presence of nails instead of claws and a well-developed opposable thumb.

A tarsier's disk-like fingertips facilitate grasping onto tree trunks after long-distance leaps. Large eyes at the front of the head and large ears are adaptations for the tarsier's nocturnal and arboreal way of life. (UPI Photo.)

A New World spider monkey uses an arm, legs, and a prehensile tail to secure his grip completely. (Photo, Robert Hermes from National Audubon Society.)

They also resemble the higher primates in such features as the structure of the brain and the adaptation of limbs for grasping but differ from them in their longer snouts, larger and more mobile ears, and relatively fixed facial expression.

Tarsiers. Like the lemur, the three living species of tarsiers, found on the islands of southeastern Asia, are well equipped for night life in the trees, possessing enormous eyes and extraordinary vision. An elongated *tarsal,* or ankle bone, from which these animals get their name, gives them tremendous leverage for jumps, enabling the tarsiers to leap from one tree trunk to another, 6 to 10 feet away. The attention tarsiers give to their offspring might be an indication of their evolutionary relationship to monkeys and man.[4]

[4] John Buettner-Janusch, *Origins of Man* (New York: John Wiley & Sons, 1966), pp. 205–209.

The Higher Primates: Anthropoids

Man's closet primate relatives are the anthropoids. They share, in varying degrees, rounded brain cases, shrunken, nonmobile outer ears, and faces with alert and versatile expressions instead of muzzles. Anthropoids also show marked differences. Accordingly, they are classified as three separate superfamilies—New World monkeys (Ceboidea), Old World monkeys (Cercopithecoidea), and apes and man (Hominoidea).

New and Old World monkeys add up to some 150 arboreal and terrestrial species. This great variety is explained by the tendency of arboreal genuses to have a greater number of species than those that live on the ground. Living in trees often prevents members of groups from mating with monkeys from other groups: the widening of a stream or thinning out of a forest may make it impossible for monkeys, whose principal means of locomotion is jumping from

tree to tree, to go any further. Isolated, they eventually evolve into a new species adapted to their particular environment.

New World Monkeys. New World monkeys are broad-nosed *(platyrrhine),* whereas their Old World relatives are flat-nosed *(catarrhine).* New World monkeys are further distinguished by their predominantly arboreal habits and their tails, which in many species are prehensile—that is, adapted for grasping and wrapping around—and which allow them to hang and swing acrobatically from branches. The tail probably developed as a "third hand," not to further the joys of tree swinging, but as an adaptation of monkeys to living conditions in the large swampy areas of South America where they were confined to a life spent entirely in the trees. Man took a liking to certain New World monkeys, notably the capuchin, and took many of them out of their jungle homes to train them as pets.

Old World Monkeys. Old World monkeys, more our evolutionary kin than New World monkeys, are particularly like man in their versatility and adaptability to changing climates. The macaque monkeys, for example, can live in tropical jungles or snow-covered mountains. Unlike the New World monkeys, which are all tree-bound, the Old Worlders range from the magnificently maned, arboreal guereza monkey to the baboons who may inhabit rocky, open country. Some species have almost totally abandoned the trees.

Arboreal Monkeys. There are physical and behavioral differences among Old World monkeys. Among the subfamily that dwells in the trees and lives on leaves are the Asian langurs and the African colobus monkeys. Their stomachs, designed to obtain maximum nutrition from what seems like a nutritionally limited bill of fare, give them a competitive advantage over other monkeys, who turn their backs on a leaf diet.

The langurs of northern India live in stable hierarchical groups of from 5 to 120 monkeys, with territories extending over one-half to 5 square miles. Young langurs are raised within the group, where infants receive considerable care from females, and young monkeys have the company of other juveniles.[5]

Terrestrial Monkeys. The other subfamily is made up of monkeys like the macaques who are equally comfortable on the ground or in the trees. They are widely distributed and roam over Asia and Africa and are even found in Gibraltar. A type of macaque, the rhesus monkey, is favored by scientists for physiological and psychological research; when they refer to "the monkey" they usually mean this particular species. In India, where the Hindus believe that all life is sacred, it is not uncommon to

[5] Phyllis Jay, "The Common Langur of North India," in Irven DeVore, ed., *Primate Behavior* (New York: Holt, Rinehart and Winston, 1965), pp. 197–249.

find effigies of the monkey god, Hanuman, in the form of macaques, and these monkeys wander through the streets unhindered by the people.

Living on the ground, but in quite a different setting from the macaques of Asia, are the various baboons of Africa; they are of great interest to primatologists because they are found in the savannas of Africa, environments presumed to be like those inhabited by early men. Because they are terrestrial, they have a fairly varied diet—vegetables, seeds, flowers, grasses, insects, and lizards are the delicacies of the baboon community. Social hierarchies generally determine where each baboon will position itself within the troop, which may have as many as 100 members.[6]

Apes and Man: The Hominoidea. Man's closest cousins in the superfamily Hominoidea are the anthropoid apes. This superfamily is divided into two distinct families—the hominids, consisting of modern and extinct forms of man, and the pongids, consisting of modern and extinct anthropoid apes. The living pongids are the chimpanzees and gorillas of Africa, the orangutans of Borneo and Sumatra, and the gibbons and siamangs of southeastern Asia.

Movies and popular literature have not been kind to the apes. In Edgar Rice Burroughs's *Tarzan of the Apes,* the ape is depicted as a brutish monster swinging from the trees to descend upon helpless humans, as it thirsts for blood. *King Kong,* a movie of the '30s, still a popular rerun on television, is about a giant gorilla who turns into a ruthless destroyer in captivity. Brutish people are called "apes" and many people continue to think of apes as indiscriminate predators.

In fact, however, apes are generally nonaggressive animals. This has been observed by various investigators who have studied them under natural conditions. Among them are John T. Emlen, Jr., and George B. Schaller who were in the jungle studying gorillas when their subjects suddenly spotted them. Startled, the gorilla leaders began to pound their chests. "The females and even the juveniles took their turns at chest beating too; a display which suggested some sort of general annoyance rather than fear or threat." After the initial shock passed, the gorillas resumed their ordinary activities. "One by one they left the huddle; some fed, a female basked in a patch of sun, a juvenile playfully swung back and forth on a liana only 80 feet from our hiding place."[7]

Gibbons. Found in the jungles of southeastern Asia, gibbons are agile and small, about 3 feet tall, weighing under 25 pounds. They are spectacular brachiators, well adapted for swinging hand over hand through the trees by virtue of their slight bodies and elongated arms and fingers. Their powerful arms can propel them more than 30 feet in one swing forward. C. R. Carpenter's pioneering studies of the gibbons' behavior and social relations give us some idea of their agility. He writes:

> The buff female . . . swung quickly through an open tree and out on a limb. As she was preparing to swing into an adjacent tree, the limb broke, leaving a stub which was about six inches long. As the limb broke and fell the gibbon recovered by turning almost in mid-air and catching the remaining stub of the branch. With extreme rapidity she swung around under and then on top of the limb and then, with only a slight loss of time and momentum, jumped outward and downward 30 feet to an adjacent tree top.[8]

[6] W. E. Le Gros Clark, *History of the Primates: An Introduction to the Study of Fossil Man* (Chicago: The University of Chicago Press, 1965).

[7] J. T. Emlen, Jr., and G. Schaller, "In the Home of the Mountain Gorilla," in Charles H. Southwick, ed., *Primate Social Behavior: An Enduring Problem. Selected Readings* (Princeton: D. Van Nostrand, 1963), p. 125.

[8] C. R. Carpenter, "A Field Study in Siam of the Behavior and Social Relations of the Gibbons, Hylobates-lar," *Comparative Psychology Monographs,* Vol. 16, No. 15 (1940), pp. 1–212.

Carpenter has also observed that they live in small family groups consisting of an adult pair and one or two immature offspring. When offspring reach adulthood, they are driven from home. Unlike most primate species, which have a male dominance hierarchy, gibbons have little sex role differentiation. A lack of secondary sex differences is thought to be the explanation.[9]

Orangutans. Unlike gibbons, orangutans are clearly recognizable as male or female. Found only on the islands of Borneo and Sumatra, the males are 4 feet tall and the females usually half that size. The orangutan, dubbed "the man of the forest" because of its thoughtful appearance, is also capable of assuming other expressions. Agile lips twist many ways in what is believed to be a form of communication. Orangutans also have large air sacs connected to the larynx which can be blown up to emit belch-like noises. They are rapidly moving towards extinction because of man's encroachment on the wilderness and destruction of the species.

Gorillas. Much of what we know about the largest of the pongids, the gorilla, has been summed up in two books by George Schaller, *The Mountain Gorilla* and *The Year of the Gorilla,* written from observations he made in the dense tropical forests of western Uganda and eastern Congo. Gorillas are large, not only in comparison with other pongids, but even when compared to man. In its natural state, the adult male weighs up to 450 pounds and the female up to 250. (Those we see in zoos are generally fatter because of their sedentary life.) They travel primarily on the ground and on all fours, in a form of locomotion known as knuckle walking, but sleep in trees on nests that they prepare with great care. Though the gorillas' arms and legs are well suited for brachiation, their size makes arboreal locomotion impractical. Consequently, when they want to travel, they descend from the trees. Social and individual behavior varies among gorillas, so that it is difficult to generalize about the ways of these gentle giants of the forest. They lead quiet, peaceful lives, using their enormous strength mainly to tear apart the vegetation they eat. Without any real natural enemies, gorillas might thrive, were it not for the humans who hunt them down and take over their forest ranges.

"Maybe you're *descended from a lemur, but* I'm *not descended from* any *lemur!"* (Drawing by W. Miller; © 1972 The New Yorker Magazine, Inc.)

Chimpanzees. The findings of molecular genetics, blood chemistry, anatomy, and behavioral studies have shown that the chimpanzee is our nearest kin. Chimpanzees are versatile animals capable of being trained to do many things. They are excellent mimics of human mannerisms and expressions. Shown how to use paints, they have painted canvases that have been taken for works of the avant garde. In their natural state, chimpanzees behave in a way that is radically different from their behavior in captivity, but even there, they show similarities to man. Recent studies have noted gestures and postures similar to man's, arising out of behavioral situations common to both species.

[9] Carpenter, "A Field Study . . . ," in Southwick, pp. 17–23.

In mid-flight, a gibbon demonstrates brachiation, an adaptation which facilitates locomotion through the trees. (Photo by A. W. Ambler from National Audubon Society.)

A good part of our information about chimpanzees in the wild has come from recent studies made by Jane Goodall. Originally a technically untrained secretary to L. S. B. Leakey, she set up camp in the Gombe Stream Chimpanzee Reserve in Tanzania. With infinite patience, she sat waiting in the jungle for the animals to grow accustomed to her presence and was rewarded after many months as the chimpanzees gradually grew less fearful and allowed her to come close and observe them. She learned a great deal, not only about the behavior of chimpanzees but also about their similarities to human beings.[10]

[10] Jane van Lawick-Goodall, "My Life among the Chimpanzees," *National Geographic* (August 1963), and *In the Shadow of Man* (Boston: Houghton Mifflin, 1971).

Chimpanzees are arboreal and terrestrial. They spend many hours in the trees eating fruit but come down to earth when moving from one feeding ground to another. They also sleep in trees on nests they prepare anew each time they bed down. The whole process of finding a suitable sleeping location—usually a horizontal fork with several branches growing out, which they bend down so that the leafy ends rest across the foundation—takes only a few minutes. The chimpanzees hold the leaves in place with their feet and, as a final touch, place some leaves under their heads as pillows. Though they take pains to find and prepare places for comfortable nests, they make no effort to seek protection from the rain. In years of observing chimpanzee behavior, Jane Goodall has never seen chimpanzees attempting to make shelters or taking advantage of any natural ones.

When chimpanzees move more than 50 yards, they do it on the ground. Their manner of locomotion is a variation of quadrupedalism, called *knuckle walking.* To support the weight of their heavy, well-developed chests, the chimpanzees use their padded knuckles to propel themselves along the ground. Occasionally, they stand and walk upright. This usually happens when they are traveling through tall grass, peering at an unusual object, or searching for a companion.

Whether on twos or fours, chimpanzees spend a good part of their day in search of food. They are primarily vegetarians and *frugivores* (fruit eaters), supplementing their diet with leaves, bark, and pith. They will occasionally eat a lizard or a small rodent, and Jane Goodall has reported that they sometimes even kill large animals. On rare occasions, she has observed them sharing the meat of monkeys, bushbucks, and bush pigs. Her observations, however, may be peculiar to the chimpanzees of the Gombe Stream Reserve, where there is not an abundance of food. Unlike the chimpanzees of the Budongo Forest, who have an abundance of available fruit and have never been seen eating meat, the Gombe Reserve chimpanzees have been forced by their environment to expand their diet. The potential of these chimpanzees has been challenged to the extent that they occasionally kill other animals and use tools as a means to gain access to food.

Jane Goodall's report of tool use by chimpanzees has answered the question of whether nonhuman primates in the wild ever fashion natural objects into tools. She saw chimpanzees using a straw or a dried stem of grass to penetrate the sealed entrances to termite nests. When the straw was withdrawn, there were termites clinging to it, which the ape would remove and eat. The process was repeated many times. When the straw became too bent, the chimpanzee would break off the bent part,

A tool-using chimpanzee inserts a stick, stripped of leaves, into a termite nest. When the stick is removed, the chimpanzee licks off the termites which cling to it. (Photo by Baron Hugo van Lawick © National Geographic Society.)

retaining the rest. When the implement became too small, he would look for another, sometimes choosing a leafy twig which had to be stripped of its leaves before it could be used. By modifying a natural object and making it suitable for a specific purpose, the chimpanzee thus attained a crude beginning to tool making. They were also seen modifying leaves by chewing them until they were absorbent and then using the mass as a sponge to sop up rainwater that otherwise could not be reached with the lips.

Man has always been considered the only tool-making animal, but Goodall's discoveries about chimpanzees appear to call for a modification of the definition. Vast differences, however, do exist: so far, no chimpanzee has been observed using one tool to make another. Recognizing the distinction between types of tool use, she writes: "The point at which tool-using and tool-making, as such, acquire evolutionary significance is surely when an animal can adapt its ability to manipulate objects to a wide variety of purposes, and when it can use an object spontaneously to solve a brand-new problem that without the use of a tool would prove insoluble."[11] Chimpanzees also lack the ability that man has to add to the existing knowledge of inventions. Learning for chimpanzees is limited to specific situations; one invention does not lead into the creation of another.

Like tool making, language has been considered the exclusive province of humans. There is now evidence that this belief, also, may be only partially correct. Beatrice and R. Allen Gardner have trained a female chimpanzee named Washoe to communicate with extraordinary effectiveness by means of some 150 of the American Sign Language hand gestures. In the wild, chimpanzees gesticulate and shout at each other all the time; for this reason the Gardners believed that sign language would be a natural form of "language" to teach them. Washoe was raised isolated from other animals and constantly surrounded by familiar persons who communicated only in sign language when in her presence. Within one year she was able to associate gestures with specific activities. For example, if thirsty, Washoe would make the signal for "give me" followed by the one for "drink." As she learned, her instructions grew more detailed. If all she wanted was water, she would place her thumb in her mouth, fingers drawn into a fist, as the sign for "drink." But if she craved soda pop, as she did more and more, she prefaced the drink signal with the sweet signal—a quick touching of the tongue with her fingers.

The education of Washoe cannot be compared to teaching a dog to bark for a biscuit; it is a much more complicated and sophisticated form of two-way communication between a human and a nonhuman. One of Washoe's handlers was able to communicate to her in signs that a large dog was waiting to harm her. She became so agitated that her hair stood on end. There was no sign or scent of a dog and the handler's face displayed no fear, yet she was able to conceptualize and react to the danger. She believed her handler implicitly, so that when he asked if she would like to go outside to play, an activity she normally relished, she flatly refused. Primatologists are interested to learn whether Washoe will teach the sign language she has mastered to her future offspring. If so, will her young pass it on to their offspring? Anthropologists are eagerly awaiting the answer.

Among chimpanzees such as Washoe, the gorillas of the Budongo forest, orangutans, and the agile gibbons, several traits characteristic of the ape family can be identified. Larger brained than the prosimians and monkeys, the apes have greater conceptual abilities; thumb and fingers are more opposable; and brachiation is a well-developed ability.

[11] Goodall, *In the Shadow of Man,* p. 240.

PRIMATE SOCIAL BEHAVIOR

So far, our discussion of the living primates has focused on individual behaviors, but in their daily activities, primates often interact. The members of the Primate order, in fact, share many social behavioral traits.

Shared Social Behaviors

Each species lives in a group, which may vary in size from parents with offspring, as among gibbons, to macaque and baboon groups numbering hundreds, to humans who may live in communities of millions. To protect the group, baboons have a rigid hierarchy which deploys a powerful front and rear guard for defense when on the move. This form of social organization may be similar to that of man's ancestors. Although man and baboon did not take the same evolutionary path, they seem to have emerged from a similar environment, the dry African savanna.

Prolonged child care and immaturity is another common primate trait. Monkey infants remain close to their mothers for at least a year; gorilla and chimpanzee infants for three to four years. A study by A. Schultz has shown that child dependency increases from prosimian to monkey, ape, and man; as a result the learning period within the group has lengthened among the higher primates.[12] (To the degree, it might be added, that modern Western man may spend up to one-third of his life going to school as part of a prolonged period of adolescence.) During their long period of infant dependency, the higher primates spend much time playing, a behavioral adaptation which we will consider more closely later in the chapter. The higher primates are also notably alike in their manual display of friendship by touching and embracing.

"By Jove, it really looks as though they've started up the ladder!" (Drawing by Ed Fisher; © 1971 The New Yorker Magazine, Inc.)

Learning in the Group

In observing most animals, laymen tend to assume that all their actions are instinctive. With regard to most primates this belief is incorrect. Much of primate behavior is learned, and the most important means for the young to acquire learning is through the social group. Of course, offspring learn from their mothers, but living within a troop enables them to learn from the other members of the troop as well. The social life of monkeys and apes, and of man as well, makes it possible for all the learning that is necessary for survival to occur. Hans Kummer has identified social structure as an asset in coping with the environment. Primates live in "a type of society which through constant association of young and old and through a long life duration, exploits their large brains to produce adults of great experience."[13] To insure survival, members of the troop must work together.

Collective Wisdom. Mothers convey to their offspring their range of individual knowledge, while the group offers a broader range of collective wisdom. For example, Washburn and Hamburg tell of a baboon being shot from a moving car after which the other baboons in the troop would not approach any car, even though they had seen cars before and never been frightened. They write: ". . . it is very unlikely all animals in the group saw the shooting; the experience of some of the animals became part of the whole group's adaptive behavior."[14] The collective wisdom of the troop prevails in primate society, and it resides in its leaders. When a dominant baboon lets out a

[12] A. Schultz, "Postembryonic Age Changes," *Primatologia,* Vol. 1, pp. 887–964.

[13] Hans Kummer, *Primate Societies, Group Techniques on Ecological Adaption* (Chicago: Aldine-Atherton, 1971), p. 38.

[14] Sherwood L. Washburn and David A. Hamburg, "The Study of Primate Behavior," in DeVore, *Primate Behavior,* pp. 3–4.

warning cry and flees, the others follow, accepting the reaction of the leader as sufficient proof of impending danger.

Tradition. In most instances, learning is passed on from the old to the young. An experiment with Japanese macaques, however, offers another explanation of how revolutionary forms of learning, like the tool use of the Gombe Stream chimpanzee, came about. The macaques on the little island of Koshima, Japan, inhabit wooded, precipitous mountains surrounded by sandy beaches and the sea. They forage exclusively in the mountains and forests, never entering the water. As an experiment to reveal adaptive potential, the researchers began to feed them by throwing sweet potatoes onto the beach. One year after the feeding began, a two-year-old female was spotted taking a potato to a brook, where she washed it in one hand and brushed off sand with the other. The technique slowly spread throughout the group and today it is an established tradition.[15] The technique "invented" and instituted by a young female has since been passed on by many mothers to their offspring.

Male adults over the age of seven never learned the behavior; in fact it is practiced by only 18 percent of the females in this adult grouping. Those who acquired potato washing behavior did so, not by observing a distant group's culinary preparations, but only after feeding with an intimate companion. Because adult and young males live on the periphery of the group, while the central part is occupied by youngsters and mothers, they had few opportunities to feed with potato washers. It is also believed that the adult males are reluctant to acquire new behavior, tending to preserve juvenile behavior traits into adulthood.

Child Rearing. During infancy, offspring already play a crucial role in primate societies. Mothers enjoy a special status and, as Irven DeVore points out, babies appear to be the most important element binding the baboon troop together: "It is scarcely possible to overemphasize the significance of the new born baboon. It becomes the center of interest, absorbing the attention of the entire troop. From the moment the birth is discovered, the mother is continuously surrounded by the other baboons who walk beside her and sit as close as possible when she rests."[16] Though the mother is an infant's most formative influence, child rearing is essentially a group activity. Other baboons are drawn to the center of the troop where the mothers congregate and tend to the young, while adolescent females look on and learn by caring for and fondling tots similar to ones that they themselves will bear.

Males, too, are attracted to the new additions. Though male baboons are dominant and often oppressive toward females, they show special kindness in the early months after birth and are extremely patient with offspring. Occasionally, when the mother of a young chimpanzee dies, a male will assume a maternal role, catering to and protecting the orphan. A dramatic example of this kind of protective behavior has been observed in the Japanese macaque monkeys. During the birth season, high-ranking adult males adopt year-old infants; they clutch, carry, and protect them, and, except for suckling, behave like mothers.

The example of the maternal males notwithstanding, infant monkeys and apes are dependent on their mothers for long periods of time. Prolonged dependence offers an evolutionary advantage in that it allows infants more time to observe, note, and learn the complex behavior essential to survival, while enjoying the care and protection of a mature teacher. The chimpanzee's ability to manipulate objects as tools is probably innate, but the actual tool-

[15] Kummer, *Primate Societies*, pp. 117–130.

[16] Irven DeVore, quoted by John E. Pfeiffer, *The Emergence of Man* (New York: Harper & Row, 1969), p. 264.

Evolution

Long necks enable giraffes to reach the top branches of trees. Through natural selection, those animals with longer necks had a better chance of surviving and reproducing, thus transmitting their genes to offspring. (Courtesy of Wildlife Photographers and Bruce Coleman Inc.)

Mutations may be adaptive, but most are potentially or actually lethal. Due to a mutation, this albino deer is at a disadvantage in its environment. Without protective coloration it can be easily spotted by predators. (Courtesy of Richard C. Finke from National Audubon Society.)

The adult male proboscis monkey's long nose may have evolved because of sexual selection, that is, females may have favored those males with larger noses. (Courtesy of R. Van Nostrand from National Audubon Society.)

The baboon's ischial callosity, *toughened skin on the behind, is an adaptation which enables primates to sit and sleep comfortably and securely in the trees.* (Courtesy of Irven DeVore.)

This orangutan is a member of the primate suborder of anthropoid apes, which contains man's closest living relatives. Note the flattened nose and eyes in the front of the head, adaptations which reflect the relative importance of vision over smell among the primates. (Courtesy of David Agee Horr.)

For protection in open environments, baboons often move in troops. Here, the troop travels down a road, the dominant males bringing up the rear. A mother and child have stopped by the side of the road and another male stands by to protect them. (Courtesy of Irven DeVore.)

The trees provide these Old World monkeys with food, shelter, and safety. Many monkey species never leave the trees: some others exploit both the ground and the trees, and still others have become wholly terrestrial. (Courtesy of Marilyn Silverstone, Magnum Photos.)

Prolonged infant dependency, allowing for physical and social maturation, is a characteristic of all primates. This baby orangutan clings to its mother and will go with her everywhere. (Courtesy of Irven DeVore.)

Man has the longest period of infant dependency. Human babies learn about themselves and their environment while still protected by their mother. (Courtesy of Irven DeVore.)

using patterns are learned, often from the mother. Goodall cites an occasion when a female with diarrhea picked up a handful of leaves to wipe her bottom. Her two-year-old infant watched closely and then twice picked up leaves and wiped her own clean behind. During infancy, chimpanzees learn how to move through the trees and on the ground and awkwardly attempt the intricacies of nest preparation, taking their first shaky steps toward mastering their physical environment.

Primate mother and child are bound together by the slow maturation process of infants, but for the first few months they are literally inseparable. The infant is either nursing or being groomed, or it is clinging to the hairs of its mother's belly. The offspring's instinct and ability to cling to the mother, coupled with her knowledge of infant care, learned from earlier observations within the group, insure the closeness of the relationship. Both make good use of their firm grasping ability when the mother moves about, for she uses all her limbs as she climbs and swings through the trees in her daily food gathering, and the infant holds on to her literally for dear life.

Under normal conditions the mother watches over her infant. She offers psychological security as well as physical protection whenever the infant is threatened from within the group. The dominant males assume the responsibility of protecting infants from outside threats, though the mother is quick to scoop her child up at the first signs of trouble.

Knowledge of the primate behavior trait of prolonged infancy has fostered a number of significant experiments which also shed light on human behavior. Dr. Harry Harlow of the University of Wisconsin has experimented, for example, on rhesus monkeys to determine the effect of maternal neglect and isolation of offspring. He found that, as a result of either inadequate mothering or isolation from other infants, monkeys may suffer from an inability to lead a normal social life. They develop aberrant sexual activities and even manifest juvenile

The infant baboon, like all newborn primates, clings to its mother for protection and transportation. (Courtesy of Irven DeVore.)

delinquency. Harlow mated the socially deprived female monkeys with well-adjusted males. When these animals gave birth, their behavior was not at all motherly, and they often totally rejected their offspring. Their abnormal behavior was offered as proof that mothering is more than instinctive. These experiments underline the importance of maternal care and attention in monkeys and, as a corollary, in human beings. From this, it may be concluded that indulging or caring for an infant is a socializing process that has developed as an adaptation among animals whose survival depends on a considerable amount of learned behavior.

Primates at Play. Like human children, young chimpanzees spend most of their time at play. They have all the natural world as a playground, and there are always playmates at their disposal. They chase around tree trunks, leap among treetops, and playfully bite and kick each other in casual wrestling matches. This kind of play is extremely useful, since it teaches the youngsters how to cope with the environment. They learn to judge which branches can hold their weight and which cannot and practice the gymnastic skills needed to jump from a high branch to a lower one. Living in a world of natural jungle gyms and monkey bars, the young primates put them to valuable use.

Play is also involved in the process of socialization, establishing each chimp's place in the group's hierarchy. Playmates learn who is strong and who is weak, whose mother is higher ranking, which playmate will be intimidated by a bluff and which will fight—information essential to the structuring of chimpanzee society. As William A. Mason points out: "there have been no detailed studies of the importance of play in the socialization process, but field workers have expressed the conviction that experience gained in play facilitates the development of communicative skills and forms the foundation of adult social relationships."[17]

The group is constantly engaged in a wide range of activities observed by the young. In this way, young chimps learn which foods are edible and which to avoid; and they learn which animals are their enemies. The interaction of the group in its day-to-day activities presents a wide variety of problems for the adults to solve and opportunities for the youngsters to observe and imitate. It is a school for survival, but not their only one. If the young primates were to give up their play to stay near the adults, they would severely hinder their behavioral development. Prolonged dependence is an asset only insofar as it assures a firm foundation on which to develop the abilities needed to cope with their challenging natural environment.

The Group and Defense

Besides contributing to the socialization of the young and the stability of the group, the group provides protection. For monkeys on the ground, safety resides in numbers. The protective role of the group was observed by C. R. Carpenter, who saw a young howler, a South American monkey, which was isolated from its group, being attacked by an ocelot. The monkey's cries were promptly answered when three males in the group came to his defense.[18]

Because of the hierarchical structure of the baboon troop an incident like the above would be unlikely to occur. Dominant adult males accompany the females with small infants and slightly older infants in the group's center. The males are prepared to dart out of the troop and act in concert to drive away the enemy. John E. Pfeiffer describes how troop organization infuses every part of baboon life:

[17] William A. Mason, "The Social Development of Monkeys and Apes," in DeVore, *Primate Behavior,* p. 528.
[18] C. R. Carpenter, "A Field Study of the Behavior and Social Relations of Howler Monkeys," *Comparative Psychology Monographs,* Vol. 10 (1934), pp. 48–168.

Figure 2
The baboon troop organizes for defense when moving through the open savanna. Dominant males protect the mothers and infants in the center, while other adult males guard the front and rear. (Courtesy of Irven DeVore.)

The boldest troop members leave the trees first, adult males who are not at the top of the social hierarchy and juveniles corresponding roughly to older teenagers in a human group. They move rapidly in a beeline as if they know exactly where they are going, and they do not look back. Other older juveniles and adult females follow: next comes the central nucleus of the troop—mothers with their infants and the youngest juveniles and the most dominant and generally the biggest and oldest males. The back part of the troop is a mirror image of the front with more older juveniles and adult females following the nucleus group and more adult males bringing up the rear.[19]

Alone, baboons are vulnerable, but as a group working together they prove formidable opponents. Their readiness to fight is often enough to drive away a predator. Kummer tells of a leopard jumping from the undergrowth into a group of baboons gathered at the edge of a waterhole. The baboons sprang back, perhaps to assemble forces. Then they turned, barking loudly, and darted toward the enemy. Under this mass assault, the leopard chose to retreat. In another example of the baboons' group strength and courage, a baboon troop was threatened by wild dogs. The large adult males immediately placed themselves between the attackers and the troop. In such an encounter, it is not uncommon for a single male to kill or maim three or four large dogs before rejoining his troop.

Though baboons are well prepared to defend themselves against enemies, they prefer to avoid a confrontation. To this end they employ an alert system—bellowing as loudly as they possibly can to frighten away a predator. The more voices the better, especially if the troop should be spread out, resting or feeding.

The baboon way of life evolved to meet the demands of living in the African savanna. Man is presumed to have evolved in the same kind of environment; hence, baboon behavior may be indicative of the behavior of early humans.

[19] Pfeiffer, *The Emergence of Man,* p. 86.

The evolutionary transition from an arboreal to a terrestrial way of life accompanied a trend toward increased brain and body size, improved sight and hearing, and the formation of permanent troops. Tight group organization against hostile animals, such as the defense formation favored by baboons, was probably the means used by early man to protect himself from predators. In a society where life is a series of emergencies, individualism is risky and the necessity for social organization is clear. Communal living was not a social option for early man, as it is not for living primates; to protect the welfare of the individual, living in a group was probably an essential adaptation.

Maintaining Territory

As social as primates are within the group, so are they antisocial toward their neighbors. They stay in a more or less fixed area of a size that varies for each species, generally remaining aloof from other groups. A fixed territory also allows mothers to devote their full attention to the needs of the infant without the distractions and problems of relocation.

Primates that live in trees can find all the nourishment they need within easy reach. Perhaps for this reason, they generally occupy smaller territories than those of terrestrial primates. On the ground, resources tend to be clustered, with the clusters often far apart. Terrestrial primates like the baboons must therefore travel farther than tree-based monkeys and must occupy larger territories to obtain sustenance from day to day.

Keeping the Group Together

The Hierarchy. The troop hierarchy and the mother-child relationship are the binding forces of the primate group. The dominance hierarchy establishes the leader and the status of every member of the troop in a descending order. Such a structure prevents rivalry from destroying the troop's cohesiveness. The relationships are fixed and are constantly reinforced during all acts, from eating and grooming to nesting. For example, a female may be chased from a comfortable nest by a dominant male, and, when food is in short supply, dominant males take precedence, thereby insuring that in a famine, troop leaders will survive and procreate.

Besides conferring privileges of rank, the dominance hierarchy is an effective means for maintaining order within the troop. From the time they are old enough to play, primates establish their social status. The structure that develops through conflict in play is subsequently maintained by threat in the form of a variety of gestures. A mere stare by a dominant male is enough to halt a fight between two juveniles or make a misbehaving infant scream as sharply as if it were struck a blow. Threats rarely lead to harm, for the threatened individual makes gestures of appeasement to show his submissiveness. Jane Goodall tells of saving herself from an attack by fleeing from a usually gentle chimpanzee who feared humans. "After all," she explains, "the most submissive thing that a subordinate chimpanzee can do is remove himself from an aggressor's presence—in other words, to run away."[20]

Friendly Behavior. Primates threatened by dominant members of their own troop almost invariably submit and usually follow up their capitulation by inching up and carefully grooming them. Grooming is more than an attempt to remove parasites; it seems to be a gesture of friendship that serves to maintain peace and cohesion in primate societies. Initiation of a grooming session may be mutual, as when two chimpanzees approach each other;

[20] Goodall, *In the Shadow of Man,* p. 196.

A baboon, threatened by a dominant male, slinks off, avoiding a fight. (Courtesy of Irven De-Vore.)

or a chimpanzee may solicit grooming by standing with its head bowed, either facing or with its back to another. Grooming is more prevalent in societies in which dominant roles are significant. This may explain the comparative infrequency of grooming among the less-regimented gorillas. Grooming among adult gorillas is primarily hygienic, concentrating on those areas the animal cannot reach itself.

When chimpanzees meet, they may groom, as has been observed in reunions between mothers and temporarily lost children; or they may react very demonstratively, hugging and kissing as they jump around together. Like many other kinds of chimpanzee behavior, the form of greeting often serves to reinforce the dominance hierarchy.

Another physical action, touching, plays an important part in chimpanzee behavior. Jane Goodall believes it is the means by which chimps reassure each other that everything is all right. Many of their communicatory gestures resemble ours: when a chimpanzee is frightened he frequently reaches out to touch or embrace a chimpanzee nearby. Like humans, chimpanzees seem reassured in times of stress by physical contact with another individual. Just as a human child cries and tugs at its mother's dress until picked up and consoled, so a chimpanzee infant whines and pulls at its mother, asking to be touched and comforted.

The Role of Sex. Sexual behavior was, until recently, believed to be more important than either the dominance hierarchy or mother-child realtionships in maintaining group cohesion. This has been disproved by research, including the observation that the troop structure remains unified even in the off-seasons of species with seasonal mating. For most of her life the female is of no sexual interest to the male, yet she is social; sexually active males are far more likely to leave the group than are the inactive females. We may conclude from this that although sex does play some part in maintaining the social structure, especially during pregnancy and lactation, evidently it does not have the cohesive power once ascribed to it.[21]

Whatever the role of sex, male and female

[21] Campbell, *Human Evolution,* p. 275.

When baboons groom one another it is more than a cleaning process. Grooming also reinforces the group's hierarchy and fosters social cohesion. (Courtesy of Irven DeVore.)

relationships are fundamental to all primates. In general, the primate male is more aggressive and dominant than the female. Though there is a definite division of roles in nonhuman primates, it is not as emphasized as in human societies, probably because in the latter there is more sexual division of labor in food getting. (In Chapter 6, we will consider the origins of this behavior.) Moreover, among primates, there is not always a one-to-one relationship. The patas monkeys band together in groups of one male and up to twelve females, and the most dominant female assists the male in maintaining order. In baboon society, however, the most dominant female is inferior to the least dominant adult male.

DISTINCTIVE HUMAN TRAITS

Despite the many anatomical and behavioral traits shared by man and the other primates, humans possess several characteristics found in no other species. It is probable that many of these traits are in some way linked to the emergence of the most distinctive of all human traits—culture.

Anatomical Differences

A number of important anatomical differences distinguish man from the other living primates.

Man is bipedal, that is, he walks erect, on two legs. Chimpanzees and gorillas walk on two legs some of the time but can hold themselves erect only when sitting or standing still. A dish-shaped pelvis, peculiar to humans, straight lower limbs, and a heeled, arched foot are related to man's bipedalism. In Chapter 6 we will consider the effects bipedalism may have had on such diverse traits as tool making, prolonged infant dependency, and sexual division of labor.

Although most primates have opposable thumbs, enabling them to grasp and examine objects, the greater length and flexibility of the human thumb makes it possible for man to handle objects with firmness and precision. In addition, man, unlike monkeys and apes, is able to carry objects without impairing his efficiency in locomotion because he is a fully bipedal walker and runner. This trait no doubt proved highly advantageous to early man when he began to hunt, carry, and possibly share food.

Human teeth are smaller than those of other primates, the result of several adaptations. Unlike other primates who have a space in the upper jaw which accommodates large lower canines, man, with his small canines, lacks a space. The dental arch and palate were also reduced, as was the jaw. In Chapter 5 we will consider several explanations for the smallness of human canines. Human jaws, unlike the jaws of other primates, flare outward at the molars. This trait has proved to be of great significance in identifying fossils as human-like or ape-like. The human jaw is a smaller, more delicate feature, with lighter bones and smaller muscles. Furthermore, the bony crests and ridges over the eyes and on the top and back of the skull, so prominent in apes and early hominids, virtually disappeared in modern man.

The human brain, particularly the cerebral cortex, is relatively much larger than that of other primates, an adaptation associated with complex tool making and the development of human culture.

Human females are capable of sexual receptivity at all times, as distinct from other primates, who are receptive only when they are in the *estrus* period, "in heat." Triggered by sex hormone secretions, estrus produces an uncontrollable sex urge and subsequent disruption in some primate groups. Its disappearance in human evolution made possible greater selectivity in mating, and the development of more emotional, individual sex relationships. This tendency was probably furthered by the development of face-to-face intercourse, another distinctively human trait.

Furthermore, man is practically hairless. Hairlessness may be an adaptation to hunting: a hairless body can rid itself of excess heat better than a fur-bearing body.

Behavioral Differences

Unlike other primates, man does not have a fixed dominance hierarchy. Weapons not only make it possible for individuals to protect themselves, they also make it impossible for any one person to establish dominance solely on the basis of physical characteristics.

Man is the only primate who possesses language—a trait which makes possible the transmission of an increasingly complex culture. Learning is also facilitated by a prolonged period of infant dependency—proportionately longer in man than in any other primate. Various other traits set man apart. His omnivorous eating habits—his taste for meats as well as vegetation—had a significant effect on the evolution of culture. Early man began to travel longer distances than other primates in search of food. The hunt influenced both technology and social organization. Like tool making, it favored the development, through natural selection, of an intelligence adapted for the storing and coordination of information: the hunter needed to remember facts about the habits of game as they varied with seasonal changes. Hunting also favored the development of sexual division of labor and food sharing. Women, who cared for children, probably remained at the home base to gather vegetation. When the bearer of food brought back more than enough for one person, the rest could be shared. Among nonhuman primates, each forages for himself after infancy. We shall consider the social consequences of human sexual division of labor in Chapter 6.

Human sleeping habits also distinguish us from the other primates. We don't sleep in trees. Perhaps our ancestors lost their perches when the forests receded, or cultural advances, in the form of weapons or fire, may have eliminated the necessity to seek nightly refuge in the trees.

Having examined man's uniqueness and the traits he has in common with the other primates, we need to determine why these traits were adaptive and what circumstances may have favored the evolution of culture in the one line of primates leading to man. The study of specifically human evolution to which we now turn will help to answer these questions.

SUMMARY

1. Although none of the living primates is a direct ancestor of man, we do share a common evolutionary history. Primate and prehuman fossils provide evidence for the pattern of man's physical evolution, and, by studying the behavior of our closest living relatives, it is possible to make inferences about man's social evolution. Studying the living primates also helps us to isolate the truly unique human physical and behavorial traits.

2. The prosimians—tree shrews, tarsiers, and lemurs—are the evolutionary antecedents of the higher primates, the anthropoids—monkeys, apes, and man. Although much lower on the evolutionary scale, prosimians have typical primate traits: grasping hands, stereoscopic vision, ability to hold the torso erect, and a small litter size with an extended period of infant dependency.

3. The anthropoids are subdivided into the New World monkeys, Old World monkeys, apes, and man. The higher primates all have hands, well adapted for grasping; stereoscopic and color vision; single births; rounded skulls; small ears set close to the skull; and mobile faces. New World monkeys are totally arboreal, unlike Old World monkeys, who are also adapted for ground living.

4. Among Old World monkeys, who adapted to a wide range of environments, there is a great diversity of anatomy and behavior. Baboons, though physically remote from man, are particularly worth studying. Their closely knit social structure, developed in a grassland habitat probably similar to that occupied by early man, may shed some light on early man's behavior patterns.

5. The anthropoid apes include the gorilla, chimpanzee, orangutan, gibbon, and siamang.

6. The gorilla, though by far the largest anthropoid, is a gentle, nonaggressive

vegetarian. Their great appetites keep groups small and widely dispersed in most ranges.

7. The chimpanzee is our nearest relative (having remarkably similar blood chemistry and molecular genetics, as well as anatomical and behavioral similarities). Chimpanzees do most of their foraging in the trees but are also adapted to the ground. They have been known to eat meat in severely overcrowded areas where vegetation is sparse. Wild chimps have also been seen to create and use tools, modifying a natural object to fulfill a specific purpose. High conceptual ability is also demonstrated by the chimpanzee's ability to learn sign language. Washoe, a chimp raised in isolation, has been taught to use 150 sign gestures of the American Sign Language to communicate with her human teachers.

8. Primates share many social behavioral traits including group living. The group is an adaptation for defense and learning. Immature primates can learn about their environment while still protected by adult group members.

9. The differences between man and the other anthropoids show us what makes man distinctive as a species. Man is totally bipedal, walking on two legs with the arms unneeded for locomotion. Man has a relatively hairless body with a more delicate bone structure, particularly in the facial area. Human females have no estrus period and the offspring have a proportionately longer dependency period.

SUGGESTED READINGS

DeVore, I. (Ed.): *Primate Behavior: Field Studies of Monkeys and Apes* (New York: Holt, Rinehart and Winston, 1965).
An important collection of fieldwork reports, covering the ecology and social behavior of major primate groups.

Itō, Y.: "Groups and Family Bonds in Animals in Relation to Their Habitat." In L. R. Aronson et al. (Eds.), *Development and Evolution of Behavior* (San Francisco: W. A. Freeman, 1970).
This article is about the dominance hierarchy in animals (popularly identified as the pecking order) and focuses on primates and integration by means of aggression. The numerical relation of males to females in various primate species is also considered in relation to social behavior.

Jay, P. (Ed.): *Primates: Studies in Adaptation and Variability* (New York: Holt, Rinehart and Winston, 1968).
A follow-up to DeVore's *Primate Behavior.*

Jolly, A.: *The Evolution of Primate Behavior* (New York: Macmillan, 1972).
An excellent and up-to-date discussion of primate behavior and its relevance to human behavior.

Kummer, H.: *Primate Societies* (Chicago: Aldine-Atherton, 1971).
An excellent examination of the social behavior of primate groups as an evolutionary adaptation for species survival. Readable and interesting, with comments on the analogies that can be drawn between human and primate social organization.

Montagu, A.: *Touching: The Human Significance of the Skin* (New York: Columbia University Press, 1971).
The subject of the book is tactile behavior; both pre- and postnatal experiences are covered and comparisons are made with nonhuman primates and other animals. Certain modes of child care to produce healthy personalities are advocated with a wide range of references from zoology, primatology, and medical and nursing science.

Schaller, G.: *The Mountain Gorilla* (Chicago: University of Chicago Press, 1963).
The first decent definitive field study of the gorilla.

5

Primate Evolution: From Early Primates to Hominids

THE RISE OF THE PRIMATES

The earliest primates, whose modern representatives are the prosimians, first appeared in the world at the beginning of the Paleocene epoch, about 64 million years ago. They were successful from that time through the Eocene epoch, up to about 38 million years ago, after which their numbers declined as the tropical forests of the world began to dwindle. Fossil evidence indicates that the prosimians evolved from small, rat-sized insectivores vaguely resembling modern tree shrews and lemurs—little, long-snouted, clawed creatures with eyes on the sides of their heads. Such animals, like other mammals, had an acute sense of smell, a characteristic that would diminish in later-evolving members of the Primate order.

The Environment

During the Paleocene, the earth went through a gradual but great upheaval. It was periodically shaken by earthquakes and volcanic eruptions. Seas that had blanketed the earth for 100 million years slowly retreated, exposing large land masses. New mountains were forming. Gradually the land dried and the swamps where dinosaurs lived began to disappear. Not adapted to the changing environment, the dinosaurs gradually became extinct over an estimated 5 million years. Eventually, in place of fetid swamps, extended areas of tropical and subtropical forests appeared from Seattle and Vancouver to southern Argentina and Chile; from London to Capetown; and from Japan to southern Australia.

The great stretches of forest offered new econiches to the evolving primates. *Econiches,* or ecological niches, are different parts of the same habitat (like a forest) that provide different resources and opportunities for adaptation. The adaptations which gradually evolved in response to tree living over 60 million years ago would have enormous consequences for further primate evolution.

Adapting to the Trees

In the trees, the early primates constantly risked injury or death from a fall. The shaky arboreal environment favored the development of new skills for locomotion and food gathering. Climbing and leaping from branch to branch required not only agility, but the ability to judge distances. Over the years, mutations that enabled the early primates to survive in the trees were perpetuated by natural selection. Thus, in time, new generations were born equipped in various ways to live in the trees.

Natural selection favored a number of changes in locomotion. Some early primates developed short forelimbs and long hindlimbs that could be used for grasping branches and tree trunks. The lemurs' ability to leap and run and the spectacular jumping prowess of the tarsiers gradually evolved. Claws, which could hinder mobility by catching in branches or penetrating the skin on the animal's palm when a branch was grasped, evolved into nailed digits, enabling the animals to get a firm grip on branches and to scurry through the trees with increased competence.

The early primates had elongated digits, and these became increasingly flexible and capable, making it possible for the animal to pick up objects and bring them closer for examination, instead of sniffing them to determine their worth, which many mammals still do. The gradual evolution of the ability to handle objects, a trait probably not possessed by terrestrial animals at the time, was an extremely important step in primate evolution, ultimately resulting in the ability to make tools.

Good eyesight was also essential in the arboreal environment, and through natural selection, eyesight improved in conjunction with improving arboreal locomotion. In time, eyes appeared closer to the front of the head instead of at the sides. With the shift in location of the eyes came a decrease in the size of the snout; the sense of smell, so vital on land for identifying unseen objects, became of lesser importance in many lineages of the evolving primates.

The primates probably evolved from a creature like this tree shrew who has claws rather than nailed fingers, a long snout, and eyes on the side of the head. (Photo, A. W. Ambler from National Audubon Society.)

Geologic Time

The accompanying chart represents the geologic time scale. Geologic time is the time that has elapsed since the formation of the earth, estimated at 4 billion years ago. To enable us to comprehend such an enormous span, geologists have divided time into a series of blocks. The largest time unit, the *era,* is subdivided into *epochs* of varying lengths. We are living in the Cenozoic era, which has been divided into the epochs listed on the chart.

Before the start of the Cenozoic, some 65 million years ago, the extinction of the dinosaurs had opened new environments for warm-blooded mammals and flowering plants. The tropical to subtropical climate of the Paleocene epoch changed to warm temperate during the Oligocene, with a temperature range similar to that of the southeastern United States. Thereafter, temperatures grew increasingly cool, culminating in glacial periods during the Pleistocene epoch. Human ancestors evolved primarily during the Miocene, Pliocene, and Pleistocene, with modern man emerging only about 30,000 years ago.

Chart 1
Cenozoic Era

EPOCHS	Starting Date (in millions of years)	Stages in Primate Evolution
Paleocene	65	Early primates radiate
Eocene	54	Maximum radiation of lemurs and tarsiers
Oligocene	35	Appearance of monkeys and apes
Miocene	30-25	Rise of the hominids: *Ramapithecus*
Pliocene	6	Hominid evolution: *Australopithecus*
Pleistocene	2.5	*Homo erectus* and *Homo sapiens*
Holocene (Recent)	10,000	

W. A. Berggren, "Tertiary Boundaries and Correlations," in B. F. Funnel and W. R. Riedel, eds., *Micropaleontology of the Ocean* (Cambridge: Cambridge University Press, 1971), pp. 693-809, p. 774.

FROM EARLY PRIMATES TO MONKEYS AND APES

The early lemurs and tarsiers thrived until about 35 million years ago, when they began to decline rapidly probably because the formerly extensive tropical forests were dwindling. As the number of tropical forest econiches decreased, other econiches opened up that favored the evolution of horses and elephants, along with other open-country mammals. Those primates that developed into monkeys and apes were probably favored by the new econiches as well.

As compared with the preceding lemurs and tarsiers, the monkeys and apes that evolved during the Oligocene[1] show a number of evolutionary changes that have implications for the

[1] David Pilbeam, *The Ascent of Man* (New York: Macmillan, 1972), p. 220.

subsequent emergence of man. There was a gradual shift of the eyes from the sides of the head to the front. The frontal position of the eyes permitted the field of vision of each eye to overlap somewhat. Thus, each eye would view an object from a slightly different angle. The result of such stereoscopic vision is depth perception.

Some living prosimians have stereoscopic and color vision, whereas experimental evidence indicates that *all* living anthropoids—New World monkeys, Old World monkeys, apes, and men—have both traits. The nocturnal tarsier, a prosimian, has stereoscopic vision but lacks color vision—surely no handicap, considering the nighttime habits of these animals. From such evidence, it is inferred that the ability to see in color and depth gradually evolved in the monkeys and apes.[2] As sight became more important than the sense of smell, the prosimian snout and dog-like muzzle

[2] John Buettner-Janusch, *Origins of Man: Physical Anthropology* (New York: John Wiley & Sons, 1966), p. 330.

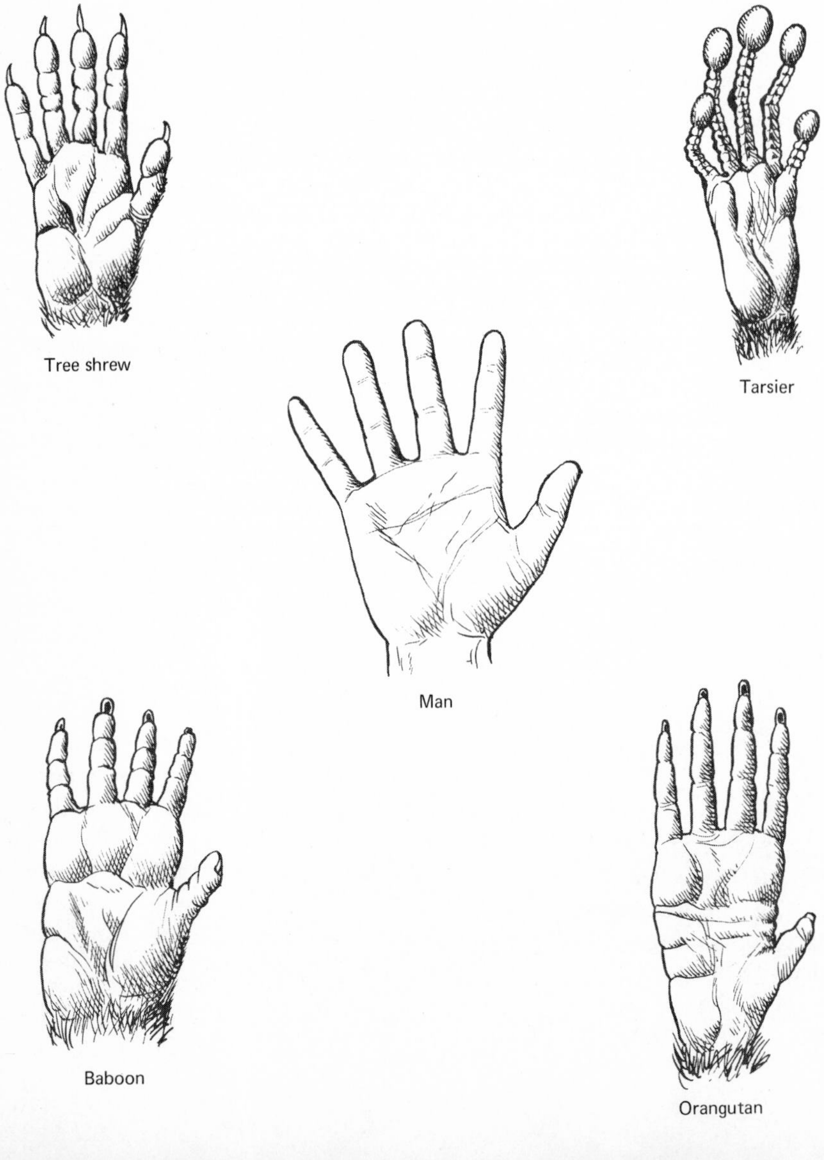

Figure 1
The evolution of primate hands included a shift from claws (retained by the modern tree shrew) to nails. The thumb became increasingly opposable, and the fingers more flexible. Lengthened fingers and palm are adaptations of the brachiating orangutan; a short thumb stays out of the way as the ape swings from branch to branch.

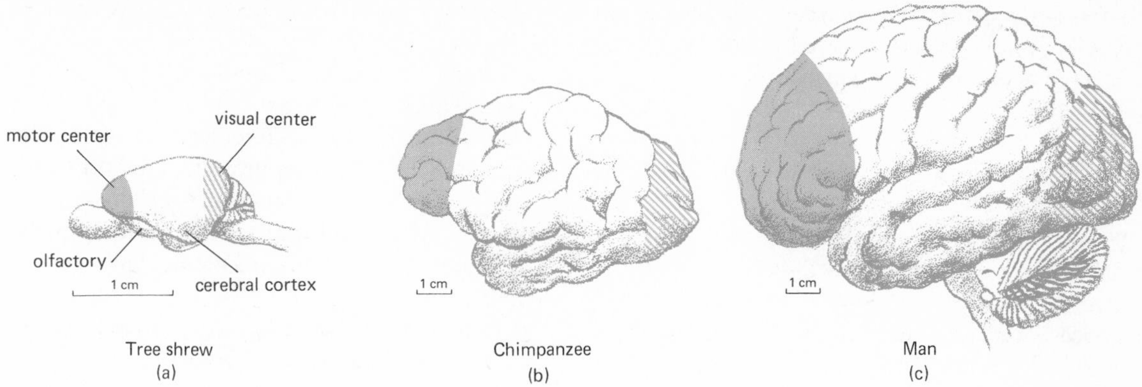

Figure 2
A comparison of primate brains. The visual center is relatively large in all primates. The motor area increases in the higher primates, and the olfactory lobe (sense of smell) decreases in relative size. The cerebral cortex became increasingly complex, as indicated by the convoluted folds. (Adapted from John Buettner-Janusch, *Origins of Man.*)

evolved into the flatter features characteristic of the monkeys and apes. And as the part of the brain that controlled sight grew larger, the area of the brain devoted to smell became relatively smaller.

Change also occurred in the formation of the teeth, presumably as a result of new dietary adaptations. The premolars developed one additional cusp, or point, on the chewing surface, and second incisors grew smaller. Molars, with their large surfaces, were already well adapted for grinding seeds and plant fibers.

Numerous adaptations had transformed the monkeys and apes into more complex animals than prosimians, with more complicated social systems. In Old World monkeys, for example, we can see tendencies for social characteristics that reached full development in man. Their life spans are longer than those of most mammals and they mature more slowly, with a longer period of infant dependency. Extended care and handling by the mother is an evolutionary advantage because the young primate can learn while still protected by a parent.

In sum, the early primates' move to the trees started a chain of evolutionary alterations through natural selection which continued over millions of years. As some of the early primates evolved into monkeys and apes, perhaps as a function of the appearance of grasslands between the forests, eyesight became more important than the sense of smell, the snout diminished, and the shape of the head became more rounded. Evolutionary changes in the hands may have facilitated new ways of locomotion and food gathering, as well as the acquisition of other new skills. Social learning probably became increasingly important for survival, setting the stage for the later emergence of human culture.

INTERPRETING THE FOSSIL RECORD

How can anyone speak about what happened millions of years ago? How do we know how the monkeys and apes differed from the prosimians? Needless to say, there is no written record of that period from which to draw the inferences that we have described. But we do have another kind of evidence for primate evolution—fossils.

What Fossils Can Tell

Fossils are the remnants or impressions of creatures that inhabited the earth millions of years ago. In the light of today's crowded dentists' offices, it may be surprising to find that the parts of the primate body most likely to be preserved are teeth. Much of the evidence for human evolution comes from teeth, which along with certain bones, are the most durable parts of the body. Dentition provides clues to evolutionary relationships, the relative sizes of animals, and, possibly, their diets. From the structure of the teeth and our knowledge of living animals, we can infer whether animals in the past were meat eaters or vegetarians. Paleontologists can infer an animal's posture and means of locomotion from unearthed limb bones and parts of the vertebral column. They can judge whether the animal was a brachiator, if it walked on all fours, or upright, or both ways.

Fossils also provide evidence about soft tissues. The form and size of muscles can be estimated by marks found on bones to which they were attached. Information about the brain and spinal cord has been inferred from imprints on the insides of skulls. From such evidence, scientists are able to surmise the relative degree of brain evolution.[3] Tunnels or grooves made by arteries on skeletel remains may indicate their relative size, from which their functions might be inferred.

By studying several fossils located at different levels in the *same* rock deposits, we can chart the various modifications of a species extending over millions of years. We can also determine approximately when a new species appeared.

Piecing together the fossil record is no easy task. The human pelvis, for example, underwent considerable evolutionary change as our ancestors became fully upright creatures, but many of the pelvic bones of our distant ancestors are still missing. The paleontologist must not only find specimens and put them in their proper order, but he must infer the course of development during geological periods from which we have few or no fossils.

Dating Fossils

Fossils alone would be insufficient as evidence without some means for determining their age and the era or epoch in which the animal lived. In dating fossils, two kinds of time are considered: an absolute point in time, such as 10,000 B.C., and a relative time—that is, identification of a fossil as younger or older than something else.

A number of methods can be used to judge the age of fossils. Some are useful only up to 10,000 years ago and are used to date artifacts found only in certain locations or confined to dating only certain materials, for instance, wood. In later chapters, several of these limited methods will be discussed more fully. Here we describe three major means for dating more ancient finds.

Potassium-argon. One frequently used method of estimating the age of a fossil is *potassium-argon dating.* This method suggests an *absolute* age but can be used only when potassium, such as volcanic ash, occurs in the rocks associated with the fossil. A radioactive form of postassium decays at an established rate and forms argon. Since the rate of disintegration is known, it is possible to determine the original animal's time of death by gauging the ratio of the potassium to argon. This method has been

[3] Bernard G. Campbell, *Human Evolution: An Introduction to Man's Adpatations* (Chicago: Aldine, 1966), p. 2.

used to date Miocene remains. Beds containing these fossils have been dated back 14.9 million years. Potassium-argon dating is far more accurate than the two relative methods described below.[4]

Relative Stratigraphy. One of the methods used to assess the *relative* age of a fossil, stratigraphy, analyzes geological layers, or *strata.* It is based on the knowledge that the lowest strata are generally the oldest (some strata may have been reversed by unusual movements of the earth's crust), and that a certain amount of sedimentation may accumulate within a specific period of time. By calculating the rate at which sedimentation accumulates and then determining the width of a stratum of rock, the age of the stratum can be estimated. The layers of rock in a region and their relationship to geological time are then recorded on a chart, or master key. After identifying the period represented by a layer, the investigator can determine the relative ages of its rocks and fossils and place them within the context of evolution. This form of measurement is crude, however, since different sediments build up at different rates of speed in different locations.

Associated Fauna. Another means used to estimate *relative* dates for strata in the earth, and hence for fossils found in them, is the evaluation of *associated fauna.*

In this method, bones and other fossil remains are studied in relation to what is known about the habitats of living species. Thus, it is assumed that extinct animals resembling the reindeer and cave bear flourished during the cold periods of prehistory, and animals like elephants and hippopotami, in warm periods. Because such organisms as mollusks, birds, and rodents are known to be extremely sensitive to climate change, fossils of similar organisms have been studied for what they can tell us about climate changes in the area of an archaeological site. This enables us to estimate when changes in climate occurred, changes that may have caused migrations or the extinction of a species that we can link to the chronology of human evolution.

Oligocene and Pliocene fossils have been dated by this method in the following manner. First, the bed in which each fossil was found is dated by its stone, mineral, and faunal content relative to a geologic time period; then this bed is cross-dated with another bed of similar age, absolutely dated. In this way, absolute dates are found for the bed under study and its fossils. For example, a fossil was found in an East African bed whose faunal content indicated that it was an Oligocene stratum. The stratum was similar to an Oligocene stratum in Wyoming dated to 20 million years ago; hence it was assumed that the African fossil was about 20 million years old. *Oreopithecus,* for instance, which may have been an early hominid, has been dated in this way to the Miocene, about 14 million years ago.

Early Primate Fossils

The fossil evidence that we have of the ancestral primates indicates that many of the varieties were similar to the tree shrews, tarsiers, and lemurs—prosimians that survive today. Monkeys and apes currently far outnumber the existing prosimians. The larger, smarter, better-coordinated monkeys and apes became the forerunners of man, surpassing the prosimians in the development of traits passed on to *Homo sapiens.*

Our information about early primates is meager. Fossils of those animals are scarce for a number of reasons: the further back in time we investigate, the less evidence is available;

[4] Garniss Curtis, "A Clock for the Ages: Potassium-Argon," *National Geographic* (October 1961), pp. 590–592.

Chart 2
Evolution of the Primates

Geologic Time	Environment	The Fossil Record and Evolutionary Changes
Paleocene starting 65 million years B.P.*	Tropical, subtropical, and warm temperate climates; uplift of land caused gradual drainage and drying of swamps and seas and expansion in new land areas of tropical and subtropical forest belts. Archaic mammals dominate, including early primates. At end of the Paleocene, evolution of primitive rabbits, armadillos, insectivores. Reptiles, birds, and mollusks present throughout.	EARLY PRIMATES Evolution of arboreal living: appearance of nails and other features adapted to living in the trees. Brain still very small. No stereoscopic vision yet.
Eocene starting 54 million years B.P.	Tropical, subtropical, and warm temperate climates with cooling trend toward end of Eocene; tropical and subtropical forest belts. Evolution of bats, ground sloths, early horses *(Eohippus),* early elephants (mastodons), camels.	LEMURS and TARSIERS Increased sophistication of arboreal adaptation: appearance of some forms with stereoscopic vision, reduced snout, grasping thumbs and big toes.
Oligocene starting 35 million years B.P.	Subtropical and warm temperate climates with cooling trend; great forest belts but expanding grasslands. Establishment of families of modern mammals: cats, dogs, raccoons, weasels, deer, antelope, bison, sheep.	OLD WORLD MONKEYS and APES *Oligopithecus* *Propliopitheus* *Parapitheus* These new primates include the direct ancestors of later monkeys and apes. Improved stereoscopic vision. Increase in relative brain size, especially visual area.
Miocene starting 30-25 million years B.P.	Warm temperate and cool temperate climates with cooling trend; relict tropical rain forests with increasing savannas. Archaic mammals disappear.	MONKEYS, APES, and HOMINIDS *Dryopithecus* *Pliopithecus* *Ramapithecus* During the Miocene, an extremely long period, the apes flourish and the hominids begin to develop (*Ramapithecus* appears sometime between 20 and 15 million years ago). As the forests dwindle, apes become rare, and the new open-country habitats are populated by hominids and many lineages of monkeys. Increase in brain size, especially cerebral cortex, visual, and motor control areas. Appearance of the opposable thumb and increased complexity of hand coordination.

W. A. Berggren, "Tertiary Boundaries and Correlations," in B. F. Funnel and W. R. Riedel, eds., *Micropaleontology of the Ocean* (Cambridge: Cambridge University Press, 1971), pp. 693-809, p. 774.

F. Clark Howell, *Early Man,* Life Nature Library (New York: Time-Life, 1965).

David Pilbeam, *The Ascent of Man* (New York: Macmillan, 1972).

*B.P. is an abbreviation for "before present."

the early primates resided in areas unfavorable for fossil preservation; they were small, and small bones and teeth are harder to locate than large ones.

Fossil Links to Old World Monkeys and Apes

Although it took perhaps 30 million years for monkeys and apes to emerge from prosimian ancestors, we have few fossils to document the evolutionary changes during this enormous time span.

Note that the New World monkeys of Central and South America split from the prosimian line farther back in time and are therefore not considered as closely related to man as Old World monkeys. New World monkeys evolved independently and had no role in human evolution. When we speak of monkey fossils, then, we are referring to Old World monkeys.

Many ancient primate fossils have been unearthed in the Fayum Depression, now wasteland on the northeastern border of the Sahara Desert. It is part of a region of the earth, stretching from the Egyptian coast of the Mediterranean to the city of Cairo, that is the richest known fossil depository for early Old World monkeys and apes. Lush, tropical forests and savannas once occupied the land surface that is now desert. Rivers flowing to the sea cut across the forests, carrying the bodies of dead animals which remained buried in layers of sand. The fossils stayed buried until an upsurge of lava cracked the earth's crust, forming folds and cliffs resembling a dimple or depression.

The abundance of fossils in this area was largely untapped until recent times. From the turn of the century to 1960 only a handful of primate remains were discovered, but since 1960 more than 200 specimens have been found on digs led by Elwyn Simons of Yale University. A member of the Simons expedition, Donald E. Savage of the University of California at Berkeley, discovered a part of a lower jaw in 1961. Since the deposits from the Fayum Depression come from the Oligocene epoch, dating from about 30 million years ago, Simons named the new primate genus represented by the jaw, *Oligopithecus.* (The suffix *pithecus* means "ape.") Its height, estimated from the size of the jawbone and teeth, was judged as no more than 12 inches. *Oligopithecus* is believed to be closely related to the evolutionary line from which living Old World monkeys developed.

When paleontologists make discoveries of small, sometimes miniscule, fragments, they must think like detectives to realize the significance of the find. They must in a positive sense be able to make mountains out of mole hills. Thus, only a fragment of a jaw was needed to distinguish *Oligopithecus* from previous finds. Most prosimians and New World monkeys have 34 or more teeth, while Old World monkeys, apes, and humans have 32. *Oligopithecus* is exceptional because it is the oldest known primate to have 32 teeth.

Importance of Teeth and Jaws. Only a piece of a jaw is sufficient to determine the number of teeth, because of the way the mouth is divided. Animals with 32 teeth have not only the same number as humans but the same tooth arrangement. The relationship is expressed in the dental formula 2:1:2:3. This formula represents the upper and lower jaws, with the mouth divided into four parts or quadrants. The numbers represent the different kinds of teeth in each quadrant: 2 incisors, 1 canine, 2 premolars, and 3 molars. The total multiplied by 4 yields 32. When a fossil is found to have this arrangement of teeth, another piece of a still incomplete puzzle has been filled in.

Sometimes the fossil evidence is not sufficient to suggest how the animal relates evolutionarily to other animals. In the case of *Oligopithecus* the dental formula is sufficient to classify it as evolutionarily related to Old World monkeys. But another Oligocene fossil discovered at Fayum, *Parapithecus,* is still surrounded by uncertainty. The fossil was found in 1911 by Schlosser and recently reexamined. Scientists still disagree over whether *Parapithecus* is related to prosimians or anthropoids (Old and New World monkeys, apes, and man). "It is so small and undistinguished that some authorities have questioned whether it was even a primate and no one at present is willing to interpret it."[5] Le Gros Clark, who disagrees, cites the shape of the teeth as the basis for his belief that the fossil is not only a primate but hominoid (of apes and man).[6]

There is general agreement, however, on the significance of *Propliopithecus,* another Fayum specimen dating from the Oligocene. It seems to be more ape-like and hence closer to man than to monkey. Again, the examination of the teeth has been crucial in identifying the fossil. *Propliopithecus*'s molars have five cusps—the same number as apes and humans in contrast to the four-cusped molars of the Old World monkeys. That small, but evolutionarily significant, difference, along with other characteristics, indicates that the lines leading to apes were already being drawn.[7] *Propliopithecus* is believed to be hominoid, at or near the beginning of the line from which man and the living apes were to emerge.

Hominoid versus Hominid. *Hominoid* in its literal translation means "man-like," but it refers to apes as well as man, as primates distinct from monkeys. *Hominid,* on the other hand, means "man-like to the exclusion of apes" and refers to those creatures who diverged from the ape-like hominoids to form the human evolutionary line. Hence, man is hominoid and hominid; apes only hominoid, and monkeys neither.

Hominoid Fossil Discoveries

The definition of these terms is essential because with the discovery of *Pliopithecus* the question became: Was a given fossil ancestral to apes or to man? The jaw of *Pliopithecus* was unearthed in France in the middle of the nineteenth century by Edouard Lartet. Subsequently, other skull fragments were found in both Europe and Africa, with skeletal portions found in Neudorf, Czechoslovakia, in 1957, forming the basis for a reconstruction.

Pliopithecus lived during the Miocene epoch about 20 million years ago. Its five-cusped molars appear to distinguish the animal as an ape whose dentition greatly resembles that of modern gibbons. We know gibbons as brachiators, yet the equal length of *Pliopithecus*'s fore- and hindlimbs, both comparatively short, seems to indicate that it was not a brachiator. What is the explanation for these contradictory traits? Evidently, it is that all traits of an animal do not evolve at the same rate. *Pliopithecus* is probably an ancestor of the gibbon, at a state of development where the teeth had already become specialized but before the adaptations for brachiation had developed.

Almost 20 years after Lartet found *Pliopithecus* he made another discovery, in 1856, at the base of the wooded hill on which the village of St. Gaudens, France, is situated. *Dryopithecus,* as it was called, flourished during the Miocene epoch roughly 15 million years ago. Dryopithecines were apparently everywhere. Their fossil remains have been found in Europe, Africa, India, and China. Like living apes and early man, but unlike monkeys, their teeth had five cusps arranged in a Y shape,

[5] C. L. Brace and Ashley Montagu, *Man's Evolution: An Introduction to Physical Anthropology* (New York: Macmillan, 1965), p. 118.

[6] W. E. Le Gros Clark, *The Antecedents of Man* (Edinburgh: Edinburgh University Press, 1959).

[7] By itself, five cusps on the molar does not necessarily indicate that *Propliopithecus* belongs in the lines leading to apes and men. After all, some elephants have five cusps on their molars.

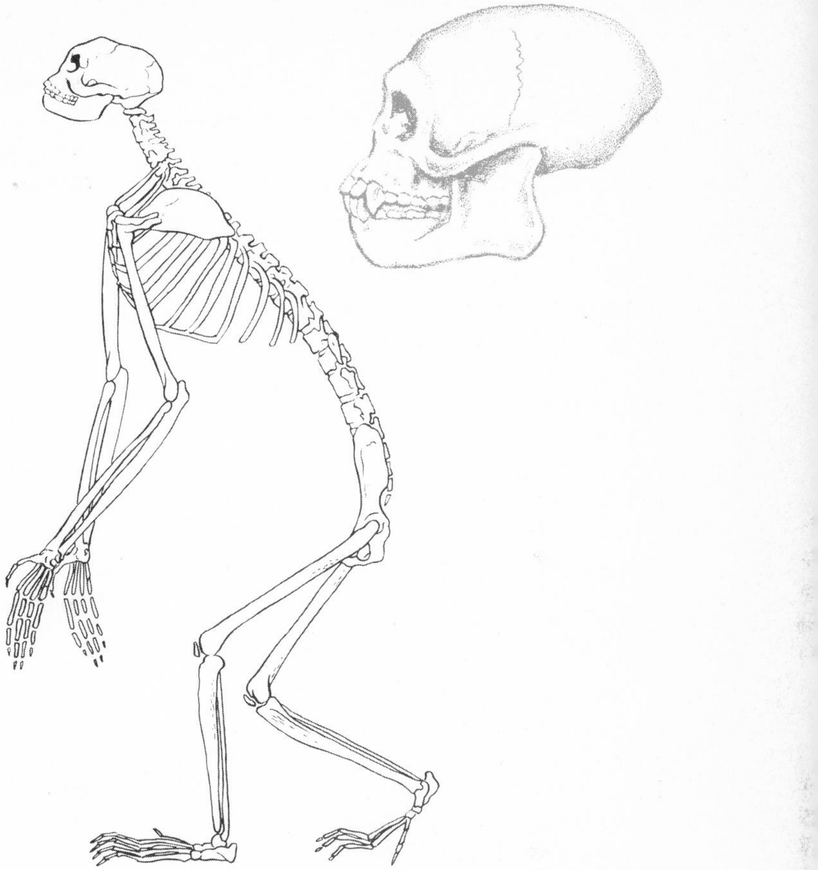

Figure 3
Reconstruction of Pliopithecus, *an ancestral gibbon who lived during the late Miocene. The similar length of the fore- and hindlimbs suggests that* Pliopithecus *probably did not brachiate, as modern gibbons do, but the heavy jaws, large canines, and sloping forehead are characteristics of modern gibbons and other apes.* (After Elwyn L. Simons, "The Early Relatives of Man," *Scientific American.*)

what has come to be known as the *Y-5 trait.* Why did this indicate they might be hominoid? Elwyn Simons has explained:

> The lower molars normally have five cusps rather than four, and the pattern of valleys that separate these bumps of enamel somewhat resembles the letter Y, with the bottom of the Y facing forward. The pattern is called Y-5. The evolutionary significance of the pattern lies in the fact that the lower molars of *Dryopithecus* and of early men typically exhibit a Y-5 pattern. Thus Y-5 is a hereditary characteristic that has persisted among the hominoids for at least 24 million years.[8]

Thus, an animal was discovered which may be ancestral to both man and the apes.[9]

[8] Elwyn L. Simons, "The Early Relatives of Man," *Scientific American* (July 1964), p. 60.

One of the most complete fossils of an early hominoid is the *Dryopithecus*-like *Proconsul,* dating back 20 million years to the early Miocene. Of this animal we have more than jaws and teeth; we also have a complete skull and limb bones. Three species of *Proconsul,* from as small as a gibbon to as large as a gorilla, are known.

The first *Proconsul* discovery was made by L. S. B. Leakey and his wife Mary on Rusinga Island in Lake Victoria, Kenya, and it created a sensation in the anthropological world. The fossils were shipped to England where their

[9] Note that the Y-5 trait alone would not positively identify a fossil as directly ancestral to man because some modern humans have *four* cusps on their molars. Later, we will consider additional characteristics that identify a fossil as a direct ancestor of man.

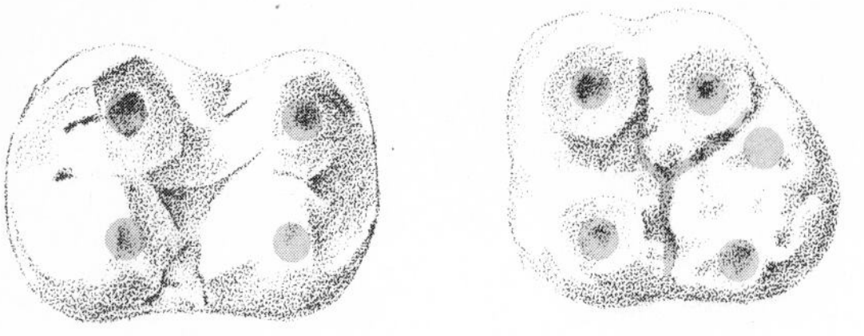

Figure 4
Molars can distinguish fossil monkeys from apes. The Old World monkey molar (left) *has four cusps, one at each corner, joined by ridges. The ape molar* (right) *has five cusps, separated by grooves which resemble the letter Y.* Dryopithecus*'s lower molars had the ape-like Y-5 pattern.* (Adapted from Elwyn L. Simons, "The Early Relatives of Man," *Scientific American.)*

close resemblance to modern chimpanzees was readily established. The affinity is indicated by the name chosen for the animal—distinguished in its simplicity from the polysyllabic tongue twisters of the other discoveries. Actually, the name is an "in" British joke—"pro" meaning "prior to" and "Consul" being the name of a famous chimpanzee in the London Zoo. The name, nevertheless, is instructive in that it identifies *Proconsul* as a predecessor of the chimpanzee and perhaps of gorillas as well. *Proconsul*'s relationship to chimpanzees and gorillas is indicated by the structure of its arms and legs, characteristic of creatures able to get about on all fours and swing in the trees.

Though *Proconsul*'s arms and legs are human-like, some authorities are uncertain that it belongs in man's line of descent. *Proconsul* is thus classified as hominoid—more like the gorilla or the chimpanzee after which it was named than like man. A comparison with the teeth and mouth of man explains why *Proconsul* is not accepted as hominid. If you run your tongue along the roof of your mouth, the palate, you will feel that it is arched. Also, notice that your teeth go back on each side in a broad curve which gradually widens as it reaches the back of the mouth. In contrast, all apes and monkeys have flat palates with a U-shaped jaw and teeth that run back in parallel rows. *Proconsul*'s molars follow the parallel row pattern, suggesting that apes were its descendants, but not humans.

Problematic Fossils: Oreopithecus **and** Gigantopithecus. Even eyewitnesses differ in their accounts of an event. Imagine, therefore, what a range of difference is possible in opinions about events never seen by historic man. Furthermore, the fossil records on which scientists must base their inferences are often fragmentary and therefore ambiguous. Conflicts consequently arise, such as the one over *Oreopithecus,* discovered in Tuscany, Italy, in 1860. For about 50 years it was thought to be a monkey; afterwards it was suggested that it was a remnant of an extinct ape. In 1958 a complete specimen in relatively good condition was discovered and hailed as a primitive hominid. Since the fossil was dated to the late Miocene or early Pliocene, it could be regarded as

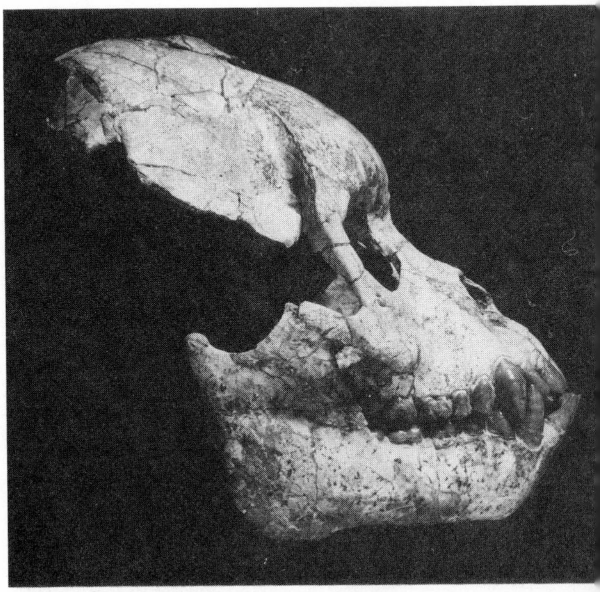

the earliest evidence of hominid life, indicating that the evolutionary lines that produced humans and apes separated between 10 and 12 million years ago.

This assumption, however, has been hotly debated. There is no general agreement about how *Oreopithecus* should be classified—whether it was ancestral to the living apes or to humans or to neither. After examining the teeth, G. G. Simpson concluded that *Oreopithecus* has too many nonhominid characteristics to be considered hominid. He concludes, rather, that it is an early ape that separated from the *Propliopithecus* line during the Oligocene, evolved on its own, and became extinct during Pliocene times. As such, it is believed to have made no direct contribution to the evolution of apes or men.[10]

Another entry into the controversy over ape-line or human-line fossils is *Gigantopithecus,* the largest known primate. G. H. R. von Koenigswald discovered teeth of this specimen in 1935, not buried in the earth, but in a most unlikely location, a Chinese pharmacy. His successful detective work resulted from more than a hunch: he knew that the Chinese believed in the therapeutic value of "dragon's teeth," which were sold from trays at pharmacies. Diligent searching through the trays rewarded von Koenigswald with the discovery of giant-sized *Gigantopithecus* molars.

Although some investigators believed they were hominid specimens, von Koenigswald maintained that the molars were ape-like. His view was confirmed by the discovery of an older, nearly intact lower jaw in northwestern India by J. R. K. Chopra of Punjab University and Elwyn L. Simons of Yale.[11] Rather than indicating a human ancestry, *Gigantopithecus*'s resemblances to man are more likely the result of the parallel evolution of traits that probably arose as adaptations to similar habitats and diets.

[10] G. G. Simpson, "The Meaning of Taxonomic Statements," in S. L. Washburn, ed., *Classification and Human Evolution* (Chicago: Aldine, 1963), pp. 21–22.

[11] Elwyn L. Simons, "Pliocene Giant," *Scientific American,* Vol. 219 (August 1968), p. 45.

The skull of Proconsul, *believed to be an ancestor of the chimpanzee and the gorilla* (left). (Courtesy of the British Museum.)

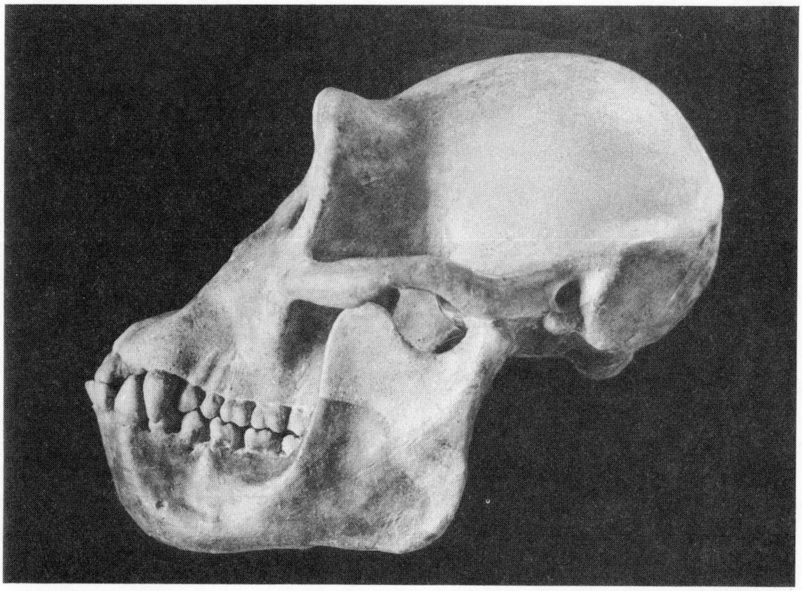

Skull of Dryopithecus, *an ancestral ape. Note the heavy brow ridges, protruding face, and large canines* (right). (Courtesy of the American Museum of Natural History.)

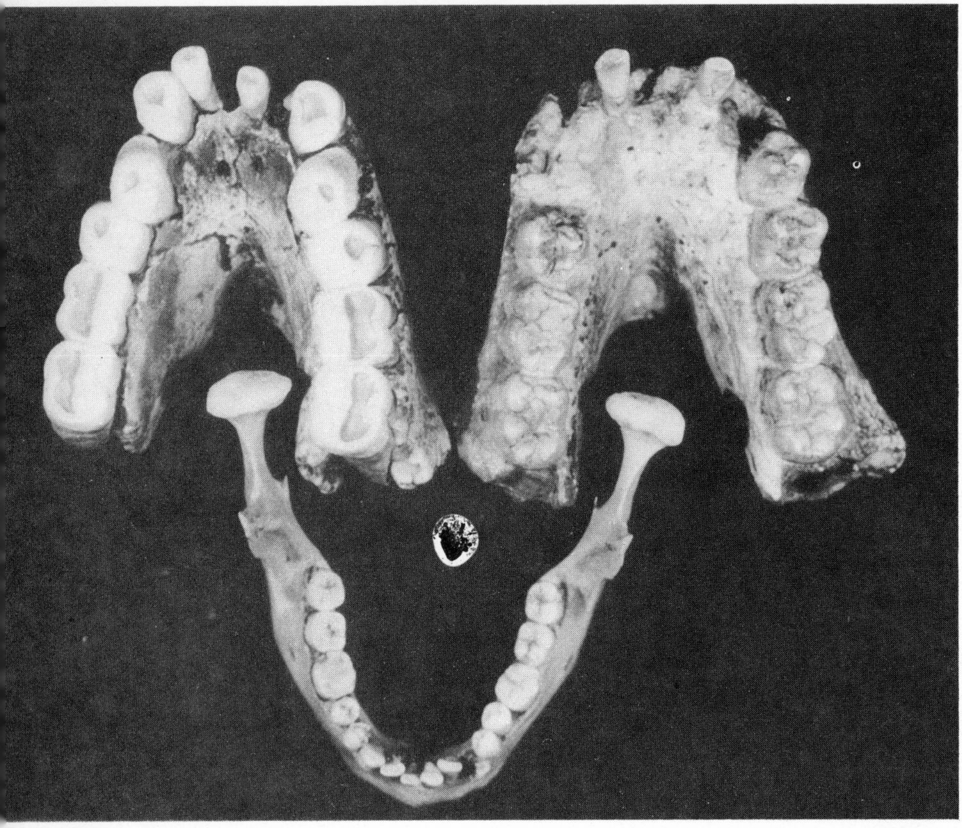

A comparison of the jaws of Gigantopithecus (top) *with a modern human jaw* (bottom). (Courtesy of F. S. Szalay.)

EMERGENCE OF THE HOMINIDS: HUMAN ANCESTORS

When hominids began to evolve about 25 million years ago, the earth was still changing (as it is today, although our lives are too short to notice how). Upheavals and eruptions produced the great mountain chains of the Alps and the Himalayas. The gases, ash, and lava thrown up by erupting volcanoes combined with increased rainfall to wear away the slopes of mountains and foothills.

During the Miocene epoch, the long stretches of Eocene and Oligocene forests, extending from the west coast of Africa to the East Indies, were gradually receding. Savannas of grass spread between the forests, and, gradually, dry, wide plains formed. The generally uninhabited areas that separated the forests from the savannas formed the econiche probably occupied by man's hominid ancestors and by many terrestrial lineages of monkeys. Ultimately, the hominids became fully terrestrial, exploiting savannas that flourished with plant and animal life between the shrinking forests. In Chapter 6, we shall see the tremendous importance that this environmental change was to have for human evolution, particularly for the emergence of human culture.

The earliest known sample of a hominid fossil is *Ramapithecus,* found by G. E. Lewis in the Siwalik Hills of India in the 1930s. The name derives from "Rama," a hero of Hindu mythology, and *pithecus,* Greek for "ape." *Ramapithecus* exhibits all the tooth characteristics—the 2:1:2:3 dental formula, the Y-5 cusp pattern, and an arched and out-curved palate—necessary to establish it as a human ancestor.

There were doubts about the relationship of *Ramapithecus* to man, since the fossil remains consisted only of a part of an upper jaw with a few teeth attached. But in 1961, L. S. B. Leakey who found *Proconsul* discovered an upper jaw in Kenya that he named *Kenyapithecus.* Subsequently, the fossil was found to resemble *Ramapithecus* so closely that it, too, became known as *Ramapithecus.* Potassium-argon dating of Leakey's find supported the conclusion that *Ramapithecus* and *Kenyapithecus* were of one genus; they are both estimated to be about 14 to 12 million years old.

The number of *Ramapithecus* fossils are few but their distribution is wide. They have been found in East Africa, northwestern India, Germany, and possibly China. These ape-like hominids appear to have moved about freely through the forests and savannas of the world. If this assumption is correct, it may imply that even very early hominids were uniquely gifted with the ability to adapt to and cope with a variety of

Range and site distribution of Dryopithecus *and* Ramapithecus. (Adapted from Elwyn L. Simons, "Some Fallacies in the Study of Hominid Phylogeny," *Science.*)

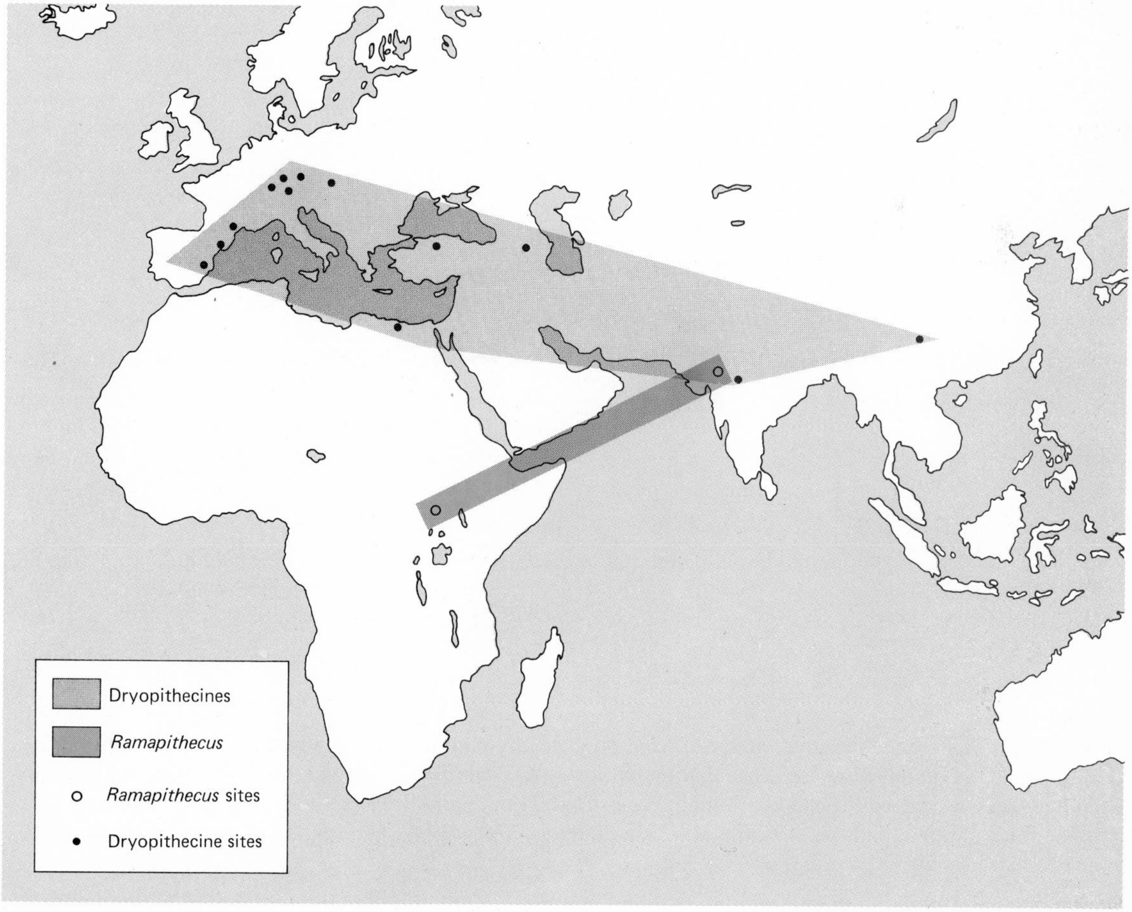

open-country environments and circumstances.

The genus *Ramapithecus* is generally conceded to be an early hominid, but its stage of advancement on the human evolutionary path is still not fully certain. Did *Ramapithecus* walk erect? As yet, no skeletal remains below the neck have been discovered, so we lack positive proof. We know that erect posture, made possible by changes in the hip, is a major aspect of physiological adaptation in human evolution. Strangely enough the teeth may provide a clue to the posture of *Ramapithecus.* This hominid has canines and incisors, but they are small compared to a contemporary ape's, and very small compared to those of the baboons. The baboons, members of the monkey family, bare their sharp canines as a threat to aggressors and, when threats fail, use them as formidable weapons. Apes and baboons also use canines to shred plants. From the shape and size of the teeth of *Ramapithecus,* John Buettner-Janusch suggests "*Ramapithecus* was probably an erect biped; . . . we may infer that the forelimbs had taken over certain tasks the front teeth perform among the apes—the grasping and tearing of vegetation."[12] Elwyn Simons notes that small teeth would have been ineffective in aggressive displays against predators. More likely, "hands played a major role in food-getting and defense. Furthermore, the extensive use of the hands implies that they walked upright, although we need a great deal more evidence before we can prove that beyond a doubt."[13] Perhaps an upright *Ramapithecus* waved a stick to ward off predators or to threaten others of his species, as some apes have been seen to do, but we can only guess at the possibility.

Another explanation for the small size of the canines of *Ramapithecus* is proposed by Clifford Jolly of New York University. He focuses

[12] Buettner-Janusch, *Origins of Man,* p. 126.

[13] Elwyn Simons quoted in John E. Pfeiffer, *The Emergence of Man* (New York: Harper & Row, 1969), p. 44.

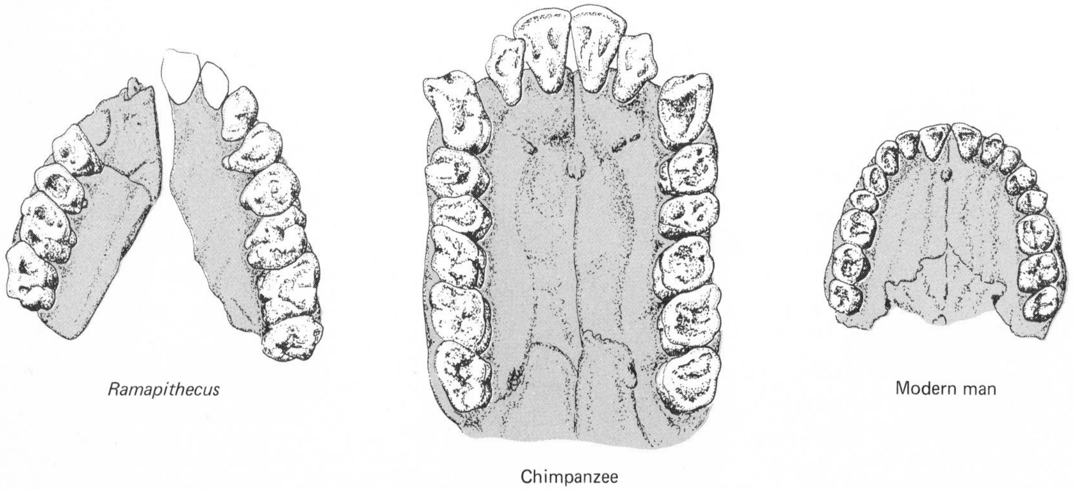

Figure 5
Ramapithecus*'s jaw, which curves out toward the back of the mouth, resembles the human jaw more closely than an ape's jaw. In both* Ramapithecus *and modern man, the tooth rows are not parallel, as they are in apes. A small canine tooth also distinguishes* Ramapithecus *from the apes and helped to identify this fossil as hominid.* (Adapted from Elwyn L. Simons, "On the Mandible of *Ramapithecus,*" *Proceedings of the National Academy of Sciences,* United States.)

on seed eating, an activity associated with open-country life and functionally consistent with hominid anatomy.

As previously noted, during the Miocene epoch, the climate was becoming more temperate, particularly in Eurasia, and a gradual change occurred in the quantity and type of vegetation available. Man's ancestors probably were gradually forced out of their forest environment with the expansion of grassy savannas. The initial adaptive shift might have come about in populations which were searching for new forests for feeding grounds. In this quest they might have had to cover varying stretches of open country. Thus, selection may have favored some of the adaptations necessary for survival away from the ancestral forest habitat. In their new habitats it became necessary to exploit seeds, instead of fruit and foliage, as a staple. A change from a fruit or foliage diet to one based on seeds would favor several ground adaptations. Their ancestors' life in the trees had already predisposed the hominids for the precise hand-eye coordination necessary for manipulating seeds. Precise opposability of thumb and forefinger was a further adaptation to picking up seeds and other small morsels. Posture too was affected. A small-object feeder might forage in a sitting position, with trunk erect and forelimbs free. Furthermore, since large canines and incisors were no longer needed for tearing and husking fruit and could block the side-to-side grinding of the jaw required for seed eating, a reduction in their size would probably be adaptive and therefore favored by natural selection.

An early hominid adapting to the eating of small objects such as seeds would presumably be subject to other physical changes as well. The outer covering of grass seeds contains phytic acid which accumulates in the intestines to form insoluble, unusable calcium in the body. It has been suggested that, in response to this condition, an increase in the bodily production of Vitamin D in the skin may have been favored in hominids, thus counteracting the effects of phytic acid by increasing the body's use of calcium. Since Vitamin D is synthesized by sunlight, exposure of a maximum amount of skin surface and, therefore, loss of body hair might also be selectively favored.[14] It is only fair to note that this explanation of our relative hairlessness is still only a speculation.

This baboon attempts to extract seeds while sitting upright, a posture which leaves his forelimbs free to manipulate the seeds. A shift from a fruit-based to a seed-based diet may have favored a similar adaptation among man's early ancestors. (Courtesy of Irven DeVore.)

The reasons for *Ramapithecus*'s reduced canines remain controversial, and whether or not he walked erect may be determined by future fossil finds. But one thing is certain: the hominids did become bipedal. Why they did, and how that adaptation may have influenced the emergence of human culture, is the subject of the next chapter.

[14] C. J. Jolly, "The Seed Eaters: A New Model of Hominid Differentiation Based on a Baboon Analogy," *Man,* Vol. 5, No. 1, pp. 5–24.

SUMMARY

1. Living primates—prosimians, New World monkeys, Old World monkeys, apes, and man—are descendants of small, originally terrestrial insectivores resembling modern tree shrews.

2. Changes in climate about 60 million years ago favored the development of forests. The prosimians began to exploit the forests as their native habitat became overcrowded.

3. Life in the trees favored the development of a hand adapted for grasping, stereoscopic vision, semierect posture, and an expanded cerebral cortex. These arboreal adaptations would prove advantageous when primates returned to the ground during subsequent geological changes.

4. Evidence for the sequence of primate evolution comes primarily from studying the fossil record. A fossil may be identified from only fragments of the teeth and jaws. Prosimians and New World monkeys have 34 teeth, while Old World monkeys, apes, and man have 32. *Oligopithecus* was easily distinguished from previous finds by its 32 teeth and is now considered the oldest known primate.

5. A fossil may be hominoid, an ancestor of both man and apes (as distinct from the Old World monkeys), or hominid, ancestral only to man. Again, the teeth play an important part in classifying fossil finds: the teeth of early man and apes have five cusps; those of Old World monkeys have four. *Propliopithecus,* an Oligocene fossil, already shows the five-cusped structure and is one of the earliest hominoids. *Ramapithecus,* a Pliocene find, has the further refinements of smaller canines and an arched and out-curved palate and is thus the earliest existing example of a hominid.

6. Without methods of dating fossil finds, such details of evolutionary progression would be lost. Stratigraphy can supply only rough, relative dates, the lowest strata usually being the oldest. Fairly accurate, absolute dates may be determined by studying the amount of disintegration of radioactive elements in the rock by, for example, the potassium-argon method. Armed with an absolute date, paleontologists can compare a fossil more fruitfully with other, undated fossils of its type and with finds of other species found in the same stratum.

SUGGESTED READINGS

Brace, C. L., and A. Montagu: *Man's Evolution: An Introduction to Physical Anthropology* (New York: Macmillan, 1965).
A basic source on physical anthropology.

Buettner-Janusch, J.: *Origins of Man: Physical Anthropology* (New York: Wiley, 1966).
The chapter on fossil primates of the Paleocene, Eocene, and Oligocene deals with the range in time and space and with the defining characteristics of primates. The language in this chapter and in the succeeding two chapters which deal with the next geological periods through the Pleistocene is somewhat technical but a glossary is available at the end of the book.

Campbell, B.: *Human Evolution: An Introduction to Man's Adaptations* (Chicago: Aldine, 1966).
A good general introductory treatment of physical anthropology.

Clark, W. E. Le Gros: *The Antecedents of Man: An Introduction to the Evolution of the Primates* (New York: Harper Torchbook, 1963).
A summary of the evolution of the primates and of their geographical areas can orient the beginning student. Specialized topics include the teeth, skull, limbs, brain, senses (eyes, ears, nose), digestive system, and reproductive system. All of these include both evolutionary evidence or inferences and comparative anatomy. The two closing chapters provide the layman with a clear picture of the relations of the primates to each other through time.

Clark, W. E. Le Gros: *History of the Primates: An Introduction to the Study of Fossil Man,* 5th ed. (Chicago: University of Chicago Press, 1966).
This book is a brief introduction to various aspects of evolution: it includes a section on the earliest primates, one on fossil apes, and several sections on human ancestors. A background is provided by an explanation of geological time and on fossil evidence.

Napier, J.: *The Roots of Mankind* (Washington, D.C.: Smithsonian Institution, 1970).
This book is for the nonspecialized reader and is concerned with the following interrelated topics on primate history: dietary habits, growth, locomotion, and ecology. The evolution and function of bipedalism are especially stressed.

Washburn, S. L.: "The Analysis of Primate Evolution with Particular Reference to the Origin of Man." In W. Howells (Ed.), *Ideas on Human Evolution* (Cambridge, Mass.: Harvard University Press, 1962).
Reviews the history of primate development up to humans with attention to adaptations. Evolution of the brain and of the locomotor system are discussed with reference to recent research.

6

Hominid Evolution and Lower Paleolithic Culture

Like a gigantic jigsaw puzzle, fossil remains have been pieced together to interpret man's evolutionary history—although there are still many missing pieces. The pieces we have are the fossil remains of early hominids, beginning perhaps with *Ramapithecus* of the late Miocene who may have walked on his two hindlimbs much of the time, continuing with *Australopithecus* of East and South Africa who certainly walked erect and probably was the first tool maker, and leading to *Homo erectus* who definitely made various kinds of stone tools and, from the neck down, looked very much like modern man. In this chapter we will discuss hominid evolution from *Australopithecus* to *Homo erectus.*

Although our knowledge of the pattern of hominid evolution is incomplete, the fossil and archaeological records suggest increasing *bipedalism,* or locomotion on the two hindlimbs, the emergence and increasing sophistication of tools made of stone, and the enlargement of the brain. In addition to discussing some possible explanations for these developments, we will also explore some of their implications for the evolution of human social behavior.

ADAPTING TO A CHANGING ENVIRONMENT

Throughout our discussion of evolution, we have noted the enormous influence of the changing environment on biological and behavioral adaptations. In primate evolution in particular, perhaps the greatest environmental influence has been the distribution of trees. Most prosimians and monkeys still live an arboreal life, the result of adaptations that began to appear about 65 million years ago. The apes, as we saw in Chapter 4, are sometimes arboreal and sometimes terrestrial, but man is one of the few primates who lives entirely on the ground. Why did this happen? For an explanation, we must examine how natural selection may have operated in conjunction with the changing arboreal environment. We shall begin by discussing probable environmental and evolutionary changes in Africa, the likely birthplace of the human lineage.

The ancestral apes emerged during the wet Miocene epoch, which produced abundant tropical rain forests. Toward the middle of the Miocene, about 13 million years ago, a drying trend began and continued into the Pliocene. The drier weather gradually diminished the African rain forests, which needed wetness and humidity to survive. Heavily forested areas slowly gave way to grasslands, or *savannas,* which thrive in arid climates. Trees did not disappear completely; they just grew fewer and farther apart, mostly along river banks. The tree-dwelling primates were not, of course, summarily dispossessed, and natural selection continued to favor better-adapted tree dwellers.

But in the new niche, the ground, characteristics that may have facilitated adaptation to ground living were favored—such as terrestrial quadrupedalism, bipedalism, improved vision, a more sophisticated brain and nervous system, and, of course, various types of social organizations to cope with life on a hostile, open terrain.

The Development of Bipedalism

Perhaps the most crucial change in early hominid evolution was the development of bipedalism, or two-legged locomotion, combined with a fully upright posture. In the opinion of many anthropologists, bipedalism was adaptive to life amid the tall grasses of the savanna. True, an upright animal is more conspicuous, but stereoscopic or depth vision, originally an adaptation to tree life, combined with an erect posture, may have made it easier to spot ground predators as well as potential prey. It has been suggested that ancestral primates "were sometimes forced to move through the tall grass between forest areas and that, since this necessitated raising their level of vision, bipedal abilities would have had selective advantages."[1] This theory does not adequately account for the development of bipedalism, however. Baboons and some other Old World monkeys live in savanna-type environments, yet although they can and do stand erect, they have not evolved fully bipedal *locomotion.*

Another theory explains bipedalism as an adaptation to new ways of food gathering consistent with terrestrial life. The dwindling forests had reduced not only living sites, but food resources as well. In their new niche, those primates who became terrestrial gathered fruits and vegetables from the ground, and they probably needed to transfer food from one locale to another. Standing on two feet freed the hands for carrying and would have been adaptive. Food carrying may also be related to the development of modified bipedalism in nonhuman primates. Jane Goodall has seen chimpanzees "loading their arms with choice wild fruits, then walking erect for several yards to a spot of shade before sitting down to eat."[2] But still, food carrying is only a part-time activity and would not necessarily favor full-time bipedalism. Other factors, then, must have been involved in the evolution from a four-legged to a two-legged animal.

Sherwood Washburn has suggested that the use of tools furthered the evolution of bipedalism: carrying tools would have prevented the hands from being used for locomotion. With increased tool use, natural selection would have favored the use of the hindlegs alone for locomotion, leaving the hands free.[3]

BIPEDALISM AND THE EVOLUTION OF CULTURE

Although the circumstances that favored the development of bipedalism are still controversial, the immensity of its impact on human evolution, and on the emergence of culture in particular, is undisputed. Not only did bipedalism influence the development of tool making and the expansion of the brain, it had profound effects on human social behavior as well. For example, the time required to care for the human infant and the early definition of male and female roles can be traced, in part, to the influence of bipedalism.

[1] Kenneth Oakley, "On Man's Use of Fire, with Comments on Tool-Making and Hunting," in S. L. Washburn, ed., *Social Life of Early Man* (Chicago: Aldine, 1964), p. 186.

[2] Jane van Lawick-Goodall, "My Life among Wild Chimpanzees," *National Geographic* (August 1963), pp. 274–308.

[3] Sherwood Washburn, "Tools and Human Behavior," *Scientific American,* Vol. 203 (September 1960), p. 69.

Bipedalism, Tool Making, and the Expansion of the Brain

The origin of tool making is still not completely understood. Grasping hands and stereoscopic vision, characteristics of man's primate ancestors, preadapted terrestrial primates for the use of tools. The ability to grasp and to perceive objects in three dimensions facilitates the use and making of tools. But the fact that nonhuman primates also have these characteristics implies that they alone cannot account for the origin of human tool making. Clearly, some other factor or factors must have also been involved.

Traditionally the development of bipedalism in hominids was thought to be crucial for the origin of tool use and tool making, since bipedalism would have freed the hands for such activities. More recently, it has been thought that the sequence was reversed—that tool use and tool making came first—and their advantages were so profound that natural selection would have favored a more complete bipedalism in a tool-using and tool-making terrestrial primate. That is, in the absence of large body size and large canines, a terrestrial primate living in a grassland environment full of predators would have been at a great disadvantage if he did not use tools at least to protect himself. Thus, those terrestrial primates that were more efficient tool users, perhaps because they were more completely bipedal, would have been able to survive in the grassland environment. It may be, however, that both of these theories are correct: bipedalism interacted with tool use and tool making, each one favoring an increase in the other. The benefits derived from efficient tool use would favor a more complete bipedalism, which in turn would free the hands even further for tool use and tool making.

Not only did tool making increase in sophistication from *Australopithecus* to *Homo erectus,* but the volume of the brain also expanded, probably in conjunction with the selective forces that adapted the hominids to open-country life. The australopithecine cranial capacity ranged from about 450 to 580 cc. The next known hominid, *Homo habilis,* had a capacity of about 600 cc. *Homo erectus*'s cranial capacity ranged from 775 to 1,300 cc. However, it should be noted that the australopithecine cranial capacity was already relatively large, considering that most of the australopithecines probably only weighed 50–100 pounds. (*Homo*

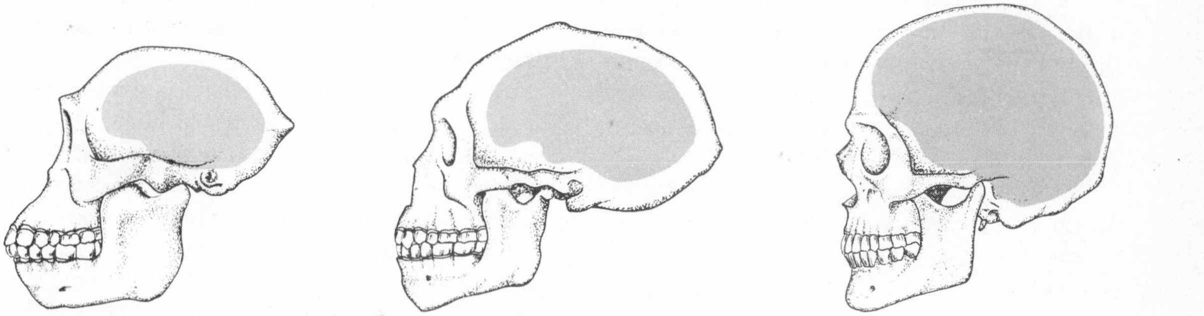

Figure 1
Comparison of the range of cranial capacities, in Australopithecus, Homo erectus, *and modern man, demonstrating the increased brain size in hominid evolution.*

erectus was about the size of modern man.) Since at least some of the australopithecines were tool makers, the emergence of tool making may have favored the expansion of the brain. Given that tool making was crucial to the survival of our ancestors in the grassland environment, natural selection may have favored not only increasing bipedalism, but also increasing motor and conceptual skills, perhaps made possible by an enlarged brain. The increasing brain size may in turn have favored the evolution of more sophisticated tool making.

Regularly patterned tools are archaeological signs of culture. This is because *culture* is defined as learned and shared patterns of behavior, thought, and feeling. Therefore, tools made according to a standard pattern and found in different places presuppose some degree of culture. There are regularly patterned, stone tool-making traditions associated with *Homo erectus,* and so anthropologists conclude that *Homo erectus* definitely had culture. Whether or not australopithecines had culture is not yet agreed upon, since many do not attribute pre–*Homo erectus* tool-making traditions to australopithecines. We shall discuss this controversy later.

Although patterns of learned behavior may be shared in the absence of language (recall the custom of washing potatoes that spread through a Japanese monkey colony), language would certainly facilitate the teaching and learning of cultural behavior. Given the absolute increase in brain size we see in *Homo erectus,* speech may have already been present. Certainly, the ability to communicate in a tool-making animal would have great adaptive advantages. It would foster the transmission of an increasingly complex culture and would favor individuals with larger brains.[4]

[4] Sherwood Washburn and Virginia Avis, "Evolution of Human Behavior," in Anne Roe and G. G. Simpson, eds., *Behavior and Evolution* (New Haven: Yale University Press, 1958), pp. 421–436.

Other Consequences of Bipedalism and Tool Making

Not only can tool making, the enlargement of the brain, and perhaps language be linked in some way to the development of bipedalism, but several other human characteristics may be related to bipedalism as well. A prolonged period of infant dependency, division of labor between men and women, and food sharing may be traceable, in part, to two-legged walking.

The human pelvis is primarily adapted for upright, two-legged walking and running. As natural selection favored increasing brain size, it also favored the widening of the female pelvis to allow larger-brained babies to be born. But there was probably a limit to how far the pelvis could widen and still be adapted to bipedalism. Something had to give, and that something was the degree of physical development of the human infant at birth: the human infant is born with cranial bones so plastic that they can overlap. (The bones at the top of the head do not even close until considerably after birth.) By being born before the cranial bones have hardened, the human infant with an enlarged brain could still pass through the mother's pelvis. But unable to cling like a monkey or an ape to its mother while nursing, the utterly dependent newborn must be carried in her free hands.

Another effect of bipedalism, perhaps a consequence of lessened maturity at birth, was the prolongation of infant and child dependency that is so distinctively human. As compared with other animals, we not only spend the longest proportion of our life span, but also the longest absolute period of time, in a dependent state. This prolongation of dependency may have also been favored by the increasing complexity of human life, which required more time spent in social learning. Thus, prolonged infant dependency has been of great significance in human cultural evolution. Dobzhansky writes:

"It is this helplessness and prolonged dependence on the ministrations of the parents and other persons that favors in man the socialization and learning process on which the transmission of culture wholly depends. This may have been an overwhelming advantage of the human growth pattern in the process of evolution."[5]

The development of hunting and division of labor by sex were other changes, related to bipedalism, that probably occurred by the time of *Homo erectus,* some 500,000 years ago. Tools made possible the development of hunting by man—for man is not naturally equipped for the killing and butchering of other animals. He did not have large canines, claws, or great size. There are definite signs of hunting found with *Homo erectus,* and australopithecines probably hunted too. (We shall consider the evidence for hunting later in the chapter.) The development of hunting, combined with the prolongation of infant and child dependency, may have fostered the development of a division of labor by sex, with the men doing the hunting, and women doing the child tending and other work closer to home. If women have to carry babies and young children, they cannot easily chase animals that may run for some distance. Since the men would have been freer to do so, they probably became the hunters early in human evolution. While the men were away hunting, the women may have gathered wild plants and hunted some wild animals within a radius that could be traversed while carrying young children. This division of labor by sex may have given rise to another distinctively human characteristic: the sharing of food.

What is the evidence that the physical and cultural changes we have been discussing occurred during the evolution of the hominids? Fossil fragments from the late Pliocene and early Pleistocene indicate that new creatures, upright-walking primates since named the australopithecines, had emerged in the shrinking African forests to roam on the plains-like savannas, then forming over much of the earth's surface. Fossil fragments dating from later in the Pleistocene indicate the appearance of the first man—*Homo erectus.* The remainder of the chapter traces the sequence of known hominid fossils and how they are associated with the development of bipedalism, brain expansion, tool making, and other aspects of cultural development.

[5] Theodosius Dobzhansky, *Mankind Evolving* (New Haven: Yale University Press, 1962), p. 196.

AUSTRALOPITHECUS AFRICANUS

Raymond Dart's Discovery: The Taung Child

In 1924, Raymond Dart, professor of anatomy at the University of Witwatersrand, in Johannesburg, South Africa, found the first evidence suggesting that an erect, bipedal hominid existed at least by the late Pliocene. Separating the bones from the matrix of a fragment found in Taung, South Africa, Dart realized that he had more on his hands than the remains of an ape. He described the experience:

> On December 23, the rock parted. I could view the face from the front, although the right side was still embedded. The creature that had contained this massive brain was no giant anthropoid such as a gorilla. What emerged was a baby's face, an infant with a full set of milk teeth and its permanent molars just in the process of erupting.[6]

By the teeth he identified the fossil as the remains of a five- to seven-year-old child. Dart named the specimen *Australopithecus africanus,* which means "southern ape of Africa."

[6] Raymond Dart, "*Australopithecus africanus:* The Man-Ape of South Africa," *Nature,* Vol. 115 (1925), pp. 195–199.

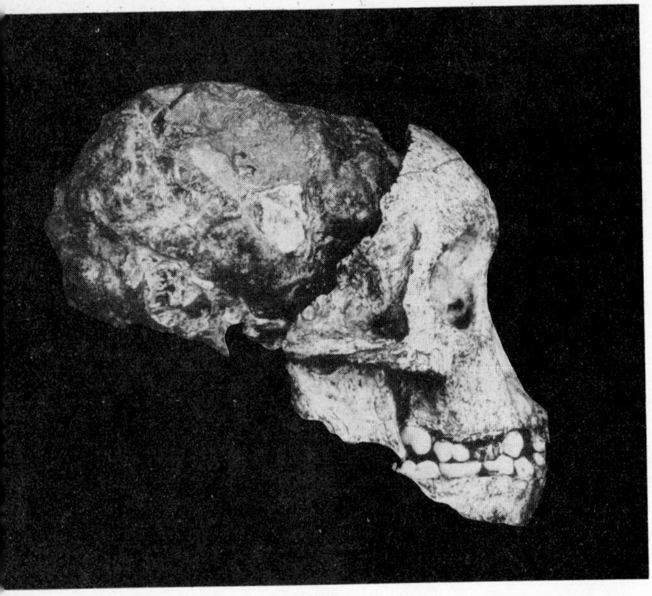

Dart's Taung child, Australopithecus africanus. *The full set of milk teeth and the erupting permanent molars enabled Dart to identify this specimen as a child.* (Courtesy, F. S. Szalay.)

Because the Taung child, as Dart's discovery was called, was found so far south, experts were perplexed. They assumed it was a type of chimpanzee whose only significance was in how it had come to a savanna, a location inappropriate for apes. Dart, however, was certain the fragment was part of a bipedal animal. He based his conclusion on the fact that the *foramen magnum,* the hole in the base of the skull through which the nerves of the spinal chord pass into the skull enroute to the brain, faced downward.

The *foramen magnum* of monkeys and apes is near the back of the skull, in a position appropriate to a more horizontal posture than man's. In the Taung child, the position of the *foramen magnum* indicates that the head was carried directly over the spine. This was enough to convince Dart that his fossil find represented the earliest known bipedalist, and a link to man. Furthermore, the Taung child's incisors and canines were short, definitely more human than ape-like.

After Dart's identification of *Australopithecus africanus* in 1924 additional *A. africanus* remains were found in South Africa in 1936, and, except for a lapse during World War II, discoveries have continued to be made. On an expedition in 1967–1968, led by F. Clark Howell of the University of Chicago, australopithecine teeth were found near Lake Omo, Ethiopia. By potassium-argon dating, they are 3,750,000 years old.[7] The accumulated evidence strongly affirms a hominid classification for the australopithecines, who lived during the late Pliocene through the middle Pleistocene.

Australopithecine Physical Traits

Since the Taung child's discovery, a half-century ago, the remains of more than 100 other australopithecines have been unearthed. From this abundant evidence a fairly complete picture of *Australopithecus africanus* can be drawn. "The brain case is rounded with a relatively well-developed forehead. Moderate brow ridges surmount a rather projecting face."[8] The estimated cranial capacity for the Taung and Sterkfontein finds is between 428 and 485 cc, not of human proportions. *Homo sapiens* have a 1,000–2,000 cc range. It is argued however that, considering the probable body weight of the australopithecines, estimated at 50–100 pounds, their brains were relatively large. But, like apes, australopithecines had large, chinless jaws and heavy, overhanging brows and ridges on top of their faces. The dental features of *Australopithecus africanus* are

[7] F. Clark Howell, "Remains of Hominidae from Pliocene/Pleistocene Formation in the Lower Omo Basin, Ethopia," *Nature,* Vol. 223 (1969), pp. 1234–1239.

[8] David Pilbeam, *The Ascent of Man* (New York: Macmillan, 1972), p. 107.

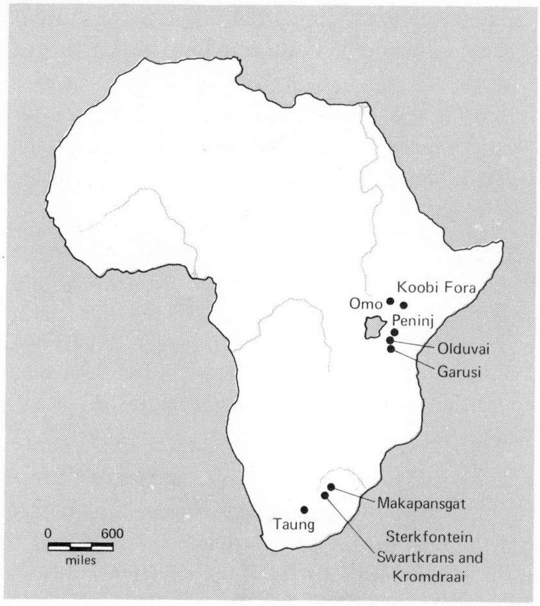

Location of major Australopithecus *sites in East and South Africa.* (Adapted from P. V. Tobias, *Olduvai Gorge,* Vol. 2.)

similar to modern man's, with broad incisors, short canines, and a parabolic dental arch. Though the premolars and molars are larger than modern man's, their form is quite similar. Presumably, function and use were also similar.

The fossil finds at Sterkfontein provide a more complete picture. *Australopithecus africanus* had relatively long arms, and the evidence of six lumbar (lower back) vertebrae suggests that these hominids did not do any knuckle walking, as knuckle walkers characteristically have only three or four lumbar vertebrae. The broad, bowl-shaped pelvis, which is very similar to the human pelvis in shape and areas for muscle attachments, provides evidence for bipedalism. In *Australopithecus africanus* and humans, the pelvis curves back, carrying the spine and trunk erect. The ape's pelvis does not curve back, carrying the spine and trunk forward.

The curve of the australopithecine spine also suggests that these hominids walked erect. The bottom part of the vertebral column forms a curve, causing the spinal column to be S-shaped. The *lumbar curve* and the S-shaped spinal column are found only in modern man and other bipeds. From this evidence, Pilbeam concludes: "*A. africanus* probably walked with toes pointed in perhaps with some swaying of the trunk, and less efficiently than man. However, this hominid was certainly a biped, and well on the way to being a fully effective one."[9]

[9] Pilbeam, *The Ascent of Man,* p. 112.

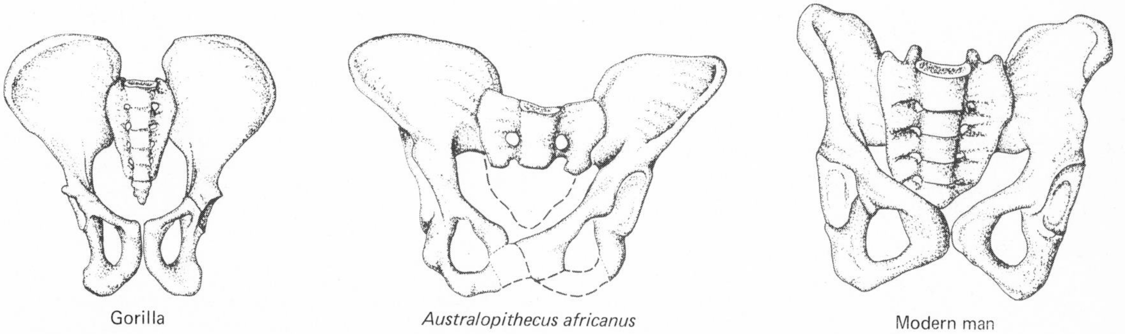

Figure 2
Comparison of the pelvis of an ape, australopithecine, and modern human. The broad, bowl-shaped pelvis of the australopithecine and man is adapted for bipedal walking. The ape's narrow, elongated pelvis carries the spine and trunk forward, not upright.

Did *Australopithecus africanus* Have Culture?

Traditional tool-use theories, as we have noted, link upright posture, reduced canines, and an open, grassland environment. *Australopithecus africanus* had each of these. Was he also, then, a tool user and maker?

No recognizable stone tools have been found with *A. africanus* remains, but Dart argued that the earliest tools were more likely to have been constructed from bone and horn than stone. At Makapansgat cave in South Africa, he found traces of many other animals in the same deposits as *A. africanus.* Of these, he wrote:

> The anatomical feature that the jaws of hyenas, baboons, wart hogs, and porcupines have in common is long, sharp teeth (lacerating canines or chisel-like incisors) such as will rip open a belly or tear out the eyes of an enemy. The ancient hunters were apparently after the tusks and teeth of these creatures for cutting tools.[10]

Dart further asserted that *A. africanus* "made the tools he wanted by splitting bones according to a definite plan."[11]

Dart's conviction that *A. africanus* not only used bone and horn tools but also fashioned them in accordance with a predesigned plan, was not shared by others. For example, Washburn viewed the many kinds of animal fragments found in the deposit with *A. africanus* as an indication that this hominid was hunted by other carnivores, such as hyenas, rather than the other way around.[12] Whether *A. africanus* was hunter or hunted remained an unresolved issue until L. S. B. Leakey's discovery of 1,750,000-year-old stone tools gave weight to Dart's conclusion.

THE TOOLS AND TOOL MAKERS OF OLDUVAI GORGE

In 1911 a German entomologist made an accidental discovery that turned out to be of great interest to anthropologists. Chasing a butterfly, he followed it into what is now known as Olduvai Gorge in Tanzania and discovered a rich source of fossil remains. In the years after World War II, L. S. B. Leakey renewed a search he had begun in the early '30s for new clues to the evolution of early man. He wrote:

> Olduvai is a fossil hunter's dream, for it shears 300 feet through stratum after stratum of earth's history as through a gigantic layer cake. Here, within reach, lie countless fossils and artifacts which but for the faulting and erosion would have remained sealed under thick layers of consolidated rock.[13]

At Olduvai Gorge in 1931 and 1932, Leakey and his wife, Mary, uncovered evidence of tool making in the form of crude stone implements dating back to the Lower Pleistocene, about 1.9 million years ago. In 1960 they discovered fragments of a child in the same level—Bed I—where they had earlier extracted stone tools of quartz and water-worn pebbles. The Leakeys concluded therefore that the tools and the child existed at the same time. Equally important was that the tools obviously had been *made.* They were not "found" tools, useful to *Australopithecus* because they happened to be there when they were needed. Discovery of a tradition of specific tools of a similar construction, over an extended period of time, indicates that culture existed in the hominid line at least as far back as 2 million years ago.

Olduvai Pebble Tools

The earliest method of making stone tools seems to have been striking a stone with another stone to remove a flake, a technique

[10] Raymond Dart, *Adventures with the Missing Link* (New York: Harper & Row, 1959), p. 48.
[11] *Ibid.*
[12] Sherwood L. Washburn, "Australopithecines: The Hunters or the Hunted?" *American Anthropologist,* Vol. 59 (1957), pp. 612–614.
[13] L. S. B. Leakey, "Finding the World's Earliest Man," *National Geographic* (September 1960), p. 424.

L. S. B. Leakey (right) *at Olduvai Gorge, Tanzania.* (Ian Berry, Magnum Photos, Inc.)

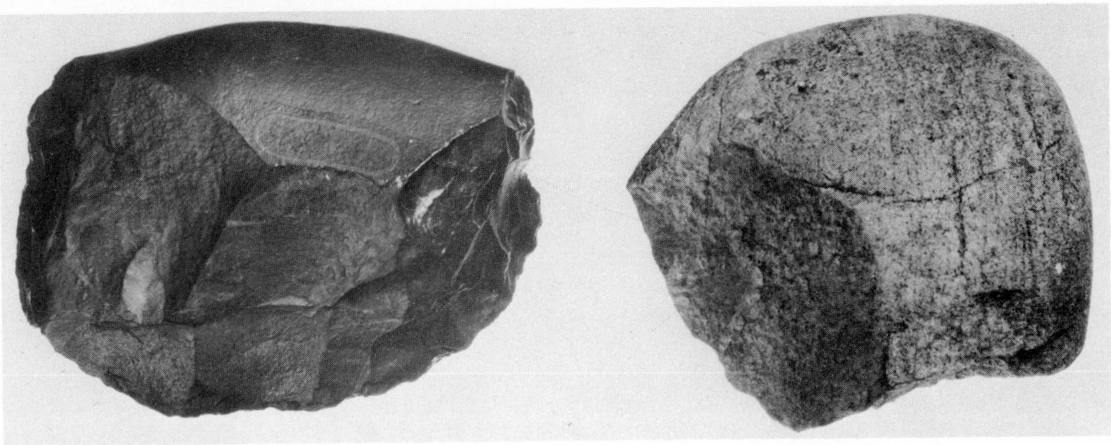

A chopper (left) *and a pebble tool* (right), *both of the Oldowan pebble tool tradition.* (Courtesy of the American Museum of Natural History.)

known as *percussion flaking.* A number of blows were struck creating a *unifacial* tool, or a tool worked on one side. Further blows struck at a right angle to the facets left by the original blows produced a *bifacial* tool (i.e., a tool worked on two sides) which could be used for chopping. The flakes struck from the pebble core could also be used. When dull, the pebble tool could be discarded and a new one quickly fashioned with a few careful blows from a hammerstone or other pebble tool.

These tools were probably used primarily in the preparation of food. Their functions might have included butchering of animals, breaking bones to extract marrow, and grinding food. Pebble tools, which can be easily hurled, may have also been among the first weapons used by hominids.[14]

Who Made the Olduvai Pebble Tools?

Digging among the seemingly limitless number of specimens at Olduvai Gorge, Mary Leakey spotted a skull fragment lodged in a rock slide in the same site as the pebble tools. The Leakeys named their specimen *Zinjanthropus boisei,* but it has since been classified as *Australopithecus.* Potassium-argon dating of this site has indicated that its contents are about 1,750,000 years old. Other tools have been found in the East Rudolph area in Kenya by Richard Leakey (the son of L. S. B. and Mary) which have been dated as far back as 2.6 million years. As of now, these latter tools are the earliest associated with hominid remains.[15]

The manufacture of tools favors high intelligence and good hand-eye coordination. Those hominids endowed with greater abilities were better adapted for survival and thus left more offspring. Through the process of natural selection, then, increased capacities for thought and manual dexterity gradually became established as definitive hominid traits.

The tools of Olduvai were believed to have been made by australopithecines until remains of *Homo habilis,* apparently a more advanced hominid, were discovered there. (We shall

[14] Jacques Bordaz, *Tools of the Old and New Stone Age* (Garden City, N.Y.: Natural History Press, 1970), p. 17.

[15] R. E. F. Leakey, "Hominid Remains and Early Artifacts from Northern Kenya," *Nature,* Vol. 226 (April 1970), pp. 223–230.

consider *Homo habilis* later in the chapter.) Which of the two kinds of hominids made the tools is still uncertain. But regardless of which hominids made the stone tools found at Olduvai Gorge, their discovery suggests that culture began to evolve well before 2 million years ago.

OTHER AUSTRALOPITHECINES

Australopithecus robustus

The fossil record is not always clear, and in the case of the australopithecines, confusion was engendered by the hominid discoveries at Kromdrai and then at Swartkrans in South Africa by Broom in 1948–1949. Today these hominids are regarded as the robust (or larger) australopithecines and called *Australopithecus robustus*. The two australopithecine species are dissimilar in several ways. As its name suggests, *A. robustus* was somewhat larger, not necessarily taller but more stockily built, weighing from 100–150 pounds. *A. africanus* was gracile, more limber, and weighed 50–100 pounds. The heads were differently shaped: *A. africanus* had a narrow and slightly domed skull, whereas the robust species had a skull cap. Because of differences in dentition and skull shape, it is inferred that their chewing apparatuses and, consequently, their diets also differed. The heavy cheekbones, large molar teeth, smaller canines and incisors, and tooth wear marks of *A. robustus* indicate that this hominid was probably an open-country vegetarian, chewing and grinding food. *A. africanus,* on the other hand, had larger canines and incisors and may have been more carnivorous or omnivorous. Both of these hominids were bipeds, but probably with different posture and gait.

Where does the robust australopithecine belong in the history of human evolution? The answer is fairly well established. Some physical

Figure 3
Manufacture of Oldowan pebble tools by the percussion method. Using a hammerstone, the tool maker strikes a blow near the edge of the pebble to break off flakes (top). *A pebble from which three flakes have been removed by blows from a hammerstone* (center). *The pebble is turned over, and two more flakes are removed adjacent to the ridges created by the three previous flake scars. The result is a crooked working edge where the ridges of the flake scars meet* (bottom). (Adapted from F. Clark Howell, *Early Man;* and Jacques Bordaz, *Tools of the Old and New Stone Age.*)

anthropologists consider *A. robustus* a later development of *A. africanus,* representing an intermediate stage in hominid evolution from *Australopithecus* to *Homo erectus.* As evidence, they note that *A. robustus* was a later arrival and that it is larger, indicative of a trend toward *Homo erectus* and *Homo sapiens.* J. T. Robinson and F. C. Howell, two of the foremost students of the original finds, suggest that *A. robustus* is *not* in the direct line of human evolution. Rather, they conclude, it is a form that developed independently and became extinct.[16] A key to Robinson's belief lies in the difference in dentition: *A. africanus* very closely resembles later hominid finds.

"Meganthropus"

No traces of an australopithecine have yet been found in Europe, but Asian digs have yielded fragments of a lower jaw of a hominid. The large size of the jaw led its discoverer to name the specimen *"Meganthropus."* The teeth however are so similar to *A. robustus* that *"Meganthropus"* may be a representative of *A. robustus.* Of special interest here is the revelation that australopithecine-like creatures might have inhabited Southeast Asia and Africa at approximately the same time. It is not known whether this happened through migration or parallel evolution, although the former is much more likely.

Homo habilis

Homo habilis is the designation for the skeletal remains of several hominids, found at Olduvai Gorge, which date from about 1.8 million years ago. There is some controversy as to its classification. Because of its similarities to *Australopithecus africanus,* some anthropologists classify this hominid as an advanced australopithecine *(Australopithecus habilis),* intermediate between *A. africanus* and *Homo erectus,* the next known hominid in the line leading to man.[17] Other anthropologists believe that since it has several traits which australopithecines lack, it should be placed in the genus *Homo (Homo habilis).* One such advanced feature is a larger cranial capacity—200 cc larger than that of *A. africanus.* But even though *H. habilis*'s cranial capacity is larger, it is still closer to that of *A. africanus* than to *Homo erectus.*

The tools found at Olduvai may have been made by *Homo habilis.* Mary Leakey concedes that "although the australopithecine may well have made simple tools to meet his requirements, I am of the opinion that the larger brained *Homo habilis* whose hand bones also indicate a degree of manual dexterity was most likely to have been responsible for the Oldowan tool assemblage."[18]

Regardless of which hominids made the Oldowan tools, it now seems clear that the australopithecines were ancestral to later forms of man. The evolutionary changes that separate the australopithecines and *Homo habilis* from *Homo erectus,* the next known hominid, are still undocumented by fossil evidence. The most notable physical distinctions between modern man and *Homo erectus* are in the characteristics of the head and the brain. Below the skull, his skeleton is identical to modern man. Except for relatively slight body differences that have developed in the different races, the changes that have occurred during the last 500,000 years have been mainly in the brain and skull.

[16] J. T. Robinson, "The Australopithecines and Their Bearing on the Origin of Man and of Stone Tool-Making," in William Howells, ed., *Ideas on Human Evolution: Selected Essays 1949–1961* (Cambridge, Mass.: Harvard University Press, 1962), pp. 279–294; F. Clark Howell, *Early Man* (New York: Time-Life, 1970), p. 44.

[17] Pilbeam, *The Ascent of Man,* p. 143.

[18] Mary D. Leakey, "A Review of the Oldowan Culture from Olduvai Gorge, Tanzania," *Nature* (April 30, 1966), pp. 462–466.

DISCOVERY OF HOMO ERECTUS: JAVA MAN

In 1891, Eugene Dubois, a Dutch anatomist digging in Java, found what he called *Pithecanthropus erectus,* meaning "erect ape man." (We now refer to this early man as *Homo erectus.*) Since the discovery was the first human-like fossil (*Australopithecus* was not discovered until the 1920s), no one was certain, not even Dubois himself, whether the animal was an ape or a man. Was it perhaps the "missing link," an animal similar to both man and ape?

The actual find consisted of a brain pan (the part of the skull above the eyes and ears) and a thighbone. For many years it was thought that the fragments were not even from the same animal. The skull was ape-like, but too large to be that of a modern ape and smaller than that of an average human, with a cranial capacity between the ape's 500 cc and modern man's 1,400 cc. The thighbone, however, matched that of modern man. Did the two fragments, in fact, belong together? The question was resolved by fluorine analysis.

Fluorine Analysis. The amount of fluorine accumulated in bones increases as they lie in the earth. But different soils contain different amounts of fluorine. Therefore, fluorine analysis cannot reveal a fossil's absolute age. If fossils from the same deposit have the same amount of fluorine, they are of the same age; if the amount differs, fluorine analysis can establish their relative ages. The skull fragment and thighbone found by Dubois were tested for their fluorine content and found to be of the same age.

A later discovery made by G. H. R. von Koenigswald in the mid-1930s, also in Java, not only confirmed Dubois's earlier speculations and extended our knowledge of *Homo erectus*'s physical characteristics but also gave us a better understanding of this early man's place in time. The oldest *Homo erectus* fossils were more ancient than Dubois's finds, implying that a form of early man resided in Java over 730,000 years ago.

Dubois and von Koenigswald made their discoveries in different parts of Java. Dubois worked at Trinil (the Trinil bed), where fossil remains were found from the mid-Pleistocene epoch; von Koenigswald dug primarily at Sangiran, in the Djetis beds, which contained fossils from an earlier part of the Pleistocene. At each site two *Homo erectus* skulls were found. The time difference indicates that there was a continuity of *Homo erectus* populations in that part of the world.

Homo erectus in China: Peking Man

Between Dubois and von Koenigswald's discoveries, Davidson Black, a Canadian anatomy professor teaching in Peking, China, found a single molar in a large cave at nearby Choukoutien. Confident that the tooth was from a hitherto unknown genus of man, he set out to excavate the area extensively. After digging carefully for two years, he found a skull in limestone which he dubbed "Peking man." Black died in 1934, and his work was carried on by Franz Weidenreich. The original finds at Choukoutien were lost during the Japanese invasion of December 1941, but Weidenreich had sent casts to the United States. From these, and from the discoveries of *Homo erectus* made since 1949, we can draw several inferences about *Homo erectus* in China.

Physical characteristics of *Homo erectus*. The Java skulls found by Dubois and von Koenigswald and the Peking skulls subsequently found by Black were similar in many respects but showed differences in cranial capacity and dental features. Since Black's time, other skull and tooth fragments of Peking man have been found, indicating that Peking man,

G. H. R. von Koenigswald points to the space in the jaw (the diastema) *of the* Homo erectus *skull found at Sangiran, Java. In apes* (gorilla skull, lower left), *the canines fit into these spaces when the jaws are closed. Modern humans* (skull at upper left), *with small canines, do not have diastemas.* (Courtesy of the American Museum of Natural History.)

typifying *Homo erectus,* was closer than Java man to modern humans. Peking man had a higher and less sloping forehead, and his cranial capacity was about 1,000 cc as compared with Java man's, which was about 900 cc. The cranial capacity of modern humans ranges from 1,000 to 2,000 cc. Because of his relatively large brain, *Homo erectus,* as exemplified by Peking man, may have been able to speak.

Peking man had a shorter, rounder palate than Java man. Thus, Peking man's face more closely resembled modern man's, but the jaw did not have a chin. The teeth in his shortened jaw were smaller than the australopithecines' and Java man's. Peking man's smaller teeth, especially his smaller canines, may be related to his use of fire, perhaps for cooking. (We shall discuss his use of fire below.) Like modern man, Peking man lacked the *diastema*—the space between the teeth to accommodate large canines—seen in the Java skull.

Since the rear part of his brain, the visual center, was as fully developed as ours, it has been assumed the *Homo erectus* could probably see as well as modern man. The center and sides of the brain—the speech, sensory, memory, and motor areas—were larger than the australopithecines' but smaller than modern man's. The comparative underdevelopment of the forebrain, that part of the brain that controls conceptual thought, also suggests that *Homo erectus*'s capacity for language and culture was probably not as well developed as modern man's.

From the neck down, *Homo erectus* was practically indistinguishable from modern man. The size of the long bones indicates that a *Homo erectus* male was about 5′6″ tall, the same height as the average European man. Because of a short, thick, and wide pelvis—identical with modern man's—*Homo erectus* is presumed to have been as able a bipedal walker and runner as modern man.

The oldest *Homo erectus* skull in China was found in the Shensi province in 1961. Encrusted

Franz Weidenreich photographed the excavation at Choukoutien, China, in 1936. Below is his reconstruction of the head and skull of a Homo erectus *woman found at the site. Note the small teeth and absence of the diastema, as in modern man, but continuous brow ridges are still present.* (Courtesy of the American Museum of Natural History.)

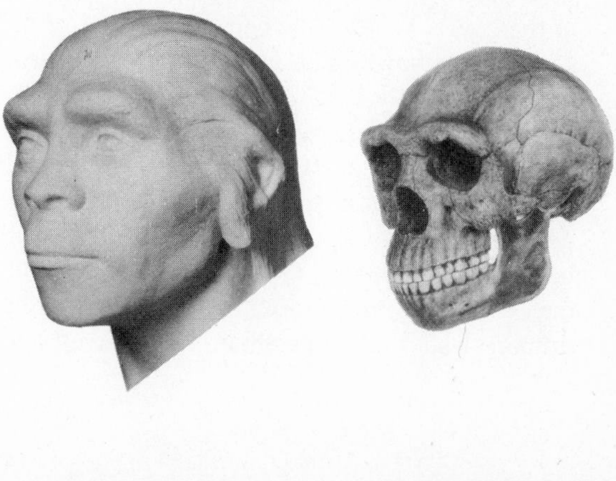

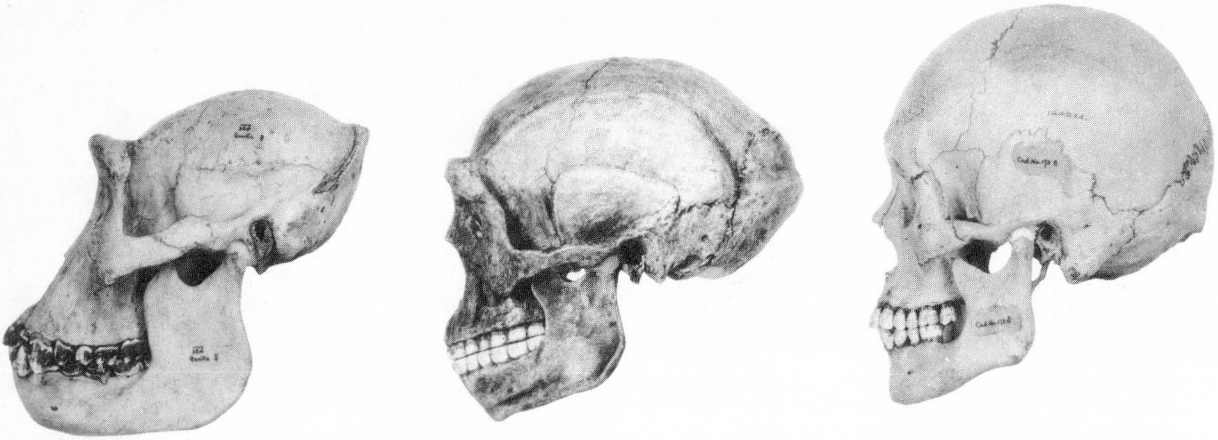

Note the large canines in the gorilla and their reduction in Homo erectus *and modern man* (left, center, and right, respectively). *The continuous brow ridges are reduced in* Homo erectus *and absent in modern man. The cranium became progressively rounder as the brain expanded. Note, too, the reduction of the flaring jaw and the gradual emergence of the chin in modern man.* (Courtesy of the American Museum of Natural History.)

in red clay, the specimen is dated as more than 600,000 years old. Despite the difficulty of determining the sex of fossils, the Lantian find, because of the size of its jawbone, is believed to be that of a female.

Culture of Homo erectus **in China.** With *Homo erectus,* for the first time, we have evidence that fire was being used. Thousands of splintered and charred animal bones found in the Choukoutien caves may have been the remains of Peking man's meals. Evidently he was a hunter who had learned how to use fire. *Homo erectus*'s ability to make fires is also evidenced by large accumulations of charcoal in the caves. Where or when the use of fire began is not known. The most reasonable guess is that naturally occurring fires, produced by volcanoes and lightning, may have been used by *Homo erectus* to sustain and start other fires.

Of tremendous importance to man's cultural development, fire making was a major step in increasing the energy under his control. Cooking with fire made animal meat, including human flesh, more digestible. The charred and split human bones found among the remains of sheep, mammoth, and ostrich in the caves of Peking man suggest that cannibalism was practiced; from the discovery of many split long bones, we can infer that Peking man ate the marrow. Brains, too, were probably part of the diet at Choukoutien: in several skulls, the *foramen magnum,* the opening at the base of the skull, had been enlarged, presumably to remove the brain within.

The stone tools associated with Peking man are very crude, consisting of flaked pebbles, crude choppers made from stone cores, and scrapers and points made from flakes. It is also possible that Peking man made wooden tools which were not preserved.

Homo erectus **in Africa, Asia, and Europe**

Hominids, almost from the beginning, but certainly from *Homo erectus* on, have been widely distributed over the Old World, as shown by fossil remains in many parts of Africa, Asia, and Europe. Evidence of the possible presence of *Homo erectus* in southern France has been found at the Escale Cave in the Durance Valley, where the remains of fire and the bones of primitive wolves and saber-toothed cats have been dated to be about 750,000 years old. In Vértesszöllös, western Hungary, fossil remains of similar structure to Peking man were unearthed. The skull, larger and more advanced in structure than Peking man's, hints that these early men may have been closer than Peking man to modern man. The fossils were found in association with hearths and chopper tools similar to those at Choukoutien.

Another fossil, a massive lower jaw with rather small teeth, found at Heidelberg, Germany, and known as Heidelberg man, has been regarded as the oldest example of *Homo erectus* in the western part of the world. However, because no other parts of Heidelberg man have as yet been found, doubts remain about its classification.

In various other parts of Europe and North Africa, remains of *Homo erectus* have been found in association with hand axes and flake tools. Compared with the pebble tools of the australopithecines, these tools are thinner, more pointed, and have a sharper cutting edge.

Social Organization and Tools of *Homo erectus*

Social Organization. The extent to which *Homo erectus* was able to control his environment was underestimated until 1960 when F. Clark Howell began excavations at Torralba and Ambrona, Spain. He found a substantial number of elephant remains and the unmistakable signs of human presence in the evidence of fire and tools. Howell suggested that early men used fire to frighten elephants into muddy bogs, where they would be unable to escape.[19]

To do this difficult task, they had to be familiar with the habits of elephants and be willing to work cooperatively in the large bands that were doubtless necessary to trap these animals. Game was probably plentiful then, as it still is in some parts of Africa. A census in 1959 of 230 square miles of Africa counted 7,400 buffaloes and 1,026 elephants, in all about 130,000 pounds of big game per square mile.[20]

Division of labor between males and females may have been well defined among *Homo erectus* populations. Women, while carrying children, were able to forage but probably depended on the males for meat supplies. Sexual division of labor, food sharing, and stronger male-female bonds probably developed, therefore, as adaptive cultural traits. Moreover, males who were able to provide the necessary provisions were doubtless favored by natural selection.

Tools. Human history is divided into three ages, according to predominant materials and techniques of tool making: the Stone Age, the Bronze Age, and the Iron Age. The Stone Age is subdivided into three periods: Paleolithic, or Old Stone Age; Mesolithic, or Middle Stone Age; Neolithic, or New Stone Age. *Homo erectus* had an early, Lower Paleolithic culture. The tool-making tradition which began in this period spanned 500,000 years. (Geologically, *Homo erectus* lived in the Pleistocene epoch. This should not be confused with the term "Paleolithic," a designation based on the remains of material culture.)

Acheulean Hand Axes. The tool-making tradition of *Homo erectus* is known as the *Acheulean,* after the site at St. Acheul, France, where the first examples were found. Using an

[19] F. Clark Howell, "Observations on the Earlier Phases of the European Lower Paleolithic (Torralba-Ambrona)," in *Recent Studies in Paleoanthropology, American Anthropologist* Special Publication, (April 1966), pp. 111–140.

[20] John E. Pfeiffer, *The Emergence of Man* (New York: Harper & Row, 1969), p. 113.

Acheulean hand ax, found at St. Acheul, France, in 1871. (Courtesy of the American Museum of Natural History.)

oblong piece of flint as his starting point, the tool maker hammered it on all sides with a small round stone, chipping more flakes off one side than the other. This produced a pear-shaped object, what we call a *hand ax,* with a pointed working edge and a broad butt end to fit into the hand. This probably served as an all-purpose tool, handy for crushing skulls as well as for hacking branches off trees. In smaller and more refined forms, the hand ax may have been used for such jobs as scraping flesh off hides to make them into leather and for preparing food. Tens of thousands of such Paleolithic tools have been found, indicating their widespread and varied use. Early Acheulean tools are said to belong to the Chellean or Abbevillian tradition (after another French site) and are cruder and more haphazard in design than the specialized creations of the later Acheulean. Both types have been found with *Homo erectus* remains. Acheulean tools have also been found in association with modern man, *Homo sapiens.*

It was in Africa, where human evolution evidently began, that tool making made its earliest progress, becoming increasingly complex.

> Beyond question, Africa continued to lead in cultural development during much of the Middle Pleistocene. . . . There is good reason for believing that the hand ax, flaked on either face to form a more or less even working edge—dominant tool of that period—developed by gradual stages from the Oldowan chopper.[21]

From Africa, the tradition may have spread to Europe, perhaps in the hands of migrating hominids.

Levalloisian Flake Tools. During the Acheulean period a new tool-making technique was developed which enabled the tool maker to produce flake tools of a predetermined size, instead of simply chipping the flakes away

[21] Graham Clark and Stuart Piggott, *Prehistoric Societies* (New York: Alfred A. Knopf, 1965), p. 49.

from the core haphazardly. In the *Levalloisian* method the tool maker first shaped the core and prepared a "striking platform" at one end. Flakes of predetermined size could then be chiseled off. Large, symmetrical flake tools were produced that may have also been used to make other tools.[22]

Levalloisian tools have been found at several African and European sites. The similarity of many of the tools found in different places attests to the accumulation and transmission of ideas and techniques from one generation to the next. As each generation built upon the knowledge of the preceding ones, tools became more sophisticated—as we have seen in our survey of human culture from the pebble-like Oldowan choppers to the hand ax and the Levalloisian flake tools.

> The manufacture of tools would in itself have demanded coordination of hand, eye, and brain which must have been of immense value in exercising man's neural apparatus. The men responsible for the magnificent hand ax of the Middle and Late Acheulean phase of culture were already well on the way to becoming *Homo sapiens*.[23]

[22] Bordaz, *Tools of the Old and New Stone Age*, pp. 31–32.

[23] Clark and Piggott, *Prehistoric Societies*, p. 54.

SUMMARY

1. The drying climate which began about 13 million years ago diminished the forests and gave rise to grasslands. This reduced the econiches for tree dwellers and created selective pressures for terrestrial adaptation, pressures which eventually led to bipedalism, improved stereoscopic vision, and the complex nervous system of modern man.
2. One of the most crucial changes in early hominid evolution was the development of bipedalism. There are several theories for its development: it increased the ability to see predators and potential prey while moving through the tall grasses of the savanna; it facilitated transferring food from one place to another by freeing the hands for carrying; tool use, which required free hands, placed increasing emphasis on using only the hindlegs for locomotion.
3. Several physical adaptations facilitated the development of tool making. Bipedalism freed the hands to grasp objects; stereoscopic, color vision increased the ability to discern objects; and the increased complexity of the brain enhanced the capacity to conceptualize and to communicate.
4. Bipedalism probably influenced the social organization of the hominids, affecting infant dependency and male and female roles. The dimensions of the pelvis and the birth canal are primarily adapted to bipedalism. Because of increased brain size, the infant must be born while still immature in order to pass through the birth canal. The infant was therefore dependent on its mother for a longer time. Females carrying children would probably be able to forage for vegetation but would be dependent on males for meat. Sexual division of labor, then, as well as the distinctively human habit of food sharing, seems to have been influenced by bipedalism.
5. The earliest definite hominids in the direct line of descent to modern man are the australopithecines, whose remains have been dated to about 2 million years ago.

They show the earliest evidence of bipedalism and tool making. The oldest tools found belong to the *pebble tool* tradition and consist of pebbles that were crudely flaked to form cutting edges.

6. Australopithecines have been divided into two species—*Australopithecus africanus* and *Australopithecus robustus*—and sometimes a third species, *Australopithecus habilis.* But this division into species is controversial. Some anthropologists believe that *A. africanus* and *A. robustus* are not two different species but part of one variable population. The *habilis* specimen is considered by some to be of the genus *Homo.*

7. *Homo erectus* is the next known hominid in the line of descent to modern man, and he is over 700,000 years old. He is more advanced than *Australopithecus,* with a larger brain capacity, fully erect bipedalism, and a more complex tool tradition.

8. The *Acheulean* tool tradition is associated with *Homo erectus.* It is composed of large hand axes made from core tools and smaller flake tools made by the *Levalloisian* method. The sequence of beds at Olduvai Gorge and the artifacts in them indicate that the more complex Acheulean tradition of *Homo erectus* was derived from the pebble tool tradition of the australopithecines.

SUGGESTED READINGS

Bordes, F. H.: *The Old Stone Age.* Trans. J. E. Anderson (New York: World University Library, 1968).
Concise, accurate, and up-to-date summary of the present state of Lower Paleolithic archaeology. It provides comprehensive coverage and an understanding of tool typologies, aided by charts, photographs, and line drawings.

Buettner-Janusch, J.: *Origins of Man* (New York: Wiley, 1966).
An introductory text in physical anthropology, amply illustrated with diagrams and tables. The book emphasizes the author's philosophy that human evolution belongs to the broader context of primate evolution. To be noted is the whole of Part I which presents a history of presapient hominids. The author traces functional developments, in particular those which are significant in the ultimate emergence of *Homo sapiens.*

Coles, J. M., and E. S. Higgs: *The Archaeology of Early Man* (London: Faber and Faber, 1970).
In this introduction to Paleolithic archaeology, the authors present an encyclopedic inventory of major sites, organized according to geographical region: Africa, Europe, Asia, the New World. Each section is preceded by a chronology of the area and a short summary of environmental factors of the Pleistocene. Understanding of tool types is aided by diagrams and illustrations.

Howell, F. C.: *Early Man* (New York: Life Nature Library, Time-Life Publications, 1964).
A vividly illustrated, readable account of human evolution from the anthropoid apes to modern man. Chapters 3, 4, and 5 cover the development of the ancient anthropoid apes, the first evidence for the use of tools, Lower Paleolithic culture, and the emergence of *Homo erectus.*

Howell, F. C., and F. Bourliere (Eds.): *African Ecology and Human Evolution* (Chicago: Aldine, 1963).
A collection of important articles in paleoanthropology, dealing with Pleistocene environments as well as physical and cultural evolution.

Napier, J. R.: *The Roots of Mankind* (Washington, D.C.: Smithsonian Institution Press, 1970).
A study of man's primate origins, understandable to the layman and student. Napier emphasizes the development of certain human features from earlier

hominid forms; for example, posture, hand development, and brain size and shape are discussed fully. Chapters 7 through 9 trace man's primate origins from ancient hominids to *Homo erectus* and modern man.

Oakley, K. P.: *Man the Tool-Maker* (Chicago: University of Chicago Press, 1967).
This brief book is a well-illustrated, basic introduction to the development, use, and implications of tools in human evolution.

Pfeiffer, J. E.: *The Emergence of Man* (New York: Harper & Row, 1969).
Traces human development from early primate origins through the early stages of *Homo sapiens* by means of skeletal and artifactual developments. Pfeiffer emphasizes early man as a hunter, supporting his view with contemporary primate studies, as well as with data from modern-day hunters and gatherers.

Pilbeam, D.: *The Ascent of Man* (New York: Macmillan, 1972).
A concisely written review of major evolutionary trends leading to the development of *Homo sapiens.* In addition to discussing the major theoretical positions regarding the processes of physical evolution, Pilbeam also presents considerable evidence for cultural evolution. The author outlines the major evolutionary stages according to the various geographical areas in which noteworthy specimens have been discovered. The book is well illustrated with drawings and photographs. Chapters 5 and 6 discuss the australopithecines and other early hominids in South and East Africa. See Chapter 7 for a discussion of the remains of *Homo erectus* found in Europe, Africa, and Asia.

7

The Emergence of Modern Man and Middle and Upper Paleolithic Culture

By the Middle Pleistocene, some 65 million years after the emergence of the earliest primates, a fully erect, tool-making population of early men and women had evolved. These hand-ax-using *Homo erectus* groups of the Lower Paleolithic age were the evolutionary forerunners of *Homo sapiens,* who would emerge during the Upper Pleistocene and who would evolve into modern man, *Homo sapiens sapiens.*

The Upper Pleistocene was a time in which glaciers periodically still covered much of Europe, Asia, and North America, as well as the mountain regions of other areas. The climate was usually very cold, especially in the northern areas near the glacial edges. However, there were also periods of glacial retreats to the north (known as *interglacials*), when the climate became warmer in Europe and other northern regions. But, even during the glacial advances, the climate in other regions, such as southwestern Asia, was not as cold as the arctic conditions near the edge of the glacier.

During one period between glacial advances (the Mindel–Riss Interglacial), the first *Homo sapiens* emerged, about 200,000–150,000 years ago. From this group Neandertal man evolved, about 80,000 years ago. The major physical change was in the size of the skull. Brain capacity had increased from an average of 970 cc for *Homo erectus* to 1,150–1,470 cc for early *Homo sapiens* to 1,300–1,600 cc for Neandertal man. Bone thickness and tooth size decreased. The forehead was still low and sloping, but not as low as that of *Homo erectus.*

A culture associated with Neandertal man is called Mousterian, after a site in France. Tools were made from a prepared core, just like the Levalloisian flake technique of *Homo erectus,* but the Mousterian flakes were lighter and smaller, conserving flint. A variety of old tool types and the appearance of new tools indicates that Neandertal man was probably exploiting a greater range of food sources than his predecessors had. Neandertal sites also supply the first evidence of belief in supernatural powers and an afterlife.

In Upper Paleolithic times, modern man *(Homo sapiens sapiens)* appeared. Again, the physical changes were mainly in the skull: brain capacity ranged from 1,000–2,000 cc; the forehead became higher and more bulging. The size of the teeth, face, and bony protuberances for the attachment of muscles decreased, as did bone thickness in general, and a chin appeared. Modern man made extensive use of the *blade technique,* which first appeared in the Middle Paleolithic. In this technique, flakes more than twice as long as they are wide (called blades) are struck off from a prepared core. The blades are lighter and smaller than Mousterian flakes, and so even more flint is conserved. There is an even greater variety of tool types than in the Mousterian, indicating an even greater specialization of tools and efficiency in the utilization of resources. The size and density of sites indicate population increases. During the Upper Paleolithic, cave paintings appear for the first time.

Thus, the trends in the Middle and Upper Paleolithic are towards lighter and smaller tools, increasing variety and specialization of tool types, increased populations, and growing interest in art and supernatural practices. Throughout the chapter, we will consider the evidence for these developments.

THE EMERGENCE OF *HOMO SAPIENS*

Early *Homo sapiens*: Steinheim, Swanscombe, and Fontéchevade Skulls

We last left *Homo erectus* more than 300,000 years ago with an Acheulean tool tradition, including hand axes made from cores and Levalloisian flake tools. For what happened during the following 200,000 years, fossil evidence is almost totally lacking. What we do know about that period can probably be held in two hands: an almost complete skull was located in Steinheim, Germany, dated between 200,000 and 150,000 years ago.[1] Another was found at Swanscombe, England, in association with Acheulean stone tools and dated to the same time. The cranial capacity of both (1,150 cc) is within the range of modern man (1,000–2,000 cc). Only the back of the Swanscombe skull has been found, but it is modern in ap-

[1] David Pilbeam, *The Ascent of Man* (New York, Macmillan, 1972), pp. 177–178.

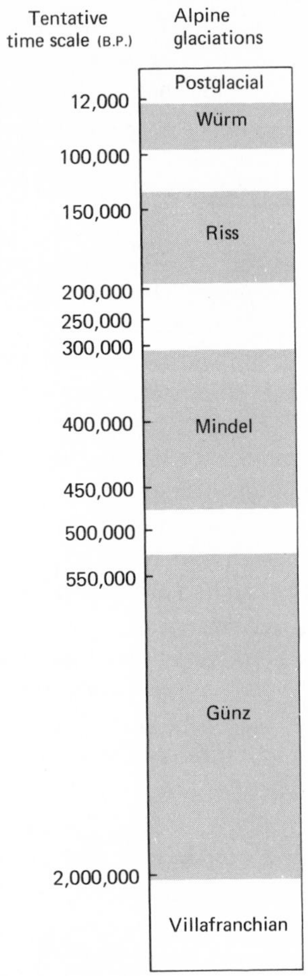

Chart 1
The accompanying diagram illustrates the chronology of the four major Pleistocene glaciations (Günz, Mindel, Riss, and Würm), when ice sheets advanced over much of the earth's surface. These were separated by three interglacials (Günz–Mindel, Mindel–Riss, and Riss–Würm), when the ice sheets retreated and the climate became warmer. A more recent picture of the glaciations suggests that each major glaciation consisted of many advances and retreats of the ice sheet, rather than one huge advance or glacial period and one large retreat or interglacial. (Richard F. Flint, *Glacial and Quaternary Geology* [New York: John Wiley and Sons, 1971], pp. 421–423, 735.)

pearance. The Steinheim find, however, has a face with heavy brow ridges and a low forehead, higher than *Homo erectus* but lower than modern man. Thus, it appears to be transitional between the two types of hominids. Carbonized vegetable matter and flint evidently exposed to fire have been discovered in association with these very early *Homo sapiens.*

Skulls between 100,000 and 70,000 years old were unearthed at Fontéchevade in southeastern France in 1947. Their cranial capacity (1,460–1,470 cc) is well within the range of modern man. The skullcap is similar to later Neandertal man: it is long and low, but there is little or no brow ridge,[2] and the bony ridge at the back of the head is absent.

Middle Paleolithic Culture of Early Homo sapiens. These early *Homo sapiens* utilized both the Acheulean and flake techniques: the Swanscombe skull was associated with Acheulean hand axes like those made by *Homo erectus,* and the Fontéchevade skull was associated with a Clactonian flake-tool tradition.

Our knowledge of the culture of these early *Homo sapiens* was practically nil until 1965, when excavations began at the site of Terra Amata, in Nice, France, along the Mediterranean Sea. The site has been dated to the end of the second (Mindel) glaciation by analysis of the fauna, flora, and tool assemblages associated with it. Because the early *Homo sapiens* date from the Mindel–Riss interglaciation, it is very probable that they were the inhabitants of the site of Terra Amata. This inference is supported by the fact that the tool assemblages associated with the early *Homo sapiens*—Acheulean hand axes and Clactonian flake tools—have also been found on the site. Along the beach, the people of the Middle Paleolithic built oval-shaped houses about 50 feet long. Twenty-one such houses were excavated. Dark circles in the earth are the remains of post holes. Burned areas containing ashes and charcoal located inside the doorways of the houses indicate the presence of hearths. A wall of rocks on the side of each hearth probably protected the fire from the northwesterly winds blowing through the house. The presence of numerous flint chips and flakes on the floor in the eastern part of each house may indicate that flint tools were manufactured there.

Bone and shell remains and analysis of coprolites (fossilized feces) found outside the house indicate that the inhabitants hunted big game, such as now-extinct elephants and rhinoceroses, wild boar, wild cattle, and stag. They also caught fish and collected shellfish and wild spring plants. In addition, pollen grains found within the coprolites are those of late-spring plants. This suggests that the inhabitants were probably nomadic hunters and gatherers, seasonally migrating to this site along the Mediterranean shore only during the spring. At the end of the season, they would move on to other regions until the next spring, when they would probably migrate back to the Mediterranean site. It appears then that the economy of these western European *Homo sapiens* centered around seasonal migrations, based upon big-game hunting, fishing, and plant collecting.[3]

Neandertal Man

The Neandertals are believed to have evolved from the early *Homo sapiens,* emerging about 80,000 years ago. Somehow, through the years, Neandertal man has become the victim of his cartoon image. Usually portrayed as a burly character, more ape than man, he is misrepresented. Actually, he might go unnoticed in a cross-section of the world's population.

[2] Pilbeam, *The Ascent of Man,* p. 178.

[3] H. deLumley, "A Paleolithic Camp at Nice," *Scientific American,* Vol. 220 (May 1969), pp. 42–50.

When the first Neandertal man was discovered on Gibraltar in 1848, little significance was attached to it. In 1856, three years prior to Darwin's publication of *On the Origin of Species,* another specimen was discovered in a cave in the Neander Valley near Dusseldorf, Germany, from which the name, Neandertal man, derives. After Darwin's revolutionary work was published, Neandertal man was acclaimed as a premodern man by evolutionists and dismissed as an oddity by doubters. The controversy centered around whether Neandertal was an early fossil man or a modern pathological freak. "A prominent anatomist reported that the fossils were those of an idiot who had suffered rickets and other bone diseases and had a violent disposition. The flat forehead and heavy brows, he explained, had been caused by blows on the head."[4]

Neandertal's position remained controversial until the discovery of two more skulls in Belgium in 1887 and numerous others throughout the world (in Europe, Morocco, Israel, Iraq, China, Indonesia, North and South Africa) after the turn of the century. Neandertal man could no longer be dismissed as an oddity, an aberration with no relation to man. Now, it was clearly marked as a widely distributed form of man.

Part of the reason for the previous relegation of Neandertal to less than *Homo sapiens* status was based on a highly respected but erroneous study of a skeleton uncovered in 1908 in southern France, near the village of La Chapelle-aux-Saints. The curvature of the spine and feet was said to suggest ape-like qualities. The specimen was therefore classified as the remains of an ape-like creature.

This misleading study was still regarded as a credible and valuable source of information about Neandertal man until 1957, when William Straus and Alec Cave examined it.[5] They concluded that the specimen was probably an elderly Neandertal male of 40 or 50 suffering from arthritis of the jaws, spine, and possibly the lower limbs. Neandertal likenesses to modern man, long overlooked because of the emphasis on the differences, could no longer be ignored, with the result that Neandertals are now classified as *Homo sapiens.*

Physical anthropologists have traditionally distinguished two kinds of Neandertals—a "classic" form ("classic" because it was found first and in Europe) and a "general" type. Classic Neandertal resembles *Homo erectus* in all

[4] John E. Pfeiffer, *The Emergence of Man* (New York: Harper & Row, 1969), p. 160.
[5] W. L. Straus and A. J. E. Cave, "Pathology and Posture of Neanderthal Man," *Quarterly Review of Biology,* Vol. 32 (1957), pp. 348–363.

Generalized Neandertal from Israel. The generalized type of Neandertal combined traits of both Homo erectus *and modern man: the skull shows an increase in cranial capacity and a more developed chin. Brow ridges are still present, but they are smaller than those of* Homo erectus.

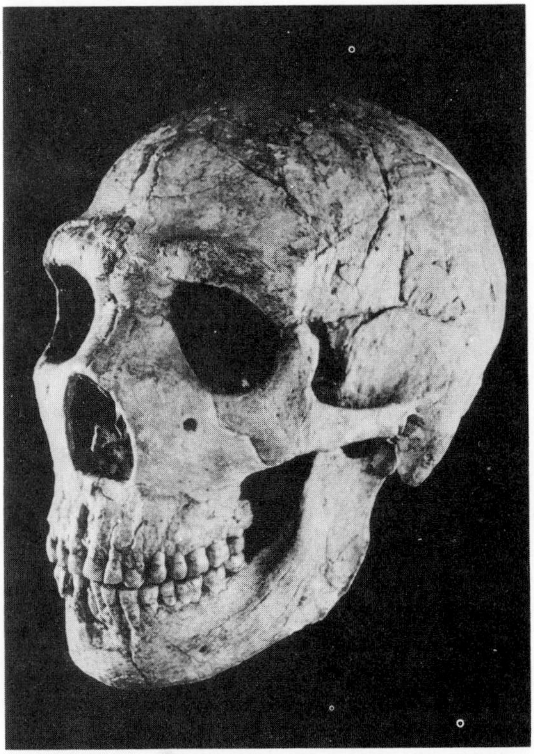

aspects except for larger cranial capacity, which ranged between 1,300 and 1,600 cc (within the range of modern man). His thick skull, heavy brow ridges, large eye sockets, broad nose, long jaw, low forehead, forward projection of the face *(prognathism),* and lack of chin all resemble *Homo erectus.* The generalized Neandertals exhibit classic Neandertal traits and *Homo sapiens sapiens* (modern man traits), such as high, bulging foreheads, small brow ridges and little or no bony ridges on the back of the head, thinner and lighter bones, and a flat face. Generalized fossils were first found in caves in the Middle East, but more recently they have been found in central and eastern Europe as well as in Africa and Java.

Classic Neandertal fossils are primarily found in western Europe, and their distinctive form is probably the result of adaptations to the glacial environment. During the time in which the Neandertals lived, glaciers extended southward over northern Europe; the climate was very cold and dry. Most of the region was ice and snow covered, and reindeer and cave bear roamed the area. Classic Neandertal man's large nose (indicated by the size of the nasal bones and aperture) may have been an adaptation to the cold temperature.

> Because of its size and construction, arteries near the nasal passages were protected from the cold. There was, therefore, no chilling of blood that went to the brain—a critical factor, since the brain cannot tolerate much variation in temperature. Another function of the large nose was to warm and moisten cold, dry air before it went to the lungs.[6]

Classic Neandertal man had a large bony ridge at the back of his head and large neck vertebrae. A bony protrusion from the body of each of the vertebrae has led paleontologists to surmise that these Neandertals had powerful back and neck muscles. Brow ridges and thick bones on the face and skull are other attachments for heavy muscles. Heavy neck muscles may have been adaptations facilitating the chewing of food and hides. Eskimos formerly used their jaws and teeth for dressing and softening skins in the process of tanning hides,[7] and the jaws and cheekbones of Eskimos are often large and heavy. Australian aborigines also have very strong jaws developed from chewing sinewy meat and hides. Alice Brues judges that Neandertal's large, heavy features—chest, skull, shoulders—helped him to retain body heat by reducing surface area relative to body mass, an adaptive characteristic considering the extreme cold they experienced.[8] The diminution of features—smaller, lighter bones and small or absent bony ridges—often found in generalized Neandertals may be a function of their more moderate environment, which did not exert the selective pressures that the extreme western European climate did upon man.

There was not much difference in the appearance of *Homo erectus* and Neandertal man. The most profound change was in the size of the brain. Increasing tool use may have favored increasing brain size, as we noted in Chapter 6. Brain enlargement, in turn, presumably facilitated conceptual thought, probably contributing to the development of more complex tool traditions. The trend in Paleolithic man towards smaller teeth and less powerful jaws is associated with the making of more and more specialized tools, for cutting and other purposes, which suggests a relaxation of selection for large teeth as cutting tools and strong jaws as leather softeners. Also, the eating of meat which was softened by cooking over fire would have relaxed the need for massive teeth and powerful, crushing jaws. But the decreasing size of the face that marks human evolution throughout the Paleolithic may not only have been a

[6] Carleton Coon, quoted in Fred T. Adams, *The Way to Modern Man* (New York: Columbia University Press, 1968), p. 250.

[7] Adams, *The Way to Modern Man,* p. 270.

[8] Alice Brues, "The Spearman and the Archer," in Yehudi Cohen, ed., *Man in Adaptation: The Biosocial Background* (Chicago: Aldine, 1968), p. 188.

function of relaxed selection in favor of robust teeth and jaws. There may also have been positive selection in favor of other characteristics associated with smaller teeth and jaws.

Rhodesian Man. Fossils of two Neandertal-like *Homo sapiens* were discovered at Broken Hill, Rhodesia, in southern Africa, dating to approximately the end of the Pleistocene. The face of Rhodesian man recalls *Homo erectus* in its appearance—huge brow ridges, wide mouth, and large eye sockets—but his brain capacity of 1,300 cc is comparable to modern man's. An oddity in the skull of Rhodesian man is a small hole on the side of the head. It resembles a surgical incision and, since the bone shows signs of healing, the cut is believed to have been made while the specimen was alive.

Solo Man. The fragments of 11 Neandertal-like skulls and two tibias were found in late Pleistocene deposits along the Solo River 6 miles from Trinil, Java. The skulls were heavy and thick; the brow ridge was heavy but discontinuous, dividing in two at the nose; brain capacity ranged between 1,035 cc and 1,255 cc, which puts the remains in the range for *Homo sapiens.* The condition of the skulls suggests cannibalism and perhaps religious ritual: the faces of all of the skulls had been cut off and the lower jaws were also missing. In all but one skull, the *foramen magnum* (the hole in the bottom of the head through which the spinal cord passes to the brain) had been enlarged, perhaps to remove the brain. The opening may have been enlarged by placing a stick or bone in the hole and pressing it against the bony sides. The bones appeared to be *in situ,* that is, in their original location. Skulls carried from one location to another by water are extremely smooth and are called *water-rolled.* The Solo skulls do not appear to have been water-rolled. Solo man and Rhodesian man are believed to be the Southeast Asian and African versions, respectively, of Neandertal man.

Neandertal Man and Modern Man. The position of Neandertal man in the evolutionary lineage leading to modern man is still debated. Experts disagree as to whether or not Neandertal is in the direct line of descent to modern man. The controversy arose primarily because from the time of the initial find in 1848 until the 1930s there was no clear, discernible fossil record of advances from a burly, barrel-chested creature whose face resembled *Homo erectus* to the chinned, high-domed features of modern men and women. It was not until the 1930s that the first generalized Neandertals were found at Mount Carmel in Israel.

Several theories attempt to explain what happened to the Neandertals. One explanation is based on the acceptance of a distinction between classic Neandertals and generalized Neandertals, the latter more closely approximating the appearance of modern man. Classic Neandertals are presumed to have been a specialized form of *Homo sapiens,* adapted to and encapsulated in the western European glacial environment, who subsequently became extinct. According to this theory, modern man would be a descendant of the generalized Neandertals.

Another view is that Neandertal man and modern man were variants of the same species and interbred.

> The archaeological and geological evidence suggests that populations from the Middle East and the Mediterranean regions moved into Europe at various times during the late middle and upper Pleistocene. There was probably considerable mixture of genes as the result of migrations. The morphological variability of the late middle and upper Pleistocene hominids of Europe reflects such movements. The Neandertals may have been absorbed and dominated culturally much as the American Indians were, beginning in the sixteenth century, by European settlers and conquerors.[9]

Interbreeding leading to the eventual assimilation of Neandertal man could also explain the discoveries at Mount Carmel where nearly a dozen individuals exhibiting both Neandertal and modern traits have been found. The possibility that Mount Carmel was the location where Neandertals were evolving into modern man is not unrecognized, though it is now generally rejected by physical anthropologists.

One theory gaining acceptance is that variety should be expected: "Just as we have racial variations in our present world, so must there have existed racial varieties of prehistoric peoples."[10] The distinction between classical and generalized Neandertals may have been a premature conclusion. Neandertals were probably not very different from us. "Brace and other modern anthropologists believe that . . . his differences fall well within the range of variation common to modern man. And, if this is true, it is possible that we can trace our development through him."[11]

To summarize then, it appears most probable that Neandertals were derived from a generalized *Homo sapiens* gene pool (e.g., the Steinheim variety of *Homo sapiens*). Because the generalized Neandertals are so widespread, it is probable that *Homo sapiens sapiens* (modern man) gradually evolved from them—the result of natural selection and adaptation to the environment. The western European Neandertals, living under extreme glacial conditions and so demonstrating adaptations to arctic conditions, were probably more isolated than other Neandertals. Physical isolation implies genetic isolation as well; this may account for less physical variation than is found in the generalized Neandertals.

Inferences about Neandertal Culture. The culture of the Neandertals, during the Middle Paleolithic, dates from 80,000 to 35,000 B.C. The culture is known as *Mousterian* and involves a new tool-making technique. With the Neandertals, we have also evidence that may indicate belief in the supernatural.

The Mousterian Technique. The Neandertal tool-making tradition, or Mousterian complex, was named after the rock shelter in Le Moustier in the Dordogne region of France. Hand axes are found on many Mousterian sites, suggesting that Neandertals probably continued the Lower Paleolithic tool traditions. Neandertals seem to have improved the Levalloisian flake technique of *Homo erectus.* In the Levalloisian technique, the core is carefully shaped by percussion flaking (i.e., it is a "prepared core") before the flake is struck off. In this way the tool maker can control the size and shape of the flake he desires, thus producing different types of tools. The Mousterian technique of producing flakes is basically the same as the Levalloisian technique: a prepared core and percussion flaking are used. But with the Mousterian technique, rather than obtaining only two or three long, large Levalloisian flakes, the tool maker flaked until the core was almost completely used up. The flakes were then retouched to make specialized tools.[12] Not only did this conserve the flint, but, since most of the core was used, it also resulted in more cutting or working edge of tool per pound of flint.

Housing. Caves, already inhabited by *Homo erectus,* also provided shelter for Neandertals. Ralph S. Solecki's discovery of Neandertal fossils in Shanidar Cave, Iraq, enables us to make some inferences about Neandertal life. This cave, apparently a good choice of housing since it has a warm southern exposure and is well protected from winter winds, moved Solecki to speculate about its past inhabitants:

> We still know comparatively little about the Big Cave of Shanidar. But standing before the deep cut that we have sliced into its floor, we can see the general outlines of that history. We see Neanderthal man crouching over a fire nearly 100,000 years ago, and looking out from a cave mouth at a valley land-

[9] John Buettner-Janusch, *Origins of Man* (New York: John Wiley and Sons, 1966), p. 151.

[10] Sharon S. and Thomas W. McKern, *Tracking Fossil Man* (New York: Praeger, 1970), p. 104.

[11] *Ibid.,* p. 110.

[12] Jacques Bordaz, *Tools of the Old and New Stone Age* (Garden City, N.Y.: Natural History Press, 1970), p. 39.

Specialized Mousterian tools: Mousterian point (left); *Mousterian side scraper* (right). (Courtesy of the American Museum of Natural History.)

> scape not too different from the one today. He goes forth to hunt tortoises, wild goats and wild pigs. . . . Apparently he does not try to tackle the swift deer or tackle the dangerous bear, wolf or leopard (at least their bones are practically absent in the deposits of Shanidar Cave). The splintered bones of his game show that he cracked open the bones to suck out every bit of marrow.[13]

Most of the homesites which have been uncovered are caves such as the site of Shanidar. However, some Neandertals lived in the open air, as evidenced by a find in Molodova, western Russia, of houses apparently made from tree trunks inserted into mammoth leg bones and covered by animal skins. Inside, there are a large number of hearths, which suggest that the structure was repeatedly occupied by the nomadic Neandertals.

Evidence of Religious Beliefs. Enough evidence exists to raise a strong possibility that Neandertal man had some belief in an afterlife. At Le Moustier, the skeleton of a boy 15 or 16 years old was found, laid out with a beautifully fashioned stone ax near his hand. With the body were charred wild-cattle bones, perhaps the remnants of a funeral feast or buried to provide sustenance for the youth in another world. Near Le Moustier, graves of three other children and two adults, possibly interred together in a family plot, were also discovered.

The degree of elaboration that could go into a burial and what may be the prehistoric precedents of some of our contemporary customs are illustrated in Shanidar Cave:

> At least one of the individuals, a man with a badly crushed skull, was buried deep in the cave with special ceremony. One spring day about 60,000 years ago members of his family went out into the hills, picked masses of wild flowers, and made a bed of them on the ground, a resting place for the deceased. Other flowers were probably laid on top of his grave; still others seem to have been woven together with the branches of a pinelike shrub to form a wreath.[14]

How can we possibly know this? We know from experience how fragile flowers are, but one part of the flower—the pollen—may be preserved.

Through pollen analysis, archaeologists have been able to infer that flowers—including ancestral forms of modern grape hyacinths, bachelor's buttons, hollyhocks, and yellow flowering groundsels—were buried with the bodies at Shanidar Cave. Pollen analysis entails microscopic identification of pollen from modern plants.

[13] Ralph S. Solecki, "Shanidar Cave," *Scientific American,* Vol. 128 (November 1957), pp. 63–64.

[14] Pfeiffer, *The Emergence of Man,* p. 171.

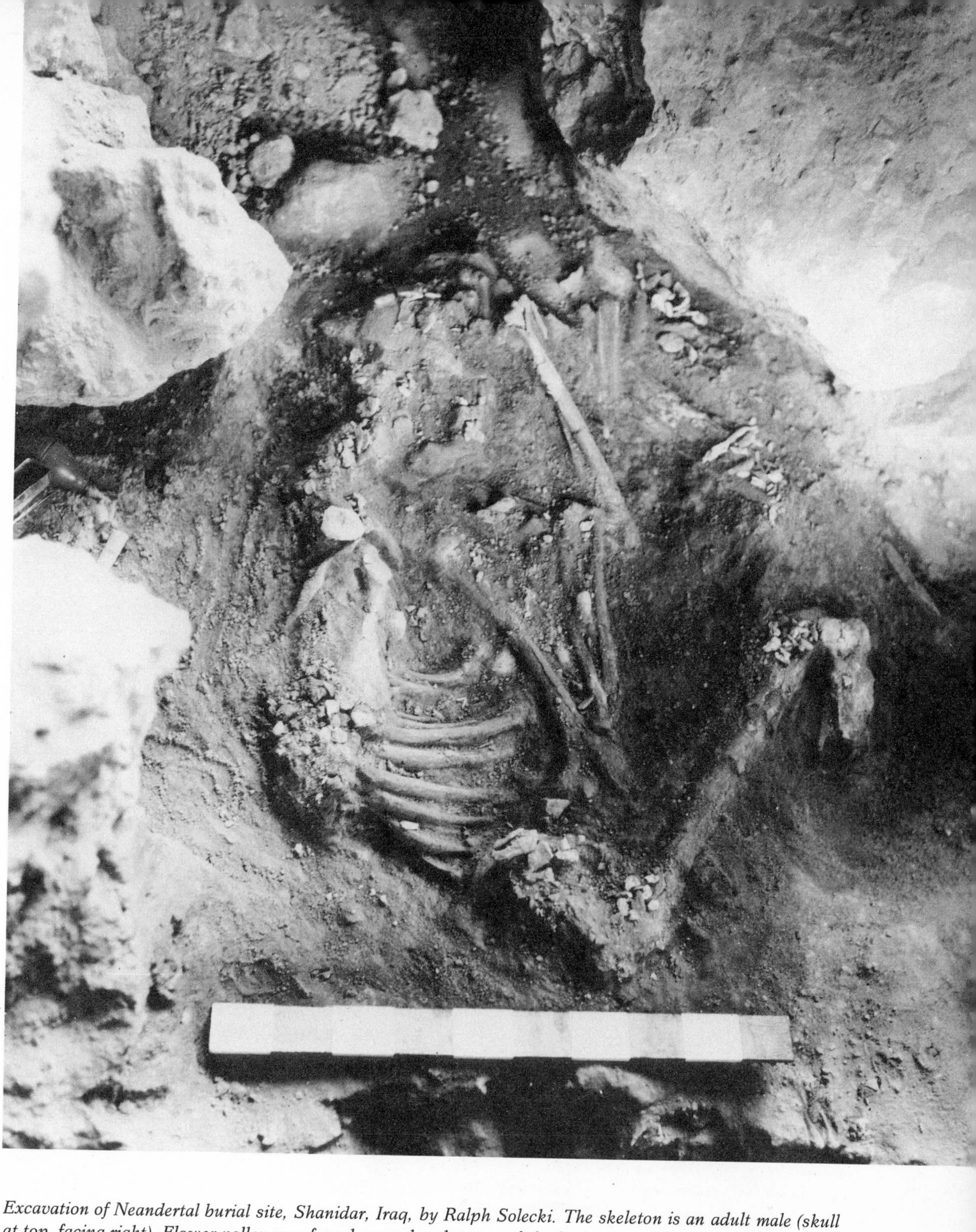

Excavation of Neandertal burial site, Shanidar, Iraq, by Ralph Solecki. The skeleton is an adult male (skull at top, facing right). Flower pollen was found around and on top of the body. (Courtesy of Ralph S. Solecki.)

When these have been identified, it is possible to take a standard number of grains from samples in a vertical stratigraphic section and count the number from each species of plant. By plotting the relative frequencies of various species through time, once can make a pollen diagram describing the changing vegetation for the area involved.[15]

The significance of the pollen in the Shanidar burial site is still controversial, but it may indicate how long ago man began to associate flowers with the rituals of death.

Funerals were probably not the only rituals. There may have been other ceremonies involving bears, which seem to have been objects of worship as well as part of the Neandertal diet. The bear cult is inferred from the circumstantial evidence of seven bear skulls, placed in a line and facing the entrance of a cave in eastern Austria. The skulls were in a rectangular vault. Another site in southern France includes a nearly complete bear skeleton and the remains of nearly 20 others in a spot marked by a unique structure as something special. The structure consisted of a rectangular pit covered by a flat stone slab weighing almost a ton. The careful placement of the bear skeletons and skulls suggests that bears were thought of as more than a source of meat, symbolizing something special to the human cave dwellers who were willing to reserve a prominent place for them in the prehistoric household.

THE EMERGENCE OF MODERN MAN AND UPPER PALEOLITHIC CULTURE

Homo sapiens sapiens

Cro-Magnon man, who emerged about 30,000 years ago, is regarded as the earliest known specimen of modern man, or *Homo sapiens sapiens.* He differed from Neandertal man in that he had a higher, more bulging forehead, much thinner and lighter bones, a smaller face and jaws, a well-developed chin, and slight or absent bony ridges over the eyes and at the back of the head. The Cro-Magnon fossil group is only one variety of *Homo sapiens sapiens.* Other fossils found in different parts of Europe, South Africa, Southeast Asia, and China suggest that the populations of modern man that lived during the Late Pleistocene were perhaps as variable as present-day populations.

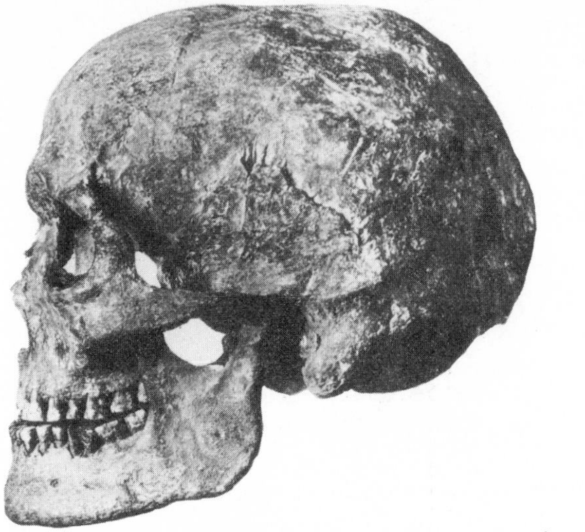

Cro-Magnon man is the earliest known specimen of Homo sapiens sapiens, *or modern man. Note the fully developed chin, increased roundness of the cranium, and the flattened facial profile.* (Courtesy of the American Museum of Natural History.)

Cro-Magnon appeared at a time of comparatively mild climatic conditions. About 28,000 years ago the glacial ice had retreated north into Scandinavia and an interval of cool-temperate climate prevailed over most of Europe. Fauna included bisons, horses, woolly rhinoceroses, musk oxen, bears, mammoths, and, especially, herds of reindeer.[16]

[15] Frank Hole and Robert F. Heizer, *Prehistoric Archeology* (New York: Holt, Rinehart and Winston, 1969), p. 247.

[16] Karl W. Butzer, *Environment and Archeology* (Chicago: Aldine, 1964), p. 379.

Upper Paleolithic Cultures

The Upper Paleolithic cultures of *Homo sapiens sapiens* date from 35,000 to 8000 B.C. The earliest known sites, dating from 35,000 B.C., have been excavated in southwestern Asia and Europe. Upper Paleolithic peoples were mainly hunters and gatherers who probably lived in nomadic bands. Studies of some sites, however, show clusters of neighboring shelters with thick, layered walls, implying that their inhabitants planned to stay for a while.

Excavations also suggest that population was increasing, an inference based on the size of the settlements. For the first time, we also see the appearance of art, including clay figurines and the famous cave paintings in France and Spain. The great variety of tool types suggests increasing specialization and more effective utilization of the environment.

Housing. Most of the Upper Paleolithic sites that have been excavated were in caves and rock shelters. However, a few open sites have also been excavated, in which evidence of dwellings was found. At two Russian sites (Gagarino on the Don and the upper level of Kostienki IV) and at the Czechoslovakian site of Dolní Věstonice, round to oval house plans with diameters of 15 to 20 feet have been excavated.[17] Their size indicates that each hut was probably inhabited by a single family.

At other Russian sites (Puskari and the lower level of Kostienki IV), dwellings were composed of rows of two or three individual family units joined together end to end, each with their own hearths.[18] In Kostienki IV, two such multiple-unit structures were excavated: one structure was about 100 feet long and 16 feet wide; the second was about 70 feet long and 16 feet wide.[19] Each rectangular-like structure contains a string of hearths along its central axis and other pits which were used for storage. A few pits contain hare bones and red ochre, which may have been used for the coloring and tanning of hare skins.[20] One of the structures has two low earthen ridges about 25 inches high,

[17] G. Clark and S. Piggott, *Prehistoric Societies* (New York: Alfred A. Knopf, 1965), pp. 75–76.
[18] *Ibid.*, p. 76.
[19] Richard G. Klein, *Man and Culture in the Late Pleistocene* (San Francisco: Chandler, 1969), pp. 170, 174.
[20] *Ibid.*, pp. 170–175.

Figure 1

Reconstruction of an Upper Paleolithic settlement at Moravia, Czechoslovakia. Huts made of skins, held in place by mammoth tusks and bones, provided shelter against the cold climate. (Adapted from G. Clark and S. Piggott, *Prehistoric Societies.*)

running across the floor and dividing it into three parts; each part is believed to be a separate unit, or room. Because the hearths are located along the central axis, and very few artifacts are found along the edges of the structures, it is believed that they had gabled roofs, the eaves of which almost touched the floors of the dwellings.[21]

Tools: The Blade Technique. Upper Paleolithic tool making appears to have its roots in the Mousterian, since Mousterian flake tools are found in many Upper Paleolithic assemblages. Numerous blade tools also appear. Blades were also found in Middle Paleolithic assemblages, but they were not widely used until the Upper Paleolithic.

In the *blade technique,* a core is prepared by shaping it with a hammerstone into a pyramidal or cylindrical form. Then a series of blades, twice as long as they are wide, are struck off until the core is used up. The blade technique used on flint in this period was more economical than previous tool-making methods. Professor Leroi-Gourhan of the Musée de l'Homme in Paris has calculated that a two-pound lump of flint yielded 16 inches of working edge using the old Acheulean core technique and produced only two hand axes. Using the more advanced Mousterian technique, a lump of equal size would yield 2 yards of working edge. The Upper Paleolithic blade technique, however, greatly surpasses the earlier methods by yielding 25 yards of working edge.[22] With the same amount of material a significantly greater number of tools could be produced with the blade technique. Getting the most out of the valuable resource was particularly important in those areas lacking large flint deposits.

Bordaz believes that the evolution of toolmaking techniques which continually increased the amount of usable edge that could be gotten out of a lump of flint was significant, since man could then spend more time in regions where flint sources were unavailable:

> Hunters and gatherers can only carry a limited amount of material with them during their seasonal migrations and hunting expeditions. With more efficient methods of knapping flint, their range could be extended farther and for longer periods of time into areas where flint was locally unavailable, of poorer quality, or difficult in access.[23]

The Upper Paleolithic is also characterized by the manufacture of large numbers of bone and antler tools. This may have been facilitated by the development of many varieties of burins. *Burins* are chisel-like stone tools used for carving, and bone and antler needles, awls, and projectile points could be manufactured with them.[24] Burins sometimes were found in Middle and Lower Paleolithic sites, but a great number and variety of burins are present only in the Upper Paleolithic. Pressure flaking also appeared during the Upper Paleolithic. In the traditional percussion method, used since Oldowan choppers were first made at least 2 million years before, the core is struck with a hammerstone to knock off the flake. In *pressure flaking,* small flakes are struck off by pressing against the core with a bone, wood, or antler tool. Pressure flaking gave the tool maker greater control in the shaping of the tool, as can be seen in the beautiful Solutrean laurel leaves made during this period.

Ideally, the study of tools should reveal not only how they were made but also how they were used. One way of suggesting what a particular tool was used for in the past is to observe the manner in which a tool is used by members of contemporary societies, preferably those with subsistence activities and environments similar to the ancient tool makers'. This is called *ethnographic analogy.* The problem with reasoning from ethnographic analogy, however, is readily apparent: we cannot be sure that the original use of a tool has not changed. For example, just

[21] *Ibid.,* pp. 171, 174.
[22] Bordaz, *Tools of the Old and New Stone Age,* p. 68.
[23] *Ibid.,* p. 57.
[24] *Ibid.,* p. 68.

because we use an implement called a toothbrush on our teeth does not mean that a much later society will also use it on their teeth. When selecting cultures that may provide the most informative and accurate comparisons, it is desirable to choose those that derive from the archaeological culture we are interested in. If the recent and archaeological cultures being compared are historically related, such as prehistoric and contemporary Pueblo cultures in the southwestern United States, there is a greater likelihood that both groups used a particular kind of tool in similar ways and for similar purposes.

The use to which a particular tool was put can sometimes also be inferred from its wear marks—scratches and nicks on the tools resulting from use. For example, S. A. Semenov has inferred that blades from a site in Siberia were used as meat knives. Only one of the edges of each blade was sharp and polished on both sides, indicating that only one edge of the blade was used. The polish, occurring on both sides of the sharp edge, indicated to Semenov that both sides of this edge of the blade had been used as a knife "to cut into a soft material into which it had been sunk, probably meat."[25] The inference that meat was the material cut is based on the observation that used tools tend to show scratches or marks which suggest in what direction the tool was moved, the tool's position on the object worked, and the kind of object worked.

The validity of this method is tested by comparing the wear marks of the prehistoric tools with those on similar tools used by contemporary people. Bordaz has described the flintworking process among present-day Australian aborigines.[26] By studying the use marks on these blades and noting the use to which they are put, we can find out if use marks correctly indicate

Solutrean laurel leaf blade. (Courtesy of the American Museum of Natural History.)

[25] S. A. Semenov, *Prehistoric Technology,* trans. M. W. Thompson (Bath, Eng.: Adams and Dart, 1970), p. 103.
[26] Bordaz, *Tools of the Old and New Stone Age,* pp. 65, 108.

their functions. For example, if the Australians use their blades as both knives and spear points, do the use marks on the knives differ from those on the spear points, and do all of the knives have the same type of use marks? When these questions have been answered, the use marks on the prehistoric tools can be compared with those on the contemporary ones. Similar marks suggest similar functions.

Another approach to making inferences about the use of ancient tools is by making them and then using them as prehistoric people may have done. One of the masters of prehistoric stone-working techniques is Don Crabtree. His efforts to recreate the handiwork of prehistoric cultures have increased our appreciation of our ancestors' abilities. By duplicating their work, Crabtree hopes to learn the "extinct skills" of the early craftsmen. His experiments with flaking different materials have indicated that prehistoric Indians in America may have heat-treated flint in order to pressure flake them more easily. Crabtree has reported:

> If I attempt to pressure flake an untreated piece of flint collected at a quarry site, the largest flake that I can detach by pressure will usually measure no more than half an inch in length. But if the same material is heated, I can easily press off flakes of more than two inches in length with a hand held flaker. In addition to improving the working qualities of silica minerals, heat treatment also produces a distinct change in the texture and lustre of these minerals, and often a change in color as well.[27]

Inventions. During the Upper Paleolithic, probably for the first time, spears were shot from a spear thrower rather than manually thrown. We know this because bone and antler *atlatls* (the Aztec word for "spear thrower") have been found at some sites. Now, propelled off a grooved board, a spear could, with less effort, be sent through the air with increased force, causing it to travel farther and hit harder. The bow and arrow, in essence a variation or miniaturization of the spear thrower, was used in Egypt and presumably elsewhere during the Upper Paleolithic. Also invented at this time were harpoons, used for fishing and perhaps for reindeer hunting.

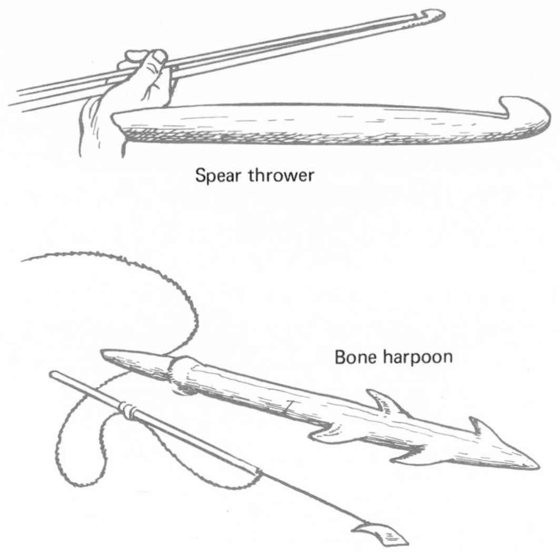

Figure 2
During the Upper Paleolithic, the spear thrower and bone harpoon were invented. (Adapted from R. J. Braidwood, *Prehistoric Men.*)

Art. The earliest discovered traces of art are from Upper Paleolithic sites. One might expect that man's early artistic efforts would be meek and crude, but the cave paintings of Spain and southern France show a marked degree of skill.

Peter J. Ucko and Andrée Rosenfeld, whose work we have heavily relied on in this section, identify three main locations of art in caves: (1) in obviously inhabited rockshelters and cave entrances, the art probably being conceived as decorations—or art for art's sake; (2) in "galleries" immediately off the inhabited area of the cave; and (3) in the inner reaches of the cave whose difficulty of access has been interpreted

[27] Don E. Crabtree and B. Robert Butler, "Notes on Experiment in Flint Knapping:1 Heat Treatment of Silica Materials," *Tebiwa,* Vol. 7, No. 1, p. 1.

by some as a sign that magical-religious activities were performed there.[28]

The subjects of the paintings are mostly animals, with few humans. Perhaps, like many contemporary peoples, Upper Paleolithic men and women believed that the drawing of a human image could cause death or injury. If that were indeed believed, it might explain why people are rarely depicted in cave art. The animal paintings rest on the bare walls, with no backdrop or incidental environmental trappings. The preponderance of animal paintings suggests that man sought to gain an advantage in the hunt. This theory is supported by evidence of chips in the painted figures, perhaps from spears thrown at them. But if hunting magic was the chief motivation for the paintings, it is difficult to explain why only few paintings show signs of being speared. If not only to gain dominance over the game, perhaps the paintings were inspired by a need to increase their supply. Cave art seems to have reached a peak toward the end of the Upper Paleolithic period when the herds of game were decreasing.

Another interpretation of Upper Paleolithic cave art has been suggested by André Leroi-Gourhan. He conducted a statistical analysis of the types of paintings and their locations within each of 66 caves. Leroi-Gourhan concluded that choice and placement of the types of paintings was not haphazard or arbitrary but had some symbolic significance. For example, female animals were usually located in the central chambers of the cave and were associated with what are considered to be female signs—enclosed circles. Male animals, located at the entrance and back of the caves, were associated with male signs—dots and barbed symbols.[29] The work of Leroi-Gourhan suggests then that the symbolism of the Upper Paleolithic cave painters may have been quite modern.

Upper Paleolithic art was not confined to cave paintings. Many shafts of spears and similar objects were decorated with figures of animals, and figurines representing the human female in exaggerated form were also found at Upper Paleolithic sites. Called "Venuses," these women are portrayed with broad hips and large breasts and abdomens. It has been suggested that the figurines may have been an ideal type or an expression of a desire for fertility, but there is no evidence to support these assumptions.

Dating Upper Paleolithic Remains

Radiocarbon Dating. Radiocarbon dating is a widely used method for dating remains up to 50,000–60,000 years old. Thus, it can be used for dating remains from the Upper Paleolithic. Radiocarbon dating stems from the principle that all living matter possesses a certain amount of a radioactive form of carbon ($Carbon^{14}$). Radioactive carbon, produced when $Nitrogen^{14}$ is bombarded by cosmic rays, is absorbed from the air by plants and by animals who eat plants. After an organism dies, no more C^{14} is absorbed. C^{14} decays at a slow but steady pace and reverts to $Nitrogen^{14}$. By "decay" we mean that a number of beta radiations are given off per minute. The rate of decay is known: C^{14} has a half-life of 5,730 years. In other words, half of the original amount of C^{14} in an organism disintegrates 5,730 years after its death; half of the remaining C^{14} disintegrates after another 5,730 years, and so on. This process continues for 50,000–60,000 years, when the amount of C^{14} left is too minute to permit accurate dating.

To discover how long the organism containing the C^{14} has been dead (i.e., how much C^{14} is left and therefore how old it is) we count the number of beta radiations given off per minute

[28] Peter J. Ucko and Andrée Rosenfeld, *Paleolithic Cave Art* (New York: McGraw-Hill, 1967).

[29] André Leroi-Gourhan, "The Evolution of Paleolithic Art," *Scientific American*, Vol. 218 (February 1968), pp. 58–70.

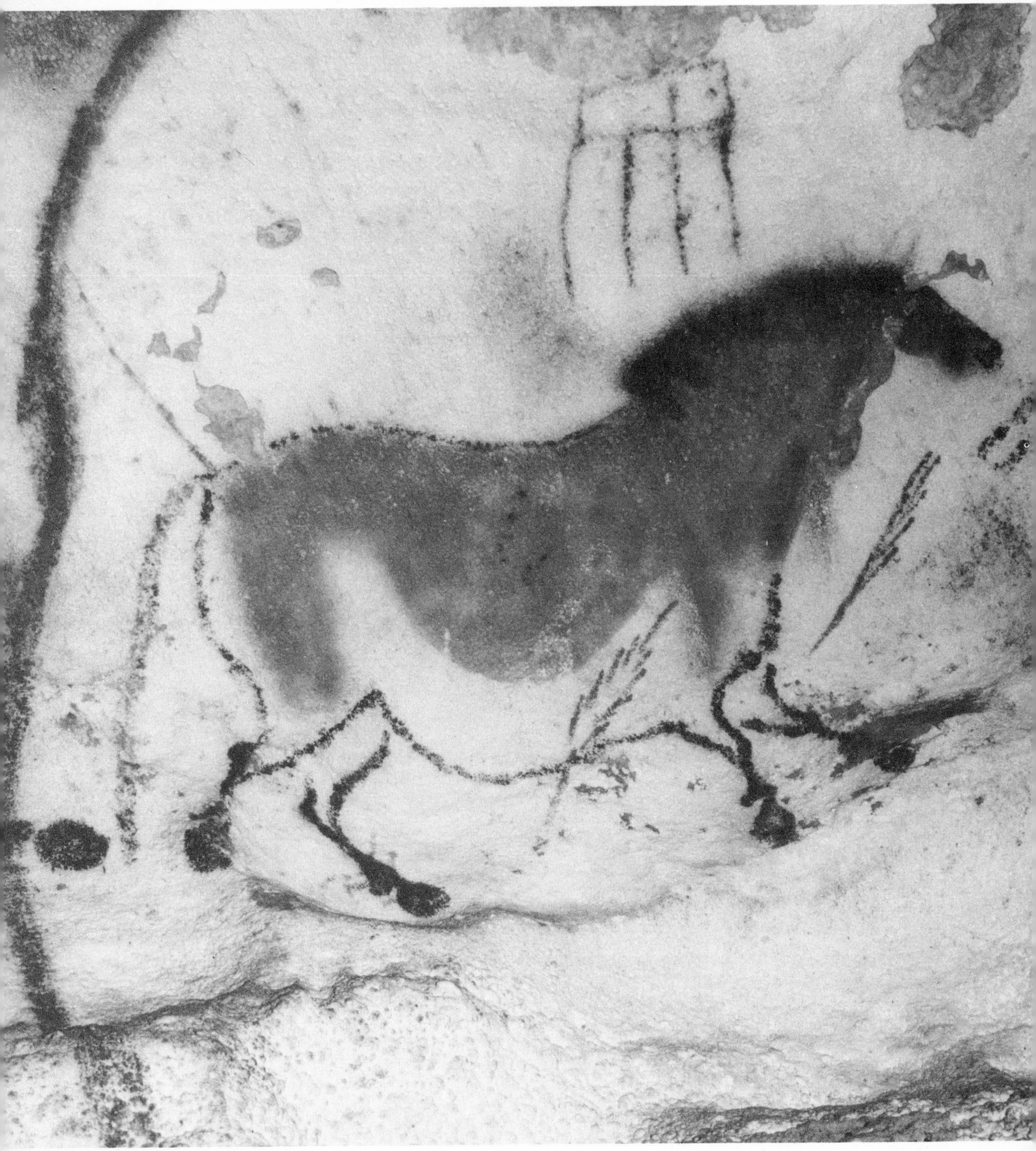

At left, a cave painting from Lascaux, France. The spear in the horse's side may have been painted in a magical attempt to ensure successful hunting. At right, a "Venus" figurine; the meaning this exaggerated female figure might have had is not known. (Left: René Burri—Magnum Photos; right: Courtesy of the American Museum of Natural History.)

per gram of material. Modern C^{14} emits about 15 beta radiations per minute, while C^{14} 5,730 years old emits only half this amount (indicating the half-life of C^{14}) per minute per gram of material. Thus, the amount of beta radiations given off per minute per gram will tell us how much C^{14} is left and therefore how old the material is. If, for example, the material emits 15 radiations per gram each minute, the organism is only recently dead, and we can date it to the present. If it gives off 7.5 radiations a minute per gram, which is half the amount given off by modern C^{14}, this means only half the C^{14} is left. Since the half-life of C^{14} is 5,730 years, the organism must be 5,730 years old.[30] In a test of this method, it was used to judge the age of parts of the Dead Sea Scrolls and wood from an Egyptian tomb, the dates of which were already known from historical records. The results based on C^{14} analysis agreed very well with the historical information.

Varve Analysis. Varve analysis is one of the oldest methods for dating remains, based on the observation that varves—annually deposited layers of silt—remain in lake basins from the run-off of melting glacial ice.

Varves are composed of a double layer with coarse sediments at the bottom and fine sediments at the top; the finer sediments settle during the winter while the lake is frozen over, and the coarser material is deposited in the summer when it is warmer and melting is increased. Varves may range in thickness from a few millimeters to more than 15 inches, though these maximum and minimum values are seldom reached.[31]

The varves are counted, each varve indicating one year of deposition. The number of varves indicates the number of years spanned. The method, however, is restricted in application because varves only accumulate near ice, and many places frozen during the Pleistocene were no longer supplied with silt once the ice retreated. Furthermore, the longest known sequence of varves goes back only 17,000 years.

Diversity of Upper Paleolithic Culture

Although we have generalized about the characteristics of the people living in the Upper

[30] Hole and Heizer, *An Introduction to Prehistoric Archeology,* p. 218.
[31] Hole and Heizer, *An Introduction to Prehistoric Archeology,* p. 236.

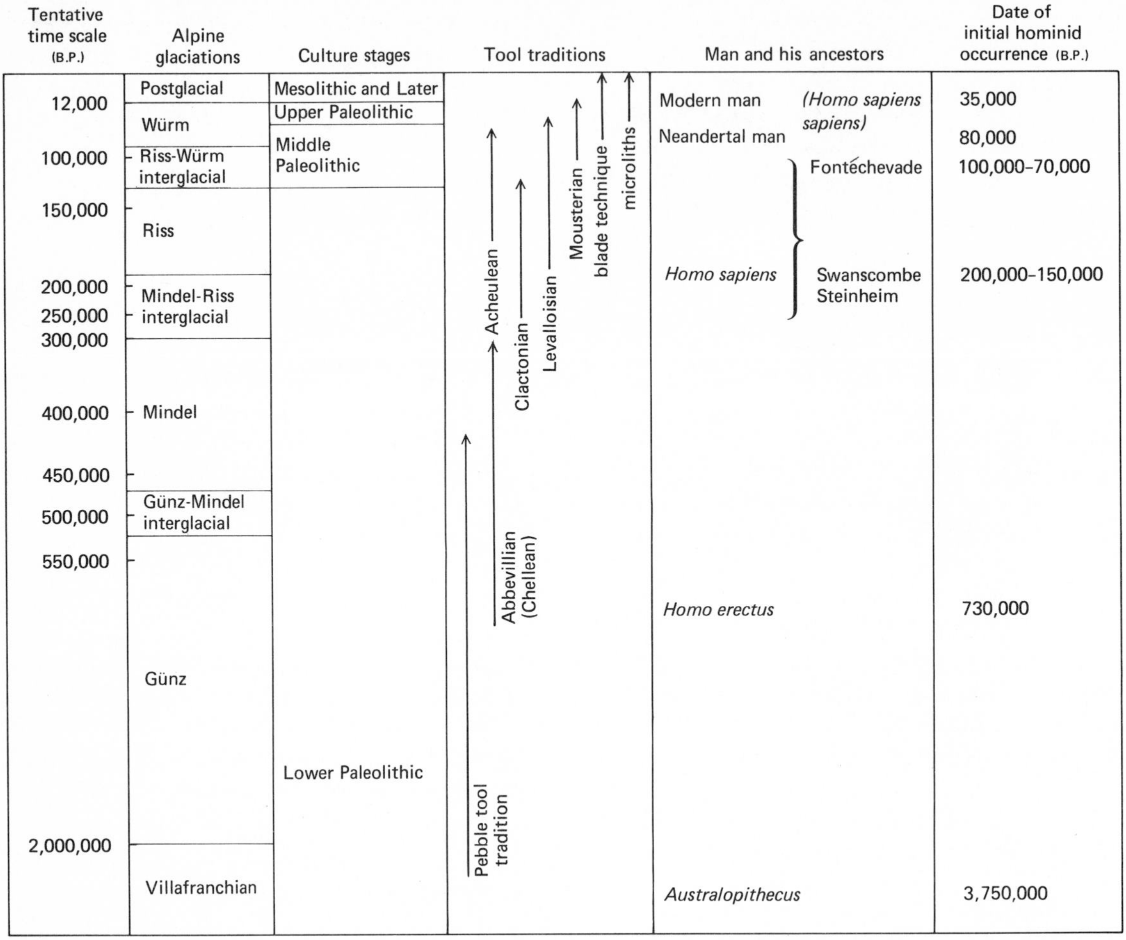

Chart 2

Hominid evolution and its relationship to Pleistocene geology and stages of culture. (Dates are from David Pilbeam, *The Ascent of Man.*)

Paleolithic, we must remember that there were many diverse groups of hunting and gathering peoples whose sites date from about 35,000 to 8000 B.C. Our knowledge of the social organization and cultural differences among these different peoples is slim. This is probably because many Old World archaeologists have not until recently been interested in making inferences about social organization from material remains. Rather, they have concentrated on establishing chronologies and classifications of tools. Recently, however, archaeologists have begun to draw and test inferences about prehistoric social organization.

One way of inferring cultural differences or similarities is to study and compare the tool kits and features (i.e., food storage pits, hearths, house remains) from various sites. These items often vary from one archaeological site to another. It is inferred that if sites share the same tool kits, they probably also share the same cultural activities (e.g., hunting camp, fishing camp, semipermanent village, quarry workshop). The converse is also true: different tool kits imply that different activities were performed at the sites. On the basis of the kinds of tools found and the nature of the site, archaeologists have distinguished a number of Upper Paleolithic cultures.

Upper Paleolithic Cultures in Europe. Based on the artifacts found at various European sites, archaeologists have identified several cultural traditions dated to the Upper Paleolithic. The European Upper Paleolithic includes the Aurignacian and Gravettian traditions, which constitute the early Upper Paleolithic, the briefer Solutrean during the middle Upper Paleolithic, and the Magdalenian of the late Upper Paleolithic.

Aurignacian. One of the oldest and most widespread Upper Paleolithic cultures is the Aurignacian. Thought to have originated in southwestern Asia, radiocarbon dating has placed its time at 35,000 B.C. Its subsequent diffusion throughout western Europe, probably through the Balkans, is suggested by the distribution of Aurignacian tools in that area. A popular tool of the period was the burin or graver, used primarily for carving wood, bone, ivory, and similar materials. The Aurignacian peoples lived in caves or rock shelters. They are credited with the earliest cave paintings in western Europe, including the older ones among the spectacular work at Lascaux, France.

The Aurignacian economy centered on herd animals—horses, mammoths, and reindeers—which provided food, skins, sinews, bones, and antlers. The hunting of these animals must have been a group effort, and the hunters may have followed the hunted in seasonal migrations.[32]

Gravettian. Spanning from 22,000 to 18,000 B.C., the Gravettian culture centered primarily in eastern and central Europe. Because they lived during a brief recession of the ice sheet during the fourth glaciation, the Gravettians were able to reside in skin-covered tents or oval huts. Fossils indicate that mammoths were widely hunted by the Gravettians, who also used the animals' bones and ivory for tools and fuel.

Gravettian artists created "Venus" figurines and pins, beads, and pendants decorated with minute geometric patterns. Evidently, the Gravettians buried their dead wearing clothing and ornaments; specimens have been found with parts of their clothing still preserved.

Solutrean. The Solutrean culture, with sites in France and Spain, dates between 18,000 and 15,000 B.C. The origin and disappearance of the Solutrean tradition is as yet unexplained. Unlike the Gravettians before them, the Solutreans lived during a very cold period in the fourth glaciation.

Solutrean flintworkers created the finest examples of Upper Paleolithic stone tools—the *laurel leaf blades.* They appear to have been made by pressure flaking, thereby giving the tool maker greater control in the shaping of the tool. Bordaz suggests several possible functions: the smaller, thicker laurel leaves may have been attached to wooden shafts and used as projectile points. Some of the larger and more finely made blades may have served a ritual function or may have been aesthetic examples of the flintworker's skill.[33] The lustrous surface and slightly greasy feel of the laurel leaf blades support the conclusion that the tools were treated with heat before flaking.[34] In the last part of the Solutrean, bone tools increased in frequency, and needles with "eyes" make their first appearance.[35]

[32] Chester S. Chard, *Man in Prehistory* (New York: McGraw-Hill, 1969), p. 151.

[33] Bordaz, *Tools of the Old and New Stone Age,* p. 76.

[34] Don E. Crabtree and B. Robert Butler, "Notes on Experiment in Flint Knapping:1 Heat Treatment of Silica Materials," *Tebiwa,* Vol. 7 (January 1964), pp. 1–6.

[35] F. H. Bordes, *The Old Stone Age,* trans. J. E. Anderson (Toronto: World University Library, 1968), p. 159.

A Magdalenian knife (left) *and two graving tools.* (Courtesy of the American Museum of Natural History.)

Figure 3

Spanish cave painting of a woman gathering wild honey. (Adapted from Hugo Obermaier, *Fossil Man in Spain.*)

Magdalenian. The last tradition of the Upper Paleolithic in Europe is the Magdalenian culture, dating from 15,000 to 8000 B.C. Magdalenians used blade tools and developed ways of conserving their stone resources by making many small blades from one stone. During Magdalenian times the number of *microliths* increased. These small, razor-like blade fragments, one inch long or less, were probably attached to wooden or bone handles to form a cutting edge. The microlithic trend extended into and gained importance in the following Mesolithic period. Barbed harpoons made from bone and antler were found at Magdalenian sites; they were probably used to hunt reindeer. During the period, the *atlatl,* or spear thrower, was invented.

With the Magdalenians, the apex of Upper Paleolithic cave art and tool decoration seems to have been reached. In addition to beautifully drawn figures, for the first time we see the use of more than one color in a painting. As we noted earlier, Magdalenians may have sought to gain control in the hunt through their art.

Upper Paleolithic Cultures in Asia and Africa. In Asia, except for some sites in the Near East and Russia, few Upper Paleolithic sites have been excavated. Sites in Syria and Israel show an increasing use of blade tools and the advent of new tool types. In the earlier stages of the Upper Paleolithic, the blades are also associated with Mousterian materials. The later stages have a number of new tools and new varieties of old tools, for example, many kinds of scrapers and burins.[36]

In North Africa, sites of the Upper Paleolithic, Aterian culture, dated from 37,000 years ago, have been found. Its flaking techniques indicate that it is derived from the Mousterian tradition.[37] Contemporary with the Aterian is a blade industry known as the Dabban, which appears to be confined to the Mediterranean coast of North Africa. Many of these sites are in caves, and they are always near either permanent or intermittent waterholes, mainly the former. As in Europe, the trend was toward smaller and lighter tools.[38]

[36] Bordes, *The Old Stone Age,* pp. 198–200.
[37] J. D. Clark, *The Prehistory of Africa* (New York: Praeger, 1970), pp. 126–128.
[38] Clark, *The Prehistory of Africa,* p. 155.

In Africa south of the Sahara, the Middle Paleolithic Rhodesian man had carried on the Acheulean hand-ax tradition of *Homo erectus.* Between 44,000 and 38,600 B.C. this tradition probably evolved into the Upper Paleolithic Sangoan–Lupemban complexes adapted to forest conditions.[39] Sangoan and its later form, Lupemban, are characterized by core tools—hand axes and picks, necessary probably for exploiting the resources of the forest environment. Also in South Africa, Upper Paleolithic sites dated between 35,000 and 20,000 years ago contain a blade industry and the remains of structures. These are semicircular arrangements of stones which may have been used to make the foundations of windbreaks.

Caves and rock shelters as well as open sites were used by Upper Paleolithic man in Africa. Clark notes that the size of the Upper Paleolithic sites indicates increasing populations. In addition, faunal remains from sites in Africa south of the Sahara suggest that Upper Paleolithic men were specializing in hunting certain animal species: at a site in South Africa, hunters concentrated on antelope, goats, bison, cattle, and deer, while in Zambia wart hog and zebra were being hunted. The range of species hunted by Upper Paleolithic man (12–49 species per site) was much greater than the range for Middle Paleolithic man (8–19 species per site).[40] "This certainly suggests that a greater significance now [during the Upper Paleolithic] attached to hunting and that more efficient and selected methods were used."[41]

Like the European and Asian Upper Paleolithic cultures, the African counterparts were hunting and gathering groups, with hunting focused on herd animals. They too seem to have migrated seasonally, living in caves, rock shelters, and open sites. The size of the camps indicates that small bands of people lived in them.

[39] *Ibid.,* pp. 110–113.

[40] Clark, *The Prehistory of Africa,* pp. 132–138.

[41] *Ibid.,* p. 141.

Upper Paleolithic Cultures in the New World. Migrations to the New World had been in progress long before the end of the Pleistocene. For periods during the Late Pleistocene, the Bering Strait, which now separates Siberia and North America, was a grassy plain over 1,000 miles wide. Asian hunters following herds of big game crossed into the New World and moved down through an ice-free corridor alongside the Rocky Mountains. Archaeologists differ on the time during which people could have entered North America. Some maintain that the corridor was open for 3,000 years—from 26,000 to 23,000 B.C. For the next 13,000 years, until 10,000 B.C., the ice barrier was presumably closed. Thereafter, new bands of migrants could have entered North America.[42] Other archaeologists suggest that man most probably entered the New World between 18,000 and 10,000 B.C.[43]

With regard to these early immigrants during the Upper Paleolithic, little is known because only a few sites have been explored. Some of the New World Upper Paleolithic peoples did use pressure flaking, and, as in Europe, bone tools, burins, blade or flake end scrapers, and leaf-shaped knives were made.

Many chopper and pebble tools have been found in the western United States, primarily in desert areas. These crudely made percussion-flaked tools resemble the core and pebble tools of the Lower Paleolithic in Southeast Asia or the core tools of the European Lower Paleolithic. The tools, however, cannot be accurately dated, because they are all surface finds; that is, they are not found where they were originally deposited.[44] In addition, in a dry, windy climate, stones may settle to a lower layer of soil as the sand beneath them is blown away. Stones that were originally on different layers, then, may all settle into earlier strata, making relative

[42] Chard, *Man in Prehistory,* pp. 141–142.

[43] Jesse Jennings, *Prehistory of North America* (New York: McGraw-Hill, 1968), pp. 43–44.

[44] Jennings, *Prehistory in North America,* pp. 65–68.

dating impossible. Radiocarbon dating has not been possible because the rocks must be associated with organic material which would yield datable carbon. Furthermore, if they are not in their original site, then any carbon close to them would give erroneous dates—the carbon would date the age of the *layer* the tools are in, not the tools. If the finds are on the surface, 1,000-year-old surface finds may be associated with 10-year-old surface charcoal. Another reason for skepticism is that the tools themselves may be naturally occurring, heat-cracked rocks. Many archaeologists, therefore, assert that a chopper-tool tradition cannot be ascribed to the early inhabitants of North America. Before this can be done, chopper tools would have to be found in strata dated, at least, to the early part of the fourth glaciation.

We can write with greater certainty about the traditions in the New World after 15,000 B.C. Apparently unique to this part of the world was the use of fluted points. These are lance-like points from which a flake is removed from the center of the point at the base, probably to facilitate attaching the point to a wooden shaft. Fluted points have been found in association with fossils of mammoths and bisons, suggesting that the early Americans were big-game hunters. The wooden handles would in all probability not be preserved, as exposure to moisture and acid in the soil would rot them away.

Three culture groups, known for their big-game hunting, have been dated to the Upper Paleolithic in the United States. Almost all of the sites are kill sites, where game had been slaughtered and butchered. Most of the sites occur along ancient lakes or creeks, where the animals probably came to drink, and at the base of cliffs, over which the herd was probably stampeded.

The Llano Culture. Dating from 9500 to 7000 B.C., this tradition is named after the "Llano Estacado," or Staked Plains of the Southwest. This region, below the range of the ice sheets, had a cool, moist climate and extensive stretches of grassland. Evidently, herds of large animals were abundant at this time. Llano tool kits are associated mainly with mammoths and mastodons and also with bisons, camels, and horses.[45] In the eastern United States, fluted points were associated with deer remains at Bull Brook in Massachusetts.[46] The Llano tool kit is best known for its Clovis fluted points, but it also includes blades and flakes, choppers, scrapers, knives, hammerstones, and bone tools.

The Folsom Culture. Most of the sites for this culture, dating from 9000 to 7000 B.C., are kill sites in the Southwest and West, where herds of extinct bison were driven over a cliff or trapped in box canyons and killed. At Folsom, New Mexico, the remains of 23 bison were found in association with Folsom fluted points. The Folsom tool kit consists of Folsom fluted points, blades, flakes, choppers, knives, gravers, scrapers, hammerstones, and a bone industry. The tools have been associated with wolf, turtle, rabbit, horse, fox, deer, and camel, but mainly with bison.[47]

Plano Culture. Dating from 7000 to 6500 B.C., the Plano culture spanned a period when the climate in the Southwest was becoming drier and temperate. The abundant lakes and marshes of the Llano tradition were diminishing. Game too was changing, as the modern bison and antelope replaced the mammoth and giant, longhorn bison. The hunting way of life continued, with local variations.

The Plano tool kit consists of unfluted lance-like knives and points. In addition to blades, flakes, choppers, drills, gravers, hammerstones, scrapers, and bone tools, milling stones have been found. Such stones were probably used to grind vegetation.[48]

[45] Jennings, *Prehistory of North America,* pp. 71–72.
[46] D. S. Byers, *Current Anthropology,* Vol. 3, No. 2 (1962), under Comments on R. Mason's, "The Paleo Indian Tradition in Eastern North America," pp. 247–248.
[47] Jennings, *Prehistory in North America,* pp. 72–88.
[48] *Ibid.,* p. 73.

SUMMARY

1. The earliest fossil remains of *Homo sapiens* were found at Swanscombe, England, and Steinheim, Germany, and are between 200,000 and 150,000 years old. The main difference between the early *Homo sapiens* and *Homo erectus* is found in the larger cranial capacity of *Homo sapiens.* Other early *Homo sapiens* remains were unearthed at Fontechevade, France. They are between 100,000 and 70,000 years old, and their cranial capacity is 300 cc larger than the earlier *Homo sapiens* at Swanscombe and Steinheim.
2. Neandertal man, whose remains date between 80,000 and 32,000 B.C., is next in the line of descent to modern man. He is believed to have evolved from the early *Homo sapiens.* There are two kinds of Neandertal—"classic" and "generalized." Classic Neandertal is similar to *Homo erectus* except in cranial capacity, which ranged between 1,300 and 1,600 cc. The generalized Neandertal finds exhibit both classic Neandertal and *Homo sapiens sapiens* (modern man) traits. Generalized Neandertals are found all over central and eastern Europe and the Middle East. The classic Neandertal is restricted to western Europe. The latter's highly specialized form is probably the result of adaptations to the glacial environment.
3. Rhodesian man from Rhodesia in southern Africa and Solo Man from Java represent two other forms of early *Homo sapiens* and are believed to be the African and Southeast Asian varieties of Neandertal man.
4. The position of Neandertal man in the evolutionary lineage leading to modern man is still debatable. Some anthropologists believe that the generalized and classic Neandertals were contemporary, the classic being a specialized adaptation to the western European glacial climate and eventually becoming extinct, while the generalized form was in the direct line of descent to modern man.
5. Neandertal man is associated with the Mousterian technique of tool making, which yielded more working edge per pound of flint than did the earlier Acheulean and Levalloisian techniques. Evidence for supernatural beliefs is also found in the Neandertal culture.
6. The earliest known variety of *Homo sapiens sapiens,* Cro-Magnon, emerged about 30,000 years ago. The differences between Cro-Magnon and Neandertal are mainly found in the skull. The Cro-Magnon fossil group is only one variety of *Homo sapiens sapiens.* Other fossils found in other parts of Europe and in South Africa, Southeast Asia, and China suggest that the populations of modern man that lived during the late Pleistocene were perhaps as variable as present-day populations.
7. The Upper Paleolithic culture of *Homo sapiens sapiens* extends roughly from 35,000 to 8000 B.C. Hunting and gathering was the primary method of food getting. Excavations suggest that population was increasing, an inference based on the size of settlements. The first evidence of art appears during this time.
8. The *blade* technique used during the Upper Paleolithic yields even more working edge per pound of flint than did the Mousterian method of tool making. *Pressure flaking* gave the tool maker greater

control over the shape of the tool. Investigators attempt to determine the functions of these tools by observing modern cultures with similar technologies and by making and using the tools themselves.

9. The function of the art found in Upper Paleolithic caves is generally thought to be magical or religious, an attempt at assuring successful hunting. Man also began to decorate his tools, and small "Venus" figurines, women with exaggerated breasts, hips, and abdomens, have also been found.

10. Based on artifacts found at various sites, archaeologists have identified several cultural traditions dated to the Upper Paleolithic in Europe: the Aurignacian and Gravettian traditions of the early Upper Paleolithic, the Solutrean of the middle Upper Paleolithic, and the Magdalenian of the late Upper Paleolithic.

11. Similar diversity has been found in Africa, the Near East, and Asia. Relatively fewer sites have been excavated in these areas and the patterns of variation are not yet as well established as the cultural developments in Europe, though the same trends towards lighter tools, conservation of flint, increased populations, and increased emphasis on hunting can be seen.

12. Upper Paleolithic groups arrived in the New World via a land bridge across the Bering Strait at least by about 12,000 years ago. The early New World cultures resemble the Upper Paleolithic cultures of Europe, Africa, and Asia in the use of blade tools, burins, bone tools, pressure flaking, and leaf-shaped knives. The early migrants to the New World were also big-game hunters, but unique to this part of the world is the use of fluted points.

SUGGESTED READINGS

Bordes, F. H.: *The Old Stone Age.* Trans. J. E. Anderson (Toronto: World University Library, 1968).
Chapters 12–19 summarize world-wide findings of the Upper Paleolithic and Chapters 12–14 present the European evidence. Artifactual materials are described and illustrated extensively.

Buettner-Janusch, J.: *Origins of Man* (New York: Wiley, 1966).
Chapter 9 is a discussion of Pleistocene fossil primates, including the problems of the Pliocene-Pleistocene border, the development of the forms *Australopithecus* and *Homo erectus,* and finally, the emergence of *Homo sapiens.*

Butzer, K. W.: *Environment and Archeology: An Ecological Approach to Prehistory,* 2nd ed. (New York and Chicago: Aldine-Atherton, 1971).
An introduction to the ecological perspective in archaeology. Butzer discusses material dealing with all aspects of the Pleistocene and post-Pleistocene periods; his unifying principle is an ecological approach to the study of prehistory. The second half of the book is particularly valuable, since it deals with Pleistocene environments in major world areas and the human cultural responses to those environments.

Coles, J. M., and E. S. Higgs: *The Archaeology of Early Man* (London: Faber and Faber, 1970).
Chapter 4 presents a purely technical discussion of developments in the stone tool technology of the Paleolithic as a whole. Most valuable chapters for the study of the Upper Paleolithic are Chapters 14–17 which present the major archaeological findings from western and central Europe as well as European Russia.

Fagan, B. M.: *In the Beginning* (Boston: Little, Brown and Company, 1972).
This introduction to archaeology summarizes the

scientific methods used to obtain the data discussed in this chapter.

Oakley, K. P.: *Man the Tool-Maker* (Chicago: University of Chicago Press, 1967).
Chapters 7 and 8 discuss refinements in Paleolithic tool assemblages and also certain general correlations which can be made between stages of anatomical development and sophistication of tool types. Chapter 9 discusses the remains of Paleolithic dwellings and the cave art of the Upper Paleolithic.

Pfeiffer, J. E.: *The Emergence of Man* (New York: Harper & Row, 1969).
Chapters 10 and 11 deal respectively with the decline of the Neandertals and the rise of modern man as well as the outstanding cultural developments of the Upper Paleolithic, including cave art and burials with grave goods.

Pilbeam, D.: *The Ascent of Man* (New York: Macmillan, 1972).
Chapter 8 discusses the hominids of the late Pleistocene, including the early *Homo sapiens* and the Neandertals, and the emergence of modern man.

8

The Development of Civilization

Prior to about 12,000 B.C., during the late Upper Paleolithic, many peoples depended upon hunting large, migratory herds of wild cattle, bison, reindeer, and mastodon. They probably lived in nomadic bands, paralleling the migratory habits of the animals on which they depended. By about 12,000 B.C., however, people, at least in some regions, began to be less dependent upon hunting and increasingly dependent upon fish, shellfish, and wild plants. The marine and riverine resources may have increased with the retreat of the glaciers, which raised the sea level and created many inlets and bays where crabs, clams, and sea mammals could be found. The warmer climate may also have been favorable to the proliferation of freshwater fish and shellfish. Probably because of this increased exploitation of local and relatively permanent resources, man became more sedentary. As sedentarism increased, preagricultural villages were founded. The cultural stage during which these developments occurred is known as the Mesolithic, or Middle Stone Age.[1]

In the next stage—the Neolithic, or New Stone Age, which began in the Near East about 11,000–10,000 years ago—man domesticated and raised or cultivated formerly wild species of animals and plants, built even more permanent settlements, and engaged in trade with distant communities for luxury items. The Neolithic also saw the first population explosion in human history. About 3000 B.C. cities first appeared in the Near East. These cities had political assemblies and kings, scribes, and specialized workshops. The specialized production of goods and services was supported by surrounding farming villages which sent their produce to the urban centers. A dazzling transformation had taken place in a relatively short time. Not only had man settled down, he had also become civilized or urbanized. (The word "civilized" refers to living in cities.) Urban societies first developed in the Near East, and somewhat later they were to develop around the eastern Mediterranean, in the Indus Valley of northwest India, in northern China, and in Mexico and Peru.

Archaeology has traced cultural developments from the Upper Paleolithic to the rise of civilization on the basis of materials excavated from long-buried campsites and villages, including tools, pottery, houses, and refuse heaps. But the boundaries separating the stages of cultural development are not always well defined. In fact, they tend to be blurred, the

[1] Lewis R. Binford, "Post-Pleistocene Adaptations," in Stuart Struever, ed., *Prehistoric Agriculture* (Garden City, N.Y.: Natural History Press, 1971), p. 27.

Upper Paleolithic shading off into the Mesolithic, the Mesolithic into the Neolithic, and so on. Thus, scholars differ somewhat over where to draw the dividing lines and over how to interpret the evidence.

INCREASE IN SEDENTARY LIFE: THE MESOLITHIC

Cultural trends arising in the Upper Paleolithic gradually became intensified, and with such intensification the Upper Paleolithic gradually passed into the Mesolithic stage of culture. For the Mesolithic European, climate may have been a key factor in effecting the transition to a new kind of existence.[2]

Late Upper Paleolithic man had lived in an environment of rolling grassy plains nourished by the water from the melting glaciers and stocked with a rich variety of animals. Immense herds of horses, bison, mammoths, and reindeer grazed and browsed in the grasslands which became more extensive as the glaciers thawed in response to a climate that was becoming more temperate. With such an abundance of excellent quarry, food was always at hand. Upper Paleolithic Europeans were largely nomadic. In those spacious, flat steppes, the animal herds roamed far and wide, and their predators, who depended upon them for subsistence, were obliged to follow suit.

But this hunting way of life lasted only for a comparatively brief time in Europe. At about 10,000 B.C., the glacial sheet began to disappear, and with its disappearance came other environmental changes. As the ice receded, the oceans rose and the waters inundated some of the richest fodder-growing coastal plains. The tundras and grasslands began sprouting trees, and, eventually dense mixed forests, mostly birch and pine, replaced the grasslands. The mammoths became extinct, and while the forested areas still teemed with big game such as wild cattle, elk, red deer, roe deer, and wild boar, it became increasingly difficult to stalk and kill the prey sheltered by the thick woods. During this time, too, the melting of the glaciers created islands, inlets, and bays and moved the sea inland, and the warming waterways began to teem with aquatic resources.[3]

In the scenario sketched for this period by archaeologists, environmental conditions in Europe were such that natural selection would favor the development of a new technology to adjust to the new environment. Thus, the Mesolithic peoples continued to hunt game but intensified their food gathering. Hunting the deer and small game inhabiting the new, dense forests probably demanded much hard work. Even more important, the density of animals per square mile decreased. Man's hunting efforts, then, were probably not very productive. No longer could he obtain large quantities of meat simply by remaining close to the huge herds of mammoths and wild cattle that had inhabited the grassy plains and tundra during Upper Paleolithic times. Thus, some archaeologists believe that the environmental changes caused man to turn from big-game hunting to the intensive collection of wild grains, mollusks, fish, and small game to fill the void created by the extinction of the mammoths and the northward migration of reindeer.[4]

Most of the Mesolithic sites are along lakes, rivers, and ocean fronts. Archaeologists became aware of the Mesolithic exploitation of aquatic resources in excavating coastal mounds, called *kitchen middens.* The refuse of Mesolithic dinners, these mounds consist of piles of shells which centuries of Mesolithic seafood-eaters had discarded. Considerable fishing equipment (hooks, net weights, and so on) and the pres-

[2] J. G. D. Clark, *Prehistoric Europe: The Economic Basis* (Stanford, Calif.: Stanford University Press, 1952).

[3] Chester S. Chard, *Man in Prehistory* (New York: McGraw-Hill, 1969), p. 171.

[4] Binford, "Post-Pleistocene Adaptations," pp. 23–25.

ence of canoes and boats indicate that the emphasis on fishing had increased since Upper Paleolithic times.

Not all archaeologists agree with this environmental theory for the shift in emphasis from hunting to the collection of aquatic resources and vegetal foods. The theory fails to explain the evidence that people had struck out in a new direction not only in Europe, where environmental changes had occurred, but also in Africa and Asia as well; in all of these latter areas, even those far from the retreating glaciers, there is little evidence of climatic change, but similar cultural trends can be observed.[5]

Preagricultural Villages

There is considerable evidence for increasing sedentarism during the Mesolithic. Houses were made of stone or heavy timber.[6] They were relatively solid and could not be easily disassembled, carried to another camp, and rebuilt. The presence of storage pits at some Mesolithic sites also implies increased sedentarism.

In accounting for the increased sedentarism of Mesolithic people, we have noted the effects of climatic and ecological changes. Man no longer needed to follow the migrating herds but rather could concentrate upon the aquatic, vegetal, and small-game resources in a local region. This situation may explain the less extensive movement of Mesolithic man. But it does not completely explain the establishment of permanent settlements. Why did people in some areas, but not in others, become completely sedentary during the Mesolithic? Again, the particular kinds of food resources exploited may have been crucial.

Even today, a traveler passing through the Anatolian Mountains of Turkey and other highland regions in the Near East may see thick stands of wild wheat and barley that grow as densely as if they had been cultivated. Wielding flint sickles, Mesolithic people could easily have harvested a bountiful crop merely from such wild stands. Just how productive this resource can be was demonstrated recently by researchers in a field experiment duplicating prehistoric conditions. Using the kind of flint-blade sickle a Mesolithic worker would have used, they were able to harvest a little over 2 pounds of wild grain in an hour. A Mesolithic family of four, working only during the few weeks of the harvest season, probably could have reaped more wheat and barley than was needed for the entire year.[7]

The amount of wild wheat harvested in the experiment prompted Flannery to conclude: "Such a harvest would almost necessitate some degree of sedentism—after all, where could they go with an estimated metric ton of clean wheat?"[8] Moreover, the stone grinding equipment would be a clumsy burden for any nomadic group. Part of the harvest would probably be set aside for immediate consumption, ground, and then cooked either by roasting or boiling. The rest of the harvest would be stored to supply food for the remainder of the year. A grain diet, then, could have been the impetus for the construction of roasters, grinders, and storage pits by the Mesolithic foragers, as well as the erection of solid, fairly permanent housing. Once the village was built, archaeologists theorize, the Mesolithic band would have been reluctant to abandon it. We can visualize the earliest preagricultural settlements clustered around such naturally rich regions, as archaeological evidence indeed suggests they were.

The Natufians of the Near East.

Eleven thousand years ago, the Natufians, a Mesolithic people living in what is now Israel

[5] Binford, "Post-Pleistocene Adaptations," p. 27.

[6] Grahame Clark and Stuart Piggott, *Prehistoric Societies* (New York: Alfred A. Knopf, 1965), p. 145.

[7] Kent V. Flannery, "The Origins and Ecological Effects of Early Domestication," in Struever, *Prehistoric Agriculture,* p. 59.

[8] Flannery, "The Origins and Ecological Effects of Early Domestication," p. 59.

and Jordan, inhabited caves and rock shelters and built villages on the slopes of Mount Carmel, Israel. At the front of their rock shelters, they hollowed out basin-shaped depressions in the rock, possibly for storage pits. Examples of Natufian villages are also found at the site of Eynan in Israel.

Eynan is a stratified site containing the remains of three villages in sequence, one atop the next. Each village consisted of about 50 circular "pit" houses. The floor of each house was sunk a few feet into the ground, so that the walls of the house consisted partly of earth, below ground level, and partly of stones, above ground level. Pit houses have the advantage of containing heat longer than houses built solely above ground. The villages appear to have had stone-paved walks; circular stone pavements ringed what seem to be permanent hearths; and the dead were interred in village cemeteries. Their tools suggest that the Natufians harvested wild grain intensively: sickles recovered from their villages have a specific sheen, which experiments have shown to be the effect of flint striking grass stems, as a sickle would be used in the cutting of grain. The Natufians are the earliest Mesolithic peoples known to us to have stored surplus crops: beneath the floors of the stone-walled houses, plastered storage pits were constructed. In addition to wild grains, the Natufians exploited a wide range of local resources.[9]

The Mesolithic in Africa. The Mesolithic stage of culture was represented in Africa by the Early Khartoum tradition which began about 5000 B.C. Like the Near Eastern Mesolithic Natufians, the Early Khartoum people had an economy based on intensified plant gathering, fishing, and hunting of a wide range of local resources. There is no evidence of domestication at their riverside sites, but fairly large village settlements and pottery indicate increased sedentarism (pottery is not generally associated in recent times with nomadic hunter-gatherers).

The Mesolithic in Northern Europe. The Mesolithic stage of culture was established in northern Europe about 5000 B.C. As in Africa, most of the sites are located along lakes and rivers. Like the Natufians and Khartoum people, the economy of the northern Europeans was based upon intensive foraging of local resources. An analysis of faunal remains and tool types suggests a diet of shellfish, fish, small mammals, and birds as well as large animals such as deer, cattle, and gazelle.

Mesolithic Technology. Technologically, Mesolithic cultures do not depart radically from Upper Paleolithic cultures. The trend toward smaller and lighter tools continues: microliths, small blades from a half-inch to 2 inches long, which occur in late Upper Paleolithic times, are now abundant. In fact, some archaeologists have singled out this technique in tool manufacture as the defining feature of the Mesolithic.[10] In place of the one-piece flint implement, Mesolithic man in Europe, Asia, and Africa equipped himself with composite tools; that is, tools made of more than one material. Microliths could be fitted into grooves in bone or wood to form arrows, harpoons, daggers, and sickles.

A Mesolithic sickle, for example, was made by inserting several microliths into a groove in a wooden or bone handle. The blades were held in place by resin. A broken microlith could be replaced like a blade in a razor. In addition to being versatile, microliths enabled the Mesolithic hunter to manufacture tools and weapons from many varieties of available stone. He was no longer limited to flint. Because he did not need the large flint nodules to make large core

[9] J. Mellaart, "Roots in the Soil," in S. Piggott, ed., *The Dawn of Civilization* (London: Thames and Hudson, 1961), pp. 41–64.

[10] Binford, "Post-Pleistocene Adaptations," p. 27.

and flake tools, he could use small pebbles of flint to make the small blades. In addition, he could use other stones which only yielded small flakes.[11]

Other Upper Paleolithic trends continued by Mesolithic man in the Near East, Africa, and northern Europe were the manufacture of bone implements and the use of the bow and arrow, which become the principal weapon. Flaked axes and adzes with edges of ground stone first appeared in the Mesolithic, especially in northern Europe, where, based on their use marks, on ethnographic analysis, and on the presence of canoes and paddles, they were probably used to make the dugout canoes and paddles.

DOMESTICATION OF PLANTS AND ANIMALS: THE NEOLITHIC

Neolithic means "new stone age," and it originally signified the cultural stage in which man invented ground stone tools and pottery. However, we now know that both of these characteristics were present in earlier times, so we cannot define the Neolithic stage of culture on the basis of these criteria. At present, archaeologists define the Neolithic in terms of the presence of domesticated plants and animals. In the Neolithic stage of culture, man began to produce his food, rather than merely collect it.

How do we know in a particular site that domestication has occurred? Domesticated plants have different characteristics than wild plants of the same types. For example, wild grains of barley and wheat have a fragile rachis (the seed-bearing part of the stem) which shatters easily, releasing the seeds. Domesticated grains have a tough rachis, which does not shatter easily.[12] In addition, wild grains have a tough husk covering the grain, while the cultivated forms usually do not, as it is often bred out of them. Domesticated species of animals also differ from the wild varieties. For example,

Tools made from microlith blades and chipped stone attached to bone and horn handles. (Courtesy of the American Museum of Natural History.)

the horns of wild goats in the Near East are shaped differently from those of domesticated goats.[13]

Differences in physical characteristics are not the only indicators of domestication. Some archaeologists believe that imbalances in the sex and age ratios of animal remains at sites suggest that domestication has occurred. For

[11] S. A. Semenov, *Prehistoric Technology,* trans. M. W. Thompson (Bath, Eng.: Adams and Dart, 1970), pp. 63, 203–204.

[12] Jack R. Harlan and Daniel Zohary, "Distribution of Wild Wheats and Barley," *Science,* Vol. 153 (September 2, 1966), pp. 1077, 1079.

[13] Kent V. Flannery, "The Ecology of Early Food Production in Mesopotamia," *Science,* Vol. 147 (March 12, 1965), p. 1252.

example, at Zawi Chemi Shanidar, in Iraq, the proportion of young to mature sheep remains is much higher than the ratio of young to mature sheep in wild herds. It is inferred that the animals were domesticated, the adults being saved for breeding purposes while the young were eaten. (If mostly young animals are eaten, and only a few animals are allowed to grow old, most of the bones found in a site will be from the young animals that were killed regularly for food.) At Jarmo, in northeastern Iraq, the proportion of males to females was much higher than in normal, wild herds of sheep, which may indicate that the females were saved for breeding and the males butchered for food.[14]

Domestication was not an easy process. Artificial, or human-planned, selection was necessary. Seeds of cereal grasses recovered from Neolithic villages, studied by the Danish botanist Hans Helbaek, tell of the prehistoric farmers' achievements in developing grains that yielded rich harvests. Sometimes, the selective process may have been inadvertent, a kind of trial-and-error separation. When wild grain ripens in the field, the seed-bearing part, or rachis, shatters easily, dispersing the seed. This is a selective advantage under wild conditions, since it is nature's method of propagating the species. Plants with a tough rachis, therefore, have a slender chance of reproducing themselves under natural conditions but are more desirable for planting. When the Neolithic farmer descended with sickles and flails on the wild stands of grain, the seeds harvested contained a high proportion of tough-rachis mutants, since these could best withstand the rough treatment of harvest processing. More consciously, perhaps, the Neolithic planters may have selected for planting any mutant grass seed that had a tough rachis and produced more and better seeds. Perhaps in this way, wild two-row barley evolved into the domestic six-row barley known to us.[15]

Livestock too were domesticated on the Neolithic farm and were also subjected to selection. There is almost no question in the minds of archaeologists that Neolithic stockkeepers bred undesirable traits out of the wild species to produce domestic varieties. The examples discussed earlier—animal bones exhumed at Jarmo which suggest that males were slaughtered while females were kept for breeding and possibly milk production and the differences between the horn shapes of wild and domestic goats—support this contention. Knowing that domestication occurred, however, does not explain *why* it occurred. Many theories have been suggested to answer this question.

Could a hunting society have transformed itself into an agricultural one because its basic food source—the great animal herds—dwindled at the close of the Upper Paleolithic age? The answer, according to some archaeologists, is yes. However, critics of this view contend that the Near East, unquestionably a region where agriculture began, experienced no such food pressures at the time. In fact, during the Mesolithic and Neolithic periods, people could have probably collected and gathered as much food from wild goats, sheep, wheat, and barley as farming could have yielded. Why, then, did they turn to domestication?

Braidwood's archaeological excavations in the Near East indicated to him that domestication began in regions where the local plants and animals were species that could be domesticated: wild sheep, goats, and grains were found in areas with the oldest farming villages.[16] In addition, Braidwood and Willey believe that people did not undertake domestication until they had learned a lot about their environment and until culture had evolved far enough for

[14] Flannery, "The Ecology of Early Food Production in Mesopotamia," p. 1253.
[15] Flannery, "The Ecology of Early Food Production in Mesopotamia," pp. 1251–1253.
[16] Gary A. Wright, "Origins of Food Production in Southwestern Asia: A Survey of Ideas," *Current Anthropology,* Vol. 12, Nos. 4–5 (October–December 1, 1971), pp. 447–477.

them to handle such an undertaking. "Why did incipient food production not come earlier? Our only answer at the moment is that culture was not ready to achieve it."[17] As Braidwood wrote earlier:

> In my opinion there is no need to complicate the story with extraneous "causes." . . . Around 8000 B.C. the inhabitants of the hills around the fertile crescent had come to know their habitat so well that they were beginning to domesticate the plants and animals they had been collecting and hunting. . . . From these "nuclear" zones cultural diffusion spread the new way of life to the rest of the world.[18]

Such an interpretation is unsatisfactory to some archaeologists because it does not suggest why culture was not "ready" earlier to achieve domestication. Another explanation of the origin of food production, which attempts to answer this question, has been offered by Kent Flannery. Flannery suggests that domestication began in areas near, but not directly within, the areas (known as *nuclear zones*) where the greatest numbers of domesticable plants and animals were found. He notes that the site of Tell Mureybat in Syria is located in a nuclear zone. Dating to about 8000 B.C., it had clay-walled houses, milling equipment, and roasting pits and was occupied by a fairly sedentary population of hunters and collectors of wild cereals. Such evidence indicates that sedentarism is possible with a hunting-gathering economy if the area is rich enough in wild cereal resources. Given this possibility, selective pressures for domestication would not be as strong in the rich nuclear zones as in the less bountiful areas adjacent to them, known as *marginal areas*. These would have had less of the potential domesticants, and the people living in such locations might have wished to increase the amount of available grain.[19] Hence, people living in the marginal areas might have been more likely to experiment with domestication than the people living in the nuclear zones.

Population Growth during the Neolithic

Simultaneous with the earliest known transition from hunting and gathering to agriculture, the population in the Near East increased greatly. The Fertile Crescent, the arc stretching from the flanks of the Zagros Mountains in Iran through Anatolia and Syria and southward to the Jordan Valley, was the area of the first population explosion in human history. The population level rose tenfold over what it had been at the end of the Paleolithic age.

Traditionally, population expansion was seen as a result of domestication: it was assumed that hunting and gathering peoples had small populations because they could not obtain enough food to support larger populations, and that domestication increased their capacity to obtain food, thereby facilitating an increase in population.[20]

Recently, the opposite view has been proposed—namely, that population growth itself stimulated the cultivation of fields and the corralling of wild animals.[21] But why did the population grow? It has been suggested that increased sedentarism may be responsible for population expansion.[22] For nomadic peoples, a

[17] R. J. Braidwood and Gordon Willey, "Conclusions and Afterthoughts," in *Courses toward Urban Life* (Chicago: Aldine, 1962), p. 342.

[18] R. J. Braidwood, "The Agricultural Revolution," *Scientific American,* Vol. 203 (1960), p. 134.

[19] Flannery, "The Origins and Ecological Effects of Early Domestication," pp. 50–60.

[20] V. Gordon Childe, *Man Makes Himself* (New York: Mentor Books, New American Library, 1951), p. 61.

[21] Ester Boserup, *The Conditions of Agricultural Growth: The Economics of Agrarian Change under Population Pressures* (Chicago: Aldine, 1965).

[22] Robert Sussman, "Child Transport, Family Size, and the Increase in Human Population Size during the Neolithic," *Current Anthropology,* Vol. 13 (April 1972), pp. 258–267; and Richard B. Lee, "Population Growth and the Beginnings of Sedentary Life among the !Kung Bushmen," in *Population Growth: Anthropological Implications* (Cambridge, Mass.: M.I.T. Press, in press).

The !Kung Bushmen of the Kalahari Desert on the move. Spacing births an average of four years apart helps to assure that a woman will not have to carry more than two children at a time. (Courtesy of Irven DeVore.)

number of small children are burdensome and awkward, since very small children must be carried by someone, usually the mother, and several such children for the same mother would be a liability when the band traveled from one campsite to another. Contemporary hunters and gatherers may increase the spacing of children, principally because of the heavy responsibilities that fall to the mother and the difficulty of carrying young children.

The !Kung Bushmen of the Kalahari Desert in Africa are hunting and gathering people whose women must carry the young on their backs or shoulders when they gather plants or move from one camp to another. Not surprisingly, Bushmen children were generally spaced an average of four years apart. But once a group becomes more sedentary, a Bushman woman can shorten the intervals between births without greatly increasing her work load. Based on these observations, Richard Lee has suggested that sedentary, agricultural communities may have been a precondition for rapid population growth during the Neolithic.[23] Thus, sedentarism may have initiated the Neolithic population explosion, which was accelerated by the development of increasingly advanced techniques of food production, such as new types of crops, larger and more fertile domestic animals, and irrigation.

[23] Lee, "Population Growth and the Beginnings of Sedentary Life among the !Kung Bushmen."

Neolithic Progress: Housing, Technology, and Trade

During the Neolithic, previously developed technological innovations became even more sophisticated, and new inventions and techniques proliferated. Never before had so much innovation been telescoped into so brief an interval as in the Neolithic.

Houses became more elaborate and more comfortable and construction methods improved. The material used in construction depended upon whether timber or stone were locally available or whether a strong sun could dry mud bricks. A modern architect might find to his surprise that bubble-shaped houses were known long ago in Neolithic Cyprus. Families in the island's town of Khirokitia made their homes in large, domed, circular dwellings shaped like beehives which had stone foundations and mud-brick walls. Often, to create more space, the interior was divided horizontally, the second floor propped firmly on limestone pillars.

Sizable villages of solidly constructed, gabled, wood houses were built in Europe on the banks of the Danube and along the rims of Alpine lakes.[24] Many of the gabled wooden houses in the Danube region were "longhouses," long, rectangular structures which apparently sheltered several family units. In Neolithic times these longhouses had doors, beds, tables, and other furniture which illustrate the close resemblance to homes in our society. We know the Danubians had furniture because miniature clay models have been found at their sites. Several of the chairs and couches seem to be models of padded and upholstered furniture with wooden frames, indicating that the Neolithic European craftsmen were creating fairly sophisticated furnishings.[25] The furnishings are the results of an advanced tool tech-

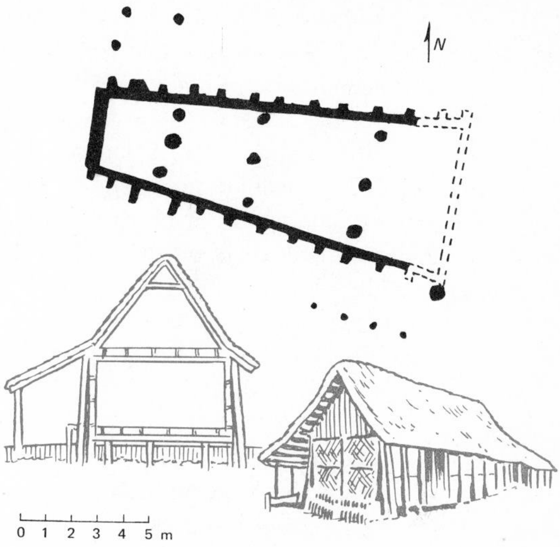

Figure 1

Plan and reconstruction of a Neolithic Danubian house. Its shape is a slight modification of the longhouse. Three rows of post holes indicate where timbers were sunk into the soil. (After W. Buttler, "Pits and Pit Dwellings in Southeast Europe.")

Figure 2

Clay models of furniture found at a Neolithic site in Bulgaria. (After G. Clark and S. Piggott, *Prehistoric Societies.*)

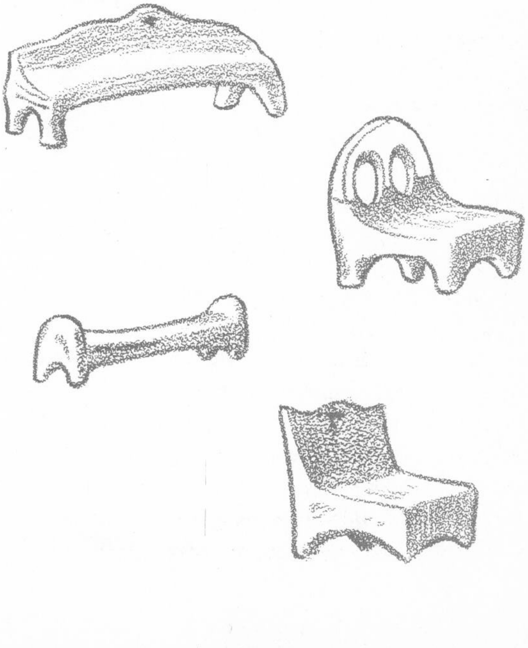

[24] Clark and Piggott, *Prehistoric Societies,* pp. 240–242.
[25] Clark and Piggott, *Prehistoric Societies,* p. 235.

nology put to use by a people who, because they were staying in one area, could use furniture.

For the first time, apparel made of a woven textile appeared. But this development was not simply the result of the domestication of flax (for linen), cotton, and wool-growing sheep. The sources of fiber alone could not produce cloth. It was the development by Neolithic society of the spindle and loom for spinning and weaving that introduced textiles. True, textiles can be woven by hand without a loom, but it is a slow and laborious process, impractical for producing garments.

For scholars tracing prehistory, pottery is an indicator of sedentarism. Nomadic hunters do not generally have ceramic vessels, which are heavy and breakable. For sedentary cultivators, however, these containers are enormously useful. Expectably, then, Neolithic sites are rich in all kinds of pottery.

At first, Neolithic ceramicists continued the older pottery tradition inherited from sedentary Mesolithic cultures, making plain earthenware suited to the many needs for utensils. They produced large urns for grain storage, mugs, cooking pots, and dishes. To improve the retention of liquid, the Near East potters were the first to glaze the earthenware's porous surface. Later, Neolithic ceramics became more artistic—designers painted colorful patterns on the vessels and shaped the clay into graceful forms.

It is very probable that virtually all of these architectural and technological innovations could not have occurred until man became fully sedentary. Nomadic hunting and gathering cultures would find it difficult to carry many material goods, especially fragile items such as pottery. Thus, many Neolithic goods would not be advantageous to the nomad, and neither would Neolithic architecture. It was only when man became fully sedentary that these goods would have provided advantages, by enabling villagers to cook and store food more effectively and house themselves more comfortably.

There is also evidence of long-distance trade in the Neolithic, as archaeologists have recently discovered: obsidian (a volcanic glass which may be ground into sharp tools) from Anatolia was being exported to sites in the Zagros mountain range of Iran and to the Levant (e.g., Israel, Jordan, Syria). Great amounts of obsidian were exported to sites about 190 miles from the source of supply: more than 80 percent of the stone tools used by residents of those areas were made of obsidian.[26] Marble was being sent from western to eastern Anatolia, and seashells from the coasts were traded to distant inland regions. Such trade suggests a considerable amount of contact between various Neolithic communities.

Early Neolithic Agricultural Settlements in the Near East

Jarmo. Jarmo, in northeastern Iraq, was settled nearly 9,000 years ago. It had about 25 houses—mud huts divided into rectangular rooms with matted floors—and a population estimated at 150. The families were farmers: the character of the charred grain kernels indicates domestication, and the fact that only about 5 percent of all the animal bones recovered at the site belong to wild species shows the extent of stockbreeding. Artifacts uncovered in Jarmo consist of tools necessary for farming—microliths for sickles used to harvest grain, querns (large, rather flat stones upon which grain is ground), mortars and pestles for pounding other plant foods, and axes and adzes for clearing and shaping trees. The people at Jarmo seem to have done some trading. Decorative seashells probably came from the nearest seacoast, the Persian Gulf, and the nearest source of the obsidian used for tools is a volcanic area about 200 miles away.

[26] Colin Renfrew, "Trade and Culture Process in European History," *Current Anthropology,* Vol. 10 (April–June 1969), pp. 156–157, 161–169.

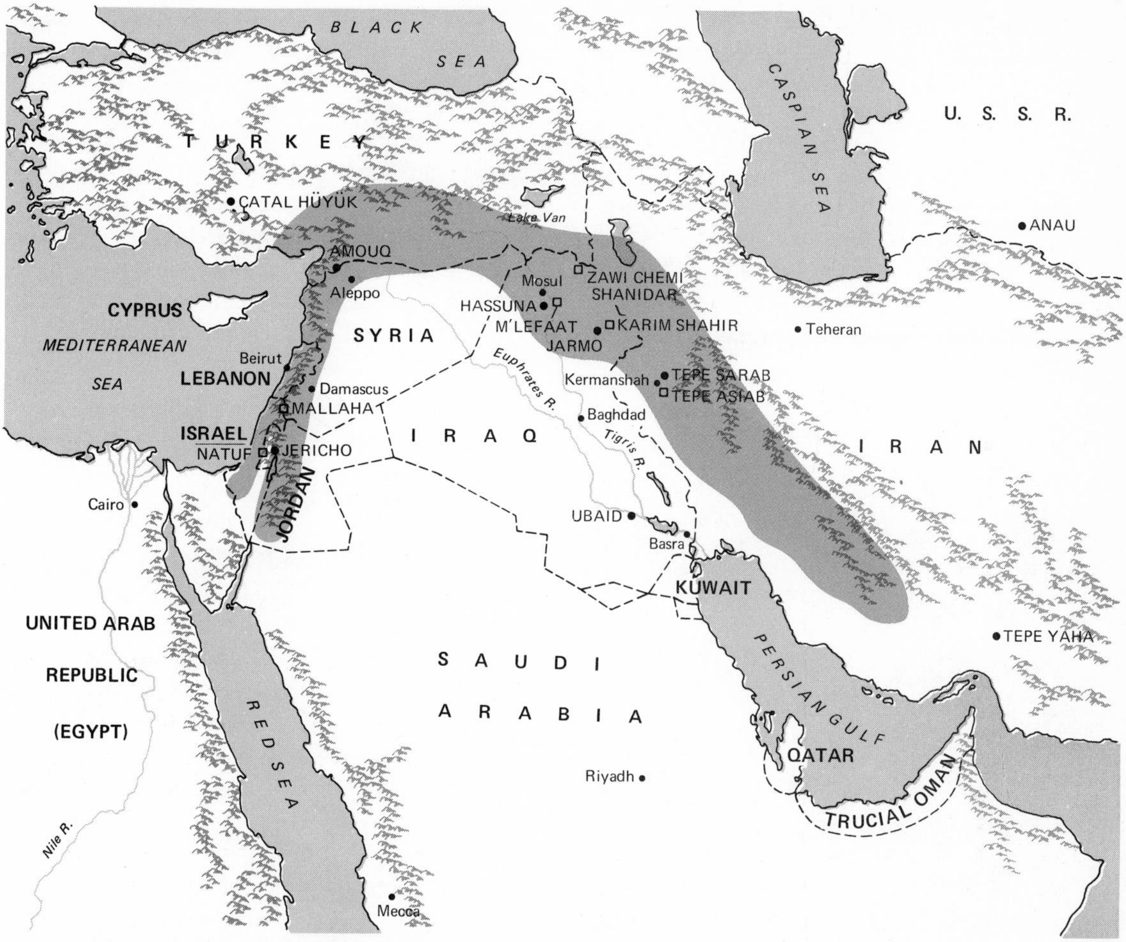

Preagricultural villages (□) and early agricultural settlements (●) arose in the fertile areas of the Near East. (Modern cities are represented by •) (Adapted from R. J. Braidwood, "The Agricultural Revolution.")

Çatal Hüyük. On a wind-swept plateau in the rugged, mountainous region of southern Turkey stand the remains of a sophisticated, mud-brick town, one of the earliest built by Neolithic people and a milestone on the road to civilization. It is known as Çatal Hüyük—*hüyük* being the Turkish word for a mound formed by a succession of settlements, one built on top of another.

Some 7,500 years ago, a people occupied this adobe town—some 200 houses have been excavated—with homes interconnected in Pueblo fashion. They decorated their walls with imaginative murals, and their shrines with symbolic statuary. The murals depict what seem to be religious scenes and everyday events. Archaeologists peeling away frescoes found layer upon layer of murals, indicating that old murals were plastered over to make way for fresh paintings. Several rooms are believed to have been shrine rooms. In those rooms, large bull murals, full-sized clay heads of cattle upon the walls, and clay bull figurines are abundant. In addition, "shrine room" murals depicted scenes of life and death, painted in red and black, respectively. Clay statuettes of a pregnant woman and a bearded man seated on a bull are also found in these rooms. Although the precise beliefs of these Neolithic people are unknown, their art and shrine rooms have given rise to a number of colorful speculations about the religion and ritual of the people of Çatal Hüyük.

Farming was well advanced at Çatal Hüyük. Lentils, wheat, barley, and peas were grown in quantities that produced surplus crops. Archaeologists were astonished by the richly varied handicrafts that the people of Çatal Hüyük produced, including beautifully carved wooden bowls and boxes. Çatal Hüyük had obsidian and flint daggers, spearheads, lance heads, scrapers, awls, and sickle blades; bowls, spatulas, knives, ladles, and spoons were made from bone. The houses contained belt hooks and toggles and pins carved from bone. Evi-

Excavation at Çatal Hüyük, a Neolithic settlement in southern Turkey. (Courtesy of Ralph S. Solecki.)

Figure 3

A reconstruction of a "shrine" at Çatal Hüyük, showing cut-out figure of a bull (left) *and rams' heads. Beneath the heads, human hands were painted.* (After G. Huxtable in J. Mellaart, *Earliest Civilizations of the Near East.*)

dence also suggests that men and women wore jewelry fashioned from bone, shell, and copper and used obsidian mirrors.[27]

Çatal Hüyük, which is located in a region with few raw materials, evidently depended on its merchants and traders to secure the rich variety of materials needed for the products popular in the town. The traders had to procure shells from the Mediterranean, timber from the hills, obsidian from volcanoes 50 miles away, and marble from western Anatolia.

Jericho. The site of Jericho is actually the town mentioned in the Bible, located in a fertile oasis north of the Dead Sea in Israel. As is true with many similar archaeological sites, Jericho marks the location of not one but several groups of people, who lived in the same area at different times. Remains of these earlier settlements—in the form of tools, bits of clothing or ornaments, houses, and so forth—are found in horizontal levels. Artifacts from the first group to settle there are found at the bottom layer; the original people may have moved or died out, or their settlement may have burned. Then, over the remains of their settlement, the next group built their settlement—and so on, with the remains of the area's most recent inhabitants closest to the top.

The earliest level is a Mesolithic village dated to 7800 B.C. Above this occupation are the remains of a Neolithic village dated to 6800 B.C. This village covered about 8 acres and contained round, semisubterranean houses with stone foundations, adobe brick walls, and wattle-and-daub roofs (twig framework plastered over with mud). Walls and floors were also plastered with mud, which probably cooled the rooms. Like the site at Jarmo, Jericho had no pottery in its lower levels.

In later levels, when the village spanned

[27] James Mellaart, "A Neolithic City in Turkey," *Scientific American,* Vol. 210 (April 1964), pp. 94–104.

about 10 acres, the residents built a heavy wall around the settlement. It was 6 feet wide with a massive stone tower 21 feet high which still stands today. The wall and tower indicate periodic conflict with enemies. It may be that the early Neolithic inhabitants were conquered by another group, as there is a distinct break in cultural continuity early in the prehistory of Jericho. That is, the cultural remains in one preceramic level of occupation are markedly different from those found in the succeeding preceramic level. Also, in the succeeding level, the adobe bricks in the house walls have a different shape than before; the houses are now built around courtyards, and the floors are covered with lime plaster.

Evidence suggests that people were often buried beneath the houses. Several of the skulls had faces molded onto them in plaster (probably a replica of the features of the deceased) with cowrie shells symbolizing the eyes. Trade is indicated, as obsidian from western Anatolia, turquoise from the Sinai Peninsula, and marine shells from the seacoast were all found at the site.

Domesticated plants or animals have not yet been found at Jericho, but the available evidence suggests they were present. Jericho was located in a fertile oasis where grains could be easily grown, and harvesting tools (sickles) and milling equipment were found at the site.

The Spread of the Neolithic

As the Neolithic complex of culture traits began to spread out in all directions from the Near East, it entered environments often much different from that region and frequently underwent changes, presumably in response to conditions within the different environments. In short, many of the new regions did not favor a simple, direct transfer of the Near Eastern cultural complex.

The tribes inhabiting the edges of the Eurasian steppes found the semiarid grasslands unsuited for agriculture but excellent for herding. Farmers in central Europe, where the arable hills were blanketed with dense forests of deciduous trees, had to clear the land before they could plant. Wild animals native to Iraq and Turkey lent themselves to domestication, while those of central Europe may not have. Furthermore, the grains of the Near East could not be introduced into a much colder and damper Europe without some acclimation and adaptation. Thus, the "Neolithic revolution" made uneven progress. Sharp divergencies emerged between areas already urbanized and functioning at a high level of technology and others lagging behind. As late as 2500 B.C., Mesolithic hunting and gathering cultures were still functioning in northern and western Europe.

But the domestication of plants and animals did prove to be viable in many regions and began penetrating them. Farming, animal breeding, and settled life proved to be the wave of the future. Neolithic communities began to appear around the northern rim of the Mediterranean basin, suggesting a spread by water (but there is always the possibility of local, independent developments in addition to diffusion). Neolithic towns sprang up in southern Europe and on the islands of Crete, Sicily, and Malta. In the sixth millennium B.C., Neolithic culture moved overland through Greece and the Balkans into Eastern Europe. By the fifth millennium B.C., Neolithic culture had penetrated the Hungarian plains and was sweeping up the Danube into western Europe. It reached England in the fourth millennium B.C. Simultaneously, Neolithic culture spread from the Near East to the North African coast.

Somewhat later, the Neolithic transformation reached China, introducing wheat, millet, cattle, and sheep into a region where three great rivers—the Huangho, Fenho, and Weishui—converge. It is believed that here the Near Eastern Neolithic encountered another cultural complex, a distinctive Southeast Asian Neolithic, and the cultures coalesced. The types of plants and animals apparently domesticated in Southeast Asia have led scholars to speculate about that area's providing an independent source of Neolithic culture. Cultivated beans, peas, cucumbers, and water chestnuts have been found in a cave in Thailand in strata dating from 10,000 to 6000 B.C. This span of time is contemporary with the emergence of domestication in the Southwest Asian area, which indicates the possibility of an independent evolution of agriculture in the southeastern part of Asia.

The Emergence of the Neolithic in the New World

Scholars long ago concluded that the American Indians descend from populations that came into the New World from northeastern Asia. Even today, Asia and North America are close geographic neighbors—only the Bering Strait separates Siberia from Alaska. We know from geology that during the Pleistocene the North American continent was periodically joined to Asia by a land corridor about 1,300 miles wide, wider, in fact, than Alaska. For thousands of years at different times during the Pleistocene, the corridor accommodated a two-way traffic of plants and animals between Asia and America. Bears, mountain sheep, bison, and mastodon crossed into America from Asia, and horses and camels passed from America to Asia.

The earliest date for Paleolithic hunting bands in America is about 12,000 years ago.[28] With them, these migrants brought Old World techniques for flaking stone to produce knives, axes, projectile points, and so on, as well as other culture traits. In Chapter 7, we noted that these early bands were big-game hunters, who exploited the wide-ranging herds of mammoth, mastodon, and bison. Following the big-game hunters were peoples whose economy was similar to that of Mesolithic groups in the Old World. These peoples were hunters, fishermen, shellfish collectors, and plant gatherers. Also, they appear to have been more sedentary than the big-game hunters, as they had adapted to the relatively restricted resources of local areas, and their economy was not based upon the exploitation of migratory big game. Such a local foraging economy is exemplified by the Archaic tradition of the North American Eastern woodlands and the Desert tradition of the American Southwest. Eventually, however, New World peoples shifted from intensive gathering to the production of vegetal foods, just as early domesticators in the Old World had.

Archaic Tradition. Emerging in the deciduous woodlands of eastern North America around 9,000 years ago—about the time when the big-game hunting economy was disappearing—the Archaic cultures were local adaptations to the deciduous forest. Their economy was based on the hunting of nonmigratory game—especially the white-tailed deer—fishing, collecting shellfish, and gathering wild plants—particularly nuts which were so prevalent in the deciduous forests. The sites served both as temporary camps and relatively sedentary home bases. The latter were possible when the local area could provide adequate gathering and hunting resources. It is suspected that several bands converged seasonally at such sites and then dispersed into smaller bands during the rest of the year.[29]

Desert Tradition. The Desert tradition of the Southwest began to emerge about 10,000 years ago. Because it was adapted to desert conditions, the culture was mainly based on the collecting of wild plants growing in certain parts of the desert. Such an economy favors seasonal

[28] W. T. Sanders and J. Marino, *New World Prehistory* (Englewood Cliffs, N.J.: Prentice-Hall, 1970), p. 26.

[29] Sanders and Marino, *New World Prehistory*, p. 29.

nomadism, groups moving from one gathering area to another. Much of the technology consists of tools for plant processing: milling stones for grinding seeds, nuts, and wild grain; choppers and scrapers for softening plant fibers; and many varieties of baskets for sifting, storing, and preparing the plant foods. A primitive maize is found in Desert tradition sites dating to between 3000 and 2000 B.C., and incipient cultivation began. But the people of the Desert tradition remained dependent on plant collecting, and the domestication of maize apparently remained incipient. Intensive foraging cultures have also been discovered in Mesoamerica and South America.[30] They emerge at about the same time as those of the Desert and Archaic traditions—about 12,000 to 9,000 years ago.

Domestication in the New World. The earliest known appearance of agriculture in America occurred in the Tehuacán Valley in central Mexico. The highland valleys of Mexico are very reminiscent of the rugged, hilly flanks of the Near Eastern mountains where the Eurasian Neolithic began. In Tehuacán between 6700 and 5000 B.C. groups of foragers began cultivating squashes and avocados; they collected wild beans, chili peppers, and amaranth seeds,[31] all potential cultigens (plants that could be domesticated). Between about 5000 and 3400 B.C., groups were cultivating corn, water-bottle gourds, amaranths, chili peppers, and several varieties of beans.[32]

Archaeologists thought that if they could find the wild ancestor of modern corn and its area of earliest domestication, they might discover the origins of New World agriculture, whether it derived from the Old World or independently evolved in America. Very tiny, wild corncobs, no larger than a cigarette filter and the ancestors of modern domesticated corn, were finally discovered in the strata of a cave in the Tehuacán Valley, dating to about 7,000 years ago.[33] This indicates that maize domestication evolved independently in the New World. Based on the number of species of domesticated plants, on the variations of those species, and on geographical distribution, it seems that domestication evolved independently in three areas of the New World: the highlands of Mesoamerica (e.g., Tehuacán); the central Andes around Peru, where cotton was domesticated about 2500 B.C.;[34] and the Caribbean lowland areas of South America, where tropical root crops, such as manioc and sweet potatoes, are thought to have been domesticated.[35]

In the Near East, people had domesticated grains such as wheat and barley, as well as vegetables such as peas and lentils. The American Indian domesticated maize, white and sweet potatoes, pumpkins, squash, lima beans, black beans, tomato, avocado, pineapple, guava, elderberry, chocolate, manioc, peanut, chili, vanilla, and plants from which they could extract edible seeds such as sunflower and amaranth. Tobacco was also domesticated in the New World.[36]

The different animal species domesticated in the New and Old Worlds also indicate the independent evolution of stockraising in the two hemispheres. That animal domestication differed in the New and Old Worlds was because different wild species were located in each region. The plains and forests of the Old World were filled with wild ancestors of most of the large animals we use today. In the New World, the Pleistocene herds of horses, mastodons, mammoths, and other large species were long

30 Sanders and Marino, *New World Prehistory,* p. 30.
31 Amaranths are weedy plants, commonly called pigweeds, which yield edible seeds.
32 R. S. MacNeish, "The Origins of New World Civilization," *Scientific American,* Vol. 211 (November 1964), pp. 29–37.
33 MacNeish, "The Origins of New World Civilization," pp. 31, 35.
34 Sanders and Marino, *New World Prehistory,* p. 48.
35 *Ibid.*
36 MacNeish, "The Origins of New World Civilization," pp. 30–35.

Corn evolved in the Tehuacán Valley of central Mexico from tiny wild corncobs, about 7,000 years ago, to modern corn, about 3,500 years ago. (Courtesy of Paul Mangelsdorf and R. S. MacNeish.)

extinct. Thus, the Neolithic peoples in America domesticated the llama, alpaca, turkey, and guinea pig.

New World Agricultural Villages and Technology. In contrast to the development of Neolithic agricultural villages in the Near East about 7000–6000 B.C., such villages did not appear in the New World until 3400 B.C. in Mexico. The earliest known village was composed of small pit houses (houses that are partly subterranean). Although pottery apparently was not made until between 2300 and 1500 B.C. in the New World (first in Mexico), the Neolithic Americans soon became proficient in ceramics. The earliest pottery was very crude and imitated the stone vessels that had been used previously. Such evidence suggests that pottery is very probably an independent invention in the New World and was not brought here by Old World groups.[37] The potter's wheel was never invented in America. Pottery was fashioned by hand, either by piling up strips of clay and molding them into a vessel, or by modeling a vessel from a lump of clay.[38] The loom was also late in coming in the American Neolithic: cotton cloth found in Peru and dated at around 2000 B.C. apparently was finger woven. Not until about 1,000 years later do we find evidence of looms and spindles in the New World.

[37] Sanders and Marino, *New World Prehistory,* p. 48.
[38] John C. McGregor, *Southwest Archaeology* (Urbana: University of Illinois Press, 1965), pp. 96–97.

Dating Neolithic Remains

Like late Paleolithic remains, Neolithic remains can be dated absolutely by Carbon-14 and relatively by the analysis of pollens and varves. Another method of absolute dating that can be used to date Neolithic remains in some areas of the world is *dendrochronology,* or tree-ring dating. This method was first applied to cultures in the North American Southwest.

Tree-ring dating is based on the fact that each year a tree adds on a layer of growth. The number of rings in a cross-section of a tree indicates how old the tree was when it was cut. The concentric rings within the cross-section are not equal in width: during years of little moisture, the tree expands with a thin layer, but during times of heavy moisture the tree grows more, adding a thicker layer. The cross-section of a tree, then, is a pattern of thick and thin rings. All the trees in a certain area will have the same pattern, as they are all subject to the same climatic conditions. A master chart of the tree-ring patterns is drawn up for a region, starting with the present and working back in time. For example, we could cut down a live tree and chart its ring pattern from the day it was cut (the present) to the day it originated. Then we could find an older tree and match its ring pattern with the oldest ring pattern on our first tree. By using progressively older trees, matching their latest ring patterns with those of the younger trees, dendrochronology provides an absolute method of dating cultural remains in some areas to a particular year within the past few thousand years.

Using dendrochronology, we can date cultural remains, such as house beams, by matching up the ring pattern in the house beam with a section of the master chart ring patterns and counting how far back the last or most central ring on the house beam (the central ring represents the year the tree was cut down and used for the house) is from the first ring on the master chart (which indicates the present). We can then find out how old the beam is.[39] Not all trees can be used in dendrochronology, since many do not have long enough life spans. Redwoods and bristle-cone pine trees are mainly used in the American Southwest, as their life spans are especially long. Certain environments, too, do not permit the use of dendrochronology. For example, in areas where there is very little variation in rainfall, there will be very little variation in ring width.

CIVILIZATION EMERGES

The hallmark of civilization is conventionally taken to be the city, perhaps because, as we noted before, our word "civilization" comes from a word meaning "city." The rise of cities in the Old and New Worlds has been called the second great revolution in human culture.[40] In the Old World, cities first appear in Mesopotamia and then in Egypt and the Indus Valley between 4000 and 2500 B.C. Mere increase in the size of a settlement does not necessarily indicate technological and economic advances beyond that of a village farming community. A city is, to be sure, larger than a village, but it also is defined by the presence of inhabitants who are engaged in specialized trades and who depend on outlying agricultural areas for food.

The rise of civilization is usually, but not always, accompanied by the appearance of other characteristics (in addition to cities), such as the invention of writing to record information, social stratification, complex political organization, craftsmen-specialists, the construction of monumental buildings, and metallurgy. Not all of these characteristics, however, always occur simultaneously. The Pre-Colombian

[39] Frank Hole and Robert F. Heizer, *An Introduction to Prehistoric Archeology* (New York: Holt, Rinehart and Winston, 1965), pp. 252–255.

[40] Robert McC. Adams, "The Origin of Cities," *Scientific American,* Vol. 203 (1960), pp. 153–168.

Incas of Peru had dazzling cities, metallurgy, astronomy, and a complex form of government—in short, a flourishing civilization—but they had no writing. (They did have a systematic way of remembering complicated information—the *quipu*, a memory device utilizing strings and knots.) In the Old World, the earliest metallurgy was based predominantly on bronze, hence the term *Bronze Age* is used to identify this era.

Sumerian Civilization

The ancient people who settled in Sumer, an arid region in Mesopotamia, found an apparently unpromising environment, stretching from ancient Baghdad to the Persian Gulf. Its soil nourished no forests, sheltered no mineral deposits or stone quarries. Yet, the settlers of Sumer were the first in the Old World to build cities. By about 3000 B.C., the Sumerians had created the first known civilization in the history of mankind.[41]

After that time, Sumer became a glittering place, culturally, intellectually, and technologically. It had great cities and imposing temples. The dozen or so city-states each consisted of a city, usually enclosed in a fortress wall, and a surrounding agricultural area. Sumer had an elaborate system for the administration of justice, codified laws, specialized government officials, and even, in the cities, functioning sewer systems. Sumerians were involved in business and trade, and the government regulated commerce. Here it seems that man first learned to write, at first to record who supplied what to whom, and later to record legends and royal chronicles. The Sumerians also devised brick making, the potter's wheel, the wheeled wagon, the plow, and the sailboat. In view of the environmental wasteland we have just described, we might ask how Sumer could have flourished in such a region. Irrigation may provide the answer.

[41] Samuel Noah Kramer, *The Sumerians: Their History, Culture and Character* (Chicago: University of Chicago Press, 1963), pp. 3–5.

Irrigation. In Sumer, the irrigation network connected to the Euphrates and Tigris rivers was a technological marvel, constructed of canals, dikes, and reservoirs.[42] Although farming would not have been possible at all in this region without at least some simple system of artificial watering, the building of a full-fledged irrigation network was very advantageous. It freed the farmer from his dependence on rainfall, which, in that semiarid environment, he could not really rely on. With irrigation, he harvested at least two crops a year. Agricultural production was also boosted by the new farming technology that originated in and spread from Sumer. Oxen were harnessed to plows and to carts that ran on wooden wheels, and a Sumerian "Farmer's Almanac" indicates that a seeder plow was invented for the purpose of planting. Threshing was done by running an animal-drawn wagon and then a special threshing sled over the grain. The most important advance in farming technology, however, was the irrigation system.

It has been suggested that labor and management for the upkeep of the irrigation system in Mesopotamia led to the formation of a political elite—overseers of the system—who eventually became the governors of the society.[43] Proponents of this view believe that the city and civilization were due in part to irrigation. Critics note, however, that the irrigation systems in the early Mesopotamian cities were generally small in scale and did not require extensive labor and management forces. That is, large-scale irriga-

[42] Kramer, *The Sumerians*, pp. 104–109.
[43] Karl Wittfogel, *Oriental Despotism: A Comparative Study of Total Power* (New Haven: Yale University Press, 1957).

Reconstruction of the Sumerian city of Ur, as it looked in 2000 B.C. *A temple can be seen in the background.* (Courtesy of the American Museum of Natural History.)

tion systems were not built until after cities had been fully established.[44] Thus, irrigation could not be the stimulus for the origin of the city and civilization. On the other hand, even small-scale irrigation systems could have resulted in unequal access to productive land and so may have contributed to the development of a stratified society. In addition, irrigation systems may have given rise to border and other disputes between adjacent groups, caus-

[44] Adams, "The Origin of Cities," p. 154.

ing people to concentrate for defense in cities that may have required at least some of the characteristics of civilization (e.g., specialized political officials, a specialized military force, and specialized craftsmen) in order to survive in such a competitive social environment.

In any case, by later times, governments had become powerful enough to organize public works projects built by slaves or laborers conscripted by the government. For example, the Greek historian Herodotus reports that 100,000 men were employed in constructing the Great Pyramid in Egypt, completed about 2600 B.C. Some 2.3 million stones were used in its construction, and some of the larger slabs weighed almost 50 tons apiece. In Sumer of the third millennium, the focal point of each of the dozen or so city-states was a grandiose temple built atop a high platform, making it visible for many miles in the Mesopotamian plain. The temple was the tallest and most important building in the city, possibly to visually reinforce the concept that the entire city was under the protection of the local deity.[45]

Writing. The practical Sumerians also invented writing, in the fourth millennium B.C.[46] and it appears in Egypt at about the same time. Although the types of writing and the materials used differ, similar conditions in Sumer and Egypt may have favored the almost simultaneous development of writing. The earliest Sumerian writings were ledgers, inventories of items stored in the temple and records of the number of livestock and other items owned by the temple.

Sumerian writing was wedge-shaped, or *cuneiform,* formed by pressing a stylus against a damp clay tablet. For contracts and other important documents, the tablet was fired to create a virtually permanent record. The Egyptian form of writing, *hieroglyphics,* appears on rolls woven from papyrus reeds. Our word "paper" comes from "papyrus."

Extensive Trade. As civilization expanded, the need for raw materials and finished products not locally available increased greatly. Importing became necessary; trade developed between peoples and nations with routes spanning continents. Copper and other metals used in Mesopotamia, the Indus Valley, and Egypt came from abroad. So did the lumber and stone used in Sumer. While watercraft had been known in earlier times, never before had the Mediterranean and the rivers of the civilization centers been so crowded now that merchant fleets were transporting goods. The vessels were sturdier and built with large cargo holds for long-distance shipping. On the land routes, goods were transported by pack animals such as mules. The wheeled wagon was not used for long-distance trade, because there were few roads, and even fewer safe ones in the Bronze Age.

Specialization and Social Stratification. The Bronze Age was a period of intense economic change, which gave rise to a new type of person—the specialist. A tablet excavated at the city of Ur in Mesopotamia documents this new era of specialization. It contains an account by two production supervisors in the workshops of a temple and a description of the various crafts that were part of the temple. There were workshops for sculptors, carpenters, jewelers, leatherworkers, basketmakers, stonecutters, blacksmiths and fullers (people who shrink and thicken cloth).[47]

The newly launched civilization of the Bronze Age, with its need for specialized occupations and the division of labor, also introduced social diversification and stratification systems under which a person's status and that of his family derived from his work and station in life. Several kinds of evidence suggest that social strati-

[45] Kramer, *The Sumerians,* pp. 73–74.
[46] Chard, *Man in Prehistory,* pp. 233–241.
[47] Kramer, *The Sumerians,* pp. 101–104.

fication had developed. First, a study of the settlements shows different sizes and types of houses, which implies different statuses for their owners. Thus, the Indus Valley homes are varied, some being very spacious and others cramped; the cramped houses appear to have been used by working men. Second, and more telling, Sumerian documents describe a fully developed system of social stratification: city-states with temples, homes, and palaces; nobles, priests, merchants, craftsmen, and farmers; free citizens, slaves, bureaucrats, and soldiers. Slaves, common in both Egypt and Sumer, were at the bottom of the social scale. Most Sumerian slaves were captives, brought back by the victorious armies as the spoils of war. Although free men might be sold into slavery as penalty for certain offenses, the term of servitude for them was fixed under Sumerian law. The metallurgist belonged to the working-class aristocracy because he possessed closely guarded trade secrets. Like the nuclear physicist in our society, the metallurgist was respected both for his arcane knowledge and because his profession was strategically important for the society.

War. If technology brought improvements in living conditions, it also brought hazards in the form of more sophisticated weapons. Whatever skirmishes had occurred among primitive tribes in the past had been small-scale feuds. With population to be found in greater concentrations, war received an impetus. Bronze gave rise to a new arms industry. In addition to horse-drawn war chariots, there were bronze spears and swords, helmets, and armor. Because tensions between the city-states were increasing, as were pressures from the barbarians east and west of Sumer, large regular armies were deployed. One of the earliest kings of the Sumerian city-states was Sargon the Great, who reportedly kept a standing army of 5,400 men. The Sumerian army was professionally drilled and consisted of infantry, charioteers, and spear bearers.

The Spread of Old World Cultures

How civilization spread out from the Bronze Age centers—Mesopotamia and Egypt—where it had first emerged, is a remarkable chapter in human history. Civilization streamed out in many directions altering life styles and transforming indigenous cultures. One factor in the spread of civilization was probably *diffusion,* the passage of a trait or trait complex from one society to another by culture contact. Such contact may be accomplished by trade and group migrations. For example, traveling merchants who were in the employ of the state helped to disperse the seeds of civilization. Civilization also spread as a result of military conquest.

Between Europe and China lie great steppe regions. These grasslands became the home of hordes of pastoral tribes. Pottery models of covered wagons found at some sites suggest that the nomads traveled in such vehicles. Mobility was important for pastoralists, who needed some contact with urban centers to acquire goods they could not produce themselves. During the second millennium B.C., Indo-European nomads overran the civilized centers of southern Asia, Europe, and the Near East. The nomads invaded northern India, Iraq, Iran, Anatolia, and later, at the eastern end of the steppes, China. These invasions, although disruptive to the indigenous civilizations, helped to spread culture traits from east to west.

Certain cultural developments probably arose as independent discoveries made in several different areas. Armenian tribes found a practical method for utilizing iron in about 1400 B.C. Iron ore deposits were far more plentiful than the copper and tin needed to make bronze. Once iron-making techniques had been mastered, iron revolutionized the manufacture of metal items. Farmers in Palestine, Greece, and Rome began using iron shovels, plowshares, hoes, and knives. Iron saws, pulleys, lathes, and other construction tools were devised. Iron also revolutionized weapons production: iron swords, spears, arrowheads, and daggers became prevalent and were acquired by barbarous hordes who used them to raid the centers of Bronze Age civilization.

Ironworking was an important factor in the development of cultures in Africa. In the first millennium B.C., the technique of ironworking spread to Egypt and from there, diffused south of the Sahara to West and East African tribes. With iron tools, Africans were able to clear the tropical forests for settlements and agriculture. The people of ancient Ghana, among the first to use iron weapons, rose to political predominance in West Africa and established a centralized government and powerful empire about A.D. 800.

The Emergence of Civilization in the New World

Although later than the emergence of civilization in the Old World centers, the peoples of Mesoamerica and the Andean region traveled a similar course. Food production increased dramatically, and the domestication of maize and other crops spread. From a cob the size of a thimble, the Indians developed a high-yield grain with its seeds encased in a thick husk, to protect it from the rigors of the threshing process.

Some of the most remarkable public buildings in the world were constructed in the Teotihuacán region of Mexico, when farmers moved from the mountains into the alluvial plain from 300 B.C. to A.D. 1. They built an irrigation system and a sprawling city that covered some 200 square miles. These were not the first New World people to use irrigation, however. Watering systems were known 2,000 years earlier in the coastal areas of Peru and in the American Southwest.

The growth of Teotihuacán closely paralleled urbanization in the Near East. The urban core area gives evidence of conscious city planning with residential districts allocated to certain craftsmen, a municipal center of public buildings and monuments, neighborhood marketplaces, and a grid pattern of streets and avenues. The imperial city of Teotihuacán, the forerunner of similar centers in other parts of Mesoamerica, stood in the shadow of the monumental "Pyramid of the Sun."

In sharp contrast, the Mayan culture to the south, based in the wooded regions of Guatemala and Yucatan, evolved into a sophisticated civilization apparently without the large population centers characteristic of civilization centers elsewhere. This may have been due to environmental characteristics that favored slash-and-burn farming and dispersed settlement. A peasantry in the habit of periodically abandoning their farms so that the forest could close in and regenerate the soil would be an unlikely base to support city life. However, the Maya did build monumental religious and civic centers. On ceremonial occasions these centers were crowded with people who streamed in from the surrounding countryside to participate, but for most of the year the centers were relatively empty (or so it would seem from the available evidence).

Cities built between A.D. 300 and 900 show Mayan architecture at its peak. Around enormous plazas containing sculpture on a monumental scale, ball courts, and altars, the Mayans built massive complexes of buildings, each with a large number of rooms. Yet the population appears to have been very sparse. Ecological studies suggest that the Mayan lowlands can only support population densities of 10–40 persons per square kilometer. Theories have been advanced to explain how so elaborate a civilization as the Mayan could have developed in the setting of a dispersed population,[48] but the question is still open—just as is the question of why Mayan society collapsed some time before the arrival of the Spaniards.

[48] Sanders and Marino, *New World Prehistory*, pp. 60–62.

A temple at the Mayan site of Tikal, dating between A.D. *300 and 900.* (Courtesy of the American Museum of Natural History.)

SUMMARY

1. About 12,000 years ago the glaciers receded causing the oceans to rise and inundate some of the coastal plains. Forest replaced the European grasslands, and large game, sheltered in these dense woods, became more difficult to stalk. This environmental change may explain why people intensified their food gathering, especially of aquatic resources, at this time. Probably because of this increased exploitation of local and relatively permanent resources, man became more sedentary. As sedentarism increased, preagricultural villages were founded. The cultural state during which these developments occurred is known as the Mesolithic.
2. The exploitation of wild grains would have required people to spend time harvesting the grains and then remain in the area for a while, as the large amount of grains harvested would be difficult to transport. The Natufians are an example of a grain-harvesting Mesolithic group. Preagricultural Natufian villages based on hunting and wheat harvesting have been found in Israel and Jordan.
3. The Mesolithic graded into the Neolithic as man domesticated and cultivated formerly wild species of animals and plants, built even more permanent settlements for a rapidly increasing population, and engaged in trade with distant communities. In the Near East, the Neolithic began between 11,000 and 10,000 years ago.
4. As the Neolithic complex of culture traits began to spread out in all directions from the Near East, it entered environments often much different from that region. The complex of Neolithic traits frequently underwent change, presumably in response to conditions within the different environments.
5. Neolithic culture spread from the Near East north into Europe, reaching England by 4000 B.C., and simultaneously spread to the North African coast. Somewhat later the Near Eastern Neolithic spread to China where it is believed to have merged with a distinctive Southeast Asian Neolithic. Scholars believe that the southeastern part of Asia may have been an independent center of domestication.
6. The New World Neolithic evolved independently of the Old World. As in the Old World, it was preceded by intensified foraging economies. Domestication seems to have occurred independently in three main areas: the Mesoamerican highlands (Mexico), Peru, and the Caribbean lowland areas of South America. The earliest known agriculture in the New World occurred in the highland valleys of Mexico between 6700 and 5000 B.C. Villages did not appear until about 3400 B.C. in Mexico and pottery was not made until later.
7. The rise of civilization, marked by the appearance of cities, was the second great revolution in human culture. Civilization is characterized by the invention of writing, social stratification, craft specialists, metallurgy, and monumental buildings. Civilizations emerged in the Old World during the Bronze Age.
8. The ancient Sumerians created the first known civilization in the history of mankind. Sumer was composed of a complex of city-states, with large, irrigated agri-

cultural areas, functioning sewer systems, an elaborate judicial-legal-governmental system, and grandiose temples. The Sumerians also had a form of writing (cuneiform) and widespread trade.

9. Civilization spread out from the Bronze Age centers where it had first emerged and developed. Diffusion by trading, conquest, and migration was an important factor in the spread of civilization. Independent discovery may also account for the development of civilization in parts of the world.

10. Although later than the emergence of civilization in the Old World centers, the peoples of Mesoamerica and the Andean region traveled a similar course. Food production increased dramatically, and the domestication of maize and other crops spread. Urbanization in the Teotihuacán region of Mexico closely paralleled that in the Near East.

SUGGESTED READINGS

Adams, R. McC.: *The Evolution of Urban Society* (Chicago: Aldine, 1966).
A discussion of ecological, social, and historical factors possibly related to the rise of urban societies in Mesopotamia and prehispanic Mexico.

Binford, L. R.: "Post-Pleistocene Adaptations," in S. R. Binford and L. R. Binford (Eds.): *New Perspectives in Archeology* (Chicago: Aldine, 1968), Chapter 16.
Begins with a brief survey of the most prominent theories of agricultural origins, with discussions of their validity. Binford goes on to outline his own theoretical position, based on demographic pressures resulting from the postglacial population expansion.

Clark, G.: *World Prehistory: A New Outline* (New York: Cambridge University Press, 1969).
A clearly written work, this brief outline presents world prehistory from the earliest human societies to the beginning of recorded history. Chapters 4–12 trace the origins of civilization, its growth and expansion over the world.

Clark, G., and S. Piggott: *Prehistoric Societies* (New York: Knopf, 1965).
Generally informative discussion of cultural development to the start of recorded history. A good reference source.

Mellaart, J.: *Earliest Civilization of the Near East* (New York: McGraw-Hill, 1966).
A condensed, informative view of the development of culture in the Near East. Excellent illustrations and very helpful chronological table of cultural correlations.

Piggott, S.: *Ancient Europe, from the Beginnings of Agriculture to Classical Antiquity: A Survey* (Chicago: Aldine, 1965).
A comprehensive text of prehistoric Europe from the incipient stages of agriculture to the start of the Christian era. Extensively illustrated, 108 pages of notes, bibliography, and index.

Sanders, W. T., and J. Marino: *New World Prehistory: Archeology of the American Indian* (Englewood Cliffs, N.J.: Prentice-Hall, 1970).
Concise introductory discussion of the New World, covering a broad scope of developmental stages from hunters and gatherers of the Great Plains to the Inca Empire. Informative culture area maps.

Sanders, W. T., and B. J. Price: *Mesoamerica: The Evolution of a Civilization* (New York: Random House, 1968).
An examination of the possible factors and processes

leading to the emergence of Mesoamerican civilization, from an ecological and evolutionary point of view. Basic concerns are population growth and competition and cooperation in the use of resources in a local ecosystem.

Weaver, M. P.: *The Aztecs, Maya and Their Predecessors: Archaeology of Mesoamerica.* (New York: Seminar, 1972).
An up-to-date survey of the culture history of the various areas of Mesoamerica, incorporating the latest archaelogical findings.

Woolley, C. L.: *Ur of the Chaldees* (New York: Norton, 1965).
A classic account of life in the ancient Sumerian city–state of Ur. The text is based on the excavation of Ur which revealed written documents as well as many artistic treasures in the form of sculpture, jewelry, and mosaics.

9

Human Variation

Throughout Part 2, we have considered the physical and cultural changes which occurred during man's evolutionary history, from his early primate origins to his creation of civilizations. But anthropologists are also concerned about groups of *living* people and how they vary both physically and culturally. In Part 3, we will discuss contemporary cultural variation in such things as food getting, marriage, political systems, religion, and the arts.

Just as different societies vary culturally, so do geographical groups vary in their frequencies of biological traits, both internal and external. The indigenous populations of certain countries look markedly different from each other. A Swede traveling in Japan, for example, would hardly be mistaken for a native. External characteristics (such as skin color, height, hair and eye form and color) are, of course, the most obvious biological variations. But populations also vary in internal biological traits, such as blood types and susceptibility to diseases. How can we explain such biological variations?

GENERAL PROCESSES OF BIOLOGICAL VARIATION

Biological variation in humans, as well as in other mammalian species, is the result of one or more of the following processes: mutation, natural selection, genetic drift, and gene flow.

Mutations and Natural Selection

Mutations, or changes in the chemistry of a gene, are the ultimate source of all biological variations. Mutations can be lethal or sublethal, reducing the reproductive rates of their carriers. They can also be beneficial, enhancing the potential for survival in a particular environment. Although most mutations are deleterious, *natural selection* favors those occasional mutations that are beneficial in a particular environment. The traits produced by those beneficial mutations become characteristic of the population. For example, in Chapter 3, we discussed the advantage dark moths had over light moths when parts of England became industrialized. Predators could not easily see the darker moths against the soot-covered trees, and these moths soon outnumbered the lighter variety.

But certain traits, such as red (versus blond or black) hair color, or thick (versus thin) lips, among human populations, may not make any difference in survival, no matter where the carriers of these traits live. Hence, as far as we know, they are neutral traits. Yet, such traits are unevenly distributed among the world's populations. Natural selection doesn't account for the distribution of neutral traits, as such traits do not seem to confer any advantages on their carriers. The differing frequencies of neutral traits in human populations may result from *genetic drift* or from *gene flow.*

Genetic Drift

Genetic drift refers to the process whereby the descendants of a small band of migrants come to have different frequencies of certain genetic traits as compared with the frequencies in the ancestral population, merely because the migrants initially and accidentally had different frequencies of those traits.

Imagine, for example, a family with ten children, all of whom exhibit a particular rare, but neutral, trait. If the family moves to New York City, that trait will remain rare; but, if they go to a tiny country hamlet, the trait may become relatively common among residents of the area in a few generations. Thus, the movement of small populations with trait frequencies that randomly differ from the frequencies found in the ancestral population may account for a number of apparently neutral traits, such as wavy or straight hair, that vary in frequency among different groups of people.[1]

Gene Flow

In Chapter 3 we noted that a gene pool is the total number of genes possessed by the members of a given population. *Gene flow* "refers to the process by which genes are introduced from the gene pool of one breeding population into the gene pool of another by reproductive sexual matings."[2] Unlike the other three evolutionary processes (mutation, natural selection, and genetic drift) which act generally to differentiate populations, gene flow tends to work in the opposite direction, making differing populations more similar over time as genes are exchanged between them. If, for example, a group of blue-eyed Scandinavians interbreeds with a population of dark-eyed Italians, the proportion of genes for blue eyes in the Italian population will increase. Hence, gene flow partially accounts for human variation—how populations resemble or differ from each other—by making some populations look similar even though they originally were quite different.

Although gene flow is often made possible by the migration of populations, the two processes may be independent—as in the case, for example, of a religious group that moves to a new place but refuses to interbreed with the natives of that area. In the United States, the Amish of Pennsylvania have tried to remain isolated. Nevertheless, some marriages do occur with non-Amish people, and reproduction introduces new genes into the population's gene pool.

Geographic isolation and the kind of social isolation practiced by the Amish are not the only factors that inhibit gene flow. Members of different economic classes—even when they live in the same geographical area and participate in the same culture—generally do not interbreed, thus tending to produce subpopulations with different gene frequencies. In the United States strong social pressure and legal measures have tended to separate Caucasian and Negro gene pools. Until recently, antimiscegenation laws were enforced against couples who chose to intermarry.

KINDS OF HUMAN VARIATION

The most noticeable biological variations among human populations are those which are on the surface—skin, hair, and eye color; body build;

[1] Theodosius Dobzhansky, *Mankind Evolving: The Evolution of the Human Species* (New Haven: Yale University Press, 1962), pp. 279–281.

[2] Laura Newell Morris, *Human Populations, Genetic Variation and Evolution* (San Francisco: Chandler, 1971), p. 409.

stature; and shape of facial features. There are also many biological variations which we do not see, such as variation in blood type and susceptibility to different diseases. Certain of these variations may now be explained as adaptations to differing physical or social environments or as consequences of other physical or cultural changes. However, there are many biological variations among human populations for which we do not yet have any explanations.

Body Build

Scientists have determined that the body build of many birds and mammals varies according to the temperature of the environment in which they live. For example, Julian Huxley, in a well-known series of studies on the puffin (a short-necked sea bird), found that the puffins in northern regions were considerably larger than those living in the south.[3] *Bergmann's rule* describes what seems to be a general relationship: the smaller-sized subpopulations of a species inhabit the warmer parts of its geographical range, while the larger-sized subpopulations inhabit cooler areas.

The studies by D. F. Roberts of variations in the mean body weights of people living in regions with widely differing temperatures have provided evidence in support of Bergmann's rule.[4] Roberts discovered that the lowest body weights were found among residents of areas with the highest mean annual temperatures and vice versa. For example, where the mean annual temperatures are 70–82° F, people weigh, on the average, only 96 to 100 pounds. Populations with average weights over 160 pounds live where the temperature averages 40° F.

[3] Julian Huxley, *Evolution in Action* (New York: Mentor Books, 1957), pp. 43–44.

[4] D. F. Roberts, "Body Weight, Race and Climate," *American Journal of Physical Anthropology,* n.s II (1953), pp. 533–558; cited in Stanley M. Garn, *Human Races,* 3rd ed. (Springfield, Ill.: Charles C. Thomas, 1971), p. 73.

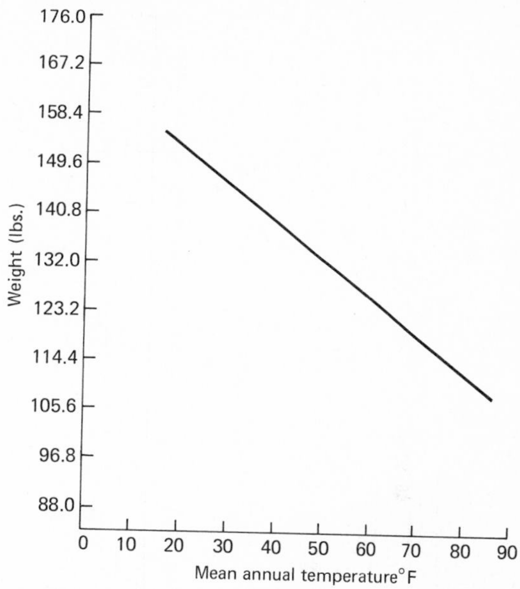

Figure 1

Graph demonstrating the relationship of mean body weight in a population to the mean annual temperature of the area in which the population is located. The graph supports the application of Bergmann's rule to human populations, demonstrating that the lower the mean annual temperature, the higher the mean body weight of the population. (After Garn, *Human Races.*)

Allen's rule describes another kind of variation in body build. This rule states that protruding body parts (particularly arms and legs) are relatively shorter in the cooler areas of a species's range than in the warmer areas.

The rationale behind these theories is that the long-limbed, lean body type that is often found in tropical regions (for example, among the Nilotic Negroes of East Africa) provides more surface area in relation to body mass and thus facilitates the dissipation of body heat. In contrast, the chunkier, shorter-limbed body type found among the residents of cold regions helps to retain body heat by reducing the amount of surface area relative to body mass.

It was once thought that the chunky build of Eskimos exemplified Bergmann's rule. But most early observers gained their impression of the Eskimo build from seeing Eskimos clad in bulky fur attire. In fact, the unadorned Eskimo body, while relatively stocky compared to some other populations, is not that stocky. Why they are not more stocky may be because the Arctic regions have not been inhabited by human beings for very long; and the Eskimo's culture, which includes igloos and warm clothing, may have halted further biological evolution in the direction of a more stocky body build. Other animal populations appear to conform more closely to Bergmann's and Allen's rules than human populations, perhaps because of recent human migrations and the masking effects of human culture.

Height

Height is a characteristic that does not vary very much in humans. Although this statement may seem somewhat rash, considering the people each of us knows who certainly vary greatly in height, the meaning of it will become clear when we consider human beings as a series of populations, rather than as individuals. Wilt Chamberlain, the 7 foot, 1 inch basketball player, is a rare exception in his own population, as he would be almost anywhere else; so is Michael Dunn, an excellent actor who also happens to be a dwarf. The average height for all humans is approximately 5 feet, 6 inches, and very few populations anywhere include appreciable numbers of people over 6 feet or under 5 feet. In Africa, for example, we can find both the small pygmies and the tall Watusi, but most Africans are neither extremely short nor extremely tall. Nevertheless, there are some differences in height between human populations that need to be explained.

We must take into consideration the fact that, since both tall and short people are found virtually everywhere, the "rules" of Allen and Bergmann (according to which people living in tropical regions should be tall, and cold-region dwellers short) cannot always be taken literally. While it may be true that many Africans have long, lean torsos and limbs which facilitate the dissipation of their body heat, there are also many who are short-limbed and stocky. Therefore, there must be a more complex relationship than we have been able to discover thus far between body height or build and climate.

Recent studies provide us with evidence to support a new viewpoint as to why people vary in height, a viewpoint that calls attention to the possibility of cultural influences on aspects of human biology regulating growth.

For example, Thomas K. Landauer and John W. M. Whiting examined the relation between certain infant care practices judged to be stressful and the stature of adult males in 80 mostly primitive societies.[5] The impetus for this study came from previous research suggesting that rats which were stressed in infancy (that is, subjected to apparently stressful treatment—such as handling, electrical shock, vibration, and temperature extremes) developed longer skeletons, longer tails, and were also somewhat heavier than nonstressed rats.

Landauer and Whiting examined, collected, and correlated data about infant care practices and adult male stature in humans. In some societies, children between birth and two years are subjected to stressful practices. These include circumcision; branding of the skin with sharp objects; the piercing of the nose, ears, or lips for the insertion of ornaments; and the molding and stretching of the head and limbs for cosmetic purposes. In these societies, the male adults are an average of more than 2 inches taller than males raised in societies which do not practice such customs.

Landauer and Whiting found it impossible to introduce controls for all the possible variables that might account for their results, but their analysis suggested that certain variables

[5] Thomas K. Landauer and John W. M. Whiting, "Infantile Stimulation and Adult Stature of Human Males," *American Anthropologist*, Vol. 66 (1964), p. 1008.

known or thought to be related to height could not account for their results. For example, genetic differences alone do not seem to account for the results linking stress to greater height. When the sample was divided into the five major geographical regions of the world (Africa, Eurasia, Insular Pacific, North and South America), they found that, although the average height in one region might be greater than that in another, within each region those societies with stress before the age of two years produced adult males who were more than 2 inches taller on the average than the males in other societies in the region who had not been stressed. Contrary to what many would expect, Landauer and Whiting found no evidence to support the view that height is related to diet.

Another cultural factor which may influence adult stature is periodic mother-infant separation. In a cross-cultural study of 69 societies, S. Gunders and J. W. M. Whiting found that males are taller in societies that practice periodic mother-infant separation than they are where such customs are lacking or minimally practiced.[6] Although this and other studies do not discount the effect of genetic inheritance on height, they do indicate that culture may modify the genetic effect.

Skin Color

Human populations obviously differ in average skin color. Many people consider skin color the most important marker of racial difference and sometimes treat others differently solely on this basis. But anthropologists, in addition to being critical of racial discrimination (for reasons we shall discuss later in this chapter), also note that skin color is not a good indicator of race. For example, extremely dark skin is found most commonly in Africa. However, there are natives of southern India whose skin is as dark as, or darker than, that of many Africans. Yet, these people are not closely related to Africans, either genetically or historically.

Nevertheless, the very fact that there are people in the world with markedly different skin colors leads us to an interesting question: How can we explain this wide range of hue? The answer appears to be extremely complex. Scientists do not yet fully understand why some people have very light skin, while others have very dark, "reddish," or "yellowish" skin. But we do have some theories that may partially account for variation in skin color.

We know that skin color is influenced by *melanin.* The more melanin there is in the skin, the darker the skin will be. Furthermore, the amount of melanin in a person's skin seems to be related to the climate in which he lives. *Gloger's rule,* frequently cited by anthropologists who hold this view, states that populations of birds and mammals living in warm, humid climates have more melanin (and, hence, darker skin, fur, or feathers) than do populations of the same species that live in cooler, drier areas. On the whole, this association with climate holds true for people as well as for birds and other mammals. Darker-skinned human populations do live mostly in warm climates (although not all residents of warm climates have dark skins). Dark pigmentation seems to have at least one specific advantage in tropical climates: melanin protects the sensitive inner layers of the skin from the sun's damaging ultraviolet rays. Therefore, dark-skinned people living in sunny areas are safer from sunburn and skin cancers than light-skinned people.

What, then, might be the advantages of a light-colored skin? Presumably, there must be some advantages; otherwise, through the process of natural selection, human populations would all tend to have relatively dark skin color. Although light-skinned people are more

[6] S. Gunders and J. W. M. Whiting, "Mother-Infant Separation and Physical Growth," *Ethnology.* Vol. 7, No. 2 (April 1968), pp. 196–206.

susceptible to sunburn and skin cancers than are darker people, the ultraviolet radiation that light skin absorbs also facilitates the body's production of Vitamin D, which is necessary for the proper growth and maintenance of bones. Too much Vitamin D, however, can cause illness. Thus, the light-colored skin of people in northern latitudes maximizes ultraviolet penetration, perhaps insuring production of sufficient amounts of Vitamin D, while the darker skin of people in southern latitudes minimizes it, preventing illness from too much Vitamin D.[7] In short, natural selection may have favored darker-skinned people in southern latitudes and lighter-skinned people in northern latitudes.

Hair and Eye Color

In contrast to variations in skin color, for which we have some possible explanations, we still know very little about why populations vary in hair and eye color. As with skin color, melanin controls hair and eye coloration. Thus, since hair and eye color vary somewhat with skin color, the former may be genetically linked to the latter and therefore partially explainable in the same ways.

Dobzhansky suggests that the prevalence of certain traits, such as hair color, within a group of people may be the result of sexual selection.[8] People tend to mate with those they regard as aesthetically pleasing, generally basing this opinion on a local tradition about what physical traits are considered more attractive. Thus, since people possessing "attractive" qualities would be more likely to marry and have children, the genes for these traits would become more prevalent in the gene pool, producing an increasingly larger percentage of individuals with particular hair colors, for example. And, since different populations may differ on what is considered attractive, they may over time develop different frequencies of hair colors. This interpretation, of course, assumes that natural selection does not operate on hair color.

The color of a person's eyes is influenced by the amount of melanin in the iris. It was once thought that since the melanin in the iris reduces the amount of light entering the pupil, dark eye color might protect the retina against possible damage from ultraviolet radiation. However, there is no evidence that low amounts of melanin are associated with visual problems.[9]

Susceptibility to Infectious Diseases

We have long been aware of the fact that certain individuals are prone to digestive disorders or to chest infections, and that individuals can actually inherit some physical disorders, such as hemophilia. Recently, it has been found that human populations also vary in their degree of susceptibility to several infectious diseases.

Certain populations seem to have developed an inherited resistance to some infectious diseases, such as tuberculosis and measles. That is, populations that were repeatedly decimated by these diseases in the past now have a high frequency of genetic characteristics which minimize effects of these diseases. As Arno Motulsky has pointed out, if there are genes that protect a person from dying when infected by one of the diseases prevalent in his area, these genes will tend to become more common in succeeding generations.[10]

[7] W. Farnsworth Loomis, "Skin-Pigment Regulation of Vitamin-D Biosynthesis in Man," *Science,* Vol. 157 (August 9, 1967), pp. 501–506.

[8] Dobzhansky, *Mankind Evolving,* p. 270.

[9] John Buettner-Janusch, *Origins of Man: Physical Anthropology* (New York: John Wiley & Sons, 1966), pp. 370–371.

[10] Arno Motulsky, "Metabolic Polymorphisms and the Role of Infectious Diseases in Human Evolution," in Morris, *Human Populations, Genetics, Variation and Evolution,* p. 223.

A field study of the infectious disease myxomatosis, in rabbits, lends support to this theory. When the virus responsible for the disease was first introduced into the Australian rabbit population, more than 95 percent of the infected animals died. But, among the offspring of animals exposed to successive epidemics of the disease, the percentage of animals who died from myxomatosis decreased from year to year. The more epidemics the animals' ancestors had lived through, the smaller the percentage of current animals that died of the disease. Thus, the data suggested that the rabbits had developed a genetic resistance to myxomatosis.[11]

Infectious diseases seem to follow a similar pattern among human populations. Tuberculosis, when it first strikes a population which has had no previous contact with the disease, is commonly fatal, but some populations seem to have inherited a resistance to death from the disease. For example, the Ashkenazi Jews in America (those whose ancestors came from central and eastern Europe) are one of several populations whose ancestors had survived many years of exposure to tuberculosis in the crowded European ghettos where they previously lived. Although the rate of infection is identical among American Jews and non-Jews, the rate of tuberculosis mortality is significantly lower among Jews than non-Jews in this country.[12] After reviewing other data on this subject, Motulsky concludes it is likely "that the present relatively high resistance of Western populations to tuberculosis is genetically conditioned through natural selection during long contact with the disease."[13]

We tend to think of measles as a childhood disease that kills virtually no one. Indeed, it is rapidly becoming a childhood disease that almost no one *gets* anymore, because we now have a vaccine against it. But when first introduced into populations, the measles virus can kill large numbers of people. In 1949, the Tupari Indians of Brazil numbered about 200 people. By 1955, two-thirds of the Tupari had died of measles, introduced by rubber gatherers in the area.[14] Large numbers of people died of measles in epidemics in the Faroe Islands (in the North Atlantic between Great Britain and Iceland) in 1846, in Hawaii in 1848, in the Fiji Islands in 1874, and among the Canadian Eskimos quite recently. It is possible that where mortality rates from measles are low, populations have acquired a genetic resistance against death from this disease.[15]

The Sickle Cell Trait and Thalassemia

Another biological variation, whose causes we are beginning to understand, is an abnormality of the red blood cells—the sickle cell trait.[16]

Sicklemia is a condition in which the red blood cells assume a crescent (sickle) shape when they are deprived of oxygen, instead of the normal (disk) shape. The sickle-shaped, red blood cells' tendency to rupture results in severe anemia. The abnormally shaped cells tend to form clumps which clog smaller blood vessels. This impairs circulation and causes pains in the abdomen, back, head, and extremities. The heart may become enlarged and brain cells may atrophy.

Sicklemia is an inherited condition for which people can be either homozygous or heterozygous. A person who is homozygous for the trait has received a sickling gene from each parent and will therefore have sickle cell anemia. Such a person almost always dies before reaching maturity; therefore, he will probably not produce any offspring.

In its heterozygous form, the offspring receives the sickle cell gene from one parent only,

[11] Motulsky, "Metabolic Polymorphisms . . . ," p. 226.
[12] *Ibid.*, p. 229.
[13] *Ibid.*, p. 230.
[14] *Ibid.*, p. 233.
[15] *Ibid.*, p. 233.
[16] *Ibid.*, p. 248.

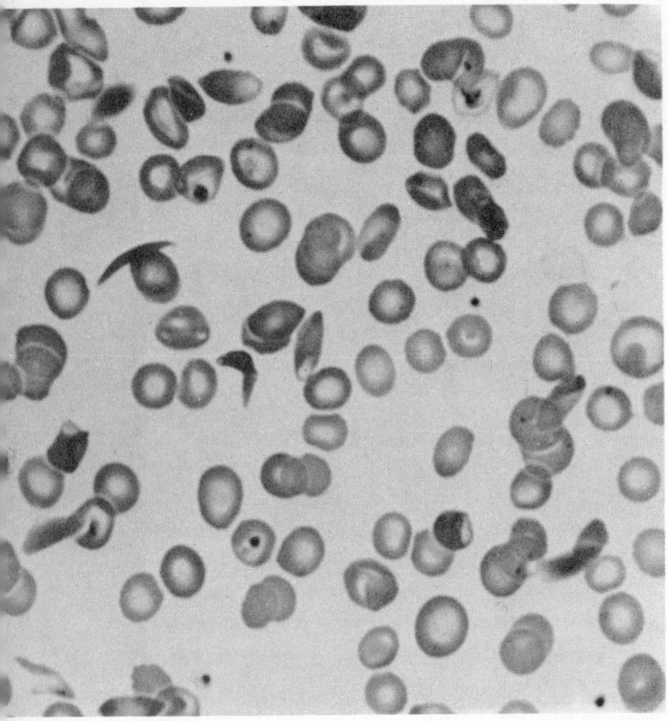

This photomicrograph illustrates the crescent-shaped red blood cells characteristic of sickle cell anemia. (Courtesy, C. Lockard Conley, M.D., Department of Medicine, The Johns Hopkins Hospital.)

and, since it is a *recessive* gene, he himself will not generally develop the condition. (In some cases, a heterozygous individual may have a mild case of anemia.) However, a heterozygous person is a "carrier," that is, he can pass on the trait, and, if he mates with a person who is also heterozygous for sicklemia, the statistical probability is that 25 percent of their children will have the homozygous form of this condition.

Since individuals homozygous for sicklemia usually die before producing offspring, each time decreasing the number of sickle cell genes in a population's gene pool, and since this gene is recessive, why hasn't sicklemia disappeared? At the very least, we would expect the condition to have become extremely rare, assuming that natural selection would have continuously weeded out this potentially lethal trait.

And yet, the sickle cell gene is still extremely common—particularly in equatorial Africa, where up to 40 percent of the population carry the trait. Ten percent of American Negroes also have the sickle cell gene. For this reason, sickle cell anemia was once thought to be a specifically "Negroid" trait. But research has shown that this is not quite the case. Sicklemia, like other red cell abnormalities, crosses "racial" lines. It is widespread in Greece, Turkey, and India. Why does the trait occur so frequently?

Recent studies indicate that the heterozygous carrier of the sickle cell trait is protected against a kind of malaria which kills many people in the regions where sicklemia is most common. Motulsky points out that the sickling trait does not necessarily keep people from contracting malaria (which is carried principally by the *Anopheles gambiae* mosquito, common in tropical areas); rather, it greatly decreases the rate of mortality from malaria which, in evolutionary terms, has the same overall effect.[17] The point is that, since persons homozygous for sicklemia die before reproducing and since many "normal" homozygous persons (those completely lacking the sickle-cell gene) die early because of malaria, individuals who are heterozygous for sicklemia are favored by natural selection in malarial regions. Hence, the sickling trait is likely to persist among certain populations until the threat of malaria entirely disappears. When that happens, the sickle-cell trait will no longer confer any advantage on its carriers.

Another common red blood cell defect is *thalassemia,* which is also found in malarial regions, but primarily around the Mediterranean, in Asia Minor, Thailand, Indonesia, and India. As with the sickle cell trait, people who have anemia caused by a double dose of

[17] Motulsky, "Metabolic Polymorphisms . . . ," p. 238.

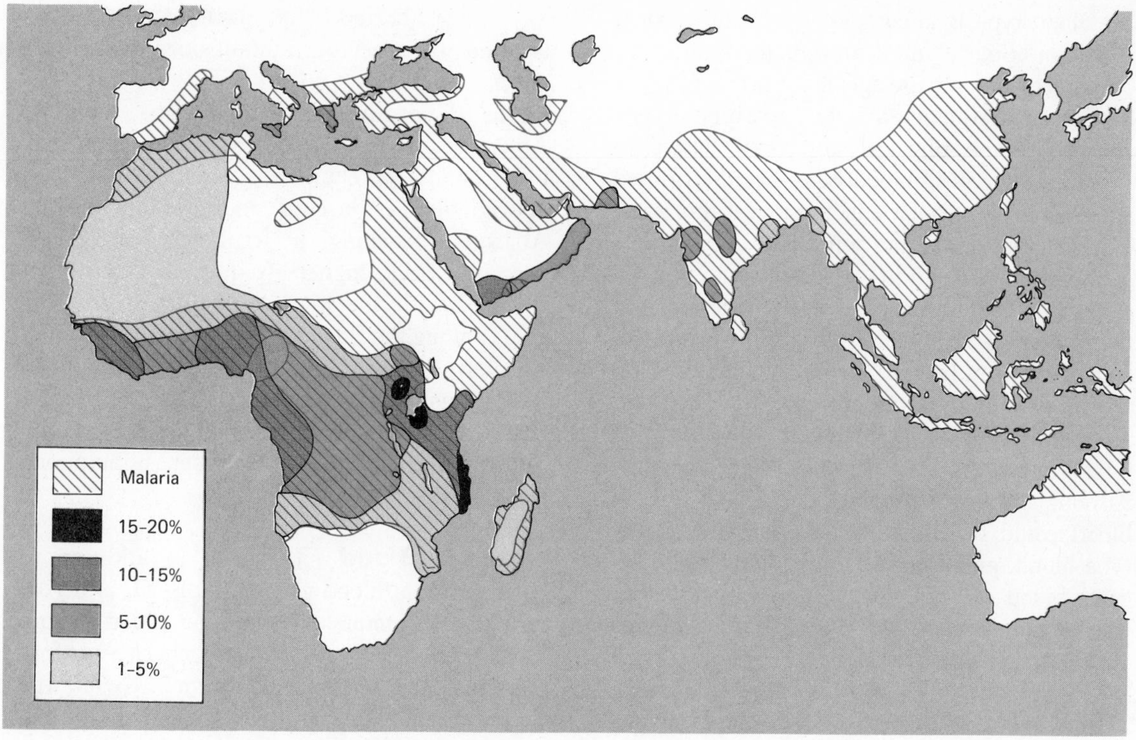

Geographical distribution of sicklemia and its relationship to the distribution of malaria.

the thalassemia gene generally die young; and heterozygous persons seem to receive some protection from malaria—which is presumed to be the reason for thalassemia's continued existence.

Blood Groups

ABO Systems. If you have ever donated blood, or had your blood tested, you probably know what blood "type" you have—it is one of the four basic blood groups: A, B, AB, and O. A person with A type blood has an antigen (called A) in his blood. Type B blood contains antigen B; AB contains both A and B antigens, and O has neither. (An antigen is a substance produced by the body which stimulates the production of antibodies.) Because we receive one blood group gene from each parent, there are six possible combinations: OO (which is type O), AA (which is A), BB (or B), AO (which is A, since the O gene is recessive), BO (which is B, for the same reason), and AB (neither A nor B is dominant over the other).

The biological importance of blood types is related to the behavior of red blood cells in blood transfusions. If a type B person is given type A blood, or vice versa, his blood cells may clump together, or clot. Therefore, the A-B-O and other blood types must be known in advance, in order to be sure that the patient receives only blood of the same type as his own.

The prevalence of A, B, or O type blood varies among different populations. For example, in Europe, type O blood occurs with 35–40 percent frequency. But in some American Indian groups, type O occurs with 90 percent frequency. Blood type B is completely absent in most North and South American Indians; it averages 15 percent among Europeans and reaches 35–37 percent frequency among the Chinese. The concern of the physical anthropologist is to explain how A-B-O blood types are distributed among human populations, but as yet this varying distribution is not understood. The frequencies of A, B, and O types are not even the same in populations supposedly belonging to the major geographical races. For example, some American Indian groups, such as the Ute, are almost all O, but others, like the Blackfoot, are mostly type A. In Europe, the incidence of type O increases from the south to the north.[18] Although it was formerly thought that O type blood could be transfused to patients of any type blood, and that AB individuals could receive blood of any type, it now appears that this is not always advisable, because bloods vary in other ways as well.

The Rh Factor. "Rh" is a chemical factor found in the blood. The Rh factor is controlled by a family of genes, with both dominant and recessive alleles, rather than by a single pair of genes. Rh becomes important when an Rh negative woman (who carries the recessive allele of each Rh gene) becomes pregnant by an Rh positive man (who carries a dominant allele of at least one of the Rh genes). Since the Rh positive condition dominates the negative one, the fetus will manufacture positive Rh substances. Although the mother's circulatory system is separate from the fetus's, some fetal blood can filter into the mother's system. When this occurs (approximately once in every 200 deliveries where the mother is Rh negative and the father positive), the mother's blood produces antibodies which may then filter back into the fetus, damaging its blood cells. This produces the condition known as *erythroblastosis fetalis,* which can cause the fetus to be aborted before birth or to die shortly after, if the newborn infant does not receive special treatment.

The Rh negative trait is rare or absent among American Indians, South Chinese, Japanese, Polynesians, Melanesians, and Australian aboriginals. It occurs more often among Africans, reaching a frequency of 20–24 percent. Still higher frequencies occur in Europe, with the highest frequency (53 percent) among the Basques of northern Spain and southern France. On the basis of this distribution, it has been hypothesized that the Rh negative trait originally developed in Europe by mutation, then spread to other populations through interbreeding.[19]

Other Blood Factors. In addition to the four main blood groups (A, B, O, and AB) and the Rh factor, various other blood factors have been discovered and are checked before transfusions. These include the MNSU, the Duffy, Diego, Kell, and Kidd factors. The frequencies of these factors also seem to vary geographically. The M group is most prevalent among American Indians, and the Diego factor is absent in whites and blacks but present in Chinese, Japanese, and in American Indians. Why this variation exists is not yet understood.

Lactase Deficiency

When educators discovered that black school children very often did not drink milk, they assumed that lack of money or of education (regarding the presumed necessity for young children to ingest a certain amount of dairy products daily) explained this behavior. These assumptions provided the impetus for establishing the school milk programs so prevalent around the country.

However, it now appears that many people

[18] Garn, *Human Races,* pp. 53–54.

[19] Dobzhansky, *Mankind Evolving,* pp. 258–259.

lack an enzyme, lactase, which is necessary to break down lactose, the sugar in milk. Without lactase, a person cannot digest milk properly, and drinking it will cause bloating, cramps, stomach gas, and diarrhea. A study conducted in Baltimore among 312 black and 221 white children in grades 1 through 6 in two elementary schools, indicated that 85 percent of the black children *and* 17 percent of the white children were milk intolerant. (Before this study, it was thought that lactase deficiency occurred only in nonwhite adults—Orientals, Indians, and Negroes.) Lactase deficiency is another human variation for which we do not yet have a verified explanation.[20]

THE CONCEPT OF RACE

Fortunately, such variations as blood type and lactase deficiency—perhaps because they are not immediately obvious—have never engendered tension among people. This is not the case, however, with some of the more obvious, external human differences.

What Is Race?

For as long as any of us can remember, countless numbers of problems—from two-man fist fights, to large-scale riots, to country-wide civil wars—have stemmed from tensions and misunderstandings among various "races." "The race problem" has become such a common phrase that most of us take the concept of race for granted, without bothering to consider what it does, and does not, really mean. We think that we know what determines a particular race, and that nothing is easier than the classification of a given individual into a standard, well-defined slot.

[20] Jane E. Brodey, "Effects of Milk on Blacks Noted," *New York Times* (October 15, 1971).

But do we really know what race is? What do we mean when we refer to the "human race?" Obviously that phrase is supposed to include all people and does not have anything to do with the concept of race. The very sloppiness of our language helps to confuse the issue of race. The "Aryan race" is best known as the group of blond-haired, blue-eyed, white-skinned persons whom Hitler wanted to dominate the world, to which end he attempted to destroy as many members of the "Jewish race" as he could. But is there an "Aryan race?" Technically, Aryans are any people who speak one of the Indo-European languages. Since the Indo-European languages include such disparate modern tongues as Greek, Hindi, Polish, Icelandic, German, Gaelic, and English, it seems obvious that only a small percentage of Aryans have either blond hair or blue eyes. Similarly, the "Jewish race" does not exist, in anthropological terms, since all kinds of people may be Jews. There are light-skinned Danish Jews and swarthy Jewish Arabs; one of the most orthodox Jewish groups in the United States is a New York City-based group composed entirely of black people.

Nevertheless, most people in this country do identify themselves with a racial group, most often one of the three races most popularly accepted: the Caucasoid (white), Negroid (black), or Mongoloid (yellow and red). Many people feel that certain biological traits are characteristic of each race, and that, although the races have become "adulterated" through miscegenation (intermarriage and interbreeding between different races), some individuals still exist who typify the "pure" Caucasoid, Negroid, and Mongoloid types. The inaccuracy of such classification is obvious: while many Caucasoids have straight hair and light skin, some have curly or quite frizzy hair and rather dark skin; Negroids do not all have wide noses or thick lips; and many people do not fit into any of the three major racial types at all.

But, racial stereotypes persist—due, in large

Racial classifications cannot be made only on the basis of skin color. Blood group analyses indicate that a young Filipino girl (left), *an Australian* (center), *and an African Negro* (right) *are members of separate races.* (Photos of Filipino and Australian, courtesy of the American Museum of Natural History; photo of African Negro, Marc and Evelyne Bernheim from Woodfin Camp and Associates.)

part, to the ease with which such obvious traits as skin color can be recognized and used to classify people. In itself, this tendency to attribute certain biological factors to all members of a supposed race, while inaccurate, is not disturbing. What is disturbing is the frequent association of the race concept with ethnocentrism and racism.

Race concepts have often been, and still are, used by certain groups in order to justify their exploitation of other groups. A blatant example of how present-day racism is linked to inaccurate concepts of race is the treatment of the American Negro. Most of the people who still justify the virtual elimination of the black person's civil rights do so because of a belief in the black's inherent (i.e., genetic) inferiority to whites. In fact, no such inferiority has been demonstrated. This racist outlook is a remnant of slavery days, when the white slaveowners assumed that their servants were inferior—and had to convince the slaves of that fact as well—in order to perpetuate the system.

The major problem with the race concept is its arbitrariness. The number of races into which the world's population can be divided depends upon who is doing the classifying, because each classifier may use different traits as the basis for his classification. All variable traits—such as skin color; blood type; hair,

nose, and lip shape—should be considered when developing a racial classification. But, unfortunately for the classifiers, many of these traits do not vary together—that is, for example, racial classifications based on blood type or skin color will not coincide completely. Even the supposedly distinguishing features of a Mongoloid person—the so-called *Mongoloid spot,* a dark patch of skin at the base of the spine which disappears as the person grows older; shovel-shaped incisor teeth; and an *epicanthic fold,* a bit of skin overlapping the eyelid—are not limited to peoples traditionally classified as Mongoloids. Southern Africa's Bushmen have epicanthic folds, for example, and Caucasoids can have "Mongoloid spots."

Thus, since the number and type of races in each classification of people depends on the traits used in the classification, and since many anthropologists base their classifications on different traits, there is no "right" and no "wrong" number of races. Boyd says there are 5; Coon recognizes 9; and Birdsell 32.[21]

Racial taxonomies in anthropology typically involve the identification of both *geographical races* and *local races.* A *geographical race* is a set of at least once-neighboring populations, which has certain distinctive trait frequencies.

[21] Dobzhansky, *Mankind Evolving,* p. 266.

Map of the world illustrating the locations of the nine geographical races. (According to Garn, *Human Races,* 3rd ed.)

Thus, the traditional trio of races (Negroid, Mongoloid, Caucasoid) would be considered geographical. Garn identifies a total of nine geographical races: European-Caucasoid and West Asiatic; Northern-Mongoloid and Eastern Asiatic; African-Negroid; Indian; Micronesian and Melanesian; Polynesian; American; and Australian.[22] A *local race* is like a *Mendelian population*—that is, a breeding population, or local group, whose members usually interbreed with each other. Garn identifies approximately 32 local races.[23]

Not only do anthropologists disagree on the number of races into which people can be classified, some even argue that there is no such thing as race. Ashley Montagu has long held this opinion, which has more recently been adopted by other physical anthropologists, including C. Loring Brace, Frank Livingstone, and Jean Hiernaux. They do not pretend that all men are the same physically; they merely point out that "race" is an artificial construct, developed by people to justify the different treatments accorded different people.

Alternative terms have been suggested, such as "ethnic group," because some feel this might discourage racial prejudice. But, clearly, the Ku Klux Klan will hate a black person just as much if his skin color is seen as an index of his "ethnic group" rather than his "race."

How Old Are Races?

Another area of strong disagreement is the question of how far back the races go in human

[22] Garn, *Human Races,* pp. 152–167.
[23] *Ibid.,* pp. 169–179.

evolution. Many anthropologists assert that races are a modern development. But others, notably Carleton S. Coon, claim that the various races diverged before *Homo sapiens* emerged.

Carleton Coon's theory of racial classification has been interpreted, perhaps unfairly, as scientific support for racism. Coon suggests that the Negroid race evolved later than the Caucasoid race, a view which has been used to explain why the Negroid people are less "advanced" culturally than white groups. Coon believes that five races have existed since pithecanthropine times, when man was still at the level of *Homo erectus.* These five races are largely geographical: Caucasoid, Mongoloid, Congoid (Pygmies and Negroids), Capoid (African Bushmen), and Australoid (aboriginals of Australia, New Guinea, and Indonesia). According to Coon, the separation into five geographic races (or subspecies) occurred during *Homo erectus*'s time, and each subspecies evolved, independently, into a separate race of *Homo sapiens.* Coon substantiates this view by labeling various pithecanthropine, Neandertaloid, and other early human fossils as "Mongoloid," "Capoid," and so forth.[24]

The opponents of Coon's viewpoint find many reasons to discredit his thesis. They say that Coon's theory depends on accepting the hypothesis that the five subspecies of *Homo erectus* survived, separately, while the species itself disappeared. This seems highly unlikely. Critics also suggest that these subspecies could have remained separate for 500,000 years only if there were infrequent gene exchanges between one subspecies and another. However, if the subspecies had remained so isolated for so long, by now they would have developed into separate species, rather than races. In any case, it is apparent that members of Coon's distinct subspecies do exchange their genes today—proving that they are not separate species. Finally, Coon's opponents stress the uselessness of attempting to determine the racial type of a human fossil, because all the relevant soft body parts (skin, hair, nose, and so forth) have disappeared. Coon's racial identifications of these early men, therefore, have to be based on such factors as facial dimensions and head and tooth shape, which are extremely variable and therefore inconclusive.

As Theodosius Dobzhansky states in his review of Coon's book, *The Origin of Races:*

> The possibility that the genetic system of living men, *Homo sapiens,* could have independently arisen five times, or even twice, is vanishingly small. A biological species can be likened to a cable consisting of many strands; the strands—populations, tribes and races—may in the course of time subdivide, branch or fuse; some of them may fade away and others may become more vigorous and multiply. It is, however, the whole species that is essentially transformed into a new species.[25]

Most anthropologists today, including Dobzhansky and Stanley M. Garn, believe that the various races of man we now identify developed quite recently. Garn writes: "How old are particular geographical races? . . . Geographical races are continually changing to the point that all geographical races are equally young." He points out, for example, that the present frequencies of the sickle cell gene in Africa are relatively recent and changing even now.

Racial and Cultural Variation: Is There a Relationship?

In the past, it was generally assumed that biological variation was related not only to the geographical location of a particular group of people but also to cultural characteristics. Even

[24] Carleton S. Coon, *The Origin of Races* (New York: Alfred A. Knopf, 1962).

[25] Theodosius Dobzhansky, *Scientific American* (February 1963), p. 170.

today, many people hold the racist viewpoint that the biological inferiority of certain races is reflected in the supposedly primitive quality of their cultures. Racists refuse to recognize that the facts of history very often contradict their theories.

Race and Civilization. Many of today's so-called underdeveloped nations—primarily in Asia, Africa, and South America—had developed complex and sophisticated civilizations long before Europe had reached beyond a crude level of technology or tribal organization. The advanced societies of the Shang dynasty in China; the Mayans in Mesoamerica; and the Africans in Ghana, Mali, and Songhay were all founded and developed by nonwhites.

Between 1523 and 1028 B.C. China already had a complex form of government; armies; and the production and storage facilities for large quantities of grain, metal tools, and weapons. A form of writing and complex religious rituals also characterized the early Chinese civilization.[26] During a span of six centuries, from A.D. 300 to 900, the Mayans were a large population with a thriving economy, who built many large and impressively beautiful cities, centered around great pyramids and luxurious palaces.[27] According to legend, the West African civilization of Ghana was founded during the second century A.D. By A.D. 770 (the time of the Sonniki rulers), Ghana had developed two capital cities—one Moslem and one non-Moslem—each with its own ruler, and both of them supported largely by Ghana's lucrative gold market. Ghana's empire was mostly destroyed by Berber tribesmen, who wanted to convert the unbelievers to Islam and to gain control of their gold. By 1076, little was left of those early African cities, at a time only ten years after Britain—then a primitive Saxon island—was invaded by William the Conqueror.[28]

Considering how long Europeans lagged behind in the development of civilization, it seems odd that modern whites should even attempt to label Africans, South Americans, and other nations as "backward" in terms of historical achievement, or "biologically inferior" in terms of capacity for civilization. But racists, both white and nonwhite, ignore the facts of history and of modern times; they refuse to believe that all races have achieved remarkable advances in civilization. Most significantly, such people refuse to believe that they can acknowledge the achievements of one race without in any way downgrading the achievements of their own. In short, there is no evidence that any racial group

"We don't consider ours to be an underdeveloped country so much as we think of yours as an overdeveloped country." (Courtesy, *Saturday Review*, January 10, 1970.)

[26] L. Carrington Goodrich, *A Short History of the Chinese People* (New York: Harper & Row, 1959), pp. 7–15.

[27] Michael D. Coe, *The Maya* (New York: Praeger, 1966), pp. 74–76.

[28] Elizabeth Bartlett Thompson, *Africa, Past and Present* (Boston: Houghton Mifflin, 1966), p. 89.

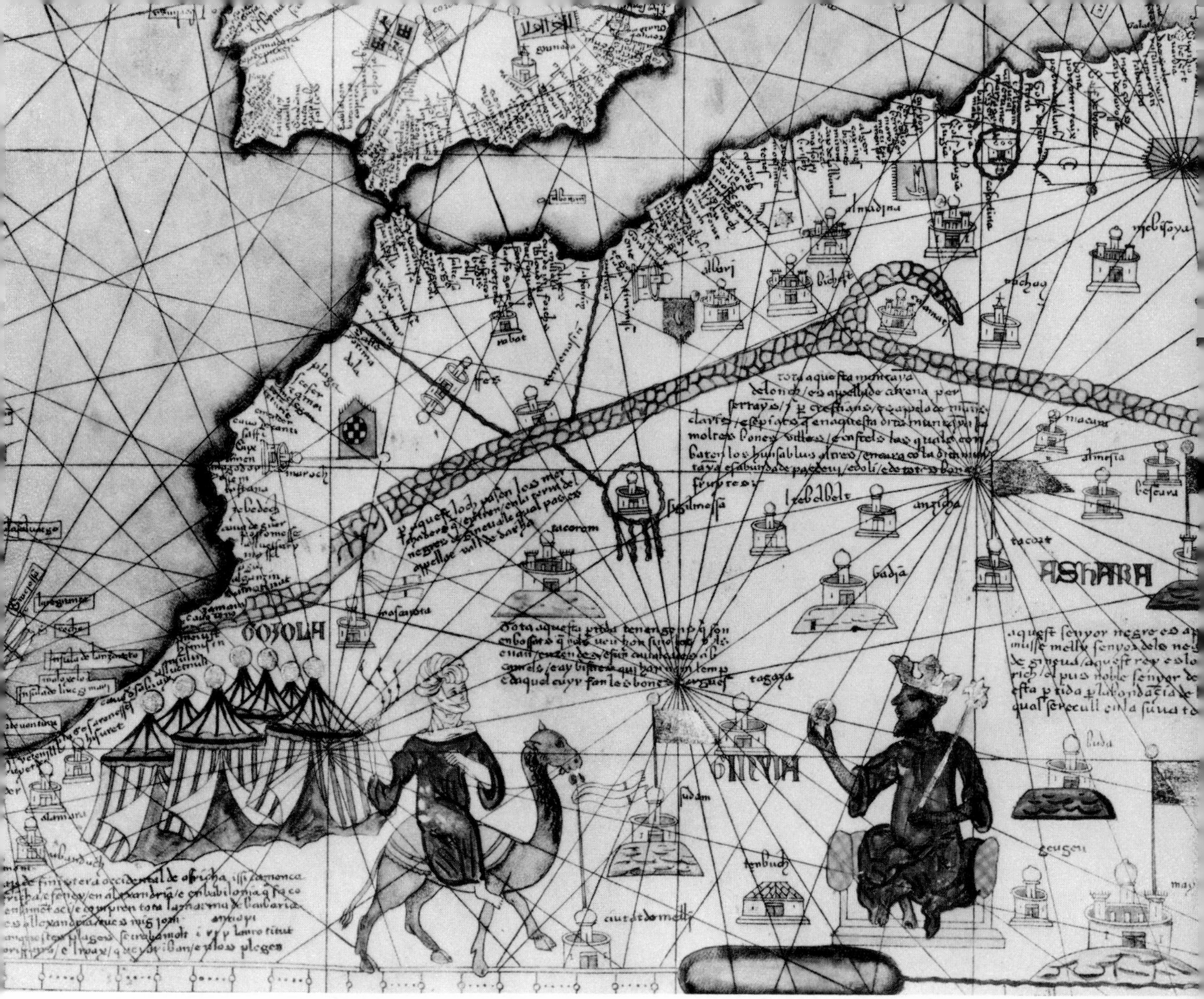

The West African kingdom of Mali flourished while Europe was in its Dark Ages. This map, drawn in 1375, shows an Arab trader coming to bargain with Mali's ruler. The writing says, "This Negro Lord is called Musa Mali, lord of the Negroes of Guinea. So abundant is the gold which is found in his land that he is the richest and most noble king in all the land." (Courtesy, The British Museum, London.)

cannot achieve an extremely high level of cultural development.

Race, Culture, and Infectious Disease. Although biological variations cannot set fixed limits on the development of a particular culture, they may strongly influence it. Earlier, we discussed how continued exposure to epidemics of infectious diseases, such as tuberculosis, measles, and poliomyelitis, can cause succeeding generations to acquire a genetic resistance to death from such diseases. But, on a short-term basis, differential susceptibility to disease may have affected the outcome of contact between different cultures. An example of this is the rapid defeat of the Aztecs by Cortez and his conquistadores. In 1520, a member of Cortez's army unwittingly transmitted smallpox to the Indians. The disease spread rapidly through the population, killing at least one-half of the Indians, who were thus considerably impaired in their fight with the Spanish.[29]

Outbreaks of smallpox repeatedly decimated many American Indian populations in North America a century or so later. In the early nineteenth century, the Massachusetts and Narragansett Indians, with populations of 30,000 and 9,000, respectively, were reduced by smallpox to a few hundred members. Extremely high mortality rates were also noted among the Crow, the Blackfoot, and other Indian groups during the nineteenth century. The germ theory alone cannot explain these epidemics. Once the European settlers realized how susceptible the Indians were to smallpox, they purposely distributed infected blankets. Motulsky calls the spread of smallpox probably "one of the first examples of biological warfare."[30]

Race and Intelligence. Perhaps the most controversial aspect of the racial distinctions made among men is the relationship, if any, between race and intelligence.

In the nineteenth century, European white supremacists attempted to find scientific justification for what they felt was the genetically inherited mental inferiority of blacks. They did this by measuring skulls. It was believed that the larger the skull, the greater the cranial capacity, and the bigger (hence, also "better") the brain.

Interest in skull measurement was first developed by a number of separate researchers from different parts of Europe who tried to determine the relative intelligence of round-headed versus narrow-headed individuals. Not surprisingly, their results were generally either inconclusive or contradictory. Paul Broca held that round-headed Frenchmen were superior in intelligence to narrow-headed Frenchmen, while Otto Ammon concluded that Baden's more intelligent residents had narrow heads. The Italian, Livi, concluded that southern Italians with round heads were of superior intelligence.

Although, fortunately, the skull-measuring mania of Broca, Ammon, and others quickly disappeared and is no longer upheld as evidence of racial superiority, the actions of these men paved the way for other attempts to justify racism. Other, more insidious and often more powerful "facts" are used today to demonstrate the presumed intellectual superiority of white people, namely, information from intelligence tests.

The first large-scale intelligence testing in this country began with our entry into World War I, when thousands of draftees were given the so-called Alpha and Beta I.Q. tests to determine their military assignments. Later, psychologists arranging the test results according to race found what they had expected—Negroes consistently scored lower than whites. This was viewed as scientific proof of the innate intellectual inferiority of blacks and was thus used to justify further discrimination against Negroes, both in and out of the army.[31]

However, Klineberg's subsequent statistical analyses of I.Q. test results demonstrated that Negroes from northern states scored higher than Negroes from the South. While dedicated racists explained that this was due to the northward migration of innately intelligent Negroes, most academics attributed the result to the influence of superior education and more stimulating environments in the North. When further studies showed that northern Negroes scored higher than southern whites, the better-education-in-the-North theory gained support—but again racists insisted such results were due to

[29] Motulsky, "Metabolic Polymorphisms . . . ," p. 232.
[30] Motulsky, "Metabolic Polymorphisms . . . ," p. 232.

[31] Otto Klineberg, *Negro Intelligence and Selective Migration* (New York: Columbia University Press, 1935); *Characteristics of the American Negro* (New York: Harper & Bros., 1944).

northward migrations by all innately intelligent whites.

As a further test of his conclusions, Klineberg gave I.Q. tests to Negro schoolgirls, born and partly raised in the South, who had spent varying lengths of time in New York City. He found that the longer the girls had been in the North, the higher their average I.Q.

In addition to providing support for the feeling that Negroes are not inherently inferior to whites, these findings suggested that cultural factors can and do influence intelligence and that I.Q. is not a fixed quantity; it can be raised by contact with an improved environment. (It should have long been obvious that biological variations alone could not account for I.Q. differences between white and black people, because it is well known that a large percentage of the Negro people in America have recent white ancestry, and many American whites have recent Negro ancestors, thus blurring the distinction between the two races.)

One of the most controversial viewpoints recently espoused on the question of how race is related to intelligence comes from a psychologist, Arthur Jensen. Jensen maintains that a person's environment has only an extremely limited influence on his I.Q. He feels that, in general, most black people cannot reach the I.Q. level of most whites, whatever changes are made in their surroundings. Jensen bases his interpretation on statistical evidence that there is approximately a 15 point difference between the average I.Q. scores of American Negroes and Caucasoids. He feels that as much as 80 percent of this gap is genetically determined and therefore cannot be modified through environmental changes.[32]

In recent years, however, increasingly less importance has been attached to I.Q. test results. Although it was once thought that the Binet test series could be of considerable value to educators, it is now widely recognized that I.Q. tests are hopelessly culture-bound. That is, an I.Q. test can measure how well a black child may compete with white children in a white school system—but nothing more. I.Q. tests cannot indicate the upper limits of a person's mental capacities, whatever his race or his environment. And studies have clearly shown that a deprived child, whether black or white, will generally have a lower I.Q. than an affluent child of either race. A child's I.Q. can increase with an improved environment; it can also decrease if environmental stimuli are decreased.

Thus, the primary objection to Jensen's findings is that I.Q. tests cannot give results that are equally valid for both black and white children. Also, since most poor black children experience more anxiety than white children in the test situation itself (a stressful examination, in a strange room, supervised by unknown and usually white people, for an unknown purpose), their test scores tend to be lower than white children more familiar with such procedures.

In an attempt to find an alternative to the Stanford-Binet series, Florence L. Goodenough, a psychologist at the University of Minnesota, developed her own I.Q. test—the Draw-a-Man test, which she felt was truly "culture-free" and "culture-fair" because it didn't use language. School children were instructed to draw a man and then were scored in terms of accuracy—that is, by how complete the man's various body parts were.[33] However, critics were quick to point out that environment was a factor even in this nonverbal testing situation. For example, Moslem Arab children scored very low with Draw-a-Man, primarily because their religion, which discourages the depiction of religious scenes in "graven images," had severely limited these children's exposure to pictorial art and thus greatly influenced their Draw-a-Man test results. After a few years' worth of experience with her Draw-a-Man test, Professor Good-

[32] Arthur Jensen, "How Much Can We Boost I.Q. and Scholastic Achievement?" *Harvard Educational Review*, Vol. 29, pp. 1–123.

[33] Otto Klineberg, *International Social Science Bulletin*, Vol. 2 (1950), pp. 460–466.

enough admitted that it was not nearly as "culture-free" as she had originally thought.

Dobzhansky emphasizes that no truly valid comparisons can be made of racially based I.Q.s until both black and white people have equal opportunities to develop their potentials. Dobzhansky stresses the need for an open society which would exist under the democratic ideal—where every person is given an equal opportunity to develop whatever gifts or aptitudes he has and chooses to develop. Dobzhansky notes that such equality of opportunity "neither presupposes nor promotes equality of ability";[34] it merely allows each person to choose any occupation for which he is qualified, both by his personal abilities and his willingness to strive.

In sum, the 1951 UNESCO (United Nations Educational, Scientific, and Cultural Organization) statement on race is still the authoritative scientific comment on the supposed influence of human biological variation on mental capacity:

> According to present knowledge, there is no proof that the groups of mankind differ in their innate mental characteristics, whether in respect of intelligence or temperament. The scientific evidence indicates that the range of mental capacities in all ethnic groups is much the same.[35]

[34] Dobzhansky, *Mankind Evolving,* p. 243.

[35] H. L. Shapiro, "Revised Version of UNESCO Statement on Race," *American Journal of Physical Anthropology,* Vol. 10 (1952), pp. 363–368.

SUMMARY

1. Biological variation in humans, as well as in other mammalian species, is the result of one or more of the following processes: mutation, natural selection, genetic drift, and gene flow.
2. Human biological variations can be both external (such as skin, hair, or eye color; body build; stature; and shape of facial features) and internal (such as blood type and susceptibility to different diseases). Certain of these variations may now be explained as adaptations to differing physical or social environments or as consequences of other physical or cultural changes. However, there are many biological variations among human populations for which we do not yet have any explanations.
3. The major problem with the concept of race is its arbitrariness. The number of races into which the world's population can be divided depends upon who is doing the classifying, because each classifier may use different traits as the basis for his classification. Racial classifiers identify both geographical and local races. A *geographical race* is a set of at least once-neighboring populations, which has certain distinctive trait frequencies. A *local race* is a breeding population, that is, a local group whose members usually interbreed with each other. Any number of races, from the traditional three geographical races (Negroid, Caucasoid, and Mongoloid) to 32 or more local races, have been identified. Race concepts have often been, and still are, used by some groups to justify their exploitation of other groups.
4. Although there is some disagreement about how far back races go in human evolution, most anthropologists assert that races are a modern development; that is, racial variations developed after *Homo sapiens* emerged.
5. Considerable evidence suggests that race is not directly related to a society's potential level of culture. White racists who refer to the "backward" and "underde-

veloped" nations of Asia, Africa, and South America often forget or ignore the fact that, historically, residents of these countries had developed complex and sophisticated civilizations long before Europe had reached beyond a crude level of technology or tribal organization. There is no evidence that any racial group cannot achieve an extremely high level of cultural development.

6. Although biological variations cannot set fixed limits on the development of a particular culture, they may strongly influence it. For example, infectious diseases, such as smallpox, when first introduced into a society can have devastating effects on its population, making conquest by another society relatively easy.

7. Perhaps the most controversial aspect of racial distinctions is the relationship, if any, between race and intelligence. Attempts have been made to prove "scientifically," through I.Q. tests and other means, the innate intellectual superiority of one race over another. However, we now recognize that we have no culture-free tests by which to measure intelligence. Furthermore, no truly valid I.Q. comparisons can be made until all people have equal opportunities to develop their potentials. There is no proof that one race is superior to another in terms of intelligence.

SUGGESTED READINGS

Dobzhansky, T.: *Mankind Evolving: The Evolution of the Human Species* (New Haven: Yale University Press, 1962).
Well-written introduction to the interaction between cultural and biological components in human evolution. Keeping the technical details and vocabulary of genetics to a minimum, Dobzhansky discusses natural selection and biological fitness in human populations by class, caste, and race.

Dunn, L. C.: *Heredity and Evolution in Human Populations* (Cambridge, Mass.: Harvard University Press, 1959).
Although it demands some biological background, this book presents a good summary of human genetics and microevolution in nontechnical language. Dunn's main areas of concern are the principles of heredity applied to human genetic data, methods and forces of evolutionary change in human populations, and the role of population genetics in explaining race formation.

Garn, S. M.: *Human Races,* 3rd ed. (Springfield. Ill.: Charles C. Thomas, 1971).
Comprehensive introduction to racial studies, with emphasis on such current research areas as race mixture, natural selection, ecology and race, disease and race, and the relationship between race, behavior, and intelligence.

Harrison, G. A., J. S. Weiner, J. M. Tanner, and W. A. Barnicot: *Human Biology: An Introduction to Human Evolution, Variation and Growth* (New York: Oxford University Press, 1964).
A detailed and technical study of all aspects of human biology. Especially useful are Sections 3, 4, and 5, which deal with biological variation in human populations, human ecology, human growth, and the effects of evolution on modern man.

Laughlin, W. S., and R. H. Osborne (Eds.): *Human Variation and Origins: An Introduction to Human Biology and Evolution* (San Francisco: Freeman, 1967).
A collection of *Scientific American* offprints, which serves as a survey of topics in human biology. Written for the beginning student, each article is prefaced with an author's summary and is generously illustrated with photographs, tables, and figures.

Morris, L. N. (Ed.): *Human Population, Genetics, Variation and Evolution* (San Francisco: Chandler, 1971).
Comprehensive collection of papers dealing with human evolution from a genetic point of view. Each section contains an introduction by the author and a selection of material by recognized authorities. Material is written clearly and interestingly, with emphasis on student understanding.

Part 3
CULTURAL VARIATION

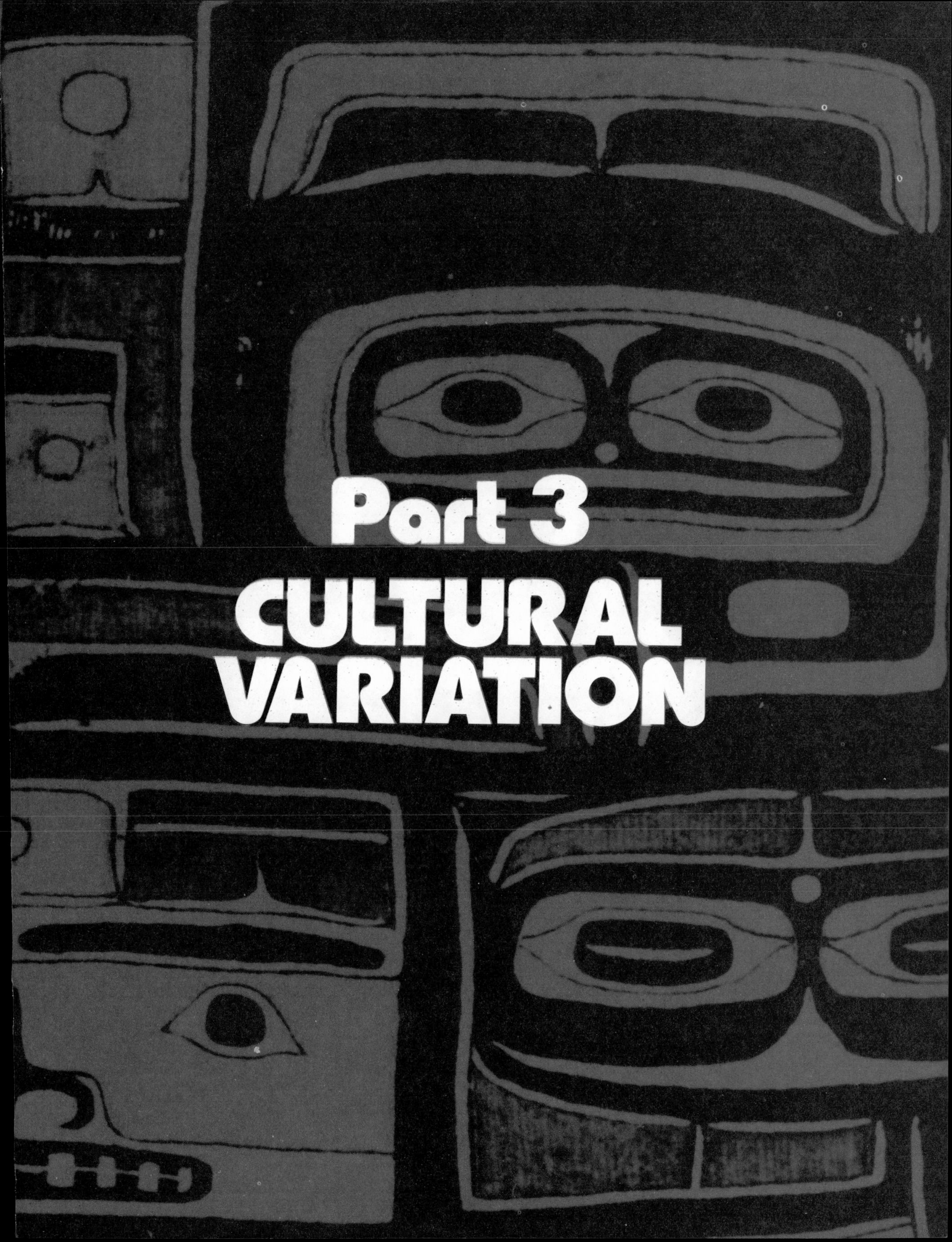

10

Theory and Method in Cultural Anthropology

People have long been interested in the customs or cultures of others, but it is only in the last 100 years or so that the study of culture has been practiced in a way that can be called scientific. Writers of picturesque travel books like Herodotus and Marco Polo recorded and commented on the exotic lifestyles of foreign peoples chiefly to entertain the literate members of their own societies. Philosophers (like Rousseau with his "noble savage") concocted pictures of primitive peoples which, though they have come to assume positions of importance in the history of ideas, bear little resemblance to reality. Beginning about 100 years ago, those who were interested in learning about other cultures realized that, if they were to produce anything of scientific value, they would have to study their subject in the same way other scientists studied theirs: by systematic and impartial observation. To describe cultures more accurately, anthropologists began to live among the peoples they were studying, so they could observe and even take part in the important events of those societies and carefully question a sampling of the natives about their customs. In other words, they began to do fieldwork.

TECHNIQUES OF FIELDWORK

Fieldwork is the cornerstone of modern anthropology. It is the means by which all anthropological information is obtained. And like laboratory work in the physical sciences, it provides the data required for the testing of theories or explanations. In American anthropology, a student is usually required to obtain data in the field and present an interpretation of those data in order to qualify for a doctoral degree. One exception to this rule occurs when a student elects to do a cross-cultural study in which he analyzes data, on a number of cultures, that have been collected by previous fieldworkers; but even in this case the importance of fieldwork remains primary.

What then are the techniques of fieldwork? Before starting out into the field an anthropologist familiarizes himself with available material on the culture he plans to study and on the problems he is particularly interested in. In studying this material, the anthropologist attempts to obtain a preliminary understanding of the society's culture. His efforts may generate ideas or possible theories about why certain customs occur, which he can investigate or test in the field.

The fieldworker may obtain information about cultural patterns in two ways: observation and interviewing. He may use one or the other, or both simultaneously, depending upon the type of information he is trying to collect. Interviewing as a technique of fieldwork is generally used to find out about customary behaviors, beliefs, and values which individuals are able and willing to talk about. It is the only technique that can be used to find out about actions or events which the anthropologist cannot observe first-hand, either because they occurred in the past or because he is excluded from witnessing them. For example, although most American Indian tribes no longer practice many of their traditional customs, anthropologists can still obtain information about former ways of life by interviewing older Indians who recall them. Interviewing can only be successfully used, however, when individuals are willing and able to verbalize about customary behaviors, beliefs, and values. Observation, on the other hand, is the only way the fieldworker can find out about unverbalized cultural patterns. People are not always able to say, for example, how far apart they typically stand from someone else when having a conversation, but such behavior patterns can be observed by the anthropologist. Observation as a technique of fieldwork also serves as a check on whether people do in fact customarily behave as they say they do.

The fieldworker must also decide how many and what kinds of people he will observe or interview. Generally, the rule is that the more obvious and widely shared a cultural pattern is, the fewer persons need to be either interviewed or observed. When great variability in cultural traits exists, however, there is a greater need for interviewing or observation of a representative sample of individuals. For example, if the fieldworker wants to know whether there is a "chief" or headman of the village, or what is the appropriate way to greet an elder, or how many wives or husbands one may have, it is generally sufficient to ask only a few *informants* (friends of the anthropologist who are relied on for information about many of the customs of the community or society under study). But if the anthropologist wants to know how many hours a day people spend in different kinds of work, he has to make a systematic study of a representative sample of individuals in order to arrive at an accurate estimate.

In spite of a great deal of prior training and reading, fieldwork is rarely easy. One of the problems is that the anthropologist comes from a different culture and, as such, is often not aware of how he ought to behave. Even if he knows what is culturally correct behavior in the field situation, it is often difficult for him to depart from what is customary for him back home. For example, the fieldworker might realize that members of the society he is studying may not have as strong a sense of the importance of being on time as he and the members of his own society have. Nevertheless, he may still feel disconcerted when informants fail to appear or are late for appointments.

Another difficulty is that the fieldworker may at first encounter resistance to his questions and his presence. After all, the people he is living with may not understand why someone would travel to their village merely to ask questions about their way of life. As a result, the fieldworker is often viewed with some suspicion, if not fear, during his first days and months in the field. Eventually, however, most fieldworkers are accepted by the peoples they are studying and begin to be regarded as friends, albeit peculiar ones.

No matter how thorough and observant the fieldworker is, he will never be able to cover all aspects of the culture he is studying. He will be forced to concentrate on certain aspects while ignoring certain others. If an anthropologist has spent several years studying the literature of his profession he will not be likely to make these choices at random; rather he will make them according to the theoretical orientation which he has obtained from his studies. That is, the school of anthropology to which he feels himself allied will govern what he notices and how he interprets his data.

THEORETICAL ORIENTATIONS

Close to 2,000 different cultures have already been described in the literature of anthropology.

This enormous wealth of information presents certain problems. The greatest difficulty is how to make sense out of all this material. How can we obtain and use anthropological data to explain or understand cultural variation?

The way in which a particular anthropologist approaches a specific question depends on his theoretical orientation. We all tend to look at things in different ways. A young, "leftist" radical and a member of the John Birch Society would attribute the causes of poverty in the U.S. to very different factors. Similarly, an anthropologist's attitude toward a particular question depends upon the school of thought to which he belongs.

While the members of a given profession do not always fit neatly into such categories, the theoretical orientations that we will describe in this chapter do represent the basic ways of thinking which govern the types of information an anthropologist collects, as well as how he organizes and attempts to interpret his data. Thus, general labels such as "functionalist" and "ethnoscientist" provide us with a way to discuss the different attitudes of various groups of anthropologists.

However, in anthropology, as in any discipline, there is a continual ebb and flow of ideas. One theoretical orientation arises and may grow in popularity, until perhaps another is proposed in opposition to it. Every theoretical orientation has its loopholes, and often one orientation capitalizes on those aspects of a problem which a previous orientation has ignored or played down. Thus, the growth of anthropological theory reflects a constant process of modification, a dynamic interchange of ideas between investigators grappling with similar problems. In our survey of the theoretical orientations that have developed since the emergence of cultural anthropology as a professional discipline we shall adhere to an approximate historical sequence, indicating for each school of thought what kinds of information or phenomena it looks to as explanatory factors.

Predetermined Evolutionism

In the early years of anthropology, the prevailing view was that the culture of every society generally develops (or evolves) in a predetermined and uniform way; that is, it was thought that most societies pass through the same series of stages, to arrive ultimately at a common end. The sources of culture change were assumed to be embedded within the culture from the beginning, and therefore the ultimate course of cultural development was internally predetermined. Two nineteenth-century anthropologists whose writings exemplify the major ideas of the theory of predetermined cultural evolution are Edward B. Tylor and Lewis Henry Morgan.

Edward Burnet Tylor (1832–1917), an Englishman, is generally considered to be the first professional anthropologist, in that he was the first person to hold a university position in anthropology. Tylor disavowed the contention of early nineteenth-century French and English writers, led by Comte Joseph de Maistre (1753–1821), that such groups as the American Indians were examples of degenerated descendants of civilized man. Tylor maintained that culture evolved from the simple to the complex, and that all societies passed through three basic stages of development—from savagery, through barbarism, to civilization.[1]

In accordance with his belief in the progressive development of human societies, Tylor maintained that contemporary societies bear differential degrees of resemblance to extinct societies. That is, he thought of contemporary societies as living fossils, in which the various previous stages of human progress were recorded or preserved. Tylor also referred to *"survivals"*—traces of primitive habits that survive in present-day cultures. The making of pottery is an example of a "survival" in the sense used by Tylor. Primitive people made

[1] Edward B. Tylor, *Primitive Culture* (New York: Harper Torchbooks, 1958, originally published in 1871).

their bowls and other implements out of clay, because it was the best material for that purpose available to them. Today, our advanced technology has provided us with several alternative materials with which to fashion stronger, longer-lasting vessels—including glass, metal, and hard plastic—so that the making of clay pottery is no longer necessary for us. Yet, even though there is no logical reason to retain the primitive form of a process we have long since improved upon, we continue making clay pots—for the good, if irrational, reason that many people prefer clay to the more advanced materials so common today.

Tylor emphasized the similarities among different peoples. He believed that there was a kind of psychic unity among all men, which allowed for parallel invention of cultural traits and therefore produced similar evolutionary histories. In other words, because of the basic similarities common to men, different societies often find the same solutions to the same problems, independently. But Tylor also noted that cultural traits may spread from one society to another, by means of simple *diffusion*—that is, the borrowing by one culture of a trait belonging to another culture as the result of contact between the two.

Another nineteenth-century proponent of predetermined cultural evolution was Lewis Henry Morgan (1818–1889). A lawyer in upstate New York, Morgan's interest in the local Iroquois Indians led him to defend their reservation in a land-grant case, as a result of which the Iroquois "adopted" Morgan, affording him a remarkable opportunity to study their customs at close quarters. In 1851, Morgan published the first full field study of an American Indian tribe, *League of the Ho-de-no-sau-nee or Iroquois.* He eventually became so involved in anthropology that he gave up law entirely.

Morgan's best-known work, *Ancient Society,* was published in 1877. In it, he divided the evolution of human culture into the same three basic stages as Tylor had done (savagery, barbarism, and civilization), but Morgan further subdivided savagery and barbarism into upper, middle, and lower segments.[2] He distinguished these stages in terms of technological achievements; for example, pottery is characteristic of Lower Barbarism, domestication of plants and animals is characteristic of Middle Barbarism, and iron tools are characteristic of Upper Barbarism. For Morgan, the cultural features characteristic of these various stages arose from a "few primary germs of thought"—germs which had emerged while man was still a savage and which developed in a predetermined manner into the "principal institutions of mankind."

Morgan postulated that the stages of technological development were associated with a sequence of different cultural patterns. For example, he speculated that the family evolved through six stages. Human society began as a "horde living in promiscuity," where there were no sexual prohibitions, and hence no real family structure. Next was the stage in which a group of brothers was married to a group of sisters and brother-sister matings were permitted. In the third stage, group marriage was practiced but brothers and sisters were not allowed to mate. The fourth stage, which evolved during barbarism, was characterized by a loosely paired male and female who still lived with other people. Then came the husband-dominant family in which the husband could have more than one wife simultaneously. Finally, the stage of civilization was characterized by the monogamous family, with just one wife and one husband who were relatively equal in status. Thus, Morgan felt that, as human society developed, its family units became progressively smaller and more self-contained. Morgan's postulated sequence for the evolution of the family, however, is not supported by the enormous amount of ethnographic data that has been collected since his time. For example, no recent society that Morgan would call "savage" has group marriage or allows brother-sister mating.

[2] Lewis Henry Morgan, *Ancient Society* (Cambridge, Mass.: Belknap Press, 1964, originally published in 1877), pp. 5–6.

Karl Marx was struck by the parallels between Morgan's evolutionism and his own theory of history. Extrapolating from Morgan's ideas, Marx and his co-worker Friedrich Engels devised a theory in which the institutions of monogamy, private property, and the state are assumed to be chiefly responsible for the exploitation of the working classes in modern industrialized societies. Marx and Engels extended Morgan's evolutionary scheme to include a future stage of cultural evolution in which monogamy, private property, and the state would cease to exist, and the "communism" of primitive society would once more come into being. Because Morgan's ideas were thus incorporated into Marxist theory, the nineteenth-century American attorney and apostle of the "civilized" profit motive is now a revered intellectual figure in the Soviet Union.

The predetermined evolutionism of Tylor, Morgan, and others of the nineteenth century is rejected today (at least outside the Soviet Union). First, predetermined evolutionist theories cannot satisfactorily account for why there is unequal development—why, for instance, some societies today are in Upper Savagery and others are in Civilization. The "psychic unity of mankind" that was postulated to account for parallel development cannot also account for differential development in time. Second and more important, we have some evidence that societies do not necessarily progress through such stages. Some societies have "regressed" or have even become extinct. Other societies may have "progressed" to civilization, but some of them have not passed through all of the postulated stages. If the sequence is not inevitable, evolution cannot be said to be predetermined, and we must look elsewhere to explain the evolution of culture.

Franz Boas. (Courtesy of the American Museum of Natural History.)

Historical Particularism

Along with the beginning of the twentieth century came the end of predetermined evolutionism's reign as the primary theoretical orientation in cultural anthropology. The leading opponent of predetermined evolutionism was Franz Boas (1858–1942), who had obtained his Ph.D. in physics at a German university with a dissertation on the color of sea water. Boas's main area of disagreement with Tylor, Morgan, and the other evolutionists was with respect to their assumption of universal laws governing all human culture. Boas pointed out that these nineteenth-century figures had insufficient data available (as Boas did himself) to be able to formulate many useful generalizations. In fact, most of the information that Tylor and Morgan used was collected from the diaries of traveling merchants, missionaries, and explorers, who could not be counted upon, according to Boas, to have the proper detached, scientific viewpoint.

Boas stressed the apparently enormous complexity of cultural variation and perhaps for this reason believed that it was premature to formulate universal laws. Boas felt that single cultural traits had to be studied in the context of the society in which they appeared. In 1896, Boas published *The Limitation of the Comparative Method of Anthropology,* which dealt with his objections to the evolutionist approach.[3] In it, Boas stated that anthropologists should spend less time developing theories based on insufficient data. Rather, it was important to collect as much data as possible, as quickly as possible, before the world's primitive cultures disappeared (as so many had already done, after contact with foreign societies). Once the body of data was gathered, then interpretations could be made and theories proposed. Thus, Boas himself made many anthropological field trips, concentrating his work on the American Indians of the northwest Pacific coast.

Boas expected that through the collection of a tremendous quantity of data, the laws governing cultural variation would emerge by themselves. According to the method advocated by Boas, the essence of science is to mistrust all expectations and to rely only on the "facts." But we now realize that no one can see or record all the "facts." What facts one records, even for the most diligent observer, depends upon what one thinks is important. Without theorizing, without ideas about what to expect, collection is meaningless—for those facts that are most important may be ignored while the irrelevant may be recorded.

[3] Franz Boas, "The Limitation of the Comparative Method in Anthropology," in *Race, Language, and Culture* (New York: Macmillan, 1940).

Although it was appropriate for Boas to be critical of previous "armchair" theorizing, his particularistic concern with an infinite number of local details did not encourage a belief in the possibility of explaining the variation that anthropologists observe. After all, if one does not believe in the possibility of causal explanations of cultural variations, one is not likely to look for them. Thus, Boas's approach is not really a theoretical orientation, since it does not tell us where to look for explanations.

Diffusionism

In the late nineteenth and early twentieth centuries, while the cultural evolutionism of Tylor and Morgan was still popular, the school of diffusionism began to take hold among anthropologists in several parts of the world. The two main schools with a diffusionist viewpoint were the British and the German-Austrian schools.

The main spokesmen for the British school of diffusionism were G. Elliot Smith, William J. Perry, and W. H. R. Rivers. They felt that most aspects of higher civilization were developed in Egypt (which was unusually advanced culturally, due to its early development of agriculture) and then diffused throughout the world, due to the contact of other peoples with the Egyptians. The British diffusionists felt that the independent parallel evolution of a particular cultural trait in two widely removed areas of the world was extremely rare. People, they believed, are inherently uninventive and invariably prefer to borrow the inventions of another culture, rather than inventing them for themselves. This viewpoint was never well accepted in the United States, and it has since been abandoned completely.

Fritz Graebner and Father Wilhelm Schmidt led the German-Austrian diffusionist school, which also held that people borrow from other cultures because they are basically uninventive. They suggested that cultural traits can diffuse in a group, as well as singly, over great distances. Schmidt and Graebner further proposed that the characteristics of the oldest culture in the world could be reconstructed by studying the traits held in common by the "ethnologically oldest" peoples—those whose way of life was the most "primitive."

Unlike the British school, which assumed that all cultural traits originated in one place (Egypt) and filtered down to cultures throughout the world, the German-Austrian school posited the existence of "culture circles" *(Kulturkreis),* or areas in which shared cultural traits could be identified. However, like the British diffusionists, the *Kulturkreis* school provided little documentation for the historical relationships they assumed.

Around this time, a separate American diffusionist school of thought also arose, led by Clark Wissler and Alfred Kroeber. Similar in method to the German-Austrian school but more modest in its claims, the American diffusionists attributed the characteristic features of a culture area to a geographical "culture center," where the traits were first developed, and from which they diffused outward. This led Wissler to formulate his age-area principle: if a given trait diffused outward from a single culture center, then it follows that the most widely distributed traits found to exist around such a center must be the oldest traits.

Although most anthropologists today acknowledge the spread of traits by diffusion, there are few who try to account for most aspects of cultural development and variation in terms of diffusion. For one thing, the diffusionists dealt only in a very superficial way with the question of how cultural traits are transferred from one society to another. This failing is a serious one since the real question is to explain why a culture accepts, rejects, or modifies a trait that one of its neighbors has. After all, societies do not always borrow from neighboring peoples—they probably do so only if they find it useful. Second, any diffusionist explanation must ultimately come up against the "chicken-and-egg" question. In other words, even if it could be demonstrated how and why a trait diffused outward from a cultural center, we would still be no closer to an explanation of how or why the trait developed within that center in the first place.

Functionalism

Bronislaw Malinowski (1884–1942) was trained in Poland as a mathematician, studied anthropology in England for four years, and then lived during World War I among the natives of the Trobriand Islands, observing and studying their way of life. By completely isolating himself from the other Europeans in the area, and by immersing himself in the language and customs of the natives, Malinowski tried to see the world from the natives' perspective, in order to better understand their culture. This is known as the *participant observer* approach to anthropological fieldwork.

Malinowski proposed a theoretical orientation called *functionalism,* which assumes that all cultural traits are useful parts of the society in which they occur.[4] In other words, the functional view of culture maintains that every customary pattern of behavior, every belief and attitude that is part of a society's culture, serves some basic function within that culture.

According to Malinowski, the function of a culture trait is its ability to satisfy some *basic* or *derived* need of the individuals in the society. The basic needs include nutrition, reproduction, bodily comfort, safety, relaxation, movement, and growth. Some aspects of the culture satisfy these basic needs. In doing so, they give rise to derived needs that must also be satisfied by the culture. For example, the

[4] Bronislaw Malinowski, "The Group and the Individual in Functional Analysis," *American Journal of Sociology,* Vol. 44 (1939), pp. 938–964.

Bronislaw Malinowski, during his fieldwork among the Trobriand Islanders (1915–1918), talks to Togugu'a, a sorcerer and informant. (Courtesy of Helena Malinowska Burke.)

culture traits that satisfy the need for food give rise to the secondary need for cooperation in food collection or production; hence societies will develop forms of political organization and social control that guarantee the required cooperation. Thus, in Malinowski's view of culture, all cultural items can ultimately be seen as satisfying a basic need for individuals.

Malinowski believed that the functional approach had an important practical value. The understanding it made possible could be put to use by those who dealt with primitive societies. As Malinowski explained it:

> The practical value of such a theory [functionalism] is that it teaches us the relative importance of various customs, how they dovetail into each other, how they have to be handled by missionaries, colonial authorities, and those who economically have to exploit savage trade, savage labor.[5]

The major objection to Malinowski's functionalism is that it cannot readily account for cultural variation. The needs which he identified are all more or less universal ones—such as the need for food—which all societies must deal with if they are to survive. Thus, while the functionalist approach may tell us that all societies need to engage in food getting, it cannot tell us why different societies engage in different food-getting practices. In other words, functionalism does not explain why certain specific cultural patterns arise to fulfill a need which might just as easily be fulfilled by any one of a number of alternative possibilities. The functionalist approach is undoubtedly useful

[5] Bronislaw Malinowski, "The Life of Culture," in G. E. Smith et al., eds., *The Diffusion Controversy* (New York: Norton, 1927), pp. 40–41.

for analyzing the workings of individual cultures, but it does not by itself suggest why different cultures have different culture traits and why culture change occurs.

Structural-Functionalism

Like Malinowski, Arthur Reginald Radcliffe-Brown, another British social anthropologist (1881–1955), based his theory of human social behavior on the concept of functionalism. But unlike Malinowski, Radcliffe-Brown felt that the various aspects of social behavior, rather than developing to satisfy individual needs, exist to maintain a society's social structure. The social structure of a society is the total network of existing social relationships.[6]

One concrete example of Radcliffe-Brown's structural-functionalist approach is his analysis of the way in which different societies deal with the tensions that are likely to develop among people related only through marriage. To reduce potential tension between in-laws, he suggests, societies may do one of two things—they may develop strict rules preventing the persons involved from ever interacting face to face (as do the Navajo, for example, among whom a man avoids his mother-in-law), or else they put the relationship on a casual, humorous basis (as Americans do, with our ever-present mother-in-law jokes). By helping to avoid conflict among the members of a family, both of these cultural traits—the Navajo rules and our jokes—contribute to the social solidarity of the societies in whose cultures they appear.

One of the major problems with the structural-functional approach is that it is difficult to determine whether or not a particular custom is in fact functional in the sense of contributing to the maintenance of the social system. In biology, the contribution an organ makes to the health or life of an animal can be assessed by removing it. But we cannot subtract a cultural trait from a society to see if it contributes to the structural maintenance of that society. It is conceivable that certain customs within the society may be neutral or even detrimental to its maintenance. We cannot assume that all of a society's customs are functional merely because the society is functioning at the moment. And even if we were able to assess whether a particular custom was functional, this theoretical orientation fails to deal with the question of why a particular society chooses to meet its social structural needs in a particular way. A given problem does not necessarily entail one particular solution—we still need to explain why one of various alternatives is chosen.

A. R. Radcliffe-Brown. (Courtesy of Fred Eggan.)

[6] A. R. Radcliffe-Brown, *Structure and Function in Primitive Society* (London: Cohen and West, 1952).

Psychological Approaches

Beginning in the 1920s, some American anthropologists began to be interested in the relations between culture and personality. The particular focus of the early studies was on the experiences of childhood and how they apparently affect adult behavior. Previously, anthropologists had not taken separate notice of child-rearing practices as a significant aspect of culture; but now, under the influence of Freud and of the educational theorist, John Dewey, anthropologists became interested in the cultural milieu of the infant or young child as an important factor contributing to the shaping of the typical adult personality.

In seminars at Columbia University in the 1930s and '40s, Ralph Linton, an anthropologist, and Abram Kardiner, a psychoanalyst, developed a number of important ideas for culture-and-personality studies. Most notably, Kardiner suggested that all the members of a society share the same basic personality structure. That is, because they would all tend to have had the same type of toilet training, childhood discipline, weaning experiences, and so on, as adults these people would tend to have certain personality traits in common.

During World War II and shortly thereafter, the culture-and-personality orientation was applied to complex societies. Most of these studies of "national character" attributed the apparent personality traits of different nations to aspects of child rearing. For example, three studies suggested that adult Japanese were compulsive because of the strict toilet training they had received.[7] Similarly, the manic-depressive swings in emotion presumed to be common among Russians were attributed by Gorer and Rickman to the practice in Soviet nurseries of swaddling infants from birth.[8] Swaddling involves the wrapping of cloth strips around the body to keep the infant's arms and legs immobile and was considered to cause anger and frustration in the infant which were later expressed in the adult as manic-depression.

Unfortunately, because it was wartime, the investigators working on Japanese compulsiveness were unable to do any fieldwork. The anthropologists studying Russian character likewise were forced to use indirect research methods. Later, when researchers were able to get first-hand data and better samplings of subjects, it was found that the conclusions of the early studies were not always reliable: for example, the Japanese were found to have toilet-training practices that were not particularly strict. In short, the early studies of national character were crude attempts to use the methods of social science to substantiate subjective generalizations about personality differences between complex societies.

As time went on, the focus of the psychological approach to cultural variation changed. While retaining their interest in Freudian theories and the relation between child training and adult personality, some anthropologists began to investigate the possible determinants of variation in child-training practices. For example, in a comparative study, Barry, Child, and Bacon suggested that the future food supply in herding and agricultural societies was best assured by adherence to an established routine, since mistakes may jeopardize a year's food supply. In most hunting and fishing societies, however, mistakes may only affect the daily food supply; as a result, adherence to routine is not as essential, and individual initiative may be stressed. As the investigators predicted,

[7] Ruth Benedict, *The Chrysanthemum and the Sword* (Boston: Houghton Mifflin, 1946); G. Gorer, "Themes in Japanese Culture," *Transactions of the New York Academy of Sciences,* Vol. 5 (1943), pp. 106–124; W. La Barre, "Some Observations on Character Structure in the Orient: The Japanese," *Psychiatry,* Vol. 8 (1945), pp. 326–342.

[8] G. Gorer and J. Rickman, *The People of Great Russia: A Psychological Study* (New York: Chanticleer, 1950).

the cross-cultural evidence indicates that agricultural societies are apt to stress obedience and responsibility in their child training, whereas hunting and fishing societies tend to emphasize independence and self-reliance.[9]

In addition to exploring the determinants of different patterns of child training, recent studies have suggested that personality traits and processes may account for the relationship between some cultural patterns. The argument here is that certain culture traits produce certain psychological characteristics which in turn give rise to other culture traits. Such a mediating influence of personality is suggested, for example, by the work of John W. M. Whiting and Irvin L. Child on cultural explanations of illness.[10] They suggest that severe punishment in child training (a cultural characteristic) may lead to an exaggerated preoccupation with that area of life (a psychological characteristic) which in turn may predispose people in that society to develop a belief that some activity in that same area of psychological conflict causes illness (also a cultural characteristic). So severe punishment for aggression in childhood may lead to conflict over the expression of aggression in adulthood, which may in turn predispose the adults to believe that aggressive behavior causes illness.

To generalize about the psychological approach in cultural anthropology, then, we may say that it seeks to explain cultural variation in child training, personality, and practices or beliefs that may be consequences of psychological factors and processes.

Later Evolutionism

The evolutionary approach to cultural development did not die with the nineteenth-century classicists, Tylor and Morgan. In the 1930s, Leslie A. White attacked the Boasian emphasis on historical particularism and championed the evolutionism of Morgan and Tylor.

Quickly labelled a "neo"-evolutionist, White rejected the term, insisting that his approach did not depart significantly from those espoused in the nineteenth century. White felt he had added nothing new to Morgan and Tylor's approach; his theories were more detailed, merely because more data were available to him.

What White did add to the classical evolutionist approach was a conception of culture as an energy-capturing system. According to his "basic law" of cultural evolution: "Other factors remaining constant, *culture evolves as the amount of energy harnessed per capita per year is increased or as the efficiency of the means of putting the energy to work is increased.*"[11] In other words, a more advanced technology gives man control over more energy (human, animal, solar, and so on), and, as a result, his culture expands and changes.

White's orientation has been criticized for the same reasons that the ideas of Tylor and Morgan were found wanting. In describing what has happened in the evolution of human culture, he assumes (along with Tylor and Morgan) that cultural evolution is strictly determined by conditions (preeminently technological ones) inside the culture. That is, he explicitly denies the possibility of environmental or historical influences on cultural evolution. The main problem with such an orientation is that it cannot explain why some cultures evolve, while others do not or even become extinct. Thus, White's idea of energy capture as the mechanism of cultural evolution begs the question of why only some cultures—not all—are able to increase their energy capture.

[9] Herbert Barry, III, Irvin L. Child, and Margaret K. Bacon, "Relation of Child Training to Subsistence Economy," *American Anthropologist,* Vol. 61 (1959), pp. 51–63.

[10] John W. M. Whiting and Irvin L. Child, *Child Training and Personality: A Cross-Cultural Study* (New Haven: Yale University Press, 1953).

[11] Leslie A. White, *The Science of Culture* (New York: Farrar, Straus and Cudahy, 1949), pp. 368–369. (Italics added.)

Julian H. Steward, another modern evolutionist, divides evolutionary thought into three schools: unilinear, universal, and multilinear.[12] Steward feels that Morgan and Tylor are examples of the unilinear approach to cultural evolution—the classical nineteenth-century orientation which attempts to place particular cultures on the rungs of a sort of evolutionary ladder. Universal evolutionists like Leslie White, on the other hand, are concerned with culture, in the broad sense, rather than individual cultures. Steward classified himself as a multilinear evolutionist—one who deals with the evolution of particular cultures and only with demonstrated sequences of parallel culture change in different areas.

Steward was concerned with explaining specific cultural differences and similarities and was critical of White's seemingly vague generalities and his disregard of environmental influences on evolution. White, on the other hand, asserted that Steward fell into the historical particularist trap of paying too much attention to particular cases.

Marshall Sahlins and Elman Service, who were students and colleagues of both White and Steward, have combined White's and Steward's views by recognizing two kinds of evolution—*specific* and *general.*[13] *Specific evolution* refers to the particular sequence of change and adaptation of a particular society in a given environment. *General evolution* refers to the general progress of human society, in which higher forms (having higher energy capture) arise from and surpass lower forms. Thus, specific evolution is similar to Steward's multilinear evolution and general evolution is similar to White's universal evolution. Although this synthesis does serve to integrate both points of view, it does not give us a way of explaining why specific cultures change or why general evolutionary progress has occurred. Unlike the early evolutionists, the later evolutionists discount predeterminism, but they do not replace it with any other mechanism supposedly determining what happens in cultural evolution.

[12] Julian H. Steward, *Theory of Culture Change* (Urbana: University of Illinois Press, 1955).

[13] Marshall D. Sahlins and Elman R. Service, *Evolution and Culture* (Ann Arbor: University of Michigan Press, 1960).

French Structuralism

One of the most influential, and controversial, viewpoints in anthropology today is that of Claude Lévi-Strauss, the leading proponent of an approach to cultural analysis called *French structuralism.* Lévi-Strauss's structuralism differs greatly from that of Radcliffe-Brown. While Radcliffe-Brown concentrated on how the elements of a society functioned as a system, Lévi-Strauss concentrates more on the origins of the systems themselves. He sees man's culture, as it is expressed in art, ritual, and the patterns of daily life, as a surface representation of the underlying structure of the human mind. To use a simple example, the color symbolism used in traffic lights can be seen as a reflection of certain predetermined patterns within the mind. We choose red as a symbol to mean "stop—danger," presumably because of its association with blood. Then, wanting a second color to convey an opposite message ("go—safe"), we choose green, which stands for growing things and is opposite red on the color wheel. Yellow, an intermediate color, is then introduced as the third term in the formula, to mean "get ready to stop—the situation is changing."[14]

Lévi-Strauss's interpretations of cultural phenomena (which tend to be far more involved and difficult to follow than the above simplified example) have concentrated on the cognitive processes of primitive people—that is, the ways in which people perceive and classify

[14] Edmund Leach, *Claude Lévi-Strauss* (New York: Viking Press, 1970), pp. 16–20.

things in the world around them. In studies such as *The Savage Mind* and *The Raw and the Cooked,* Lévi-Strauss suggests that even technologically primitive groups often construct elaborate systems for the purpose of classifying plants and animals not only for practical purposes but out of a need for such intellectual activity.

Lévi-Strauss has been influenced greatly by the work of those linguists who attempt to reconstruct the underlying thought patterns behind human speech. He applies this approach to the analysis of myth, in an effort to uncover the universal patterns which may underlie the legends and folktales of different societies. He has also done a great deal of work on how a society's culture is reflected in its cooking practices. For example, he considers roasting a more primitive method of food preparation than boiling, since roasting is merely the direct exposure of food to an open fire, while boiling requires a container and water.

Lévi-Strauss's structuralism has been criticized, chiefly by American and British anthropologists, for its concentration on abstruse, theoretical analyses at the expense of solid, ethnological observation and evidence. It is not always clear how a particular structuralist interpretation was derived, and in the absence of any systematically collected supporting evidence it is left to the reader to decide whether or not the interpretation seems plausible. Thus Lévi-Strauss's studies, though highly suggestive and often eloquently written, have come to be regarded by many as vague and untestable, self-contained intellectual constructs with little explanatory value.

Claude Lévi-Strauss. (Photo by Henri Cartier-Bresson, Magnum.)

Ethnoscience

While Lévi-Strauss's structuralist approach involves intuitively grasping the rules of thought that may underlie a given culture, a "new" ethnographic approach, known as *ethnoscience,* attempts to derive these rules from the logical analysis of ethnographic data, kept as free as possible from contamination by the observer's own cultural biases.

The approach of ethnoscience is similar to Lévi-Strauss's—in that both are influenced by the methodology of structural linguistics—but there the similarity ends. Rather than collecting data according to a predetermined set of anthropological categories, the ethnoscientist seeks to come to an understanding of the natives' world from their point of view. Based on what he has discovered about the natives through studying their language and particularly the words they use to describe what they do, the ethnoscientist tries to formulate the rules which generate acceptable behavior in the culture—rules which are comparable to the grammatical rules that generate the correct use of language.

Many ethnoscientists think that if we can discover the rules that generate correct cultural behavior, we can explain much of what people do and why they do it. Probably to a great extent individuals do act generally according to the conscious and unconscious rules they have internalized. Thus, discovering the cultural rules can partially explain behavior. However, we would still need to understand why a particular society has the particular cultural rules it has. Just as a grammar does not explain how a language came to be what it is or how it changes, so the ethnoscientific discovery of cultural rules does not explain culture change and variation.

Cultural Ecology

It is only relatively recently that the influence of environment upon culture has begun to be taken seriously. For many anthropologists, environment is seen as having only a limiting effect on culture—that is, certain activities are prohibited in certain climates (such as agriculture in the Arctic), but beyond this kind of limitation, environment has been viewed as having no direct influence on culture.

Julian H. Steward was one of the first to advocate the study of cultural ecology—the analysis of the relationship between a culture and its environment. Steward felt that the explanation for some aspects of cultural variation could be found in the adaptation of societies to their particular environments. But rather than merely hypothesizing that the environment did or did not determine cultural variation, Steward wished to resolve the question empirically—that is, he wanted to carry out investigations to substantiate his viewpoint.[15]

Steward, however, felt that cultural ecology must be separated from biological ecology (the study of the relationships between organisms and their environment). More recent cultural ecologists like Andrew P. Vayda and Roy A. Rappaport[16] wish to incorporate principles of biological ecology into the study of cultural ecology, in order to make a single science of ecology. According to this view, cultural traits, just as biological traits, are subject to natural selection and can be considered adaptive or maladaptive. Environment, then, including the physical and social environment, affects the development of culture traits in that

> individuals or populations behaving in certain different ways have different degrees of success in survival and reproduction and, consequently, in the transmission of their ways of behaving from generation to generation.[17]

Consider how culture and environment interact among the Tsembaga, who live in the interior of New Guinea.[18] The Tsembaga are horticulturists, living mainly on the root crops and greens they grow in their home gardens; they also raise pigs, which serve many useful functions. Although the pigs are seldom eaten, they keep residential areas clean by consuming garbage, and they help prepare the soil for planting by rooting in the future gardens. Small numbers

[15] Julian H. Steward, "The Concept and Method of Cultural Ecology," in *Theory of Culture Change,* pp. 30–42.

[16] Andrew P. Vayda and Roy A. Rappaport, "Ecology: Cultural and Noncultural," in James H. Clifton, ed., *Introduction to Cultural Anthropology* (Boston: Houghton Mifflin, 1968), pp. 477–497.

[17] *Ibid.,* p. 493.

[18] See Roy A. Rappaport, "Ritual Regulation of Environmental Relations among a New Guinea People," *Ethnology,* Vol. 6 (1967), pp. 17–30.

of pigs are easy to keep—they run free all day, returning at night to eat whatever substandard tubers were found in the course of gathering the humans' daily rations. Thus pigs, which require a minimum of maintenance, serve both as janitors and cultivating machines.

But problems arise when the pig herd grows large. There are often not enough substandard tubers, so pigs must be fed human rations. Eventually, the people must work to supply their pigs with food. Similarly, although a small number of pigs will clean up yards and soften the soil in the gardens, a large herd is likely to consume garden crops. Pigs can even break up communities—if one person's pig invades a neighbor's garden, the garden owner often retaliates by killing the offending pig. In his turn, the dead animal's owner may kill the garden owner, the garden owner's wife, or one of his pigs. As the number of such feuds increases, people began to put as much distance as possible between their pigs and other people's gardens.

So, in order to cope with the problem of pig overpopulation, the Tsembaga have apparently developed an elaborate cycle of rituals which involve the slaughter of large numbers of surplus pigs. The pigs can then be distributed, in the form of pork—a valuable commodity—to friends, and to ancestors (who, the Tsembaga believe, will grant them strength and courage, in return for pork offerings). Thus, a cultural practice (ritual pig feasts) can be viewed as an adaptation to environmental factors that produce a surplus pig population; the feasts also reduce conflict in the society.

APPLYING THEORETICAL ORIENTATIONS

When one is familiar with the general characteristics of the major theoretical orientations, he can begin to apply them to concrete situations. Specifically, how may an anthropologist's theoretical orientation influence his approach to a particular problem?

As an example, we will examine the approaches taken by representatives of various schools of thought to the following problem: Why do some societies have male initiation ceremonies? Needless to say, none of the following interpretations is necessarily correct. We merely refer to them to show more concretely how different theoretical orientations give rise to different interpretations of the same problem.

Some, but not all, societies have special ceremonies marking the initiation of adolescent boys into manhood. These rites generally involve some "hazing" of the initiates; often they must fast, wear certain types of clothing, or perform particular tasks, in order to gain admission into the world of adult men. Painful experiences such as circumcision are also common in initiation ceremonies.

A psychological interpretation of male initiation rites has been proposed by Roger Burton and John W. M. Whiting.[19] They suggest that, in societies in which boys typically sleep with their mothers for the first few years of their lives (to the exclusion of their fathers, who often are prohibited from having sexual relations with the mother for at least a year after a child's birth), boys are apt to develop an initial feminine identification. Subsequently, when boys find out that men exercise control in their society, they learn to identify with males—but their initial identification with females creates conflict for them. Initiation rites, according to Burton and Whiting, serve psychologically to emphasize male identity (a boy

[19] Roger V. Burton and J. W. M. Whiting, "The Absent Father and Cross-Sex Identity," *Merrill-Palmer Quarterly of Behavior and Development,* Vol. 7, No. 2 (1961). This paper modifies an earlier interpretation presented in J. W. M. Whiting, R. Kluckhohn, and A. Anthony, "The Function of Male Initiation Ceremonies at Puberty," in E. Maccoby, T. M. Newcomb, and E. L. Hartley, eds., *Readings in Social Psychology,* 3rd ed. (New York: Holt, Rinehart and Winston, 1958), pp. 359–370.

According to one theory of economic development, a society's level of development depends upon the agricultural potential of its physical environment. Thus, in an environment with no agricultural potential, such as the arctic environment shown here, economic development would be prohibited. (Courtesy of the American Museum of Natural History.)

is considered a man after the initiation ceremony) and therefore resolve the conflict in identification.

A functional approach to male initiation ceremonies can be illustrated by Frank W. Young's studies.[20] Young suggested that male initiation rites are functionally necessary to maintain the solidarity of adult males in societies that have strong male organizations. Young feels that the drama and elaborate details surrounding these rites call attention to the status change of the young boys who are being accepted into the group of men and instill in them the will to cooperate with their peers and elders. Because of the emphasis placed on the young initiates' change in status, the boys quickly learn their new roles as adults—thus maintaining the solidarity and cooperation among the society's adult men which is necessary for them to function as hunters, warriors, and fully participating members of male organizations. Young also hypothesizes that the greater the society's level of male solidarity, the more elaborate and dramatic their male initiation rites.

As another example of how different theoretical orientations generate different approaches to the same question, one could consider the literature on the following problem: Why do societies vary in their level of economic development?

Betty Meggers takes an ecological approach to this problem. Her studies of certain areas in South America and of European history suggested to her that "the level to which a culture can develop is dependent upon the agricultural potentiality of the environment it occupies."[21] According to Meggers, there are four types of environment—those with no agricultural potential, those with limited agricultural potential, those that have increasable agricultural potential, and those with limitless agricultural potential. These types are presumed to determine the level of economic development attainable for the people living in them.

[20] Frank W. Young, *Initiation Ceremonies: A Cross-Cultural Study of Status Dramatization* (New York: Bobbs-Merrill, 1965).

[21] Betty Meggers, "Environmental Limitations on the Development of Culture," *American Anthropologist*, Vol. 56 (1954), pp. 801–824.

Some anthropologists have looked to a society's technological system in an effort to explain the level of economic development. A society which depends upon manpower as its primary source of energy, as is the case in this Indian village, will be substantially limited in its level of economic development. (Photo by Marilyn Silverstone, © 1966 Magnum Photos.)

Another answer to the question of economic development might take a psychological approach. One such theory suggests that a society whose members have acquired a strong psychological need for achievement may experience a rapid rate of economic growth. For example, the need for achievement may be linked to economic development in the United States. (Photo by Cornell Capa, © 1970 Magnum Photos.)

For Leslie White, it is the society's technological system that is mainly responsible for its evolutionary status and hence its level of economic development.[22] We have already mentioned White's belief that "culture evolves as the amount of energy harnessed per capita per year is increased, or as the efficiency of the instrumental means of putting the energy to work is increased." According to this principle, then, the earliest, most primitive cultures of mankind had very unproductive economies because they were dependent upon the meager energy resources of the human body. But, with the technological revolution that occurred in agriculture, including the domestication of plants and animals, and the development of scientific knowledge sufficient to tap natural deposits of coal, oil, and natural gas, the amount of energy available for culture building was greatly increased. Thus, improved technology allowed for an increased level of economic development.

A different kind of approach to the question of economic development is taken by psychologist David C. McClelland.[23] He suggests that differences in economic development among various societies must be explained not in terms of external factors, but rather in terms of men's motives and values—since these are what ultimately determine a society's level of economic achievement. McClelland identifies "the need for achievement" as a primary force in human life, referring to it as *n* Achievement. This is a desire to excel—whether the activity is sculpture, selling insurance, or farming—not for the sake of money, social recognition, or prestige, but rather to acquire a feeling of personal accomplishment. Thus, McClelland suggests that a society which has a large proportion of people with high *n* Achievement will subsequently experience a high rate of economic growth. In other words, cultural variation in the level of economic development is attributed by McClelland to variation in the strength of a psychological motive, the need to achieve.

GENERATING EXPLANATIONS

We have seen how different theoretical orientations may lead to different interpretations of cultural phenomena. But whatever an anthropologist's theoretical bent, the process of coming up with an explanation is never a simple matter. After all, a general theoretical orientation is just that—a general guide to where we might look for answers; it does not by itself suggest a particular answer to a particular question.

How then does an anthropologist develop a theory to explain some cultural phenomenon? It is difficult to specify any one procedure that is guaranteed to produce a theory, because coming up with a theory requires a creative act of imagination, and no discovery procedure by itself necessarily generates the creative act. Too much dependence on a particular theoretical orientation may in fact be detrimental, since it may blind the investigator to other possibilities. A more important factor in generating a theory may be the investigator's belief that it is possible to do so. A person who believes that something is explainable will be more apt to notice possibly connected facts, as well as to recall possibly relevant considerations, and put them all together in some explanatory way.

We can, however, point to some procedures that have helped anthropologists to produce explanations of cultural phenomena. These procedures seem to fall into two types: an anthropologist may be helped by analyzing a particular society in which he or she has done fieldwork (we refer to this as *single-case analy-*

[22] Leslie White, "Energy and the Evolution of Culture," in *The Science of Culture.*

[23] David C. McClelland, *The Achieving Society* (New York: Van Nostrand, 1961).

sis); or, he may try to come up with a theory by a *comparative study* of more than one society.

In analyzing a single case, the anthropologist may be interested in explaining a particular custom. If he is still in the field, he may ask informants why they practice (or think they practice) the custom. Sometimes such inquiries will elicit a plausible explanation. But more often than not, the informants may merely answer: "We have always done it that way." The investigator may then make a kind of mental search through other features of the society or its environment which he thinks may be connected with the custom he is interested in explaining. If possible, the anthropologist might try to view the situation historically, to see if the custom appeared more or less recently. If that is the case, he might try to find out what other possibly explanatory conditions appeared just prior to that time.

An anthropologist may also generate an explanation by comparing different societies which share the characteristic he is interested in explaining, in order to determine what other characteristics regularly occur along with it. He will also consider societies in which the characteristic is lacking, because the possible cause of that characteristic should be absent in those societies. If an anthropologist discovers that a characteristic regularly occurs in different cultures along with certain other features, he may be reasonably sure that he has narrowed down the possible causes of that characteristic.

It must be remembered, however, that the investigator is not a computer; he does not search through all of the conceivable characteristics shared by different cultures. The investigator usually looks only at those traits which he thinks can be plausibly connected. Here is where one's theoretical orientation generally comes into play, since that orientation usually points to the importance of a particular set of factors.

TESTING EXPLANATIONS

The task of increasing scientific understanding is not impeded by a shortage of interpretations. In any field of investigation, theories are generally the most plentiful commodity, apparently because of the human predisposition to try to make sense of the world. The scientist, however, is interested in theories that work, that are capable of predicting behavior. It is necessary, then, to have some procedures that enable us to select, from among the many theories that may be available, those that are more likely to be correct. "Just as mutations arise naturally but are not all beneficial, so hypotheses [theories] emerge naturally but are not all correct. If progress is to occur, therefore, we require a superfluity of hypotheses and also a mechanism of selection."[24] In other words, generating a theory or interpretation is not enough. We need some reliable method of testing whether or not that interpretation is likely to be correct. After all, an interpretation that is not correct does not really add to our understanding. In fact, it may detract from our efforts to achieve understanding by misleading us into thinking that the problem is already solved.

The strategy of all kinds of testing in science is to predict something one would expect to find if a particular interpretation is correct, and then to conduct some investigation to see if the prediction is borne out. If the prediction is not borne out, the investigator is obliged to accept the possibility that the interpretation is wrong. If, however, the prediction holds true, then the investigator is entitled to say that there is some evidence to support his theory. Thus, conducting research that is designed to test expectations derived from theory allows us to eliminate some interpretations and to accept others, at least tentatively.

[24] Peter Caws, "The Structure of Discovery," *Science*, Vol. 166 (December 1969), p. 1378.

TYPES OF RESEARCH IN CULTURAL ANTHROPOLOGY

Cultural anthropologists conduct their research using several different methods, each method having certain advantages and disadvantages with respect to the goals of generating and testing theory. The types of research in cultural anthropology can be classified according to two criteria: (1) the spatial scope of the study (analysis of a single society, analysis of a number of societies in a region, or analysis of a world-wide sample of societies); and (2) the temporal scope of the study (historical versus nonhistorical). The combination of these criteria yields the table below which identifies each of the major types of research conducted in cultural anthropology.

Ethnography

We have already noted that ethnography, the description and analysis of a single society on the basis of fieldwork, provides the essential data for all studies in cultural anthropology. Therefore, a comparison of societies in a given region, or on a world-wide basis, requires that there be ethnographic data on each society in the sample.

With regard to the goal of generating theory, ethnography with its in-depth, first-hand, long-term observations provides an investigator with a wealth of descriptive materials on a wide range of phenomena. Thus, it may stimulate thinking about how different aspects of the culture are related to each other and to features of the environment. The ethnographer in the field has the opportunity to get to know the total context of a society's customs by asking people about those customs and by observing those phenomena which appear to be associated with them. In addition, if the ethnographer begins to think of an explanation of some custom, he can pursue that hunch by collecting new information related to it. In this sense, the ethnographer is similar to a physician who is trying to understand why a patient has certain symptoms. Like the physician who obtains information about a patient's overall physical condition in order to see if his initial diagnosis is correct, the ethnographer often formulates an explanation and then collects further data in order to substantiate it.

Although ethnography is extremely useful for generating explanations, it is not generally sufficient for testing hypotheses. For example, the ethnographer may think that a particular society practices polygyny (one man married to two or more women simultaneously) because it has a smaller number of men than women. But he could not be reasonably sure that he is right unless the results of a comparative study of a sample of societies showed that an imbalanced sex ratio in favor of women was generally associated with polygyny. After all, the fact that one society has both conditions could be an historical accident—that is, not due to any nec-

	Single Society	*Region*	*World-wide Sample*
Nonhistorical	Ethnography	Controlled Comparison	Cross-cultural Research
Historical	Ethnohistory	Controlled Comparison	Cross-historical Research

essary connection between the two conditions.

The only way in which analysis of a single case can be used to test a theory is if that case serves to refute a theory which purports to be universal. Thus, Margaret Mead's fieldwork in Samoa (as reported in *Coming of Age in Samoa,* 1928) was sufficient to lead to rejection of the theory that adolescence must necessarily be accompanied by psychological stress.

Nonhistorical Controlled Comparison

In a nonhistorical controlled comparison, the anthropologist compares ethnographic information for a number of societies which are found in a particular region—societies which presumably have similar histories and which occupy similar environments. The anthropologist who conducts a regional comparison is apt to be familiar with the complex of cultural features associated with that particular region—features which may give him a good understanding of the context of the phenomenon he is interested in explaining. However, his knowledge of the region under study is probably not as great as the ethnographer's knowledge of a single society. But the anthropologist's understanding of local details is greater in a regional comparison than in a world-wide comparison, which, because of its global scope, prevents the investigator from knowing a great deal about any one of the societies being compared.

The controlled comparison is not only useful for generating explanations, but it is also useful for testing explanations. Since the anthropologist has a number of societies to work with—some of which have the characteristic he is trying to explain and some of which do not—he can be more confident than with a single case analysis that the conditions he thinks are related may in fact be so, at least in the region investigated. However, we must remember that two or more conditions may be related in one region for reasons which are peculiar to that region. Therefore, an explanation that is supported in one region may not pertain in others.

Cross-cultural Research

Although it is possible to generate interpretations on the basis of world-wide comparisons, by looking for differences between those societies with and those without a particular characteristic, perhaps the most common use of world-wide comparisons has been to text explanations. The cross-cultural researcher first identifies conditions which should generally be associated if a particular theory is correct and then looks at a world-wide sample of societies to see if the expected association generally holds true. The advantage of cross-cultural research is that—provided the sample has been more or less randomly selected—the conclusion drawn is probably applicable to all societies. In other words, in contrast to the regional comparison, whose results may or may not be applicable to other regions, the results of a cross-cultural study are presumably applicable to all societies and all regions.

As we have already noted, the greater the number of societies that are examined in a study, the less likely it is that the investigator will have detailed knowledge of the societies involved. Hence, if a cross-cultural test does not support a particular explanation, the investigator may not know enough about the societies involved to know how to modify his interpretation or come up with a new one. In this situation, the anthropologist may reexamine the details of one or more particular societies in order to stimulate fresh thinking on the subject. Another limitation of cross-cultural research, as both a means of generating and of testing explanations, is that one can only test those explanations for which the required information is generally available in ethnographies. When one is interested in explaining something that has not been generally described, it is necessary to resort to some other research strategy which allows the investigator to collect his own data.

Types of Historical Research

Ethnohistory, or studies based on descriptive materials about a single society at more than one point in time, provides the essential data for historical studies of all types, just as ethnography provides the essential data for all nonhistorical types of research. Ethnohistorical data may consist of sources other than ethnographic reports by anthropologists; the materials of ethnohistory may include accounts by explorers, missionaries, traders, and government officials.

In terms of generating and testing hypotheses, studies of societies over time tend to be subject to the same limitations as studies confined to a single time period. Like their nonhistorical counterparts, studies which concentrate on a single society observed through time are likely to generate a number of hypotheses, but they do not generally provide the opportunity to establish with reasonable certainty which of those hypotheses are correct. Cross-cultural historical studies (of which we have a few examples thus far) suffer from the opposite limitation; they provide ample means for testing hypotheses through comparison but are severely constrained (because of the necessity of working with second-hand data) in their ability to generate hypotheses derived from the available data.

However, there is one advantage to historical studies of any type. The goal of theory in cultural anthropology is to explain variation in cultural patterns. This means specifying what conditions will favor one cultural pattern rather than another. Such specification requires us to assume that the supposed causal or favoring conditions antedated the pattern to be explained. Theories or explanations, then, imply a sequence of changes over time, which are the stuff of history. Therefore, if we want to come closer to an understanding of those factors that account for the cultural variations we are interested in, we should ideally examine historical sequences in order to determine whether the conditions we think caused various phenomena truly antedate those phenomena and thus might be more reliably said to have caused them. If we are able to examine historical sequences, we may be able to insure that we do not put the cart before the horse.

The major impediment to historical research is that collecting and analyzing historical data, particularly when it comes from the scattered accounts of explorers, missionaries, and traders, is a tedious and exasperating task. Such accounts may be incomplete, inaccurate, or insufficiently clear. Therefore, it may be more efficient to test explanations nonhistorically first, in order to eliminate some interpretations. Only when an interpretation survives a nonhistorical test should we look to historical data to test the presumed sequence.

SUMMARY

1. Fieldwork is the cornerstone of modern anthropology, being the means by which all anthropological information is obtained. The fieldworker obtains information about cultural patterns in two ways: observation and interviewing. Yet no matter how thorough the fieldworker is, he will never be able to cover all aspects of a culture. The aspects of a culture the anthropologist will concentrate on are governed by his theoretical orientation.

2. The prevailing theoretical orientation in anthropology during the nineteenth century was based on the belief that culture

generally evolves in a predetermined way—that is, all societies were believed to pass through the same series of stages, to arrive ultimately at a common end. Two proponents of this early theory of predetermined evolution are Edward B. Tylor and Lewis Henry Morgan.

3. The leading opponent of predetermined evolution during the early twentieth century was Franz Boas, who rejected the way in which early evolutionists had assumed universal laws governing all human culture. Boas stressed the importance of collecting as much anthropological data as possible, after which the laws governing cultural variation would supposedly emerge by themselves.

4. The diffusionist approach, popular in the late nineteenth and early twentieth centuries, was developed by two main schools—the British and the German-Austrian. In general, diffusionists believed that most aspects of higher civilization had emerged in culture centers from which they then diffused outward.

5. Functionalism as an approach in anthropology, proposed by Bronislaw Malinowski, holds that all culture traits serve some useful function in the society in which they occur. According to Malinowski, the function of a culture trait is its ability to satisfy some basic or derived need of the individuals in the society.

6. Unlike the functional approach of Malinowski, the structural-functional approach of A. R. Radcliffe-Brown maintains that the various aspects of social behavior, rather than developing to satisfy individual needs, exist to maintain a society's social structure—that is, its total network of social relationships.

7. Another theoretical orientation in anthropology which began in the 1920s—the psychological approach—seeks to explain cultural variation in child-training practices, personality, and practices or beliefs that may be consequences of psychological factors and processes.

8. In the 1930s, the evolutionary approach to cultural development was revived by Leslie A. White, who proposed that "culture evolves . . . as the efficiency of the means of putting energy to work is increased." Other anthropologists, such as Julian H. Steward, Marshall Sahlins, and Elman Service, have also expounded evolutionary viewpoints in recent times.

9. One of the most influential, and controversial, viewpoints in anthropology today is that of Claude Lévi-Strauss, the leading proponent of French structuralism. Essentially, Lévi-Strauss sees man's culture, as it is expressed in art, ritual, and the patterns of daily life, as a surface representation of the underlying patterns of the human mind.

10. While Lévi-Strauss's approach involves intuitively grasping the rules of thought that may underlie a given culture, a "new" ethnographic approach, known as ethnoscience, attempts to derive these rules from the logical analysis of data—particularly the words people use to describe their activities. In this way, the ethnoscientist endeavors to formulate the rules which generate acceptable behavior in the culture.

11. Another theoretical orientation in anthropology, cultural ecology, seeks to understand the relationship between man's environment and his culture. Cultural traits, then, may be adaptive or maladaptive given a particular environment.

12. Cultural anthropologists conduct their

research using several different methods. The types of research in cultural anthropology can be classified according to two criteria: (1) the spatial scope of the study (analysis of a single society, analysis of a number of societies in a region, or analysis of a world-wide sample of societies); and (2) the temporal scope of the study, (historical versus nonhistorical). The basic research methods, then, are ethnography and ethnohistory, historical and nonhistorical controlled comparisons, and historical or nonhistorical cross-cultural research.

SUGGESTED READINGS

Casagrande, J. B. (Ed.): *In the Company of Man: Twenty Portraits by Anthropologists* (New York: Harper & Row, 1960).
A collection of papers in which anthropologists discuss their experiences with field informants. The field experiences are clearly and interestingly described, and the caliber of material makes this book valuable for professional anthropologists as well as for students and laymen. The papers cover a wide geographical range and deal with societies ranging in complexity from hunting and gathering groups to pastoralists and peasants.

Freilich, M. (Ed.): *Marginal Natives: Anthropologists at Work* (New York: Harper & Row, 1970).
A collection of papers, presenting creative attempts by individual anthropologists to construct fieldwork designs. The editor divides the various methodological approaches into two basic categories: adapting to a new cultural environment and solving a research problem.

Golde, P. (Ed.): *Women in the Field: Anthropological Experiences* (Chicago: Aldine, 1970).
This group of papers deals in general with women's experiences as anthropologists in the field and in particular with their unique problems as women in a male-dominated field. The editor has attempted to focus on three main points of view in each paper: the personal and subjective, the ethnographic, and the methodological and theoretical.

Harris, M.: *The Rise of Anthropological Theory* (New York: Thomas Y. Crowell, 1968).
A critical review of the history of anthropological theory from 1750 to the present. The author discusses the social context and personalities involved in the different theoretical orientations.

Jongmans, D. G., and P. C. W. Gutkind (Eds.): *Anthropologists in the Field.* Non-European Societies, 6. (Assen: Van Gorcum, 1967).
A well-organized collection of papers which provides a complete and honest portrayal of the work of the ethnographer, whose problems often cannot be solved by means of the usual experimental scientific techniques. The editors have also included papers dealing with anthropological problems that may be caused by the ethnographer's moral position and by the fact that the understanding of a particular society usually reflects the experience of the individual ethnographer in the field.

Manners, R. A., and D. Kaplan (Eds.): *Theory in Anthropology: A Sourcebook* (Chicago: Aldine, 1968).
A massive compilation of readings on anthropological theory, with selections culled from leading theorists of the distant and recent past.

Moore, F. (Ed.): *Readings in Cross-Cultural Methodology* (New Haven: HRAF Press, 1966).
A collection of recent and classic papers on the theory and method of cross-cultural research. The editor has selected his materials on the basis of their contribution to the understanding of this approach's history, problems, and attempted solutions.

Naroll, R., and R. Cohen (Eds.): *A Handbook of Method in Cultural Anthropology* (Garden City, N.Y.: Natural History Press, 1970).
In this large collection of specially written articles, the editors and more than 40 other anthropologists and behavioral scientists explain how research in cultural anthropology should be planned and carried out. Topics covered range from the fieldwork process to problems and methods of comparative research.

Pelto, P. J.: *Anthropological Research: The Structure of Inquiry* (New York: Harper & Row, 1970).
An introduction to the collection of reliable data in cultural anthropology. Techniques of observation and measurement are emphasized. A bibliography for further study accompanies each chapter.

Spindler, G. D. (Ed.): *Being an Anthropologist: Fieldwork in Eleven Cultures* (New York: Holt, Rinehart and Winston, 1970).
A series of reports by 13 anthropologists describing how they and their families adapted to life in 11 different cultural situations. The papers are case studies, in which both subjective problems of field study and methodological problems and techniques are discussed. For the benefit of students in anthropology, the papers were selected on the basis of differences in theoretical and methodological positions, as well as variation in location and type of fieldwork.

11 Language and Culture

Few of us can remember the moment when we first became aware that words signify something, yet that moment is a milestone not simply in the acquisition of language but of all the complex, elaborate behavior that constitutes our culture. Without language, the transmission of complex traditions would be virtually impossible, and each person would be trapped within his own world of private sensations.

To recapture that instant when language became meaningful, we must rely on those like Helen Keller, who came to language late. Miss Keller, left deaf and blind by illness at the age of 19 months, gives a moving personal account of the afternoon on which she first established contact with another human being, through words:

> She [my teacher] brought me my hat, and I knew I was going out into the warm sunshine. This thought, if a wordless sensation may be called a thought, made me hop and skip with pleasure.
>
> We walked down the path to the well house, attracted by the fragrance of the honeysuckle with which it was covered. Someone was drawing water and my teacher placed my hand under the spout. As the cool stream gushed over one hand she spelled into the other the word *water,* first slowly, then rapidly. Suddenly I felt a misty consciousness as of something forgotten—a thrill of returning thought; and somehow the mystery of language was revealed to me. I knew then that *w-a-t-e-r* meant the wonderful cool something that was flowing over my hand. That living word awakened my soul, gave it light, hope, joy, set it free! There were barriers still, it is true, barriers that could in time be swept away.
>
> I left the well house eager to learn. Everything had a name, and each name gave birth to a new thought. As we returned to the house every object which I touched seemed to quiver with life. That was because I saw everything with the strange, new sight that had come to me.[1]

Against all odds, Helen Keller had come to understand the essential function which language plays in all societies, namely, that of *communication.* The word *communicate* comes from the Latin verb *communicare,* to share, to impart that which is *common.* We communicate by agreeing, consciously or unconsciously, to call an object, movement, or abstract concept by a common name. For example, speakers of English have all agreed to call the color of grass *green* even though we have no way of comparing precisely how two people actually experience this color; whatever I see as green and whatever you see as green remain part of our uncommunicable private experience. What we share, then, is the agreement to call this sensa-

[1] Helen Keller, *The Story of My Life* (New York: Dell, originally published in 1902), p. 36.

tion *green.* Any system of language consists of publicly accepted *symbols* by which we try to share private experience.

Man's communication is obviously not limited to spoken language. He communicates directly through body stance, gesture, and tone of voice; indirectly through systems of signs and symbols, such as algebraic equations, musical scores, painting, code flags, and road signs. But for all of the competing systems of communication available to man, we must recognize the overriding importance of language. It is the primary transmitter of culture from generation to generation; it is the vehicle man employs to share and to transmit his complex configuration of attitudes, beliefs, and patterns of behavior.

Animal Communication

Systems of communication are not unique to man. Other animal species communicate in a variety of ways. One way is by sound: a bird may communicate by a call that a territory is his and should not be encroached upon; a squirrel may utter a cry which leads other squirrels to flee from danger. Even some insects communicate by sound. For example, scientists have isolated five distinct types of calls among grasshoppers, including sexual and alarm calls.

Another means of animal communication is by odor. The gypsy moth signals her availability to the male by excreting a special chemical. A dead ant releases a chemical on its death, whereupon its fellows carry it away to the compost heap. Apparently the communication is highly effective: a healthy ant painted with the death chemical will be dragged to the funeral heap again and again.

Another means of communication, body movement, is used by bees to communicate the location of food sources. Von Frisch discovered that the black Austrian honeybee—through a choice of round dance, wagging dance, or a short, straight run—could communicate not only the precise direction of the source of food but also its distance from the hive.[2]

Human communication is not limited to spoken language; in all societies man also communicates in signs and gestures. Here a Nigerian policewoman signals stop to oncoming traffic, and a Bushman hunter uses sign language to silently indicate the presence of a secretary bird. (Photo of Bushman courtesy of Irven DeVore; Photo of policewoman by Marc and Evelyne Bernheim from Woodfin Camp and Associates.)

Although primates use all three methods of communication—sound, odor, and body move-

[2] K. von Frisch, "Dialects in the Language of the Bees," *Scientific American* (August 1962), p. 3.

ment—sound is the method that most concerns us here. The great apes exhibit a variety of call systems, from the relatively limited system of the gibbon to the more comprehensive one of the chimpanzee. But no matter how many calls a species of ape might possess in its repertory, each call is mutually exclusive. One call might be a request for female companionship, another, a warning of danger; the ape cannot combine parts of the two calls to obtain a third call which will combine the two messages. His system of communication, in other words, is *closed.*

Several people have attempted to teach chimpanzees human speech. One couple, who adopted a baby chimp to raise with their own newborn son, abandoned the project a year later when it became obvious that the human child was imitating the ape, not the ape the child. Keith and Cathy Hayes recorded that they were able to elicit only four recognizable words after years of effort.[3]

Perhaps the most complex system of communication the chimp is able to learn is a system of signs. In 1967 Adriaan Kortlandt reported that chimps had learned hand gestures

[3] Emily Hahn, "Chimpanzees and Language," *New Yorker* (April 24, 1971), p. 54.

which signify "Come with me," "May I pass?" "You are welcome," "Stop!" and "Be off!" among others.[4] Using this insight, Allen Gardner and Beatrice Gardner succeeded in teaching the American Sign Language (A.S.L.) to their chimpanzee Washoe. The amazing extent of Washoe's ability to use the 150 signs she had learned was recorded when she was with other chimpanzees on an island and noticed that the humans across the water were drinking iced tea. "She kept signing, 'Roger ride come gimme sweet eat please hurry hurry you come please gimme sweet you hurry you come ride Roger come give Washoe fruit drink hurry hurry fruit drink please.' . . . A plane flew over just then, and Washoe mentioned that, too. She signed, 'You me ride in plane.'"[5]

The Origins of Language

There has been much speculation as to how early man developed his language system, with special attention to the question of how selection may have favored an *open* language—in which utterances can be combined to produce new meanings—as opposed to a closed system of discrete calls. Hockett and Ascher have suggested a possible chain of events.[6] As a starting point in their argument, they cite the major climatic changes in East Africa, beginning in the late Miocene, which led to a drastic reduction in the number of trees. The ensuing competition for space and food forced some primate species onto open ground (relinquishing their former territory to those protohominoids who were to become the fathers of the apes). Those that survived in the new, more open environment were the ancestors of man. Hominid bipedalism probably developed around this time, with consequences for carrying and ultimately for speech as well. The forearms were no longer needed primarily for holding oneself in trees or restricted to the limited carrying possibilities of tree dwellers. The mouth was no longer required for carrying at all. The forearms could now be employed for transporting food and weapons over long distances, while the mouth was freed for chatter.

Hockett and Ascher suggest that the final stage in the development of an open language must have come about through a blending of two calls to produce a new call, in response to new communication requirements of the early hominids who were now living in open country and perhaps dependent upon tool use for survival. How this development occurred is open to question. What is certain is that a call system of communication was eventually changed to a system based upon small units of sound which can be put together in many different ways to form meaningful utterances. An ape has one sound, or call, for greetings. But a human can combine *h* and *i* to say *hi,* the human can then use *h* in *howdy, hurry, help,* etc., and use *i* in *ice, ivory,* etc.

The movement from calls to language, which may have taken millennia in the evolution of man, takes but a few years for children. Nonetheless, the acquisition of language by children may offer some insights into the origins of speech. Although a specific language, like other cultural patterns, is learned and shared, the process by which a child acquires the structure, or grammar, of language seems to be inborn and therefore precultural, a consequence presumably of the organization of the human brain. A child seems to be equipped from the outset with the capacity to learn any language, to reproduce all of the sounds used by the world's languages. The language the child learns is, perforce, that spoken by his parents, and because this language is a system of shared patterns, it can be re-formed into an infinite variety of expressions and be understood by all who share these

[4] Hahn, "Chimpanzees and Language," p. 54.
[5] Hahn, "Chimpanzees and Language," p. 98.
[6] C. F. Hockett and R. Ascher, "The Human Revolution," *Current Anthropology,* Vol. 5 (1964), pp. 135–168.

patterns. In this way T. S. Eliot can form a sentence never before formed, "In the room the women come and go talking of Michelangelo,"[7] and the sense of his sentence, though not necessarily his private meaning, can be understood by fellow speakers of English.

The child's acquisition of the structure and meaning of language has been called the most difficult intellectual achievement of his life. If that is so, it is pleasing to note that he accomplishes it with relative ease and vast enjoyment. What has been called a "difficult intellectual achievement" may in reality be a natural response to the capacity for language which is one of his genetic characteristics. For all over the world children begin to learn language at about the same age—in no culture do children wait until they are seven or ten to learn language. By 12 or 13 months the child is able to name a few objects and actions. In addition, he seems able to grasp the underlying grammar; he is able to make one key word stand for a whole sentence: "out!" for "take me out for a walk right now"; "bottle!" for "I want my bottle now."

His progression to two-word sentences at about 18 months clearly indicates his possession of a basic sense of grammar. Of all the possible two-word combinations (some of which would make no sense, such as "sun-water" or "car-dog") he chooses grammatical sentences structured around a key word, such as "see" ("see daddy," "see horse," "see water") or "bye-bye" ("bye-bye moon," "bye-bye car"). He seems to acquire the grammar with little or no teaching from his parents, who concentrate on vocabulary. Grammar in fact seems to be of first importance, as evidenced by the five-year-old who, confronted with the unfamiliar "Gloria in Excelsis" sang quite happily "Gloria eats egg-shells." To make the words fit the structure of English grammar was more important than to make the words fit the meaning of the Christmas pageant.

Psycholinguists have become aware of the inadequacy of the usual learning methods—imitation, practice, reinforcement—to explain the child's early acquisition and creative use of grammatical structure. Noam Chomsky, a prominent theoretician of grammar, posits a "language acquisition device" in the brain, as innate to man as are the call systems of the other animals. As the forebrain evolved, this "language acquisition device" became part of man's biological inheritance. Whether this "device" in fact exists is not yet clear. But we do know that the actual development of individual languages is not biologically determined, for all human beings would speak the same brain-generated language if language were simply a biological attribute. Instead, about 6,000 mutually unintelligible languages have been identified.

"Primitive" Languages

Intuitively, one might suppose that languages of nonliterate peoples would be much less developed than languages spoken by technologically advanced, literate peoples. But this is in no sense true. The sound systems, vocabularies, and grammars of technologically primitive peoples are in no way inferior to those of more complex societies such as our own.

Of course, the Australian aborigine will not be able to name the sophisticated machines used in our society; his language, however, has the potential for doing so. All languages possess the amount of vocabulary that their speakers need, and they expand in response to modernization or other cultural changes. Moreover, the language of a technologically primitive people, while lacking terminology for some of our conveniences, may have a rich vocabulary to deal with events or natural phenomena that are of particular importance in that society.

[7] T. S. Eliot, "The Love Song of J. Alfred Prufrock," in *Collected Poems. 1909–1962* (New York: Harcourt Brace Jovanovich, 1963).

Contrary to common notions, the grammars of those languages spoken by technologically primitive peoples are also equal in complexity to our own. Some of these languages, as we shall see, recognize distinctions that cannot be easily expressed in English. The Indian who speaks so badly on our TV Westerns—omitting articles and other niceties—may in reality be heir to a language with more verb tenses or pronouns than our own.

DESCRIPTIVE LINGUISTICS

The average person expects to be disoriented in a foreign country if he does not know the language. Even an anthropologist who is trained in linguistics is a little confused when he arrives to do fieldwork among a people who speak a language unknown to him. But within a short time, the anthropologist's training in linguistics will enable him to begin discovering the rules of that language, for every language has rules or principles that determine what sounds are used, and in what combinations or sequences, to convey meaning.

In order to study the great diversity of human languages, linguists have had to develop ways of describing languages that would make it possible to compare languages systematically. In everyday communication we may talk about verbs and nouns and parts of speech, but the linguist cannot compare languages in those terms because many languages do not convey verbal or other meanings as English does. So linguists have had to invent special descriptive concepts, such as phoneme and morpheme, to permit them to describe all languages in the same systematic and comparable terms.

Phonemes

From the exceedingly wide variety of possible human sounds, each language has selected some sounds or *phones* and ignored others. The linguist studying a language will notice which speech sounds occur and which are used most frequently. Once he has identified the phones, he will identify how sounds are grouped by the speakers of the languages into *phonemes.* The phoneme is a class of slightly varying sounds which do not make any difference in meaning to the speaker of the language. In other words, if one phone of a phoneme class is substituted for another phone of the same class, the speaker will not say that the meaning of the utterance is different.

The way in which sounds or phones are grouped into phonemes varies from language to language. In English, the sound of the *t* in *take* is regarded as the same sound as that of the *t* in *steak.* Although they are different phones (one is aspirated, or followed by a puff of breath, and the other is not) they belong to the same phoneme in English, because we do not distinguish between them. In Chinese, however, the two types of *t*'s are linguistically significant and constitute a basis for distinguishing between different words; therefore, in Chinese these two phones are said to belong to two different phonemes.[8] Similarly, in English the sound of *l* in *lake* is considered quite different from the sound of *r* in *rake;* the two phones belong to different phonemes. In Chinese, however, *l* and *r* could be used interchangeably in the initial position in a word without making a difference in meaning; in Chinese, then, these two phones belong to the same phoneme.

As the anthropologist begins to analyze the phonemes of a language, he will attempt to write them down. Undeniably this would be a very troublesome undertaking were he restricted to using his own alphabet, for he would have no easy way of noting sounds that were not distinguished in his own alphabet. To surmount this difficulty, linguists have developed the

[8] Thomas Pyle, *The Origins and Development of the English Language* (New York: Harcourt Brace Jovanovich, 1964), p. 51.

International Phonetic Alphabet (IPA), which provides a symbol for every sound that occurs in every known language. Using this alphabet, the linguist is able to record the utterances which he must analyze to arrive at a list of phones and phonemes used in a language.

Estimates of the number of phonemes used in the world's languages vary from around 15 (some Polynesian dialects) to just under 100 (some languages of the Caucausus); English has 46 phonemes. Languages differ, then, in the number and kinds of sounds they use, as well as in the ways those sounds are grouped into phonemes.

Morphemes

A structural description of a language includes an analysis of units of meaning. The smallest unit of language that has a meaning is a *morph.* One or more morphs with the same meaning make up a *morpheme.* For example, the prefix *in-* as in "indefinite," and the prefix *un-* as in "unclear," are morphs that belong to the morpheme meaning "not." A morph or morpheme should not be confused with a word. Although some words are single morphs or morphemes (for example, "for" and "giraffe" in English), many words are built upon a combination of morphs, generally prefixes, roots, and suffixes. Thus "cow" is one word but the word "cows" contains two meaningful units: a root *(cow)* and a suffix (pronounced like *z*) meaning more than one.

It seems likely that the intuitive grasp which a child has of the structure of his language includes a recognition of morphology: once he learns that the morph /-z/ added to a noun-type word indicates more than one, he plows ahead with *mans, childs;* once he grasps that the morpheme class /-t/ or /-d/ added to the end of a verb indicates that the action took place in the past, he applies this concept generally and invents *runned, drinked, costed;* he sees a ball roll near*er* and near*er,* and he transfers this to a kite which goes upp*er* and upp*er.* From his mistakes as well as his successes we can see that he understands the regular uses of morphemes. By the age of seven, he has mastered many of the irregular forms as well—that is, he learns which morphs of a morpheme are used when.

The child's intuitive grasp of the dependence of some morphemes on others corresponds to the linguist's recognition of *free* morphemes and *bound* morphemes. A free morpheme has meaning standing alone—that is, it can be a separate word. A bound morpheme displays its meaning only when attached to another morpheme. The phrase "attached to" is rather loosely applied. The morph /-t/ of the bound morpheme meaning "past tense" is actually attached to the root *walk* to produce *walked,* but how should we consider the morpheme *the* in relation to man in *The man walked? The* has no meaning by itself, but it is grammatically significant. *The* must precede a noun. In the sentence "The man walked," *The* and *-ed* are bound; *man* and *walk* are free morphemes.

Grammar

The grammar of a language consists of *morphology*—the ways in which morphemes are combined to form words—and *syntax*—the ways in which words are arranged to form phrases and sentences. English relies heavily on syntax to convey meaning, whereas some other languages rely more heavily on morphology.

Syntax. In any language there are rules that govern the ways in which words may be arranged to form meaningful utterances. As we have seen, the child seems to grasp these rules intuitively. He says, "I want my green dog," not, "Want dog my green I." Except in his use of pronouns ("Me want my green dog" is a common error), it does not really occur to him to structure his sentences in any way other than according to the rules of syntax in English. In languages such as English, which have lots of "free morphemes," the order of morphemes (or, the order of the words) may be crucial for meaning. "The dog bit the child" has a different meaning from "The child bit the dog." In such languages, one order may be correct whereas the opposite order is "incorrect." Thus the American says "light coffee" but not "coffee light," while the Frenchman says "cafe blanc" but not "blanc cafe." An analysis of one of Lewis Carroll's nonsense sentences in *Alice in Wonderland* points up the extent to which syntax alone is meaningful in English:

'Twas brillig, and the slithy toves did gyre
and gimble in the wabe

Simply from the ordering of words in the sentence, we can surmise which part of speech a word is, as well as its function in the sentence. "Brillig" is an adjective; "slithy" an adjective; "toves" a noun and subject of the sentence; "gyre" and "gimble" verbs; and "wabe" a noun and the object of a prepositional phrase. Of course, an understanding of morphology helps too. The *-y* ending on "slithy" is an indication that it is an adjective, and the *-s* ending on "toves" tells us that we most probably have more than one of these creatures.

The way in which English words are put together seems so natural to the native speaker that he is usually surprised to discover how differently speakers of other languages form their sentences. For example, the speaker of English would translate "I would like" into French as "je voudrais" and think that he is saying the same thing. Yet the English phrase contains three words, three morphemes; the French contains two words, four morphemes. "Je voudrais" translates literally as "I like would I"; the four morphs are *je/ voudr/ ai/ s.*

Morphology. The connection between the two elements of grammar—syntax and morphology—is apparent from the expressions in the table below; not only can the arrangement of words be expected to convey meaning, so does the ordering of morphs within a word. The potential of morphology for expressing complex relationships is rather impressive. Turkish, for example, has ten orders of suffixes that may be added to a verb to express such grammatical meanings as passive voice, negation, obligatory action; with any given root, more than 3,000 verb forms are possible. In some languages the order in which morphemes are bound affects meaning. For example, in Luo (a language of East Africa) the same bound morpheme may mean the subject or object of an action. If it is the prefix to a verb, it means the subject; if it is the suffix, it means the object.

In many kinds of languages, the meaning of an utterance does not depend much, if at all, on the order of either morphemes or words. Rather the part of speech (object, adjective, and so on) may be indicated by some alteration of or addition to the root morph. For example, in German there are so-called case endings or declensions that indicate parts of speech. So the verb and even the subject and object may appear at different places in the sentence, but the meaning of the sentence will be clear because the verb, noun, and object are indicated by different suffixes.

Compare the following English words with the equivalent French, Wishram, and Takelma expressions.*

English.	He will give it to you.
French.	Il vous (or te) le (or la) donnera. he-you (or thee)-him (or her)-to give will he
Wishram.	ačimlúda will-he-him-thee-to-give-will
Takelma.	?òspink will give-to-thee-he or they in the future.

*Wishram is a Chinookan dialect of the Columbia River region; Takelma is an all-but-extinct Indian language of southwestern Oregon.

The main point about grammatical variation among languages is that meaning is not always, or even usually, conveyed, as in English, by the way morphemes or words are ordered. If order is not significant, then something has to be done to the morphs to indicate what the utterance means. In some languages, for instance, what is considered a sentence in English is a single word, made up of bound morphs which are altered in various ways (internally or by prefixes or suffixes) to indicate the meaning of the sentence-word.

Transformational Grammar. For much of its history, linguistics has concerned itself with descriptive and prescriptive grammars, both of which concentrate on the sound and structure of given sentences. However, the approach of transformational grammar, originated by Noam Chomsky of M.I.T., attempts to examine both *surface structure,* or the appearance of a sentence, and *deep structure,* the underlying relationship which presumably determines how the sentence was formulated. In other words, transformational grammar presents a model that explains the various ways that elements in the language system may be structured. Because Chomsky's system uses complex representations of symbolic logic and because it is still the subject of much controversy among linguists, we will not present his method in any detail. What is important to understand is that transformational grammar tries to see all the elements of a language, semantic as well as structural, as a total system with characteristic ways of operation. It does not take for granted that what *looks* similar must *be* similar, and it shows that what looks different may have underlying structures in common.

The deep-structure approach of transformational grammar may provide a means of finding corresponding processes in all the disparate languages of man. If similar processes are found in comparing the deep structures of historically unrelated languages, we shall be able to conclude that there are some universals underlying the great diversity of human language. Chomsky would attribute these universals to a language faculty which is part of "the structure of the mind." In other words, Chomsky suggests that universals would point to a physical basis of linguistic patterning that is nonetheless expressed in a myriad of forms.

HISTORICAL LINGUISTICS

Whereas descriptive linguists are concerned with analyzing the sound and structure of a language, historical linguists are interested in discovering how languages change over time. Naturally, written works are the best records of such change. For example, the following passage from Chaucer's *Canterbury Tales,* written in the English of the fourteenth century, has recognizable elements but is different enough from modern English to require a translation:

A Frere ther was, a wantowne and a merye,
A lymytour, a ful solempne man.
In alle the ordres foure is noon that kan
So muchel of daliaunce and fair langage.
He hadde maad ful many a mariage
Of yonge wommen at his owene cost.
Unto his ordre he was a noble post.

Ful wel biloved and famulier was he
With frankeleyns over al in his contree,
And eek with worthy wommen of the toun;
For he hadde power of confessioun,
As seyde hymself, moore than a curat,
For of his ordre he was licenciat.

(Geoffrey Chaucer,
The Canterbury Tales, 1: 208–220)

A Friar there was, wanton and merry,
A limiter, a full solemn [very important] man.
In all the orders four there is none that knows

So much of dalliance [gossip] and fair
  [engaging] language.
He had made [arranged] many a marriage
Of young women at his own cost.
Unto his order he was a noble post [pillar].
Full well beloved and familiar was he
With franklins [wealthy landowners]
  all over his country,
And also with worthy women of the town;
For he had power of confession,
As said himself, more than a curate
  [parish priest],
For of his order, he was a licentiate
  [licensed by the Pope].

From this comparison we can see a number of changes: some words, like "eek," have passed out of our vocabulary, and, of course, a great many are spelled differently from today. In some cases, meaning has changed: "full," for example, would be translated today as "very." What is less evident is that changes in pronunciation, or *phonology,* have occurred. For example, the *g* in "marriage" was pronounced *zh,* as in the French from which it was borrowed, whereas now it is pronounced like the *g* in "George" which is more in accordance with standard English phonemics.

The Comparative Method

Some changes in language follow discernible patterns, which enable linguists to observe relationships between divergent tongues. By comparative analysis of cognates and grammar, historical linguists test the notion that certain languages are related—that is, they derive from a common ancestral language, or protolanguage. The goals are to reconstruct the features of the protolanguage, to hypothesize how the daughter languages separated from the protolanguage or from each other, and to establish the approximate dates of such separations.

It is through the comparison of languages that the probable derivation of many modern languages, including English, has been hypothesized. As early as 1786, Sir William Jones, an Englishman serving as a judge in Calcutta, noticed similarities between Sanskrit, Greek, and Latin and claimed that they must be derived from a single source. In 1822, Jacob Grimm, one of the brothers Grimm, formulated rules to describe the sequences of phonetic change from Sanskrit (which he believed to be closest to the original Indo-European tongue) to later languages such as Greek, Latin, German, and English. Using *cognates* (words of similar sound and meaning) he observed changes like the one from *p* to *f* (Sanskrit "pitar," English "father"; Sanskrit "pat," English "foot"). From these he derived laws of phonetic change for this language family.

Close examination of cognates denoting certain plants and animals also has suggested that the ancestral home of Proto-European was somewhere in northern Europe. Paul Thieme notes that cognate names for certain trees of northern Europe, such as the oak and birch, are found in most of the modern Indo-European languages, whereas cognates for the more southern trees, such as the olive, fig, and cypress, are not found as frequently. Moreover, the modern Indo-European languages contain no cognates for tiger, elephant, or any of the animals characteristic of Asia or India; however, they do contain cognate words for creatures distributed throughout northern and central Europe—including the wolf, salmon, and bear. From such evidence Thieme has placed the center of dispersion for Indo-European languages as in the area south of the Baltic Sea, encompassing the Vistula, the Oder, and the Elbe rivers. Migration to the east produced the Baltic and Slavic languages; to the west, Germanic and Romance languages; to the south the Indic and Iranian. This theory is by no means confirmed, and other linguists have argued for other centers of dispersion, including southern Russia, Scandinavia, and southwestern Asia.[9]

Once the linguist identifies the common

parent of several languages, he is usually interested in dating the times of divergence between the daughter languages. Through such research, he may be able to shed some light on the origin and movements of a given people—information which may then be pieced together with relevant findings from archaeology, physical anthropology, and historical documents to reconstruct some of the details of the history of particular peoples and cultures.

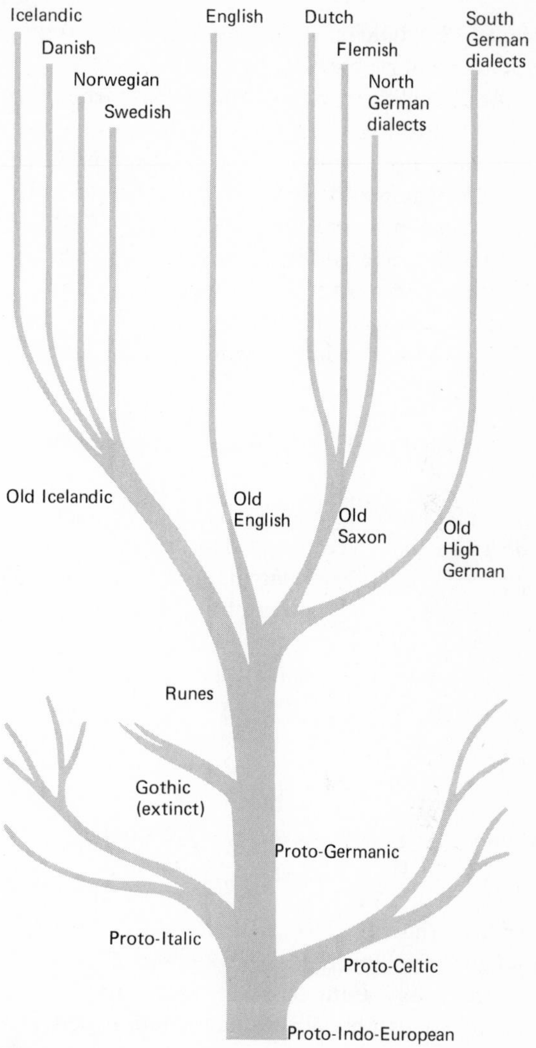

Figure 1

The Germanic languages developed from a common ancestral Proto-Germanic language, which had previously derived from Proto-Indo-European.

Glottochronology

One method for establishing a date for the divergence between two languages is *glottochronology.* This method is based on the assumption that a language replaces about 19 percent of its basic vocabulary over 1,000 years. In other words, a language retains about 81 percent of its basic vocabulary over that period of time. Linguists have arrived at this rate of retention of basic vocabulary by examining changes in languages for which we have written records going back several thousand years. The basic vocabulary of a language consists of a list of words for things, like parts of the body, that are universal in human experience and consequently are not likely to be replaced in response to changes in geographical location or culture. If we assume that this rate holds true for languages for which we have no written records, then we can estimate the date of divergence of two languages which appear to be related by calculating the percentage of basic vocabulary shared between them. Both languages should retain about 81 percent of their parent language per 1,000 years, but if their respective speakers are not in contact they will probably not retain the same 81 percent. Statistically, then, the percentage of words shared between related languages should be closer to 81 percent of the 81 percent, or 66 percent, after 1,000 years of divergence. In other words, should we discover that two languages share 66 percent of their basic word lists, we could say that their ancestral speech communities probably separated about 1,000 years ago. If they retained 59 per-

[9] Paul Thieme, "The Comparative Method for Reconstruction in Linguistics," in Dell Hymes, ed., *Language in Culture and Society* (New York: Harper & Row, 1964), pp. 585–598.

cent, we would say that they probably separated centuries earlier.

Applying the glottochronological method to basic word lists in modern languages, one can estimate, for example, that the split between the Germanic and Romance branches of Indo-European must have occurred about 1000 B.C. Of course, not all linguists are in agreement with all of the assumptions of glottochronology; nevertheless the technique has enlarged the possibilities of research into cultural history.

Processes of Linguistic Divergence

The historical or comparative linguist hopes to do more than record and date linguistic divergence. He seeks to explain it: just as the physical anthropologist may attempt to develop explanations for human variation, so may the linguist investigate the possible causes of linguistic variation. When groups of people speaking the same language lose communication with one another because they become either physically or socially separated, they begin to accumulate small changes in phonology, morphology, and grammar (which occur continuously in any language). Eventually, if the separation continues, the two former dialects of the same language will become separate languages—that is, mutually unintelligible. (This process is analogous to the geographic isolation between gene pools, which in time may result in the reproductive isolation that marks the emergence of new species.)

Even when geographic isolation is not complete, there may still be a great deal of dialect differentiation because of social barriers to communication between neighboring areas. Northern India provides an excellent example. Three thousand years ago Aryan invaders speaking an Indo-European language conquered northern India and that language became dominant. In succeeding years the language began to diversify into regional dialects. Variations in topography and climate played a part in the partial isolation of the incipient dialect groups, but the most powerful influence was the emergence of largely self-supporting and semi-isolated villages and regions. So one language was transformed, in the course of time, into hundreds of local dialects. Today, the inhabitants of each village understand the dialects of the surrounding villages and, with a little more difficulty, the dialects of the next farther circles of villages. But slight dialect shifts accumulate village by village, and over the space of 1,000 miles it seems as if different languages are being spoken at opposite ends of a region. Yet at no boundary is there such an abrupt change of language that neighboring villagers cannot converse easily.[10]

Whereas isolation brings about divergence between speech communities, contact results in greater resemblance. This is particularly evident when contrast between mutually unintelligible languages introduces "borrowed" words, usually naming some new item borrowed from the other culture—tomato, canoe, sputnik, and so on. Bilingual groups within a culture may also introduce foreign words especially when the mainstream language has no real equivalent: thus "siesta" has come into English, and "le weekend" into French.

Contiguous cultures present possibilities for extensive borrowing. For example, the Norman conquest of England introduced French as the language of the new aristocracy. It was 300 years before the educated began to write in English. During this time the English borrowed words wholesale from French and Latin, and the two languages—English and French—became more alike than they would otherwise have been. About 50 percent of the English general vocabulary has been borrowed from French.

In those 300 years of extensive borrowing,

[10] John J. Gumperz, "Speech Variation and the Study of Indian Civilization," *American Anthropologist,* Vol. 63 (1961), pp. 976–988.

the grammar of English remained relatively stable. It lost most of its inflections or case endings, but it adopted none of the French grammar. In fact, borrowing of grammar is extremely rare; Sapir, a pioneer in American linguistics, believed it to be nearly impossible, although there may be cases of grammatical borrowing in India, where three language families have come to exist side by side. Interestingly enough, borrowing by one language from another can make the borrowing language more different from its sister languages (those derived from a common ancestral language) than it would otherwise be, just as gene flow into a population can make it more different biologically from related populations. English, as a result of the French influence, looks quite different from its sister languages—German, Dutch, and Scandinavian—with which it is actually most similar in terms of phonology and grammar.

RELATIONSHIP BETWEEN LANGUAGE AND CULTURE

Some attempts to explain the diversity of languages have focused on the possible interaction between language and other aspects of culture. On the one hand, if it can be shown that a culture may affect the structure and content of its language, then it would follow that linguistic diversity derives at least in part from cultural diversity. On the other hand, the direction of influence between culture and language might work in reverse; the linguistic structures might affect other aspects of the culture. Both of these possibilities have been explored by anthropologists.

Cultural Influences on Language

One way a society's language may reflect its corresponding culture is in lexical content, or vocabulary. Which experiences, events, or objects are singled out and given simple or single-morph names may be a result of cultural characteristics. For example, Brent Berlin and Paul Kay have investigated why different societies vary in the number of simple color terms their languages have. Based on their study of first 20, and later over 100, different languages, Berlin and Kay found that some languages only have simple words to denote, roughly, dark and light; these languages express other colors by combining terms, such as "fresh leaf" for green or "cut orchid fibers" for yellow. Berlin and Kay suggest that there is a fixed sequence by which color categories are added to a language and that the evolution of color terminology in a language parallels the evolution of the culture in its economic and technological aspects.[11] This finding may indicate that cultural complexity influences lexical content.

The vocabulary of a language may also reflect everyday distinctions that are important in the society. It appears that those aspects of the environment or culture which are of special importance to people will receive greater attention in their language. Even within a single society speaking the same language there may be lexical variation from one region to another or between different subcultures. An adult farmer in the American Midwest may know three simple words for boat—boat, ship, canoe—and a few compound variations such as rowboat, sailboat, motorboat, steamship. Yet a six-year-old child who lives on Long Island Sound may be able to distinguish many kinds of sailboats, such as catboat, ketch, yawl, sloop, schooner, as well as subclasses of each, such as bluejay, sunfish, weekender.

As the domains that we choose to name may vary even for two speakers of the same language, the difference in how and what we name

[11] Brent Berlin and Paul Kay, *Basic Color Terms: Their Universality and Evolution* (Berkeley: University of California Press, 1969).

Culture seems to influence language, particularly in terms of vocabulary. The Garo language of northeastern India, for example, has different words to indicate the various kinds of carrying that are important in that culture. (Photograph by Marilyn Silverstone, © 1965 Magnum Photos.)

appears even more startlingly between languages. For instance, English has three common words—"bring," "take," and "carry"—for transporting an object, either animate or inanimate, from one place to another. The Garo language of northeast India has instead one term *ra* for inanimate objects and one term *rim* for animate objects. Affixes *ang* and *ba* can be added to either root to indicate direction away from or toward the speaker. Garo has no general term for *carry* but instead has words for different kinds of carrying: "ol-" means specifically "to carry something in a basket that is held in a strap over the forehead"; "itchil-" means "to carry on the head"; "ripe-" means "to carry on the shoulder," as one might carry a log; "ke-" means "to carry in a bag that hangs from a strap over the shoulder"; "detom-" means "to carry in the arms." It seems that the Garo language focuses on particular categories or actions that are important in Garo culture.[12]

There are many interesting examples of "focal areas" in different cultures being reflected in their respective vocabularies. In a study of the Kwakiutl, a coastal Indian tribe of the Pacific Northwest, Franz Boas showed that Kwakiutl geographical terms reflect their awareness of the importance of hunting, fishing, and other food-gathering activities essential to their survival. Locations on land are given names such as "having-blueberries," and "having-hunter's-lodge"; areas of coastal waters are described as "having-difficult-currents," "having-spring-salmon."[13] One might compare the importance of river crossings to the early English, who designated Ox-ford and Cam-bridge—names which have lost their original meanings in modern times.

Most of the examples we could accumulate would show influence of the culture in naming things visible in the environment. Evidence for cultural influence on the grammatical structure of a language is less extensive and convincing. Harry Hoijer draws attention to the verb categories in the language of the Navajo, a traditionally nomadic people. These categories center largely on the reporting of events, or "eventings" as he calls them. Hoijer notes that "in the reporting of actions and events, and the framing of substantive concepts, Navajo emphasizes movement and specifies the nature, direction, and status of such movement in considerable detail." For example, Navajo has one category for eventings that are in motion and another for eventings that have ceased moving. Hoijer concludes that the emphasis on events incessantly in the process of occurring reflects the Navajo's own nomadic experience over the centuries, an experience reflected in their myths and folklore.[14]

We would probably be mistaken, however, to overemphasize the possibility of culture as a determinant of linguistic structures. Some evidence to the contrary exists. Goodenough has found, in his study of property relationships on Truk, an atoll in the Caroline Islands of the central Pacific, that grammatical distinctions in forming the possessive do not parallel Trukese concepts of ownership. Although there are several very important concepts of ownership, leasehold, or gift in Trukese culture, the language offers only a single affix to the noun, denoting "my."[15] Thus, it appears on the basis of present knowledge that culture may often influence vocabulary, but seldom grammar.

Linguistic Influences on Culture

Sapir-Whorf Hypothesis. There is no general agreement among ethnolinguists—those

[12] R. Burling, *Man's Many Voices* (New York: Holt, Rinehart and Winston, 1970), pp. 10–13.

[13] Franz Boas, *Geographical Names of the Kwakiutl Indians* (New York: Columbia University Press, 1934).

[14] Harry Hoijer, "Cultural Implications of Some Navaho Linguistic Categories," *Language*, Vol. 27 (1951), pp. 111–120.

[15] Ward H. Goodenough, *Property, Kin and Community on Truk* (New Haven: Yale University Press, 1951), pp. 61–64.

anthropologists who are interested in the relationship between language and culture—that linguistic elements may influence culture. The Sapir–Whorf hypothesis is one formulation of the basic issue. Edward Sapir has asserted that language is not merely a symbolic inventory of man's environment and experience but is a force in its own right; it "actually defines experience for us by reason of its formal completeness and because of our unconscious projection of its implicit expectations into the field of experience."[16]

What, then, is the evidence for language as a modifying influence upon other aspects of culture? Can linguistic structure affect patterns of perception, thought, belief, and behavior? Edward Sapir went so far as to suggest that language, in some ways, possesses despotic powers. In a discussion of conceptual categories in different languages, he made the point that categories such as number, gender, tense, mode, and a host of others "are not so much discovered in experience as imposed upon it because of the tyrannical hold that linguistic form has upon our orientation in the world."[17]

The concept of *forced observation* concerns itself with a similar hypothesis. Forced observation is often used to describe certain features of grammar which seem to compel a person to express reality in a particular way. English provides an example. The English language has tenses; Chinese does not. An English speaker is accustomed, one might even say *forced,* to specify whether an event occurred in the past, is occurring now, or will occur in the future. Not so the Chinese. It might follow, therefore, that an English speaker is being "programmed" by his language structure toward a different time perspective than the Chinese.

The possible effect of language on culture has been investigated by Benjamin Lee Whorf, first Sapir's student and subsequently his colleague. Whorf was particularly interested in the ways a language might structure a people's conceptions of space and time and he set out to compare Hopi with Standard Average European (S.A.E.) usage. In essence, he discovered that S.A.E. usage objectified time, made it finite, and spoke about it in spatial terms (as in "three hours *long,*" or "a stretch of time"). The Hopi language does not include such spatial terminology. For the Hopi, time is not a motion or a quantity but simply a "getting later of everything that has ever been done." The S.A.E. structure facilitates our thinking of "summer" or "September" or "morning" as actually containing such and such quantities of time. But this is not the case in Hopi linguistic structure. A Hopi says "when it is morning" (not "in the morning") and "summer is only when conditions are hot" (not "summer is hot").[18]

The implications of Whorf's findings are intriguing. On the one hand, S.A.E. objectification of time may favor materialistic thought patterns. Its conception of time as extending into the past and into the future in equal, spacelike units facilitates thinking of time in pro rata quantities (as in wage calculations), and may be partially responsible for the high value we place on speed and other quantifiable experiences. On the other hand, for the Hopi, who see time as "a getting later of everything that has ever been done," the language seems to favor an emphasis on repetition or the accumulation of experience (in contrast to the S.A.E. usage in which time is "spent" or "saved" or "borrowed").

Despite such suggestive evidence, the influence of language on culture is far from completely understood. Particularly confusing are the instances in which groups share a language

[16] Edward Sapir, "Conceptual Categories in Primitive Languages," *Science,* Vol. 74 (1931), p. 578.
[17] Sapir, "Conceptual Categories in Primitive Languages," p. 578.

[18] John B. Carroll, ed., *Language, Thought, and Reality: Selected Writings of Benjamin Lee Whorf* (New York: Wiley, 1956), pp. 65–86.

but not the same culture. For example, the Apache, mounted hunters of the Southwest desert, speak a language very similar to the languages spoken by Indians in Alaska and northwestern Canada, yet the Apache world view and culture seem to be as distant from those of their northern relatives as their geographical location. Conversely, a people need not share a language in order to have similar cultures. The Hopi and Zuñi Indians of the American Southwest have very similar cultures, yet they speak languages that are not only mutually unintelligible but also belong to different language families.

THE ETHNOGRAPHY OF SPEAKING

Linguists have traditionally studied language as a system of rules governing what is considered acceptable speech in a particular society. Recently, however, some linguists have begun to study variations in how people actually use their language when speaking. On the one hand, we may deal with language as a socially shared system of symbols, generated by a similarly shared system of rules; and on the other hand, we may deal with how people customarily speak differently in different social contexts. This second type of linguistic study, called *sociolinguistics,* is concerned with the ethnography of speaking—that is, cultural and subcultural patterns of speaking and how they vary in different social contexts.

The sociolinguist may ask, for example, what kinds of things does one talk about in casual conversation with a stranger. A foreigner may know English vocabulary and grammar well but may not know that one typically chats to a stranger about the weather, or where one comes from, and not about what one ate that day or how much money one earns. A foreigner may be familiar with much of the culture of an American city, but if he divulges the state of his health and feelings to the first person who says "How are you," he has much to learn about American small talk.

The way in which people address one another is also of interest to sociolinguists. In English, the forms of address are relatively simple. One is called either by a first name or by a title (such as Mrs., Dr., or Professor) followed by a last name. But how do American speakers of English actually address one another? A study by Roger Brown and Marguerite Ford indicates that terms of address vary with the nature of the relationships between the speakers.[19] When first names are used reciprocally, it is generally an indication of informality or intimacy between two people. When the title and last name are used reciprocally, it is usually an indication of a more formal or business-like relationship between people who are roughly equal in status. Nonreciprocal use in English is reserved for speakers who recognize marked difference in status between themselves. This difference can be a function of age (as when a child refers to her mother's friend as Mrs. Miller and is in turn addressed as "Sally"), or it can be drawn along occupational lines (as when a person refers to his boss by title and last name and is in turn addressed as "John"). In some cases, generally between men, the use of the last name alone represents a middle ground between the intimate and the formal usages.

Forms of address in some cultures reveal much about the status of the person addressed. Among the Nuer of the Sudan, a person's sex, relative age, and family group can be expressed by choosing among a variety of names. Each person is given a personal name soon after birth which is used by his paternal relatives and close friends in the paternal village. He

[19] Roger Brown and Marguerite Ford, "Address in American English," *Journal of Abnormal and Social Psychology,* Vol. 62 (1961), pp. 375–385.

is given another name by his maternal grandparents which is used by his mother's family and close friends. At his initiation, a boy is given an ox and acquires an ox-name (the name of the ox) which members of his peer group may then use instead of his personal name. A girl may choose an ox-name from the bull calf of a cow she milks; the name is used only by her age-group friends, often at dances where boys and girls call out their friends' ox-names with other titles suggesting friendship. On formal occasions, a person may be greeted by his father's relatives by the paternal clan name or by his mother's relatives by the maternal clan name. A man may be addressed as "son of" followed by his father's personal name or as "father of" followed by his eldest child's name. A young person may address any elderly man as *gwa,* father, and an older man may call a young man *gatda,* my son. A woman may choose a cow-name from a cow she milks, or she may be called "mother of" followed by her eldest child's name.[20] Although much of the same information can be expressed through the English system of given names, nicknames, surnames, hyphenated names, and generic terms such as sonny, Miss, sir, and ma'am, the Nuer system of address is more structured and considerably more informative than the English. Why this may be so is presumably related to how Nuer and English speakers differ in their social organization.

In most languages one's choice of vocabulary seems to indicate the social status of the user. Clifford Geertz, in his study of Javanese, has shown that the vocabularies of the three rather sharply divided social groups—peasants, townsmen, and aristocrats—reflect their separate positions. For example, the word "now" will be expressed by a peasant as *saiki* (considered the lowest and roughest form of speech), by a townsman as *saniki* (considered somewhat more elegant), and by an aristocrat as *samenika* (the most elegant form).[21]

Some languages possess variations in speech style or vocabulary based on sex. For example, sex differences in language use have been noted for some American Indian societies in Canada, California, and South America and in some societies in Thailand and Siberia. Mary Haas has analyzed the speech of men and women in Koasati, a Muskogean language of southwestern Louisiana. She found, for example, that differences appear in certain indicative and imperative verb forms. One of Mary Haas's male informants characterized the speech of the women as "easy, slow, and soft. It sounds pretty." As the men of the tribe do not use women's speech, it seems we may assume that they associate it with women's role in society.[22] (Female readers will be encouraged to learn that the young women of the tribe have begun to adopt men's speech.)

Variations in language use based on age appear more frequently in the world's languages than variations based on sex. For instance, a special vocabulary, "baby talk," is often used for communicating with children. In certain languages, English for instance, use of "baby talk" varies with parental choice and ingenuity: some parents/elders use words such as *choo-choo, woof-woof,* or *ta-ta;* others do not. The Comanche Indians, on the other hand, have developed a special baby talk which forms a uniform and distinct part of their language. About 40 words and phrases have been supplied by Casagrande; these words cover general topics of communication. For instance, "*koko:* stands for 'fruit, candy, cookies; any snack between meals; give me . . .'; *nana:* stands for 'it might hurt, get away; blood; sore, hurt.'[23] These words and phrases have three

[20] E. E. Evans-Pritchard, "Nuer Modes of Address," *The Uganda Journal,* Vol. 12 (1948), pp. 166–171.

[21] Clifford Geertz, *The Religion of Java* (Glencoe, Ill.: Free Press, 1960), pp. 248–260.

[22] Mary R. Haas, "Men's and Women's Speech in Koasati," *Language,* Vol. 20 (1944), pp. 142–149.

[23] Joseph B. Casagrande, "Comanche Baby Talk," *International Journal of American Linguistics,* Vol. 14 (1948), pp. 11-14.

points in common with those for baby talk in most languages: they represent whole sentences; they use simple sounds; and they depend upon repetition of those sounds.

Baby talk is initiated by adults in order to help the child begin to learn the language. Looked at from another point of view, it is one instance of the way one person changes his speech as the social context changes. John Fischer's study of children in a semirural New England village indicates another instance of changing the mode of speech to fit the social context. Although one might expect that children below the age of 11 would not have acquired an awareness of proper formality in conversation, Fischer found that they responded to the degree of formality of a situation by changing their speech. Their varying use of the *-ing* and *-in* verb suffixes showed that the children consistently preferred the *-ing* ending in more formal contexts. For example, the *-ing* suffix would be used with formal verbs such as *correcting, visiting,* or *criticizing,* whereas *-in* would be used with informal verbs such as *hittin, swimmin,* or *chewin.*[24]

The field of sociolinguistics has only recently emerged. At the present time, sociolinguists seem to be primarily interested in describing variation in the use of a language. Eventually, however, sociolinguistic research may enable us to understand why such variation in language use exists. Why, for example, do some societies use many different status terms in address? Why do other societies use modes of speaking that vary with the sex of the speakers? It may be possible to understand structural aspects of linguistic change when we understand more about how language use is related to the social context; for as social contexts in a society change, so might the structure of language tend to change.

[24] John L. Fischer, "Social Influences on the Choice of a Linguistic Variant," *Word,* Vol. 14 (1958), pp. 47–56.

SUMMARY

1. The essential function which language plays in all societies is that of *communication.* Although man's communication is not limited to spoken language, language is of overriding importance because it is the primary vehicle through which human culture is shared and transmitted.
2. Systems of communication are not unique to man. Other animal species communicate in a variety of ways—by sound, odor, body movement, and so forth. Primates also communicate, but their system of communication is closed; that is, the ape cannot combine parts of two calls to obtain a third call which will combine the two messages.
3. A structured description of a language usually begins with an analysis of sounds and how they are grouped. From the wide variety of possible human sounds, each language has selected some sounds or *phones* and ignored others. How sounds are grouped into *phonemes* also differs from language to language. The phoneme is a class of slightly varying sounds which do not make any difference in meaning to the speaker of the language.
4. A structural description of a language also includes an analysis of units of meaning. The smallest unit of language that has a meaning is a *morph.* One or more morphs with the same meaning make up a *morpheme.* A morph or morpheme,

however, should not be confused with a word. Although some words are single morphs or morphemes, many words are built upon a combination of morphs, generally prefixes, roots, and suffixes.

5. The grammar of a language consists of *morphology*—the ways in which morphemes are combined to form words—and *syntax*—the way in which words are arranged to form phrases and sentences. English relies heavily on syntax to convey meaning, whereas some other languages rely more heavily on morphology.

6. Historical linguists are interested in discovering how languages change over time. By comparative analysis of cognates and grammar, historical linguists test the notion that certain languages derive from a common ancestral language, or protolanguage. The goals are to reconstruct the features of the protolanguage, to hypothesize how the daughter languages separated from the protolanguage or from each other, and to establish the approximate dates of such separations.

7. Linguistic divergence can occur through various processes. When groups of people speaking the same language lose communication with one another because they become either physically or socially separated, they begin to accumulate small changes in phonology, morphology and grammar. Eventually, if the separation continues, the two former dialects of the same language will become separate languages—that is, mutually unintelligible.

8. Whereas isolation brings about divergence between speech communities, contact results in greater resemblance. This is particularly evident when contact between mutually unintelligible languages introduces "borrowed" words, usually naming some new item borrowed from the other culture.

9. Some attempts to explain the diversity of languages have focused on the possible interaction between language and other aspects of culture. On the one hand, if it can be shown that a culture may affect the structure and content of its language, then it would follow that linguistic diversity derives at least in part from cultural diversity. On the other hand, the direction of influence between culture and language might work in reverse: the linguistic structures might affect other aspects of the culture. Both of these possibilities have been explored by anthropologists.

10. Recently some linguists have begun to study variations in how people actually use their language when speaking. This type of linguistic study, called *sociolinguistics,* is concerned with the ethnography of speaking—that is, cultural and subcultural patterns of speaking and how they vary in different social contexts.

SUGGESTED READINGS

Bolinger, D.: *Aspects of Language* (New York: Harcourt Brace Jovanovich, 1968).
An introduction to linguistics that discusses phonetics, phonemics, morphology, semantics, dialect, and language change, as well as topics that are rarely included in an introductory text—for example, written language, the dictionary, and methods of learning a second language.

Burling, R.: *Man's Many Voices: Language in Its Cultural Context* (New York: Holt, Rinehart and Winston, 1970).
A clearly written introduction to issues of current interest in anthropological linguistics. The book provides coverage of such topics as componential analysis, semantics, the effect of social setting on language, Black English, verse and linguistic games, and nonhuman versus human communication.

Giglioni, P. P.: *Language and Social Context* (London: Nicholls, 1972).
An anthology of articles in sociolinguistics. Topics include the sociology of language, language and class, socialization and social structure, and language conflicts and change.

Gleason, H. A.: *Introduction to Descriptive Linguistics* (New York: Henry Holt and Company, 1955).
A beginning text in linguistics. Maps, charts, and a workbook aid understanding of such subjects as articulatory and acoustic phonetics, English phonemics, morphology, syntax, communication theory, speech variation, and language classification.

Greenberg, J. H.: *Anthropological Linguistics: An Introduction* (New York: Random House, 1968).
A nontechnical treatment of the fundamental nature and goals of anthropological linguistics. Greenberg discusses phonology, grammatical theory, linguistic change, types of language classifications, language universals, and dialects.

Hockett, C. F.: *A Course in Modern Linguistics* (New York: Macmillan, 1958).
A general introduction to linguistics, covering such subjects as phonology, grammar, morphology, dialects, linguistic prehistory and geography, and language acquisition. At the end of each chapter is a set of problems and a recapitulation of new terminology.

Hoijer, H. (Ed.): *Language History* from *Language* by Leonard Bloomfield (New York: Holt, Rinehart and Winston, 1965).
A reprint of Chapters 17–27 of Bloomfield's *Language* (1933), the classic, authoritative, and still relevant introduction to the fundamental theory and methodology of historical linguistic research.

Hymes, D. (Ed.): *Language in Culture and Society: A Reader in Linguistics and Anthropology* (New York: Harper & Row, 1964).
A collection of 69 articles that discusses the wide range of anthropological interest in language. Hymes prefaces each of the 10 sections with an introduction.

Lehmann, W. P.: *Historical Linguistics: An Introduction* (New York: Holt, Rinehart and Winston, 1962).
An introduction to historical linguistics emphasizing methods of gathering and analyzing linguistic data. Discussion of language classification is aided by maps.

Lyons, J.: *Introduction to Theoretical Linguistics* (New York: Cambridge University Press, 1968).
An introduction to the concepts and practices of modern linguistic theory from the generative-transformational viewpoint. Emphasis is on semantics, syntax, and the philosophical and historical background of modern linguistics.

Wardhaugh, R.: *Introduction to Linguistics* (New York: McGraw-Hill, 1972).
A detailed and technical introduction to linguistics. Glossary, diagrams, illustrations, and a workbook aid understanding of such subjects as communication theory, phonetics, morphology, meaning, language, change, generative-transformational grammar, and social and geographical dialects.

12
Food Getting

While it may be true that man does not live by bread alone, without bread he cannot live at all. Thus, throughout his history, man has spent much of his time in the search for food. As a society that does its foraging in supermarkets we tend to lose sight of the fact that our way of getting food is a recent phenomenon. During man's 2 million years on earth, 99 percent of the time he has obtained food by more fundamental methods—gathering wild plants, hunting wild animals, and fishing. Richard B. Lee and Irven DeVore have noted that of the 80 billion men who have ever lived, 90 percent have been hunter-gatherers and 6 percent agriculturalists. As part of an industrial society, we are among the remaining 4 percent.[1]

In the overall picture of man's development, the search for food has taken precedence over other activities important to survival. Reproduction, social control (the maintenance of peace and order within the group), defense against external threat, and the transmission of knowledge and skills to future generations—none could have taken place without food-derived energy. Once man's belly was filled he could put his mind to interests other than food, including devising ways to satisfy his developing needs.

Anthropologists, therefore, have shown great interest in the relatively few hunting-gathering societies still available for study. To the extent that such groups have clung to their traditional ways of life, they bear witness to circumstances that were once the lot of all men.

FOOD COLLECTION

Food collection may be generally defined as all forms of *subsistence technology* in which food getting is dependent on naturally occurring resources—that is, on wild plants and animals. Whether the primary activity of a food-collecting society is gathering, hunting, or fishing depends on the nature of the habitat: its climate, terrain, and food resources.

We must bear in mind that food collecting began to be supplanted by food production (farming and herding) about 10,000 years ago, and that recent hunter-gatherers cannot be regarded as typical of those in the distant past. Remaining hunting-gathering societies, estimated in 1966 as including some 30,000 people in a world population of 3,300,000,000[2] live in the marginal areas of the earth—whereas early

[1] Richard B. Lee and Irven DeVore, eds., *Man the Hunter* (Chicago: Aldine, 1968), p. 3.

[2] John E. Pfeiffer, *The Emergence of Man* (New York: Harper & Row, 1969), p. 312.

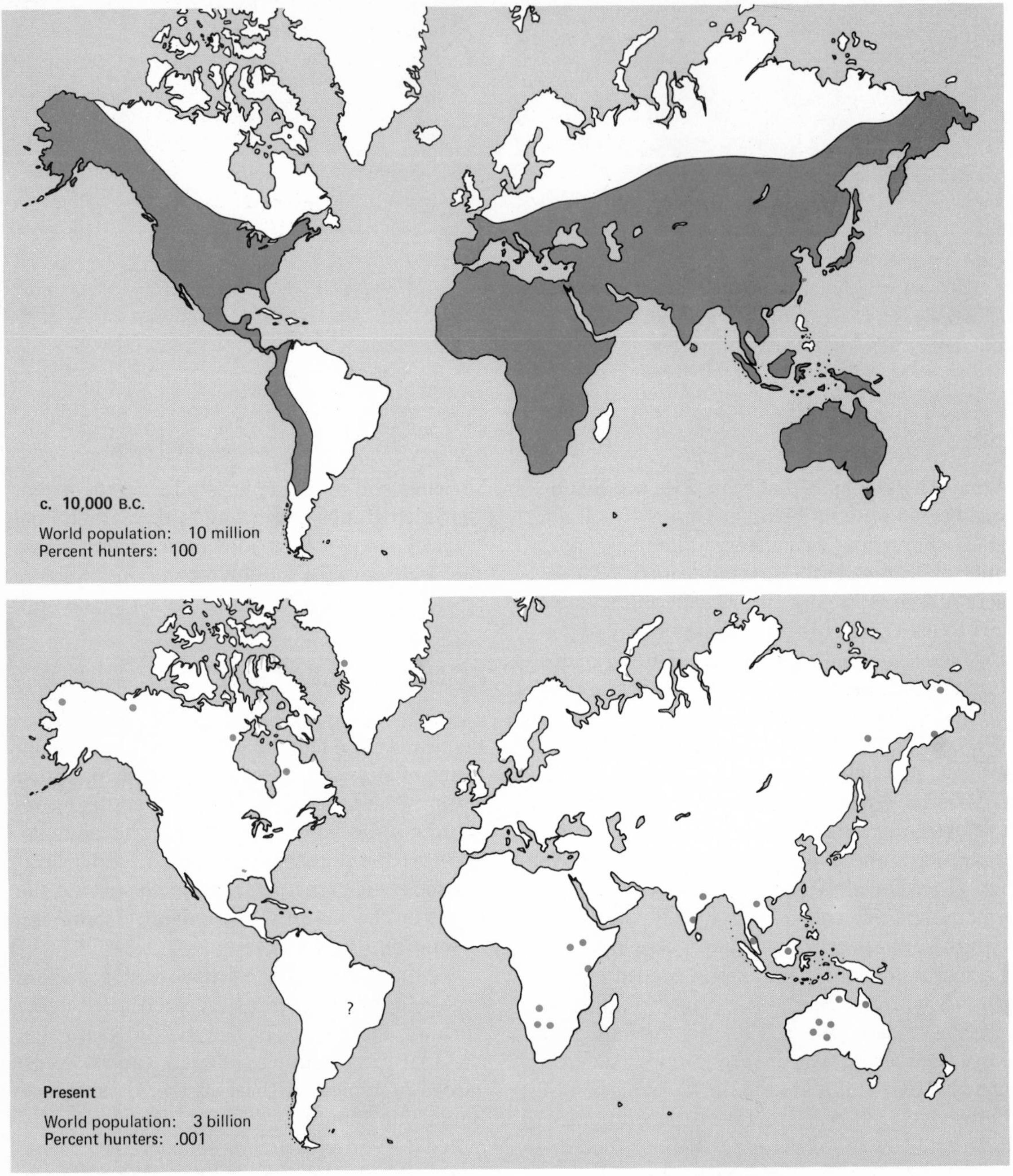

About 10,000 years ago, all men depended upon food collection. Today, hunter-gatherers comprise only a small fraction of the world population, and they inhabit marginal areas of the earth.

hunter-gatherers lived in almost all environments including some very bountiful ones. Today they are found only in deserts, the Arctic, and in thick tropical forests, habitats that do not allow easy exploitation even by modern technology. Each of the following three examples of food-collecting societies is situated in a distinctively different environment.

The Australian Aborigines. The Ngatatjara aborigines of Western Australia have been extensively studied as one of the few remaining examples of a society that still makes and depends on the use of stone tools.[3] They live on the edge of the Gibson Desert, a terrain so inhospitable as to have kept out white settlers. Rainfall there is usually less than 8 inches per year and temperatures rise above 120° F in summer; permanent water holes are widely separated by hundreds of square miles of sand, scrub, and rock.

The aborigines' day begins just before dawn, to the cries of parrots and other birds of the region. Each person eats breakfast from a separate supply of food prepared the night before. All day, except when the noonday heat is excessive, the search for food goes on, ending just before dark, when the women prepare food for the evening meal and the next morning, and large fires are lit to keep the *mamu,* or night cannibal spirits, away.

In the search for food, the men and the women go their separate ways. The women, however, are more productive as food collectors, providing about 70 percent of the total quantity. In the cool hours of the morning and again in the afternoon, they depart carrying wooden bowls full of drinking water on their heads and babies strapped to shoulders or hips, as the older children walk alongside. They return with their bowls full of berries or roots they have turned up with their digging sticks. Meanwhile, the men hunt, usually in pairs or small groups. Ambush is the preferred method of hunting in the heat of the summer (though big game might be stalked over long distances should a good opportunity present itself). Ordinarily, a blind is erected in scrub near a water hole, or a fresh soak hole is dug out of a dried creek bed and the blind placed on an overlooking bank. The men lie patiently in the blind, hoping for a chance to hurl a spear at an emu or a kangaroo. They often have to settle for much smaller game, however, such as rabbits, lizards, and snakes.

The whole band spends the midday period resting, gossiping, and making tools. A common tool is the adze flake, a stone scraper with a thick, sharp edge. The edge is made by removing tiny chips with a hammerstone,[4] a wooden stick, or the teeth. This last technique requires teeth that have been worn flat at the crowns, providing an even working platform, and exceptionally strong jaw muscles—both developed from years of chewing tough, sinewy meat and biting bark off trees.

The Ngatatjara aborigines are a nomadic people—that is, they move their campsites frequently in search of food. Aborigine campsites may be isolated and inhabited by only a small number of people. Or they may be clustered in groups, the total camp complex including up to about 80 persons. The aborigines never place their camp next to a water hole. Rather they establish it at least 300 to 400 feet away. To be closer would frighten game off and might cause tension with neighboring bands, who also wait for game to come to the scarce watering spots. The aborigines use scrub, low trees, and shrubs for summer shade and winter windbreaks, and they do not exert themselves at the hottest times of the day to avoid unnecessary thirst and fatigue.

The Copper Eskimos. This group of Eskimos, so called because they fashion tools by cold hammering copper nuggets, numbered

[3] The discussion of the Australian aborigines is based on Richard A. Gould, *Yiwara: Foragers of the Australian Desert* (New York: Scribner's, 1969).

[4] See Richard A. Gould, "Chipping Stones in the Outback," *Natural History* (February 1968).

between 700 and 800 people in 1913–1916, when they had not yet been significantly affected by contact with Westerners.[5] Today, they live in bands of about 50 persons each, in the vicinity of Coronation Gulf, in the Canadian Arctic, a difficult habitat by any standards. Winter lasts nearly 9 months, with temperatures frequently between -30° and -50° Fahrenheit, and the sun is not seen for weeks at a time. Only during a brief summer interval do mean daily temperatures rise above the freezing point. The land surface is treacherous in winter; in summer, it is often boggy and difficult to cross because of the heavy thaw.

Much more than Australian aborigines, Copper Eskimos are governed by the season. In winter they depend on seals, and an occasional polar bear, for their food supply. Accordingly, each hunter establishes himself and his family on the pack ice offshore, or next to it, in groups of related families. The method of hunting is called *maupok,* meaning "he waits," and so he does, next to a seal's breathing hole. He stands or sits, in absolute quiet and at peak attentiveness, sometimes for hours at a time, until the seal surfaces to breathe. Then he thrusts a harpoon into it, as deep as possible, and waits until his catch is exhausted, to insure that he does not lose it or the harpoon under the ice; finally he enlarges the hole in the ice and hauls the animal out.

Seals are indispensable to the Eskimos in winter. For many months, especially in the last half of the season, seal meat will form the staple, if not the only, food. Seal blubber provides clear-burning cooking and lighting oil, and seal skin is used for a variety of items including ice boots, kayaks, oil storage bags, and buckets.

With the coming of spring, the Copper Eskimos split up into smaller groups and move onto the shore. Fishing becomes important; lean caribou are hunted not only for their meat but for the largely undigested vegetables in their stomachs, which are pulled out and eaten raw, on the spot, by the hunters. By summer, the groups have moved on again and have redivided. Small bands of hunters head inland after the full-grown caribou, which are usually captured by entrapment in a bog or in a gully. Some of the meat is dried in strips and preserved. The hides are softened by prolonged chewing and made into tents and clothing by the women. Older

The Arunta tribesmen of Central Australia, the Copper Eskimos of the Arctic, and the Pygmies of the Ituri forest in the Congo all exploit very different environments. Yet all share the hunter-gatherer way of life. (Courtesy of the American Museum of Natural History.)

[5] Diamond Jenness, *The People of the Twilight* (Chicago: University of Chicago Press, 1959). Describes fieldwork done as part of the Thule (Danish) expedition between the years 1913–1918.

folk and most of the women and children pass the summer at the fishing camps, catching and drying salmon, lake trout, and other fish.

In the fall, after the southward-bound caribou have been hunted, the Copper Eskimos settle down to await the formation of the pack ice. Usually there are ample supplies of meat and dried fish, so most of the time is utilized in preparing winter clothing, in repairing or manufacturing dogsleds, harpoons, lances, and similar articles. The skill, ingenuity, and craftsmanship of the Eskimos is particularly evident in their snow houses or *igloos*. These are built from snow blocks, cut from firm drifts with copper (or bone) knives. The blocks are shaped with the inside edge beveled so that the igloo will taper inward and upward to a dome, with the whole edifice being consolidated by a key block. Indeed, as Elman Service notes, "modern industrial science has been unable to surpass some of the devices for arctic living which the Eskimos have used for many centuries."[6]

The Mbuti Pygmies. So far we have discussed food-collecting societies in two harsh and contrasting habitats. The Mbuti Pygmies offer another contrast, since the thick, tropical Ituri Forest they inhabit in the Congo offers more benign conditions than those faced by the Australian aborigines or Eskimos.[7]

The Mbuti live in bands of three to 30 families, each band occupying a hunting-gathering territory of several hundred square miles of forest. Barriers, such as rivers and ravines, that limit the movement of game, also restrict the band. There is an ample supply of edible plants, and game is usually abundant. So plentiful are food resources that the Pygmies have coined the proverb that the only hungry Pygmy is a lazy Pygmy.

Mbuti bands vary in size depending on whether they hunt with nets or bows and arrows, net hunters forming larger groups than archers. In a net-hunting community, each family possesses a net about 300 feet long. On arrival at the hunting ground, families fasten their nets together. The bands then separate into sexes, with men and boys forming a large semicircle while the women and girls go a short distance into the forest and form another semicircle. When the men give a signal, the women move in the direction of the nets, beating the undergrowth with branches and letting out a distinctive cry. Animals running away from the women fall into the nets and are killed with spears. If they are too large for the women to carry back to the camp, they are cut up and the meat is parcelled out on the spot.

[6] Elman R. Service, *Profiles in Ethnology,* rev. ed. (New York: Harper & Row, 1963), p. 69.

[7] The discussion of the Mbuti Pygmies is based on Colin Turnbull, *Forest People* (New York: Simon and Schuster, 1961), and an article by him in James L. Gibbs, Jr., ed., *Peoples of Africa* (New York: Holt, Rinehart and Winston, 1965), pp. 275–315.

Archers work on a smaller scale than net hunters. Usually several men set out immediately after dawn to locate game. They climb trees and either wait for animals to pass nearby or lure them by imitating their calls. Archers rely on poison for their killings, so their bows do not have to be very powerful or aimed at vital parts.

The forest supplies most of the Pygmy's general needs. Arrows and spears are fire-hardened; slit bamboos and reeds serve as elementary cutting tools; thorny brambles are especially effective as root and vegetable scrapers. Animal sinews are made into bow strings, and leaves and vines into clothing and poison for arrows.

Possible Cultural Consequences of Food Collecting. Despite differences in terrain, climate, and food-collecting technology, Australian aborigines, Eskimos, Pygmies, and most other hunter-gatherers seem to have certain cultural patterns in common. Most have small communities, sparsely populated territories, and a nomadic life style with no permanent settlements. Individual land rights are not generally recognized. Communities are unstratified and have no specialized political officials, authority within each local unit residing with the older males of the group. Division of labor is based mostly on age and sex. If the primary food source is hunting, men do most of the work; if gathering, then the burden shifts to the women.[8]

Although it may seem that the hunting-gathering way of life is difficult, there is evidence that it is not necessarily grueling or insecure. For example, making a living seems to be relatively easy for the !Kung Bushmen of the Kalahari Desert of southern Africa. Because the Bushmen can collect an adequate amount of food with only a few hours' work a day, they

[8] Data from Robert B. Textor, comp., *A Cross-Cultural Summary* (New Haven: HRAF Press, 1967); and Elman R. Service, *The Hunters* (Englewood Cliffs, N.J.: Prentice-Hall, 1966).

are left with ample leisure time. Moreover, their old people live in security, unlike those in some other hunting-gathering societies, where the elderly are eliminated after they have ceased to contribute labor.[9] In general, the hunting-gathering way of life may simply be less productive than the agricultural way of life, not less secure. The lower level of productivity among food collectors means that fewer people can be supported in a given territory.

FOOD PRODUCTION

Roughly between 9500 and 7500 B.C. certain peoples, in widely separated geographical locations, made the revolutionary changeover to *food production;* that is, they began to domesticate plants and animals. With domestication, man acquired control over certain natural processes, such as animal breeding and seeding, which allowed him some choice in where and when food resources were provided. Over the centuries, food production began to supplant food collection as the predominant mode of subsistence. Today, most peoples in the world depend for their food upon some combination of domesticated plants and animals.

Horticulture

Horticulture is farming carried out with relatively primitive tools and methods. Small amounts of land are worked at one time, mostly with handtools, since neither draft animals, the plow, nor irrigation are usually employed. There are two kinds of horticulture. Extensive or shifting cultivation is a method in which land is worked for short periods, then left to regenerate for some years before used again; generally, the slash-and-burn method of clearing fields for cultivation (described below) is employed. The other method of horticulture is more or less continuous cultivation of root and tree crops.

The Jivaro. The Jivaro have long fascinated the world with their practice of shrinking and preserving human heads. They number perhaps 20,000 and live in small village groups along the eastern slopes of the Andes, a tropical rain forest region of difficult access. Understandably, they have had little contact with the world beyond this terrain.[10]

The Jivaro depend for subsistence on garden produce, particularly the manioc root. This large, starchy tuber, rather like a parsnip in color and texture, is made into a flour, or into a slightly fermented drink called *nijimanche.* The Jivaro cultivate maize, sweet potatoes, squash, cotton, and tobacco. Plants such as bananas and papayas are planted but need no tending.

The men are responsible for the initial clearing of a "garden" or vegetable plot in the jungle, the women for its cultivation. Clearing is done by the slash-and-burn method. The undergrowth is first cut away from a given area, then rings are cut in the bark of the smaller trees so that they will weaken and topple. Only the larger trees are cut down by hand, a formidable undertaking because of the exceptional hardness of the wood. After trees and brush have lain for several months of the dry season, they are set afire. The resulting plot is cultivated with digging sticks and used for a short time by the community, until soil exhaustion requires a move to other sites, which are similarly prepared.

Hunting also plays a useful role in the economy; indeed, the men spend a considerable

[9] Richard B. Lee, "What Hunters Do for a Living, or, How to Make Out on Scarce Resources," in Lee and DeVore, *Man the Hunter,* p. 39.

[10] See Service, *Profiles in Ethnology,* Ch. 9.

The Amahuaca Indians of Peru practice slash-and-burn agriculture. Men and boys cooperate in clearing the forest for cultivation. Even a giant kapok tree is felled. (Photograph by Cornell Capa, © Magnum Photos.)

amount of time pursuing game and fishing. Monkeys and birds are hunted with blowguns and poisoned darts, larger animals with lances as well. Fish are usually poisoned in man-made pools.

The economy of the Jivaro is essentially self-sufficient. All food is locally consumed, and spinning and weaving are done from indigenous materials. With the exception of a few items, such as steel axes (largely introduced by missionaries), all implements are made by the Jivaro from local materials. This self-sufficiency is reflected in the society as a whole. The Jivaro are proud, independent people, who are still as determined to avoid, and if need be to fight off, cultural incursions as they were long ago when the Incas and the Spaniards attempted to penetrate their territory.

The Kpelle. Another horticultural society, the Kpelle, numbers about 86,000 persons who live in "townships" in the central and western provinces of Liberia.[11] Theirs is a tropical forest habitat, characterized by a relatively small area of virgin forest and a proportionately larger area of secondary bush. There are two distinct seasons: a rainy season from May to October, during which Kpelle lands may receive as much as 175 inches of rain in one year, and a dry season. The average monthly temperature for the year averages about 77–79° Fahrenheit.

Rice forms the principal subsistence and cash crop, the manioc root taking second place. Garden vegetables, including okra, eggplant, and tomatoes, are also produced. Like the Jivaro, the Kpelle use the slash-and-burn mode of farming, and a high level of participation is obtained from the whole community.

Men and women together clear the jungle growth, which is set afire just before the rainy season, so that the ashes can be beaten into the earth as a fertilizer. In July, during the rainy season, the women plant the rice seeds. Then, for a period of about two weeks, practically the whole population of a town will sleep near the newly planted land to keep birds from plundering the germinating seeds. The women weed the rice beds; the men build granaries for use in October and December. After the crop has been painstakingly cut stalk by stalk, it is left to dry in the sun for some weeks to prevent dampness and spoilage.

The Kpelle horticultural technology seems to have reached so high a level of productivity and general sophistication that further advance could only come from a change to intensive agriculture. Specialization of labor is fairly advanced: iron is utilized for tools (the blacksmith being one of the more important specialists), clay is used for pots, and wood for furniture and figurines. Food surpluses are traded for cash, which is then used to buy new clothes and equipment.

Possible Cultural Consequences of Horticulture. The cultures of horticultural peoples tend to vary appreciably according to the relative richness of their environments and their opportunities for cultural borrowing. In most horticultural societies, however, simple farming techniques have tended to insure a more plentiful food supply than is generally available to hunting and gathering peoples. Consequently, horticulture is generally able to support larger, more densely populated communities. The way of life is generally more sedentary, although communities may move after a number of years to farm a new series of plots. In contrast to most hunter-gatherers, some horticulturists exhibit the beginnings of social differentiation. For example, there may be part-time craftsmen or part-time political officials; and there may be certain members of a kin group who have more status than others.

Intensive Agriculture

Intensive agriculture is chiefly characterized by the technological aspects that are missing in

[11] Gibbs, *Peoples of Africa,* pp. 197–240.

horticulture. These are the use of the plow and other improved farming implements, draft animals (and, in later stages of development, machines), fertilizers, and irrigation and other water storage techniques.

Rural Greece. The village of Vasilika is situated at the foot of Mount Parnassus on the Boeotian plain and in recent times comprised some 220 inhabitants.[12] Three kinds of crops are raised during the year: those for home consumption, those for sale, and those for feeding the livestock. Only the first two categories concern us here.

Grapevines and wheat are cultivated for domestic use. Wine is produced for household use only; thus, grapevines take up relatively little acreage. Pruning and hoeing, regarded as men's work, start off the agricultural year in March. Wine making, begun in September after the cereal harvest, involves the whole family. Everyone goes to the fields to gather the grapes into large baskets, which are carried to the farmhouse by pack animals. There, the leaves are removed, the fruit trampled by the men, and the newly pressed grape juice, or *must,* is transferred to barrels. After samples have been analyzed by a chemist in the nearby town, the recommended quantities of sugar and alcohol are added, and the barrels are sealed and allowed to stand.

Wheat fields are usually horse-plowed in October and November; sowing is done by hand. The crop is harvested the following summer, generally by machine. Wheat constitutes the staple village food, eaten as bread, as a cereal (called *trakhana*), or as noodles. It is also commonly bartered for other food items, such as fish, olive oil, and coffee.

Cotton and tobacco are raised for cash income. The growing of cotton in this dry plains country depends on irrigation, which has been aided by the development of efficient diesel pumps that distribute the water from the high local water table. The real work in the cotton fields begins after the spring plowing and seeding, when the young plants have to be hoed and mulched, a task mostly done by women. Irrigation, which begins in July, is men's work. It is usually done three times a season and involves the clearing of shallow ditches, mounting of pumps, and channelling of water, a procedure which often requires working well into the summer night. Cotton picking, which starts in October, is considered women's work. For picking, as well as for the hoeing and harvesting, a farmer with more than five acres usually calls in hired labor from neighboring villages and pays them cash wages. The cotton ginning is carried out by centrally located contractors, who are paid on the spot with 6 percent of the produce. Most of the returned seed is used for the following year's planting, the remainder being pressed into cakes to serve as supplementary fodder for the ewes at lambing time. Tobacco realizes a larger cash income than does cotton, and it fits well into what otherwise would be slack periods in cultivation.

Animal husbandry plays a relatively minor role. Each farmer has a horse or two for the heavy draft work, a mule or donkey, two dozen sheep or so, and some fowl.

Farmers at Vasilika are responsive to modern developments; they are prepared to experiment to a certain extent, especially with mechanization. Where the acreage under work warrants, tractors are hired. Specialists are regularly called upon to handle harvesting, cotton ginning, and the like. Indeed, the Greek farmer is content to be a farmer—and not one whit more—relying totally on the skills of others to repair his roof, maintain his water pump, or provide the mechanical know-how for his production.

Rural Vietnam: The Mekong Delta. Khanh Hau is a village situated along the flat Mekong Delta comprising about 600 families

[12] The discussion of rural Greece is based on Ernestine Friédl, *Vasilika: A Village in Modern Greece* (New York: Holt, Rinehart and Winston, 1962).

In the Mekong Delta of South Vietnam, wet rice cultivation is practiced, using extensive systems of irrigation. Here two women cultivate a paddy with hand-driven rotary hoes. (Courtesy of the United Nations.)

in the late 1950s.[13] The delta area has a tropical climate with a rainy season that lasts from May to November; as a whole, it has been rendered habitable only by extensive drainage operations.

Wet rice cultivation is the principal agricultural activity of Khanh Hau. It is complex, specialized, and involves three interacting components: an extensive system of irrigation and water control; a variety of specialized equipment, including the plow, waterwheels, threshing sledges, and winnowing machines; a clearly defined set of socioeconomic roles—from those of landlord, tenant, and laborer to those of rice millers and rice merchants. Descriptions of the technology of rice growing indicate how much organization, cooperation, and specialization is required.

In the dry season, the farmer decides what sort of rice crop he will plant—whether of long (120 days) or short (90 days) maturation, and whether glutinous or not, the choice depending upon the capital at his disposal, the current cost of fertilizer, and the anticipated demand. The seedbeds are prepared as soon as the rains have softened the ground in May; the soil is turned over and broken up as much as six separate times, with two-day intervals for "airing" between each operation. While the soil is being plowed and harrowed in this way, rice seeds are soaked in water for two days, so as to encourage sprouting, and before the seedlings are planted, the paddy is plowed once more and harrowed twice in two directions at right angles.

Planting is a delicate, specialized operation usually requiring speed; it is performed by hired male labor. But efficient planting is not enough to guarantee a fair crop. Proper fertilization and irrigation are equally important. In irrigating, steps must be taken to ensure that water levels will remain at exactly the proper depth over the entire paddy. Water is distributed by means of scoops, wheels, and mechanical pumps. All the community cooperates in giving this operation care and diligent control. The crop is harvested, threshed, winnowed, and dried when it ripens during the period from late September to May. Normally, the rice is sorted into three portions; one is set aside for use by the household in the following year, one for payment of hired labor and other services (such as loans from agricultural banks), and one for cash sale on the market.

The villagers also cultivate garden produce, raise pigs, chickens, and the like, and frequently engage in fishing. The village economy usually supports three to four implement makers and a much larger number of carpenters.

Possible Cultural Consequences of Intensive Agriculture. In contrast to horticultural societies, societies with intensive agriculture are more likely to have towns and cities, a high degree of craft specialization, and more complex political organization. Women in intensive agricultural societies generally contribute less to subsistence than women in horticultural societies, perhaps because intensive agriculture involves plowing and the handling of large draft animals. Yet in spite of the fact that intensive agriculture is generally more productive than horticulture, intensive agricultural societies are more likely to face food shortages.[14] Perhaps this is because intensive agriculture—mainly practiced in nontropical areas where rainfall can be unreliable—is more vulnerable to severe drought which can hurt, and even destroy, the entire food supply.

Pastoralism

Pastoralism is a relatively rare form of subsistence technology practiced by nomadic people

[13] This discussion is based on Gerald Cannon Hickey, *Village in Vietnam* (New Haven: Yale University Press, 1964), pp. 135–165.

[14] Data from Textor, *A Cross-Cultural Summary.*

in which food getting is based largely upon the maintenance of large herds of animals. It is especially associated with such terrain as steppes, rolling hills, grasslands, and the like—areas of low rainfall where cultivation is difficult without (or even with) irrigation, but where grasses are plentiful enough to support herds of animals.

The Basseri. The Basseri are a tribe of tent-dwelling, pastoral nomads numbering about 16,000 and living in southern Iran.[15] The Basseri principally raise sheep and goats, though donkeys and camels are employed for draft work, and the more wealthy men have horses for riding. Theirs is a dry, arid habitat with average rainfall of no more than 10 inches a year. However, the mountains to the north trap water in the form of snow, and this enables the growth of considerable vegetation in mountain pastures when the snow melts.

Their pastoral way of life is based upon a regular, migratory exploitation of the grazing lands within their territory, which overall measures about 15,000 square miles. In winter, when the mountains in the north are snow covered, the plains and foothills to the south offer extensive pasturage. During the spring, grazing is excellent on a plateau near the center of the territory, and by summer, when most of the lower-lying pastures have dried up, sufficient food for the herds may be found in the mountains at an altitude nearly 6,000 feet above sea level.

Annual migrations are so important to the economy of the Basseri—as well as to other groups of pastoral nomads in southern Iran—that there has developed the concept of *il-rah,* or "tribal road." A major pastoral tribe, such as the Basseri, will have its traditional route and schedule. The route refers to the localities in the order they are visited and follows the existing passes and lines of communication; the schedule regulates the length of time each location will be occupied and depends on the maturation of different pastures and the movements of other tribes. The *il-rah* is regarded, in effect, as the property of the tribe—local populations and authorities recognize the tribe's right to pass along roads and uncultivated lands, to draw water from public wells, and to pasture their flocks on public land.

The Basseri generally herd sheep and goats together, with one shepherd responsible for flocks of 300 to 400 animals. Milk and its by-products are the most important products, followed by wool, hides, and meat. The tribe's diet consists mainly of milk (especially favored in its various sour forms), cheese, and fresh meat (mostly female lambs and kids), as well as flour, dates, sugar, and tea, obtained principally through trade.

Wool and hides are important to the economy of the Basseri. Both are traded, but they are of even greater use within the tribe. The Basseri are skilled spinners and weavers, especially the women, much of whose time is spent at these activities. Saddle bags and pack bags are woven on horizontal looms from homespun wool and hair, as are carpets, sleeping rugs, and the characteristic black tents made of panels of woven goat hair. Woven goat hair provides an exceptionally versatile cloth: for winter use, it retains heat and repels water; in summer, it insulates against heat and permits free circulation of air. Lambskin hides also serve many purposes; plucked and turned inside-out, they are made into storage bags for water, buttermilk, sour milk, and other liquids.

Hunting and gathering play no major role in the Basseri economy (though hunting is a popular sport among the men). Agriculture and, especially, trading are important. The wealthier Basseri practice agriculture indirectly, buying pieces of land along the *il-rah* and paying peasants to grow crops for them. However, most tribesmen must obtain through trade the

[15] The discussion of the Basseri is based on Frederick Barth, *Nomads of South Persia* (Oslo: Universitetsforlaget, 1964; New York: Humanities Press).

necessities and luxury items that are not produced within the community. The staple items they sell are butter, wool, lambskins, rope, and, occasionally, livestock.

The Lapps. The Lapps live and move with their reindeer herds in that part of northwestern Scandinavia called Fennoscandia, an area where Finland, Sweden, and Norway share common frontiers. It is a typical arctic habitat: cold, windswept, and dark for much of the year. Though the Lapps gradually have come under modern cultural influences in the twentieth century, theirs is still very largely a pastoral form of life.[16]

The Lapps herd their reindeer either intensively or extensively, using the latter method most often today. In the intensive system, the herd is constantly under observation as it moves westward from its winter to its summer

[16] The discussion of the Lapps is based on Ian Whitaker, *Social Relations in a Nomadic Lappish Community* (Oslo: Utgitt av Norsk Folksmuseum, 1955); and also T. I. Itkonen, "The Lapps of Finland," *Southwestern Journal of Anthropology,* Vol. 7 (Spring 1951), pp. 32–68.

Pastoral nomadism is a form of food-getting technology usually limited to marginal areas where other means of making a living would be difficult or impossible. In the barren regions of northern Scandinavia, a Lapp reindeer herd surrounds the owner's tent during migration from one pasture to another. (Courtesy of Fred Bruemmer.)

feeding areas, and back east again. The Lapps live with their animals at all times and always know the number of animals in their charge. Intensively herded reindeer and other animals are accustomed to human contact. Hence, the summer corralling of the females for milking and the breaking-in of the ox-reindeer for use as draft animals are not difficult tasks. Herds are usually small enough to be managed easily.

The extensive system allows less surveillance but encompasses larger herds. Under this system the reindeer are allowed to move through their seasonal feeding cycles watched only by one or two "scouts," the other Lapps staying with the herd only when it has settled in its summer or winter habitat. Milking, breaking-in, and corralling in general are more arduous in the extensive system because the animals are less accustomed to humans. However, this method of herding shares an important characteristic with the intensive system: it is the reindeer that decide when and where to move to obtain sustenance. The herders simply follow after them.

Even under the extensive system, which theoretically permits Lapps to engage in subsidiary economic activities such as hunting and fishing, the reindeer herd is the essential, if not the only, source of income. A family may possess as many as 1,000 head of reindeer but, more usually, the figure is half that number. Studies show 200 as the minimum number of reindeer needed to provide for a family of four to five adults.

The Lapps hunt to add variety to their diet, but the staple is bull reindeer meat; the females are kept alive for breeding purposes. Bulls are slaughtered in the fall, after the mating season. Meat and hides are frequently sold or bartered for food and other necessities.

Possible Cultural Consequences of Pastoralism. Pastoralism is a highly specialized form of food production involving the care of large animal herds. It has survived today mostly in habitats which cannot support cultivation but can provide sufficient pasture for a herd on the move, as well as secondary hunting-gathering opportunities. Even though they are nomadic, pastoral societies tend to be more stratified and have more social differentiation—for instance, craft specialization—than those dependent upon food collection. Individuals or families may own property, particularly animals, but herding is often organized by groups of families. There is also an interdependence between the pastoral group and agricultural groups in the area. This involves trade, which generally plays an important role, since a pastoral economy is often not self-sufficient. Finally, as in the case of intensive agriculturalists, pastoralists, are vulnerable to food shortages, possibly because their nontropical environments are subject to fluctuations in rainfall.[17]

CAUSES OF FOOD-GETTING DIVERSITY

Of great interest to anthropologists is the question of why different societies have different methods of food getting. Archaeological evidence suggests that major advances in food getting—such as the domestication of plants and animals—have been independently invented in many areas of the world. Moreover, these advances have spread outward from the original areas, rather like ripples from a stone dropped in a pool. Yet, in spite of comparable inventions and their subsequent diffusion or spread by migration, there still is wide diversity in the means by which man obtains food. How is this to be explained?

Environmental Influences

In examining the effects of physical environment on food getting, we are first faced with a

[17] Data from Textor, *A Cross-Cultural Summary.*

problem of definition. There is no one indisputable way of defining a physical habitat, but many anthropologists favor the kind of geographical focus exemplified by Preston James's classification of the world's land surface into eight principal types.[18] Using the twin criteria of natural vegetation and surface features, James distinguishes between dry lands (deserts), tropical forests, Mediterranean scrub forests, mid-latitude mixed forests, grasslands, boreal forests, polar lands, and mountain lands.

Dry Lands. Dry lands are the desert regions of the world. They comprise 18 percent of the total land surface but are occupied by only 6 percent of the earth's population. Contrary to popular belief, few parts of these areas are entirely barren or rainless. The typical landscape includes a cover of low shrubs and grasses.

James groups dry lands into five principal locations: North African and Asian, of which the Sahara, Arabian, Turkestan, and Gobi deserts are examples; North American, including northern Mexico, Arizona, New Mexico, southern California, and the Great and Wyoming basins; South American coastal deserts of Peru and western Argentina; South African, including the Namib and Kalahari deserts; and Australian, such as the Great Sandy, Gibson, and Great Victoria deserts.

Shortage of water has hampered the agricultural development of dry lands, except where there are *oases*—small, fertile areas where crops can be grown with a simple technology—or rivers that could be tapped by irrigation. Some of the major ancient civilizations, in fact, emerged in river valleys of dry land regions, such as in Mesopotamia and along the Indus valley. In dry land regions without an oasis, the existing technology has determined the living pattern. When the technology is simple, food getting may take the basic hunting-gathering form, as exemplified by the Australian aborigines or the Kalahari Bushmen. Or, with irrigation, it can take the intensive agricultural form, as exemplified by cultivation in Israel. Horticulture is apparently not possible in dry land areas, although pastoralism may be.

Tropical Forest Lands. Tropical forests occupy 10 percent of the earth's land surface and are inhabited by 28 percent of the world population. These are areas with abundant rainfall. But despite the attractiveness of lush vegetation and brilliant colorings, tropical forest lands do not usually offer favorable environments for intensive agriculture, perhaps because heavy soaking by rain may quickly deplete cleared land of certain minerals. Horticulture, with shifting cultivation and slash-and-burn preparation, as exemplified by the Jivaro, is generally practiced in such environments. In the past, however, hunting and gathering economies were found frequently in tropical forest areas. And today, there are a few areas (for example, the Mekong Delta of South Vietnam) whose tropical forests were cleared and prevented from growing up again by the use to which the cleared land was put—rice cultivation in paddies. Tropical forest lands cover the Amazon Basin and parts of the Guianas, extending to southern Brazil; they form much of the Congo Basin, with fingers reaching into Liberia and Sierra Leone; they stretch from northeastern India, along the Malay Peninsula to Indonesia, Melanesia, and northern Australia, and are also in parts of Burma, Thailand, and Vietnam.

Mediterranean Scrub Forests. Mediterranean scrub forests comprise 1 percent of the earth's land mass and are occupied by 5 percent of the world population. These areas are usually located between mountains and coasts and are characterized by mild, rainy winters and hot, dry summers. Besides occurring along the Mediterranean itself, such areas are found primarily in middle Chile, between Coquimbo and Concepcion, and in North Amer-

[18] Preston E. James, *A Geography of Man,* 3rd ed. (Waltham, Mass.: Blaisdell, 1966).

ica, between Los Angeles and Oregon. They provide an excellent habitat for human beings at any level of technology. California was populated by hunting-gathering peoples long ago, as were parts of Greece and Italy long before the emergence of Athens and Rome.

Mixed Forest Lands. Although only 7 percent of the earth's land surface is classified as mixed forest, 42 percent of the world population lives in such regions. The surface features of these areas vary, containing mixed coniferous (cone-bearing evergreens) and broadleaf forests, rolling hills and low mountain ranges, large fertile plains and river valleys. The climate tends to be milder along the seashores, harsher in the interior. Principal regions are North America, Europe north of the Mediterranean zone, most of China north of the tropics, Korea, and Japan. In prehistoric times, this kind of habitat supported only a small population, largely because stone technologies were not sufficient to clear the forest of thick-trunked hardwoods. When bronze and iron tools came into existence, however, the mixed forest lands were cleared and became so productive that large populations now live in such regions.

Grasslands. Grasslands occupy 19 percent of the earth's land surface and are inhabited by 10 percent of the world population. These regions may be *steppes* (having dry, low grass cover), *prairies* (with taller, better-watered grass), or *savannas* (tropical grasslands). They are found extensively in North Africa, Mongolia, Manchuria, Russia, and North America, as well as elsewhere. The grassland habitat favors large game and hence both hunter and pastoral technologies, except where a machine technology makes intensive agriculture possible, as in parts of the United States and the Soviet Union today.

Boreal Forest Lands. Only 1 percent of the world population lives in boreal land forests, which occupy 10 percent of the global land surface. Mainly coniferous, and not so dense as those of the tropics, these heavily wooded areas are found throughout the Northern Hemisphere in most of Canada, Alaska, Siberia, and Scandinavia. Rainfall is low, though little of it is lost through evaporation. The terrain is a difficult one for food growing.

Polar Lands. Although polar lands comprise 16 percent of the earth's surface, only 1 percent of the total world population lives in these inhospitable regions. The type of land surrounding the North and South poles varies from *tundras,* which have brief summer seasons (about six weeks), to heavily glaciated areas. The food resources of this habitat include few plants; thus, as we have seen, the Eskimos subsist largely by fishing and hunting.

Mountain Lands. Mountains occupy 12 percent of the earth's land surface and are inhabited by 7 percent of the world population. James indicates that the world is "tied together" by more or less continuous chains of high mountains. From a core in Southeast Asia, these extend on three axes: one through southern Asia and southern Europe to North Africa and the Atlantic coast of Africa; another via Tibet, across western China, Siberia, and down the west coasts of North and South America; and the third, partially submerged, across the Pacific Basin. Mountain lands vary in climate and terrain (and thus in habitat) according to elevation. Although today no mountain regions are inhabited by food collectors, it is not clear whether this was also true in the past, particularly before the domestication of plants and animals. In any case, mountain lands may currently be occupied by pastoralists and intensive agriculturalists.

Given this classification of habitats, what conclusions can we draw about the influence of environmental factors on food getting? Cross-cultural evidence indicates that neither food collection nor food production is significantly associated with any particular type of habitat.[19] In other words, hunter-gatherer societies are found in a variety of habitats: Australian Aborigines in dry lands, the Copper Eskimos in the North American polar regions, the Mbuti Pygmies in the tropical forests of Africa. Similarly, food producers exploit several different habitats, as we have seen in the Peruvian rain forests cultivated by the Jivaro using slash-and-burn techniques, the Mediterranean scrub forests intensively farmed by the Greek peasant, the Mekong Delta, a former tropical forest region, farmed intensively by the Vietnamese, and the Iranian dry land region supporting the pastoral Basseri. Certain very general patterns are suggested, however, in comparisons between specific means of food production and specific types of habitat. Approximately 80 percent of all societies that practice simple agriculture are in the tropics, whereas 75 percent of all societies that practice intensive agriculture are *not* in tropical forest environments.[20] This may be because the soil-depleting effects of high rainfall in tropical regions and/or the difficulty of weeding where vegetation grows so quickly hinder the development of intensive agriculture.[21] Pastoralism also is not often found in tropical forest regions.[22] This is not surprising since a dense jungle is hardly a likely spot to herd animals.

From the information available, anthropologists generally agree that the physical environment by itself has a limiting rather than a strictly determining effect on the major types of subsistence. In other words, some environments may not permit certain types of food getting, although allowing a number of others. The type of food getting that can be practiced in a particular kind of environment depends upon the level of technological development, as dramatically illustrated by the history of the Imperial Valley, a dry land region in California. The complex systems of irrigation used there now have made it one of the most productive regions in the world; but about 400 years ago this same valley could support only hunting and gathering groups who subsisted on wild plants and animals.

[19] Data from Textor, *A Cross-Cultural Summary.*

[20] Data from Textor, *A Cross-Cultural Summary.*

[21] For an argument supporting the "weeding" explanation, see Robert L. Carneiro, "Slash-and-Burn Cultivation among the Kuikuru and Its Implications for Cultural Development in the Amazon Basin," *Antropologica,* Supplement No. 2 (September 1961).

[22] Data from Textor, *A Cross-Cultural Summary.*

Other Influences on Food Getting

Recognizing the physical environment may limit the major types of food getting, we still need to ask why certain food-getting techniques are practiced in areas where other techniques are also possible. For example, in some environments, both hunting and gathering and cultivation are possible, yet cultivation has generally supplanted food collection throughout the world. We have already discussed various theories about the origin of agriculture in Chapter 8. Because the changeover to cultivation is important for our understanding of contemporary variation in food getting, we shall briefly review some of those theories.

The growth of population has come to be recognized as an unmistakably consistent trend beginning in prehistoric times. As we are often reminded, population puts pressure on the food resources of all societies at all times, but especially upon those which are expanding; indeed, the term "population explosion" is widely used today. It is not surprising, therefore, that the relation between population growth and subsistence technologies has been closely studied.

Most societies, regardless of the type of food-getting technology, have probably been sensitive to population pressure. In the Fertile Crescent, as an example, it appears that, by about 8000 B.C., population growth had outstripped the food supply. Some groups may have been

The level of technological development has a significant effect on the type of food getting practiced in a particular environment. With the use of complex systems of irrigation, the Imperial Valley in California, a dry land area, has become one of the most productive regions in the world. (Photo by Georg Gerster, Rapho Guillumette Pictures.)

forced to move into areas that they were less able to exploit given the existing level of technology. At some time thereafter, the slowly developing realization that food collection was not sufficient to guarantee the desired food supply probably provided the stimulus for the first, tentative steps toward food production. Because the region was amply stocked with a species of wild wheat that proved adaptable to a wide range of conditions, a new technology was possible. And that new mode of subsistence—food production—was developed by at least some groups in the region. Later on, when cereal surpluses accrued, they may have been fed to wild goats and sheep, animals that were adaptable to domestication. Similar crises of subsistence may have caused the parallel development of food-production technologies in northwestern India, northern China, Mexico, Southeast Asia, and West Africa.

The view that demographic factors gradually *caused* the agricultural revolution has only recently gained currency among anthropologists. Previously, the emphasis was on the reverse: population increase was regarded as the *product* of improved food-getting methods. A stimulus and response mechanism was seen to operate between technology and demography: as domesticated plants, the plow, the irrigation trench, and the like were introduced and their effects felt, population expanded.

Michael Harner is an exponent of the view that increasing population brought on agricultural advances.[23] Harner has set out to explain how agricultural societies evolved and, more particularly, how they acquired their particular social structures. Working with a computer and using a sample of 1,170 societies, he has identified "the demand on subsistence resources resulting from both the density of population and its level of technology in relation to a specific environment" as the prime mover in cultural change.[24] In his model, the key moment comes when a food-collecting community has utilized the food resources of its habitat to the point where it has reached "the limit of population density." It is then obliged to supplement its usual sources of food supply with new, domesticated ones. At first, the proportion of cultivated plants to wild plants is low, but gradually the proportion is increased as each new step in domesticating food resources stimulates an expansion in population.

Harner sees a parallel tendency in the development of the social organization of the community. He argues that it soon becomes apparent to the society that as the source of food becomes more domesticated, the risk of famine increases because of the possibility of crop failure. Consequently, there is a higher value on organization, supervision, and control than there was in the former hunter-gatherer economy. A new "class" or element in society emerges to assume the "command" function, and it has a vested interest in continuing the new developments. While fostering a gradual dependence on cultivated food resources, it succeeds in making the society increasingly dependent on the new "ruling" elites, and both trends become progressively more difficult to reverse.

Kent V. Flannery's suggestions are of special interest here because they refer to possible causes of the agricultural revolution in the Near East—the area in which the agricultural revolution first occurred.[25] Flannery argues that hunter-gatherer societies have little incentive to seek the greater productivity associated with agriculture. Far from laboring in the shadow of starvation, man the hunter is able to maintain a favorable caloric intake, with a surprisingly low labor output. Among the !Kung Bushmen, for example, less than three days' foraging per week normally produces food amounting to over 2,100 calories per day. Further, when left relatively undisturbed in their habitats, populations in hunter-gatherer economies stabilize at a level below that of "resource exhaustion."

Only a major "disturbance" sufficient to reduce existing food resources can project a food-collecting economy out of its "orbit," says Flannery. One possibility—that of major environmental change—has to be dismissed for lack of sufficient evidence. Another possibility—that of demographic change—is strongly suggested by the available archaeological data.

Flannery draws on the insights of the archaeologists, Lewis R. and Sally R. Binford, to theorize how the cultural "breakthrough" occurred. In the Near East, he says, there was

[23] Michael J. Harner, "Population Pressure and the Social Evolution of Agriculturalists," *Southwestern Journal of Anthropology,* Vol. 26 (1970), pp. 67–86.

[24] *Ibid.,* p. 68.

[25] Kent V. Flannery, "Origins and Ecological Effects of Early Domestication in Iran and the Near East," in Peter J. Ucko and G. W. Dimbleby, eds., *The Domestication and Exploitation of Plants and Animals* (Chicago: Aldine, 1969), pp. 73–97.

already a "mosaic" of optimal habitats—those having a high population-carrying capacity—bordering on less favorable ones.

> It is the optimal habitats which are regional growth centers; it is in them that populations rise, followed by buddings-off and emigrations of daughter groups before the carrying capacity has been strained. They are the "donor systems"; the marginal habitats are the "recipient systems." And it is in the marginal habitats that the density equilibrium would most likely be periodically disturbed by immigrations of daughter groups, raising populations too near the limited carrying capacity.[26]

Thus, according to this theory, it was along the margins of the areas of population growth, not in the central areas, that demographic pressures probably contributed to the agricultural revolution.

Both Harner and Flannery have argued that demographic changes may have given rise to the development of agriculture. They have also suggested that as man the cultivator expanded his agricultural activity, so, proportionately, did he create social and environmental conditions which would effectively prevent a return to his previous hunting-gathering state.

An interesting addition to the demographic argument has recently been offered by both Richard B. Lee and Robert Sussman.[27] They suggest that with the development of sedentary communities, populations increase because women no longer have to carry their children great distances and therefore do not have to space births as widely. Lee's and Sussman's observations are only a preliminary indication of a possible correlation between increased sedentariness and a higher birth rate. But if such a correlation is confirmed, it will strongly reinforce Flannery's belief that the seminomadic, hunting and gathering stage, because it causes demographic pressure on food resources, is crucial to the initial momentum of the agricultural revolution.

Although we may have some understanding of why domestication originated, we still need to explain why it generally supplanted food collection as the primary mode of subsistence. It cannot be assumed that food collectors would automatically adopt food production as a superior way of life once they understood the process of domestication. After all, domestication may entail more work and provide less food security than the food-collecting way of life.

The spread of agriculture may perhaps be linked to the need for territorial expansion. As sedentary, food-producing populations grew—their birth rates being higher than those of nomadic peoples—they may have been forced to expand into new territories. Some of this territory may have been vacant, but much of it was probably already occupied by food collectors. Although food production is not necessarily easier than food collection, it is generally more productive; and greater productivity means that more people can be supported in a given territory. In the competition for land between the faster-expanding food producers and the food collectors, the food producers may have had a significant advantage—they had more people in a given area. Thus, the hunter-gatherer groups were more likely to lose out in the competition for land. Some groups may have adopted cultivation, abandoning the hunter-gatherer way of life in order to survive. Other groups, which remained food collectors, may have been forced to retreat into areas not desired by the cultivators. Today, the small number of hunter-gatherers that remain inhabit areas which are not particularly suitable for cultivation—dry lands, dense tropical forests, and polar regions.

[26] Flannery, "Origins and Ecological Effects," p. 74.
[27] Richard B. Lee, "Population Growth and the Beginnings of Sedentary Life among the !Kung Bushmen," in Brian Spooner, ed., *Population Growth: Anthropological Implications* (Cambridge, Mass.: MIT Press, in press); also Robert Sussman, "Child Transport, Family Size, and the Increase in Human Population during the Neolithic," *Current Anthropology,* Vol. 13 (April 1972), pp. 258–267.

SUMMARY

1. The need to ensure an adequate food supply is basic to the survival of all societies. Food collection or hunting and gathering—dependence on naturally occurring plants and animals—is the oldest of man's food-getting technologies. Today, however, only a small fraction of the world population practices it, and those societies tend to inhabit marginal environments. More advanced technologies have taken over the bulk of the available land resources.
2. The aborigines of central Australia (desert lands), the Copper Eskimos (polar lands), and the Mbuti Pygmies (tropical forest lands) exemplify that hunting and gathering cultures can be found in a number of different physical habitats. Nevertheless, hunting and gathering societies have some important characteristics in common. They are generally nomadic, with populations being relatively small in number and low in density. The division of labor is usually along age and sex lines only; personal possessions are limited, most resources being communally held; economic relations are based on sharing. The community is a band of related families, with vaguely defined leadership; social stratification is generally unknown.
3. Roughly between 9500 and 7500 B.C. certain peoples, in widely separated geographical locations, made the revolutionary changeover to food production; that is, they began to domesticate plants and animals. Over the centuries, food production began to supplant food collection as the predominant mode of subsistence. Today, most peoples in the world depend for their food upon some combination of domesticated plants and animals.
4. Horticulturists, such as the Jivaro and the Kpelle, practice simple agriculture: their technology includes only simple tools and farming methods. The slash-and-burn technique is frequently used to clear areas for cultivation. The food supply of horticulturists is generally sufficient to support larger, more densely populated communities than can be fed by food collection. The way of life is generally more sedentary, although communities may move after a number of years to farm a new series of plots. In contrast to most hunter-gatherers, some horticulturists exhibit the beginnings of social differentiation.
5. Intensive agriculture is chiefly characterized by the technological aspects that are missing in horticulture. These are the use of the plow and other improved farming implements, draft animals (and, in later stages of development, machines), fertilizers, and irrigation and other water storage techniques. In contrast to horticultural societies, societies with intensive agriculture are more likely to have towns and cities, a high degree of craft specialization, and more complex political organization. Women in intensive agricultural societies generally contribute less to subsistence than women in horticultural societies, perhaps because intensive agriculture involves plowing and the handling of large draft animals. Yet in spite of the fact that intensive agriculture is generally more productive than horticulture, intensive agricultural societies are more likely to face food shortages.
6. Pastoralism is a subsistence technology based on the care of large herds of animals. It is a highly specialized adaptation to marginal land areas. The Basseri and

the Lapps represent variations of pastoralism, the essential features of which are: a nomadic way of life; clearly defined seasonal areas of pasturage and access routes; and somewhat more complex sociopolitical systems than are found among hunter-gatherer groups.

7. It is generally agreed that the physical environment exercises a limiting rather than determining influence on the major types of food-getting technology. But, although an area can support several food-getting techniques, one form usually becomes dominant. Population pressure in marginal areas may explain the emergence of cultivation in the Near East. Competition for land may explain the spread of food producers at the expense of food collectors, since food producers can generally support more people in a given territory and therefore may have generally had a competitive advantage in their confrontations with food collectors.

SUGGESTED READINGS

Barth, F.: *Nomads of South Persia: The Basseri Tribe of the Kamseh Confederacy.* Universitets Etnografishe Museum, Oslo, Bulletin No. 8. (Oslo, Norway: Oslo University Press, 1961).
Description and analysis of one variety of pastoral nomadism. The author discusses the relationship between subsistence and sociopolitical organization, and interaction between the nomadic herders and sedentary groups in the area.

Lee, R. B., and I. DeVore (Eds.): *Man the Hunter* (Chicago: Aldine, 1968).
The outcome of a 1966 symposium of the same name, this volume includes papers on the social organization, demography, and ecology of hunter-gatherers. Prehistoric hunter-gatherers and the role of hunting and gathering in the evolution of human culture are also discussed.

Leeds, A., and A. P. Vayda (Eds.): *Man, Culture and Animals: The Role of Animals in Human Ecological Adjustments.* Publication No. 78 of the American Association for the Advancement of Science. (Washington, D.C.: American Association for the Advancement of Science, 1965).
A collection of papers dealing with the complex feedback relationship between environment and culture. The papers cover a wide range of subsistence patterns, from hunters and gatherers to modern cattle ranching. All the authors share the attitude that culture is related to its surrounding natural environment.

Service, E.: *The Hunters* (Foundations of Modern Anthropology Series. Englewood Cliffs, N.J.: Prentice-Hall, 1966).
An introduction to the basic features of the hunting-gathering way of life. The book also includes an ethnographic appendix with descriptions of many hunting and gathering societies, as well as selected readings on the subject.

Struever, S. (Ed.): *Prehistoric Agriculture* (Garden City, N.Y.: Natural History Press, 1971).
An up-to-date sourcebook which focuses on the problems involved in explaining the rise of agriculture. Part II should be of particular interest, because it presents hypotheses to explain the beginnings of agriculture and its consequences in various parts of the world. The book also includes an extensive bibliography.

Ucko, P. J., and G. W. Dimbleby (Eds.): *The Domestication and Exploitation of Plants and Animals* (Chicago: Aldine, 1969).
An excellent collection of papers on the determinants of the transition to food production.

Zeuner, F. E.: *A History of Domesticated Animals* (New York: Harper & Row, 1963).
This work is intended to serve as a text on the history of animal domestication. The author attempts to draw together paleontological as well as archaeological evidence from specific sites.

13

Economic Systems

When we think of economics, we think of things and activities involving money. We think of the costs of goods and services like food, rent, haircuts, and the price of movie tickets. We may also think of factories and farms and other business enterprises that produce the goods and services we need or think we need. However, many societies (indeed, most that are known to anthropology) do not have money or the equivalent of the American factory worker who stands before a moving belt for eight hours, tightening identical bolts that glide by him, for which he is given bits of paper he may exchange for food, shelter, and other goods or services.

All societies, however, do have an economic system, whether or not they use money. All societies have customs regulating the access to natural resources, customs for transforming those resources through labor into necessities and other desired items, and customs for distributing (and perhaps exchanging) goods and services.

THE ALLOCATION OF PRODUCTIVE RESOURCES

Land Resources

Every society has access to surrounding natural resources—land, water, plants and animals, minerals—and every society has a system for determining who has access to those resources. Our own society is based on a system of private ownership of natural resources. Land is divided into precisely measureable units; it is the invisible borders of land units that determine what parcels of land may be bought, owned, and sold in Western societies. Small plots of land and the resources on that land may be owned by individuals absolutely and may be sold, given away, or sometimes even destroyed at the owner's wish. Large plots of land are generally collectively owned. The "owner" may be a government agency, as when the National Park Service owns land on behalf of the entire population of the United States, or a corporation, a private collective of shareholders.

The ownership of a resource such as water in industrial societies is harder to regulate than land, since water follows laws of its own. Water for private use is generally controlled by the government. But the question of who has access to rivers and lakes is treated differently in different countries. France has recently made all its beaches public, declaring in effect that the ocean is not a resource which could be owned by an individual. As a result, all the hotels and individuals who had fenced off portions of the best beaches for their exclusive use had to remove the fences. In the United States, many beaches are privately owned and people do not always have access to the shores of their country.

Yet regardless of some variation concerning which resources are said to be privately owned and which are publicly owned, all Western societies base their allocation of land resources on a concept of property ownership. In the United States, property ownership entails: a more or less exclusive right to use land resources in whatever way the owner wishes; and the right to sell, give away, or destroy those resources. Of course, these two privileges of ownership—the right to use resources and the right to dispose of them—are not absolute, even in our own society. At times we do not have exclusive rights to dispose of our property as we wish. Our land, for example, may be taken by the government for use in the construction of a highway; we may be paid compensation, but we cannot usually prevent confiscation. Similarly, our right to use of land is not absolute. We cannot burn our homes, nor can we use them as brothels or munitions arsenals. In short, even in our highly individualistic system of ownership, property is not entirely private.

Individual ownership of land, or ownership by a group of unrelated shareholders, is alien to the thinking of most hunter-gatherers or most horticulturists. To be sure, they often have collective ownership, but such ownership is always by groups of related people (kinship groups) or by territorial groups (bands or villages).

The absence of a concept of private ownership of natural resources among hunter-gatherer societies is probably because the survival of the band is best assured by every member having access to all the resources in the band's territory. To the hunter-gatherer, land itself has no intrinsic value; what is of value is the presence of game and wild plant life. If game moves away or food resources become less plentiful, the land is correspondingly less valuable. Therefore, the more the wild food supply is susceptible to fluctuations in a particular locale, the less desirable it is to parcel out small areas of land to individuals, and the more advantageous it is to make land ownership communal.

The Hadza of Tanzania, for example, do not consider that they have exclusive rights over the land in which they hunt. Any member of the band can hunt or gather where he likes, and encroachment on their territory by settlements and by the government has not been protested. Each person hunts and gathers primarily for himself. Whatever he finds he eats; and if anything is left he carries it back to camp.[1]

The allocation of natural resources that most closely approaches "ownership" among hunter-gatherers occurs in some societies in which the harvest of one fruit or nut tree or a clump of trees is allocated to one family by tradition. Such was the case in the Andaman Islands in the Indian Ocean.[2] However, rather than being true ownership of a tree, this assignment of trees was probably only an extension of a division of labor by families. It would be a waste of time and effort (and probably not productive enough per capita) if the whole band gathered from a single tree, so the traditional right to harvest by a family or an individual may have been favored for reasons of efficient work organization. The family is still obligated to share the fruit or nuts so acquired with families who collected little or nothing. And at the time when fruit is ripe on one person's tree, it is ripe or every other tree in the vicinity.

The territory of one hunter-gatherer band is typically surrounded by that of other bands. In most hunter-gatherer societies, the communal ownership of land is extended to provide some degree of access to members of neighboring bands. Among the !Kung Bushmen, the right of "hot pursuit" is honored, and one band is al-

[1] James Woodburn, "An Introduction to Hadza Ecology," in Richard B. Lee and Irven DeVore, eds., *Man the Hunter* (Chicago: Aldine, 1968), pp. 49–55.

[2] A. R. Radcliffe-Brown, *The Andaman Islanders* (Cambridge: Cambridge University Press, 1933), p. 41.

lowed to follow its game into the territory of its neighbors. The sharing of water is perhaps most characteristic of the Bushmen's attitude toward the allocation of natural resources. Members of one band, as a matter of courtesy, must ask permission of a neighboring band to use a waterhole in the other's territory; as a matter of tradition, the headman of a Bushman band cannot refuse. The best test of how the system works comes when water is scarce in all territories, when a particularly dry summer has reduced all the waterholes. We might think that, under such circumstances, the Bushmen would tighten control of their waterholes, thus monopolizing the small supply for themselves, but this is not the case. When supplies are limited, the obligation to share is even stronger. The reasoning is quite sound: if they help their neighbors when they most need help, then they themselves can ask for help when they most need it. To share out of plenty is a pleasure; to share out of little is a necessity.

Among the Anbara, an Australian aborigine community of about 135 people, groups of kinsmen or clans had nonexclusive claims on particular stretches of land. Six clans, each with its own land area, formed the community. For example, one of the clans, the Mararagidf, felt a close tie to a certain land area, often claiming that they had been born there and wished to die there. They hunted and built traps on their clan territory, but they had the whole Anbara area to hunt in as well, and the other clans could enter their territory at will. In other words, the six clans camped together and roamed the entire territory at will, but each clan had an emotional tie to its own land.[3]

When a group of hunter-gatherers lives in a microenvironment so plentiful that it will support the members all year round, the group may actually live most of the year in a fixed community. Under these conditions, some rights to certain sites may be established. For instance, when the Haida of the Northwest Pacific coast moved to their summer fishing grounds, the chief often had first rights to a particularly good fishing site. However, when he had caught what he needed, he was obligated to offer the site to others.

Like hunter-gatherers, most horticulturists seem to require a flexible system for allocating land resources. This may be because rapid depletion of the soil necessitates letting some of the land lie fallow for several seasons, or abandoning old garden plots completely and moving on to new areas after a few years. Such a shifting system of landholding is necessary among many horticultural groups, because land cannot be cultivated indefinitely; therefore, like most hunter-gatherers, horticulturists generally require more land than they can actually use at any one time. There is no point in claiming permanent access to land that, given the level of technology, is not permanently usable.

In horticultural societies, individuals may be allocated land to use, but they do not generally own the land in our sense of the term "ownership." For instance, a man on Truk, a central Pacific atoll, may plant a breadfruit tree, which matures in 15 years and produces for 150 years, and the tree is considered to be his. Yet he cannot sell it. He may assign the use of it to his children, but, if he does not, the tree reverts to other members of his kin group upon his death. Similarly, he may clear a plot of land for his own use and he maintains the right to use that garden as long as he works it. But the plot is under the same kind of agreement as the tree. If he stops working the land, someone else in his kin group may ask to take it over.[4]

The Siane of New Guinea have a system of clan ownership of farming land. The climate allows the land to be farmed all year, but the method of farming exhausts the land after about

[3] L. R. Hiatt, "Ownership and Use of Land among the Australian Aborigines," in Lee and DeVore, *Man the Hunter,* pp. 99–102.

[4] Ward H. Goodenough, *Property, Kin, and Community on Truk* (New Haven: Yale University Publications in Anthropology, 1951).

three harvests. The plot is then allowed to lie fallow for 15 years, so that a village needs at least ten times as much land as it uses each year. Every male clan member has a right to use plots of land, and he has the assurance that he cannot be driven from the land. The clan, on the other hand, has the assurance that, because each man is a member of the clan, no one person has the power to dispose of the jointly held wealth of the kin group.

The concept of land as an extension of the tribe—as reflecting the needs and the makeup of the tribe—is based on the belief that it is the moral right of every man to have food to eat and that it is unthinkable for one man to ignore another's hunger. Land is a right, not a privilege.

The territory of pastoral nomads far exceeds that of even the most ambitious horticultural societies. Since their wealth depends upon two elements—mobile herds and fixed pasturage and water—they must combine the adaptive potential of both the hunter-gatherers and the horticulturists. Like the hunter-gatherers they must know the potential of their territory, which can extend as much as 1,000 miles, so that they are assured a constant supply of grass and water. And like the horticulturists, after they graze an area clean they must move on and let that land lie fallow until the grass renews itself. Also like the horticulturists they depend for their subsistence upon human manipulation of a natural resource—animals as opposed to the horticulturist's land.

Grazing lands are communally held among many pastoral nomads. Although the chief may be designated "owner" of the land, his title is merely a symbolic statement that the territory is the domain of the nomadic community. Such a community may have to make two types of agreements with outside groups concerning the allocation of natural resources: agreements with other nomadic groups about the order in which the land they both graze is to be used, and agreements with settled agriculturists about rights to graze unused fields or even to clear a harvested field of the leftover stubble.

Among pastoral nomads, animals are the wealth of the people. Since a certain number of animals per family is necessary for survival, a family which drops below the minimum allowing self-sufficiency becomes a drain on the balance of the economy. If other families divide their herds to share with them, they too are likely to approach the edge of pastoral bankruptcy; therefore, pastoralists tend not to share animals. A family which loses its herd must usually drop out of the nomadic life and settle in some village until it can replenish its stock and rejoin the nomads.[5]

Among the pastoral Somali of the eastern horn of Africa, control of land resources is obtained through force. The Somali make no claim to own the land they graze. Their right to graze depends upon their force of numbers. This tenure-by-force applies also to wells which they have dug. Even though on leaving an area they may close the well, brand the cover and surround it with a thorn fence as evidence of ownership, they recognize that continued ownership depends upon power to enforce it. The Somali have no fixed, traditional route but claim the right to graze wherever they have the force to ensure that right.[6]

The early herders of the American West met some of the same difficulties that pastoralists have always met concerning land resources. There was competition over land use between cattle herders and sheep herders and between herders and agriculturists. But herders in the American West cannot be called nomads or pastoralists, for just as the discovery of land-renewal methods—manure or compost fertilizers—led to permanent settlements and continual land use by intensive agriculturists, so the employment of cowboys to move herds periodically led to permanent settlements of herders.

The continuing use of one area of land season

[5] Marshall D. Sahlins, *Tribesmen* (Englewood Cliffs, N.J.: Prentice-Hall, 1968), pp. 32–39.

[6] I. M. Lewis, *A Pastoral Democracy* (New York: Oxford University Press, 1961), pp. 47–126.

Pastoral nomads, like these Turkish herdsmen, travel over large areas of land which are generally considered the communal territory of the group. Individual families, however, usually own their animals. (Courtesy of the American Museum of Natural History.)

after season is one of the factors on which permanent possession of land is based. Under the Homestead Act of 1862, if a man cleared a 160-acre piece of land and farmed it for five years, the federal government would consider him the owner of the land. The similarity to the method by which the chief in some societies is obligated to assign a parcel of land to anyone who wished to farm it for his own needs is clear; the difference is that once the American homesteader had become the owner of his land, he could dispose of it as he wished and could sell it or give it away.

This concept of private ownership of land resources—including the right to use resources and the right to dispose of them—is common among intensive agriculturists, for whom land is relatively scarce. Once private ownership of land has become established, then the property owners use their economic, and hence political, power to pass laws which favor property owners. Thus, in the early years of the United States, only property owners could vote.

The nearly absolute control which a property owner apparently has over the use and disposal of his property is offset by the real absoluteness with which he can lose his property—generally through government action as the penalty for being unable to pay his taxes or to pay a debt or because the government decides to take it for some public purpose (usually with some compensation to the owner) under the right of eminent domain. Thus, a family which had farmed its land for 100 years could lose it irrevocably in one year, often as a result of events over which the family had no control—a national economic depression, a drought which caused a bad year, a change in climate like the one which created the Oklahoma dust bowl, or the economic stagnation following the Civil War.

Tools and Technology

Man is not the only tool user; some of the apes also devise and use tools. But all human societies have methods of tool making and traditions of tool use which are allocated within the society and passed on to the next generation. A society is restricted in its tool use by its way of living. Hunter-gatherers and pastoralists must limit their tools and artifacts to what they can comfortably carry with them. Possessions hamper their movements. Settled people can accumulate more.

The tools most needed by hunter-gatherers are weapons for the hunt, digging sticks, and receptacles for gathering and carrying. Most hunters know the bow and arrow; Andaman Islanders used them exclusively for hunting game and large fish. Australian aborigines developed two types of boomerang, a heavy one for a straight throw in killing game and a light returning one for playing games or for scaring birds into nets which had been strung between trees. The Semang of Malaya used poisoned darts and blowguns. The Congo Pygmies still trap elephants and buffalo in deadfalls and nets, and several hunters work together in devising traps for game. Of all hunter-gatherers, the Eskimos have probably the most sophisticated weapons, including the harpoon, compound bow, and ivory fish hooks; but the Eskimo also has relatively fixed settlements with more available storage space, and the dog team and sledge for transportation.[7]

Among hunter-gatherers, tools are considered to belong to the person who made them. But there is no way of gaining superiority over others through possession of tools. This is because whatever resources for tool making are available to one are available to all; every man can fashion the same weapons; every woman can make her own digging stick. In addition, the custom of sharing applies to tools as well as to food; if a member of the band asks to borrow a spear that another person is not using, that person is obligated to lend it to him. The spear, however, is still considered the personal property of the man who made it, and the man who kills an animal with it may be obligated to share the kill with the owner of the spear.

Among the Andaman Islanders, whatever a person made was his personal property. Even if others had helped him make it, it was still exclusively his. A husband had no right over his wife's property. However, gift giving was so common that possessions changed hands frequently.[8]

The !Kung Bushmen have few possessions—bows and arrows, spears, digging sticks, receptacles for carrying, and so on. According to E. M. Thomas,

> A Bushman will go to any lengths to avoid making other Bushmen jealous of him, and for this reason the few possessions that Bushmen have are constantly circling among the members of their groups. No one cares to keep a particularly good knife too long, even though he may want it desperately, because he will become the object of envy.[9]

The Bushmen have adapted a few of the objects from their natural environment for their use; for instance, ostrich eggshells are used for catching rainwater and animal stomachs are fashioned into water bags; a hollow reed with a grass filter is used for sucking water from underground sources. Knowledge of how to find scarce underground water in the desert is as much a tool in the Bushmen's society as knowledge of how to construct and use the bow and arrow. Such knowledge is shared as surely as a tangible weapon.[10]

To the Hadza the importance of the bow and arrow as a hunting weapon is superseded by its importance as a gambling stake. Every man

[7] Elman R. Service, *The Hunters* (Englewood Cliffs, N.J.: Prentice-Hall, 1966), pp. 10–11.

[8] Radcliffe-Brown, *The Andaman Islanders,* p. 41.

[9] Elizabeth Marshall Thomas, *The Harmless People* (New York: Alfred A. Knopf, 1959), p. 22.

[10] Service, *The Hunters,* p. 101.

Food Getting

In food-collecting societies, such as the !Kung Bushmen of the Kalahari Desert, division of labor is based primarily on age and sex. Men are responsible for hunting; using spears and bows and arrows as weapons, they often track game for many miles. (Courtesy of Irven DeVore.)

The mongongo nut is the most important single food in the Bushman diet. Women and children collect hundreds of mongongo nuts each day, and then pound the hard outer shell with rocks to obtain the kernel. It is not surprising that one Bushman, when asked why the group did not turn to agriculture, answered: "Why should we plant, when there are so many mongongo nuts in the world?" (Courtesy of Irven DeVore.)

Although it may appear that the hunter-gatherer way of life is difficult, it is not necessarily grueling or insecure. The Bushmen can obtain a sufficient amount of food with only a few hours' work each day; consequently, ample leisure time remains. (Courtesy of Irven DeVore.)

Horticulture is farming conducted with relatively primitive tools and methods. On the New Hebrides Islands of the southwestern Pacific, crops are cultivated with hand tools in small garden plots. (Photo by Kal Muller, Woodfin Camp and Associates.)

Intensive agriculture is primarily characterized by technological aspects that are absent in horticulture. Draft animals and the plow, for instance, are used in cultivating these fields in the countryside surrounding Yenan, China. (Photo by Marc Riboud, Magnum Photos.)

Irrigation and other water-storage techniques are also frequently employed in intensive agriculture. On the Indonesian island of Bali, terracing is used to aid in irrigating the rice fields. (Photo by Thomas Höpker, Woodfin Camp and Associates.)

In complex, industrialized societies, agriculture becomes highly mechanized. In the United States, agricultural productivity is so high that a relatively small number of farmers can supply enough food to support a population of over 200 million. (Photo by Erich Hartmann, Magnum Photos.)

Domesticated animals are also an important source of food in many societies. Pastoralism is a relatively rare form of subsistence technology; it is practiced by nomadic peoples whose livelihood is based primarily on maintaining large herds of animals. Pastoralism is especially associated with habitats, such as that of these Bakhtiari nomads of Iran, in which cultivation would be difficult. (Photo by Tony Howarth, Woodfin Camp and Associates.)

Cattle herding is the basis of subsistence among the Masai of the Sudan. Milk is a dietary staple, and fresh blood, rich in protein, is also consumed. Here a group of Masai men draw blood from the neck of an animal. (Photo by Stanley Washburn.)

An industrialized society such as our own usually derives its food supply from both intensive agriculture and herding. In many parts of the United States, for example, cattle raising is a large-scale industry. (Photo by Erich Hartmann, Magnum Photos.)

possesses metal-headed arrows for big-game hunting but is often unwilling to use them for hunting, since they are prized for gambling. During the dry season, when more time is spent gambling than hunting, an arrow may change hands hundreds of times during a day.[11]

Pastoralists, like hunter-gatherers, are somewhat limited in their possessions, for they too are nomadic. But unlike most hunter-gatherers, pastoralists can use their animals to carry some possessions. Each family owns its own tools, clothes, and perhaps a tent, as well as its own livestock. The livestock are the source of other needed articles, for the pastoralists often trade their herd products for the products of the townspeople. "Of the totality of objects contained in a nomad's home—be he a Kurd of West Iran or a Gujar in North Pakistan—only a small fraction have been produced by himself or his fellow nomads; and of the food such a family consumes in a year only a small fraction is pastoral products."[12]

Horticulturists, on the other hand, are generally more self-sufficient than pastoralists. The knife for slashing and the hoe or stick for digging are the principal farming tools, and they are usually of such simple construction that each man can make his own. What a man makes is considered his own, yet he is obligated to lend his tools to members of his family. In Truk society, a person has first use of his canoe and of his farming implements. Yet if a close kinsman needs the canoe and finds it unused, he may take it without permission. A distant kinsman or neighbor must ask permission if he wishes to borrow any tools, but the owner may not refuse him. If he were to refuse, he runs the risk of being scorned and of being refused if he were to need tools later.

The more complicated the construction of a tool the more likely it is to be made by specialists, which means that its acquisition will be made by trade or by money purchase. If a horticulturist wishes to acquire a metal hoe, he must produce a cash crop in addition to his subsistence crop. Any kinsman who helps in the production of the cash crop will be considered part-owner of the tool that is purchased, and he will

Among hunter-gatherers, tools are considered to belong to the person who made them, although the custom of sharing applies to tools as well as food. The bow and arrow used by this Andaman Islander is probably one of the few possessions he owns. (Courtesy of the American Museum of Natural History.)

[11] Woodburn, "Hadza Ecology," pp. 53–54.
[12] Fredrik Barth, "Nomadism in the Mountain and Plateau Areas of South West Asia," in *The Problems of the Arid Zone* (Paris: UNESCO, 1960), p. 345.

have a right to its use as well as a say in its disposal.

However, in industrialized societies, when the tool in question is a diesel-powered combine which requires a large amount of capital for its purchase and upkeep, the man who has supplied the capital is likely to regard it as private property and to regulate its use and its disposal as he alone desires. Thus, among intensive agriculturists, tool making is a specialized activity; those who make farming tools and machinery may not know how to use the tools and may never have seen a farm. A farmer may not have the capital to purchase the machine he needs, so he may have to borrow from a bank; he must then use the machine to produce enough surplus to pay for its cost and upkeep, as well as, ideally, for its replacement. He will therefore use it himself or allow family members or hired farmhands to use it on his crops, or he may rent it to neighboring farmers during slack periods to obtain a maximum return on his investment. He may even allow his tenants to use the machine for their own crops, but only in return for a part of their harvest.

In some intensive agricultural societies, several small farmers may form a machine cooperative in order to purchase together what they could not afford singly. In that case, each has the right to use the machine on his own land, but he may not rent, sell, or loan it without permission of the others.

Some capital equipment is too expensive for even a cooperative to afford; a government may then allocate tax money collected from all to benefit some productive group: airports to benefit airlines, roads to benefit trucking firms, dams to benefit power companies. Such resources are collectively owned by the whole society, but they are subject to strict rules, including additional payment, for use. Other man-made productive resources in industrial societies, such as factories, may be jointly owned by shareholders who purchase a portion of a corporation's assets in return for a proportionate share of its earnings.

The Organization of Work

Organization of work varies from society to society. The type of society and the methods of food getting are so interrelated that it is difficult to separate the two. Yet work organization can be seen to depend upon two distinct factors: type of tools available and type of work.

The tools available obviously affect the way work is organized: a ten-acre field can be plowed by one man on a tractor, or several men with ox and plow, or many men or women with hoes. The type of work is equally important: one Eskimo may wait for hours on the ice by a seal's breathing hole, but it takes many men cooperating to catch a whale; one Pygmy can stalk an eland alone, but it takes many men to capture an elephant. One man may build some kitchen steps, but it takes many men to build a skyscraper.

The Division of Labor. Division of labor by sex is a universal economic characteristic. Early in life, children learn the tasks that will later be assigned to them as adults. Even in our own society, where children generally do few chores, little girls may be given a chore which prepares them for "women's" work, such as drying or washing dishes or making beds; little boys might be assigned tasks which prepare them for "men's" work, such as cutting the lawn or carrying out the rubbish. Similarly, among the !Kung Bushmen, little girls learn to help their mothers in the tasks assigned to women—gathering, cooking, setting up shelters. Boys, on the other hand, are encouraged to acquire the skills they will need as men in hunting. Their play includes making toy weapons and using them to capture small animals such as lizards and insects.

In all societies, there appear to be regular patterns in the assignment of male and female roles. In general, men undertake more strenuous work and are allotted tasks that involve leaving home. Thus, hunting in most primitive societies is men's work, as is the herding of large animals, clearing fields, plowing, and so forth. Women, on the other hand, are more frequently assigned lighter tasks that can be performed in or near the home. Accordingly, women in most primitive societies do the gathering, water carrying, cooking, cleaning, and so on.[13]

The reasons for these regularities in the division of labor by sex are somewhat understandable on the basis of biological differences between men and women. Because men, on the average, are physically stronger than women, it seems likely that men would undertake the heavier chores, leaving the lighter tasks for women. In addition, because women bear children and must care for infants (who are normally breast-fed), they generally perform tasks that will not take them far from home. Men, on the other hand, are typically free to engage in work that ranges farther afield. The division of labor between men and women is probably more pronounced in societies where labor is typically more strenuous and involves leaving home—those, for example, that depend upon the hunting of large game or the herding of large animals.

Although these patterns in the division of labor by sex hold true generally, there still are other variations in the organization of work in different societies. Among the Hadza, all members of the band gather, the women for themselves and their children, the men for themselves. And among the Ainu of northern Japan, women often hunt small animals or join in the cooperative hunt of a large animal, although they are seldom allowed to hunt large game alone.[14] In horticultural societies, too, various tasks—other than agricultural work—seem to be arbitrarily assigned as men's work or women's work. Weaving is men's work in The Congo, men's and women's work in parts of India, and women's work in peasant Ireland. Milking is men's work among the Swazi but women's work among the Nuer of the Sudan.

In industrialized societies, the division of labor on the basis of sex is probably not as dependent on physical strength and mobility, as in primitive societies. Most likely, this is because, with increased mechanization, physical strength becomes less important in assigning tasks. In addition, women in the industrial world are better able to free themselves from the duties of child care and thus gain greater economic mobility. Therefore, it may be that many of the traditional distinctions between men's and women's work can be eliminated.

Age is also a universal basis for division of labor. Clearly, children cannot perform as much work as adults; usually, however, they are required to assist in the tasks assigned to adults. In many primitive societies, boys and girls contribute a great deal more in labor than do children in our own society. They help, for example, in such chores as child care, weeding, harvesting, and so forth.

In some societies, work groups are formally organized on the basis of age. Among the Nyakyusa of southeastern Africa, for example, cattle are the principal form of wealth; boys from 6 to 11 herd the cattle for their parents' village. The boys join together in herding groups to tend the cattle of their fathers and of any neighboring families which do not have a son of herding age.[15]

Kinship ties are an important basis for work organization in most primitive societies. The organization of a work party to assist a family member is characteristic of horticulturists and of the few hunter-gatherer societies that are fairly settled. In horticultural societies, a man may request help from all the members of his family in clearing a field. After cultivation, a large hoeing party might also be assembled to which all male relatives and their special friends will be invited; the invitation cannot be re-

[13] See George Peter Murdock, "Comparative Data on the Division of Labor by Sex," *Social Forces,* Vol. 15 (1937), pp. 551–553.

[14] Hitoshi Watanabe, "Subsistence and Ecology of Northern Food Gatherers with Special Reference to the Ainu," in Lee and DeVore, *Man the Hunter,* pp. 69–79.

[15] Monica Wilson, *Good Company: A Study of Nyakyusa Age Villages* (Boston: Beacon Press, 1961).

In most primitive societies, kinship ties are an important basis of work organization. Here a group of related Kikuyu women cooperate in clearing a field. (Marc and Evelyne Bernheim from Woodfin Camp and Associates.)

fused. House building is a family occupation among the Haida of the Northwest Pacific coast. Brothers may build a house, after which the stationary house posts belong to the family, but individual planks which were split and put in place belong to the man who worked them. Each brother can then take his planks to their summer grounds where smaller lean-tos are used for shelter, then back to the main house for winter. Generally, it is the duty of the organizer of the work party to provide a feast for the workers; it is his further duty to join in the work parties of those who require his help.

In pastoral societies, too, organization of work along kinship lines is widespread. Among the Somali, for example, a herding group may consist of brothers and their sons and all wives, unmarried daughters, and small children. Those members of the tribe who decided to settle on farmland apportioned within the British Protectorate did so as larger kin groups, not as individuals. As a result, the former cooperating pastoral kin groups became equally cooperative farming villages, depending upon kin affiliation for land and other forms of economic help.[16]

[16] Lewis, *A Pastoral Democracy*, pp. 107–109.

Kin groups as work organizing units are not as important in industralized countries, as they are in most of the primitive world. The economic advantage of having a large family has been reversed; children are a drain on family resources rather than a source of family wealth. Individual families may still continue to work together in performing certain tasks, but whenever large work parties are needed—in factories, businesses, government, construction—they are unlikely to be composed of people related to each other.

Specialization of Labor. In societies with relatively simple technologies there is little specialization of labor. Most of the knowledge and skills of making a living are shared and utilized by all the adult men and women. With the advance of technology and the ability of society to produce surplus food, more and more people become freed from subsistence work to specialize in some other work: canoe builder, weaver, priest, potter, artist.

A day in the life of a hunter-gatherer, for instance, would be quite varied, involving a large number of skills. A man must know how to make his own traps and weapons as well as how to use them to catch a large variety of animals. A woman must be an amateur biologist, able to identify and gather edible food. Both know how to cook, dance, and sing. Each working day is somewhat different from the others.

In contrast to hunter-gatherers, horticultural societies may have some part-time specialists. Such specialization is possible because increased productivity frees time from subsistence activities. Some people may devote special effort to perfecting a particular skill or craft—pottery making, weaving, house building, doctoring—and in return for their products or services are given food or other gifts. Among some horticultural groups, the entire village may specialize in making a particular product which they then trade to neighboring peoples.

With the development of intensive agriculture, full-time specialists—potters, weavers, blacksmiths—begin to appear. The trend toward greater specialization reaches its peak in industrialized societies, where workers develop

With the development of intensive agriculture, full-time specialists, such as potters and weavers, begin to appear. Specialization reaches a peak in industrialized societies. Here a young girl specializes in making coffee pots in a Japanese ceramics factory. (Photo by Henri Cartier-Bresson, Magnum Photos.)

skills in one small area of the economic system. The meaninglessness of much of industrialized work was depicted by Charlie Chaplin in the film *Modern Times:* when he left the factory after repeatedly tightening the same kind of bolt all day, he could not stop his arm from moving as if it were still tightening bolts.

One might expect that specialization of labor would produce more leisure time; after all, a specialist is more efficient at his work and can accomplish it more quickly. But this is probably not true. Somewhat surprisingly, people with simpler technologies and less specialization seem to have more leisure.[17] Why might this be so? Perhaps it is because peoples with simpler technologies are more limited by the potentialities of the natural environment, whereas peoples with complex technologies are less limited. For example, it would not be beneficial for hunter-gatherers to kill more animals or collect more wild plants than they can consume at a given time. First, they cannot keep or preserve them; and second, they may reduce the next season's supply of food by overhunting or overgathering this season. With complex technology, however, one can apparently produce more and more (although we are now beginning to realize that there are limits to production even in industrialized societies). Complex technology, for instance, means the development of higher yield grains, improved fertilizers, and more efficient machinery, which results in greater output. The possibility of improving one's economic position by producing more and storing the surpluses (in freezers or as money in the bank), encourages people to work harder. Consequently, leisure time probably decreases with the development of advanced technology.

Forced Labor. The work discussed thus far has all been voluntary labor—voluntary in the sense that no formal organization exists within the society to force a person to work and to punish him for not working. Social training and social pressure, however, are generally powerful enough to induce labor. Yet in both hunter-gatherer and horticultural societies, a man who can stand being the butt of jokes about laziness will still be fed. At most he will be ignored by the other members of the group. There is no reason to punish him and no way to coerce him.

More complex societies include in their systems of organization ways of forcing people to work for the authorities—be they king, chief, or state. An indirect form of forced labor is taxation. If a man's tax is 37 percent of his income (the average percentage of total earnings which the various levels of government take in the United States) then he is working about 4 months out of 12 for the state. If he decides not to pay the taxes, they will be taken from him or he can be put in prison.

Money is the form of tax payments in a commercial society. A politically complex but nonmonetary society requires other ways to pay taxes—either man-hours of labor or a certain percentage of what is produced. The corvée, a system of required labor, existed in the Inca empire in the central Andes prior to the Spanish conquest. Each commoner was assigned three plots of land to work: a temple plot, a state plot, and his own plot. The enormous stores that went into the state warehouses were used to feed the nobles, the army, the artisans, and all other state employees. If labor became overabundant, the people were still kept occupied; it is said that one ruler had a hill moved to keep some laborers busy. In addition to subsistence work for the state, each Inca commoner was liable to taxation by man-hours under a draft system. Men were subject to obligations for military service, as personal servants to the nobility, and for all public service work.[18]

Under the feudal organization of Europe, the

[17] Service, *The Hunters,* pp. 12–13.

[18] Julian H. Steward and Louis C. Faron, *Native Peoples of South America* (New York: McGraw-Hill, 1959), pp. 122–125.

landowner of an estate could require that a certain percentage of a serf's harvest or a certain number of days' work on the lord's estate be given in exchange for the lord's protection. The lord could also exact military service and personal servitude in his manor house. In addition, the serf could not leave the land he was born on. He belonged to the land; the land did not belong to him.

Tenant farming is a degenerate form of feudal farming. The popular song "I Owe my Soul to the Company Store" clearly expresses the helplessness and hopelessness of the debt-ridden tenant. In return for a house or shack and some acreage to farm, the tenant farmer owes a proportion of the harvest to the owner. The owner generally manages—through manipulation of the price for the tenant's crop, through a system of cash loans to the tenant with high interest, and through the provision of a company store through which the tenant must buy his staple goods at exorbitant prices—to keep the tenants working his farm as economically forced labor. If he tries to leave without paying these debts engineered by the owner, the owner can use the power of the state to make him pay. On the other hand, if he becomes obsolete through the introduction of mechanized farming, the owner can use the power of the state to make him leave.

The draft is a form of corvée in that a certain period of service is required, and failure to serve can be punished by a prison term or voluntary exile. Emperors of China, in order to provide defense, had the Great Wall built along the northern borders of the empire. The wall extends over 1,500 miles, and thousands of laborers were drafted to work on it.

Slavery is perhaps the most extreme form of forced work, especially in societies in which the slave has no civil rights and can be bought and sold at will. He need be given only minimum subsistence in return for his labor, and the owner can use the power of the state to keep him from leaving.

DISTRIBUTION OF GOODS AND SERVICES

Goods and services are distributed in all societies by systems which, however varied, can be classified into three general types: reciprocity, redistribution, and market exchange. The three systems often coexist in one society. For instance, when our market exchange system became shaky during the depression of the 1930s, a theater in Virginia dropped money as the medium of exchange and operated as Barter Theater, exchanging the evening's entertainment for a bag of potatoes or a slice of ham. Within a single society, however, one system of distribution usually predominates; that type of system seems to be associated with the society's food-getting technology and, more specifically, its level of productivity.

Reciprocity

The term *reciprocity* refers to giving and taking without the use of money; it ranges from pure gift giving to equalized barter to self-interested cheating. In other words, reciprocity may take three forms: generalized reciprocity, balanced reciprocity, and negative reciprocity. The expectation in reciprocity (which may or may not be conscious) is that what one gives is eventually returned, although not necessarily right away or by the same person or involving the same object or service originally given.

Generalized reciprocity is gift giving without any immediate return or conscious thought of one. A distribution system built around generalized reciprocity is like the indirect interdependencies in the world of nature. Each thing in nature provides something without expecting an equal or immediate return. Plants provide oxygen; animals provide carbon dioxide. An oak tree provides free room and board for a squirrel; the squirrel helps establish a few oak offspring by burying some acorns and promptly forgetting where. Berry bushes manufacture prized food for birds; birds help propagate more berry bushes by depositing undigested seeds throughout the area. In the end, it all evens out.

Generalized reciprocity, then, is that form of reciprocity in which the distribution of goods and services evens out in the long run. The hunter who succeeds today gives away much of his catch to other members of the community, with the sure knowledge that he will not succeed every day, but that some other hunter will share with him, will reciprocate, tomorrow.

Generalized reciprocity sustains the family in all societies. Parents give food to children because they want to, not because the child may reciprocate years later. Of course, it is usually the case that someone—often the child who has grown up—will feed the parents when they are too old to make their own living. In this sense, all societies have some kind of generalized reciprocity. In our own society, the child who refuses to reciprocate, to support his parents in their old age, is sometimes called hard-hearted, but there is no legal obligation on the child's part to care for his aged parents.

The !Kung Bushmen call "far-hearted" anyone who does not give gifts, and who does not reciprocate when given gifts. The practice of giving is not evidence of altruism but is entrenched in the Bushmen's awareness of social interdependence. The !Kung remember quite well the gift-giving activities of everyone else in their own and other bands and express their approval or disapproval openly. The necessity to reduce tensions, to avoid jealousy and anger, to keep all social relations peaceful, not only within their own band but between all !Kung bands, creates continuing cross-currents of obligation to friendship that are maintained, renewed, or established through the generalized reciprocity of gift giving. Two examples, one of meat sharing and the other involving the sharing of a gift from an ethnographer, suggest how generalized reciprocity evens things out among the !Kung.

Reciprocity is the predominant mode of economic distribution in most hunter-gatherer societies. The sharing of food among the !Kung Bushmen, for example, results in a generalized reciprocity, since what people give and receive evens out in the long run. (Courtesy of Irven DeVore.)

Lorna Marshall recounts the division of an eland which was brought in when five bands and several visitors were camping together, over 100 people in all. The owner of the arrow which had first penetrated the eland was by custom the owner of the meat. He first distributed the forequarters to the other two hunters who had aided in the kill. After that the distribution was dependent generally upon kinship, as each owner of meat shared with his wives' parents, his wives, children, parents, siblings, and they in turn shared with their kinsmen; 63 gifts of raw meat were recorded, after which further sharing of raw and cooked meat was begun. Since each large animal is distributed in the same way, the sharing of such food over the years results in a generalized reciprocity which evens out what people receive. Kinship seems to determine who participates in the sharing of food; maintaining peaceful relations and friendship are the motivations behind other gift giving.

It is undesirable among the !Kung for some people to possess something valuable, for that would create jealousy, or perhaps even conflict. As an example, when Marshall left the band which had sponsored her in 1951, she gave a present of enough cowrie shells to make a necklace, one large shell and 20 small ones, to each woman in the band. When she returned in 1952, there were no cowrie-shell necklaces and hardly a single shell in the band, but the individual cowrie shells appeared by ones and twos in the ornaments of the people of neighboring bands.[19]

Balanced reciprocity is more explicit and short-term in its expectations of return than generalized reciprocity—in fact, it involves a straightforward, immediate or limited-time trade. Even though a Bushman may well have his heart set on a friend's cooking pot when he gives his friend a spear and three arrows and may even ask for the pot after a few months have passed and the friend has not reciprocated, the exchange is still marked as gift giving, and the bond of friendship established by the gifts remains more important than the gifts themselves. In balanced reciprocity, the exchange is often motivated by desire or need for the objects, and the exchange is impersonal.

The Bushmen, for instance, do not trade with other Bushmen, but they do trade with the Bantu. Although the Bantu usually have the advantage, the Bushmen can reach satisfactory trades with the Tswana Bantu: a gemsbok hide for a pile of tobacco; five strings of beads which the Bushmen make from ostrich eggshells for a spear; three small skins for a good-sized knife.[20]

Balanced reciprocity covers not only goods but actions. The work parties of the Kpelle constitute an example of balanced reciprocity since equal labor is expected in return and the date of the return work party is generally fixed rather closely as required by the needs of planting and harvest. A cooperative work party, or *kuu,* may contain from 6 to 40 persons, generally either related somehow to the leader or friends of one of the members. Each farmer rewards their hard day's work by providing a feast and sometimes rhythmic music to work by, so that in reality two kinds of reciprocity coexist: the rather unequal return of food for a day's work, which will all even out in the long run, and the work party's equalized work on each member's farm which is balanced within a short term.[21]

Balanced reciprocity can be seen in action in much of our Christmas gift giving. Two friends or relatives will try to exchange presents of fairly equal value, based on calculations of what last year's gifts cost. If a person receives a one-dollar present when he expects a twenty-five-dollar present, he will be hurt, perhaps angry. On the other hand, if he receives a five-hundred-dollar present when he expects a twenty-five-dollar present, he may well be dismayed, even suspicious. If he receives a magazine subscription indicative that his friend no longer bothers

[19] Lorna Marshall, "Sharing, Talking and Giving: Relief of Social Tensions among !Kung Bushmen," *Africa,* Vol. 31 (1961), pp. 239–241.

[20] Marshall, "Sharing, Talking and Giving," p. 242.

[21] James L. Gibbs, Jr., "The Kpelle of Liberia," in *Peoples of Africa* (New York: Holt, Rinehart and Winston, 1965), p. 223.

to select a gift just for him, he will no doubt balance off this fading friendship by a return subscription of equal value.

Negative reciprocity is an attempt to take advantage of another for one's self-interest. For instance a !Kung Bushman related to Marshall that he had been forced by a Herero to trade the shirt and pants she had given him as a parting gift for a small enamel pan and a little cup.[22] Self-interest extends beyond uneven trade to raiding and other forms of theft. It is the basis of the "something for nothing" attitude of the gambler, the motivation of the con man who sells the Brooklyn Bridge to a stranger in town, the reality behind the phrase *caveat emptor*—let the buyer beware.

According to Sahlins, the three kinds of reciprocity—generalized, balanced, and negative—constitute a continuum of exchange in primitive societies associated with kinship distance. Generalized reciprocity is the rule for family members and close kinsmen. Balanced reciprocity is generally practiced among equals who are not closely related. A tribesman who would consider it demeaning to trade with his own family will trade with neighboring tribes; the desire to satisfy both parties is the desire to maintain peaceful relations between two groups. Negative reciprocity is practiced against strangers and enemies.[23]

Reciprocal Exchange Relations and Disposing of Surplus Goods. Reciprocity as a means of distributing goods and services cannot be isolated as a purely "economic" act; gift giving and sharing of food are always bound up in social relations. However, some kinds of exchange provide other benefits, among them the means for getting rid of unneeded and unstorable surpluses.

Even generalized reciprocity among hunter-gatherers has the advantage, in addition to strengthening social relations, of distributing highly spoilable food before it becomes uneatable. For instance, among the Ngatatjara aborigines of Australia, small game such as rabbit need not be shared but will be eaten by the hunter and his family. Only large game, principally emu and kangaroo, must be divided among various classes of kin.[24] When a surplus occurs, however, which either cannot be consumed or otherwise used, a people must decide how to get rid of it. Trade with other groups is an obvious solution. Through trade, a society can dispose of those goods which they have in great abundance and obtain those goods which are scarce in their own territory. Since trade transactions between neighboring people may be crucial to survival, it is important to maintain good relations. Various societies have developed methods of peaceful exchange.

The Semang, jungle hunter-gatherers of the Malay Peninsula, have engaged in a "silent trade" with the settled Malay agriculturists. In the belief that no personal relations at all are good relations, the Semang leave their surplus jungle products at an agreed-upon place near a village and return later to take whatever has been left by the villagers, usually salt, beads, or a metal tool.[25]

The Trobriand Islanders have worked out an elaborate scheme for the trade of food and other items, with the people of neighboring islands. Such trade is essential, for some of the islands are small and rocky and cannot produce enough food to sustain the inhabitants; as a result, they specialize instead in canoe building, pottery, and so on. Other islands produce far more yams, taro, and pigs than they need, yet the trade of such necessary items is carefully hidden beneath the panoply of the *Kula* ring, a ceremonial exchange of valued shell ornaments.

[22] Marshall, "Sharing, Talking and Giving," p. 242.

[23] Marshall D. Sahlins, "On the Sociology of Primitive Exchange," *The Relevance of Models for Social Anthropology,* Association of Social Anthropologists, Monograph #1 (New York: Praeger, 1965), pp. 149–158.

[24] Richard A. Gould, *Yiwara: Foragers of the Australian Desert* (New York: Scribner's, 1969), pp. 16–19.

[25] Service, *The Hunters,* p. 107.

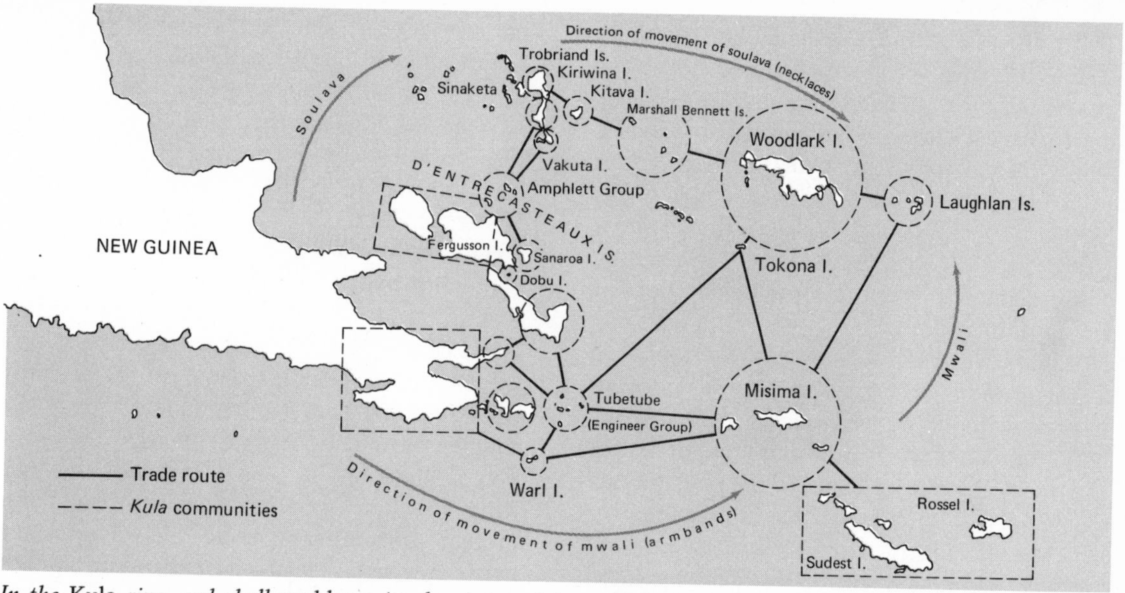

In the Kula *ring, red shell necklaces* (soulava) *travel in a clockwise direction, while white shell armbands* (mwali) *travel in a counterclockwise direction. The solid lines show the overseas trade routes. The dotted circles identify the* Kula *communities, and the dotted squares show the areas indirectly affected by the* Kula.

Two kinds of ornaments are involved: white shell armbands *(mwali)* which travel around the circle of islands in a counterclockwise direction, and red shell necklaces *(soulava)* which travel in a clockwise direction. The possession of one or more of these ornaments allows a man to organize an expedition to one of his trading partners on another island. An expedition takes up to six months to prepare, including the repair of canoes and the collection of items of trade. The high point of an expedition is the ceremonial giving of the valued *Kula* ornaments. Each member of the expedition receives a shell ornament from his trade partner and remains for two or three days as guest of his partner. That is when the real trading goes on. Some of the exchange takes the form of gift giving between trading partners; there is also barter between expedition members and others on the island. By the time the visitors leave, they have accomplished a year's trading without seeming to. (One is reminded of the recent ceremonial exchange of musk oxen and pandas, valued because rare, yet practically useless, between the United States and China; immediately thereafter the real trade of goods began between the two countries.)

Trading within the *Kula* ring is based on mutual trust. Trade partnerships are lifelong and ensure hospitality and aid as well as trade. A commoner will have a few partners to the south and a few to the north; an old chief may have as many as 100 in each direction. Maintaining the *Kula* ring achieves several advantages for the Trobriand Islanders. First, surplus goods are traded with ease and enjoyment, the expedition taking on the flavor of adventure rather than business. Second, the traditions of the islands remain alive. Much myth, romance, ritual, and history are linked with the circulating ornaments, especially the larger, finer pieces, which are well known and recognized as heirlooms.

Third, the establishment of trade partnerships seems to reduce social tensions and hostilities among the various island communities. Fourth, the *Kula* ring allows wide ownership of valuables. Instead of being able to possess one valued object permanently, a man is able in his lifetime to possess many valued things for a year or so, each object on its receipt awakening enthusiasm in a way that one lifelong possession could not do.[26]

Many Melanesian societies have established a system of dispensing surplus goods, especially pigs, without trade. Pigs are the principal manifestation of wealth and also a major source of protein in the people's diet. The ostentatious display of wealth is one of the motivations behind the holding of a pig feast in which 50, 100, or even, as reported on one occasion, 2,000 pigs are slaughtered as evidence of social status.[27]

Vayda, Leeds, and Smith have suggested that these enormous pig feasts, though apparently wasteful, are just one of the outcomes (and relatively infrequent ones at that) of a complex of cultural practices that are highly advantageous. As noted by economists, a society cannot maintain its population at a level which can be supported by the food available during years of bumper crops, nor even by the average expected production; it must limit its population to the food supply of its years of minimum production, even if these years occur only once in a generation. In addition the society must overplant each year in anticipation of a drought which would sharply limit production; but this overplanting results in overproduction during average and exceptionally good years. The Melanesians provide for just that contingency by overplanting yams and taro for their three harvests a year. Since these root crops do not keep well over long periods, the surplus is fed to pigs, which become, in effect, food-storing repositories. Pigs are then available for needed food during lean years as well as for the usual feasts during any year.

The state of too much of a good thing results when several years of good crops cause the pig population to increase to menacing proportions; that is, menacing to the yam and taro patches. One of these massive feasts is then held which, whatever its ostensible reason, results in sharply delimiting the pig population and keeping the country from being overrun by pigs. This solution of "banking" surplus food results in equalizing the food consumption, especially the protein consumption, of all the villages that participate in the feasts over the years and in assuring food for lean years as well as good years.[28]

Reciprocal Exchange as a Leveling Device. The accumulation of wealth in the hands of one man or one family is often viewed with alarm, as among the Swazi of South Africa, who claim that any man who owns too many cattle must be using witchcraft to obtain them. All of his cattle might then be taken away from him and slaughtered to provide a feast for the people. In order to prevent this confiscation, a rich man often lends out his cattle to people who have only a few so that they are the practical owners while he remains the true but nonadvantaged owner. The effect, then, is to distribute surpluses of cattle more evenly among the people.

Some societies have developed other reciprocal exchange practices, even more subtle than the Swazi accusation of witchcraft, that

[26] Bronislaw Malinowski, "*Kula:* The Circulating Exchange of Valuables in the Archipelagoes of Eastern New Guinea," *Man,* No. 2 (1920), pp. 97–105.

[27] Richard C. Thurnwald, "Pigs and Currency in Buin: Observations about Primitive Standards of Value and Economics," *Oceania,* Vol. 5 (1934), pp. 119–141.

[28] Andrew P. Vayda, Anthony Leeds, and David B. Smith, "The Place of Pigs in Melanesian Subsistence," in Viola E. Garfield, ed., Proceedings of the 1961 Annual Spring Meeting of the American Ethnological Society, Symposium: *Patterns of Land Utilization and Other Papers,* pp. 69–74.

Among the Northwest Pacific coast Indians the potlatch served as a means of both disposing of surplus food and leveling wealth. Here Indians of British Columbia display the objects to be given away at a potlatch. (Courtesy of the American Museum of Natural History.)

apparently prevent the accumulation of wealth by a few people. The Northwest Pacific coast Indians have a mechanism that serves both as a way of disposing of surplus food and as a means of leveling wealth. Any kin group or village may have an abundance of food (principally salmon and other kinds of fish) during some seasons. Although they have techniques for preserving such surpluses for a number of months, which allow them to store food for the winter months, a man also had the option of taking surplus food to his in-laws in another village where that food might be scarce; in return he would receive a gift of wealth. Later, when his in-laws brought surplus food to him, he would return the gift of wealth. Thus, exchange between in-laws of surplus foods for objects of value made it theoretically possible for a man to store his surplus indefinitely. If, through these exchanges and similar exchanges with nonkin, he accumulated more wealth than he could use, he could convert the wealth into prestige by giving a *potlatch,* a feast in which large quantities of food were consumed and great numbers of other objects given away. Sometime later, the chiefs or other men who had been given gifts at the potlatch would reciprocate by mounting their own potlatches. When contact with European diseases brought about a huge decrease in population, and fur trade introduced by the Europeans made the accumulation of wealth even easier, the Northwest Pacific coast Indians intensified their surplus-controlling potlatches in a frantic but vain effort to maintain the traditional system by which wealth was distributed and leveled. Finally, after a period during which the potlatches became so extravagant that enormous quantities of wealth were being destroyed at the feasts, the Canadian authorities prohibited potlatching.[29]

The device of "storing" surpluses of food by trading them for nonperishable items of value was adopted by the Pomo Indians of central California. A village which had an overabundance of fish or acorns might invite another village to a trade feast. In return for surplus fish or acorns, the guests would give the host village a certain number of beads. Before the journey, the chief of the guest village would procure from each man as many strings of beads as possible, and, following a few days of feasting at the host village, would trade the beads for the supply of surplus fish or acorns. Each member of the visiting village would be given an equal share of the food no matter how many beads he had contributed. But the members of a village would not be invited to a feast unless they brought beads to trade, and they could not obtain beads unless they had given food away themselves sometime in the past. Thus, giving away food and receiving beads in return served as a means of storing "social credit" for times of scarcity. At a later date, when food was scarce in the former host village, the population could use the beads they had acquired to obtain food from another village which had a surplus. The trade feasts, then, had the effect of equalizing the consumption of food not only within a village but over a fairly widespread area.[30]

A dislike, even fear, of the accumulation of wealth is apparent from these several examples. It seems that many societies in the primitive or noncommercial world maintained their more or less egalitarian social systems by preventing or minimizing unequal accumulation of wealth. However, reciprocal exchange is only one of the leveling devices which such societies may adopt.

Redistribution

Redistribution is the accumulation of goods by a particular person or in a particular place for the purpose of subsequent distribution. The federal government in the United States, for example, collects a portion of national income and subsequently distributes it as our public officials deem best to construct schools, highways, and hospitals, to aid the poor, disabled, and elderly, to compensate government officials and other personnel for their work.

Although redistribution is found in all societies, it becomes an important mechanism of distribution only in societies with political hierarchies—that is, with chiefs or other specialized officials and agencies. In all societies, there is some redistribution, at least within the family. Members of the family pool their labor or products or income for the common good, and food as well as other items are redistributed to all family members regardless of the amount each has contributed. But beyond the family there is little or no redistribution in many societies. Particularly in hunter-gatherer and horticultural societies, which generally lack specialized political officials, the major mechanism of distribution is reciprocity, not redistribution. It

[29] Wayne Suttles, "Coping with Abundance: Subsistence on the Northwest Coast," in Lee and DeVore, *Man the Hunter,* pp. 64–67.

[30] Andrew P. Vayda, "Pomo Trade Feasts," in George Dalton, ed., *Tribal and Peasant Economies* (Garden City, N.Y.: Natural History Press, 1967), pp. 494–500.

seems, then, that redistribution on a territorial basis emerges when there is a political apparatus to coordinate centralized collection and distribution.

An account of redistribution is given of eighteenth-century Creek Indians:

> [When] all the grain is ripe, the whole town again assembles, and every man carries off the fruits of his labour, from the part [of the town field] first allotted to him, which he deposits in his own granary. . . . But previous to their carrying off their crops from the field, there is a large crib or granary, erected in the plantation, which is called the King's crib; and to this each family carries and deposits a certain quantity, according to his ability or inclination, or none at all if he so chooses, this in appearance seems a tribute or revenue to the mico [chief], but in fact is designed for another purpose, i.e., that of a public treasury, supplied by a few and voluntary contributions, and to which every citizen has the right of free and equal access, when his own private stores are consumed, to serve as a surplus to fly to for succour, to assist neighboring towns whose crops have failed, accommodate strangers, or travellers, afford provisions or supplies, when they go forth on hostile expeditions, and for all other exigencies of the state; and this treasure is at the disposal of the King or mico; which is surely a royal attribute to have an exclusive right and ability in a community to distribute comfort and blessings to the necessitous.[31]

The account makes redistribution sound like an ideal arrangement in which the whole community benefits from its own efforts. But variations in the pressure of the people upon the chief, in the power of the chief, in the number of specialists the chief supports before he begins to redistribute the remainder, these factors all affect how fairly the chief may redistribute. And in many cases, it was the chief who apparently was the most "unfairly" treated. Identifying the chief in some American Indian villages became something of a joke among early ethnographers who reported that they looked about for the poorest man; apparently the demands of redistribution were so great that the chief gave away everything he could accumulate and was left with prestige alone.

Not so with all societies that practice redistribution. In the African state of Bunyoro in western Uganda, for example, the King (called the *Mukama*) retained much of the wealth for himself and his close kinsmen. The *Mukama* had the authority to grant the use of land and all other natural resources to his subordinate chiefs, and they in turn to the common people. In return, everyone was required to give to the *Mukama* large quantities of food, crafts, and even labor services. The *Mukama* then redistributed these goods and services, in theory at least, to all the people. The *Mukama* was praised with names that emphasized his generosity: *Agutamba* (he who relieves distress) and *Mwebingwa* (he to whom the people run for help). But it is clear that much of what the king redistributed did not find its way back to the common people who produced the bulk of the goods. Instead, the wealth was largely distributed according to rank within the state. A large part was bestowed on the *Mukama*'s own close kinsmen, who collectively comprised an aristocratic class. Part was also given to members of the royal household who personally attended the king, and another part allotted as a mark of royal favor to those who had performed services for the *Mukama,* particularly military services.[32]

Redistribution systems vary, then, from relative equality of all members of a community to gross inequality. At one extreme, illustrated by the Buin of Melanesia, "The chief is housed, dressed, and fed exactly like his bondsman. . . . The stratification, therefore, can only be discovered by close observation of the behaviour and customs, and by obtaining confidential

[31] William Bartram, *The Travels of William Bartram,* ed. Francis Harper (New Haven: Yale University Press, 1958), p. 326.

[32] John Beattie, *Bunyoro: An African Kingdom* (New York: Holt, Rinehart and Winston, 1960).

information."[33] Even though the chief owns most of the pigs, everyone shares equally in the consumption of the wealth. At the other extreme, a wealthy Indian landowner may live in luxury while the lower castes, dependent upon him for redistribution, live in poverty.

Market Exchange

The development of market exchange (commercial or monetary exchange) probably occurs when food-getting technology becomes so efficient that surpluses of food are regularly produced. When the surplus food supply can be counted on to be more or less dependable, more efficient methods of disposing of the surplus appear to be favored, methods that are more efficient than Melanesian pig feasts, Northwest Pacific coast potlatches, and Pomo trade feasts. Market or commercial exchange is the third method of distributing goods and services within a population and between populations. As an increased food supply becomes guaranteed, more and more people are released from subsistence activities to specialize in various activities—crafts, religion, warfare, and so on. No doubt direct barter of food for services or food for artifacts was employed fairly early (as it still is in relatively unproductive economies). But barter, as a personal transaction between two people or groups, succeeds most easily when the two know each other and there is sufficient mutual trust to arrive at a fair exchange. Moreover, barter or balanced reciprocity can be relied upon as a method of distributing surplus goods and services only if you are always assured of finding someone who has an excess of what you want to obtain, and a shortage of what you want to give away. It should be expected, then, that when many different craft and labor specialists want to trade what they have a surplus of, it might be difficult and time-consuming, if not completely hopeless, to try to find a suitable barter partner. Thus, it seems that market or commercial exchange (involving what we call "money"—for which nearly all goods and services can be exchanged) emerges when an economy develops to the point that surplus food is regularly produced by those engaged in food production, the population has accordingly become fairly dense (and includes many people whom one does not know), and there are many craft and labor specialists who need (as do the food producers) what others have to offer.

In many societies, however, money is not the all-purpose medium of exchange we take for granted in our own society. For many people, whose level of food production per capita is not sufficient to support a large population of non-producers of food, there is often what is called "special-purpose money"—objects of value for which only some goods and services can be exchanged on the spot or through a balanced reciprocity. In some parts of Melanesia, pigs are assigned value in terms of "shell money"—lengths of shells strung together in units each roughly as long as the distance covered by a man's outstretched arms; according to its size, a pig will be assigned a value in tens of such units up to 100.[34] But such shell money cannot be exchanged for all the goods or services that one might need. A Northwest Pacific coast Indian could exchange food (but not most other goods or services) for a "gift of wealth" (such as blankets); the gift was his receipt which entitled him later to an equal amount of food (but little else). The Pomo Indians of California used strings of beads in the same way.

Whether these objects should actually be called "money" is a matter of some dispute among anthropologists. Some define money according to the functions and characteristics of the general-purpose money used in our own and other complex societies. According to this

[33] Thurnwald, "Pigs and Currency in Buin," p. 125.

[34] Thurnwald, "Pigs and Currency in Buin," p. 122.

definition, money performs the basic functions of serving as a medium of exchange, a standard of value, and a store of wealth. In addition, money is said to be characterized by certain general features: it is nonperishable; it is transportable; and it is divisible, so that transactions can be made when the goods being purchased differ in value. If this definition is used as the criterion of "true money," then the objects used in limited or special-purpose exchange in other societies are not money. Other anthropologists, however, contend that an item used in exchange need not serve all the functions and have all the characteristics associated with money in an industrialized society in order to be considered "money."

George Dalton has suggested that special- and general-purpose money can be distinguished in terms of the kinds of distribution system in which they operate—particularly marketless systems, those with peripheral markets only, and those with money-dominated, peasant markets.

In *marketless societies,* reciprocity (mostly generalized) and some redistribution are the major forms of distribution. Special-purpose money—goats, cattle, spears, pig tusks, shells—may occasionally be used but only for particular purposes such as funeral and marriage gifts.

Peripheral market societies, the Trobriand Islands, for instance, generally follow the practices of marketless societies; but in addition they have established marketplace sites at which some products are traded, either with special-purpose money or by barter (balanced reciprocity). These markets are called "peripheral" because they account for only a small part of the society's output of goods and because land and labor are never traded there. Two kinds of special-purpose shell money—Dap and Kö—are used by the Rossel Islanders. Dap shells are divided into 22 main values, Kö into 16 values. Generally, payments are made in some combination of Dap and Kö. Each value of Dap is designated for a special kind of purchase such as a basket. The five most valued classes are used only on important occasions of generalized and balanced reciprocity: for instance, one shell is part of the bridewealth gift to the bride's kin; one is exchanged for pigs when a chief sponsors a pig feast. The special-purchase money is a symbol of the transaction, but the transaction is a socially determined one. For example, a man cannot "buy" a wife with the bridewealth Dap shell; the marriage is arranged by the two families, and the proper Dap shell merely formalized the agreement.[35]

Societies with *money-dominated, peasant markets* include land and labor among the goods and services which can be bought or sold. Peasants, however, although depending upon the market to trade certain goods and services, usually produce by themselves most of what they need to live. In this sense peasants differ from farmers in our own society who rely upon the marketplace to exchange their crops for almost all the goods and services they need.

Most people in peasant societies use general-purpose money as a means of assigning relative value to the goods and services they trade. General-purpose money is a universally accepted medium of exchange which is used for commercial transactions—buying and selling—as well as for noncommercial transactions—paying taxes or fines, personal gifts, giving to religious and other charities. General-purpose money provides a way of "condensing" wealth, to use Malinowski's term: pesos are easier to carry around than a cartload of potatoes; a checkbook is handier than a herd of cattle. In addition, general-purpose money acts also as a store of wealth.[36]

[35] W. E. Armstrong, "Rossell Island Money: A Unique Monetary System," *The Economic Journal,* Vol. 34 (September 1924), pp. 423–429.

[36] George Dalton, "Primitive Money," *American Anthropologist,* Vol. 67 (1965), pp. 44–65.

In market distribution, exchange of goods and services involves the use of money. In this marketplace in Algeria, a wide range of products are traded. (Photo by Marc Riboud, © 1970 Magnum Photos.)

The market town of Pátzcuaro in Mexico illustrates the dependence of the people of the surrounding countryside on the market and the ability of the market to support large numbers of middlemen and other specialists. "Support," however, refers only to a minimum level since the market area exists in an economy of what Kaplan calls "shared poverty." The population of the market town is 12,000; of the surrounding area, 14,000; and of the lake district several miles around, 70,000. Most of the rural areas are agricultural, with increasing populations but no increase in land. Some villages have concentrated on their own craft specialties, which reflect a traditional division of labor among several communities, so that each village practices a monopoly over a particular craft, such as pottery, basketry, weaving, wood carving, and so on. The principal market is held once a week, smaller markets on three other days; subsidiary markets are held in surrounding villages. About 75 percent of the market produce is food, about 20 percent locally produced artifacts, about 5 percent imported manufactured goods. The market is the only supplier of food for the town dwellers, and the only source of cash income for the rural inhabitants. Prices are flexible and subject to bargaining; they do not include labor as a price factor, for all producers are households and labor is therefore "free." The large number of people who are supported by the agricultural efforts of the rural inhabitants, plus the lack of goods for export which might bring new money into the area, serve to keep the population dependent upon the market as it is organized.[37]

Peasant communities often retain leveling mechanisms to limit the accumulation of wealth. One such mechanism in the regional market area of Amatenango in Guatemala is the honorary post of *alférez*. Four young men from rich families must take the posts each year; their families must then spend large amounts feasting local groups. The system serves to redistribute some wealth and also to support the market system by requiring purchases of food and of local crafts—special large cooking pots, benches, and other goods.[38]

In addition to societies with money-dominated, peasant markets, market exchange also occurs in the industrialized societies of the modern world. In these societies, commercial exchange in markets and elsewhere dominates the economy, prices and wages being regulated, or at least significantly affected, by the forces of supply and demand. In a modern industrial economy, which may involve international as well as national "markets" (not necessarily actual marketplaces but opportunities and occasions for commercial exchange), almost everything has a price, stated in the same money terms—natural resources, labor, goods, services, prestige items, religious and ceremonial items. Reciprocity is reserved for family members and friends or is hidden behind the scenes in business transactions. Redistribution, however, is an important mechanism of distribution and is practiced in the form of a taxation and the use of public revenue for transfer payments and other benefits to low-income families—welfare, social security, health care programs, and so on. But the market or commercial exchange is the major way goods and services are distributed.

[37] David Kaplan, "The Mexican Marketplace Then and Now," in June Helm, ed., Proceedings of the 1965 Annual Spring Meeting of the American Ethnological Society, *Essays in Economic Anthropology,* pp. 86–92.
[38] Manning Nash, *Primitive and Peasant Economic Systems* (San Francisco: Chandler, 1966), p. 79.

SUMMARY

1. All societies have economic systems regardless of whether or not they use money. All societies have customs for regulating access to natural resources, for transforming those resources through labor into necessities and other desired items, and for distributing (and perhaps exchanging) goods and services.
2. Regulation of access to natural resources is a basic factor in all economic systems. In our own society, portions of land are owned by individuals, groups, or government agencies; our right of ownership includes the right to use land as well as the right to dispose of it. In contrast, hunter-gatherers generally own land com-

munally. Among horticulturists land is frequently held in common by a kin group, but the right to use the land is allocated to individual families. Pastoral nomads range over large tracts of land which are generally considered the communal territory of the group; animals, however, are considered family property and are not usually shared.

3. The allocation of tools and technology is also part of any economic system. Hunter-gatherers and pastoralists must limit their tools and artifacts to what they can carry with them. Settled people can accumulate more. Hunter-gatherers and horticulturists tend to share tools such as weapons, knives, digging sticks, hoes, and so forth, while nomads tend to keep possessions within the family. Among intensive agriculturists, tool making is a specialized activity. Owners tend to regard tools as private property, unless the capital required for their purchase is greater than any single person can afford; in such a case tools and other facilities may be bought and used collectively, or, in some cases, provided by government agencies.

4. Organization of labor varies from society to society according to different criteria. Division of labor by sex is nearly universal. Some jobs are apportioned according to biological differences based on sex; usually males hunt and herd large animals while women care for children, cook, gather, and so forth. In many primitive societies, large jobs, such as house building and field clearing, are accomplished through the cooperative efforts of a kinship group. In industrialized societies cooperation of kin groups is not as prevalent as in primitive societies. Generally, the more technically advanced a society is, the more surplus food is produced, freeing members to engage in specialized work. The trend toward increasing specialization reaches a peak in industrialized society with its assembly-line work. In some societies, work may be forced rather than voluntary. Taxation, the feudal system, tenant farming, the military draft, and slavery are all forms of forced labor.

5. Goods and services are distributed in all societies by systems which can be classified into three types: reciprocity, redistribution, and market exchange. *Reciprocity* refers to giving and taking without the use of money and may take three forms: generalized reciprocity, balanced reciprocity, and negative reciprocity. Generalized reciprocity is gift giving without expectation of immediate return. Members of a society freely give goods and services to one another, trusting that all will come out even in the end. In balanced reciprocity individuals exchange goods and services whose values they calculate as roughly equal. In contrast to generalized reciprocity, the value of the goods or services exchanged is more important than the bond of friendship developed by the exchange. Negative reciprocity is generally practiced with strangers or enemies. One individual attempts to cheat the other or force him to exchange something valuable for something worth less.

6. *Redistribution* refers to the accumulation of goods by a particular person or in a particular place for the purpose of subsequent redistribution. Redistribution is found in all societies, but it becomes an important mechanism of distribution only in societies with political hierarchies. Redistribution systems may be equal or unequal. Either the redistributor (i.e., chief) may be driven to poverty by trying to provide for the needs of his people, or he may use collected goods for personal aggrandizement at the expense of the people.

7. *Market exchange* develops when food-getting technology becomes so efficient that surpluses of food are regularly pro-

duced. Market exchange is distinguished from reciprocity in that an all-purpose medium of exchange (money) is used to make transactions. Markets operate efficiently in areas of relatively dense population where people are not always personally acquainted; this is because trust and friendship is not an important factor in market exchange. Market exchange is common among peasant communities and, on a much vaster scale, in our own industrialized society.

SUGGESTED READINGS

Belshaw, C. S.: *Traditional Exchange and Modern Markets* (Englewood Cliffs, N.J.: Prentice-Hall, 1965).
An attempt to explore the relationship of the economic system to the social and political organization, with particular attention paid to problems of growth and modernization. The topics discussed include the economy and society, gift exchange and reciprocity, monetized peasant marketing, and conditions of modernization in a market economy.

Bohannan, P., and G. Dalton (Eds.): *Markets in Africa* (Evanston, Ill.: Northwestern University Press, 1962).
A collection of articles on the development and effects of markets in eight African societies.

Dalton, G. (Ed.): *Tribal and Peasant Economies: Readings in Economic Anthropology* (Garden City, N.Y.: Natural History Press, 1967).
A collection of papers on tribal and peasant economies. The selection is intended to demonstrate the theoretical split between the "substantivists" and the "formalists"—those who believe that economic theory cannot be applied to the study of primitive societies versus those who believe it can.

Firth, R. (Ed.): *Themes in Economic Anthropology* (New York: Tavistock, 1967).
This collection of ten essays includes six theoretical papers dealing with the relevance of economic concepts and models to the study of economic anthropology and four case studies based on fieldwork.

LeClair, E. E., Jr., and H. D. Schneider (Eds.): *Economic Anthropology: Readings in Theory and Analysis* (New York: Holt, Rinehart and Winston, 1968).
A compilation outlining the main issues of the substantivist/formalist controversy, focusing on methodological as well as controversial issues. The underlying theme is that the economic system reflects diverse aspects of the society's culture.

Nash, M.: *Primitive and Peasant Economic Systems* (San Francisco: Chandler, 1966).
A concise work which summarizes the facts and conflicting theoretical positions of economic anthropology. The author briefly discusses such topics as the meaning and scope of economic anthropology; the general character of primitive and peasant economies; nonmonetary economic systems; and the effects of modernization on primitive and peasant economies.

Sahlins, M. D.: "On the Sociology of Primitive Exchange," in M. Banton (Ed.), *The Relevance of Models for Social Anthropology* (New York: Praeger, 1965).
Sahlins's paper discusses the concept of reciprocity, including generalized, balanced, and negative reciprocity. He discusses the influence of balanced exchange on the cultures of primitive societies in their relations with more advanced societies.

Sahlins, M. D.: *Tribesmen* (Englewood Cliffs, N.J.: Prentice-Hall, 1968).
Chapter 3, dealing with the ecology and subsistence economies of tribesmen, is of particular interest in the context of economic anthropology.

Service, E. R.: *The Hunters* (Englewood Cliffs, N.J.: Prentice-Hall, 1966).
A discussion of hunter-gatherer societies based upon data from the most extensively documented hunting and gathering groups.

Wolf, E. R.: *Peasants* (Englewood Cliffs, N.J.: Prentice-Hall, 1966).
A theoretical basis for the study of peasant societies. Primary emphasis is on the definition of peasants in terms of economic factors and the continual effort required by such groups to balance limited resources against constantly competing demands, both biological and social.

14

Social Stratification

A long-enduring value in American society is the belief that "all men are created equal." This does not mean that all people are assumed to be equal in wealth or status, but rather that all are equal under the law, enjoying equal rights. In a complex society, such as our own, it is unlikely that absolute equality could ever exist. Modern industrial societies are stratified—that is, they are characterized by unequal access to advantages, whether they be economic resources or prestige.

Whether stratification exists in all societies is a matter of some dispute. The position of many sociologists is stated by Kingsley Davis and Wilbert Moore: "Starting from the proposition that no society is 'classless,' or unstratified, an effort is made to explain, in functional terms, the universal necessity which calls forth stratification in any social system."[1] Sociologists who take this position have based their conclusions on the observation of some inequality in all societies, for even the most simple societies include differences in advantages based upon age or sex or ability. Some sociologists, then, equate all types of inequality with stratification.

Unlike many sociologists, anthropologists contend that truly egalitarian societies exist—societies in which access to economic resources, and to prestige or higher status, is available to all. In the anthropological view, most hunter-gatherer societies are egalitarian. Natural resources—food, water, materials for tools and shelter—are equally available to all. Moreover, in a society of hunter-gatherers, accumulation of food is unnecessary, indeed futile without storage techniques. Therefore, status cannot be achieved by amassing wealth in the form of food surpluses. The only status attainable by food-getting is achieved by giving food away. As a result, prestige, based on generosity, is also equally available to all.

Anthropology has contributed to the study of social stratification by broadening the scope of study and shifting the focus from the inequality inherent in human beings to the principles by which societies regulate these inequalities in the distribution of status and economic rewards. A society in which economic resources are equally available to all and every status position is open to every member of a particular age-sex group is an egalitarian society, anthropologists conclude. Human inequality may be universal; social stratification is not.

[1]Kingsley Davis and Wilbert Moore, "Some Principles of Stratification," in Celia Heller, ed., *Structured Social Inequality: A Reader in Social Stratification* (New York: Macmillan, 1969), p. 496.

VARIATION IN STRUCTURED INEQUALITY

A society with institutionalized or socially structured unequal access to economic resources and prestige is a stratified society. Some societies may limit access only to prestige or status positions; others may limit access to both economic resources *and* status positions. Thus, three types of societies can be distinguished: egalitarian societies; rank societies; and class/caste societies. Egalitarian societies have no structured unequal access to economic resources or to status positions. They are unstratified. Rank societies do not have structured unequal access to economic resources; but they do have structured unequal access to status positions. Rank societies, then, are partially stratified. Class/caste societies have structured unequal access to both economic resources and to status positions. They are completely stratified. The table below summarizes these three types of societies.

Egalitarian Societies

Egalitarian societies occur not only among hunter-gatherers; simple agriculturists and pastoralists may also be egalitarian. It is important to keep in mind that *egalitarian* does not mean that all people within such a society are the *same.* There will always be differences in age, sex, and in such abilities or traits as hunting, perception, health, creativity, physical prowess, attractiveness, and intelligence. Morton H. Fried has defined "egalitarian" as meaning that within a given society "there are as many positions of prestige in any given age-sex grade as there are persons capable of filling them."[2] For instance, if a man can achieve status in a society by fashioning fine spears, and every man in the society fashions such spears, then every man acquires status as a spear maker. If status is also acquired by carving bones into artifacts, and only three men are considered expert carvers of bones, then only those three achieve status as carvers. But the next generation might produce eight spear makers and twenty carvers. In the egalitarian society, the number of prestigious positions is adjusted to fit the number of qualified candidates; we would therefore say that it is not a stratified society.

	Structured Unequal Access to:	
Type of Society	*economic resources*	*status positions*
Egalitarian	no	no
Rank	no	yes
Class/caste	yes	yes

There are, of course, differences in status and prestige arising out of differences in ability, so that even in an egalitarian society differential prestige exists. However, although some men may be better hunters or more skilled artists than others, there is still equal *access* to status positions. Any prestige awarded by achievement of status as a great hunter, for instance, is neither transferable nor inheritable. Because a man is a great hunter, it is not assumed that his sons are also great hunters. The egalitarian society keeps inequality at a minimal level.

In an egalitarian society, the differences in prestige that do exist are not related to economic differences. Egalitarian societies depend heavily on *sharing,* which insures equal access to economic resources in spite of differences in acquired prestige. For instance, in some egalitarian societies, status is achieved through hunting, but even before the hunt begins, how the animal will be divided and distributed among the members of the band has already been decided according to the norms of the culture. Thus, the culture works to separate the status achieved—recognition as a

[2] Morton H. Fried, *The Evolution of Political Society* (New York: Random House, 1967), p. 33.

great hunter—from actual possession of the wealth, in this case, the slain animal.

The Mbuti Pygmies of central Africa provide an example of a society almost totally equal: "Neither in ritual, hunting, kinship nor band relations do they exhibit any discernible inequalities of rank or advantage."[3] Hunting bands have no leaders; recognition of the achievement of one person is not accompanied by privilege of any sort. Economic resources, such as food, are communally shared, and even tools and weapons are frequently passed from person to person. Only within the family are rights and privileges somewhat differentiated.

!Kung Bushman society is only slightly more complex, since each band has a headman. But the position of headman has no power or other advantage associated with it; the headman serves merely as a unifying symbol. A stranger must ask permission of the headman to take water from the band's water hole, a symbolic gesture which the headman cannot refuse. The headman is neither the leader of the hunt nor the chief decision maker. In fact, all men hunt, and all share in decisions that affect the band.

Egalitarian conditions, moreover, are not

[3] Michael G. Smith, "Pre-Industrial Stratification Systems," in Neil J. Smelser and Seymour Martin Lipset, eds., *Social Structure and Mobility in Economic Development* (Chicago: Aldine, 1966), p. 152.

In egalitarian societies all persons have equal access to both status positions and economic resources. Among the members of a !Kung Bushman band, for example, there is no visible difference in prestige or wealth. Although the second man from the right holds the position of headman, he has no power, nor does he enjoy any other advantages. (Courtesy of Irven DeVore.)

unique to hunter-gatherer groups. Societies dependent upon simple agriculture or herding may also be egalitarian. For example, certain East African societies with age-sets—that is, groups of males differentiated by age—can also be classified as egalitarian. As each new age-set is established among the young, each other group moves up a notch, gaining more prestige and additional rights, such as the right to marry, the right to go on raids, the right to be a councilman or ritual leader. The inequalities within the society at any one time are apparent, but each age-set is automatically promoted so that all rights, duties, and privileges are available equally to all men during their lifetimes—illustrating the basis on which a society is defined as egalitarian. Systems by which status can be achieved may vary, but all status positions in such a society are open to everyone within the qualifying age-sex group. This criterion does not apply to rank societies.

Rank Societies

Societies with social *ranking* generally practice agriculture or herding, but not all agricultural or pastoral societies are ranked. Ranking is characterized by structured unequal access to prestige and status. Such access is often reflected in the position of chief, a rank to which only some members of a specified group in the society can succeed. The chief retains the symbolic unifying role of headman, as among the Bushmen, but in the practical role of food distributor he has added prestige; he receives a portion of the harvest and of the hunt, which he redistributes to the rest of the group.

Redistribution of food by the chief symbolizes that the wealth is communally held. Although the chief may be designated "owner" of the land, the people always retain the right to use the land. The chief in a rank society does not possess greater access to economic resources, nor is he generally excused from labor; quite the contrary, sometimes he has to work extra hard to retain his position. In some Polynesian societies, for instance, the chief was designated "manager" of the labor of others, seeing to it that the people did not neglect their fields nor shirk giving food for him to redistribute to the community.[4] In rank societies the chief maintains his status and prestige by his generosity. According to our own societal values, the chief may appear impoverished, but by those of his society, he has high status because of his ability to give wealth away, not keep it.

In most rank societies the position of chief is at least partially hereditary. The criterion of superior rank in some Polynesian societies, for example, was geneological. Usually the eldest son succeeded to the position of chief, and different kinship groups were differentially ranked according to their geneological distance from the chiefly line.

An example of a rank society is the Swazi of South Africa. Hilda Kuper reports that the Swazi are a horticultural society who invest their chief with "ownership" of the land.[5] The staples of their diet are maize and millet, produced cooperatively by men and women. Farming supplies the staple foods of the Swazi, although herding is a more prestigious occupation. Nevertheless, only 10 percent of Swazi land is given to cultivation; cattle grazing claims 75 percent of the land.

Among the Swazi, the chief is recognized as the lineal descendant of the first ruler of the tribe. He is selected according to the rank of his mother; both are treated with great deference, addressed with extravagant titles, and wear elaborate regalia. Members of the chief's lineage are called the "Children of the Sun," and collectively they comprise a distinct social

[4] Marshall Sahlins, *Social Stratification in Polynesia* (Seattle: University of Washington Press, 1958), pp. 6–8.

[5] Hilda Kuper, *A South African Kingdom: The Swazi* (New York: Holt, Rinehart and Winston, 1963).

In rank societies there is differentiated access to status positions but not to economic resources. Among the Dey of Liberia, the chief is clearly accorded greater prestige, but the house in which he lives (shown here) is no different than those of other villagers. (Courtesy of the American Museum of Natural History.)

elite. Other members of the society are ranked according to their relationship to the chief.

All Swazis, however, regardless of their rank, do the same kinds of work, live in the same kinds of houses, and eat the same foods. The superior rank of the chief is evident by the many cows in his possession and by his right to organize work parties. Sharing is the principal way goods are distributed, and the chief shares (or redistributes) more than others. A man who accumulates too many cattle is in danger of public retaliation unless he shares them or lets others use them. If he does not, he may be accused of wizardry and his cattle may be killed and eaten. This is a cultural means of preventing the accumulation of wealth. Labor, too, is shared and a work party from a particular age-set might be called upon to help a family undertaking a construction job.

Although the Swazi have managed to retain much of the economic and social base of their traditional rank society, the money economy of the white colonizers has begun to alter their way of life. About 12,000 Swazi males are now employed as unskilled laborers; about 1,000 women work at farming or as domestics.

Unique among rank societies were the nineteenth-century northwest Pacific coast Indian tribes. Their economy was based on food collecting, but huge catches of salmon—which were preserved and stored for year-round consumption—permitted them to support fairly large and permanent communities. In many ways, the northwest coast societies were like food-producing societies, including their development of social ranking. Still, the principal means of proving one's status among the northwest coast Indians was by giving wealth away, and a chief celebrated solemn rites by grand feasts, called *potlatches,* at which he gave a gift to every guest.[6]

Class Societies

In class societies, as in rank societies, there is structured unequal access to prestige. But unlike rank societies, class societies are also characterized by structured unequal access to economic resources—that is, not every type of person has the same chance to obtain land, animals, money, or other economic benefits. Anthropologists are interested in how and why access to economic resources became unequal. Some have suggested that population pressure on resources might have played some role in its development.[7]

C. K. Meek offers an example of how population pressure in northern Nigeria may have led to economic stratification. Land use at one time was obtained by asking the chief for the use of the land and presenting him with a token gift in recognition of his status. But by 1921, the reduction of available land had led to a system under which applicants offered the chief large payments for scarce land; as a result of these payments, farms came to be regarded as private property and differential access to such property became institutionalized.[8]

However economic stratification came into existence, it has dominated the globe in the relatively short space of 10,000 years. Economically stratified societies range from extremely rigid caste systems to more flexible systems. We will consider the class system of the United States first.

Class System. A class is a category of persons who have about the same chance to obtain economic resources, as well as prestige. During the last 50 years, study after study has been made of classes in American towns. Sociologists have produced such profiles as "Yankee City," "Middletown," "Jonesville," and "Old City," all of which support the premise that the United States has distinguishable though somewhat "open" social classes. Both Warner's "Yankee City"[9] and the Lynds' "Middletown"[10] produced the conclusion that the social rank of a family generally correlated with the occupation and wealth of the head of the family.

Towns in America have been described as having as few as two and as many as eleven social classes, but generally from four to six classes are recognized. In Warner's "Yankee City," 99 percent of the 17,000 inhabitants were studied and classified over a period of several years. Warner concluded that six groups emerged strongly enough to be called classes. They are summarized by characteristic traits in Table 1.

The way members of the top and bottom classes see each other has also been observed and recorded. Table 2 summarizes such percep-

[6] Philip Drucker, *Cultures of the North Pacific Coast* (San Francisco: Chandler, 1965), pp. 56–64.

[7] See Fried, *The Evolution of Political Society,* pp. 201–202.

[8] C. K. Meek, *Land Law and Custom in the Colonies* (London: Oxford, 1940), pp. 149–150.

[9] W. Lloyd Warner and Paul S. Lunt, *The Social Life of a Modern Community* (New Haven: Yale University Press, 1941).

[10] Robert S. Lynd and Helen Merrell Lynd, *Middletown* (New York: Harcourt, Brace, 1929); and *Middletown in Transition* (New York: Harcourt, Brace, 1937).

Table 1
American Social Classes: "Yankee City"

% of Income	*% of Population*		
45% for top 20% of the population	1.4	Upper Upper:	"old family"; usually possessing wealth, but sometimes poor, active in charities, Episcopal or Congregational church, exclusive clubs, endogamous.
	1.6	Lower Upper:	newly rich, imitate the U-U class and long to marry into the class above them.
	10.2	Upper Middle:	professional men or store owners, active in civic affairs, respectable; they long to be accepted by the groups above them, but almost never are.
	28.1	Lower Middle:	white collar workers, respectable home owners, school teachers; looked down upon by all above them; some members of recently integrated groups, such as Irish, Italians, French-Canadians, are in this group.
	32.6	Upper Lower:	"poor but honest workers," spend most of their income on food and rent.
5% for bottom 20% of the population	25.2	Lower Lower:	other classes believe they are lazy, shiftless, sexually proficient, and promiscuous. In reality, they are simply poor.

Summarized from W. Lloyd Warner and Paul S. Lunt, *The Social Life of a Modern Community* (New Haven: Yale University Press, 1941), p. 88.

Table 2
Perceptions of Social Classes

Upper-Upper Classified the Town		*Lower-Lower Classified the Town*
"Old aristocracy"	U-U	
"Aristocracy," but not "old"	L-U	"Society" or the "folks with money"
"Nice, respectable people"	U-M	
"Good people," but "nobody"	L-M	"Way-high-ups," but not "Society"
"Po' whites"	U-L	"Snobs trying to push up"
	L-L	"People just as good as anybody"

Allison Davis, Burleigh B. Gardner, and Mary R. Gardner, *Deep South: A Social-Anthropological Study of Caste and Class* (Chicago: University of Chicago Press, 1941), p. 65.

tions as they were revealed in a study of a town in the American South. The people at the top grouped the bottom two classes together and the people at the bottom grouped the top three classes together, suggesting that the greater the social distance between groups, the more likely it is that a group will lump together those other groups which are furthest away in the class hierarchy. Groups tend, however, to distinguish between other groups just above or just below themselves.

A person's identification with his social class is a process which begins quite early in life. The residence area chosen by one's parents, one's church, school, school curriculum, clubs, sports, college (or lack of college), marriage partner, and occupation are all influential in socializing us into a particular status group. White American society is, on the whole, an open society; that is, it is possible, through

Class societies are characterized by unequal access to both prestige and economic resources. In Great Britain, for example, wealthy aristocrats are clearly distinguished from working-class people. (Photograph by David Hurn, © 1967 Magnum Photos.)

effort, to move from one class to another. A university education is the easiest means of moving upward. A lower-class person may become "resocialized" at the university, which separates him from his parents and enables him gradually to learn the speech, attitudes, and manners characteristic of the higher status class he wishes to join. So successful is this process that a student from a lower class who moves into a higher class may find himself ashamed to take his new friends to his parents' home.

Although social class in America is not fully determined at birth, Americans have a strong tendency to stay within the class into which they were born and to marry within that class. Identification with a particular status group and the roles of that group begins in early childhood. The seven-year-old daughter of a farm laborer, for example, may be assigned the role of farm helper; she will have few rights and her duties would include feeding the chickens, gathering the eggs, milking the cow, and harvesting certain crops. In contrast, the seven-year-old daughter of a wealthy businessman may be assigned the role of debutante-in-training. Her duties would include learning to ride, to play tennis and the piano, and to sit through concerts and teas; among her rights would be the right to be shown respect by the servants of the house, the right to a large variety of choice foods, the right to a room or a suite of her own, the right to private tutors. It is sometimes hard to distinguish rights from duties: she would have a right to a variety of foods, but as a duty, she might learn to eat caviar, *paté de foie gras,* and raw oysters.

By the time each of these girls is 20 she will have passed through many roles. At this point the farmhand's daughter and the debutante would stand an equal chance of achieving the role of wife, but a highly unequal chance of achieving the role of wife of a millionaire. Each would be likely to marry someone of her own status at birth.

Class boundaries, even though vague, have been established by custom and tradition; and these have sometimes been reinforced by the enactment of laws. Many of our laws deal with protection of property and thus tend to favor the upper and upper-middle classes. The poor, in contrast, seem to be perennial losers in our legal system. The crimes which the poor are most likely to commit are dealt with quite harshly in our judicial system; and poor people rarely have the knowledge or the money to secure effective legal counsel.

American society is an excellent example of a relatively open class structure which gradually grew more closed. The reasons are fairly obvious. The availability of vast quantities of land in the West opened opportunities to European colonizers to rise to a higher social class by becoming landowners. When the country ran out of land, a pattern was established that has become typical of industrial countries: the economy shifted from an agricultural base to an industrial base; the population shifted from rural to urban; and positions in the top ranks of business and government were increasingly filled by sons of the elite.[11]

Japan is another highly industrialized country. A study by Edward Norbeck reveals that the modern, relatively open class system in Japan developed only within the last 100 years. Previously the system had been almost completely closed, being composed of a merchant class, a class of farmers, the warrior class or *samurai,* and the nobility at the top of the social hierarchy. The recent urbanization of Japan perhaps accounts for the development of a more open class system. A study in 1960 of the upper-class business elite showed that 8 percent came from lower-class and 31 percent from middle-class backgrounds.[12] This social mobility was achieved chiefly by means of successful passage through the highly competitive university system. The fact that the Japanese class system is not completely open, however, is indicated by the 61 percent of the business elite who came from the relatively small upper class. The tendency to retain high status even through changing times is clear.

Caste Systems. In stratified societies, people generally remain for life in the status group in which they are born. In a caste system, however, one's position in society is *completely* ascribed or determined by birth; upward mobility is prohibited either by law or custom or both and marriage is restricted to members of one's own caste.

India is by far the best known example of a caste society. Studies of India often concentrate upon the injustices of the system. It should be remembered, however, that an Indian studying our own culture might well be amazed at certain injustices—one man may refuse to hire another because he does not like his haircut; one man may fire another who has worked for 23 years for the same company. It is not that one system is more just or unjust than the other, but simply that injustice takes different forms in different societies.

A question basic to all stratified societies, and particularly to a caste society, was posed by John Ruskin: "Which of us . . . is to do the hard

[11] W. Lloyd Warner and James C. Abegglin, *Occupational Mobility in American Business* (Minneapolis: University of Minnesota Press, 1955).

[12] Edward Norbeck, "Continuities in Japanese Social Stratification," in Leonard Plotnicov and Arthur Tuden, eds., *Essays in Comparative Social Stratification* (Pittsburgh: University of Pittsburgh Press, 1970).

In caste societies status and economic positions are ascribed at birth. This untouchable woman is assigned the task of cleaning bathrooms in a Bombay apartment building; the Brahman, in contrast, is a professor of metaphysics in Sanskrit. (Photographs by Marilyn Silverstone, © 1964 Magnum Photos.)

and dirty work for the rest—and for what pay? Who is to do the pleasant and clean work, and for what pay?"[13] This question has been answered in Indian society by the maintenance of a rigidly constructed caste system or hierarchy of statuses whose underlying basis is economic; it involves an intricate system of exchange of goods and services.[14]

Who is to do the hard and dirty work for the rest of society is clearly established: a large group of untouchables forms the bottom of the hierarchy. Among the untouchables are subcastes such as the *Camars,* leathers workers, and the *Bhangis,* sweepers. At the top of the hierarchy, performing the pleasant and clean work of priest, are the *Brahmans.* Between these two extremes are literally thousands of castes and subcastes. Each caste is traditionally associated with an occupation. For example, in a typical village the potter makes clay drinking cups and larger water vessels for the entire village population. In return, the principal landowner gives him a house site and supplies him twice yearly with grain. Some other castes owe the potter their services; the barber cuts his

[13] John Ruskin, "Of King's Treasuries," in John D. Rosenberg, ed., *The Genius of John Ruskin: Selections from His Writings* (New York: George Braziller, 1963), pp. 296–314.

[14] See Oscar Lewis with the assistance of Victor Barnouw, *Village Life in Northern India* (Urbana: University of Illinois Press, 1958).

hair, the sweeper carries away his rubbish, the washer washes his clothes, the *Brahman* performs his children's weddings. The barber serves every caste in the village except the untouchables; he is in turn served by half the others. He has inherited the families he works for along with his father's occupation. He also receives a house site from the principal landowner and, at each harvest, all the grain he can lift. All castes help at harvest and at weddings for additional payment, sometimes including a money payment of one rupee.

This is, in fact, an idealized picture of the caste system of India showing the system as it was designed to work. In reality it operates to the advantage of the principal landowning caste—sometimes the *Brahmans,* and sometimes other castes—and it is not carried on without some resentment and signs of hostility shown toward the ruling caste by the untouchables and many of the other lower castes. The resentment does not appear to be against the caste system as such; the lower castes instead exhibit bitterness at their own low status and strive for greater equality. For instance, one of the *Camars'* traditional services is to remove dead cattle from which they can have the meat to eat and the hide to tan for their leatherworking. But since handling dead animals and eating beef are both regarded as unclean acts, the *Camars* of one village refused to continue this service, thus losing a source of free hides and food in a vain attempt to lose their unclean status.

Since World War II, the economic basis of the caste system in India has been undermined somewhat by increased cash payment for services. For instance, the son of a barber may be a teacher during the week, for a cash salary, and confine his haircutting as an exchange service to weekends. However, he still remains in the barber caste *(Nai)* and marries within that caste, thus reinforcing the social effects of caste.

Perpetuation of the caste system is ensured by the power of those in the upper castes, who derive three main advantages from their position: economic gain, gain in prestige, and sexual gain. The economic gain is most immediately apparent. An ample supply of cheap labor and free services is maintained by the threat of sanctions: withdrawing the use of the house site, refusing access to the village well or to common grazing land for animals, or expulsion from the village. Prestige is also maintained by the threat of sanctions; the higher castes expect deference and servility from the lower castes. The sexual gain is less apparent, but equally real. The high-caste male has access to two groups of females, his own caste and lower castes, while keeping high-caste females free of the contaminating touch of low-caste males and allowing low-caste males access only to low-caste women. Moreover, the constant reminders of ritual uncleanness serve to keep the lower castes "in their place." Higher castes do not accept water from untouchables, or sit next to them, or eat at the same table.

A caste system, then, is a hierarchy of economic classes in which all status is ascribed and permanent, and marriage outside one's caste is forbidden. Although few areas of the world have developed a caste system like that of India, there are caste-like features in some other societies. For example, there is the caste-like status of blacks in the United States, whose status is partially determined by the ascribed characteristic of skin color. Until recently, there were laws in some states prohibiting a black from marrying a white. Even when interracial marriage does occur, children of the union are often regarded as having lower status, even though they might have blonde hair and fair skin. In the South, where treatment of blacks as a caste was most apparent, whites have traditionally refused to eat with blacks, or, until recently, to sit next to them at lunch counters, on buses, and in schools. Separate drinking fountains and toilets have reinforced the idea of ritual uncleanness. The economic advantages and gains in prestige enjoyed by whites are well documented; white males have also had sexual advantages since the days when concubinage was practiced with black slave women and later with "free" black women.

Another example of a caste group in class society is the *Eta* caste of Japan. Unlike the blacks in America, the *Eta* caste is physically indistinguishable from Japanese higher classes. It is an hereditary, endogamous group, comparable to India's untouchables. In the old estate system, the *Eta* were a caste of about 400,000, segregated from other Japanese by place of residence, by denial of rights of citizenship, and by elaborate ritual. When the estate system broke down, they not only remained at the bottom of the hierarchy, but their ranks swelled to between 1 and 3 million as a result of the downward mobility that accompanied the decline in the farm population. Their occupations are traditionally those of farm laborer, leatherworker, basket weaver; their standard of living, very low.

In Rwanda, a country in east central Africa, a longtime caste system was overthrown, first by an election, then by a short revolution, in 1959–1960. Three castes had existed, each distinguished by physical appearance and occupation from the others. The ruling caste, the *Tutsi,* were very tall and lean; they comprised 16 percent of the population and practiced the prestigious occupation of herding. The agricultural caste, the *Hutu,* were shorter and stockier; as 85 percent of the population, they produced most of the country's food. The *Twa,* comprising 1 percent of the population, were a pygmy group of hunter-gatherers who formed the lowest caste. It is believed that the three castes derive from three different language groups, who came together because of migration and conquest. Later, however, they came to use a common language, although remaining endogamous and segregated by hereditary occupation. When the middle caste united to demand more of the rewards of their labor, the king and many of the *Tutsi* ruling caste left the country. The *Hutu* then established a republican form of government, although the forest-dwelling *Twa* are still generally excluded from full citizenship. Rwanda is an example of a caste society that may be in the process of becoming a class society.

Slavery. Slaves are persons who do not own their own labor, and as such they represent a class. Slavery has existed in various forms in many times and places, regardless of race and culture. Sometimes it has been a closed or hereditary system, sometimes a relatively open one. In different slave-owning societies, slaves have had different rights.

In ancient Greece slaves were often conquered enemies. Since city-states were constantly conquering one another, and rebelling against former conquerers, slavery was a threat to every human being. Following the Trojan War, the transition of Hecuba from queen to slave was marked by her cry, "Count no mortal fortunate, no matter how favored, until he is dead."[15] Nevertheless, the Greek slave was considered a human being, and he could even acquire some status along with his freedom. For example, the daughter-in-law of Hecuba, Andromache, was taken as slave and concubine by one of the Greek heroes, and when his legal wife produced no children, Andromache's slave son became heir to his father's throne. Although the slave had no rights under law, once freed either by the will of the master or by purchase, he and his descendants could become assimilated into the dominant group. In other words, slavery in itself was not seen as the justified position of inferior people; it was regarded, rather, as an act of fate that relegated a victim to the lowest class in society; in a sense, "the luck of the draw."

Among the Nupe, a society in central Nigeria, slavery was of quite another tenor.[16] The methods of obtaining slaves as part of the booty of warfare, and later by purchase, were similar to those of Europeans; but the position of the slave was quite different. Mistreatment of slaves was rare. Male slaves were given the same opportunities to earn money as other dependent males in the household—younger brothers, sons, or other relatives. A slave might be given a garden plot of his own to cultivate, or he might be given a commission if his master were a craftsman or a tradesman. Slaves could acquire property, wealth, and even slaves of their own. However, all a slave's belongings went to the slave's master on the death of the slave.

Among the Nupe, *manumission,* the granting of freedom, was built into the system of slavery. If a male slave could afford the marriage payment for a free woman, the children of the resulting marriage were free; the man himself, however, remained a slave. Marriage or concubinage were the easiest ways out for a woman. Once she had produced a child by her master, both the slave woman and the child had free status. The woman, however, was only figuratively free; if a concubine, she had to remain in that role. As might be expected, the family trees of the nobility and the wealthy were liberally grafted with branches descended from slave concubines.

The most fortunate slaves among the Nupe were the house slaves. They could rise to positions of power in the household, as overseers and bailiffs, charged with law enforcement

[15] Euripides, *The Trojan Women.*

[16] S. F. Nadel, *A Black Byzantium: The Kingdom of Nupe in Nigeria* (London: Oxford University Press, 1942). The Nupe abolished slavery at the beginning of this century.

For many years after the Civil War, the "badges of slavery" remained in the United States. In public places in the South, for example, blacks were required to drink from separate water coolers and use segregated rest rooms. (Photo by Russell Lee, Library of Congress, Prints and Photos Division, F.S.A. Collection.)

and judicial duties. (Recall the Old Testament story of Joseph, who was sold into slavery by his brothers; Joseph became a household slave of the pharaoh and rose to the position of second in the kingdom because he devised an ingenious system of taxation.) There was even a titled group of Nupe slaves—the Order of Court Slaves—who were trusted officers of the king and members of an elite. Slave status in general, though, was the bottom of the social ladder. In the Nupe system, few slaves, mainly princes from their own societies, ever achieved membership in the titled group of slaves.

In the United States, slavery originated as a means of obtaining cheap labor, but the slave soon came to be regarded as deserving of his status because of his alleged inherent inferiority. Since the slaves were black, some whites justified slavery and belief in the black man's inferiority by quoting fragments of religious writings ("they shall be hewers of wood and drawers of water"). The slave could not marry or make any other contract, nor could he own property. In addition, his children were also slaves, and the master had sexual rights over the female slaves. Because the status of slavery was determined by birth in the United States, slaves constituted a caste. Thus during the days of slavery, the United States had both a caste and a class system. And even after the abolition of slavery, as we have noted, some caste-like elements remained.

THE EMERGENCE OF CLASS SOCIETY

Anthropologists are not certain why social stratification developed. Nevertheless, they are reasonably sure that higher levels of stratification emerged relatively recently in human history. This generalization is made because a number of recent cultural developments are associated with stratification. For example, most societies which are primarily dependent on agriculture or herding have social classes.[17] Because agriculture and herding developed within the past 10,000 years, we may assume that most hunter-gatherers in the distant past lacked social classes. Other cultural factors associated with class stratification also indicate a relatively recent emergence: fixed settlements, political integration beyond the community level, the use of money as a medium of exchange, and the presence of at least some full-time specialization.[18]

It appears, then, that social stratification increases with the level of productivity. Gerhard Lenski, however, has suggested that the 10,000-year-old trend toward ever increasing inequality is recently being reversed. He argues that inequalities of power and privilege in industrial societies—measured in terms of the concentration of political power and the distribution of income—are less pronounced than inequalities in preindustrial, complex societies. Lenski offers several reasons to justify this theory. Technology in industrialized societies is so complex, he argues, that those in power are compelled to delegate some authority to their subordinates in order for the system to function effectively. In addition, a decline in the birth rate in industrialized societies, coupled with the need for skilled labor, has pushed the average wage of workers far above the subsistence level, resulting in greater equality in the distribution of income. Finally, Lenski suggests that the spread of democratic ideology and particularly its acceptance by elites has significantly broadened the political power of the lower classes.[19] However, whether or not Lenski's argument is correct, and the evolutionary trend toward greater inequality is in fact being reversed, remains to be corroborated.

The kind of stratification system a particular society develops seems to be associated with certain factors. Caste systems, for example, seem to be characterized by intensive agriculture and the relatively undeveloped use of money as a medium of exchange.[20] This is exemplified by the situation in India, where castes exchange goods and services in a culturally prescribed way without money entering into the transactions. In fact, compensation for services is typically delayed over time; the barber, for instance, must wait until harvest time before he receives grain from the landowner in "payment" for his services. Slavery, too, seems to be associated with particular conditions; it is generally found in societies in which warfare is prevalent—understandably, since physical force is the principal means of acquiring slaves.

Thus we see that social stratification is linked with other cultural phenomena. Yet the specific determinants of stratification are still a matter of conjecture. Marshall Sahlins, on the basis of his study of Polynesian societies, has suggested that an increase in agricultural productivity results in social stratification.[21] According to Sahlins, the degree of stratification is directly related to the production of a surplus, made possible by greater technological efficiency. The higher the level of productivity and the larger the surplus, the greater will be the scope and complexity of the distribution system, and this in turn enhances the status of the chief who serves as redistributing agent. Sahlins argues that the differentiation between distributor and producer inevitably gives rise to differentiation in other aspects of life:

> First, there would be a tendency for the regulator of distribution to exert some authority over produc-

[17] Data from Robert B. Textor, comp., *A Cross-Cultural Summary* (New Haven: HRAF Press, 1967).
[18] Data from Textor, *A Cross-Cultural Summary.*
[19] Gerhard Lenski, *Power and Privilege* (New York: McGraw-Hill, 1966), pp. 308–318.
[20] Data from Textor, *A Cross-Cultural Summary.*
[21] Sahlins, *Social Stratification in Polynesia.*

tion itself—especially over productive activities which necessitate subsidization, such as communal labor or specialist labor. A degree of control of production implies a degree of control over the utilization of resources, or, in other words, some pre-eminent property rights. In turn, regulation of these economic processes necessitates the exercise of authority in interpersonal affairs; differences in social power emerge.[22]

Gerhard Lenski's theory of the causes of stratification is similar to that of Sahlins. Lenski, too, argues that production of a surplus is the initial stimulus in the development of stratification, but he focuses primarily on the conflict that arises over control of that surplus. Lenski concludes that the distribution of the surplus will be determined on the basis of power—thus, inequalities in power enable unequal access to economic resources and simultaneously give rise to inequalities in privilege and prestige.[23]

Future research may provide more definite answers as to why social stratification emerges, and why systems of stratification vary in different societies.

[22] Sahlins, *Social Stratification in Polynesia,* p. 4.
[23] Lenski, *Power and Privilege.*

SUMMARY

1. Whether social stratification exists in all societies is a matter of dispute. Some sociologists contend that stratification is universal because certain inequalities exist in all societies. Anthropologists, however, argue that truly egalitarian societies exist—societies in which access to economic resources and to prestige and higher status is equally available to all.

2. The presence or absence of structured unequal access to status positions and economic resources can be used to distinguish three types of societies. Egalitarian societies have no structured unequal access to economic resources or to status positions. They are unstratified. Rank societies do not have structured unequal access to economic resources; but they do have structured unequal access to status positions. Rank societies, then, are partially stratified. Class/caste societies have structured unequal access to both economic resources and to status positions. They are completely stratified.

3. However economic stratification came into existence, it has come to dominate the globe. Economically stratified societies range from class systems, which have some mobility between classes, to caste systems, which are extremely rigid, caste status being ascribed and fixed permanently at birth.

4. Slaves are persons who do not own their own labor, and as such they represent a class, and sometimes even a caste. Slavery has existed in various forms in many times and places, regardless of race and culture. Sometimes slavery is a rigid and closed or hereditary system; sometimes it is a relatively open one. In different slave-owning societies, slaves have different rights.

5. Social stratification appears to have emerged relatively recently in human history; this conclusion is based on evidence that a number of recent cultural developments are associated with stratification. Gerhard Lenski, however, has

argued that the 10,000-year-old trend toward ever increasing inequality is being reversed in industrial societies.

6. Anthropologists are not certain why social stratification developed. The theories of stratification proposed by Marshall Sahlins and Gerhard Lenski both link the emergence of stratification to increases in productivity and the production of a surplus.

SUGGESTED READINGS

Fried, M. H.: *The Evolution of Political Society* (New York: Random House, 1967).
Beginning with definitions of commonly used terms and drawing from several disciplines, the author attempts to develop a comprehensive theory of ranking, social stratification, and the state.

Genovese, E. D.: *The Political Economy of Slavery* (New York: Pantheon, 1965).
A series of studies that examine the political and economic reasons for the existence of slavery in the southern United States. Part One discusses the conditions in the South and the conflicts between North and South over slavery; Part Two delves into the systems of southern agriculture; Part Three analyzes how slavery hindered the Industrial Revolution; and Part Four concludes with a history of slavery, its expansion and effect on the social, economic, and political life of the United States.

Heller, C. (Ed.): *Structured Social Inequality* (New York: Macmillan, 1969).
This collection includes articles dealing with the theory of stratification, types of stratification, and social mobility. The editor provides a general introduction to the literature on social stratification, as well as an overview of the articles on each major topic covered.

Hutton, J. H.: *Caste in India: Its Nature, Function and Origins,* 4th ed. (London: Oxford University Press, 1963, first published in 1946 by Cambridge University Press).
A wide-ranging book, which covers various aspects and functions of the Indian caste system and which includes theoretical material on the origins of castes.

Leach, E. R. (Ed.): *Aspects of Caste in South India, Ceylon, and Northwest Pakistan* (Cambridge: Cambridge University Press, 1960).
A collection of five essays, beginning with a discussion of the definition of caste by Leach and followed by four essays on local variants of the caste system.

Lenski, G.: *Power and Privilege* (New York: McGraw-Hill, 1966).
A survey of the evolution of stratification theory. Basing his organization on Hegel's theory that each idea generates an opposite one and that these eventually coalesce into a new theory, the author reviews the various theories from ancient times to the present and seeks in this way to advance the development of stratification theory.

Nieboer, H. J.: *Slavery as an Industrial System* (The Hague: Martinus Nijhoff, 1900).
In this classic study, the author analyzes the facts of and the causes for the regional distribution of slavery. Using a variety of hunting and fishing societies, pastoral groups, and agricultural groups for his sample, Nieboer suggests that slavery is related to economic conditions.

Plotnicov, L., and A. Tuden (Eds.): *Essays in Comparative Social Stratification* (Pittsburgh: University of Pittsburgh Press, 1970).
Eleven lectures by anthropologists, discussing various cultures in the light of different models of stratification systems.

Sahlins, M.: *Social Stratification in Polynesia* (Seattle: University of Washington Press, 1958).
An analysis of stratification in Polynesia, suggesting that the degree of social stratification varies with the level of productivity.

Tuden, A., and L. Plotnicov (Eds.): *Social Stratification in Africa* (New York: Free Press, 1970).
The eleven essays in this book deal with slavery, caste, and class in several areas of Africa.

15

Sex, Marriage, and the Family

Marriage and the family are virtually universal institutions in human societies and are intimately related to each other through sex. Although sex is generally involved in marriage and is certainly involved in the creation of families, we also know that it is even more pervasive than that.

Since sex is a biological drive, it is not surprising that it is found in all societies. Why marriage (and the resulting families produced) is nearly universal is a somewhat more perplexing problem—one that we shall attempt to deal with in this chapter. But the universality of sex, and the near-universality of marriage and the family, does not indicate that they are the same everywhere. On the contrary, there is much variation from society to society in the degree of permitted sexual activity before marriage, outside of marriage, and even within marriage. There is also great variation in how one marries, whom one marries, and how many one marries. The only cultural universal about marriage regulations is that people are not permitted to marry (or to have sexual intercourse with) their parents, brothers, or sisters. Who belongs to the family varies too; the family often includes other individuals than just a man, a woman, and their immature offspring—a family may include two or more related married couples and their children.

SEX

A Hopi, speaking to an ethnographer, reported:

> Next to the dance days with singing, feasting, and clown work, love-making with private wives was the greatest pleasure of my life. And for us who toil in the desert, these light affairs make life more pleasant. Even married men prefer a private wife now and then. At any rate there are times when a wife is not interested, and then a man must find someone else or live a worried and uncomfortable life.[1]

The president of the University of California, Clark Kerr, reported in *Time* magazine: "I find that the three major administrative problems on a campus are sex for the students, athletics for the alumni and parking for the faculty."[2]

These comments, made by very different people, living in very different cultures, both testify to the intensity and the ubiquity of the sex drive in human beings. The fact that Clark Kerr speaks of sex as a problem suggests something that anthropologists have long been aware of: no known human society has permitted its members to indulge in *unrestrained* sexual activity.

[1] Leo W. Simmons, *Sun Chief* (New Haven: Yale University Press, 1942), p. 281.
[2] *Time* (November 17, 1958), p. 42.

All societies regulate the sexual activity of their members, within and without marriage. As their cultures differ, so naturally do their approaches to sex. Some are permissive, others restrictive; some frown upon premarital sexual intercourse, others upon extramarital activity; some allow one or both. Our own culture has traditionally been rather restrictive, insisting upon a blanket prohibition of all sexual relations outside marriage, though recently more permissive attitudes seem to be gaining acceptance.

Sexually Permissive and Restrictive Cultures

A cross-cultural review of the range of attitudes toward childhood sexuality and pre- and extramarital sex reveals that societies vary from permissive to restrictive, but not necessarily with total consistency. For example, some societies are permissive with adolescents, but not at all so with married people.[3] Why some societies are more permissive and others more restrictive regarding sex is not yet fully understood.

Childhood Sexuality. The sexual curiosity of children is met with a tolerant and open attitude in many societies. Among the Hopi Indians of the American Southwest, for example, parents often masturbate their children. When the children themselves masturbate, the parents pay no attention; all childhood sexual behavior is viewed permissively, although certain restrictions may be imposed at the onset of puberty.[4]

On the other hand, in a Pacific island society (called East Bay to protect confidences), "great concern for sexual propriety" is demonstrated.[5] Children are discouraged from touching their genitalia in public, the boys through good-natured ridicule, the girls by scolding. Strict modesty training begins as soon as children can walk; girls especially are closely supervised by their mothers. From about the fifth year, children have learned not to touch the other sex at all and have become sensitive to lapses in modesty, which they frequently point out to one another. Boys must always remain a certain distance from a female.

Premarital Sex. The degree to which sex before marriage is approved or disapproved varies greatly from society to society. The Trobriand Islanders, for example, condone and, in fact, encourage premarital sex, seeing it as an important preparation for later marriage roles. Both boys and girls are given complete instruction in all forms of sexual expression at the onset of puberty and are then allowed plenty of opportunity for intimacy. Some societies not only allow premarital sex on a casual basis but specifically encourage trial marriages between adolescents. Among the Ila-speaking peoples of Africa, girls are given houses of their own at harvest time where they may play at being man and wife with the boys of their choice. It is said that among these people virginity does not exist beyond the age of ten.[6]

On the other hand, there are many societies in which premarital sex is adamantly discouraged. For example, among the Tepoztlan Indians of Mexico, from the time of a girl's first menstruation, her life becomes "crabbed, cribbed, confined." No boy is to be spoken to or encouraged in the least way. To do so would be to court disgrace, to show oneself to be crazy or mad.

> The responsibility of guarding the chastity and reputation of one or more daughters of marriageable

[3] Clellan S. Ford and Frank A. Beach, *Patterns of Sexual Behavior* (New York: Harper & Row, 1951), p. 83.

[4] Ford and Beach, *Patterns of Sexual Behavior,* p. 188.

[5] William Davenport, "Sexual Patterns and Their Regulation in a Society of the Southwest Pacific," in Frank A. Beach, ed., *Sex and Behavior* (New York: John Wiley and Sons, 1965), pp. 164–174.

[6] Ford and Beach, *Patterns of Sexual Behavior,* p. 191.

age is often felt to be a burden by the mother. One mother said she wished her fifteen-year-old daughter would marry soon because it was inconvenient to "spy" on her all the time.[7]

In many Moslem societies, a girl's premarital chastity is tested after her marriage. Following the wedding night, blood-stained sheets are displayed as proof of the bride's virginity.

Extramarital Sex. In their cross-cultural survey of sexual behavior, Ford and Beach found that among 139 societies, 61 percent were found to forbid a married woman from engaging in extramarital sex.[8] In many of these societies, men are punished for seducing married women, but concern is mainly focused on female marital fidelity. Sometimes the prohibition on such liaisons is a religious one. In Islamic countries, for example, the Koran prohibits all sexual activity outside wedlock. So does the Bible, wherever Christianity still exerts influence upon society.

In many of these restrictive societies there is quite a difference between the restrictive code and actual practice. The Navajo forbid adultery, but the rule is loosely honored: "married men under 30 attain . . . 27 percent [of their sexual outlet] in other heterosexual contacts. . . . In men between 30 and 40 [this] drops to 19 percent, between 40 and 50 to 12 percent, over 50 to 4 percent."[9] And while American society prohibits extramarital sex in theory, Kinsey's studies showed that three-quarters of the married men interviewed admitted to wanting extramarital coitus, while over one-third experienced it.[10]

A substantial number of societies openly accept extramarital relationships. Among the Toda of India there is no censure of adultery; indeed, "immorality attaches to the man who begrudges his wife to another."[11] The Chukchee of Siberia, who often travel long distances, allow a married man to engage in sex with his host's wife, with the understanding that he will offer the same hospitality when the host visits him.[12]

Sexual restrictions often have religious origins. These Moslem women in Afghanistan must cover themselves in public places. (Marc Riboud, Magnum Photos.)

[7] Oscar Lewis, *Life in a Mexican Village: Tepoztlan Revisited* (Urbana, Ill.: University of Illinois Press, 1951), p. 397.

[8] Ford and Beach, *Patterns of Sexual Behavior,* p. 115.

[9] Clyde Kluckhohn, "As an Anthropologist Views It," in A. Deutsch, ed., *Sex Habits of American Men* (Englewood Cliffs, N.J.: Prentice-Hall, 1948), p. 101.

[10] Ford and Beach, *Patterns of Sexual Behaviors,* p. 117.

[11] *Ibid.,* p. 113.

[12] *Ibid.,* p. 114.

Sex within Marriage. There is as much variety in the way coitus is performed as there is in sexual attitudes generally. Privacy is a nearly universal requirement, but where an American will usually find this in the bedroom, many other peoples are obliged to go out into the bush. The Siriono of Bolivia seem to have no option, for there may be as many as 50 hammocks 10 feet apart in their small huts.[13] However, different cultures may interpret privacy in different ways. In some cultures, coitus often occurs in the presence of others who may be sleeping or simply looking the other way.

Time and frequency of coitus are also variable. While night is generally preferred, some people such as the Rucuyen of Brazil and the Yapese of the Pacific Caroline Islands specifically opt for day, and the Chenchu of India believe that a child conceived at night may be born blind. People in most societies abstain from intercourse during menstruation and at least during part of pregnancy. The Lesu, a people of New Ireland, an island off New Guinea, prohibit all members of the community from engaging in sex during the time between the death of any member and his burial.[14] Some societies prohibit sexual relations before various activities, such as hunting, fighting, planting, brewing, and iron smelting. Our own society is among the most lenient regarding restrictions on coitus within marriage, with rather loose restraints imposed only during mourning, menstruation, and pregnancy.

Reasons for Sexual Restrictiveness

Generally, societies which restrict sexuality in one area are also restrictive in other areas. Thus, most societies which restrict sexual expression by young children punish pre- and extramarital sex.[15] Why are some societies less sexually permissive than others?

Although we do not as yet understand the reasons why, we do know that greater sexual restrictiveness tends to occur in more complex societies—societies that have hierarchies of political officials, part-time or full-time craft specialists, cities and towns, and class stratification.[16] It may be that as social inequality increases, and different groups of people have differential wealth, people become more concerned with preventing their children from marrying "beneath them." Permissive premarital sexual relationships might lead a person to become attached to someone who would not be considered a desirable marriage partner. Even worse (from the family's point of view), such "unsuitable" sexual liaisons might result in pregnancy which might make it impossible for a girl to marry "well." To control mating, then, is to control property.

MARRIAGE

Although many people have questioned the necessity and advantages of marriage, the fact remains that almost all societies we know of have had the custom of marriage. And, if there is a universal rule-of-thumb regarding sexual practices, it is that all societies permit sexual activity within marriage.

What Is Marriage?

Marriage is a *socially approved sexual and economic union* between a man and a woman which is presumed, both by the couple and by others, to be more or less permanent, and which

[13] Ford and Beach, *Patterns of Sexual Behavior,* p. 69.
[14] Ford and Beach, *Patterns of Sexual Behavior,* p. 76.
[15] Data from Robert B. Textor, compiler, *A Cross-Cultural Summary* (New Haven: HRAF Press, 1967), p. 12.
[16] *Ibid.,* p. 13.

subsumes reciprocal rights and obligations between spouses, and between spouses and their future children.[17]

It is a socially approved sexual union in that a married couple is not obliged to be discreet about the sexual nature of their relationship. A woman might say "I want you to meet my husband," but she could not say "I want you to meet my lover" without causing social feathers in most societies to ruffle. Marriage is presumed to be permanent in that the couple, at least in the beginning, intends it to last "until death do us part." Although the marriage may ultimately be dissolved by divorce, couples in all societies begin marriage with permanence in mind. Implicit too in marriage are reciprocal rights and obligations. These may be more or less specific and formalized regarding matters of property, finances, and child rearing, but, in any case, marriage implies that both partners will fulfill certain responsibilities considered appropriate in their society.

Marriage entails both a sexual and an economic relationship:

> Sexual unions without economic co-operation are common, and there are relationships between men and women involving a division of labor without sexual gratification, e.g., between brother and sister, master and maidservant, or employer and secretary, but marriage exists only when the economic and the sexual are united into one relationship, and this combination occurs only in marriage.[18]

As we shall see later, the event which marks the commencement of marriage varies in different societies. In our own society, a wedding ceremony of either a religious or civil nature is necessary before a relationship is recognized as a "marriage" (except in cases of common law marriages), but this is not the case in every culture. A Winnebago bride, for example, knows no such formal ritual. She goes with her man to his parents' house, takes off her "wedding" clothes and finery, gives them to her mother-in-law, receives a plain set in exchange, and that is that.[19]

"If there really were transmigration of souls, wouldn't it be fabulous if we both came back married to each other?" (Drawing by Hoff, © 1972 The New Yorker Magazine, Inc.)

The Nayar Exception

There is one society in which marriage as we have defined it did not exist. Until late in the nineteenth century, the Nayar, a high-ranking caste group in southern India, seem to have treated sex and economic relations between men and women as things separate from marriage. At about the time of puberty, Nayar girls took ritual husbands, the union being publicly established in a ceremony during which the husband tied a gold ornament around the neck of his bride. But from that time on he had no more responsibility for her. Generally he never saw her again.

[17] William N. Stephens, *The Family in Cross-Cultural Perspective* (New York: Holt, Rinehart and Winston, 1963), p. 5.

[18] George P. Murdock, *Social Structure* (New York: Macmillan, 1949), p. 8.

[19] Stephens, *The Family in Cross-Cultural Perspective,* pp. 170–171.

Customarily, she lived in a large household with her family, where she was visited over the subsequent years by a number of other "husbands." One might be a passing guest, another a more regular visitor; it did not matter, providing he met the caste restrictions. He came at night and left the following day. If a regular visitor, he was expected to make certain small gifts of cloth and betel nuts, hair and bath oil. If the father of her child, or one of a group who might be, he was expected to pay the cost of the midwife. But at no time was he responsible for the support of the woman or their child. Rather, her blood relatives retained such responsibilities.[20]

Whether or not the Nayar had marriage depends of course on how we choose to define marriage. Certainly, Nayar marital unions involved no regular sexual component or economic cooperation; nor did they involve important reciprocal rights and obligations. According to our definition, then, the Nayar did not have marriage. However, rather than classify Nayar society as "marriageless," Kathleen Gough chooses to redefine marriage as follows: "Marriage is a relationship established between a woman and one or more other persons, which provides that a child born to the woman (legitimately) is accorded full birth-status rights common to normal membership of his society or social stratum."[21] According to this definition, all societies we know of (including, now, the Nayar) have marriage.

Why Is Marriage Nearly Universal?

Since all, or almost all, societies practice marriage as we have defined it, we might assume that the custom is highly adaptive. Clearly, marriage would not exist in so many societies if it were not highly advantageous in all of them. Several interpretations suggest that marriage is so widespread because it solves certain problems found in all societies: how to share the work efforts of men and women; how to care for infant children; and how to minimize sexual competition.

Economic Benefits. Most societies have a division of labor by sex, along the following lines:[22]

Males	*Females*
hunt and fish	gather and plant food
herd	carry water
cut lumber	cook
quarry	make and repair clothing
work with metal	make pottery

The origins of sexual division of labor may be traceable to biology and to systems of food getting which do not allow an individual to feed himself or herself completely. In Chapter 6 we noted that the dimensions of the female pelvis may make her a less efficient runner and hunter than the male. And since hunting is a widespread human practice which often involves traveling long distances, a difficult task for a female with a nursing infant or a young child, biological considerations may have made it more efficient for men to hunt. Women could contribute to subsistence in other, less strenuous ways which do not involve being too far from home, such as gathering and preparing food. And as men are often hunting away from home, women would more naturally take on the primary responsibility for child care. Even in nonhunting economies, this type of division of labor is continued; men seem to engage in the more strenuous tasks, or those which often take them away from home—such as herding large animals, deep-water fishing, and plowing—

[20] E. Kathleen Gough, "The Nayars and the Definition of Marriage," *Journal of the Royal Anthropological Institute,* Vol. 89 (1959), pp. 23–34.

[21] Gough, "The Nayars," p. 33.

[22] George P. Murdock, "Comparative Data on the Division of Labor by Sex," *Social Forces,* Vol. 15, No. 4 (1937), pp. 551–553.

whereas women engage in less strenuous activities closer to home.

Given this type of division of labor, it is necessary for men and women to share the products of their labor. Marriage would be one way of solving this problem. However, we must ask whether marriage is the only solution. This seems unlikely, since the hunter-gatherer rule of sharing could be extended to include all the products brought in by both men and women; or a small group of men and women might be pledged to cooperate economically. Thus, while marriage may solve the problem of sharing the fruits of division of labor, a sexual division of labor by itself does not seem to explain the universality of more or less permanent mating through marriage.

Prolonged Infant Dependency. Human infants have the longest period of infant dependency of any primate. Not only does a child require a great deal of care until he is biologically mature, but, being a "cultural animal," the human child needs to acquire the requisite amount of traditional knowledge and skills, the beliefs, values, and behaviors of his culture. The child's prolonged dependence generally places the greatest burden on the mother, who in most societies is the main child tender. This probably limited the woman's capacity to hunt, herd, or move great distances from home. Occupied with child care, the female had to be supplied by men with food for both herself and her children. Although marriage is a solution to this problem, permanent mating is still not completely explained. After all, there is no apparent reason why a *group* of men could not supply meat for a group of women and children.

Reduced Sexual Competition. Unlike other primates, the human female is more or less continuously receptive to sexual activity. Some have suggested that continuous female sexuality may have created a serious problem in that it may have fostered considerable sexual competition between males for females. It is argued that society had to prevent such competition to survive, that it had to develop some way of minimizing competition between males for females in order to reduce the chance of lethal conflict. Again, permanent paired mating is *a* solution—but it is not so clear why it is the only possible solution.

Couldn't sexual competition be regulated by cultural rules other than marriage? For instance, society might haye adopted a rule whereby men and women circulated among all of the opposite-sexed members of the group, with each person staying a specified length of time with each partner. Such a system presumably would also solve the problem of sexual competition. However, if individuals normally came to prefer other individuals, a person might be reluctant to give up someone he becomes particularly attached to (even if only temporarily) and be jealous of others' relations with that person. Because of such preferences and jealousies, competition might still be a problem. So, perhaps, more or less permanent mating may be the only practical solution to the condition of continuous female sexuality, and, at the same time, it could guarantee needed economic cooperation between men and women.

How Does One Marry?

The ways in which marriages are made can vary considerably. Some cultures have no ceremonies; some have relatively minor ones; some have highly elaborate ones, usually involving a succession of events phased over a number of days or months. In addition, marriages in many societies involve economic transactions of various types. We will consider both the ceremonial and the economic aspects of marriage below.

Ceremonial Aspects of Marriage. Among the Takamuit Eskimos, the betrothal is considered more important than the marriage and is arranged between the parents at or be-

In Bulgaria, a Karakachan bride wears an elaborate veil as the members of her wedding party look on. (United Press International Photo.)

fore the time their children reach puberty. Later, when the youth is ready, he moves in with his betrothed's family for a trial period. If all goes well, that is, if the girl gives birth to a baby within a year or so, the couple is considered married. At this time, the wife goes with her husband to his camp.[23]

Consistent with the general openness of their attitudes to sexual matters, a Trobriand couple, when they want to marry, advertise the fact "by sleeping together regularly, by showing themselves together in public, and by remaining with each other for long periods at a time."[24] When a girl accepts a small gift from a boy, she demonstrates that her parents favor the match. Before long, she moves to the boy's house, takes her meals there, and accompanies her husband all day. Then, the word goes round that the couple is already married.[25]

The Kwoma of New Guinea practice a trial marriage followed by a ceremony which makes the couple husband and wife. The girl lives for a while in the boy's home. When the boy's mother is satisfied with the match and knows that her son is too, she waits for a day when he is away from the house. Until this time, the girl has been cooking only for herself, while the boy's food has been prepared by his womenfolk. Now the mother has the girl prepare his meal. The young man returns and begins to eat his soup. As the first bowl is nearly finished, his

[23] Nelson H. Graburn, *Eskimos without Igloos* (Boston: Little, Brown, 1969), pp. 188–200.

[24] Bronislaw Malinowski, *The Sexual Life of Savages in North-Western Melanesia* (New York: Halcyon House, 1932), p. 77.

[25] Malinowski, *The Sexual Life of Savages in North-Western Melanesia,* p. 88.

mother tells him that his betrothed cooked the meal, and his eating it means that he is now married. At this news, the boy customarily rushes out of the house, spits out the soup, and shouts: "Faugh! It tastes bad! It is cooked terribly!" A ceremony then makes the marriage official.[26]

Feasting is a common element of many elaborate wedding ceremonies. It expresses publicly the importance of the two families being united by marriage. The Reindeer Tungus of Siberia set a wedding date after protracted negotiations between the two families and their larger kin groups. Go-betweens assume most of the responsibility. The wedding day opens with the two kin groups, probably numbering as many as 150 people, pitching their lodges in separate areas and offering a great feast. After the groom's gifts have been presented, the bride's dowry is loaded onto reindeer and carried to the groom's lodge. There the climax of the ceremony takes place. The bride takes the wife's place, that is on the right-hand side of the entrance, and members of both families sit around in a circle. The groom enters and follows the bride around the circle, greeting each guest, while the guests, in their turn, kiss the bride on the mouth and hands. Finally the go-betweens spit three times on the bride's hand, and the couple are formally man and wife. More feasting and revelling brings the day to a close.[27]

In many cultures, marriage includes ceremonial expressions of hostility. A common form is the trading of insults between kin groups, such as occurs on the Polynesian atoll of Pukapuka. Mock fights are found in many cultures. On occasion, the hostility can have really aggressive overtones, as among the Gusii of Kenya.

> Five young clansmen of the groom come to take the bride and two immediately find the girl and post themselves at her side to prevent her escape, while the others receive the final permission of her parents. When it has been granted the bride holds onto the house posts and must be dragged outside by the young men. Finally she goes along with them, crying and with her hands on her head.[28]

But the battle is not yet over. Mutual antagonism continues right onto the marriage bed, even up to and beyond coitus. The groom is determined to display his virility, his bride equally as determined to test it. "Brides," LeVine remarks, "are said to take pride in the length of time they can hold off their mates." Men can also win acclaim. If the bride is unable to walk the following day the groom is considered a "real man."[29]

Two marriage practices almost guaranteed to engender hostility are capture and elopement. Wife capture and elopement are certainly expedient, but they run the risk of alienating the "wronged" kinfolk. Both practices often preclude the economic and social cooperation which usually develops between families after a marriage; moreover, the couple's children usually do not have the social status of those of more conventional marriages.

Among the Arunta of Australia, for example, actual elopement, which occurs only when there is parental resistance to a marriage, leads to retaliation and may begin a feud. Captive marriage may be a by-product of a raid connected with such a feud.[30] North Alaskan Eskimos even promote capture. A girl, especially if she is considered unusually beautiful, is quite likely to be captured, often to become the second wife of a wealthy man. The fact that she may already happen to be married is not a

[26] J. W. M. Whiting, *Becoming a Kwoma* (New Haven: Yale University Press, 1941), p. 125.

[27] Elman R. Service, *Profiles in Ethnology* (New York: Harper & Row, 1963), p. 104.

[28] Robert A. LeVine and Barbara B. LeVine, "Nyansongo: A Gusii Community in Kenya," in Beatrice B. Whiting, ed., *Six Cultures* (New York: John Wiley and Sons, 1963), p. 65.

[29] LeVine and LeVine, "Nyansongo," p. 65.

[30] Baldwin Spencer and F. J. Gillen, *The Arunta: A Study of a Stone Age People,* Vol. 1 (London: Macmillan, 1927), p. 466

deterrent. Again, if a girl refuses to marry or for too long plays off one man against another, her family may encourage one of them to abduct her, saying: "This is what she has been wanting."[31]

Economic Aspects of Marriage. "It's not man that marries maid, but field marries field, vineyard marries vineyard, cattle marry cattle." In its down-to-earth way, this German peasant saying indicates that marriage in many societies involves economic considerations. In our society, economic considerations may not be explicit—however, a person (and his or her family) may consider how the intended spouse will benefit economically. In many other societies, there is an explicit economic transaction that takes place before or at the time of the marriage. The economic transaction may take several forms.

Bride Price. If the groom or his kin give money or goods to the bride's kin, we call it bride price (or bride wealth). This usually gives the groom the right to marry a girl and the right to her children. In many parts of the world, this is still the usual way of obtaining a wife. In 60 percent of the societies in Murdock's *World Ethnographic Sample* the groom's kin customarily pay a bride price; in 50 percent of those societies, a "substantial" bride price is paid.[32] Payment can be made in a number of different currencies. Livestock and food are two of the more common. Among the Swazi of southern Africa,

> The number of cattle varies with the girl's rank: twelve head is the current rate for commoners, princesses command fifteen and more. A boy's father should provide the animals for his son's first wife, and subjects contribute for their chief's main wife.[33]

The Gusii of Kenya, the Nyakyusa of Tanzania, and the Tiv of West Africa also pay in cattle; the Siane of New Guinea and the Ifugao of the Philippines provide pigs; the Navajo and Somali pay in horses. Food is used by the Hopi and Arapesh; the Kwakiutl pay in blankets.

The Subanun of the Philippines have an expensive bride price. They compute the sum as several times the annual income of the groom *plus* three to five years of bride service (described below).[34] Among the Manus of the Admiralty Islands off New Guinea, a groom requires an economic backer—usually an older brother or an uncle—if he is going to marry, but it will be years before he can pay off his debts. Depending on the amount of the bride price agreed upon, payments are concluded at the time of the marriage or continue for years afterwards.[35]

Despite the connotations bride price may have for us, it does not reduce a woman to a slave. Actually, she acquires prestige for herself and her family, perhaps compensating them for the loss of her services, and those of her future children. Indeed, the fee paid can serve as a security—for should the marriage fail through no fault of her own, and the wife return to her kin, the price might not be returned; on the other hand, the wife's kin may pressure her to remain with her husband, even though she does not want to, because her kin do not want to or are unable to return the bride price.

Bride Service. About 13 percent of the 565 societies in the *World Ethnographic Sample* have this custom. Generally, bride service requires the groom to work for his bride's family, sometimes before the marriage is finalized,

[31] Robert F. Spencer, "Spouse-Exchange among the North Alaskan Eskimo," in P. Bohannan and J. Middleton, eds., *Marriage, Family, and Residence* (Garden City, N.Y.: Natural History Press, 1968), p. 187.

[32] Data tabulated in Allan D. Coult and Robert W. Habenstein, *Cross Tabulations of Murdock's* World Ethnographic Sample (Columbia, Mo.: University of Missouri Press, 1965).

[33] Hilda Kuper, "The Swazi of Swaziland," in James L. Gibbs, Jr., ed., *Peoples of Africa* (New York: Holt, Rinehart and Winston, 1966), p. 487.

[34] Charles O. Frake, "The Eastern Subanun of Mindanao," in G. P. Murdock, ed., *Social Structure in Southeast Asia. Viking Fund Publications in Anthropology,* No. 29, 1960.

[35] Margaret Mead, *Growing Up in New Guinea* (London: Routledge & Kegan Paul, 1931), pp. 206–208.

sometimes afterwards. Bride service varies in duration—in some societies it lasts for only a few months, in others it lasts as long as several years. Among the North Alaskan Eskimos, for example, the boy worked for his in-laws after the marriage was arranged. To fulfill his obligation, he might simply catch a seal for them. The marriage might be consummated at any time while he was in service.[36] In some societies, bride service supplements bride price, thereby reducing the amount, or even may be substituted for the bride price.

Exchange of Females. Only 16 societies (or about 3 percent of the societies in the *World Ethnographic Sample*) have this custom, whereby a sister or female relative of the groom is exchanged for the bride. For example, among the Tiv of West Africa, women are exchanged between the two families or kin groups involved.

Gift Exchange. This customary mode of marriage is reported for 15 societies (or about 3 percent of the societies in Murdock's sample). In gift exchange, the two kin groups about to be linked by marriage exchange gifts of about equal value. For example, among the Andaman Islanders as soon as a boy and girl indicate their intention to marry, their respective sets of parents cease all communication and begin sending gifts of food and other objects to one another through a third party. This arrangement continues until the marriage is completed and the two kin groups are united.[37]

Dowry. A *dowry* is a substantial transfer of goods or money from the bride's family to the married couple or the groom's family. Payment of dowries was common in Medieval and Renaissance Europe, where the size of the dowry often determined the desirability of the daughter. Only 4 percent of the societies in Murdock's sample offer dowries, but the custom is still practiced in parts of Eastern Europe and in parts of southern Italy and France, land often being the major item provided by the bride's family.

Among the Rājpūts of India, the dowry includes money paid to the groom-to-be and, in lesser amounts, to members of his family and some of his servants. Expensive jewelry, kitchen utensils, clothing, and bedding are also included. The dowry is a major expense for the bride's family, who often begin collecting the items when the girl is an infant. After the marriage, the dowry is displayed for the benefit of the husband's female relatives, who inspect the bride as well.[38]

In only a small number of societies is compensation paid, even indirectly, to the groom's kin. If there are economic aspects to marriage, almost always it is the bride's kin who are compensated (by bride price, bride service, sister exchange). Why should this be? Murdock has shown that compensation to the bride's kin generally occurs when the bride moves away from home to live with or near the groom's kin. He suggests that the economic considerations transferred to the bride's kin are to compensate them for the loss of the bride's services, which now belong to the groom's kin.[39] And since it is much more frequently the case that the bride moves away from home and goes to live with or near the groom's kin (rather than vice versa), it is perhaps not so surprising that if marriage involves economic considerations at all, they will most frequently go the bride's kin.

Restrictions on Marriage: The Universal Incest Taboo

Hollywood and its press agents notwithstanding, marriage is not always based solely on mutual love, independently discovered and expressed by the two life partners-to-be. Nor is it based on sex alone. But even where love and

[36] Robert F. Spencer, "Spouse-Exchange among the North Alaskan Eskimo," p. 136.

[37] A. R. Radcliffe-Brown, *The Andaman Islanders* (London: Cambridge University Press, 1922), p. 73.

[38] Leigh Minturn and John T. Hitchcock, *The Rājpūts of Khalapur, India* (New York: John Wiley and Sons, 1966), pp. 57–59.

[39] Murdock, *Social Structure,* p. 20.

A TABLE OF

KINDRED AND AFFINITY,

WHEREIN WHOSOEVER ARE RELATED ARE FORBIDDEN IN SCRIPTURE AND OUR LAWS TO MARRY TOGETHER.

A Man may not marry his	*A Woman may not marry with her*
1 GRANDMOTHER,	1 GRANDFATHER,
2 Grandfather's Wife,	2 Grandmother's Husband,
3 Wife's Grandmother.	3 Husband's Grandfather.
4 Father's Sister,	4 Father's Brother,
5 Mother's Sister,	5 Mother's Brother,
6 Father's Brother's Wife.	6 Father's Sister's Husband.
7 Mother's Brother's Wife,	7 Mother's Sister's Husband,
8 Wife's Father's Sister,	8 Husband's Father's Brother,
9 Wife's Mother's Sister.	9 Husband's Mother's Brother.
10 Mother,	10 Father,
11 Step-Mother,	11 Step-Father,
12 Wife's Mother.	12 Husband's Father.
13 Daughter,	13 Son,
14 Wife's Daughter,	14 Husband's Son,
15 Son's Wife.	15 Daughter's Husband.
16 Sister,	16 Brother,
17 Wife's Sister,	17 Husband's Brother,
18 Brother's Wife.	18 Sister's Husband.
19 Son's Daughter,	19 Son's Son,
20 Daughter's Daughter,	20 Daughter's Son,
21 Son's Son's Wife.	21 Son's Daughter's Husband.
22 Daughter's Son's Wife,	22 Daughter's Daughter's Husband,
23 Wife's Son's Daughter,	23 Husband's Son's Son,
24 Wife's Daughter's Daughter.	24 Husband's Daughter's Son.
25 Brother's Daughter,	25 Brother's Son,
26 Sister's Daughter,	26 Sister's Son,
27 Brother's Son's Wife.	27 Brother's Daughter's Husband.
28 Sister's Son's Wife,	28 Sister's Daughter's Husband,
29 Wife's Brother's Daughter,	29 Husband's Brother's Son,
30 Wife's Sister's Daughter.	30 Husband's Sister's Son.

The incest taboo exists in all cultures, including twentieth-century England, as this page from an Anglican prayer book illustrates. (Courtesy, Ann Novotny.)

sex are contributing factors, regulations apply which determine whom one may or may not marry. A number of considerations are usually involved, not least of all, the economic and the prestigious. But perhaps the most rigid regulation, found in *all* cultures, is the incest taboo.

The *incest taboo* refers to the prohibition of sexual intercourse or marriage between mother and son, father and daughter, and brother and sister. No society we know of has generally permitted sexual intercourse within the nuclear family (mother, father, and children). However, there have been societies in which incest was permitted within the royal family (but not generally in the rest of the society). The Incan and Hawaiian royal families were two such exceptions to the universal incest taboo, but probably the most famous example is provided by Cleopatra of Egypt.

It seems clear that the Egyptian aristocracy and royalty indulged in father-daughter and brother-sister marriages. (Cleopatra was married to two of her younger siblings at different times.)[40] The reasons seem to have been partly religious—the Pharaoh, as god, could not marry a commoner—and partly economic, for marriage within the family kept the royal property undivided.

Despite the practices of the ancient Egyptians, incestuous relationships have traditionally been felt to contravene primary human instincts. But if this is so, why then would societies *forbid* incest, and why is this taboo applied universally? A number of explanations have been suggested.

Childhood Familiarity Theory. This explanation, suggested by Westermarck, was given a wide hearing in the early 1920s. Westermarck argued that people who have been brought up together since earliest childhood, such as siblings, would not be sexually attracted to each other. This theory was subsequently rejected because there was evidence that children *were* sexually interested in their parents and siblings. However, two recent studies have suggested that there may be something to Westermarck's theory, that it may well be generally true that individuals lose sexual interest in people they grow up with.

Yonina Talmon investigated marriage patterns among the second generation of three, well-established, collective communities in

[40] Russell Middleton, "Brother-Sister and Father-Daughter Marriage in Ancient Egypt," *American Sociological Review,* Vol. 27, No. 5 (October 1962), p. 606.

Israel *(kibbutzim).*[41] In these collectives, children live with their peer group in separate quarters from their family; they are in constant interaction with their peers, from birth to maturity. The study reveals that, among 125 couples, there was "not one instance in which both mates were reared from birth in the same peer group,"[42] despite parental encouragement of marriage within the peer group. The same situation pertains regarding nonmarital sexual relations, and the reasons given by members of the same age group are quite specific. "They firmly believe that over-familiarity breeds sexual disinterest." One kibbutz member told Talmon, "we are like an open book to each other. We have read the story in the book over and over again and know all about it."[43] Kibbutz children live in large groups, and Talmon's evidence reveals not only the onset of disinterest and even sexual antipathy among children reared together, but a correspondingly heightened fascination with newcomers or outsiders, particularly for their "mystery."

Arthur Wolf's study of the Chinese in northern Taiwan also supports the theory that childhood familiarity produces sexual disinterest.[44] Wolf focused on a community still practicing the Chinese custom of *t'ung-yang-hsi,* or "daughter-in-law-raised-from-childhood."

> When a girl is born in a poor family . . . she is often given away or sold when but a few weeks or months old, or one or two years old, to be the future wife of a son in the family of a friend or relative which has a little son not betrothed in marriage. . . . The girl is called a "little bride" and taken home and brought up in the family together with her future husband.[45]

[41] Yonina Talmon, "Mate Selection in Collective Settlements," *American Sociological Review,* Vol. 29 (August 1964), pp. 491–508.
[42] *Ibid.,* p. 492.
[43] *Ibid.,* p. 504.
[44] Arthur Wolf, "Adopt a Daughter-in-Law, Marry a Sister: A Chinese Solution to the Problem of the Incest Taboo," *American Anthropologist,* Vol. 70 (1970), pp. 864–874.
[45] Wolf, "Adopt a Daughter-in-Law," p. 864.

Wolf's evidence indicates that this arrangement is associated with sexual difficulties when the childhood "couple" later marries. Informants implied that familiarity results in disinterest and lack of stimulation.

Although it may then be true that children brought up together are not very interested in each other sexually, this still does not satisfactorily account for the existence of the incest taboo, which involves parents as well as siblings. And if childhood familiarity *does* reduce sexual interest, why is it necessary to have a taboo on incest? That is, why not simply rely on natural disinclinations?

Freud's Psychoanalytic Theory. Freud's approach offers a possible explanation for the taboo. He suggests that the incest taboo is a reaction against the unconscious existence of incestuous desires. Freud suggested that the son is attracted to his mother (and the daughter to her father) and, as a result, feels jealousy and hostility toward his father. But these feelings cannot continue, for they might lead the father to retaliate; therefore, they have to be renounced, or repressed. Usually they are repressed or made unconscious. But the desire to possess the mother continues to exist in the unconscious, and the horror of incest is a reaction to or a defense against the forbidden unconscious impulse. Although Freud's theory may account for the horror felt about incest, his theory does not account so well for the origin of the taboo. Indeed, it seems to assume at the outset that incest is forbidden; otherwise, there would be no reason for the son or daughter to repress their incestuous desires.

Family Disruption Theory. This theory, often associated with Malinowski, can best be summed up as follows: sexual competition among family members would create so much rivalry and tension that the family could not function as an effective unit. Since the family must function effectively for society to survive, society has to curtail competition within the family. The incest taboo is thus imposed to keep the family intact.

But there are inconsistencies in this approach. Society could have shaped *other* rules about the sexual access of one member of the family to another which would also eliminate potentially disruptive competition. Also, why would brother-sister incest be so disruptive? As we noted, such marriages *did* exist in ancient Egypt. Brother-sister incest would not disrupt the authority of the parents, if the children were allowed to marry when mature. The family disruption theory, then, does not seem to adequately explain the origin of the incest taboo.

Cooperation Theory. This theory, proposed by the early anthropologist Edward B. Tylor and elaborated by Leslie A. White, emphasizes the value of the incest taboo as a device to promote cooperation among family groups, thus helping communities to survive. As Tylor sees it, certain operations necessary for the welfare of the community can only be accomplished by large numbers of people working together. In order to break down suspicion and hostility between family groups, thus making such cooperation possible, early man developed the incest taboo in order to insure that individuals would marry members of other families. The ties created thereby would then serve to hold the community together. Thus Tylor explains the incest taboo as primitive man's answer to the choice "between marrying out and being killed out."[46] Although there may very well be advantages to marriage outside the family, we need to ask ourselves whether the incest taboo is necessary to promote cooperation with outside groups. Is it not possible, for example, that families could have required some of their members to marry with outside groups if they thought it necessary for survival and could have permitted incestuous marriages when such alliances were not needed? Thus, although the incest taboo might enhance cooperation between families, the need for cooperation does not adequately account for the existence of the incest taboo in all societies, as other customs might also promote alliances between families.

[46] Leslie A. White, *The Science of Culture* (Farrar, Straus and Giroux, 1949), p. 313.

Inbreeding Theory. One of the oldest explanations for the incest taboo, this theory focuses on the potentially harmful consequences of inbreeding, or marrying within the family. That is, people within the same family are likely to carry the same harmful recessive genes and thus inbreeding will tend to produce offspring who are more likely to die early of genetic disorders than the offspring of unrelated spouses. For many years this theory was rejected because it was thought that inbreeding need not be harmful—after all it works well with animals and seems not to have produced defective offspring among the Hawaiian, Incan, and Egyptian royal lineages, if Cleopatra is anything to go by. However, we now have a good deal of evidence, from humans as well as other animals, that inbreeding is generally deleterious. Genes that arise by mutation are generally harmful and recessive, and therefore offspring of close relatives may inherit a double, and possibly lethal, dose of the recessive gene. Recently, a group of behavioral scientists suggested that for species with widely spaced births and few offspring, natural selection would favor some mechanism that prevents inbreeding. Inbreeding is probably particularly deleterious among animals (like man) that produce few offspring at a time, since such species can ill afford many unnecessary deaths. (Animal breeders sometimes obtain beneficial effects with inbreeding, but they usually do not care about the death rate or the high risk of defective offspring.) In man, therefore, natural selection may have favored groups with the incest taboo—a cultural prohibition—since they would have had higher reproductive rates than groups without the taboo.[47] Whether or not people actually recognized the harmfulness of inbreeding, the demographic consequences of the incest taboo may account for its universality, reproductive and hence competitive advantages accruing to groups practicing the taboo. Unlike the family disruption theory and the cooperation theory, for which we might envision cultural solutions other than the incest taboo to obtain the desired effect, the taboo is the only possible solution to the problem of inbreeding. At the same time, such a taboo provides a way of avoiding family disruption and favors social cooperation among families.

Whom Should One Marry?

Every child in our society probably knows the story of Cinderella—how a poor, down-trodden but lovely girl accidentally meets, falls in love with, and eventually marries a prince. It is a charming tale, but as a guide to mate choice in our society it is quite misleading. The majority of marriages simply do not occur in so free and coincidental a way in any society, our own included. Aside from the familiar incest taboo, society often has rules restricting marriage with other persons, as well as preferences about which other persons are the most desirable mates. In other words, every culture tells people what kinds of people they cannot marry and what kinds they can—and sometimes even exactly whom they should marry.

Even in a modern, urbanized society such as ours, where mate choice is, theoretically, free, people tend to marry within their own geographical area and class. For example, studies made in America over the last 20 years reveal that over one-half of all urban marriages occurred between people living less than a mile from one another.[48] Since neighborhoods are frequently made up of people from similar class backgrounds, it is unlikely that many of these alliances were Cinderella stories.

Arranged Marriages. In an appreciable number of societies, marriages are completely arranged—negotiations being handled by the immediate families or by go-betweens. Sometimes betrothals are completed while the future partners are still children, formerly the custom in much of Hindu India, China, Japan, and eastern and southern Europe. Implicit to the arranged marriage is the conviction that the joining together of two kin groups to form new social and economic ties is too important to be threatened by free choice and romantic love.

An example of a marriage arranged for reasons of prestige comes from Ford's study of the Kwakiutl Indians of British Columbia. Ford's informant described his marriage as follows:

> When I was old enough to get a wife—I was about 25—my brothers looked for a girl in the same position that I and my brothers had. Without my consent, they picked a wife for me—Lagius' daughter. The one I wanted was prettier than the one they chose for me, but she was in a lower position than me, so they wouldn't let me marry her.[49]

Exogamy and Endogamy. Marriage partners often must be chosen from *outside one's own kin group or community:* this is known as a rule of *exogamy.* Exogamy can take many forms: it may mean marrying outside a particular group of kinsmen or outside a particular village or group of villages. This often results in spouses coming from quite a distance away. For example, Rani Khera, a village in India, had 266 married women coming from about 200 different villages averaging between 12 and 24 miles away, and 220 local women went to 200 neighboring villages to marry. As a result of these exogamous marriages, Rani

47 David F. Aberle et al., "The Incest Taboo and the Mating Patterns of Animals," *American Anthropologist,* Vol. 65 (1963), pp. 253–265.

48 William J. Goode, *The Family* (Englewood Cliffs, N.J.: Prentice-Hall, 1964), p. 30.

49 Clellan S. Ford, *Smoke from Their Fires* (New Haven: Yale University Press, 1941), p. 149.

Among Indian Hindus, many marriages are still arranged. (Marilyn Silverstone, Magnum Photos.)

Khera, a village of 150 households, is linked with 400 other nearby villages.[50]

A rule of *endogamy* obliges a person to marry *within his or her culturally defined group.* The caste group of India—legally abolished but still a social force—has traditionally been endogamous. The higher castes believed that marriage with lower castes would "pollute" them, and such unions were strictly forbidden. Caste endogamy is also found in some parts of Africa. In East Africa, a Masai warrior will never stoop to marry the daughter of an ironworker, nor will a ruling-caste Tutsi (from Rwanda in East Central Africa) so much as think of joining himself to the family of a hunting caste Twa.

Cousin Marriages. Our kinship system does not differentiate between *types* of cousins. In many other systems such distinctions are of great significance, particularly in regard to first cousins, because they define which cousins are marriageable (or, in some cases, which cousins are preferred mates) and which are not. So, for example, a few societies allow or even prefer marriage with a cross-cousin but prohibit marriage with a parallel-cousin. Most societies, however, prohibit marriage with all types of first cousins.

Cross-cousins are children of siblings of the opposite sex. For example, a child's cross-cousins are his *father's sister's* or his *mother's brother's children. Parallel-cousins* are children of siblings of the same sex. A person's parallel-cousins then, are his *father's brother's children* or his *mother's sister's children.* The Chippewa Indians used to practice cross-cousin marriage as well as cross-cousin joking: with his female cross-cousins, the Chippewa brave was expected to exchange broad, risque jokes; not so with his parallel-cousins, where a severe propriety was the rule. Generally, in societies where cross-cousin, but not parallel-cousin, marriage is allowed, there often is a joking relationship between a man and his female cross-cousin, in contrast to the formal and very respectful relationship he maintains with his female parallel-cousin. Apparently, the joking relationship signifies the possibility of marriage, whereas the respect relationship signifies the extension of the incest taboo to parallel-cousins.

Levirate and Sororate. The *levirate* is the custom whereby a man marries his brother's widow. In the *sororate,* a woman marries her deceased sister's husband. These customs generally apply to secondary marriages—that is, they are practiced after a primary marriage has been terminated by the death of one of the spouses.

Among the Chukchee of Siberia, the levirate means that the next oldest brother becomes the successor. He cares for the widow and children, assumes the sexual privileges of the husband, and unites the deceased's reindeer herd with his own, keeping it in the name of his brother's children. If there are no brothers, the widow passes on to a cousin. Generally, the Chukchee regard the custom more as a duty than as a right. The nearest relative is obliged to care for a woman left with children and a herd.[51] Among the Murngin of Australia, the economic burden of a large household can be such that an elder brother might wish to foster a leviratic marriage even before his death.

> If *wawa* (Elder Brother) has four or five wives, he may say to a single *yukiyoyo* (Younger Brother), "You see that one, you take her and feed her." *Yukiyoyo* says, if *wawa* is an old man, "No, you are an old man, I'll wait until you die, then I'll have them all." *Wawa* replies. "No, you take her now, *yukiyoyo.* I have many wives and you have none."[52]

[50] W. J. Goode, *World Revolution and Family Patterns* (New York: Free Press, 1963), p. 210.

[51] Waldemar Bogoras, "The Chukchee," Pt. 3, *Memoirs of the American Museum of Natural History,* Vol. II, 1909, in Stephens, *The Family in Cross-Cultural Perspective,* p. 195.

[52] W. Lloyd Warner, *A Black Civilization* (New York: Harper & Row, 1937), p. 62.

How Many Does One Marry?

We are accustomed to thinking of marriage as involving just one man and one woman at a time *(monogamy),* but most societies in the world allow a man to be married to more than one woman at the same time *(polygyny).* Polygyny's mirror image, one woman being married to more than one man at the same time *(polyandry),* is practiced in very few societies. Polygyny and polyandry are the two variants of *polygamy,* or plural marriage. *Group marriage,* more than one man being married to more than one woman at the same time, sometimes occurs but is not generally customary in any known society. The table below illustrates these four different forms of marriage, where △ represents male; O, female; and =, marriage.

Form of Marriage		*Males*	*Females*
Monogamy		△ =	O
Polygyny	Polygamy	△ =	O + O . . .
Polyandry	Polygamy	. . . △ + △ =	O
Group marriage		. . . △ + △ =	O + O . . .

Monogamy. There was a time when Westerners seriously believed that monogamy was the end product of civilization. Polygyny was considered base and uncivilized. However, monogamy is not necessarily a hallmark of civilization, nor polygyny of barbarism.

Only about one-quarter of the 565 societies in Murdock's *World Ethnographic Sample* are "strictly monogamous," but the majority of people living in societies permitting or preferring polygyny often practice monogamy, because no society habitually has twice as many marriageable women as men.

Polygyny. Although it is not practiced in Western and other highly industrialized societies, polygyny is found in many societies throughout the world. Murdock's *World Ethnographic Sample* reports that over 70 percent of societies practice it, and there is ample evidence for its existence in our own cultural background. The Old Testament has many references to it, Kings David and Solomon being just two examples of men polygynously married.

We have defined polygyny as the marriage of one man to more than one woman. Note that we only call marriage polygynous when the plural marriages are contemporaneous, not successive. Polygynous marriages are socially recognized marriages, "involving residental co-habitation and economic co-operation as well as sexual association."[53]

Polygyny in many societies is a mark of a man's high wealth or status, since generally only the very wealthy and the leaders (who are rich in any case) can, and are expected to, support a number of wives. This situation still exists in some Moslem (especially Arabic-speaking) societies. However, in other societies, where women are important contributors to the economy, greater wealth may be obtained by having more than one wife.

Among the Siwai, a society in the South Pacific, status is achieved through feast giving. Since pork is the main dish at these feasts, the Siwai link pig raising with prestige. Moreover, pigs are beloved pets to the Siwai:

> When Siwai natives call their pigs by name, grin with pleasure as the beasts troop in squealing, carefully set out food for them in baskets and discuss their merit with noticeable pride, it becomes apparent to an observer that these people look upon their pigs as pets. . . . Even granted that a man must occasionally butcher a pig to celebrate an event, he rarely ever uses a pig which he, himself, has raised.[54]

This great interest in pigs sparks an interest in wives, since, in Siwai society, women raise the food needed to raise pigs.

[53] Murdock, *Social Structure,* p. 26.

[54] Douglas Oliver, *A Solomon Island Society* (Cambridge, Mass.: Harvard University Press, 1955), pp. 352–353, as quoted in Stephens, *The Family in Cross-Cultural Perspective,* pp. 54–55.

A Yoruba king in western Nigeria is greeted by some of his 156 wives. The two older women were wives of the present king's father and are cared for by the young king. (Marc and Evelyne Bernheim from Woodfin Camp and Associates.)

It is by no mere accident that polygynous households average more pigs than monogamous ones. Informants stated explicitly that some men married second and third wives in order to enlarge their gardens and increase their herds.[55]

[55] Oliver, *A Solomon Island Society,* pp. 348–349, as quoted in Stephens, *The Family in Cross-Cultural Perspective,* p. 55.

Thus, while having many wives does not in itself confer status among the Siwai, the increase in pig herds that may result from polygyny is a source of prestige for the owner.

One does not need to be a marriage counsellor with monogamous experience to appreciate that a household with multiple wives is likely to be troublesome. Sinu, a Siwai, describes his plight:

> There is never peace for long in a polygynous family. If the husband sleeps in the house of one wife, the other one sulks all the next day. If the man is so stupid as to sleep two consecutive nights in the house of one wife, the other one will refuse to cook for him, saying: "So-and-so is your wife; go to her for food. Since I am not good enough for you to sleep with, then my food is not good enough for you to eat." Frequently the co-wives will quarrel and fight. My uncle formerly had five wives at one time and the youngest one was always raging and fighting the others. Once she knocked an older wife senseless and then ran away and had to be forcibly returned.[56]

Although jealousy among co-wives is generally a problem in polygynous societies, it seems to be lessened if one man is married to two or more sisters *(sororal polygyny)*. It seems that sisters, having grown up together, are more likely to get along and cooperate as co-wives than are co-wives who are not also sisters *(nonsororal polygyny)*. Polygynous societies often have the following customs or rules which presumably lessen jealousy among co-wives:

1. Co-wives who are not sisters tend to have separate living quarters; sororal co-wives almost always live together. Among the Plateau Tonga in Africa, who practice nonsororal polygyny, the husband shares his personal goods and his favors among his wives, who live in separate dwellings, according to principles of strict equality. The Crow practice sororal polygyny, and co-wives usually share the same tepee.[57]
2. Co-wives have clearly defined equal rights in matters of sex, economics, and personal possessions. For example, the Tanala of Madagascar require the husband to spend a day with each co-wife in succession. Failure to do so constitutes adultery and entitles the slighted wife to sue for divorce and alimony of up to one-third of the husband's property. Furthermore, the land is shared equally among all the women, who expect him to help with its cultivation when he visits them.[58]
3. Senior wives often have special privileges. The Tonga of Polynesia, for example, grant to the first wife the status of "chief wife." Her house is to the right of her husband's and is called "The House of the Father." The other wives are called "small wives" and live to the left. The chief wife has the right to be consulted first, and her husband is expected to sleep under her roof before and after a journey. Although this rule might seem to enhance the jealousy of the secondary wives, later wives are usually favored somewhat because they tend to be younger and more attractive. By this custom, then the first wife may be compensated for her loss of physical attractiveness by increased prestige.

A potential for discord and jealousy exists not only among a man's wives, but among his children as well. Not surprisingly, the emotional ties between child and mother are deeper than those between child and father, and the resentment of a co-wife toward her younger counterpart may also be felt by her children. If the children of one wife seem to be receiving favored treatment from their father, rivalry may develop among the other siblings.

In view of the problems that seem to accompany polygyny, how can we account for the fact that it is so widespread? Linton[59] suggests that polygyny derives from the general primate urge to collect females; but then why wouldn't all societies practice polygyny?

Another explanation of polygyny is that it

[56] Oliver, *A Solomon Island Society,* pp. 223–224, as quoted in Stephens, *The Family in Cross-Cultural Perspective,* p. 58.
[57] Stephens, *The Family in Cross-Cultural Perspective,* pp. 63–67.
[58] Ralph Linton, *The Study of Man* (New York: Appleton-Century-Crofts, 1936), pp. 184–187.
[59] Linton, *The Study of Man,* p. 183.

may occur most frequently in societies which practice long postpartum (after birth) sexual prohibitions.[60] In these societies, a couple must abstain from intercourse until their child is at least a year old. John Whiting suggests that couples may abstain from sexual intercourse for a long time after birth because of health reasons. A Hausa woman reported:

> A mother should not go to her husband while she has a child she is suckling. If she does, the child gets thin; he dries up, he won't be strong, he won't be healthy. If she goes after two years it is nothing, he is already strong before that, it does not matter if she conceives again after two years.[61]

The baby's illness seems to be *kwashiorkor,* a disease common in tropical areas which is probably caused by protein deficiency. By observing a long postpartum sex taboo, there are fewer births; therefore, each child is nursed longer and receives more protein from the mother's milk. The likelihood of a child contracting kwashiorkor is thereby reduced. Consistent with Whiting's interpretation is the fact that presumably low-protein societies (whose principal crops are root and tree crops, such as taro, sweet potatoes, bananas, and breadfruit) tend to have a long postpartum sex taboo. Societies with long postpartum sex taboos also tend to be polygynous. Perhaps, then, a man's having more than one wife is a cultural adjustment to the taboo. As a Yoruba woman said:

> When we abstain from having sexual intercourse with our husband for the 2 years we nurse our babies, we know he will seek some other woman. We would rather have her under our control as a co-wife so he is not spending money outside the family.[62]

[60] J. W. M. Whiting, "Effects of Climate on Certain Cultural Practices," in Ward H. Goodenough, ed., *Explorations in Cultural Anthropology* (New York: McGraw-Hill, 1969), pp. 511–544.
[61] Whiting, "Effects of Climate on Certain Cultural Practices," p. 518.
[62] Whiting, "Effects of Climate on Certain Cultural Practices," p. 516–517.

Although we may agree that men might seek other sexual relationships during the period of a long postpartum sex taboo, it is not clear why polygyny is the only possible solution to the problem. After all, it is conceivable that all of a man's wives might be subject to the postpartum sex taboo at the same time. Furthermore, there are always sexual outlets outside marriage.

Another explanation of polygyny is that it may be a response to an imbalanced sex ratio, such that women outnumber men. Although no society we know of has twice as many women as men (so that all adults can be married polygynously), this does not mean that less than 2 to 1 imbalances do not exist. An imbalanced sex ratio may occur because of the prevalence of warfare in such societies. Given that almost all adults are married in noncommercial societies, polygyny may be a way of providing spouses for surplus women. Indeed, there is some evidence that societies with imbalanced sex ratios in favor of women tend to have both polygyny and high male mortality in warfare. Conversely, societies with balanced sex ratios tend to have both monogamy and low male mortality in warfare.[63]

Polyandry. Murdock's *World Ethnographic Sample* includes only four societies (less than 1 percent of the total) where *polyandry,* or the marriage of several men to one woman is practiced. Polyandry can be *fraternal* (when the husbands are brothers), or *nonfraternal.*

Tibetans and the Toda of India practice fraternal polyandry. Marriage arrangements are quite unambiguous—the wife of one brother is accepted as the wife of all of them, even of a brother who is born after the wedding itself. For the Toda, paternity does not reside with the biological father (which anthropolo-

[63] Melvin Ember, "Warfare, Sex-Ratio, and Polygyny." Paper presented at annual meeting of the American Anthropological Association, Toronto, November 1972.

gists refer to by the Latin term *genitor*) but with the social father (Latin, *pater*) whose status is confirmed with a ceremony in the seventh month of pregnancy. Generally, the family lives in the same dwelling, but in Tibet each husband has his own room if the household is sufficiently wealthy. The men decide when their wife will visit each of them.

Two possible explanations for polyandry are female infanticide, which would limit the number of women in society, and the possible need to keep landholdings above a minimum size (thus favoring the pooling of husbands' property). Among the Toda and Tibetans, female infanticide is practiced.[64] and polyandry may therefore be a response to an imbalanced sex ratio in favor of men. (Why female infanticide is practiced in the first place is not clear.) Among the Tibetans, the landholdings of a part of the population are so small and fixed that further subdivision (normally among brothers) is not feasible. It is among this group that polyandry is practiced. Polyandry, especially since it is fraternal, keeps the land undivided and in the same family.[65]

Group Marriages. Group marriages are not customary in any society. When they do occur, as among the Marquesans of the South Pacific and the Toda, they seem to develop out of polyandrous marriages. For example, if a polyandrously married wife has not produced a child, another wife may be coopted with a view to remedying the situation.

The Reindeer Chukchee regard group marriage as a means of security.

> Not to be connected with such a [group] union, means to have no friends and good-wishers, and no protectors in case of need; for the members of a marriage group stand nearer to one another than even relations in the male line.[66]

[64] Stephens, *The Family in Cross-Cultural Perspective,* p. 45.

[65] Melvin C. Goldstein, "Stratification, Polyandry, and Family Structure in Central Tibet," *Southwestern Journal of Anthropology,* Vol. 27, No. 1 (Spring 1971), pp. 65–74.

THE FAMILY

The family is a social unit, consisting minimally of a married couple and the children that couple may have. Families, as we define them, are as nearly universal as marriage. This is not surprising in view of the fact that nearly all societies have marriage, and immature offspring usually live with at least one parent.

The members of a family (particularly the parents and their young children) usually share a *common residence* and acknowledge certain reciprocal rights and obligations, especially regarding economic activity. A person generally belongs in his life to at least one family—a family of *orientation*—the one he is born into. Later, upon marrying, a person forms a new family—a family of *procreation.*

The family provides a learning environment for children. While no animal is able to care for itself at birth, man is exceptional in that he is still not able to do so many years afterwards. This is because, biologically, man matures late, he has few if any inborn or instinctive responses to simplify his adjustment to his surroundings, and he has to learn a repertoire of beliefs and habits (which are mostly cultural) to become a functioning adult in his society. A family cares for and protects children while they acquire the cultural behavior, beliefs, and values necessary for their own and their society's continuance.

The Extended Family

Though we are accustomed to the family consisting of a married couple and their young children (called the *nuclear family*), this is not the most typical family arrangement. The *extended family* is the most common form known

[66] Bogoras, "The Chukchee," as quoted in Stephens, *The Family in Cross-Cultural Perspective,* p. 48.

to anthropology. It consists of two or more monogamous, polygynous, or polyandrous families linked by a blood tie. Most commonly, a married couple and one or more of their married children live in the same house or household. The constituent nuclear families are linked through the parent-child tie. However, an extended family is sometimes composed of families linked through a sibling tie; this variant is called a *joint family*. For example, such a family may consist of two married brothers, their wives, and their children. Extended families may be quite large—containing many nuclear families and including three generations.

Extended Family Life. In a society composed of extended families, marriage does not bring as pronounced a change in life style as it does in our nuclear family culture, where the couple moves to a new residence and forms a new and basically independent family unit. In extended families, the newlyweds are assimilated into an existing family unit. Margaret Mead describes such a situation in Samoa:

> In most marriages there is no sense of setting up a new and separate establishment. The change is felt in the change of residence for either husband or wife and in the reciprocal relations which spring up between the two families. But the young couple live in the main household, simply receiving a bamboo pillow, a mosquito net and a pile of mats for their bed. . . . The wife works with all the women of the household and waits on all the men. The husband shares the enterprises of the other men and boys. Neither in personal service given or received are the two marked off as a unit.[67]

The young couple in Samoa, as in other societies with extended families, generally has little decision-making power over the governing of the household. Often, the responsibility of running the household rests with the senior male. Nor can the new family usually accumulate its own property and become independent; it is a part of the larger corporate structure.

> So the young people bide their time. Eventually, when the old man dies or retires, *they* will own the homestead, they will run things. When their son grows up and marries, he will create a new subsidiary family, to live with them, work for the greater glory of *their* extended-family homestead, and wait for them to die.[68]

The extended family is thus more likely to perpetuate itself as a social unit than the independent nuclear family. In contrast to the independent nuclear family, which by definition disintegrates with the death of the senior members (the parents), the extended family is always adding junior families (monogamous and/or polygamous) that eventually become the senior members when their elders die.

Possible Reasons for the Extended Family. The extended family is the form of family found in the majority of the world's societies,[69] but not all societies have extended families. How can we explain this variation? Since extended families tend to be found in societies with sedentary, agricultural economies and tend to be absent in hunting-gathering societies, it has been suggested that economic factors may play a role in determining family type. The perpetuating extended family may be a social mechanism that prevents economically ruinous subdivision of family property in societies where property is important. Property ownership is generally more important among food producers than among hunter-gatherers, and this might account for the relationship between type of economy and type of family. In addition, the necessity for mobility in hunter-gatherer societies may make extended families less likely in such economies. During certain seasons, the community may be obliged to sub-

[67] Margaret Mead, *Coming of Age in Samoa* (New York: William Morrow, 1928), as quoted in Stephens, *The Family in Cross-Cultural Perspective,* pp. 134–135.

[68] Stephens, *The Family in Cross-Cultural Perspective,* p. 135.

[69] Coult and Habenstein, *Cross Tabulations of Murdock's* World Ethnographic Sample.

A Sikh extended family in Delhi, India. (Marilyn Silverstone, Magnum Photos.)

divide into nuclear families which scatter into other areas.[70]

Economic factors may also help to explain the dominance of the nuclear family in modern industrial societies. The industrial society resembles a hunting and gathering one in that there is little need for maintaining permanent ownership and control over land from generation to generation. That is, in both kinds of societies mobility is emphasized: the hunter pursues game, and the adult in an industrial society pursues a job. Moreover, in industrial societies, there is money—a commodity that is easily inherited and transferred—which may substitute for land as a form of security. Thus, the independent nuclear family may be adaptive for both the simple nomadic and complex industrial society.

[70] M. F. Nimkoff and Russell Middleton, "Types of Family and Types of Economy," *The American Journal of Sociology,* Vol. 66, No. 3 (November 1960), pp. 215–225.

SUMMARY

1. Although all societies regulate sexual activity to some extent, some are much more permissive than others. Some societies allow both masturbation and sex play among children, while others strictly forbid these acts. Some societies allow premarital sex while others do not. Some allow extramarital sex in some situations while others forbid it. While it is true that most societies are largely either restrictive or permissive about sex, in some cases there are different rules for different age groups. In general it seems that as social inequality increases, so does sexual restrictiveness.
2. Nearly all societies known today practice some form of marriage. Marriage is a socially approved sexual and economic union between a man and a woman which is presumed to be more or less permanent, and which subsumes reciprocal rights and obligations between spouses, and between spouses and their children. Marriage may be so widespread because it is adaptive. It promotes division of labor between men and women, thus contributing to efficiency.
3. The social recognition of marriage varies greatly; there may be highly elaborate ceremonies or none at all. Variations include childhood betrothals, trial marriage periods, feasting, elopement, and outright abduction.
4. Marriage arrangements often include an economic element. The most common form is bride price, in which the groom or his family give an agreed-upon amount of money or goods to the bride's family. Bride service exists when the groom works for the bride's family for a specified period. In some societies, a female from the groom's family is exchanged for the bride, and in others, gifts are exchanged between the two families. Dowry is a payment of goods or money by the bride's family to the married couple or to the groom's family.
5. No society allows marriage or sex between brothers and sisters, mothers and sons, or fathers and daughters.
6. Every culture tells a person whom he cannot marry and whom he can and sometimes even whom he should marry. In quite a few societies, marriages are completely arranged by the couple's kin groups. Implicit to the arranged marriage is the conviction that the joining of two kin groups to form new social and economic ties is too important to be threatened by

free choice and romantic love. Some societies have rules of *exogamy* which require marriage outside one's own kin group or community—while others have rules of *endogamy* requiring marriage within one's group. Although most societies prohibit all first-cousin marriages, many permit or prefer marriage with *cross-cousins* (children of siblings of the opposite sex) and *parallel-cousins* (children of siblings of the same sex). Many societies have customs providing for the remarriage of widowed persons. The *levirate* is the custom whereby a man marries his brother's widow. The *sororate* is when a woman marries her deceased sister's husband.

7. We think of marriage as involving just one man and one woman at a time *(monogamy),* but most societies allow a man to be married to more than one woman at a time *(polygyny). Polyandry*—the marriage of one woman to several husbands—is very rare.

8. Our society is characterized by the independent *nuclear family.* In most societies, however, the *extended family,* consisting of two or more families linked by a blood tie, is the rule. Extended families are most often found in agricultural societies. This is probably because the extended family allows for greater continuity of land ownership.

SUGGESTED READINGS

Bohannan, P., and J. Middleton (Eds.): *Marriage, Family and Residence* (Garden City, N.Y.: Natural History Press, 1968).
A collection of papers on kinship covering a wide range of ethnographic materials. The editors have divided the work into six sections: incest and exogamy; marriage; marriage forms; the family; residence and household; and special problems in the formulation of generalizations and theory in the study of kinship.

Fox, R.: *Kinship and Marriage: An Anthropological Perspective* (Baltimore: Penguin Books, 1967).
An introduction to problems and theory in the study of kinship and marriage. Chapters 1 and 2 are of particular relevance to the present chapter.

Geiger, H. K. (Ed.): *Comparative Perspectives on Marriage and the Family* (Boston: Little, Brown, 1968).
A collection of papers dealing with different cross-cultural approaches to the study of marriage and family life. Includes the editor's critical assessment of these various approaches. The introduction contains Geiger's own theory of conjugal stability and family universality.

Goode, W. J.: *World Revolution and Family Patterns* (New York: Free Press, 1963).
Review of the character of the family under conditions of social change, particularly under the influence of industrialization. Goode discusses factors of social organization, which can encourage, or result from, industrialization: the rise of the nuclear family; the lessening of parental authority; decline of bride price or dowry; lessening of control of the husband over the wife; and greater equality in the distribution of inheritance.

Murdock, G. P.: *Social Structure* (New York: Macmillan, 1949).
A classic cross-cultural analysis of variation in social organization. Chapters 1, 2, 9, and 10—on the nuclear family, composite forms of the family, the regulation of sex, and incest taboos and their extensions—are particularly valuable.

Nimkoff, M. F. (Ed.): *Comparative Family Systems* (Boston: Houghton Mifflin, 1965).
Chapters 1–4 provide a summary of recent studies dealing with variation in family organization. The ethnographic papers which follow describe the family in a variety of social systems. The concluding chap-

ters deal with the role and function of the family in modern society.

Radcliffe-Brown, A. R., and D. Forde (Eds.): *African Systems of Kinship and Marriage* (New York: Oxford University Press, 1950).
A classic work dealing with kinship and social structure in African societies. The important role of the kinship system in simple societies is emphasized in the editors' introduction, which also discusses the general principles of African kin and marriage patterns.

Stephens, William N.: *The Family in Cross-Cultural Perspective* (New York: Holt, Rinehart and Winston, 1963).
A descriptive survey of the family, marriage, sex restrictions, mate choice, and other topics.

16

Marital Residence and Kinship

In American society, and in much of western Europe, a young couple usually establishes a place of residence apart from their parents or other relatives when they marry, if they have not already moved away before that. Our society is so oriented toward this pattern of marital residence, *neolocal* (new place) *residence,* that it seems to be the obvious and natural one to follow. Upper-income families in the United States, perhaps because they are financially able, begin earlier than usual to train their children to live away from home by sending them to boarding schools at thirteen or fourteen. In the army or at an out-of-town college, young adults learn to live away from home most of the year yet may still return "home" for vacations. In any case, when a young person is married, or otherwise established, he or she generally lives apart from his family.

So familiar is neolocal residence to us that we tend to assume that all societies must practice the same pattern. Quite the contrary. Of the 565 societies in Murdock's *World Ethnographic Sample,* only about 5 percent practice neolocal residence.[1] About 95 percent of the world's societies have some pattern of residence whereby a new couple settles within or very close to the household of the parents, or some other close relative, of the groom or the bride.

PATTERNS OF MARITAL RESIDENCE

In societies in which newly married couples customarily live with or near kin, there are several residence patterns that might be established. Because children in all societies are required to marry outside the nuclear family (because of the incest taboo), and because couples in almost all societies live together after they are married (with a few rare exceptions), it is not possible for an entire society to practice a system in which all married offspring reside with their own parents. Some children, then, have to leave home when they marry; but which children remain at home and which reside elsewhere? The four most prevalent patterns in which married couples live with or near kinsmen are:

1. *Patrilocal residence:* the son stays and the daughter leaves, so that the married couple lives with or near the husband's parents (67 percent of all societies)[2]

[1] Allan D. Coult and Robert W. Habenstein, *Cross Tabulations of Murdock's* World Ethnographic Sample (Columbia: University of Missouri Press, 1965).

[2] Percentages calculated from Coult and Habenstein, *Cross Tabulations of Murdock's* World Ethnographic Sample.

2. *Matrilocal residence:* the daughter stays and the son leaves, so that the married couple lives with or near the wife's parents (15 percent of all societies)
3. *Bilocal residence:* either the son or the daughter leaves, so that the married couple lives with or near either the husband's parents or the wife's parents (7 percent of all societies)
4. *Avunculocal residence:* both sons and daughters normally leave; but the son and his wife settle with or near his mother's brother (4 percent of all societies)

A fifth pattern of residence, of course, is neolocal, in which the newly married couple does not live with or near kin:

5. *Neolocal residence:* both son and daughter leave; married couples live apart from the relatives of either spouse (5 percent)

Patrilocal Residence

The most frequent residence pattern is clearly the patrilocal: either the son brings his bride to his father's household (forming or joining a patrilocal extended family or an even wider group of kin), or the couple sets up their own household near the husband's parents (forming a patrilocal independent nuclear family).

Among the Tiv of northern Nigeria,[3] when a son marries, his wife generally comes to live with him within his father's compound or household, forming a patrilocal extended family. The organization of the compound revolves around the oldest male, known as the "great father," who is the head of the extended family. (When the father dies, the eldest son becomes the head of the household.) The Tiv compound or extended family, then, includes the oldest male and his brothers, their wives and unmarried children, along with their married sons and their wives and children. The head of the compound usually has a reception hut, where he entertains guests, and a sleeping house for each wife. Also within the compound is a sleeping house for the wife of each younger brother or son who is married.

Each compound is called by the name of the compound head; it is said to be "in the palm of his hand." He has authority over plans for new buildings, bride prices, disputes, and punishment. The men of the compound give a portion of the money they earn from trading, weaving, and selling crops to the head of the extended family. In addition to exercising his authority over others in the compound, the head is said to determine the character and the moral atmosphere of the compound.

Matrilocal Residence

In matrilocal residence, a husband comes to live with or near his wife's parents. This is the general pattern of residence among the people of Truk, a group of small volcanic islands in the Pacific.[4] Before 1900, the Trukese lived in large houses, each of which contained a number of related women, their husbands and unmarried children, and any married daughters with their husbands and children. In the dwelling, each married woman had a separate sleeping compartment for herself, her husband, and their small children. The girls of the household who had reached puberty but were not yet married slept in their own separate compartment. Unmarried young men of the household slept in a separate building that may have also served as a canoe house. Thus, the man who went to live with his new wife in her household joined a group there that probably included the parents, married sisters, and other more distant kinswomen of his wife.

[3] Laura Bohannan and Paul Bohannan, *The Tiv of Central Nigeria* (London: International African Institute, 1953).

[4] David M. Schneider, "Truk," in David M. Schneider and Kathleen Gough, eds., *Matrilineal Kinship* (Berkeley: University of California Press, 1961), pp. 202–233.

The most frequent pattern of marital residence is patrilocal, in which a son brings his bride to live in or near his father's household. Among the patrilocal Kassem of northern Ghana, a family compound has a sleeping hut for each wife (the cylindrical dwellings painted with abstract designs) and several granaries (the conical buildings covered by straw roofs). (Photo by Marc and Evelyne Bernheim from Woodfin Camp and Associates.)

After 1900, the large Trukese dwelling houses were no longer built. Instead, the group that used to live together in one house now live in a cluster of smaller houses, each containing one, or at most two or three, related women and their families. In other matrilocal societies, as in some patrilocal, the married couple does not join a household with kinsmen. Rather, the couple may simply locate their house near kinsmen.

Bilocal Residence

In societies with bilocal residence, we find many couples living with or near the husband's kin and many couples living with or near the wife's kin. This is the pattern of residence generally found today in the villages of American Samoa, a group of islands in the South Pacific.[5] The village is generally located behind a stretch of beach. From the seaside, one sees an array of large houses, each spaced some distance from the immediately neighboring ones, strung out parallel to the water. Each large house is normally occupied by the head of an extended family. Smaller houses stand behind each large house and are occupied by the other members of

[5] The description of residence in American Samoa is based upon M. Ember's fieldwork during 1955–1956.

the extended family. Each house, large or small, is generally a single elliptical or circular room without walls, with a roof of thatch, and a perimeter of posts spaced a few feet apart. There are usually as many houses per extended family as there are constituent nuclear families. Since a couple may live either with the husband's or wife's parents, depending upon where there is more land available for cultivation, some of the extended families in a village will be patrilocal, some will be matrilocal, and some will be bilocal (where both a brother and sister may be living with their families). Thus, because either a son or daughter may remain after marriage, the extended family may include any combination of married siblings and their nuclear families.

Not all societies with bilocal residence have extended families. For example, among the !Kung Bushmen of South Africa, bilocal residence means that a married couple may be living with the husband's parents' band or with the wife's parents band. However, each couple resides as a separate unit within the band.

Avunculocal Residence

In societies with avunculocal residence, most couples live with or near the husband's mother's brother. Although this pattern of residence may appear strange to members of our own society, it begins to make more sense when we realize that societies with avunculocal residence always have kin groups in which the mother's brother is the major authority figure—a pattern of authority which will be discussed later in this chapter.

Often in avunculocal societies a boy will leave his parents' house even before his marriage and live with his mother's brother. For example, among the Haida of British Columbia, a boy moved to his maternal uncle's house at about the age of ten. The uncle assumed charge of the boy's training in fishing, hunting, canoe building, war, and so forth, and was his sole disciplinarian. Even when the boy grew up and married, he was still subject to the uncle's authority. In the case of the Haida, the young man brought his bride to live with him in his mother's brother's house.[6] In other avunculocal societies, however, the young man and his bride may simply live near his maternal uncle.

Neolocal Residence

We are already familiar with how neolocal residence works, for in our own society we are accustomed to living apart from all kin. In fact, some married couples in our society try to live as far away as possible from either spouse's parents or other kin. For many of us, the desire to be independent of kin is so overriding that we may be reluctant even to attend family affairs such as christenings, weddings, and funerals.

Explanations of Variation in Residence

Why is it that in some societies couples live separately from kin, whereas in most societies couples live near, if not with, kin? Many anthropologists have suggested that neolocal residence is somehow related to the presence of a money or commercial economy. They argue that when people can sell their labor or their products for money, they can buy what they need to live, without having to depend on kin. Since money (unlike crops and other foods in a world largely without refrigeration) is not perishable, it can be stored for exchange at a later time. Thus, a money-earning family can resort to its own savings during periods of unemployment or disability. This is not possible in nonmoney economies, where people must depend upon relatives for food and other necessities if for some reason they cannot obtain their own food. There is

[6] George Peter Murdock, "Kinship and Social Behavior among the Haida," *American Anthropologist,* Vol. 36 (1934), pp. 355–385.

some cross-cultural evidence that supports this interpretation: neolocal residence tends to occur in societies with commercial or market exchange, whereas societies without money tend to have patterns of residence that locate a couple near or with kin.[7]

As we have seen, most societies of the world have patterns of marital residence that locate married couples with or near kin. But why in some societies does a married couple live with the husband's parents and in others with the wife's parents? Traditionally it has been assumed that, in societies where married children live near or with kin, residence would tend to be patrilocal if males contribute most to the economy, and matrilocal if women contribute most to the economy. However plausible this assumption might seem, the cross-cultural evidence does not support it. Where men do most of the subsistence work, residence is no more likely to be patrilocal than matrilocal; and where women do an equal amount or more of the subsistence work, residence is no more likely to be matrilocal than patrilocal.[8]

Another factor that more accurately predicts whether residence will be matrilocal or patrilocal is the type of warfare practiced in a society. In most societies, neighboring communities or districts are often enemies—hostilities breaking out every once in a while between such groups. This type of warfare may be called internal, since the fighting occurs between groups speaking the same language. In other societies, the warfare that occurs is never within the same society, but only with other language groups. This pattern of warfare may be referred to as purely external. Cross-cultural evidence suggests that in societies where warfare is at least sometimes internal, residence is almost always patrilocal rather than matrilocal. This is perhaps explained by the concern in such societies over keeping sons close to home in order to help in defense. Since women do not usually comprise the fighting force in any society, having sons reside at home after marriage might be favored as a means of maintaining a loyal and quickly mobilized fighting force close at hand. In contrast, residence is more often matrilocal than patrilocal when warfare is purely external.[9] Under such circumstances, apparently, families need not fear attack from neighboring districts or communities, and it may not be so essential for the sons to reside at home after marriage. If, in societies with purely external warfare, the women do most of the work, families might want their daughters to remain home after marriage, and hence the pattern of residence would be matrilocal. The need to keep sons at home after marriage when there is internal warfare may take precedence over any considerations based on division of labor. It is perhaps only when internal warfare is nonexistent that a female-dominant division of labor may give rise to matrilocal residence.[10]

In contrast to societies in which married couples live with the husband's kin *or* with the wife's kin, in societies that practice bilocal residence a married couple goes to live with or near *either* the husband's parents or the wife's parents. Elman Service has suggested that bilocal residence is likely to occur in societies which have recently suffered a severe and drastic loss of population, due to the introduction of new infectious diseases.[11] As we noted in Chapter 9, contact with Europeans resulted in the depopulation of many non-European populations because they lacked resistance to the Europeans' diseases. Given that couples need to live with

[7] Melvin Ember, "The Emergence of Neolocal Residence," *Transactions of the New York Academy of Sciences,* Vol. 30 (December 1967), pp. 291–302.

[8] Melvin Ember and Carol R. Ember, "The Conditions Favoring Matrilocal versus Patrilocal Residence," *American Anthropologist,* Vol. 73 (June 1971), pp. 571–594.

[9] Ember and Ember, "Conditions Favoring Matrilocal versus Patrilocal Residence," pp. 571–594.

[10] Ember and Ember, "Conditions Favoring Matrilocal versus Patrilocal Residence."

[11] Elman R. Service, *Primitive Social Organization* (New York: Random House, 1962), p. 137.

some set of kinsmen in order to make a living in noncommercial societies, it seems likely that couples in depopulated, noncommercial societies might have to live with whichever spouse's parents (and other relatives) are still alive. In other words, such societies generally could not maintain a *unilocal* (one place) residence pattern, as in matrilocal, patrilocal, or avunculocal residence; instead, they would generally find it necessary to practice bilocal residence (or, more generally, some combination of two or more patterns of unilocal residence). This interpretation seems to be supported by the cross-cultural evidence: recently depopulated societies tend to have bilocal residence or frequent departures from unilocality, whereas societies that are not recently depopulated tend to have one or another pattern of unilocal residence.[12]

The final pattern of marital residence—avunculocal residence, in which a married couple lives with or near the husband's mother's brother—is found (although infrequently) in several parts of the world, including North and South America, the Pacific, and Africa. Thus, avunculocal residence is not at all geographically limited in scope. Although it is associated with matrilineal descent (which will be discussed shortly), anthropologists do not as yet understand the conditions under which avunculocal residence develops.

THE STRUCTURE OF KINSHIP

The fact that most societies have residence patterns which locate people with or near kinsmen suggests that kinship connections are very important in most societies. In noncommercial societies particularly, kinship connections structure many areas of social life—from the kind of access one has to productive resources, to the kind of political alliances which are formed between communities and larger territorial groups, to whom one can and cannot marry. In some societies, in fact, kinship connections have an important bearing on matters of life and death.

Recall the social system described in Shakespeare's *Romeo and Juliet.* The Capulets and the Montagues were groups of kin in lethal competition with one another, and the fatal outcome of Romeo and Juliet's romance was related to that competition. Although Romeo and Juliet's society had a commercial economy (but not, of course, an industrialized one), the political system of the city they lived in was a reflection of the way kinship was structured: sets of kin of common descent lived together, and the various kin groups competed (and sometimes fought) for a prominent or at least secure place in the political hierarchy of the city-state. If a near-modern commercial society could be so structured by kinship, one can imagine how much more important kinship connections and kin groups are in many noncommercial societies that lack political mechanisms—such as "princes" and councils of lords—to keep the peace and initiate other activities on behalf of the community. It is no wonder, then, that anthropologists often speak of the web of kinship as providing the main structure of social action in many primitive or noncommercial societies.

Rules of Descent

If kinship is important in most societies, particularly noncommercial societies, there is still the question of which kin one depends on. After all, if you kept track of all your relatives, distant as well as close, there would be an unmanageably large number of members in each person's network of kin. Consequently, in most societies where kinship connections are important, there is some rule that allocates each person to a particular and definable set of kin, perhaps because

[12] C. R. Ember and M. Ember, "The Conditions Favoring Multilocal Residence," *Southwestern Journal of Anthropology* (in press).

smaller sets of kin can have clearer and firmer ties than infinitely large sets of kin. These rules affiliating individuals with sets of kin are called *rules of descent*. By the particular rule of descent operating in his society, a person can know more or less immediately to whom he can turn in an emergency, as well as who will support him in his daily work or during the important events in his life, such as marriage or the death of a close relative.

There are only a few known rules of descent that affiliate individuals with different sets of kin:

1. *Bilateral* (two-sided) *descent* affiliates an individual more or less equally with his or her mother's and father's relatives of all types.
2. *Patrilineal descent* (the most frequent rule) affiliates an individual with kinsmen of both sexes related to him or her *through men only;* in each generation, then, children belong to the kin group of their father.
3. *Matrilineal descent* affiliates an individual with kinsmen related to him or her *through women only;* in each generation, then, children belong to the kin group of their mother.
4. *Ambilineal* (or *cognatic*) *descent* affiliates an individual with kinsmen related to him or her through men *or* women. In other words, some people in the society affiliate with a group of kinsmen through their fathers, and others through their mothers; consequently the descent groups show both female and male genealogical links.
5. *Double descent* affiliates an individual for some purposes with a group of matrilineal kinsmen and for other purposes with a group of patrilineal kinsmen; thus, two rules of descent, each traced through links of one sex only, are operative at the same time.

Bilateral Descent

The bilateral rule of descent affiliates an individual with a group of close kinsmen more or less equally on his father's and mother's side.

Because the kindred is an ego-centered group in a bilateral system of descent, the kindreds are different for different people. Thus, although the relatives gathered here might represent the entire kindred for some members of this American family, other members will have somewhat different kindreds. (Photo by Kim Wells for *Life* Magazine.)

Consequently, this rule does not by itself exclude any relatives from membership in one's set of kinsmen. In practice, however, a bilateral rule of descent affiliates a person only with close relatives on both his father's and mother's side. This network of close relatives is called a *kindred.* In our own society, we can think of this group of kinsmen as including the people we might invite to weddings, funerals, or some other ceremonial occasion. The kindred, however, is not usually a very definite group. As anyone who has been involved in the planning of a wedding invitation list knows, a great deal of time may be spent deciding which relatives one ought to invite and which ones can be legitimately excluded. The boundaries of the kindred, then, are often fuzzy; no one is usually sure of how "close" relatives have to be to get invited, and how far away they have to be to warrant exclusion. Societies with bilateral descent differ in how distant relatives have to be before they are lost track of or before they are not included in ceremonial activities. In societies like our own, in which kinship is relatively unimportant, fewer relatives are included in the kindred. In other bilateral societies, however, where kinship connections are somewhat more important, more relatives would be included in the kindred.

The distinctiveness of the bilateral system of descent is that, aside from brothers and sisters, no two people belong to exactly the same kin group. The kindred contains close relatives spreading out on both the father's and mother's sides, but the members of your kindred are affiliated only by way of their connection to you. Thus, the kindred is an *ego-centered* group of kin. Since different people (aside from brothers and sisters) have different mothers and fathers, one's first cousins will have different kindreds, and even one's own children will have a different kindred from oneself. For example, you would probably include your aunts and uncles in your kindred, but to your children these aunts and uncles would be great-aunts and great-uncles and might not be close enough to them to be included in their kindred. Because the kindreds are ego-centered and therefore are different for different people, the kindred is not generally a perpetuating group—that is, it does not continue in existence after the death of the focal member (yourself). In our society, the kindred usually comes together only on certain occasions and then only temporarily. Moreover, one's kindred never reassembles after one's death.

Unilineal Descent

Both the matrilineal and patrilineal rules of descent are *unilineal* rules, in that a person is affiliated with a group of kinsmen through descent links of one sex only—either through males only or through females only. As Figure 1 indicates, in patrilineal systems the children in each generation belong to the kin group of their father; their father, in turn, belongs to the group of his father, and so on. An individual is affiliated, then, through descent links of the male sex only: although a man's sons and daughters are all members of the same descent group, affiliation with that group is transmitted only by the sons to their children. In matrilineal systems, on the other hand (see Figure 2), children in each generation belong to the kin group of their mother. Descent, therefore, is traced through the female sex only: although a woman's sons and daughters are all members of the same descent group, only her daughters can pass on their descent affiliation to their own children.

Unilineal rules of descent affiliate an individual with a line of kinsmen related to him back in time and into the future. By virtue of this line of descent (whether or not it passes consistently through males or females), some very close relatives are excluded. For example, in a patrilineal system, your mother and your mother's parents do not belong to your patrilineal group. But your father and his father do. So some of your

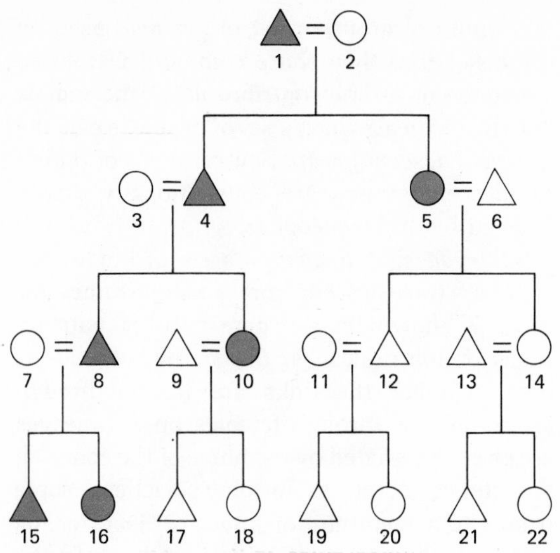

Figure 1 *Patrilineal Descent*
Individuals 4 and 5, who are the children of 1 and 2, affiliate with their father's patrilineal kin group, represented by the color light brown. In the next generation, the children of 3 and 4 also belong to the light brown kin group, since they take their descent from their father who is a member of that group. However, the children of 5 and 6 do not belong to this patrilineal group, since they take their descent from their father who is a member of a different group. That is, although the mother of 12 and 14 belongs to the light brown patrilineal group, she cannot pass on her descent affiliation to her children; and since her husband (6) does not belong to her patrilineage, her children (12, 14) belong to their father's group. In the fourth generation, only 15 and 16 belong to the light brown patrilineal group, since their father is the only male member of the preceding generation who belongs to the light brown patrilineal group. In this diagram, then, 1, 4, 5, 8, 10, 15, and 16 are affiliated by patrilineal descent; all the other individuals belong to other patrilineal groups.

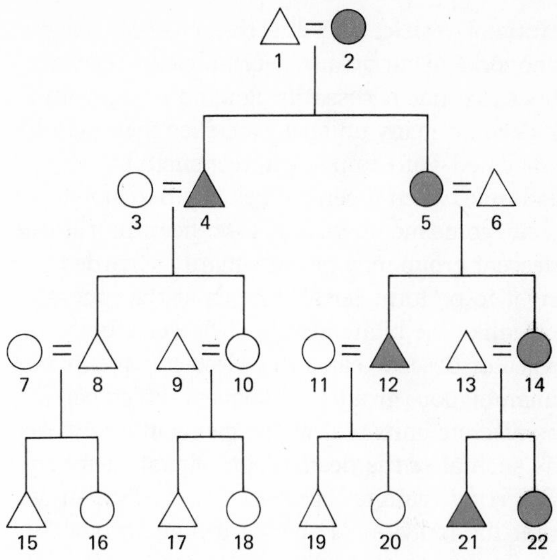

Figure 2 *Matrilineal Descent*
Individuals 4 and 5, who are the children of 1 and 2, affiliate with their mother's kin group, represented by the color light brown. In the next generation, the children of 5 and 6 also belong to the light brown kin group since they take their descent from their mother who is a member of that group. However, the children of 3 and 4 do not belong to this matrilineal group since they take their descent from their mother who is a member of a different group; their father, although a member of the light brown matrilineal group, cannot pass his affiliation on to them under the rule of matrilineal descent. In the fourth generation, only 21 and 22 belong to the light brown matrilineal group, since their mother is the only female member of the preceding generation who belongs. Thus, individuals 2, 4, 5, 12, 14, 21, and 22 belong to the same matrilineal group. This rule of descent generates a group that is the mirror image of the group generated by a patrilineal rule.

closest relatives are not members of your descent group. In your own generation, some cousins are excluded, and in your children's generation, even your own children may be excluded as well as some of your nieces and nephews. However, although unilineal rules of descent exclude certain types of relatives from membership in one's kin group (just as practical considerations restrict the effective size of kinship networks in our own society), the excluded relatives are not necessarily ignored or forgotten. Indeed, in many unilineal societies they may be entrusted with important responsibilities. For example, when a person dies in a patrilineal society, some members of his mother's patrilineal descent group may be customarily accorded the right to perform certain rituals at the funeral.

Unlike the bilateral rule of descent, unilineal rules of descent can form clear-cut and hence unambiguous groups of kinsmen, which can act as discrete units and which can continue to act as such after the death of individual members. Referring again to Figures 1 and 2, one can see that the individuals shaded in light brown belong to the same group with no ambiguity—an individual in the fourth generation belongs to the group just as much as one in the first generation. If you imagine that this group has a name, say, the Hawks, then one knows immediately whether or not he is a Hawk. If he is not a Hawk, then he belongs to some other group instead, for each person belongs only to one line. This fact is important if kin groups are to act as discrete or nonoverlapping units. It is difficult for people to act together unless they know exactly who should get together. And it is easier to act together as a group if you only belong to one such group. In a bilateral system, in contrast, not only is it not always clear where the boundary of the kindred is, but one person may belong to many different kindreds, his own and other's (children's, cousins', and so forth). Consequently, it is not surprising that the kindred only gets together temporarily for ceremonial occasions. Societies with unilineal descent, on the other hand, usually have groups of unilineal kin acting as units over time—sometimes owning land, sometimes performing rituals together, sometimes fighting together.

Types of Unilineal Descent Groups.

In a society with unilineal descent, people usually refer to themselves as belonging to a particular unilineal group or set of groups based on the belief that they share common descent in either the male line (patrilineal) or the female line (matrilineal). Such a set of people is called a *unilineal descent group.* Several types of unilineal descent groups are conventionally distinguished by anthropologists.

Lineages. A *lineage* is a set of kin whose members trace descent from a common ancestor through known links. There may be patrilineages or matrilineages, depending, of course, upon whether the links are traced through males only or through females only. Lineages are often designated by the name of the common ancestor or ancestress. In some societies, people belong to a hierarchy of lineages. This means that they first trace their descent back to the ancestor of a minor lineage, then to the ancestor of a larger and more inclusive major lineage, and so on.

Clans. A *clan* (also called a *sib*) is a set of kin whose members believe themselves descended from a common ancestor or ancestress, but the links back to that ancestor cannot be specified; in fact, the ancestor may not even be known. Clans or sibs are often designated by an animal or plant name (called a *totem*), which may have some special significance for the group and at the very least provides for group identification. Thus, if someone says he or she belongs to the Bear, Wolf, or Turtle group, for example, others will know whether or not that person is a clansman.

Although it may seem strange to us that an animal or plant should be a symbol of a kin group, animals as symbols of groups are familiar in our own culture. Football and baseball teams, for example, are often named for animals (Detroit Tigers, Los Angeles Rams, Philadelphia Eagles, Atlanta Falcons); voluntary associations such as men's clubs are sometimes called by the name of an animal (Elks, Moose, Lions); boys in our society may become cub scouts or eagle scouts. Entire nations may be represented by an animal, as the American Eagle, the British Lion, or the Russian Bear; and political parties also adopt animals as symbols, witness the Democratic donkey and the Republican elephant.[13]

The use of a totem (an animal or plant name) to refer to one's clan or sib is common in societies with unilineal descent groups. The word "totem" itself comes from the Ojibwa American Indian word *ototeman,* meaning "he is a relative of mine." In some societies, people have to observe taboos relating to their clan totem. For example, clan members may be forbidden to kill or eat their totem. However, this is not the case in all societies with totems.

The reasons for choosing animals and, very infrequently, plants, to represent clans is problematic. Lévi-Strauss suggests that particular qualities of animals strike the human imagination, perhaps even the unconscious, as somehow representative of features important to the survival and even the behavior of clan ancestors—qualities such as vitality, aggressiveness, slyness, restlessness, or eternal unpredictability.[14]

Phratries. A phratry is a unilineal descent group composed of a number of supposedly related clans or sibs. As with the clan, the descent links in phratries are also unspecified.

Moieties. When a whole society is divided into two large unilineal descent groups, we call each of the two groups a moiety. (The word "moiety" comes from a French word meaning "half.") The people in each moiety believe themselves to be descended from a common ancestor, although they cannot specify how.

Although we have distinguished several different types of unilineal descent group, this by no means implies that all unilineal societies have only one type of descent group. Although some have only one type of group, many societies have two or more types in var-

Many Northwest Pacific coast Indian societies constructed totem poles representing animals associated with their kin groups. Shown here are Beaver and Eagle totem poles of the Tlingit Indians. (National Museum of Canada, Ottawa, Canada.)

[13] George Peter Murdock, *Social Structure* (New York: Macmillan, 1949), pp. 49–50.

[14] Claude Lévi-Strauss, *Totemism* (Boston: Beacon Press, 1962).

ious combinations. For example, some societies have lineages and clans; others may have no lineages but clans and phratries; and still others may have clans and moieties but not phratries or lineages. Aside from the fact that if a society has phratries it must also have clans (since phratries are combinations of clans), all combinations of descent groups are possible.

Patrilineal Organization. Patrilineal organization is the most frequent type of descent system. The Kapauku Papuans, a people living in the Central Highlands of western New Guinea, are an example of a patrilineal society with many types of descent groups.[15] To a Kapauku, the hierarchy of groups to which he is affiliated by virtue of the patrilineal descent system plays an extremely important part in his life. All Kapauku belong to a patrilineage, a patriclan which includes his lineage, and a patriphratry which includes his clan.

The male members of a patrilineage, all the living males who can trace their actual relationship through males to a common ancestor, constitute the male population of a single village or, more likely, a series of adjoining villages. In other words, the lineage is a territorial unit. The male members of the lineage live together by virtue of a patrilocal rule of residence and a fairly stable settlement pattern—a son stays near his parents and brings his wife to live in or near his father's house, while the daughters leave home and go to live with their husbands. Over a long period of time, if the group lives in one place, the male descendants of one man live in the same territory. If the lineage is large, it may be subdivided into sublineages—people tracing their descent from one of the sons of the lineage ancestor. The male members of the sublineage live in a contiguous block of territory within the larger lineage territory. Often the sublineage constitutes an entire village, which normally contains about 120 people.

The members of the same patrilineage address each other affectionately, and within this group law and order is maintained by a headman. Killing within the lineage is considered a serious offense, and if any fighting takes place within the lineage it is with sticks, rather than with lethal weapons such as spears. Not surprisingly, since sublineage members are even more closely related, they have an even greater feeling of unity than members of the lineage. The sublineage headman tries to settle any kind of grievance within the sublineage as quickly and as peacefully as possible. Externally, sublineage members are responsible for the actions of their fellows. Consequently, if a fellow sublineage-mate has committed a crime, all the members may be considered responsible, and their property may be seized; or, if a fellow sublineage-mate kills another, any member of the sublineage may be killed in revenge.

The Kapauku also belong to larger and more inclusive patrilineal descent groups—clans and phratries. All the people of the same clan believe that they are related to each other in the father's line, but they are unable to say how they are related. Tradition has it that the clans were formed by the Creator, who related each clan to a totem plant or animal. If a member of the patriclan eats his plant or animal totem, it is believed that he will become deaf. A Kapauku is also forbidden to marry anyone from his or her clan; in other words, the clan is exogamous. It is believed that marriage to someone of one's own clan will cause harm to the entire clan and will lead to the death of the culprits.

Unlike the members of the patrilineage, the male members of the patriclan do not all live together; in fact, a clan's male members may be scattered all over Kapauku territory. Thus, the lineage is the largest group of patrilineal

[15] Leopold Pospisil, *The Kapauku Papuans* (New York: Holt, Rinehart and Winston, 1963).

Among the Kapauku Papuans, clans are exogamous —that is, individuals are required to marry outside their own clan. Here the patrilineage of the bride (right) *confronts the patrilineage of the groom concerning payment of a bride price.* (Courtesy, Leopold Pospisil.)

kinsmen that is localized. The lineage is also the largest group of kinsmen that acts together politically: among clan members there is no mechanism for resolving disputes, and members of the same patriclan (who belong to different lineages) even go to war with one another.

The most inclusive patrilineal descent group among the Kapauku is the phratry, each phratry being composed of two or more clans. The Kapauku believe that the phratry was originally one clan, but in a conflict between brothers of the founding family, the younger brother was expelled and formed a new clan. The two resulting clans are, of course, viewed as patrilineally related since their founders are said to have been brothers. The members of a phratry observe all the totemic taboos of the clans which belong to that phratry. However, unlike the clan, which is exogamous, members of the same phratry but of different clans may marry.

The Kapauku are an example of a unilineal society with many types of descent groups. That is, they have lineages with demonstrated kinship links and two kinds of descent groups with unknown descent links (clans and phratries).

The Tiv of northern Nigeria,[16] on the other hand, are a patrilineal society with lineages only. But the lineages are not all of one level or scale of inclusiveness; since the Tiv reckon their patrilineal descent very far back—indeed, back to the supposed founder of the whole society—their lineages are included one within another, minimal lineages forming branches of more inclusive or maximal lineages, and so on. The lineage system underlies the territorial and political organization of the Tiv. (The political implications of this type of lineage organization will be discussed more fully in Chapter 18.)

If one were to view Tivland from the air, he would see a settlement pattern of scattered compounds or extended family households; there would be nothing corresponding to what we would call a community. However, the male members of a patrilineage and their families generally live in the same territory, just as the Kapauku do. But in contrast to the Kapauku, the Tiv have a hierarchy of more and more inclusive descent groups (lineages) each of which tends to be a territorial unit. The smallest lineage whose male members occupy a contiguous territory is referred to as a *minimal segment.* Males in this segment may trace their patrilineal descent from an ancestor perhaps four to six generations removed, and the segment

[16] The description of the Tiv is based on Bohannan and Bohannan, *The Tiv of Central Nigeria.*

may include from 160 to 1,000 people. These minimal lineage segments are themselves embedded in larger patrilineal segments—the most closely related minimal lineage segments tending to occupy contiguous territories. As shown in Figure 3, the circles numbered 1, 2, 3, and 4 represent minimal patrilineal segments, each minimal segment tracing descent patrilineally to its respective ancestor (1, 2, 3, or 4). But 1 and 2 together trace their descent from A, even further removed in time; and 3 and 4 trace their descent from B also further back in time. The members of lineages A and B also tend to live near one another. But the genealogical hierarchy does not end here. For the larger patrilineages A and B are also embedded in a still larger patrilineage I. This system of descent reckoning extends so far back in time that the entire Tiv society considers itself to be descended from the same ancestor. Thus, to some extent, the division of the Tiv into a hierarchy of lineage segments corresponds roughly to how they are distributed territorially.

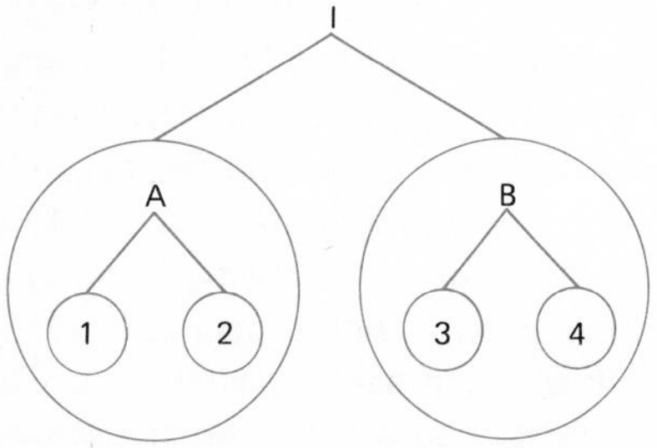

Figure 3 *Segmentary lineage system.*

Because of the number of patrilineages a Tiv belongs to, it is almost impossible to say precisely what functions lineages perform, for it depends upon which lineages one is talking about, and what special circumstances are operative. In fact, one can almost say that the importance of any particular lineage at any given moment depends upon the conflicts it is involved in. Generally, the closer two groups are related genealogically, the more likely they are to be on friendly terms; and the more distantly related, the more likely they are to be hostile. Moral values, too, tend to be associated with genealogical distance. For example, it is considered morally bad for a man to steal within his minimal segment. On the other hand, stealing between lineage segments related 9 to 12 generations back is to be expected—and it is also expected that the victim will kill the thief. Between the minimal segment and the larger lineage segments there is a gradation of moral restrictions that, roughly, vary inversely with increasing genealogical distance. However, this general rule by no means suggests that the Tiv do not have conflicts between closely related patrilineages. As will be discussed in Chapter 18, the Tiv type of lineage structure, called a *segmentary lineage system,* provides a person with different levels of alliance which become activated in different ways depending upon the nature of one's opposition.

Matrilineal Organization. Although societies with matrilineal descent seem in many respects like mirror images of their patrilineal counterparts, there is one important way in which they differ. That difference has to do with who exercises authority in matrilineal systems. In patrilineal systems, descent affiliation is transmitted through males and it is also the males who exercise authority in the kin groups. Consequently, in the patrilineal system, the lines of descent and of authority converge. In a matrilineal system, however, while the line of descent passes through females, females rarely exercise authority in their kin groups—usually males do. Thus, unlike the patrilineal system, the lines of authority and descent do not converge.[17] Although it is not quite understood why this is so—that is, why females rarely exercise political authority even in matrilineal systems—nevertheless, it seems to be an ethnographic fact. In any case, since males exercise authority in the kin group, one's mother's brother becomes an important authority figure, for it is one's mother's brother that is one's closest male matrilineal relative in the parental generation. One's own father does not belong to one's own matrilineal kin group (since one is required to marry outside the kin group) and thus has no say in kin group matters.

The divergence of authority and descent in a matrilineal system has some effect on community organization and marriage within the community. Most matrilineal societies practice matrilocal residence: daughters stay at home after marriage and bring their husbands to live with them; sons leave home to join their wives. But the sons who are required to leave will be the ones who eventually exercise authority in their kin groups. This presents somewhat of a problem. If the men go too far away from their parents' homes it will be difficult for them to exercise authority in their kin groups; moreover, the fact that they move to where their wives live means that the males of the kin group, the decision makers, will be scattered. The solution which seems to have been arrived at in most matrilineal societies is that, although the males move away to live with their wives, they usually do not move away too far, and; indeed, they often marry women who live in the same village. Thus matrilineal societies tend not to be locally exogamous—that is, they do not marry only people from outside the village—whereas patrilineal societies are often locally exogamous.[18]

The matrilineal organization on Truk illustrates the general pattern of authority in matrilineal systems.[19] The Truk have both matrilineages and matriclans. The matrilineage is a property-owning group, whose members trace descent from a known common ancestor in the female line. The female lineage members and their husbands occupy a cluster of houses located on the matrilineage's land. The property of the lineage group is administered by the oldest brother of the group. He allocates the productive property of his matrilineage and directs the work of the matrilineage members. The oldest brother of the lineage also represents the group in dealings with the district chief and all outsiders, and he must be consulted on any matter that affects the descent group. There is also a senior woman of the lineage, who exercises some authority but only insofar as the activities of the women are concerned. She may supervise the women's cooperative work (they usually work separately from the men) and may supervise the management of the household.

Within the nuclear family, the father and mother have the primary responsibility for raising and disciplining their children. However, when a child reaches puberty, the father's right to discipline the child or exercise authority over him ceases. The mother still continues to exercise her right of discipline, and her brother may interfere in this respect. A woman's brother rarely interferes with his sister's child before puberty, but after puberty he may exercise some authority, especially since he is an elder in the child's own matrilineage. On Truk, men rarely move far from their natal homes. As Goodenough has pointed out: "Since matrilocal residence takes the men away from their home lineages, most of them marry women whose lineage houses are within a few minutes' walk of their own."[20]

[17] David M. Schneider, "The Distinctive Features of Matrilineal Descent Groups," in Schneider and Gough, *Matrilineal Kinship,* pp. 1–35.

[18] M. Ember and C. R. Ember, "The Conditions Favoring Matrilocal verus Patrilocal Residence."

[19] Schneider, "Truk."

[20] Ward H. Goodenough, *Property, Kin and Community on Truk* (New Haven: Yale University Publications in Anthropology, 1951), p. 145.

Although there are some differences between the patrilineal and matrilineal systems, there are still many similarities. In both types of systems, there may be lineages, clans, phratries, and moieties and any combination of these. These kin groups, in either matrilineal or patrilineal societies, may perform any number of functions—they may regulate marriage, they may come to each other's mutual aid either economically or politically, and they may perform rituals together.

Functions of Unilineal Descent Groups. Unilineal descent groups tend to be found in societies in the middle-range of cultural complexity. In other words, societies with food production as the basis of subsistence are more likely to have unilineal descent systems than are food collectors;[21] highly commercialized and industrialized food-producing societies, like food collectors, also tend to lack unilineal descent groups. In the middle-range societies, then, unilineal descent groups often have important functions in the social, economic, political, and religious realms of life.

Regulating Marriage. In unilineal societies, one is not usually permitted to marry within any of his own unilineal descent groups. That is, the incest taboo is usually extended to all members of one's largest kin group—whether it be lineage, clan, phratry, or moiety. In some unilineal societies, however, marriage may be permitted within more inclusive kin groups but prohibited within smaller kin groups; and in a few societies, marriage within the kin group is actually preferred. But, in general, the incest taboo in unilineal societies is extended to all supposed unilineal relatives. For example, on Truk, which has matriclans and matrilineages, a person is forbidden by the rule of descent-group exogamy to marry anyone from his or her matriclan; and since the matrilineage is included within the matriclan, the rule of descent-group exogamy also applies to the matrilineage. Among the Kapauku, who have patriphratries, patriclans, and patrilineages, the largest descent group that is exogamous is the patriclan. The phratry may once have been exogamous, but the exogamy rule no longer applies to it. It is traditionally assumed in anthropology that rules of exogamy for descent groups may have developed because the alliances between descent groups that are generated by such rules may be selectively favored under the conditions of life faced by most unilineal societies.

Economic Functions. The strength of the claim to mutual aid on the basis of kinship usually diminishes the more distant the kinship ties become. Thus, members of a man's household or lineage are almost always required to side with him in any quarrel or lawsuit, to help him establish himself economically whether that entails starting a garden plot or a herd of animals, to contribute to the bride price or a fine, and to support him in life crises such as births, initiation ceremonies, marriages, or deaths. One's claim on the members of one's clan is usually not as strong, though a clan may begin a blood feud with another clan over a single individual's crime of murder or theft. Clan members among the Nayar had to share ritual pollution following a birth or death within the clan. The Chinese clans required that poor members be fed and that the higher education of bright students be financed. Where the clan is widely dispersed, the claim to mutual aid may be limited to the provision of hospitality to travelers.

Mutual aid often extends to economic cooperation on a regular basis. The lineage often acts as the corporate landowner. So, for example, house sites and farm land are owned by a lineage among the Tiv, the Trukese, and the Kapauku. Farm tools, fishing tools, and canoes can also be owned jointly. In addition to working together for subsistence, lineage members support each other in larger enterprises, such as clearing virgin bush or forest for farm land, but particularly in sponsoring feasts, potlatches, curing rites, and ceremonial occasions such as births, initiations, marriages, and funerals.

[21] Data from Robert B. Textor, compiler, *A Cross-Cultural Summary* (New Haven: HRAF Press, 1967).

Members of a Kapauku patrilineage cooperate in constructing a dance house for a pig feast. The sponsor of the feast is the man in the foreground. (Courtesy, Leopold Pospisil.)

Money earned—either by harvesting a cash crop or by leaving the community for a period of time to work for cash wages—is sometimes viewed by the lineage as belonging to all; in recent times, however, young people in some places have shown an unwillingness to part with their money, viewing it as different from other kinds of economic assistance.

Finally, economic aid is generally provided by descent groups to a person who is too old or infirm to provide for himself. However, in times of food shortage, the old and infirm may suffer. In Truk society, a man may plant breadfruit trees (which take 15 years to mature and produce for 150 years) for his children, while retaining residual rights to a portion of the food in his old age. But he does not always get that portion. The contract between parents and children—"I will feed you when you are too young to get your own food, and you will feed me when I am too old to get mine"—is broken by some people in all societies.

Political Functions. The word "political," as members of an industrialized society use the term, generally does not apply to the rather vague powers that may be entrusted to a headman or the elders of a lineage or clan. However, such persons may have the right to assign land for use by a lineage member or clansman, even if this right is purely symbolic and does not include the power to refuse land. Headmen or elders may have the power to attempt to settle disputes between two members within a lineage, although they generally lack power to force a settlement. And they may act as intermediaries in disputes between a member of their own and a member of an opposing kin group.

Certainly one of the most important political functions of unilineal descent groups is their role in warfare—the attempt to resolve disputes within and without the society by violent action—for in middle-range societies the organization of such fighting is often in the hands of descent groups. The Tiv of northern Nigeria, for instance, know quite well which lineages they will fight with and which lineages they will fight against, which merit only a stick fight and which must be attacked with bows and arrows. If a man from an unfriendly lineage is caught taking food from a Tiv garden at night, the owner may kill him. The dead man's lineage retaliates by killing one person from the garden owner's lineage, which also retaliates, and so on *ad infinitum.*

In no society is murder allowed within the smallest type of descent group. On the other hand, killing outside the lineage or the clan may be regrettable, but it is not viewed as a crime. It is interesting to note then that the murder of a brother, Cain's murder of Abel, because of favoritism, is the first crime mentioned in the Bible; it was punished by ostracism. Greek law viewed murder of a family member as an unforgivable, heinous crime, yet mythology recounts family murder after family murder: Agamemnon, his daughter; Medea, her brother; Heracles, his wife and children. Perhaps the underlying basis for the strong prohibition of murder within a family exists because that is where murder is most likely to occur, as present statistics continue to bear out.

~~*Religious Functions.*~~ A clan or even a lineage may have its own religious beliefs and practices. Whatever their actual form, religious belief and practice seems to have at least one universal function—to work out man's place in the world by providing reassurance and explanations, no matter how implausible, for events which people cannot understand.

The Tallensi of West Africa revere and try to pacify their ancestors. They see life as we know it as only a part of human existence; life existed before birth and will continue to exist after death. The ancestors of their descent groups have changed their form but have retained their interest in what goes on within the society. They can show their displeasure by bringing sudden disaster or minor mishap; they can show their pleasure by bringing unexpected good fortune. But people can never tell what will please them—ancestral spirits are above all unpredictable. Thus, the Tallensi try to account for unexplainable happenings by attributing them to the ever-watchful ancestors. Belief in the presence of ancestors also provides security; if a man's ancestors have survived death, so will he. The Tallensi religion is a descent-group religion. They are not concerned with other people's ancestors; it is only one's own ancestors who plague one.[22]

The Hopi clans control their religion. Each clan sponsors one of the festivals each year and is the guardian of the paraphernalia and the ritual. Any masks or other objects used at the festival are stored during the year in the principal clan house. A festival is not exclusive to one clan; all Hopi clans participate and each clan is host to at least one festival. The Hopi accept clan responsibility for ceremonies as part of the will of the spirits or deities; each clan is said to have been assigned its ritual role before the emergence of Hopi people from the underworld. The Hopi religion is a tribal religion in which the unity of the people is evidenced by the interdependence of the clans, each being responsible

[22] M. Fortes, *The Web of Kinship among the Tallensi* (New York: Oxford University Press, 1949).

for one of the festivals, each being a significant part of the whole.[23]

The Nayar castes of central Kerala in India are part of an ancient culture which was trading by sea as early as 800 B.C. Not only do various castes possess their own temples, but separate lineages within castes have their own shrines. Nayar temples were dedicated to Bhagavadi, the goddess of war, epidemic, land, and fertility, the goddess being named differently by each lineage. This household goddess was believed to control sickness and other misfortunes, and lineage members were expected to perform daily temple rites to her as well as to sponsor annual festivals in her honor.[24]

The lineage of Abraham had a family religion which was carried on to become the clan religion of the 12 sons of Jacob. A patrilineal society, they recognized only a male deity, and the men did not allow women to worship in the inner temple. Being nomadic, they constructed a portable shrine which they could take with them for their daily rites. They believed their deity had especially chosen their family to succeed, but that he would not hesitate to show his disapproval of them or of others by such acts as sending floods or destroying cities.

Development of Unilineal Systems. Unilineal kin groups often play very important roles in the organization of many societies. But not all societies have unilineal kin groups. In societies which have complex systems of political organization, it would seem that political officials and agencies take over many of the functions that might be played by kin groups, such as the organization of work, warfare, and the allocation of land. However, not all societies that lack complex political organization have unilineal descent systems. Why, then, do some societies have unilineal descent systems and others do not?

It is generally assumed that unilocal residence (patrilocal or matrilocal) is necessary for the development of unilineal descent. Patrilocal residence, if practiced for some time in a sedentary society, will generate a set of patrilineally related males who live in the same territory; and matrilocal residence over time will similarly generate a localized set of matrilineally related females. It is no wonder, then, that matrilocal and patrilocal residence are cross-culturally associated with matrilineal and patrilineal descent, respectively.[25]

But although unilocal residence might be necessary for the formation of unilineal descent groups, it is apparently not the only condition required. First, many societies with unilocal residence lack unilineal descent groups. Second, merely because related males or related females live together by virtue of a patrilocal or matrilocal rule of residence, it does not necessarily mean that the related people will actually view themselves as a descent group and function as such. Thus, it appears that other conditions are needed to supply the impetus for the formation of unilineal descent groups.

There is some evidence that unilocal societies that engage in warfare are more apt to have unilineal descent groups than unilocal societies without warfare.[26] It may be, then, that the presence of fighting in societies lacking complex systems of political organization may provide an impetus to the formation of unilineal descent groups—for unilineal descent groups provide individuals with unambiguous groups of persons that can fight or form alliances as discrete units.[27] One distinguishing feature of unilineal

[23] Fred Eggan, *The Social Organization of the Western Pueblos* (Chicago: University of Chicago Press, 1950).
[24] Kathleen Gough, "Nayar: Central Kerala," in Schneider and Gough, *Matrilineal Kinship,* p. 330.
[25] Data from Textor, *A Cross-Cultural Summary.*
[26] C. R. Ember, "Warfare and Unilineal Descent." Paper presented at the annual meeting of the American Anthropological Association, New York City, 1971.
[27] The importance of warfare and competition as a factor in the formation of unilineal descent groups is suggested by Service. *Primitive Social Organization;* and Marshall D. Sahlins, "The Segmentary Lineage: An Organization of Predatory Expansion," *American Anthropologist,* Vol. 63 (1961), pp. 332–345.

descent groups is that there is no ambiguity about your membership. It is perfectly clear whether you are a descendant of a particular person or not; and it is also perfectly clear whether you belong to a particular clan, phratry, or moiety. It is this feature of unilineal descent groups that enables them to act as discrete units, mostly perhaps in warfare.

Bilateral descent, in contrast, is ego-centered, and every person, other than siblings, has a slightly different set of kinsmen to rely on. Consequently, in societies with bilateral descent it is often ambiguous as to who one can turn to and who has responsibility for aiding another. Such ambiguity, however, might not be a liability in societies with no warfare.

Whether the presence of warfare is in fact the major condition responsible for transforming a unilocal society into a society with unilineal descent groups is still open to question. But however unilineal descent groups come into being, we know that unilineal descent groups often take on importance in many spheres of activity, and it may be that some of these spheres other than warfare are responsible for their formation.

Ambilineal Systems

Ambilineal descent affiliates an individual with kinsmen related to him or her through men *or* women, as illustrated in Figure 4. In other words, some members of the society affiliate with a group of kinsmen through their fathers, others through their mothers. Consequently, the descent groups show both male and female genealogical links. Societies with ambilineal descent groups are far less numerous than unilineal or even bilateral societies. However, ambilineal societies resemble unilineal ones in many ways. For instance, the members of an ambilineal descent group believe they are descended from a common ancestor, though frequently they cannot specify all of the genealogical links; the descent group is commonly named and may have an identifying emblem or even totem; land and other productive resources may be owned by the descent group; myths and religious practices are often associated with the group; and marriage is often regulated by group membership, just as in unilineal systems, though kin group exogamy is not nearly as common in ambilineal as in unilineal systems. Moreover, ambilineal societies resemble unilineal ones in having various levels or types of descent groups: ambilineal societies may have lineages and higher orders of descent groups, distinguished (as in unilineal systems) by whether or not all the genealogical links to the supposed common ancestor are specified.[28]

The Samoans of the South Pacific are an example of an ambilineal society.[29] There are two types of ambilineal descent groups in Samoa, corresponding to what would be called clans and subclans in a unilineal society. These ambilineal groups are both exogamous. Associated with each ambilineal clan is one or more chiefs. The group takes its name from the senior chief; subclans, of which there are always at least two, may take their names from junior chiefs. The man (or, rarely, woman) who becomes a chief of a clan or subclan is selected by those members of the group who attend a special meeting for that purpose.

The distinctiveness of the Samoan ambilineal descent system, as compared with unilineal descent systems, is that because I may be affiliated with an ambilineal group through my father or mother (and my parents, in turn, could be affiliated with any of their parents' groups), there are a number of ambilineal groups I could belong to. Affiliation with a Samoan descent group is optional and a person may theoretically

[28] William Davenport, "Nonunilineal Descent and Descent Groups," *American Anthropologist,* Vol. 61 (1959), pp. 557–572.

[29] The description of the Samoan descent system is based upon M. Ember's 1955–1956 fieldwork. See also Melvin Ember, "The Nonunilinear Descent Groups of Samoa," *American Anthropologist,* Vol. 61 (1959), pp. 573–577; and Davenport, "Nonunilineal Descent and Descent Groups."

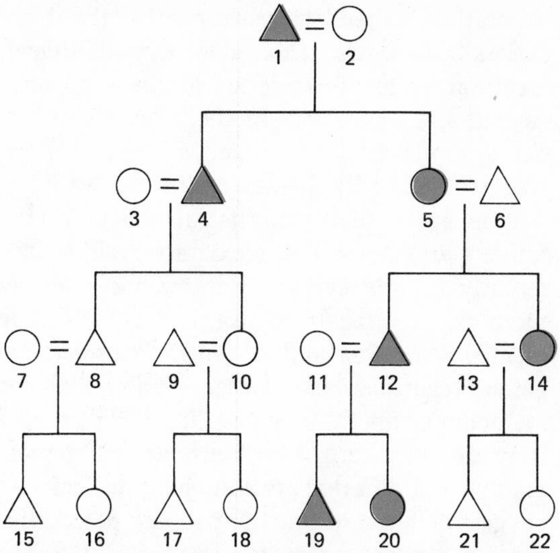

Figure 4 *Ambilineal Descent*
A hypothetical ambilineal group of kinsmen is indicated by the color light brown. Members 4 and 5 belong to this group because of a male link, their father (1); members 12 and 14 belong because of a female link, their mother (5); and members 19 and 20 belong because of a male link, their father (12).

affiliate with any or all of the ambilineal groups he is related to through his parents. In practice, however, a person is primarily associated with one group—the ambilineal group whose land he actually lives on and cultivates—although he may participate in the activities (house building, for example) of several ambilineal groups. Since a person may belong to more than one ambilineal group in Samoa, the society is not divided into discrete kin groups, in contrast to unilineal societies where each person belongs to only one descent line. Consequently, the core members of each ambilineal group cannot all live together (as they could in unilineal societies), since each person belongs to more than one group and cannot live in several places at once.

Not all ambilineal societies have multiple descent group membership as occurs in Samoa. In some ambilineal societies a person may belong (at any one time) to only one group, and in such cases the society can be divided into discrete, nonoverlapping groups of kin.

KINSHIP TERMINOLOGY

Most individuals have an enormous number of relatives. Our society, like all other societies, refers to a number of different kinsmen by the same *classificatory* term. Our kinship terminology is so much a part of our everyday usage that most people probably never stop to think about why we name relatives the way we do. For example, we call our "mother's brother" and "father's brother" (and often "mother's sister's husband" and "father's sister's husband") by the same term—"uncle." It is not that we are unable to distinguish between our mother's or father's brother or that we do not know the difference between *consanguineal kin* (blood kin) and *affinal kin* (kin by marriage); rather it seems that in our society we do not find it necessary to distinguish between our various types of "uncles" in most conversations.

However natural our system of kinship classification may seem to us, countless field studies by anthropologists have revealed that societies differ markedly in how they group or distinguish relatives under the same or different terms. Why different societies have such different systems of classifying relatives is of great interest to anthropology, because these systems shed light on the varying ways societies organize themselves with respect to kinship. The major systems of kinship terminology are the Omaha system, the Crow system, the Iroquois system, the Hawaiian system, and the Eskimo system.

Omaha System

The Omaha system of kin terminology is named after the Omaha Indian tribe of North America, but this system of kin terminology is found in many societies around the world, usually those with patrilineal descent.[30]

[30] The association between the Omaha system and patrilineality is reported in Textor, *A Cross-Cultural Summary.*

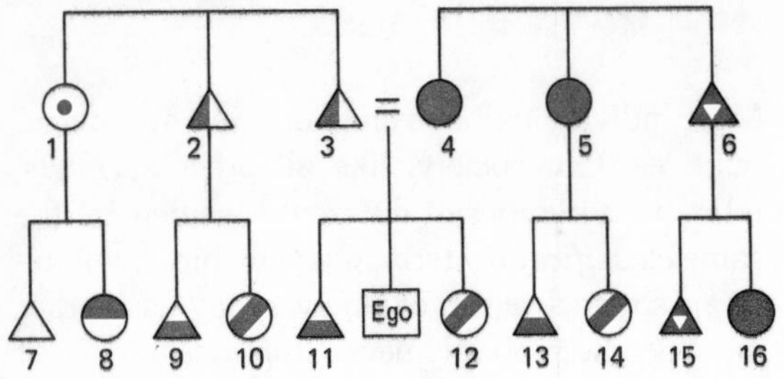

Note: Kin types referred to by the same term are marked in the same way.

Figure 5

Omaha kinship terminology system.

By referring to Figure 5, one can see immediately which types of kin are lumped together in an Omaha system. First, father and father's brother (numbers 2 and 3) are both referred to by the same term. This contrasts markedly with our way of classifying relatives, in which no term that applies to a member of the nuclear family (father, mother, brother, sister) is applied to any other relative. What could account for the Omaha system of lumping? One interpretation is that father and father's brother are lumped in this system because most societies in which this system is found have patrilineal kin groups. Father's brother and father are both in the parental generation of my patrilineal kin group and may behave toward me similarly. My father's brothers also probably live near me, since patrilineal societies usually have patrilocal residence. The term for father and father's brother, then, might be translated "male member of my patrilineal kin group in my father's generation."

A second lumping (which at first glance appears similar to the lumping of father and father's brother) is that of mother and mother's sister (numbers 4 and 5), both of whom are called by the same term. But more surprisingly, mother's brother's daughter (number 16) is also referred to by this same term. Why should this be? If we think of the term as meaning "female member of my mother's patrilineage of *any* generation," then the coverage of the term makes more sense. Consistent with this view, all the male members of my mother's patrilineage of any generation (mother's brother, number 6; mother's brother's son, number 15) are also referred to by the same term.

It is apparent, then, that relatives on the father's and the mother's side are grouped differently in this system. For members of my mother's patrilineal kin group I lump all male members together and all female members together regardless of their generation; but for members of my father's patrilineal kin group I have different terms for the male and female members of different generations. Murdock has suggested that a society lumps kin types, rather than separating them terminologically, when there are more similarities among them than differences.[31]

Using this principle, and recognizing that societies with an Omaha system usually are patrilineal, my father's patrilineal kin group is the one to which I belong and in which I have a great many rights and obligations. Consequently, persons of my father's generation are likely to behave quite differently toward me than persons of my own generation. Members of my patrilineal group in my father's generation are likely to exercise authority over me and I am required to show them respect; members of my patrilineal group in my own generation are those I am likely to play with as a child and to be friends with. Thus, in a patrilineal system, persons on my father's side belonging to different generations are likely to be distinguished. On the other hand, my mother's patrilineage is relatively unimportant to me in a patrilineal system: I do not belong to my mother's patrilineal group (since I take my descent from my father); and because residence is probably patrilocal, my mother's relatives do not even live near me. Thus, inasmuch as my mother's patrilineal relatives are relatively unimportant

[31] Murdock, *Social Structure,* p. 125.

in such a system, they become similar enough to be lumped together.

Finally, in the Omaha system, I refer to my male parallel-cousins (my father's brother's son, number 9, and my mother's sister's son, number 13) in the same way I refer to my brother; and I refer to my female parallel-cousins (my father's brother's daughter, number 10, and my mother's sister's daughter, number 14) in the same way I refer to my sister. Considering that my father's brother and mother's sister are referred to by the same terms I use for my father and mother, this lumping of parallel cousins with siblings is not surprising. If I call my own mother's and father's children (other than myself) "brother" and "sister," then the children of anyone whom I also call "mother" and "father" ought to be called "brother" and "sister" as well.

Crow System

The Crow system, named after another North American Indian tribe, has been called the mirror image of the Omaha system. The same principles of lumping kin types are employed, except that since the Crow system is associated with matrilineal descent,[32] the individuals in your mother's matrilineage (which is your own) are not lumped across generations, whereas the individuals in your father's matrilineage *are* lumped across generations. By comparing Figure 5 with Figure 6, we find that the lumping and separation of kin types is much the same except that the lumping across generations in the Crow system appears on the father's side rather than on the mother's side: I call both my mother and my mother's sister by the same term (both female members of my matrilineal descent group in my mother's generation); I

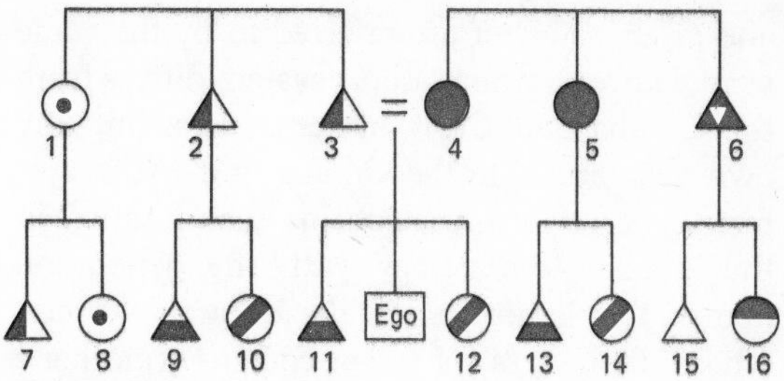

Figure 6

Crow kinship terminology system.

call my father, my father's brother, and my father's sister's son by the same term (all male members of my father's matrilineal group in *any* generation); I call my father's sister and my father's sister's daughter by the same term (both female members of my father's matrilineal group); and I refer to my parallel-cousins in the same ways I refer to my brother and sister.

Iroquois System

The Iroquois system, named after the Iroquois Indian tribe of North America, is similar to both the Omaha and Crow systems in the way in which I refer to relatives in my parents' generation. That is, my father and my father's brother are referred to by the same term, and my mother

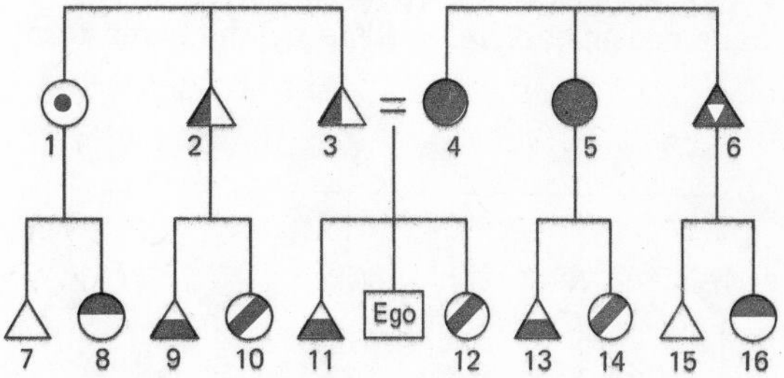

Note: Although not shown in this diagram, in the Iroquois system, parallel cousins are sometimes referred to by different terms than one's own brother and sister.

Figure 7

Iroquois kinship terminology system.

[32] The association between the Crow system and matrilineality is reported in Textor, *A Cross-Cultural Summary.*

and mother's sister are referred to by the same term. However, the Iroquois system differs from the Omaha and Crow systems regarding my own generation. In the Omaha and Crow systems, one set of cross-cousins was lumped in the kinship terminology with the generation above. This is not true in the Iroquois system, where both sets of cross-cousins (mother's brother's children and father's sister's children) are referred to by the same terms, distinguished by sex. That is, mother's brother's daughter and father's sister's daughter are both referred to by the same term; and mother's brother's son and father's sister's son are also referred to by the same term. Parallel-cousins always have different terms from cross-cousins and are sometimes, but not always, referred to by the same terms as one's brother and sister.

The Iroquois kinship system is exceedingly widespread geographically and accompanies all kinds of descent systems. Why it is so widespread and under what conditions it develops are still unanswered questions.

Hawaiian System

The Hawaiian system of kinship terminology is the least complex in that it uses the smallest number of terms. In this system, all relatives of the same sex in the same generation are referred to by the same term. Thus, all my female cousins are referred to by the same term as my sister; all my male cousins are referred to by the same term as my brother. Everyone known to be related to me in my parent's generation is referred to by one term if female (including my mother) and by another term if male (including my father).

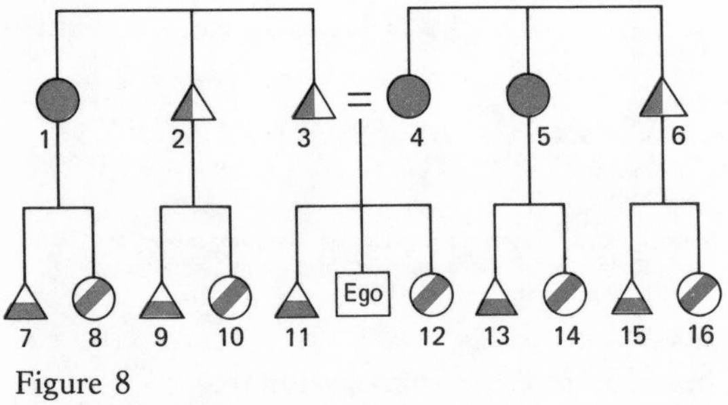

Figure 8
Hawaiian kinship terminology system.

The Hawaiian system is associated with ambilineal descent.[33] In an ambilineal society, a person might be affiliated with an ambilineal group through his mother *or* his father at any given moment in time. If this is so, then any of my mother's or father's brothers or sisters might belong to my kin group. This creates similarity between all of my parents' siblings and might account for the lumping of persons in the parental generation. Furthermore, if people related to me in my parent's generation are called by the same terms I use to refer to my mother and father, then all of their children would tend to be referred to by the same terms as my own brother and sister. And, since any of my cousins might also be in my ambilineal kin group, they also would tend to be referred to by the same terms as my brother and sister.

Eskimo System

Although the Eskimo system is so named because it is found in some Eskimo societies, it also is the terminological system which the United States and many other commercial societies have.

The distinguishing features of the Eskimo system are that all cousins are lumped together under the same term but distinguished from brothers and sisters, and all aunts and uncles are generally lumped under the same terms but distinguished from mother and father. Unlike all the other systems we have discussed, in an Eskimo system no other relatives are generally referred to by the same terms used for members

[33] This association is reported in Textor, *A Cross-Cultural Summary.*

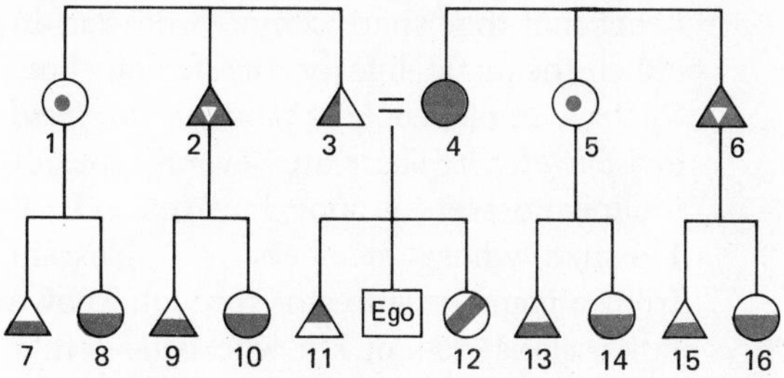

Note: In some Eskimo systems the cousin term may vary according to sex.

Figure 9
Eskimo kinship terminology system.

of the nuclear family—mother, father, brother, and sister. Perhaps this is because in societies with any of the other terminological systems, some kind of lineal descent group (either unilineal or ambilineal) is usually important—and such descent groups usually entail important roles for nonnuclear family members. Eskimo kinship terminology is not generally found where there are unilineal or ambilineal descent groups; the only kin group that may be present is the bilateral kindred.[34] The kindred in a bilateral descent system is an ego-centered group. Although relatives on both my mother's and my father's side are equally important, my most important relatives are generally the closest. This is particularly true in our type of society where the nuclear family generally lives alone, separated from, and not particularly involved with, other relatives except on ceremonial occasions. Since the nuclear family is most important, we would expect to find that the kin types in the nuclear family are distinguished terminologically from all other relatives. And since the mother's and father's side are equally important (or unimportant), it makes sense that we use the same terms (aunt, uncle, and cousin) for both sides of the family.

[34] Data from Textor, *A Cross-Cultural Summary.*

SUMMARY

1. In our own society, as in much of western Europe, a young couple usually establishes a place of residence apart from their parents or relatives when they marry. This pattern of marital residence, called *neolocal* (new place) *residence,* is relatively rare. About 95 percent of the world's societies have some pattern of residence whereby the new couple settles within or very close to the household of the parents, or some other close relative, of the groom or the bride.

2. The four most prevalent patterns in which married couples live with or near kinsmen are:
   a. *patrilocal residence:* the married couple lives with or near the husband's parents (67 percent of all societies);
   b. *matrilocal residence:* the married couple lives with or near the wife's parents (15 percent of all societies);
   c. *bilocal residence:* the married couple lives with or near *either* the husband's parents or the wife's parents (7 percent of all societies);
   d. *avunculocal residence:* the son and his wife settle with or near his mother's brother (4 percent of all societies).

3. Kinship connections are extremely important in most societies, particularly noncommercial societies. In most societies where kinship connections are important, there is some rule that allocates each person to a particular and definable set of kin, perhaps because smaller sets of kin can have clearer and firmer ties than infinitely large sets of kin. These rules affiliating individuals with sets of kin are called *rules of descent.*

4. There are only a few known rules of descent that affiliate individuals with different sets of kin:
   a. *bilateral descent:* affiliates an individual more or less equally with his mother's and father's relatives;
   b. *patrilineal descent:* affiliates an individual with kinsmen of both sexes related to him or her *through men only;* in each generation, then, children belong to the kin group of their father;
   c. *matrilineal descent:* affiliates an individual with kinsmen related to him or her *through women only;* in each generation, then, children belong to the kin group of their mother;
   d. *ambilineal* (or *cognatic*) *descent:* affiliates an individual with kinsmen related to him or her through men *or* women. In other words, some people in the society affiliate with a group of kinsmen through their fathers, and others through their mothers; consequently the descent groups show both female and male genealogical links;
   e. *double descent:* affiliates an individual for some purposes with a group of matrilineal kinsmen, and for other purposes with a group of patrilineal kinsmen; thus, two rules of descent, each traced through links of one sex only, are operative at the same time.
5. With unilineal descent (patrilineal or matrilineal), people usually refer to themselves as belonging to a particular unilineal group or set of groups based on the belief that they share common descent in either the male line or the female line. Such a set of people is called a *unilineal descent group.* There are several types of unilineal descent groups: lineages, sets of kinsmen whose members trace descent from a common ancestor through known links; clans, sets of kin who believe they are descended from a common ancestor but cannot specify the genealogical links; phratries, groups of supposedly related clans; and moieties, large unilineal descent groups without specified links to the supposed common ancestor when there are only two such groups in the entire society.
6. Unilineal descent groups tend to occur in societies in the middle range of cultural complexity—that is, in food producing (as opposed to food collecting) societies, but not commercialized and industrialized ones. In such societies unilineal descent groups often have important functions in the social, economic, political, and religious realms of life.
7. Societies differ markedly in how they group or distinguish relatives under the same or different kinship terms. Why different societies have such different systems of classifying relatives is of great interest to anthropology, because these systems shed light on the varying ways societies organize themselves with respect to kinship. The major systems of kinship terminology are the Omaha system, the Crow system, the Iroquois system, the Hawaiian system, and the Eskimo system.

SUGGESTED READINGS

Fox, R.: *Kinship and Marriage: An Anthropological Perspective* (Baltimore: Penguin Books, 1967).
An introduction to social organization. Beginning with a history of anthropological studies of marriage and the family, Fox then outlines the development of issues and theories. Emphasis is on the parallels and relationships between theories.

Murdock, G. P.: *Social Structure* (New York: Macmillan, 1949).

A cross-cultural analysis of variation in a number of aspects of social organization, including the family and marriage, kin groups, kinship terminology, the incest taboo and its extensions, and the regulation of sex. There is also an appendix offering a method for reconstructing the evolution of social organization in many societies around the world.

Radcliffe-Brown, A. R., and D. Forde (Eds.): *African Systems of Kinship and Marriage* (New York: Oxford University Press, 1950).
A collection of essays describing the character and significance of kinship in some selected African societies. The ethnographic chapters provide detailed information on various aspects of kinship in the selected societies.

Schneider, D. M.: *American Kinship: A Cultural Account* (Englewood Cliffs, N.J.: Prentice-Hall, 1968).
A description and analysis of American kinship as primarily a system of symbols. Schneider focuses on such fundamental issues of debate and study as the relatedness of spouses, the varying degrees of relatedness in distant consanguineal kin, and the basis of the kinship system.

Schneider, D. M., and K. Gough (Eds.): *Matrilineal Kinship* (Berkeley: University of California Press, 1961).
An extensive collection of theoretical and descriptive papers on matrilineal kinship. An introductory paper by Schneider discusses various theoretical issues. The ethnographic studies illustrate the various cultural expressions of matrilineal descent systems. In the final chapters, Gough and Aberle discuss how the ethnographic materials may relate to three main variables: subsistence methods, productivity of subsistence technology, and political development.

Schusky, E. L.: *Manual for Kinship Analysis,* 2nd ed. (New York: Holt, Rinehart and Winston, 1971).
A brief manual explaining kin-type notation and genealogical tables and types of kin terms. The author also presents the established concepts and terminology of patterns of descent and residence. A bibliography of current trends in kinship studies is provided for the interested student.

17

Associations and Interest Groups

Samuel Johnson, the eighteenth-century English author, was once asked to describe Boswell, his gregarious companion and biographer. "Boswell," he boomed, "is a very clubable man." Johnson did not mean that Boswell deserved to be attacked with bludgeons; he was alluding to Boswell's fondness for all sorts of clubs and associations, a fondness which he shared with many of his contemporaries. The tendency of man to form associations is not unique to eighteenth-century England. At all times and in all areas of the world, we find evidence of man's "clubability."

This chapter will examine the kinds of nonkinship groups that are formed in different societies, how they function, and what general purposes they serve. The organizations that concern us here have the following characteristics in common: (1) exclusive membership; (2) membership based on commonly shared interests or purposes; (3) some kind of formal, institutional structure; and (4) a clearly discernible sense of mutual pride and belonging. Contemporary American society has an abundance of "interest groups"—to use the terminology of the political scientist—that exemplify these general characteristics. The membership of the American Pork Producer's Association is exclusive in that it is limited to farmers who raise hogs; the physicians who belong to the American Medical Association clearly share common interests and purposes; the United Auto Workers has its own constitution and bylaws; and the members of the Veterans of Foreign Wars can be said to feel mutual pride and a sense of belonging.

Interest groups such as these vary in size and social significance. They also differ in two other important ways. One way is whether membership is voluntary or not. In Great Britain, for instance, a person may choose to join the military or stay out of it (as of 1972); in South Vietnam he has no such choice. Similarly, in the United States all persons are free to join a major political party; in the Soviet Union, party membership is restricted. Interest groups also differ in their prerequisites or qualifications for membership. These "qualities" or criteria for membership fall into three general categories: (1) *universally ascribed qualities*—those one is born with and thus acquires automatically (such as age and sex); (2) *variably ascribed qualities*—those acquired at birth but not found in all persons of a given age-sex category (such as ethnicity or region of birth); (3) *achieved qualities*—those the individual acquires by doing something.

Table 1 summarizes types of associations according to the criteria of recruitment and qualifications for membership. The specific conditions that favor the development of a particular type of organization may vary. However, nonvoluntary groups with universally ascribed membership—that is, age-sets and men's associations—tend to be found in relatively unstratified or egalitarian societies. In contrast, voluntary associations, with variably ascribed or achieved membership qualifications, appear to be found mostly in stratified societies. Presumably, this is because stratified societies are composed of people with different, and often competing, interests.

Table 1
Types of Nonkinship Organization

Membership Criteria	*Recruitment* Voluntary	Nonvoluntary
Universally ascribed		Age-sets Unisex associations
Variably ascribed	Ethnic associations Regional associations	Conscripted army
Achieved	Examples: Occupational associations Political parties Special interest groups Secret societies Military clubs	

NONVOLUNTARY ASSOCIATIONS

Age-Sets

All societies utilize a vocabulary of *age terms* just as they utilize a vocabulary of kinship terms. As we, for instance, distinguish between "brother," "uncle," and "cousin," so do we also differentiate "infant," "adolescent," and "adult." Age terms refer to categories based on age, or *age grades*. Thus, an age grade is simply a category of persons who happen to fall within a particular, culturally distinguished age range.

Age-set, on the other hand, is the term used to describe a group of persons of similar age and sex who move through some or all of life's stages together. For example, all the boys of a certain age range in a particular district might simultaneously become ceremonially initiated into "manhood"; later in life the group as a whole might become "warriors," and still later "elders." In societies with an age-set system, entry into the system is generally nonvoluntary and is based on the universally ascribed characteristics of sex and age.

In most noncommercial or primitive societies, kinship forms the basis of the organization and administration of the society. However, there are some societies in which age-sets cross-cut kinship ties and form strong supplementary bonds. Three such societies are the Karimojong, the Nandi, and the Nyakyusa of Africa.

Karimojong Age-Sets. The Karimojong are a tribe numbering some 60,000, predominantly cattle herdsmen, who occupy about 4,000 acres of semiarid country in northeastern Uganda. Their society is especially interesting because of its organization into combinations of age-sets and generation-sets, groupings which provide "both the source of political authority and the main field within which it is exercised."[1]

A Karimojong age-set comprises all men in each local group who have been initiated into manhood in a span of about five to six years; a generation-set consists of a combination of five such units, covering 25 to 30 years. Each generation-set is seen as "begetting" that which immediately follows it, and, at any one time, two generation-sets are in corporate existence.

[1] Neville Dyson-Hudson, *Karimojong Politics* (Oxford: Clarendon Press, 1966), p. 155.

The senior unit—whose members perform the administrative, the judicial, and the priestly functions—is closed; the junior unit—whose members serve as warriors and policemen—is still recruiting. Once all the age-sets in the junior generation-set are closed, it will be ready (actually impatient) to assume the status of its senior predecessor. Eventually, grumbling but realistic, the elders will agree to a succession ceremony, moving those who were once in a position of obedience to one of authority.

The Karimojong age system, then, consists of a cyclical succession of four generation-sets, in a predetermined continuing relationship: (1) the *retired generation-set,* consisting of elders, who have passed on the mantle of authority, most of the five age-sets within the retired generation-set being depleted, if not defunct; (2) the *senior generation-set,* all closed age-sets, which actively exercise authority; (3) the *junior generation-set,* which is still recruiting members and, although obedient to elders, has administrative powers; and (4) the *noninitiates,* who are starting a generation set.

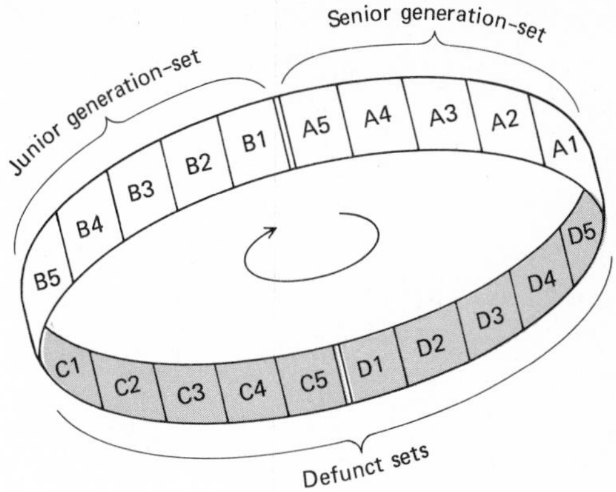

Figure 1

The Karimojong age system is composed of four distinct generation-sets (labeled A, B, C, and D in this diagram), which succeed each other cyclically; each generation-set, in turn, is subdivided into five age-sets. At any one time, there are two extant generation-sets—one is senior (A) and closed; and the other is junior (B) and still recruiting members—and two defunct generation-sets.

The significance of the age- and generation-sets in Karimojong society gives particular importance to initiation into manhood. Initiation ceremonies are elaborate and fall into three parts, all supervised by the elders. The first part, called "spearing the ox," takes place in a ceremonial enclosure. Each initiate spears a beast from his family's herd and dismembers it, according to a set pattern. The head and neck are carried away by the women for use in the later stages of the ceremony; the stomach sacs are carefully laid out unopened. The oldest tribal elder present and the local senior generation-set leader then slit the sacs with a spear and anoint each initiate with the semidigested food which spills out, blessing him with the words, "Be well. Grow old. Become wealthy in stock. Become an elder."

In the second part of the ceremony, called "eating the tongue," the meat previously taken away by the women is boiled in clay pots and served to the men of the senior generation-set in the settlement, who bless the initiate and his family. The final part, called "cooking the stomach," takes place in the cattle corral, where a feast is held. The elders, the other adult men, and the initiates all sit and eat, each group in a separate circle. Before the initiation ceremony began, each boy was required to shave his head; after it, he is allowed to let his hair grow. Once it is sufficiently long, he plasters it with mud and ties it back with a chain—the tangible symbol of his adult status.

Once initiated, a boy has become a man, with a clearly defined status and the ultimate certainty of exercising full authority together with his set partners. Indeed, a Karimojong is not expected to marry—and is certainly barred from starting a family—until initiated. The initiation ceremony itself illustrates the essential political and social characteristics of the age-set system. Without the authority of the elders, the ceremony cannot be held;

throughout the proceedings, their authority is explicit. The father-son relationship of adjacent generation-sets is emphasized, for fathers are initiating their sons.

Nandi Age-Sets. The Nandi, cattle herders and agriculturists of western Kenya, provide another example of how age-sets may be organized.[2] As soon as he is born, the young Nandi male is a member of an age-set—that of the uninitiated. As he grows he will pass through initiation, symbolized by circumcision, the warrior stage, and finally, if he lives long enough, through four more stages of "elderhood." The Nandi warrior-set theoretically holds the greatest authority in the system. It has the training, the means, and the power to carry out essential military operations—though, in modern times, the occasion for demonstrating these qualities does not arise. There are altogether seven age-sets, which succeed each other in strict rotation. However, the focus is upon three of the seven: (1) the set composed of men about to become elders; (2) the set composed of men about to become warriors; and (3) the set composed of boys about to become initiated.

Initiation ceremonies take place about every 15 years. Participation in the ceremony by initiates symbolizes their changed status—the move forward from boyhood to responsible adulthood. Boys are usually circumcised in their mid- to late teens, although, if the family is wealthy enough, ten-year-old boys may participate in the ceremonies. The ritual of circumcision places much emphasis on the qualities of fortitude and physical toughness expected of a warrior. The ceremonies as a whole are carried out under the supervision of, and by the authority of, the warrior set.

The initiates are separately housed, under the elderly men assigned to watch over them for the six-month initiation period. The initiation begins with a morning ceremony in which the boys' heads are anointed with a mixture of water, milk, and salt and shaved. The boys are given a strong purge and their clothes are taken away and replaced with girls' clothing. The next evening, after a dance ceremony, they hear the circumcision knife being sharpened outside of their huts, while warriors joke about the knife's eagerness to do its work. Later, during a procession, warriors beat them with nettles and drop hornets on them, as tests of endurance. Then each initiate has to confess his past misdeeds.

The circumcision itself is done in two steps. After a cut is made, each boy's face is scrutinized for signs of cowardice, and if he shows no fear, the rest of the operation is performed. To ease the pain which causes many initiates to faint, cold water is applied to the wound. Afterwards, the initiates remain in seclusion for six months, wearing male apparel again, and during this time are taught their duties as warriors. Finally, a feast celebrates their achievement of adult status.[3]

Nyakyusa Age-Villages. The Nyakyusa, who live on the northwest shores of Lake Nyasa in the southeastern part of Africa, supply what might be termed the extreme example of age-set organization.[4] In this society, members of an age-set actually build a village together and settle down to live in it, later donating land to their sons so that the process may continue. Age-villages, like those of the Nyakyusa, are quite rare today.

Between the ages of 5 and 11, Nyakyusa boys sleep in their parents' homes and care for the family cattle. Since the cows of 10 or so neighboring families are herded together, the boys tending them begin to form close attachments,

[2] See G. W. B. Huntingford, *The Nandi of Kenya: Tribal Control in a Pastoral Society* (London: Routledge and Kegan Paul, 1953).

[3] A. C. Hollis, *The Nandi: Their Language and Folklore* (Oxford: Clarendon Press, 1909), pp. 52–57.

[4] Monica Wilson, *Good Company: A Study of Nyakyusa Age-Villages* (Boston: Beacon Press, 1963).

Young boys of the Madingo tribe in Gambia undergo initiation into manhood. An adult male, dressed in a frightening costume, makes threatening gestures toward the boys with a knife. (Photograph © Arthur Tress, distributed by Magnum Photos.)

having spent all their days together for about six years. At about 12 years of age, the boys begin hoeing in their fathers' fields and hand over the cattle herding to their younger brothers. At this age, they depart from their parental homes and live in a village of their own, returning to their own homesteads only for meals. Gradually, as their younger brothers mature and join the village, it grows until at some point its members decide to close admittance.

The age-village is now complete, though its members still work their fathers' fields and eat their fathers' food. Upon reaching the age of 25 or so, the young men marry, bringing their wives into their own village and setting up their own homes. Each young man now receives his own fields from his father and eats food prepared by his wife instead of his mother. Eventually, the entire village assumes an autonomous life. After about a decade, when a number of such villages are established in the territory, the fathers ceremonially hand over full political authority to their sons and, as old men, step aside.

What is particularly interesting in the Nyakyusa system is its blending of family and age-set. When still quite young, the Nyakyusa male has already become accustomed to non-family social arrangements; and long before he becomes a father, with family obligations of his own, he is a fully involved participant in his own age-village, with particular communal and social responsibilities.

Unisex Associations

Unisex, as used here, has quite a different meaning from its current usage in our own society, where it signifies something that is suitable for both sexes. Rather, the word "unisex" is used here to describe a type of association that restricts its membership to one sex, most often male. Sex as a qualification is directly related to the purpose of the unisex association; in general, this purpose is to strengthen the concept of male superiority and offer men a refuge from females. In primitive societies, men's associations are similar to age-sets, except that there are only two sets, or stages: mature males, who are association members, and immature males, who are nonmembers. Today such associations are still found in New Guinea and other Melanesian islands.

Women in most primitive or noncommercial societies have few associations. Perhaps this is because the men in primitive societies are generally dominant in the kinship, property, and political spheres of life. And there is also the possibility that anthropologists, for the most part men, have given women's associations less attention than men's associations.

Unisex associations or clubs are also a feature of modern, industrialized society. The Boy Scouts and the Kiwanis, the Girl Scouts and the League of Women Voters are cases in point. Admission to these clubs, however, is voluntary and often not solely based on ascribed criteria, as are the nonvoluntary unisex associations in primitive societies.

Mae Enga Bachelor Associations. The Mae Enga are a group of about 30,000 sedentary horticulturists living in the New Guinea highlands. Their society has received a great deal of attention from anthropologists for its practice of sexual segregation—indeed for the strain of active hostility to women which runs through its culture.[5] It is the custom for Mae men to live in a separate, communal house. Up to the age of five, a young boy is permitted to live in his mother's house, although he is unconsciously aware of the "distance" between his father and mother. As he grows older, this awareness is made explicit by his father and elder clansmen. It is undesirable, he is told, to be so much in the company of women; it is better that he join the menfolk in their house and in their activities. As the boy grows up, the need to avoid contact with women is made abundantly clear to him. Their menstrual blood especially, if not countered by magic rites, can "pollute" a man, "corrupt his vital juices so that his skin darkens and wrinkles as his flesh wastes, permanently dull his wits, and eventually lead to a slow decline and death."[6]

Since Mae culture regards a woman as, to say the least, potentially unclean, it enforces strict codes of male-female deportment—codes designed to safeguard male integrity, strength, and possession of crops and other property. So strict are these regulations that many young men are reluctant to marry. However, the elders do try to impress upon the young men their duty to marry and reproduce. The men's association attempts to regulate the male's sex relation-

[5] M. J. Meggitt, "Male-Female Relationships in the Highlands of Australian New Guinea," *American Anthropologist* (Special Issue, 1964), pp. 204–224.
[6] *Ibid.*, p. 207.

ships. The association is said to have several purposes: to cleanse and strengthen their members; to promote their growth; to make them comely to women; and, most important, to supervise contact between the sexes so that ultimately the "right" wives are procured for the men, and the "right" children born for the clan.

By the time he is 15 or 16, a Mae youth has joined the village bachelor's association. He agrees to take scrupulous care neither to copulate with a woman nor to accept food from her hands. As a club member, he will participate in the *sanggai* rituals. Bachelors, under the supervision of senior club members, go into seclusion, in a club house deep in the forest, to undergo "purification." During four days of "exercises" (rather similar in aim to those of a religious retreat), he observes additional prohibitions to protect himself from all forms of sexuality and impurity. For instance, pork is denied him, as women have cared for the pigs; and he may not look at the ground during excursions into the

Men of Papua, New Guinea, gather together in front of the village men's house. (Courtesy of the American Museum of Natural History.)

forest, lest he see feminine footprints or pig feces. His body will be scrubbed, his dreams discussed and interpreted. Finally, together with his club, now restored to purity and reprotected at least for a while against contamination, he will participate in organized dances and feasting with his chosen lady.

In Mae society, then, it would seem that the battle of the sexes has decisively been won by the men, though at the price, it might well be argued, of some repression and internal tension. How, therefore, does Mae bachelor organization fit into the general social context? What sort of function does it fulfill? On an individual level, bachelor associations may strengthen and attempt to reaffirm a man's feeling of masculinity. On a community level, the association organizes the fighting strength of the village. The *sanggai* festivals afford the entire clan an opportunity to display its size, solidarity, and magnificence to its enemies, whom on other occasions it fights. Hostility toward women may not be surprising in view of the fact that a man's wife and mother come from neighboring clans (the Mae villages being exogamous) which are perpetually in conflict with his own; male-female hostility, then, seems to reflect the broader, interclan hostility. The Mae have a succinct way of describing the situation: "We marry the people we fight."[7]

Men's houses, and occasionally women's, are found among many peoples, especially in Melanesia, Polynesia, Africa, and South America. Men's associations generally involve bachelors, although older, married men will often come by to instruct the youngsters, and pass on the benefits of their experience. In more militant days, men's houses acted as fortresses and arsenals—even as sanctuaries to protect fugitive criminals. By and large, they serve to strengthen—certainly to symbolize—male power and solidarity. As do age-sets, men's clubs provide ties which cut across and supplement kinship bonds. Hence, they permit a given group of men in a given society to act in concert towards the realization of mutually agreed-upon objectives, irrespective of kin relationships.

[7] Meggitt, "Male-Female Relationships," p. 218.

VOLUNTARY ASSOCIATIONS

Regional Associations

Regional associations are clubs which bring together migrants from a common geographical background. Membership is based on the variably ascribed criterion of common regional origin. Regional associations are characteristic of rural to urban population movements *within* a particular country. In the United States, for example, migrants from rural Appalachia have formed such associations in Chicago and Detroit. Many of these have become vocal political forces in municipal government.

William Mangin has described the role of regional associations in helping rural migrants to adapt to urban life in Lima, Peru.[8] During the 1950s, Mangin closely studied a group of migrants from the rural mountains, the *serranos* from Ancash. Typically these *serranos,* about 120,000 in number, live in a slum-like urban settlement called a *barriada.* The *barriada* is not officially recognized by the national government or the city authorities; accordingly, it lacks all such normal services as water supply, garbage removal, and police protection. Its inhabitants have left their rural birthplace for reasons generally typical of such population movements, be they in South America or West Africa. These reasons are generally social and economic, related to population and land pres-

[8] William P. Mangin, "The Role of Regional Associations in the Adaptation of Rural Migrants to Cities in Peru," in Dwight B. Heath and Richard N. Adams, eds., *Contemporary Cultures and Societies of Latin America* (New York: Random House, 1965), pp. 311–323.

sure. However, the higher expectations associated with the big city—better education, social mobility, wage labor—are also compelling considerations.

Typically, also, the *serranos* from Ancash have formed a regional association, as have literally dozens of migrant groups, not only in Lima, but in the other coastal cities and in regional capitals. Club membership is open to both sexes. Men generally control the executive positions, and club leaders are often those men who have achieved political power in their home towns. Women, who have relatively less economic and social freedom, nevertheless take an important part in club activities.

The *serrano* regional association performs a number of services for its members. First, it lobbies the central government on matters of community importance—for example, the provision of sewers, clinics, and similar public services. This requires a club member to follow a piece of legislation carefully through the channels of government to make certain it is not forgotten or abandoned somewhere along the line. Second, the *serrano* association assists in acculturating newly arrived *serranos* to the conditions of urban life in Lima. The most noticeable rural traits—coca-chewing, hair style, and clothing peculiarities—are the first to go, with the men generally able to adapt faster than the women to the new conditions. The association similarly provides opportunities for fuller contact with the national culture. And finally, the group organizes social activities, such as *fiestas,* acts as the clearing house for information transmitted to and from the home area, and supplies a range of other services to help the migrant adapt to his new environment while still retaining connections with his birthplace.

In general, as Mangin's study reveals, regional clubs help to integrate their members into a more complex, urban environment, although occasionally they serve to aggravate local rivalries—especially those based on individual interest groups in the home town. But since club membership is voluntary, it is not uncommon for a dissatisfied group to break away to establish its own club.

Ethnic Associations

There are many types of ethnic interest groups; generally they are urban-based. Membership in these associations is based on the variably ascribed characteristic of ethnicity. Ethnic associations are particularly widespread in West Africa, where accelerated cultural change—reflected in altered economic arrangements, in technological advances, and in new urban living conditions—has weakened kinship relations and other traditional sources of support and solidarity.[9]

Tribal unions are frequently found in Nigeria and what is now Ghana. These are typical of most such associations in that they are extraterritorial (that is, they recruit members who have left their tribal locations), have a formal constitution, and have been formed to meet certain needs arising out of the conditions of urban life. One such need is to keep members in touch with their traditional cultures. The Ibo State Union, for example, in addition to providing mutual aid and financial support in case of unemployment, sickness, or death, performed the service "of fostering and keeping alive an interest in tribal song, history, language and moral beliefs and thus maintaining a person's attachment to his native town or village."[10] Some tribal unions collect money to improve conditions in their ancestral homes, education being a popular area of concern. Others publish

[9] See Kenneth Little, *West African Urbanization* (New York: Cambridge University Press, 1965); and Claude Meillassoux, *Urbanization of an African Community* (Seattle: University of Washington Press, 1968).

[10] Kenneth Little, "The Role of Voluntary Associations in West African Urbanization," *American Anthropologist,* Vol. 59 (1957), p. 582.

Kikuyu tribeswomen, who have migrated to the city of Nairobi, Kenya, and formed a union of street sweepers, march in the Independence Day parade. (Marc and Evelyne Bernheim from Woodfin Camp and Associates.)

newsletters that report members' activities. Most unions have a young membership that exercises a powerful democratizing influence in tribal councils, and the organizations provide a springboard for those with national political aspirations.

"Friendly societies" differ from tribal unions in that their objectives are more limited, confined for the most part to mutual aid. Such a club has been formed by the wives of Kru migrants in Freetown, Sierra Leone. Kru men normally go to sea, still a hazardous occupation. The club is classified into three grades. An admission fee of one guinea (about $3 in 1972) permits entry into the lowest grade. Elevation to higher grades depends on further donations. Upon the death of the member or her husband, the family receives a lump sum commensurate with her status in the club. The Yoruba Friendly Society in Nigeria uses another common approach to mutual aid. At regular intervals all members contribute a fixed sum, and the total is given to one member at a time. In this way, significant amounts of capital are available, in rotation, for each member to buy trading stock, expensive new clothes (to keep up appearances in a government post, for example), or even pay a bride price.

West African occupational clubs also fall into the ethnic category. They are African versions of trade unions, organized along tribal as well as craft lines. Their principal concern is the status and remuneration of their members as workers. The Motor Drivers' Union of Keta, in what is now Ghana, was formed to fund insurance and legal costs, to contribute to medical care in case of accident or illness, and to help pay for funeral expenses.

Finally, clubs that concentrate on entertainment and recreation are very common in West Africa. The dancing *compin* of Sierra Leone are typical. This is how Little describes them:

> This is a group of young men and women concerned with the performance of "plays" of traditional music and dancing and with the raising of money for mutual benefit. . . . A "play" is generally given in connection with some important event, such as the close of Ramadan, or as part of the ceremonies celebrating a wedding or a funeral. The general public as well as the persons honored by the performance are expected to donate money to the compin on these occasions. Money is also collected in the form of weekly subscriptions from the members.[11]

Some observers have suggested that the widespread incidence of ethnic associations in West Africa has amounted to virtually a resurgence of tribalism, albeit on a more sophisticated scale. The presence of such interest groups in urban areas has indeed seemed to slow the development of national identity and loyalty. On the other hand, the evidence indicates that such clubs serve important adaptive and integrative functions, for men and women both, as do regional associations in other areas of the world. To quote Little again: "Their combination of modern and traditional traits constitutes a cultural bridge which conveys, metaphorically speaking, the tribal individual from one kind of sociological universe to another."[12]

Military Associations

Military associations in primitive societies may be compared to our own American Legion or Veterans of Foreign War posts: they all seem to exist to unite the members through their common experiences as warriors, to glorify the activities of war, and to perform certain services for the community. Membership in such associations is usually voluntary and based upon the achieved criterion of participation in war. Among the American Plains Indians, military societies were common. The Cheyenne Indians, for example, were renowned for the courage of their warriors. Their military societies were not

[11] Little, "The Role of Voluntary Associations," pp. 586–587.
[12] *Ibid.*, p. 593.

ranked by age, being open to any boy or man ready to go to war.[13]

Originally, the Cheyenne had five military associations: the Fox, the Dog, the Shield, the Elk (or Hoof Rattle), and the Bow-string (or Contrary) which was annihilated by the Pawnee in the mid-nineteenth century. Later, two new associations were established, the Wolf and the Northern Crazy Dogs. While the various clubs may have had different costumes, songs, and dances, they were alike in their internal organization, each being headed by four leaders who were among the most important war chiefs of the tribe.

Several of the Cheyenne military societies selected four virgin daughters of tribal chiefs to serve as "maids of honor." The girls participated in the clubs' ceremonies and sat with the war chiefs during council meetings. Women, although having no political authority, were highly respected among the Cheyenne; the maids of honor of the military societies were looked upon as reflecting the ideals of female chastity and deportment. So important was the virtue of female chastity among the Cheyenne that a defiled maid of honor was believed to bring bad luck to the warriors of the association. As a result, the Dog and Contrary societies were unwilling to take the risk of having maids of honor affiliated with their clubs.

Secret Societies

Secret societies are characterized principally by limited membership and secret rituals, which are generally believed to increase the supernatural power of the members. As a rule, those who are not members, or who have attained only the lowest rank within the society, are told only enough about the society to arouse fear and command respect. Those who advance through various degrees of initiation increase their social and political influence as they increase their supernatural expertise.

The *Poro* is a rather well-known secret society, with voluntary membership open to all males, contingent upon passing of a series of grueling physical tests.[14] It flourishes in Liberia, among the Kpelle, and in Sierra Leone, among such tribes as the Mende and the Temne. Since the Poro has features typical of most secret "clubs," it is worth examining in some detail.

The corporate identity of the Poro is personified by a figure named in various ways: the Grand Master, the Forest Thing, the *namu.* When *namu* makes a public appearance, usually to presage a meeting of the society, he is always masked, wears regalia and a costume, is accompanied by attendants, and speaks in a musical falsetto. His emergence from the forest causes great dread and anxiety. Noninitiates and women rush to seclude themselves within their homes. Should an uninitiated boy catch sight of *namu* he is taken away at once to undergo initiation; a woman is considered likely to die of poisoning.

The intense fear aroused by the Poro is a reflection of two basic attributes credited to the society. First, it is believed that the Poro is close to the spirits of its deceased members. These spirits are thought to exert enormous influence both in canalizing supernatural powers and in acting as intermediaries between God and man. Second, the Poro is said to possess certain powerful medicines. These potions can be employed to further the interests of the society, but they can also be applied to the world at large, especially to bring disaster, should certain norms be disregarded or precepts disobeyed.

As a result, the Grand Master is held in great awe, and respect is always shown to the Poro. This deference has direct sociopolitical conse-

[13] E. Adamson Hoebel, *The Cheyenne: Indians of the Great Plains* (New York: Holt, Rinehart and Winston, 1960).

[14] See Kenneth Little, "The Political Function of the Poro," *Africa,* Vol. 35 (October 1965), pp. 349–365, and Vol. 36 (January 1966), pp. 62–71.

Members of the Ku Klux Klan, a well-known secret organization in the United States, wear hooded costumes when appearing in public. (Photograph by Constantine Manos, © 1968 Magnum Photos.)

quences. It makes it easier for the society to enforce obedience to certain social restrictions—for instance, the prohibition of incest and arson. In addition, awe of Poro strengthens the hands of political authority, since it is well known that chiefs occupy high levels within the Poro's hierarchy.

The Poro's initiation ceremonies employ procedures typical of those adopted by many secret societies. The aim is to turn an initiate first into a "good Poro man" and, second, into a useful member of the community. This means a period of attendance—it used to be between three and four years but has now been much shortened—

at a "bush school" situated in a secluded part of the forest. There, each initiate must abandon his former status in favor of a new, Poro identity; he must undergo severe, psychological "experiences" designed to etch deeply into his mind the sacredness and secrecy of Poro rituals; and he must learn the tribal history of his people as well as the skills he will need to attain a position in community life.

Secret societies undeniably have greatly influenced the political traditions of West Africa, though their very secrecy has made precise documentation hard to obtain. They bolster the authority of the chiefs and help maintain a code of social behavior. In recent years, secret societies have contributed effectively to opposition movements against colonial authority.

In industrialized societies, secret associations have had as prominent a role. Freemasonry, for example, exerted a powerful influence in much of Europe in the late eighteenth and nineteenth centuries, though in recent times its influence has greatly diminished. In our own society, the Ku Klux Klan is a well-known example of a secret organization. The Klan keeps its membership and its rituals secret; Klansmen wear hooded costumes and their insignia of office when appearing in public and have often used violence to impress the society's policies on society in general. In some parts of the South, particularly in the past, politicians and civic figures gained stature from their membership in the Klan.

Our examination of voluntary associations is not complete without a passing mention of such organizations as trade unions, charitable organizations, political parties, bridge clubs, and various other associations, of which there are tens of thousands in our own and other complex societies. In all of these voluntary organizations, the qualities required for membership are "achieved" rather than ascribed or determined by birth. Generally, clubs of this category are more numerous where the society is larger and more diversified. They serve to bring together those sets of people with common interests, aspirations, or qualifications. Opportunities to work for what are regarded as worthwhile social goals, or self-improvement, or to satisfy a need for new and stimulating experiences are among the many motivations for joining clubs. Not the least is identification with a corporate body, and through it, the acquisition of status and influence.

CONDITIONS ASSOCIATED WITH GROUP FORMATION

Anthropologists are not content to provide descriptions of the structure and operation of human associations; they also seek to understand why different types of associations develop. What, for example, may account for the development of age-set systems?

S. N. Eisenstadt's comparative study of African age-sets leads him to the hypothesis that when the kinship group fails to carry out functions important to the integration of society—such as political, educational, and economic functions—age-set systems arise to fill the void. Age-set systems provide a workable solution to the society's need for functional divisions among its members because: (1) age is a criterion that can be applied to all members of society in the allocation of roles; and, (2) since age relationships have no contractual bonds to begin with, there is no obstruction to setting up standards of behavior based on age.[15]

It is not at all clear why age-set systems arise to fill the void left by lack of kinship organization. Many societies have kin structures that are limited in their scope, yet by no means all, or even the majority of them, have compensated by adopting an age-set system.

[15] S. N. Eisenstadt, "African Age Groups," *Africa,* Vol. 24 (April 1954), p. 102.

B. Bernardi, in his critical evaluation of Nilo-Hamitic age-set systems,[16] takes a similar but broader view than Eisenstadt of the factors contributing to the development of age-set systems. Bernardi suggests that age-set systems arise in societies with: (1) lack of central authority; (2) a history of territorial rivalry; and (3) dispersed kin groups. When all three factors are present, he argues, the need for a mechanism of territorial integration is supplied by an age-set system.

Still another explanation is advanced by Robert LeVine and Walter Sangree, who offer the concept of "adjusted diffusion" in answer to the question: "Why have some Bantu-speaking peoples adopted age-group organization and associated rituals from their non-Bantu neighbors, while other Bantu peoples in the same region have not?"[17] LeVine and Sangree suggest that age-set systems may have been borrowed by numerically small groups under pressure from large groups. Such was the case with the Tiriki. Their survival at stake, the Tiriki were able to find a non-Bantu group, the Terik, that was prepared to assist them; but they had to agree first to adopt the Terik's kind of age organization in order to combine forces with them. LeVine and Sangree suggest that larger groups, which were more capable of defending their own interests, had no reason to borrow age-sets.

In dealing with voluntary associations whose membership is of the "variably ascribed" type (that is, acquired at birth but not found in all persons of a given age-sex category), it is difficult to say exactly what causes them. There is evidence to suggest that voluntary associations become more numerous (and more important) as the society harboring them advances in technology, complexity, and scale. No definitive explanation for this answer is yet available, but the following trends seem to be sufficiently established to merit consideration.

First, there is the factor of urbanization. Developing societies are becoming urban in character, and as their cities grow, so do the number of people separated from their traditional kinship ties and local customs. It is not surprising, then, that the early voluntary associations should be mutual aid societies, established first to take over kin obligations in case of death, and later broadening their benefits in other directions. In this respect, the recent associations in the "third world" of the developing African societies closely resemble the early English laboring associations. These clubs also served to maintain the city migrant's contacts with his former traditions and culture. Similarly, the regional associations in Latin America resemble the regional associations of European immigrants to the United States; such associations also seem to arise in response to the migrant's or immigrant's needs in the new home.

Second, there is an economic factor. Migrants and immigrants try to adapt to the new economic conditions, and group interests in the new situations have to be organized, promoted, and protected.

Why, then, do "variably ascribed" associations tend to be replaced by clubs of the "achieved" category in highly industrialized societies? Perhaps the strong focus on specialization in industrialized societies is reflected in the formation of specialized groups. Perhaps the emphasis on achievement in industrialized societies is another contributing factor. Perhaps, too, the trend toward a standardized uniformity, encouraged by mass marketing and the mass media, is progressively weakening the importance of regional and ethnic distinctions, with the result that the more broadly based organizations are replaced by more narrowly based associations, more responsive to particular needs which are not being met by the institutions of mass society.

[16] B. Bernardi, "The Age-System of the Nilo-Hamitic Peoples," *Africa,* Vol. 22 (October 1952), pp. 316–332.

[17] Robert A. LeVine and Walter H. Sangree, "The Diffusion of Age-Group Organization in East Africa," *Africa,* Vol. 32 (April 1962), pp. 97–110.

SUMMARY

1. Clubs or interest groups are a persistent feature of almost all human societies. They may be defined as associations of individuals which are exclusive within a larger society, have membership based on common aims, some sort of institutional structure, and a sense of mutual pride and belonging. Membership varies according to whether it is voluntary or not, and according to whether the qualities of members are universally ascribed, variably ascribed, or achieved.
2. Age-set systems are examples of nonvoluntary, universally ascribed associations. They are composed of age- and generation-sets which are cyclical in operation and which usually put emphasis on initiation and succession rituals. Generally they serve to establish useful categories of authority and influence in societies whose members are often widely dispersed or in which there is a lack of effective centralized direction.
3. Regional and ethnic organizations are voluntary, variably ascribed associations. Both usually occur in societies where technological advance is accelerating, bringing with it economic and social complexity. Despite a variety of types, regional and ethnic associations have in common an emphasis on (*a*) helping the members adapt to new conditions; (*b*) keeping them in touch with local traditions; and (*c*) promoting improved living conditions in local areas.
4. It is not easy to arrive at more than an approximation of the possible determinants of any type of association. It has been suggested by some that age-sets may arise to fill sociopolitical voids, where kinship groups are not effective. Others argue that certain African peoples may have adopted age-sets for external, strategic reasons. Voluntary associations of all sorts seem to be caused by the onset of "modern" conditions, especially urbanization, economic change, and diversity, and their psychological and sociological consequences.

SUGGESTED READINGS

Bernardi, B.: "The Age System of the Nilo-Hamitic Peoples" (*Africa,* Vol. 22, October 1952), pp. 316–332.
Theoretical discussion of why age systems occur in some societies and not in others.

Eisenstadt, S. N.: *From Generation to Generation: Age Groups and Social Structure* (Glencoe, Ill.: Free Press, 1956).
A comparative and theoretical analysis of age groups in different societies. Chapters II through V give a detailed presentation of age groupings in a wide variety of societies, as well as classifications of types and functions.

Huntingford, G. W. B.: *The Nandi of Kenya* (London: Rutledge and Kegan Paul, 1953).
General discussion of the political structure of this group. Particular attention is paid to the importance of age-sets as the basis for political organizations.

LeVine, R. A., and W. H. Sangree: "The Diffusion of Age-Group Organizations in East Africa" (*Africa,* Vol. 32, April 1962), pp. 97–110.
Theoretical description of the diffusion of age-sets in East Africa and the reasons for this diffusion.

Lowie, R. H. *Primitive Society* (New York: Boni and Liveright, 1920).

A classic, comparative work, discussing various elements of social organization. Chapter 10, "Associations," and Chapter 11, "Theory of Associations," contain comparative discussions of clubs and age groups in primitive societies.

Meillassoux, C.: *Urbanization of an African Community* (Seattle: University of Washington Press, 1968). Interesting description of the changing structure of Mali society, particularly in terms of the decline of voluntary associations as important centers of power. Such associations continue to exist in Mali but are subordinated and in opposition to the new party system.

Prins, A. H. J.: *East African Age Class Systems* (Groningen, Djakarta: J. B. Wolters, 1953).
Primarily a descriptive work dealing with three East African societies that have age-set systems.

Wilson, M.: *Good Company: A Study of Nyakyusa Age-Villages* (Boston: Beacon Press, 1963).
A monograph describing the social organization of the Nyakyusa, among whom villages are founded by members of a single age-set.

18

Political Organization: Social Order and Disorder

For most Americans, the term "political life" has many connotations. It may, for example, call to mind the executive branch of government, from the President on a national level to the mayor on a local one; legislative institutions from Congress to the city council; administrative organs from federal government departments to local agencies. It may also evoke thoughts of political parties and interest groups, as well as certain common political activities such as lobbying, campaigning, and voting. In other words, when people living in the United States think of political life, they may think first of the complex process by which authoritative decisions (often called "public policies") are arrived at and implemented.

But "political life" has a still wider range of meaning in America, as in many other countries. It may also bring to mind ways of preventing or resolving trouble cases and disputes both within and without our society. Internally, a complex society, such as our own, may employ mediation or arbitration for resolving an industrial dispute, a police force for preventing crimes or tracking down criminals, courts and the penal system for dealing with law breakers as well as with social conflicts in general. Externally, such a society may establish embassies in other nations and develop and utilize its armed forces both as a way of maintaining its security and as a means of supporting its domestic and foreign interests. All these are political organizations and activities and are mechanisms which complex societies have developed in order to establish social order and to minimize—or at least deal effectively with—social disorder.

Many societies, however, do not have political officials or courts or armies; nor do they have individuals or agencies formally responsible for making and implementing policy or for resolving disputes. Does this mean that they have no political life? If we mean political life as we know it in our own society, then the answer has to be that they do not. But, if we look beyond our complex formal institutions and ask what functions these institutions perform, we find that all societies have customs or procedures which result in policy making and the resolution of disputes—ways and means of creating and maintaining social order and coping with social disorder.

A straightforward, working definition of the term "political"—one which may be applied to all societies—is not easy to frame, for the differences between forms of political organization are great. In general, though, one can say that "political" refers to customary behaviors, as well as beliefs and attitudes, which pertain to policy making and its execution (creating and maintaining social order) and to conflict resolution (minimizing social disorder). These customs are initiated by, or on behalf of, a distinct territorial group; the territorial groups involved may range from neighborhoods and hamlets to villages, towns, cities, regions, nations, and even groups of nations.

VARIATIONS IN POLITICAL ORGANIZATION

Elman Service has suggested that societies can be classified into four principal types of organization: bands, tribes, chiefdoms, and states.[1] We shall examine how political life is organized in each type of society in order to obtain a general view of how societies vary in the ways they try to create and maintain social order and minimize social disorder.

Band Society

Band societies are composed of a number of fairly small, usually nomadic groups of people. Each band is self-sufficient and autonomous, the band usually being the largest group that acts politically. Since most contemporary food collectors are organized as bands, some anthropologists contend that band organization characterized nearly all societies before the development of agriculture, or until about 10,000 years ago.

Band organization may differ from society to society. Different environmental conditions and food-collecting technologies may make one band somewhat different from another, both in internal and in external arrangements. One band may contain a larger number of people than another band; some bands live closer to other bands (thus having more structured relations with them). But there are several features which almost all bands have in common.

First and foremost, band societies are generally at the hunter-gatherer (or collecting) level of food-getting technology. This means that food has to be "found," either prodded out of the earth, taken out of the water, or hunted down, wherever nature has placed it. Consequently, almost all bands are nomadic. They move from place to place, in a regular, seasonal pattern, following migratory game or exploiting seasonally varying plant or animal life, taking their few possessions with them.

Bands are typically small in size, and band societies are low in population density. Julian Steward has estimated that population density among band societies ranges from a maximum of about one person per 5 square miles to a minimum of one per 50 or so square miles.[2] The primary factor determining the exact size of a band is probably its relative productivity and the sort of food-collecting technology employed. The Guayaki of the Amazon basin number about 20 individuals in their local bands; the Semang of the Malay Peninsula, 50; the Patagonian Tehuelche of South America, 400–500, perhaps the largest of all.[3] Band size often varies by season, the band breaking up or recombining according to the quantity of food resources available at a given time and place. Eskimo bands, for example, are smaller in the winter when food is hard to find and larger in the summer when there is sufficient food available to feed a larger group.

Band societies are generally egalitarian: all individuals of a particular age-sex category have equal access to prestige and resources. Typically, the concept of private property is alien to band society; if there is any concept of resource

[1] Elman R. Service, *Primitive Social Organization: An Evolutionary Perspective* (New York: Random House, 1962).

[2] Julian Steward, *Theory of Culture Change* (Urbana: University of Illinois Press, 1955), p. 125.

[3] Morton H. Fried, *The Evolution of Political Society* (New York: Random House, 1967), p. 68.

ownership—ownership of land for instance—that resource is thought to belong to the group as a whole. Thus, among hunting and gathering peoples, sharing of virtually all resources is the rule. All members of the group, for example, share in the distribution of game that is killed, even though all members were not directly involved in the hunt.

Band political organization is generally informal. Characteristically, there is no real means of organizing politically beyond the individual band. "There is no separate political life and no government or legal system above the modest, informal authority of family heads and ephemeral leaders."[4] Such "modest informal authority" as does exist within the band can be seen in the way that decisions affecting the entire group are made.

Since the formal, permanent office of "leader" generally does not exist within band societies, decisions—such as when camp has to be moved, how a hunt is to be arranged, when a ritual ought to be performed, or what sort of relationship should be adopted with a nearby

[4] Service, *Primitive Social Organization,* p. 109.

Eskimo bands generally lack a permanent leader with formal authority. Decisions, such as how a whale hunt is to be arranged and how the meat is to be divided, are either agreed upon by the community as a whole or made by the "best qualified" member. (Courtesy of the American Museum of Natural History.)

group—are either agreed upon by the community as a whole or made by the "best qualified" member, depending upon the sort of activity that requires planning or carrying out. Leadership, when it is exercised by an individual, is not the consequence of "bossing" or of throwing one's weight about. Each band may have its informal headman, or its most proficient hunter, or its old man most accomplished in rituals, and so on. He may be one and the same person, he may be several persons, but he, or they, will have gained status through the community's recognition of his skill, good sense, and humility. In writing of the Andaman Islanders, Radcliffe-Brown describes the basis of leadership in band societies:

> Beside the respect for seniority there is another important factor in the regulation of the social life, namely the respect for certain personal qualities. These qualities are skill in hunting, . . . generosity and kindness, and freedom from bad temper. A man possessing them inevitably acquires a position of influence in the community.[5]

Leadership, in other words, stems not from power but from influence, not from office but from admired personal qualities.

Among Eskimo bands, each settlement may have its headman, who acquires his influence because the other members of the community recognize his good judgment and superior skills. The headman's advice concerning the movement of the band and other community matters is generally heeded, but he possesses no permanent authority and no sanctions of any kind. Among the Iglulik Eskimos, for example, leadership exists only in a very restricted sense.

> Within each settlement . . . there is as a rule an older man who enjoys the respect of the others and who decides when a move is to be made to another hunting center, when a hunt is to be started, how the spoils are to be divided, when the dogs are to be fed. . . . He is called *isumaitoq,* "he who thinks." It is not always the oldest man, but as a rule an elderly man who is a clever hunter or, as head of a large family, exercises great authority. He cannot be called a chief; there is no obligation to follow his counsel; but they do so in most cases, partly because they rely on his experience, partly because it pays to be on good terms with this man.[6]

This lack of fixed authority is characteristic of political organization at the band level. A man will not acquire or maintain influence unless he has the abilities needed by the rest of the band.

Although the position of headman is often hereditary among the !Kung Bushmen, the authority of the headman is extremely limited and the position itself offers no apparent advantages and is not actively sought after. Like all Bushmen, the headman fashions tools and shelters, carries his possessions, and hunts for food. No regalia or special honors distinguish him from the other members of the band. Indeed, the !Kung headman goes out of his way not to be envied for his possession of material goods.

While the authority of the !Kung headman is tenuous, he nevertheless has certain, at least symbolic, duties. He is generally held responsible for the way the band makes use of its food resources, although most of his decisions will be dictated by nature, long-standing custom, or consensus of band members. If there is theft by some person not affiliated with the band, he is expected to cope with the problem, and his consent is necessary for an outsider to be admitted to the band. Yet despite his customary duties, the !Kung headman is not necessarily the leader of the band. If he lacks the special abilities needed to lead in a given situation, the band turns to another person quite informally. No man of influence within the band, however, has formal authority or receives special privileges. At most, he is first among equals, at the least,

[5] A. R. Radcliffe-Brown, *The Andaman Islanders* (Glencoe, Ill.: The Free Press, 1948), p. 45.

[6] Therkel Mathiassen, *Material Culture of the Iglulik Eskimos* (1930), as quoted in E. M. Weyer, *The Eskimos: Their Environment and Folkways* (New Haven: Yale University Press, 1932), p. 213.

as one was overheard to say, "All you get is the blame if things go wrong."[7]

Tribal Society

The tribe is similar to the band in its egalitarian nature, its lack of political hierarchies and dominant classes, and its informal leadership patterns. Its technological base, however, is more advanced, for tribal societies generally are food producers. Because the tribe's food-getting technology is more productive, its population density is generally higher, its local groups larger, and its way of life more sedentary than the hunter-gatherer band's.

What principally distinguishes tribal from band political arrangements is the presence of some associations (such as clans, age-sets, religious or military societies) which can potentially integrate more than one local group into a larger whole. Such multilocal political integration, however, is not permanent, and it is informal in the sense that it is not headed by political officials. Frequently, the integration is called into play only when an external threat arises; when the threat disappears, the local groups revert to self-sufficiency. In other words, a tribal society lacks a permanent multilocal political authority; situations do arise which call for intergroup cooperation of some kind, but they are transitory, and a new situation may well require the coordination of quite different groups.[8]

Yet it is inaccurate to consider tribes as no more than temporary collections or aggregations of bands. While a tribe may seem a fragile social entity when compared to a state, the special associations which integrate local groups into a larger political entity make for a substantial difference between a tribe and a band. Such integration, which can be potentially called into play at any time, does not exist in band society.

Kinship Bonds. Frequently, pan-tribal associations are based upon kinship ties. Clans are the most common pan-tribal kinship group. In some societies, clan elders have the right to try to settle disputes between clansmen, or to attempt to punish wrongs committed against them by members of different clans. In addition, kinship bonds often tend to unite members of the same descent group during periods of warfare; in many societies the organization of warfare is the responsibility of the clan.[9]

The segmentary lineage system is another type of pan-tribal integration based on kinship, although the geographical distribution of the segmentary lineage system is more limited than that of clanship. The whole society (tribe) is composed of like segments or parts, each similar to the other in structure and function. As the society grows, it develops more segments of the same type. Every local segment, however, belongs to a hierarchy of lineages, each one stretching further and further back genealogically; the hierarchy of lineages, then, unites the many segments into larger and larger genealogical groups. The closer two groups are genealogically, the greater their general closeness. In the event of a dispute between members of different segments, people more closely related to one contestant than to another take the side of their nearest kinsman.

Although it is not based on kinship, a newly established but expanding university provides a good example of the workings of a segmentary lineage system. Initially the university is composed of a few departments (sgements), and as it grows more of these are established, each acknowledging links to the original core body. The departments of chemistry and physics, both representing the natural sciences, can be

[7] Lorna Marshall, "!Kung Bushmen Bands," in Ronald Cohen and John Middleton, eds., *Comparative Political Systems* (Garden City, N.Y.: Natural History Press, 1967), p. 41.

[8] Service, *Primitive Social Organization,* pp. 114–115.

[9] Service, *Primitive Social Organization,* p. 126.

expected to have a closer rapport than those of political science and fashion merchandising, whose only "genealogical link" is with the university as a whole. Yet when different issues are at stake, different coalitions form. For example, the chemistry department might have a major dispute with the physics department over the use of certain laboratory facilities. But in the interdepartmental "infighting" for budgets, one can expect the departments representing the natural sciences to exhibit a common front against those representing the social sciences and, on a higher level, those comprising the college of arts and sciences to oppose those comprising the college of business administration.[10]

The Tiv of northern Nigeria offer a classic example of a segmentary lineage system, a system which links all of the Tiv into one genealogical structure. The Tiv are a large and still expanding tribe, numbering 800,000 in 1958. Figure 1 is a representation of the Tiv segmentary lineage structure. As Paul Bohannan explains:

> The lineage whose apical ancestor is some three to six generations removed from living elders and who are associated with the smallest discrete territory *(tar)* I call the minimal segment; . . . it can vary in population from 200 people to well over a thousand. . . . The territory of a minimal segment adjoins the territory of its sibling minimal segment. Thus, the lineage comprising two minimal segments also has a discrete territory, and is in turn a segment of a more inclusive lineage, and of its more inclusive territory. In Fig. 1, the whole system can be seen: the father or founder of segment *a* was a brother of the founder of segment *b.* Each is a minimal segment today, and each has its own territory. The two segments taken together are all descended from *1,* and are known by his name—the children of *1.* In the same way, the territory of lineage *1,* made up as it is of the combined minimal territories *a* and *b,* combines with the territory of lineage *2,* made up of the combined minimal territories of *c* and *d,* to form territory *A,* occupied by lineage segment *A,* all descended from a single ancestor "A." This process is extended indefinitely, right up to the apex of the genealogy, back in time to the founder who begot the entire people, and outwards in space to the edges of Tivland. The entire 800,000 Tiv form a single "lineage" *(nongo)* and a single land called *Tar Tiv.*[11]

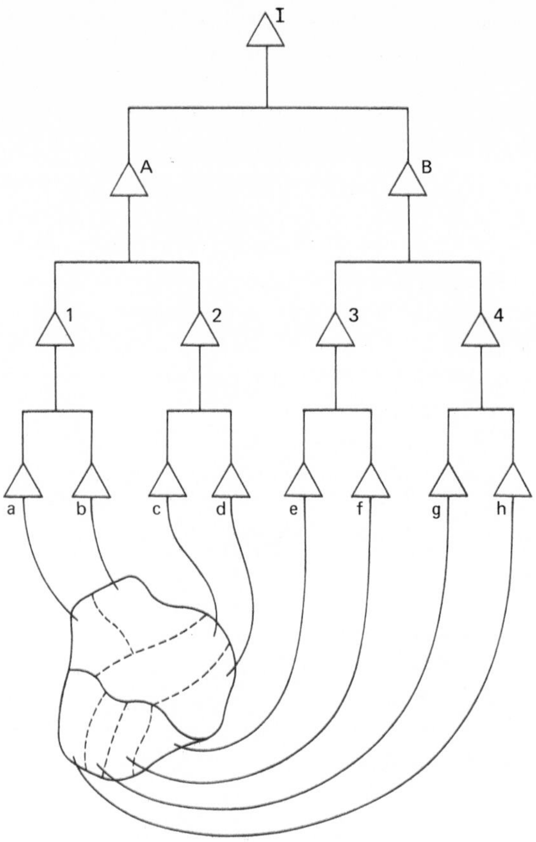

Figure 1
Tiv lineage segments and their territories.

Tiv lineage organization is the foundation of the political organization. A look at Figure 1 helps to explain how. A dispute between lineages (and territories) *a* and *b* remains minor,

[10] Marshall D. Sahlins, "The Segmentary Lineage: An Organization of Predatory Expansion," *American Anthropologist,* Vol. 63 (1962), p. 338.

[11] Paul Bohannan, "The Migration and Expansion of the Tiv," *Africa,* Vol. 24 (1954), p. 3.

since no more than "brother" segments are involved. But a dispute between *a* and *c* now involves lineages *1* and *2* as well, with the requirement that *b* assist *a,* and *d* support *c.* This process of mutual support, often called *complementary opposition,* means that segments will unite only in a confrontation with some other group. Groups that will fight with each other in a minor dispute might coalesce at some later time against a larger group.

Externally, the system is effective because it enables individual lineage segments to call on ever-increasing support when faced with border troubles. Indeed, within the society (between segments), conflicts, especially in border areas, are often turned outwards, "releasing internal pressure in an explosive blast against other peoples."[12]

Tiv segmentary lineage arrangements are not, however, quite so massive or so powerful as they seem. The combinations we have described are temporary, forming and dissolving as the occasion demands. Sahlins sums up the limitations as follows:

> The segmentary lineage system is self-liquidating. It is advantageous in inter-tribal competition, but having emerged victorious it has no longer *raison d'être* and the divisive tendencies of tribal polity reassert themselves.[13]

Age-Set Systems. Age-sets are pan-tribal groupings in which age and not kinship is the basis for political organization. Age-set systems have already been described in Chapter 17; the discussion here is restricted to political aspects of age-set systems.

Societies with age-set systems initiate their members either at birth or at about the age of puberty; not to become a member of an age-set means to remain "disenfranchised," excluded from all significant political decisions. One set (or group of sets) is usually in a position of authority, having replaced the set immediately preceding it; when it must retire in due course, it is replaced by the set immediately following it. Membership in the senior set bestows tribal-wide office in so far as each elder has authority because he belongs to the set which collectively holds authority on behalf of the whole tribe.

Senior set members represent the tribal whole as individuals in their own localities, exercising authority in matters of war (generally raiding), administration, and ritual. As is the case with segmentary lineages, times of particular crisis may join all the members of a senior age-set together; but, as soon as the normal situation is restored, the group will reseparate into its individual local components.

The Karimojong, a society characterized by age-sets, are a people of northeastern Uganda who depend on cattle herding and agriculture for their livelihood. Their political community includes elders who direct day-to-day affairs, large herd owners whose wealth enables them to have a say in certain activities, and initiated adult males whose responsibility it is to implement policy once it has been decided. Initiation into an age-set, and public acceptance of tribal customs, means that a Karimojong will ultimately become an elder and perhaps a leader of his local community.

The Karimojong age-set system has an important bearing on the practical, day-to-day content of tribal life. As herdsmen, Karimojong adults are often widely separated from their usual settlements. Herders will meet, mingle for a while, then go their separate ways, but each man may call upon other members of his age-set wherever he goes. The age-set system is important among the Karimojong because it immediately allocates to each individual a place in the universal ranking system and, thereby, establishes for him an appropriate pattern of response. A quarrel in camp will be settled by the representatives of the senior age-set present, regardless of which section of the tribe they may belong to.

[12] Sahlins, "The Segmentary Lineage," p. 342.
[13] *Ibid.,* p. 345.

Age-sets are a pan-tribal grouping that may form the basis of political organization. Among the Karimojong, elders are respected for their ability to intercede with the deity on behalf of the tribe. Here a group of elders gathers at a public ritual. (Courtesy Neville Dyson-Hudson.)

Karimojong elders are respected for their practical knowledge and experience, but they are particularly credited with the gift of being able to intercede with the deity on behalf of the tribe—a gift which they demonstrate at regular public rituals. Age has granted them

> experience of how and when the deity is best approached. Their impending death (relative to most members of the society) puts them in closer proximity to the boundaries of natural and supernatural. Most important, the deity is accessible to them, and generally amenable to their requests, more so than in the case of other men.[14]

Rituals serve political ends through prayers for economic security and betterment for each Karimojong. Elders can use their supernatural power as punishment; the severe drought and disease which swept through the tribe in the late nineteenth century is explained as being the consequence of the senior generation-set's displeasure with, and punishment of, its juniors.[15]

In theory, all Karimojong political leaders are equal in status; in fact, wealthy herd owners are usually able to exercise a telling influence over policy. Owners of large herds often have a number of wives and can count upon the support of numerous affinal groups. In addition, they are often owed a debt of gratitude in many communities for assistance rendered during times of food scarcity.

Political leaders are not elected from among the elders, nor are they appointed; they obtain their position informally. Usually a man's background and the capacity he has demonstrated

[14] Neville Dyson-Hudson, *Karimojong Politics* (Oxford: Clarendon Press, 1966), p. 213.
[15] *Ibid.,* p. 217.

in public debate over a period of time will result in his being considered "spokesman" by the men of his neighborhood. His function is to announce to the people what course of action seems required in a particular situation, to initiate that action, and then to coordinate it after it is begun. Although a spokesman may act as a decision maker in council, he does not necessarily take the lead in implementing decisions. Be it a cattle raid, a negotiation, or a ritual, the person chosen to lead is the one judged the most likely to achieve success.

Most political leaders exercise their authority within the local sphere because the pastoral nature of the Karimojong economy, with its dispersed bands and movement from one feeding ground to another, offers no viable alternative. However, from time to time an elder may acquire the status of a prophet and be awarded respect and obedience on a tribal scale; he is called on to lead sacrifices (to avert communal misfortune), to undertake rain making (to bring prosperity), and so on. Yet even a prophet's prestige and authority do not mean that he assumes a position of overlord or chief.

Chiefdoms

A chiefdom differs from a tribe in several important ways. Whereas a tribe has associations that can informally integrate more than one community, a chiefdom has a formal authority structure integrating multicommunity political units. Generally, the population of a chiefdom is more dense than that of a tribe, and the community is more permanent, partly as a consequence of its higher economic productivity.

The position of chief, which is sometimes hereditary and generally permanent, bestows high status on its holder. Chiefdoms are mostly rank societies, the chief and his family often having structured greater access to prestige. But some chiefdoms have developed simple class systems; that is, those most closely related to the chief, or those working closely with him in administration, constitute a kind of nobility with greater access to economic resources.

An important responsibility of most chiefs is that of redistributing agent. The goods and services produced by the society are often accumulated by the chief who reallocates them to the people. Generally, the chief also serves as coordinator of various activities. The chief may plan and direct the use of public labor, sometimes with significant economic consequences; he may supervise religious festivals, often acquiring religious status as a result; and he may be responsible for the security of the society and directing military activities.

In South Pacific chiefdoms, the ruler exercised authority in most of these areas. On the island of Fiji, for example, the chief was responsible for the redistribution of goods and the coordination of labor.

> The paramount [chief] could summon the community's labor on his own behalf, or on behalf of someone else who requested it, or for general purposes. . . . Besides his right to summon labor he accumulated the greater proportion of the first fruits of the yam crop . . . and he benefited from other forms of food presentation, or by the acquisition of special shares in ordinary village distribution. . . . Thus, the paramount would collect a significant part of the surplus production of the community and redistribute it in the general welfare.[16]

The Tahitians had a history of large-scale warfare, with chiefs coordinating land and naval forces in thrusts and counter-thrusts. Tahitian society was clearly ranked—from the preeminence accorded to the families of the paramount chiefs, who were believed to have exceptional spiritual power, down in various gradations to the lowest status of the general

[16] Marshall Sahlins, *Moala: Culture and Nature on a Fijian Island* (Ann Arbor: University of Michigan Press, 1962), pp. 293–294.

Although tribal societies have no formal chief, leadership still exists. Here a Masai elder addresses the younger men of the tribe. (Photo by Marc and Evelyne Bernheim from Woodfin Camp and Associates.)

populace. Many of the early missionaries to Tahiti regarded the Tahitian chiefs as despots, because of the great deference and tribute paid to them by the common people. In fact, however, the chiefs did not really have tyrannical control over the daily lives of the islanders.

Some Bantu societies of southern Africa were also chiefdoms. In many of these there were at least two distinct social classes, often referred to by different names meaning "nobles" and "commoners." The "nobility" could be distinguished by their close kinship ties to the chief. Among the Tswana and the Ndebele, social stratification was even more developed, each tribe also having a separate servant class. There was substantial mobility, however, between classes. A commoner, for example, might achieve political influence by demonstrating bravery in warfare, sound judgement, or a knowledge of law.[17]

These Bantu chiefs had a wide range of duties and responsibilities. Commonly referred to as the "father" or "herdsman" of the tribe, the chief made decisions in all matters of public policy—those regarding the management of internal affairs as well as those concerning external relations. The chief was also responsible for resolving disputes among the people, providing justice for injured parties, and punishing wrong-doers. In some cases, the chief had the privilege of making new laws, subject to the approval of the people. Other duties of these Bantu chiefs included control over the allocation of land use, deciding when crops should be planted and when they should be harvested, organization of large collective hunts, creating new age-sets, mobilizing the people for defense, and conducting important religious ceremonies and magical rites.[18]

The State

A state, according to a simple definition, is "an autonomous political unit, encompassing many communities within its territory and having a centralized government with the power to collect taxes, draft men for work or war, and decree and enforce laws."[19] State societies, then, have a complex, centralized political structure, with a wide range of permanent institutions having legislative, executive, and judicial functions, and inevitably a large bureaucracy. Central to the definition of the state-type of society is the concept of legitimate force to implement policies both internally and externally; in state societies, the government holds a monopoly on the legitimate use of physical force.[20] Such a monopoly of physical force can be seen in the development of formal and specialized instruments of social control: a police force, a militia, a standing army. Of course, the rulers in the state do not maintain the social order by force alone; the people must believe, at least to some extent, that those in power have a legitimate right to govern their activities. If the people think otherwise about their rulers, history suggests that those in power may eventually lose their ability to maintain control.

In addition to their strictly political features, states are characterized by class stratification and hence restricted access to basic economic resources. State societies are generally supported by a system of intensive agriculture, the high productivity of which presumably allows for the emergence of cities, a high degree of economic and other kinds of specialization, commercial exchange (distribution of goods and services involving the use of money), and extensive foreign trade.

Ancient Rome was a complex state society that dominated the Mediterranean and Near East for hundreds of years. Roman society was clearly stratified, with the patricians, who controlled the bulk of the wealth and influence, sharply distinguishable from plebians (common folk). The Romans made productive use of favorable agricultural conditions in Italy, and intensive agricultural methods were employed in the provinces, especially in Egypt, southern Gaul (France), and Spain. Roman commerce was world-wide (as the term was defined in those days), and its money was the principal medium of exchange around the entire Mediterranean and within much of Europe.

[17] I. Schapera, *Government and Politics in Tribal Societies* (London: C. A. Watts, 1956), pp. 56–60.
[18] Schapera, *Government and Politics in Tribal Societies,* pp. 68–74.
[19] Robert L. Carneiro, "A Theory of the Origin of the State," *Science,* Vol. 169 (August 21, 1970), p. 733.
[20] See Max Weber, *The Theory of Social and Economic Organization,* trans. A. M. Henderson and Talcott Parsons (New York: Oxford University Press, 1947), p. 154.

Politically, Rome had a complex of institutions. During her imperial phase, which lasted for the first three centuries A.D., emperor and senate acted together in governing the Roman world, though the emperor tended to concentrate on foreign and military affairs, while the senate dealt with domestic matters. Roman government employed a large bureaucracy, controlled communications, deployed substantial army and navy units, and made its power felt both internally and externally. To be a Roman citizen was considered no small honor, and the legitimacy and the sovereignty of the Roman state went more or less unquestioned for half a millennium.

State society is not unique to Western civilization. The kingdom of Nupe in Central Nigeria is an old and highly centralized political unit. As is characteristic of state societies generally, Nupe society is quite rigidly stratified. At the top of the social system is the king, or *Etsu.* Beneath the king, members of the royal family form the highest aristocratic class; they are called *ena gitsuzhi,* "the ones who will become *Etsu.*" Next in rank are two other classes of nobility—the local chiefs and the military leaders. At the bottom of the social hierarchy are the commoners, who have neither rank, nor power, nor any share in political authority.

The Nupe state is composed of two types of territorial units: those towns and villages which are part of the royal domain and therefore under direct rule of the king, and those which are designated as fiefs and are under the control of local lords. The state, however, has supreme authority over all local magistrates and lords. Although the people of a village may select their own chief, the king has the right to confirm such appointments, as well as the power to depose all local rulers, including the lords.

The Nupe king possesses ultimate authority in many judicial matters. Minor disputes and civil cases are handled by the local village councils, but serious criminal cases are the prerogative of the king. Such cases, referred to as "crimes for the king," are brought before

In state societies, the government holds a monopoly on the legitimate use of physical force, as can be seen in the development of specialized instruments of social control—a police force, a militia, an army. Here Parisian police look on as student demonstrators participate in a sit-in. (United Press International Photo.)

the royal court by the king's local representatives. It is the king and his councillors who judge the cases and determine suitable punishments.

The most powerful influence of the state over the Nupe people was in the area of taxation. The king had the power to impose and collect taxes from every household. Payment was made either in money (cowrie shells originally, and later British currency) or certain gifts, such as cloth, mats, and sometimes slaves. Much of the revenue collected was kept by the king, the remainder being shared with his local representatives and lords. In return for the taxes they paid, the people received security—protection against invasion and domestic disorder.[21]

Factors Associated with Variation in Political Organization

The classification of types of society into band, tribe, chiefdom, and state implies an evolutionary trend from simpler to more complex forms of political organization; from small-scale local autonomy to large-scale regional unification; from a few, ephemeral, and informal political leaders to large numbers of permanent, specialized political officials; from the absence of political power to a monopoly of public force by a central authority. Service and others have suggested that this evolutionary trend in political institutions may be associated with similar trends in other social realms, such as:

1. *Technology:* from food collection (hunting and gathering) to intensive food production (agriculture and animal husbandry)
2. *Population:* from small, local groups to large communities, and from low to greater population density
3. *Social status:* from egalitarian society, to rank society, and finally to class-differentiated society
4. *Economic distribution:* from major emphasis on reciprocity in the distribution of goods and services, to redistribution, and finally to market or commercial exchange, using money as the principal medium of exchange

These suggested associations (summarized in Table 1) seem to be confirmed by the available

[21] S. F. Nadel, "Nupe State and Community," *Africa,* Vol. 8 (1935), pp. 257–303.

Table 1
Suggested Trends in Political Organization and Other Social Characteristics

	Highest Level of Political Integration	*Specialization of Political Officials*	*Predominant Mode of Subsistence*	*Community Size and Population Density*	*Social Differentiation*	*Major Form of Distribution*
Band	Local group	Little or none, informal leadership	Hunting and gathering	Very small communities, very low density	Egalitarian	Reciprocity
Tribe	Sometimes multilocal	Little or none, informal leadership	Extensive (shifting) agriculture and/or herding	Small communities, low density	Egalitarian	Reciprocity
Chiefdom	Multilocal	Some specialized political officials	Extensive or intensive agriculture and/or herding	Large communities, medium density	Rank	Redistribution
State	Multilocal, often entire language group	Many specialized political officials	Intensive agriculture and herding	Cities and towns, high density	Class and caste	Market exchange

cross-cultural evidence. In regard to the relation between the level of subsistence technology and political complexity, a cross-cultural study employing a small random sample of societies found that the greater the importance of agriculture in a society the larger the population which is politically unified, and the greater the number and types of political officials.[22] A massive cross-cultural survey reports a similar trend: the more intensive the agriculture, the greater the likelihood of state organization; and conversely, societies with no more than local political institutions are likely to depend on hunting, gathering, and fishing.[23] With regard to community size, M. Ember's study also suggests that the larger the leading community, the wider the range of political officials in the society.[24] Textor, too, presents a similar finding in that societies with state organizations tend to have cities and towns, whereas those with only local political organization are more likely to have communities with an average population of less than 200 persons.[25] Cross-cultural research also tends to confirm that societies with higher levels of political integration are the more likely to exhibit social differentiation, especially in the form of class distinctions.[26]

Does this evidence provide us with an explanation as to why political organization varies? Clearly, the data indicate that several factors are associated with political development, but exactly how those factors are related is not yet known. Several anthropologists, however, have suggested some theories.

Morton Fried represents those theorists who link the rise of the state to advances in food-production technology, which in turn is presumed to be responsible for increased population.[27] Fried suggests that increasing population tends to put pressure on economic resources, so that social stratification (differential access to resources) eventually develops. In the nonstate society of Tikopia, an island in Melanesia, for example, population increased by about 35 percent between 1929 and 1952, bringing famine in its train and also a fundamental change in the system of land tenure—a change which increased the emphasis on land ownership as opposed to community use of land.[28] Thus demographic pressure is presumed to result in increasing restriction on access to basic resources and in the growth of social distinctions; eventually the state, with its monopoly on the legitimate use of force, emerges as a means of maintaining the system of stratification.

Like Fried, Robert Carneiro recognizes the importance of food-getting technology but sets it into a somewhat different context. The primary weight is given to the scarcity of agricultural land in areas of "environmental circumscription," by which Carneiro means areas where mountains, seas, or deserts delimit the land that simple farming peoples could occupy and cultivate. As land shortages in such areas become more acute, warfare presumably increases, and defeated political units are subordinated to the victor. The end result, according to Carneiro, is that a circumscribed area becomes unified under a single, centralized political authority, complex enough to be termed a state. Accompanying such centralization would be changes in the internal political structure of the emerging state. Because conquered peoples must be administered, a specialized group of administrators, responsible for collecting taxes, organizing labor, building roads, and so on, should tend to develop. Finally, Carneiro sug-

[22] M. Ember, "The Relationship between Economic and Political Development in Nonindustrialized Societies," *Ethnology,* Vol. 2 (April 1963), pp. 228-248.

[23] Data from Robert B. Textor, comp., *A Cross-Cultural Summary* (New Haven: HRAF Press, 1967).

[24] Ember, "The Relationship between Economic and Political Development in Nonindustrialized Societies."

[25] Data from Textor, *A Cross-Cultural Summary.*

[26] Raoul Naroll, "Two Solutions to Galton's Problem," *Philosophy of Science,* Vol. 28 (January 1961), pp. 15–39.

[27] Fried, *Evolution of Political Society.*

[28] Raymond Firth, *Social Change in Tikopia* (New York: Macmillan, 1959).

gests, these administrators, along with the rulers and warriors, form an upper class which uses the taxes collected from conquered villages to support themselves and maintain the state system that has evolved.[29]

Future research that systematically tests such theories of state formation may enable anthropologists to determine which theory is most valid.

RESOLUTION OF CONFLICT

Political organization implies more than the making of policy, its administration, and enforcement. It also generally refers to the resolution of conflict, which may be accomplished peacefully by adjudicating disputes, negotiating compromises, or by the threat of social sanctions. But if such procedures fail or are not possible because of the absence of mediating procedures, then disputes may erupt into violent conflict. When violence occurs within a political unit in which disputes are usually settled peacefully, we conventionally refer to such violence as crime. When the violence occurs between groups of people from separate political units, groups between which there is no effective procedure for settling disputes, we usually call such violence warfare.

Peaceful Resolution of Conflict

Most modern, industrialized states have formal institutions and offices such as police, district attorneys, courts, and penal systems for dealing with minor disputes and more serious conflicts that may arise in society. All of these institutions generally operate according to codified laws—that is, a set of written (and therefore explicit) rules stipulating what is permissible and what is not. Transgression of the law by an individual gives the state the right to take action against him. Whatever that action might be, implicit in it is the threat of force, a threat which is reserved only to the duly constituted institutions, offices, and officials of the state. Thus, the state has a monopoly on the legitimate use of force in the society, for it alone has the right to coerce its subjects into agreement with its regulations, customs, political edicts, and procedures.

Many societies, however, lack such specialized offices and institutions for dealing with conflict—indeed, they would seem, at first impression, to lack systems of law. Yet, since all societies have peaceful, regularized ways of handling at least certain disputes, some anthropologists speak in terms of the universality of law. E. Adamson Hoebel, for example, states that:

> Each people has its system of social control. And all but a few of the poorest of them have as a part of their control system a complex of behavior patterns and institutional mechanisms that we may properly treat as law. For, "anthropologically considered, law is merely one aspect of our culture—the aspect which employs the force of organized society to regulate individual and group conduct and to prevent, redress or punish deviations from prescribed social norms."[30]

Thus, a decision not only resolves a particular dispute but also sets a precedent and represents an ideal for other people to follow in the future. Law, then, whether informal as in simple societies, or formal as in complex societies, provides a means of dealing peacefully with whatever conflicts develop.

Peaceful Resolution of Conflicts: Community Action. Societies have found various ways of peacefully resolving disputes. One such way involves action on the part of

[29] Carneiro, "A Theory of the Origin of the State," pp. 733–738.

[30] E. Adamson Hoebel, *The Law of Primitive Man* (New York: Atheneum, 1968), p. 4, quoting S. P. Simpson and Ruth Field, "Law and the Social Sciences," *Virginia Law Review*, Vol. 32 (1946), p. 858.

the community as a whole. Eskimo societies, for example, frequently resolve disputes through community action. Rarely numbering more than a dozen or so families, the Eskimo community has a social organization that is quite simple. Within local groups, kinship ties are not particularly emphasized, and the family is regarded as autonomous in most matters. Eskimos believe that spirits—particularly if displeased—can determine much of a man's fate, and consequently, they carry out their daily tasks within a complex system of taboos. This system of taboos is so extensive that some have suggested that the Eskimos have no need for a formal set of laws.

Nevertheless, conflicts do take place and have to be resolved. Accordingly, there are "principles" which act as guides to the community in settling trouble cases. Failure to heed a taboo, or the orders of a shaman, leads to expulsion from the group, since the community cannot accept a risk to its livelihood. The man who fails to share his goods voluntarily will find them confiscated and distributed to the community, and he may be executed in the process. A single case of murder, as an act of vengeance (usually because of the abduction of a wife, or as part of a blood feud), does not concern the community, but repeated murders do. Boas gives a typical example:

> There was a native of Padli by the name of Padlu. He had induced the wife of a native of Cumberland Sound to desert her husband and follow him. The deserted husband, meditating revenge . . . visited his friends in Padli, but before he could accomplish his intention of killing Padlu, the latter shot him. . . . A brother of the murdered man went to Padli to avenge the death . . . but he also was killed by Padlu. A third native of Cumberland Sound, who wished to avenge the death of his relatives was also murdered by him.
>
> On account of these outrages the natives wanted to get rid of Padlu, but yet they did not dare to attack him. When the *pimain* (headman) of the Akudmurmuit learned of these events he started southward and *asked every man in Padli whether Padlu should be killed. All agreed;* so he went with the latter deer hunting . . . and . . . shot Padlu in the back.[31]

Informal Adjudication without Power. Community action is not the only way that societies without codified laws peacefully resolve disputes. Some societies have informal adjudicators who resolve trouble cases, although such adjudicators do not have the formal power needed to enforce their decisions. One such society is the Nuer of East Africa.

The Nuer are a pastoral and horticultural people, who live in villages grouped into tribal sections. Each section is an informal political unit, with its own machinery for settling disputes. However, if a section has a large population, residing over a wide area, it may well be a long time before certain disputes are cleared up. On the higher, intersectional level there is little chance of bringing feuding sections to a quick settlement, and few means of apportioning blame or of assessing damages exist, other than war.

Within a single community, however, disputes are more easily settled by the use of an informal adjudicator called the "leopard-skin chief." This man is not a political chief but a specialist mediator, whose position is hereditary, has religious overtones, and makes its holder responsible for the social well-being of the section.

Matters such as cattle stealing rarely come to the attention of the leopard-skin chief; the parties involved usually prefer to settle in their own private way. But if, for example, a murder has been committed, the culprit will go at once to the house of the leopard-skin chief. Immediately the chief cuts his arm so that the blood flows; until the cut has been made the murderer may not eat or drink. If the murderer is afraid of vengeance by the slain man's family, he will remain at the house of the leopard-skin chief,

[31] Franz Boas, *Central Eskimos* (Bureau of American Ethnology, Annual Report 6, 1888), p. 668.

Societies have found various ways of peacefully resolving disputes. A council of men among the Bakhtiari nomads of Iran meets to decide the fate of a man who stole an animal. (Photo by Tony Howarth from Woodfin Camp and Associates.)

which is considered sanctuary. Then, within the next few months,

> The chief elicits from the slayer's kin that they are prepared to pay compensation to avoid a feud and he persuades the dead man's kin that they ought to accept compensation. During this period neither party may eat or drink from the same vessels as the other, and they may not, therefore, eat in the house of the same third person. The chief then collects the cattle—till recently some forty to fifty beasts—and takes them to the dead man's home, where he performs various sacrifices of cleansing and atonement.[32]

[32] E. E. Evans-Pritchard, "The Nuer of the Southern Sudan," in M. Fortes and E. E. Evans-Pritchard, eds., *African Political Systems* (New York, London: Oxford University Press, 1940), p. 291.

The chief acts throughout as a go-between. He has no authority to force either of the parties to negotiate, and he has no power to enforce a solution once it has been arrived at. He is, however, able to take advantage of the fact that, because both parties to the dispute belong to the same community and are anxious to avoid a blood feud, they are usually willing to come to terms.

Oaths and Ordeals. Still another way of peacefully resolving disputes is through oaths and ordeals. Oaths and ordeals both involve appeals to supernatural power. An oath, however, is the act of calling upon a deity to bear witness to the truth of what one says, while an ordeal is a means used to determine guilt or innocence by submitting the accused to dangerous or painful tests believed to be under supernatural control.[33]

Oaths, as one would expect, vary widely in content according to the culture in which they are found. The Rwala Bedouin, for example, do the following:

> In serious disputes the judge requires the *msabba* oath, so called from the seven lines drawn with a saber on the ground. The judge first draws a circle with a saber, then its diameter; then he intersects with five vertical lines, inviting the witness to step inside and, facing south, to swear: "A false oath is the ruin of the descendants, for he who [swears falsely] is insatiable in his desire [of gain] and does not fear for his Lord."
>
> Scarcely is the oath finished when the witness jumps out of the circle and, full of rage, runs at his opponent, who has made him swear. The people present at the trial have to surround and hold him until he calms down.[34]

Ordeals fall into several types. A common one, found practically in every part of the world, is the scalding ordeal. Among the Tanala of Madagascar, the accused person, having first had his hand carefully examined for protective covering, has to reach his hand into a cauldron of boiling water and grasp, from underneath, a rock which is suspended there. He then plunges his hand into cold water, has it bandaged, and is led off to spend the night under guard. In the morning his hand is unbandaged and examined. If there are blisters, he is guilty. Another common type of ordeal involves the taking of poison; obviously, to survive is to establish one's innocence. Yet another is the water ordeal:

> The suspected criminal or criminals, together with their accuser, were led to the bank of a river. Their hands and feet were tied with cords, and in this condition they were thrown into the river. The person whose body remained on the surface of the water was regarded as the guilty one, and was consequently punished. The people believed that the body of a culprit was always rejected by the river, and that the innocent one was kept by the water. Consequently, the person whose body remained under the water was considered innocent.[35]

Oaths and ordeals have also been practiced in Western societies. They were both common, for example, in medieval Europe; and even today, in our own society, vestiges of oaths can be found: children can be heard to say "Cross my heart and hope to die," and witnesses in courts of law are expected to swear on the Bible.

Why do some societies use oaths and ordeals? It has been argued that ordeals may render more than a mere chance verdict. Concerning the scalding ordeal, for example, Roberts suggests that there may be some relationship between the anxiety raised in a guilty person and severe blistering on the hand. But, whether or not oaths or ordeals can establish guilt or innocence, we have to ask why some societies use them, while others do not. Roberts suggests that oaths and ordeals are found in fairly complex societies where there are relatively well-developed political institutions, yet ones in which political officials lack sufficient power or would make themselves unnecessarily vulnerable, were they to attempt to make and enforce judicial decisions. In other words, in many parts of Africa, as well as in medieval Europe, ruling cadres had problems with succession and with maintaining continuous social control. To put their prestige and influence on the line behind every important judicial verdict

[33] John M. Roberts, "Oaths, Autonomic Ordeals, and Power," in Clellan S. Ford., ed., *Cross-Cultural Approaches: Readings in Comparative Research* (New Haven: HRAF Press, 1967), p. 169.

[34] Alois Musil, *The Manners and Customs of Rwala Bedouins* (New York: The American Geographical Society, Oriental Exploration Studies, No. 6, 1928), p. 430.

[35] Alexander Grigolia, *Custom and Justice in the Caucasus: The Georgian Highlanders* (1939), as quoted in Roberts, "Oaths, Autonomic Ordeals, and Power," p. 171.

was dangerous and impracticable. Hence the resort to an appeal to the gods, which proved to be "an important device allowing weak authority to maintain control at a reasonably low cost."[36] In contrast, smaller and less complex societies have no need for elaborate mechanisms to acertain guilt; in such societies everyone is aware of what crimes have been committed and who the guilty party is.

Codified Law and the Courts. Codified laws and courts as a means of peacefully resolving disputes are used in our own society. But such mechanisms are not limited to modern industrialized states. The Ashanti of West Africa, for example, had, from the late seventeenth to the early twentieth centuries, a complex political system with elaborate legal arrangements. The Ashanti state was a military-based empire possessing legal codes that resembled those of many ancient civilizations.[37]

The most effective sanction underpinning Ashanti law and its enforcement was the intense respect, almost religious deference, accorded to the wishes of the ancestors and also to the elders as custodians of the ancestral tradition. Ashanti law was based on a concept of Natural Law—a belief that there is an order of the universe whose principles law makers should follow in the decisions they make and in the regulations they design. Criminal and religious law merged in that crimes were regarded as sins against the ancestral spirits, especially acts of homicide, cursing the chief, cowardice, and sorcery. In Ashanti court procedure, elders examined and cross-examined witnesses as well as parties to the dispute; there were also quasi-professional advocates, and appeals against a verdict could be made directly to the chief. Particularly noteworthy was the emphasis placed on intent when assessing guilt. Drunkenness constituted a valid defense for all crimes except murder and cursing the chief, and a plea of insanity, if proved, was upheld for all offenses. Ashanti punishments could be severe, physical mutilation such as slicing off the nose or an ear—even castration in sexual offenses—being often employed. However, fines were more frequently imposed, and often those sentenced to death were allowed to commute their punishment to banishment and confiscation of goods.

What is it that leads some societies to have codified systems of law and others not? One explanation advanced by E. Adamson Hoebel, A. R. Radcliffe-Brown, and others is that in small, closely knit communities there is little need for formal, legal guidelines because competing interests are minimal. In addition, possible transgressors are easily spotted in a small community and therefore find it difficult to avoid criticism. Thus, members of such societies are highly dependent upon favorable public opinion, for chronic transgressors may be subject to banishment from the community—a punishment often tantamount to death. In other words, simple societies need little codified law because there are relatively few matters to quarrel about and because the general will of the group is sufficiently well known and demonstrated frequently enough to deter transgressors.

This point of view is corroborated in Richard Schwartz's study of two contemporary Israeli settlements. For example, in one communal kibbutz a young man aroused a good deal of community resentment because he had received an electric tea kettle as a gift. It was the general opinion that he had overstepped the code about not having personal possessions, and he was so informed. Accordingly, he gave the kettle to the communal infirmary. Schwartz comments: "No organized enforcement of the decision was threatened, but had he disregarded the expressed will of the community, his life . . . would have been made intolerable

[36] Roberts, "Oaths, Autonomic Ordeals and Power," p. 192.
[37] Hoebel, *The Law of Primitive Man,* Ch. 9.

by the antagonism of public opinion."[38] In this community, where people worked and ate together, not only did everyone know about transgressions, but a wrong-doer could not escape public censure. Thus, in such a community, public opinion was an effective sanction. In another Israeli community, however, where individuals lived in widely separated houses and worked and ate separately, public opinion did not work as well in resolving conflicts. Not only were community members less aware of problems, but they had no quick way of making their feelings known. As a result, they established a judicial body to handle trouble cases.

Unlike small, closely knit communities, in larger, more heterogeneous and stratified societies, disputes are likely to be more frequent and at the same time less visible to the public. Individuals are generally not so dependent on other community members for their well-being and hence are less likely to know of or care about other people's opinions. It is in such societies that codified laws and formal authorities for resolving disputes may develop—in order perhaps that disputes may be settled impersonally enough so that the parties can accept the judicial decision and social order can be restored.

A good example of how more formal systems of law develop is the experience of towns in the American West at the end of the nineteenth century, during the gold rush period. Such communities were literally swamped by large numbers of total strangers. The story is often reenacted in TV westerns. The local townsfolk, having no control (authority) over these intruders because the strangers had no local ties, looked for ways to deal with the troublesome cases that were always flaring up. According to the TV Western version of this problem, a first attempt at a solution was to hire gunslingers—also strangers—to act as peace officers or sheriffs, but this usually failed. Eventually towns succeeded in having federal authority send in marshals backed by federal power. Another related problem was how to prevent innocent people from getting killed. This led to efforts to gain acceptance for judges, court trials, and the efficacy of peaceful resolution of conflicts.

Is there some evidence to support the theory that codified law is only necessary in larger, more complex societies? Based on a large, world-wide sample of societies, Textor reports that codified law is associated with political integration beyond the local level. With particular reference to the way murder cases are handled, it seems that, in societies with only local political organization, such cases are dealt with informally, without a specialized official. In societies with multilocal political units, murder cases tend to be adjudicated by specialized political authorities.[39]

Violent Resolution of Conflict

People are likely to resort to violence when regular, effective, alternative means of resolving a conflict are not available. When violence occurs between political entities such as communities, districts, or nations, some form of warfare is the result. The aim of the antagonists in each case is to control the situation so that they can obtain a particular objective—revenge for a killing, access to food, animals, raw materials, land, or markets—or to prevent someone else from gaining those objectives. The type of warfare, of course, varies in scope and in complexity from society to society. Sometimes a distinction is made between feuding, raiding, and large-scale confrontations.

Feuding. Feuding is a state of recurring hostilities between families or groups of kins-

[38] Richard D. Schwartz, "Social Factors in the Development of Legal Control: A Case Study of Two Israeli Settlements;" *Yale Law Journal,* Vol. 63 (February 1954), p. 475.

[39] Textor, *A Cross-Cultural Summary.*

men, usually motivated by a desire to avenge an offense against a member of the group—insult, injury, deprivation, or death. The most characteristic feature of the feud is that responsibility to avenge is carried by all members of the kin group; the killing of any member of the offender's group is considered appropriate revenge, since the kin group as a whole is considered responsible. In the absence of a centralized authority with the capacity to intervene and to stop the dispute, a feud can fester for years, even being passed on from one generation to the next. Nicholas Gubser tells us of a feud within a Nunamiut Eskimo community, caused by a husband's killing of his wife's lover, which lasted for decades. The Nunamiut take feuds seriously, as do many societies, especially when murder has been perpetrated. When a man is killed, Gubser writes:

> The closely related members of his kindred do not rest until complete revenge has been achieved. The immediate relatives of the deceased . . . recruit as much support from other relatives as they can. Their first action, if possible, is to kill the murderer, or maybe one of his closest kin. Then, of course, the members of the murderer's kindred are brought into the feud. These two kindreds may snipe at each other for years.[40]

Sometimes a full-scale battle takes place, as when the inland Nunamiut are drawn into a feud with coastal Eskimos over the abduction of a woman, after her kinsfolk learn that she has been mutilated or possibly killed.

Raiding. Raiding may be defined as a short-term use of force, usually carefully preplanned and organized, to realize a limited objective, usually the acquisition of goods, animals, or other forms of wealth belonging to another (often a neighboring) community. Raiding is especially prevalent in pastoral societies, in which cattle, horses, camels, and so forth, are prized and one's own herd can be augmented by theft. Raids are often organized by temporary leaders or coordinators whose authority may not endure beyond the planning and execution of the venture. Raiding differs from feuding in that it can more readily be terminated, temporarily or permanently, by recognized methods, such as truce or negotiated settlement.

Lloyd Briggs's study of the various tribes of the Sahara reveals the major role raiding can play in the economy of a nomadic community. The Chaamba, for example, had elevated raiding "practically to the level of an industry" by the time the French arrived and put a stop to it.[41] The Tuareg economy depended for at least one-quarter of its wealth on raiding, the objectives being both booty and slaves. The raiding performed by such tribes as the Chaamba and the Tuareg is an example of the high level of planning, coordination, and execution a raiding society may be able to achieve. Here is how Briggs describes one such operation:

> Success depended, of course, on the element of complete surprise, and on speed and efficient team work in collecting booty and getting away with it well ahead of the enraged victims bent on speedy vengeance. Also the target had to be far from the raiders' home territory [to make pursuit and counter raids difficult]. For this reason raiders usually directed their operations against some nomad camp three or four hundred miles away from home.

They would head out by the least known and traveled routes, zigzagging about for days on the way home to throw off pursuit, traveling at night and over the roughest, the most barren country.[42]

Large-Scale Confrontations. Both feuding and raiding usually involve relatively small numbers of persons and almost always

[40] Nicholas J. Gubser, *The Nunamiut Eskimos: Hunters of Caribou* (New Haven: Yale University Press, 1965), p. 151.

[41] Lloyd Cabot Briggs, *The Tribes of the Sahara* (Cambridge, Mass.: Harvard University Press, 1960), p. 203.

[42] Briggs, *The Tribes of the Sahara,* p. 121.

Among the Dani of central New Guinea, warfare is characterized by formal battles. The two sides meet at an agreed-upon battle site to set up their lines and commence fighting with spears, sticks, and bows and arrows. (Photo by Karl Heider, © 1968 by the Film Study Center, Harvard University.)

an element of surprise. Because they are generally attacked without warning, the victims are often unable to muster an immediate defense. Large-scale confrontations, in contrast, involve a large number of people, with both sides planning strategies of attack and defense.

Large-scale warfare is usually practiced among societies with intensive agriculture or industrialization, for such societies possess a sufficiently advanced technology to support specialized armies, military leaders, strategists, and so on. However, large-scale confrontations are not limited to state societies alone. Among the Dugum Dani of central New Guinea, for example, warfare is widespread.

The military history of the Dani, with its shifting alliances and confederations, is reminiscent of that of Europe, although Dani battles of course involve far fewer fighters and less sophisticated weaponry. Among the Dani, long periods of ritual warfare are characterized by formal battles which are announced through a challenge sent by one side to the opposing side. If the challenge is accepted, the protagonists meet at the agreed-upon battle site to set up their lines. Fighting with spears, sticks, and bows and arrows begins at mid-morning and continues until nightfall or rain. There may also be a rest period during the midday heat during which both sides shout insults to one another or talk and rest among themselves. The front line of battle is composed of about a dozen active warriors and a few leaders. Behind them is a second line, still within arrow range, which is composed of those who have just left the forward line or are preparing to join it. The third line, outside arrow range, is composed of noncombatants—males too old or too young to participate and those recovering from wounds. This third line merely watches the battle taking place on the grassy plain. On the hillsides far back from the front line, some of the old men help to direct ancestral ghosts to the battle by gouging a line in the ground that points in the direction of the battlefield.[43]

Yet as "total" as large-scale confrontations may be, even warfare has cultural rules governing its conduct. Among the Dani, for instance, no fighting occurs at night, and weapons are limited to simple spears and bows and arrows. Similarly, in state societies, governments will sign "self-denying" pacts, restricting the use of poison gas, germ warfare, and so forth. Unofficially, private arrangements are common. One has only to glance through the memoirs of national leaders of the two world wars to become aware of locally arranged truces, visits to one another's front positions, exchanges of prisoners of war, and so on.

Anthropologists have in recent years become interested in examining the relationships between types of warfare and types of political organization. Keith Otterbein, for example, in a cross-cultural study of some 46 societies, found that the higher the level of political centralization, the more advanced the degree of military sophistication; in other words, chiefdoms and states are more likely to have complex military establishments, with a professional army and a hierarchy of military authority, than are bands and tribes. In addition, societies with complex political organizations are likely to have higher casualty rates and to wage war in order to gain political control over other groups. However, although military sophistication seems to increase with political development, the frequency of warfare seems to be no greater in complex states than in simple band societies.[44]

[43] Karl Heider, *The Dugum Dani* (Chicago: Aldine, 1970), pp. 105–111.

[44] Keith F. Otterbein, *The Evolution of War* (New Haven: HRAF Press, 1970).

SUMMARY

1. All societies have customs or procedures which result in policy making and the resolution of disputes—ways of creating and maintaining social order and coping with social disorder—although such customs vary from society to society.
2. Band societies are composed of a number of fairly small, usually nomadic groups of people. Each band is self-sufficient and autonomous, the band usually being the largest group that acts politically. Bands are generally at the hunter-gatherer level of food-getting technology and are egalitarian in their social organization. In terms of political leadership, authority within the band is informal.
3. The tribe is similar to the band in its egalitarian nature, its lack of political hierarchies and of dominant classes, and its informal leadership patterns. A tribal society, however, is generally supported by food production, has a higher population density, and is usually more sedentary. Tribal society is defined by the presence of some associations (such as clans, age-sets, religious or military societies) which can potentially integrate more than one local group into a larger whole.
4. A chiefdom differs from a tribe in that while a tribe has associations which can informally integrate more than one community, a chiefdom has a formal authority

structure integrating multicommunity political units. Generally, the population of a chiefdom is more dense than that of a tribe, and the community is more permanent, partly as a consequence of its higher economic productivity. The position of chief, which is sometimes hereditary and generally permanent, bestows high status on its holder. Chiefdoms are mostly rank societies, but some have developed simple class systems. An important responsibility of most chiefs is that of redistributing agent.

5. A state is a political unit comprised of many communities and having a centralized government with the authority to make and enforce laws, collect taxes, and draft men for military service. In state societies the government holds a monopoly on the legitimate use of physical force. In addition, states are generally characterized by class stratification, intensive agriculture (the high productivity of which presumably allows for the emergence of cities), commercial exchange, a high degree of economic and other kinds of specialization, and extensive foreign trade.

6. Since all societies have regularized ways of peacefully resolving disputes, some anthropologists speak in terms of the universality of law. Societies have found various ways of peacefully resolving disputes. One such way involves action on the part of the community as a whole; another is through the use of informal adjudicators, although such adjudicators do not have power to enforce their decisions; still another way is through oaths and ordeals; and finally, in societies such as our own, disputes are peacefully resolved generally through the use of codified laws and courts.

7. People are likely to resort to violence when regular, effective, alternative means of resolving a conflict are not available. When violence occurs between political entities such as communities, districts, or nations, we generally speak of warfare. The type of warfare, of course, varies in scope and in complexity from society to society. Sometimes a distinction is made between feuding, raiding, and large-scale confrontations.

SUGGESTED READINGS

Balandier, G.: *Political Anthropology.* Trans. from the French by A. M. Sheridan Smith (New York: Random House, Pantheon Books, 1970).
A review of anthropological studies of political organization, both theoretical and field studies. Topics discussed include the role of social stratification in political organization, links between the political and the sacred, and the development of the state.

Banton, M. (Ed.): *Political Systems and the Distribution of Power.* Association of Social Anthropologists of the Commonwealth, Monograph 2 (New York: Praeger, 1965).
A collection of papers, by British and American anthropologists, discussing current developments in political anthropology. The writers emphasize research models rather than specific interpretations and tend to concentrate on political change or stability through time.

Bohannan, P. (Ed.): *Law and Warfare: Studies in the Anthropology of Conflict.* American Museum Sourcebooks in Anthropology (Garden City, N.Y.: Natural History Press, 1967).
A sourcebook providing articles and selections from monographs mainly on primitive law and warfare but also on disputes in complex societies. The first quarter of the book is devoted to papers on law; the rest is devoted to papers on war and other settlement of disputes.

Cohen, R., and J. Middleton (Eds.): *Comparative Political Systems.* American Museum Sourcebooks in Anthropology (Garden City, N.Y.: Natural History Press, 1967.)
A collection containing both classic and recent anthropological writings on the problems involved in the study of non-Western political systems. The papers describe hunting-gathering societies, decentralized societies, and state societies, with strong emphasis placed throughout on the process of political development and change.

Fortes, M., and E. E. Evans-Pritchard (Eds.): *African Political Systems* (New York, London: Oxford University Press for the International African Institute, 1940).
A classic collection of papers on political organization in Africa. Two types of political system are distinguished, those with and those without central authority, and examples of each are described.

Fried, M. H.: *The Evolution of Political Society: An Essay in Political Anthropology* (New York: Random House, Random House Studies in Anthropology 7, 1967).
In this theoretical work, the author begins with general remarks on the anthropology of political organization and goes on to describe differences between kinds of societies in terms of their political structures. He defines four main types of societies in terms of their political organization: egalitarian, ranked, stratified, state.

Fried, M. H., M. Harris, and R. Murphy (Eds.): *War: The Anthropology of Armed Conflict and Aggression* (Garden City, N.Y.: Natural History Press, 1968).
A collection of essays, most of which deal with specific field experiences. Some of the topics discussed are: the unique quality of human as opposed to animal aggression; the ecological effects of warfare; the sociocultural effects of war; the reduction of conflict by the overlapping of institutional affiliations within the larger society.

Hoebel, E. A.: *The Law of Primitive Man* (Cambridge, Mass.: Harvard University Press, 1954).
Discusses systems of social control in technologically simple societies and attempts to establish a working definition of law in terms of fundamental rights and duties of people in all societies. The book is divided into three parts: the theoretical and methodological background for the study of primitive law; discussion of legal systems among the Eskimo, Plains Indians, Trobrianders, and Ashanti; law and society—the relationship of law to religion and magic, its social functions, and development through time.

Nader, L. (Ed.): *The Ethnography of Law (American Anthropologist* Special Publication, Vol. 67, No. 6, Pt. 2, December 1965).
A collection of papers on the anthropological study of primitive law. The editor's introduction presents an overview of the general topic.

Otterbein, K.: *The Evolution of War: A Cross-Cultural Study* (New Haven: HRAF Press, 1970).
In this cross-cultural study of primitive warfare, the author relates variation in warfare to degree of cultural, particularly political, complexity.

Service, E. R.: *The Hunters* (Englewood Cliffs, N. J.: Prentice-Hall, Foundations of Modern Anthropology Series, 1966).
A brief introduction to the hunting-gathering way of life, with material on such societies from fieldwork on five continents. Chapter 4 discusses the preservation of order and the use of seniority, rank, and custom in resolving conflict and maintaining authority.

Service, E. R.: *Primitive Social Organization: An Evolutionary Perspective* (New York: Random House, Random House Studies in Anthropology, AS 3, 1962).
A classification of primitive social organization into band society, tribal society, and chiefdoms, presenting the criteria by which these levels are defined and suggesting possible reasons for their development.

Swartz, M. J. (Ed.): *Local-Level Politics: Social and Cultural Perspectives* (Chicago: Aldine, 1968).
A collection of 17 case studies, most dealing with Africa and India, but also dealing with Melanesia and the circumpolar area. Local political systems are presented as living structures in which the actors either succeed or fail to adapt to conditions in a changing world.

Swartz, M. J., V. W. Turner, and A. Tuden (Eds.): *Political Anthropology* (Chicago: Aldine, 1966).
A collection of essays on political systems around the world. Many of the essays deal with aspects of change; others have been written with the idea of comparative study and future generalization. Of particular interest is the introductory essay by the editors which gives an introductory definition of the "political" in society and analyzes some key issues in political anthropology.

19
Religion and Magic

As far as we know, all societies have possessed beliefs which we group under the term "religion." These beliefs vary from culture to culture and from year to year; but whatever the variety of beliefs in things supernatural, we will define *religion* as any set of attitudes, beliefs, and practices pertaining to *supernatural power,* whether it be forces, gods, spirits, ghosts, demons, or any other imagined power.

We divide phenomena into the natural and the supernatural, but not all languages or cultures make such a neat distinction. Moreover, what is considered supernatural—powers that are not human or subject to the laws of nature—varies from society to society. Some of the variations are determined by what a society regards as natural law. For example, some illnesses in our society are believed to result from the natural action of germs and viruses. In other societies (and for some people in our own society) illness may be believed to result from supernatural forces, and thus it is a part of religious belief. Beliefs about what is or is not a supernatural occurrence also vary within a society at a given time or over time: floods, earthquakes, volcanic eruptions, comets, and epidemics were once thought in Judaeo-Christian traditions to be evidence of supernatural powers intervening in human affairs. It is now generally agreed that they are simply natural occurrences. Yet as recently as 1833, a particularly vivid meteor display caused thousands of intelligent Americans to ascend available hills to wait for the imminent end of the world at the hands of the supernatural. Thus, the line between the natural and the supernatural appears to vary according to the current state of belief about the causes of things and events in the observable world.

In many cultures, what we would consider religious is embedded in other aspects of everyday life. To say that it is often difficult to separate the religious (or economic or political) from other aspects of culture is just another way of saying something we have noted before: simpler cultures have little or no specialization and hence the various aspects of culture we distinguish (for example, in the chapter headings of this book) are not as separated and easily recognized as in complex cultures like our own. However, it is sometimes difficult even for us to agree whether a particular custom of our own is religious or not. After all, the categorizing of beliefs as religious or political or social is a relatively new custom. The ancient Greeks, for instance, did not have a word for religion but had many concepts concerning the behavior of their gods and concerning their expected duty to the gods. When a people's duties to its gods are linked with duty to its princes, it is difficult to separate religious ideas from political ideas. As an example of our own difficulty in labeling a particular class of actions or beliefs "religious" or "social," consider our beliefs about wearing clothes. Is our belief that it is necessary to wear them, at least in the company of nonlovers, religious or something else? Recall that in Genesis the wearing of clothes, or figleaves, is distinctly associated with the loss of innocence: Adam and Eve, after eating the apple, covered their nakedness. Accordingly, when American missionaries in the nineteenth century discovered the Pacific islands, they forced the women to wear more clothes, particularly to cover their sexual parts. Were the missionaries' ideas about sex "religious" or "political," or perhaps both? When British government officials discovered carvings showing positions for sexual intercourse in Hindu temples, they covered them up or destroyed them. Did they do so for religious reasons?

UNIVERSALITY OF RELIGION

Religious beliefs are evident in all known present cultures and inferred from artifacts found associated with *Homo sapiens* at least since Neandertal times. Artifacts have been found in Neandertal graves, suggesting a belief in an afterlife. Sculptures of females whose secondary sex characteristics are emphasized, which may have been fertility charms, have been found at widely separated archaeological sites. Cave paintings in which the predominant images are animals of the hunt may reflect a belief that the image had some power over events, that hunting could be made more successful by the making of images showing success in hunting. Megaliths, huge monuments of stone, were erected, generally to mark burial sites, in parts of the Middle East and throughout Europe. The details of religions practiced in the far distant past cannot always be recovered, but evidence of ritual treatment of the dead suggests that early man believed in the existence of supernatural spirits and that he tried to communicate with and perhaps influence them.

Given both the assumption of prehistoric religion and the evidence of the universality of religion in historic times, the subject of religion has been the focus of much speculation, research, and theorizing. As long ago as the fifth century B.C., Herodotus made fairly objective comparisons between the religions of the 50 or so societies he visited, noting many similarities among their gods and pointing out evidence of diffusion. Scholars, theologians, historians, and philosophers, for the 2,500 years since then, have speculated about religion; some have claimed superiority for their own form of religion, some have derided the naïve simplicity of others' beliefs, and some have expressed scepticism concerning all beliefs.

Speculating about which religion may be superior is not an anthropological concern. What is of interest to anthropologists is why religion is found in all societies. Anthropologists, sociologists, and psychologists have all offered theories to account for the universality of religion. These theories seem to fall into three groups—the psychological, the sociological, and a mixture of the two. The psychological theories generally account for the universality of religion as a way of reducing anxiety or as a way of satisfying a cognitive need for intellectual understanding. The sociological theories generally account for the universality of religion as a reflection of society and its social conditions.

Tylor's Theory

Edward Tylor is generally credited with having constructed the first inclusive theory of religion.

He noted the similarities of many contemporary religions such as Islam and Christianity to ancient "pagan" religions, especially the widespread belief in a soul. He assumed that the belief stemmed from speculation about such states as dreams and trances and death; the dead, the distant, those in the next house, and animals seem real in dreams and trances. This life-like appearance suggests a dual existence for all things—a physical, visible body and a psychic, invisible soul—a religious belief which Tylor called *animism.*[1]

Thus, in this view, religion stems from an intellectual curiosity concerning things not fully understood and perhaps is also a generalization from such mental states as dreaming.

Psychological Theories

There are a number of psychological theories which attempt to explain the universality of religion by pointing to religion as a way of reducing anxiety and uncertainty felt by all individuals. Variants of this theory stress different kinds of anxiety. One of these theories, put forth by Malinowski, is that religion is a response to anxieties and uncertainties which affect individuals personally and, as a consequence, threaten to disrupt the social group. The principal disrupter is death itself: "man affirms his convictions that death is not real nor yet final, that man is endowed with a personality which persists even after death, and that there are forces in the environment which can be tuned up and propitiated to the trend of human hopes and desires."[2] Other uncontrollable sources of disaster, especially drought and illness, combined with the general anxiety about death, cause men to create rituals which affirm their social unity in the face of social disruption by seeking to control the supernatural forces they created.

Psychoanalytic theories suggest that anxiety stems from early childhood experiences. Freud's theory is that religion springs from the unresolved Oedipus complex, the sexual love for the mother and simultaneous fear and hate for the father. As a result, the feared father becomes, unconsciously, the feared god, and it is the guilt of people who cannot accept their desire and their hatred that leads them to exalt and to fear a god. Freud considers religion a neurotic need which all people would grow out of as mankind matured. Jung, on the other hand, considers religion to be therapeutic. Recognizing the anxieties that man is prey to as a result of his socialization experiences, he suggests that religion provides help for the resolution of inner conflicts and the attainment of maturity.

All psychological theories agree on one thing: whatever its origins or purposes, its beliefs or rituals, religion serves to reduce anxiety and uncertainty, which are common to all men.

Sociological Theories

Sociological theories suggest that religion stems from society and societal needs. Emile Durkheim recognized that it is the society, not the individual, which distinguishes between *sacred* and *profane* things. There is nothing in an object—a piece of wood, a stone, a statue—to make it automatically sacred; it must therefore be a symbol. But of what? Durkheim suggests that a sacred object symbolizes the social fact that society considers something sacred. In other words, religion is a social artifact, symbolizing what a society considers sacred, and the most sacred thing to any society is itself. Durkheim cites the symbolic use of totems by the tribes of central Australia as an example of how religion symbolizes society. The people

[1] Edward B. Tylor, "Animism," in W. A. Lessa and E. Z. Vogt., eds., *Reader in Comparative Religion,* 3rd ed. (New York: Harper & Row, 1971), pp. 10–19.

[2] Bronislaw Malinowski, "The Group and the Individual in Functional Analysis," *American Journal of Sociology,* Vol. 44 (May 1939), p. 959.

are organized into clans, each clan having its own totem, the symbol of the clan. The totem is the focus of the religious rituals of the clan and thus becomes symbolic both of the clan and its spirits. It is the clan, or the society as a whole, on which we are dependent for survival, with which we identify, which exercises power over our actions as well as our thoughts, which we must affirm in communal ritual.[3]

Swanson accepts Durkheim's belief that certain aspects or conditions of society generate the responses that we call religious. More explicitly, Swanson suggests that a belief in spirits derives from the kinds of "sovereign" groups in a society. These sovereign groups are those that have original or independent jurisdiction (decision-making powers) over some sphere of life: the family, the clan, the village, the state. Just like the sovereign groups in a society, the spirits are invisible, live longer than men, and have purposes and goals that supersede those of an individual. In fact, from the point of view of the individual, social groups to a great extent dictate one's behavior: one is born into families, kin groups, and societies and experiences, through these institutions, almost invisible pressure to act according to stated and unstated social norms. Swanson suggests that the spirit world man invents personifies the family and other decision-making groups which are found in society and which have power over him. Man experiences the demands of the groups, accepts the purposes of the groups, and re-creates the *nature* of his groups in his spirits.[4]

Other Theories

Other theories of the origin of religion combine psychological and sociological approaches to suggest that religion is a response to strain or deprivation felt by individuals resulting from events in society. Thus, when the society is stable, as it can be for hundreds of years, its efforts and its energy are employed to maintain its equilibrium. But when the stability of a society is threatened, either by internal dissension or by outside force, the society may "revitalize" itself by various means—perhaps by way of a new cult, sect, denomination, or religion. Aberle argues that relative deprivation, whether economic or social, is the cause of the stress which generates new religious movements.[5] Wallace suggests that the threat of societal breakdown forces people to examine new ways to survive; it is the hope they gain from these new ways, not deprivation—for people can live for centuries in deprivation—which leads them to revitalize their society.[6] This theory will be discussed further at the end of the chapter.

VARIATION IN RELIGIOUS BELIEFS

Although there is no general agreement about why men need religion, or about how they first came to invent spirits, gods, and other supernatural beings and forces, there is general recognition of the enormous variation in details of religious belief and practice. Societies differ in the kinds of supernatural beings or forces which they create, in the character of their supernatural beings, in the structure or hierarchy of the organization of those beings, what the beings actually do, and what happens to men after death. Variation exists also in the ways in which the society interacts with the

[3] Emile Durkheim, "The Elementary Forms of the Religious Life," in Lessa and Vogt, *Reader in Comparative Religion,* pp. 28–36.

[4] Guy E. Swanson, *The Birth of the Gods* (Ann Arbor: University of Michigan Press, 1969), pp. 1–31.

[5] David Aberle, "A Note on Relative Deprivation Theory as Applied to Millenarian and Other Cult Movements," in Lessa and Vogt, *Reader in Comparative Religion,* pp. 528–531.

[6] Anthony Wallace, *Religion: An Anthropological View* (New York: Random House, 1966), p. 30.

supernatural, for example, whether everyone has equal access to the supernatural, or whether specialists act as intermediaries between people and the supernatural, and whether the communication is supplicative or manipulative.

Types of Supernatural Forces and Beings

Supernatural Forces. The supernatural is sometimes believed to be a *force* which has no person-like character. The supernatural, impersonal force called *mana,* after its Malayo-Polynesian name, inhabits some objects but not others, some people but not others. We can compare mana to the power that a golfer may attribute to some of his clubs but, unhappily, not to all. A ballplayer may think that a certain shirt or pair of socks has supernatural power or force and that he will score more points when he wears them. A four-leaf clover has mana; a three-leaf clover does not. One farmer in Polynesia places stones around his field; his crops are bountiful; the stones have mana. During a subsequent year the stones may lose their mana and his crops will be poor. People may also be believed to possess mana, as, for example, the chiefs in Polynesia were said to. However, such power was not necessarily permanently possessed; chiefs who were unsuccessful in war or other activities were said to have lost their mana. One potter in a village has mana and so makes the best pots. The best canoeist, the mightiest warrior, and the successful hunter are all believed to have mana.

Folktales often refer to objects in which supernatural force—not necessarily mana, sometimes even an evil force—lodges and then acts automatically: a slipper, a goose, a porridge pot, a lamp, a monkey's paw, a pair of boots. Marrett, feeling that Tylor's theory of animism advocated a process too sophisticated to have been the first idea of religion, suggested that *animatism,* a belief in supernatural forces, preceded the creation of spirits.

Wallace distinguishes mana from taboo by pointing out that things containing mana are to be touched whereas taboo things are not to be touched, for their power can cause harm. Taboos surround food not to be eaten, places not to be entered, animals not to be killed, people not to be touched sexually, people not to be touched at all, and so on. Any person who is the victim of misfortune may unwittingly have violated a taboo. He may have to search his memory for evidence, just as a person who is a victim of neurosis today may search his memory in order to discover the sources of his neurosis. Untouchability is used to separate various castes in India. When a caste taboo is violated, as when a barber cuts the hair of a high-caste man, the man is then ritually unclean until he performs the ritual which cleanses him. The Hebrew tribesmen were forbidden to touch a woman during menstruation or for seven days following. An Australian aborigine could not eat the animal which was his totem, and for many centuries a Catholic could not eat meat on Fridays.

Supernatural Beings. Supernatural beings fall within two broad categories: those of nonhuman origin, such as gods and spirits, and those of human origin, such as ghosts and ancestral spirits. Chief among the beings of nonhuman origin, *gods* are named personalities. They are often anthropomorphic, conceived in the image of man, although they are sometimes given the shapes of other animals or celestial bodies such as the sun or moon. They do not generally take the shape of trees, flowers, stones, or other innately passive things. The gods are believed to have created themselves; some of these then created or gave birth to other gods. Some are seen as creator gods, but not all people include the creation of the world as one of the acts of the gods.

Creator gods often, after their efforts at

creation, retire; having set the world in motion, they are not interested in its day-to-day operation. Other creator gods remain interested in the ordinary affairs of human beings, especially of one small, chosen segment of humanity. Whether a society has a creator god or not, the job of running the creation is often left to lesser gods. The Maori of New Zealand, for example, recognize three important gods: a god of the sea, a god of the forest, and a god of agriculture; they call upon each in turn for help and try to get the gods to share their knowledge of how the universe runs. The gods of the ancient Romans, on the other hand, specialized to such a high degree that there were three gods of the plow, one god to help with the sowing, one for weeding, one for reaping, one for storing grain, one for manuring, and so on.

Beneath the gods in prestige, but often closer to men, are multitudes of unnamed spirits. Some may be guardian spirits for people. Some, who become known for particularly efficacious work, may be promoted to the rank of named gods. Some spirits, known to, but never invoked by, the people, are of the hobgoblin type who delight in mischief; they can be blamed for any number of small mishaps. Others take pleasure in deliberately working evil for men.

Ghosts and *ancestor spirits* are among the spirits who were once human. The belief in some cultures that everyone has a soul—or several souls—and that the soul survives after death, leaves a great deal of room for interpretation of what a person's soul does after death. Some societies believe that the spirits of the dead remain nearby and remain interested in their living kin.

Swanson suggests, and found in his cross-cultural study of 50 societies, that a belief in ancestral spirits is likely to be found where kin groups are important decision-making groups. The kin group is an entity which exists over time, into the past as well as into the future, in spite of the deaths of individuals.[7] The dead feel concern for the fortunes, the prestige, and the continuity of their kin group as strongly as the living. As a Lugbara elder put it: "Are our ancestors not people of our lineage? They are our fathers and we are their children whom they have begotten. Those that have died stay near us in our homes and we feed and respect them. Does not a man help his father when he is old?"[8]

The Lugbara recognize two types of dead—ancestors and ghosts. The multitude of nameless forebears, including also childless members of the clan, by all lines of descent, male and female, are called *a'bi* or ancestors. One shrine embraces them all. Named ancestors, those recently dead and therefore still individually interested in the behavior of living kin, are called *ori,* ancestor spirits or ghosts. Each ghost has a shrine of his own. A man whose father is dead may have the power to "invoke the ghosts" to cause illness or other misfortune to a member of the clan, especially a younger member, whose behavior threatens clan solidarity. If a man strikes, swears at, shouts at, deceives, lies to, or quarrels with a kinsman or is a poor guardian or a disrespectful heir, the elder of the clan may invoke the ghosts to bring sickness to the deviant clan member. If a woman quarrels with her husband, or strikes him, or denies him sex, she may have the ghosts invoked against her. This veneration of the dead has several effects upon the society. It keeps serious fights from developing within the family: the living may grumble at the behavior of the young, but they leave punishment of that behavior up to the ancestors. The man who eats rich foods and does not invite his kinsman to share, the man who shows off his agility at a dance and impresses the girls while his kinsman stands alone, the young man

[7] Swanson, *The Birth of the Gods,* pp. 97–108.

[8] John Middleton, "The Cult of the Dead: Ancestors and Ghosts," in Lessa and Vogt, *Reader in Comparative Religion,* p. 488.

In New Guinea, a Gururumba tribesman kills a pig to pacify a ghost. It is believed that the ghost is causing illness in one of the women seated in the foreground. (Courtesy of the American Museum of Natural History.)

who lords it over his seniors, these objects of envy may not be reproached directly but may have the ghosts invoked against them. The invocation of the ghosts is particularly useful when there is a power struggle for authority within the lineage or clan; the man who wins will claim the favor of the ghosts. If illness is caused by the ghost, a sacrifice is made if the patient recovers. An animal is sacrificed, the family has a small feast, the now-penitent one is anointed and blessed and his sin forgotten. In other words, having been the object of the family's indignation, he is now the object of their concern and pleasure; he is accepted; like the prodigal son, he is chastened and restored to the family.[9]

Character of Supernatural Beings

Whatever the types of gods or spirits believed in, the ones in a given culture tend to have certain personality or character traits. They may be unpredictable or predictable, aloof from or interested in human affairs, helpful or punishing. Why do the gods and spirits in a particular culture exhibit certain character traits rather than others?

We have some evidence from cross-cultural studies suggesting that the character of supernatural beings may be related to the nature of child training. Thus, Spiro and D'Andrade suggest that the god/human relationship is a projection of the parent/child relationship, in which case child-training practices might well be relived in dealings with the supernatural. A society in which parents are nurturant tends to have nurturant gods. For example, if when the child cried or waved his arms about or kicked, he was nutured by his parents, then he would grow up expecting to be nurtured by the gods when he performed a similar ritual, that is, when he prayed, lifted his arms to the gods, danced, and so on. On the other hand, if his parents punished him, or sometimes punished and sometimes rewarded him, he would grow up expecting the gods to behave capriciously toward humans.[10] Lambert, Triandis, and Wolf, in another cross-cultural study, found that societies with some hurtful or punitive child-training practices are likely to believe that their gods are aggressive and malevolent; on the other hand, societies with less punitive child training are more likely to believe that the gods are benevolent.[11] It is worth noting, in this respect, that some cultures represent the father/child pattern in their own terminology, referring to the god as "father" and to themselves as his "children."

Structure or Hierarchy of Supernatural Beings

The range of social structures in human societies from egalitarian to highly stratified is matched by a comparable range in the supernatural world. Some societies have a number of gods or spirits with or without any special jurisdictions and the gods are not ranked; one has about as much power as another. On the other hand, some societies have gods or spirits that are ranked in prestige and power in both the natural and supernatural worlds.

Religions in which there is one high god and all other supernatural beings are subordinate to or are alternative manifestations of this supreme being are called *monotheistic.* For instance, the Hindu believes in five great gods—Siva, Krishna, Rama, Vishnu, and Lakshmi—who are subordinate to the all-encompassing god—the *One*—into which all humanity is evolving in anticipated spiritual union, or oneness. A *polytheistic* religion recognizes many important gods.

The idea that all religions are projections of man's various political systems, that rituals introduce new members of the society to political realities by way of ideographs of the family, the clan, the tribe, the nation, or the state has been examined by Swanson who suggests that an association exists between political com-

[9] Middleton, "The Cult of the Dead: Ancestors and Ghosts," pp. 488–492.

[10] Melford E. Spiro and Roy G. D'Andrade, "A Cross Cultural Study of Some Supernatural Beliefs," *American Anthropologist,* Vol. 60 (1958), pp. 456–466.

[11] William W. Lambert, Leigh Minturn Triandis, and Margery Wolf, "Some Correlates of Beliefs in the Malevolence and Benevolence of Supernatural Beings: A Cross-Societal Study," *Journal of Abnormal and Social Psychology,* Vol. 58 (1959), pp. 162–169.

plexity and monotheism. More specifically, he shows evidence from a cross-cultural study that a belief in a high god is likely to be found where the political system has three or more levels of decision-making groups. That is, the structure or hierarchy of supernatural beings seems to parallel the structure or hierarchy of political authority. In his study of 50 societies, he discovered that of the 20 which had three or more distinct types of sovereign groups—for instance, family, clan, and chief—17 possessed an idea of a high god. Of the 19 societies which had fewer than three decision-making groups, only two had a high god.[12] Consistent with this idea are findings which show that a high god is generally found in societies with higher levels of political development and in societies dependent upon food production rather than upon food collecting.[13]

Consistent with Swanson's findings, there are societies in which the gods associated with families or clans of high status are themselves awarded high status. In Palauan society, for instance, each clan had its ancestor spirits and acknowledged the existence of all other clans' spirits, which were potentially dangerous. Each clan also worshipped a male and a female god who had names and titles similar to clan titles. The ranking clan in a village was believed to hold its position because of the superiority in rank of its gods, who naturally helped their own clan. Thus the leading clan's gods were respected by all the clans of the village, and their shrine was given the place of honor in the center of the village and was larger and more elaborately decorated than other shrines.[14]

Intervention of the Gods in Human Affairs

According to Clifford Geertz, it is when faced with his ignorance, with pain, and with the unjustness of things that man explains events by the intervention of the gods.[15] Thus in Greek religion, the direct intervention of Poseidon as ruler of the seas prevented Odysseus from getting home for ten years. The direct intervention of Yahweh caused the great flood which killed most of the people at the time of Noah. The Trobriand Islanders explain conception as the intervention of the gods. When contemplating pain, illness, and death, the Nyakyusa blames the spirits of the dead; the Christian says "it is the will of God"; the Maori searches his memory for a taboo he has violated which has brought this punishment through the spirit's intervention; a Zande looks for some neighbor or relative who might wish to cause illness or death with the help of some supernatural intervention. The unjustness of things, the knowledge that the good suffer and the evil prosper, is explained by the Christian belief that the good will get their reward after death and the evil will then be punished; the projected intervention comes after death. The Greek gods intervened to bring bad fortune to Oedipus, which was undeserved because he did not know that he was breaking two fundamental taboos—murder of a near relative and incest. The Greek gods often interfered with life on earth by raping mortal women and leaving them with superchildren. The fate of these extraordinary children, often possessors of special insight or great power, was generally a life of sorrow, undeserved suffering, and early death. The intervention of evil spirits is apparent in witchcraft beliefs and in many cases of demonic possession.

The brief accounts above are of unasked-for divine interference, with the exception of cases

[12] Swanson, *The Birth of the Gods,* pp. 55–81.

[13] Robert B. Textor, compiler, *A Cross-Cultural Summary* (New Haven: HRAF Press, 1967).

[14] H. G. Barnett, *Being a Palauan* (New York: Holt, Rinehart and Winston, 1960), pp. 79–85.

[15] Clifford Geertz, "Religion as a Cultural System," in Michael Banton, ed., *Anthropological Approaches to the Study of Religion,* Association of Social Anthropologists Monographs, No. 3 (London: Tavistock Publications, 1965).

of witchcraft. There are numerous examples of requests for divine intervention, either for good for oneself and friends or for evil for others. All request prayers are appeals for divine intervention, for a god to change the course of things, to make 2 + 2 = 5. Gods are asked to intervene in the weather and make the crops grow, to send fish to the fisherman and game to the hunter, to find lost things, to accompany travelers and prevent accidents, to stop the flow of lava down the side of a volcano, to remove the pimples from an adolescent's face, to stop a war, and so on. Generally, as science presents more and more rationally acceptable causes for things—high-pressure area, germs, earth fault, gravity—then educated people the world over see fewer and fewer events as due to the intervention of the gods. But isolated villages, small towns, and peasant communities, no matter what religions they profess, still see the intervention of gods as an everyday possibility.

The gods do not intervene in all societies. To be sure, in some they cannot keep their hands out of human affairs; in others, they are not the slightest bit interested; and in still others they interfere only occasionally. We have little research on why gods are believed to interfere in some societies and not in others. However, we have some evidence as to the kinds of societies in which the gods take an interest in the morality of human behavior.

Swanson's study suggests that a relationship exists between the intervention of the gods in the moral behavior of people and varying degrees of wealth within the society. In a society in which wealth is unequally distributed, specifically in a society which has either private ownership of property, considerable debt relations, or stratified social classes, the gods are likely to intervene in human affairs by creating sanctions against behavior which threatens the status quo of the society. Both a person's health on earth and his pleasures or tortures in the afterlife thus are prescribed by the gods in stratified societies.[16] It may be that supernatural support of moral behavior is particularly useful in societies with inequalities that tax the ability of the political system to maintain social order and minimize social disorder.

Life after Death

It is comforting for many people to believe that life is somehow more than the body, that the body possesses a soul which continues its life after the body has died. In cultures with a belief in the soul, there is considerable variation in what happens to the soul after death. The Lugbara see the dead joining the ancestors of the living and staying near the family homesite; they retain an interest in the behavior of the living, both rewarding and punishing them. The Zuni think that the dead join the past dead, the Katcinas, at a Katcina village at the bottom of a nearby lake. They lead a life of singing and dancing and bring rain to the living Zuni; they are also swift to punish the priest who fails in his duty or the people who impersonate them in masks during the dance ceremonies.[17] The Chamulas have merged the ancient Mayan worship of the sun and moon with the Spanish conquerors' Jesus and Mary. Their vision of life after death contains a blending of the two cultures: all souls go to the underworld where they live a human-like life except that they are incapable of sexual intercourse. After the sun travels over the world, it travels under the underworld, so that the dead also have sunlight. Only murderers and suicides are punished, being burned by the Christ/sun on his journey. Life after death is then an inverted form of life: life is up, death is down; life produces new life, death is sterile; daylight and darkness are inverted for the dead; the sun

[16] Swanson, *The Birth of the Gods,* pp. 153–174.

[17] Ruth Benzel, "The Nature of Katcinas," in Lessa and Vogt, *Reader in Comparative Religion,* pp. 493–495.

travels counterclockwise for the living, clockwise for the dead.[18]

Christians separate their dead after death, sending the unsaved to everlasting punishment and the saved to everlasting reward. Accounts differ, but hell is often associated with torture by fire and heaven with mansions. Several societies see the dead returning to earth to be reborn. The Hindus accompany this pattern of reincarnation with justification of one's caste in this life and eventual release from the pain of life by attaining *Nirvana,* inclusion into "the One."

VARIATION IN RELIGIOUS PRACTICE

Beliefs are not the only elements of religion that vary from society to society. There is also variation in how people deal with the supernatural: there may or may not be intermediaries between god and man and the manner of approach to the supernatural varies from supplication (requests, prayers, and so on) to manipulation.

It is permissible in all religions for an individual to approach the supernatural. But in some societies the contact with the supernatural is more on an individual basis than in others. For instance, the young Crow Indian before reaching manhood would seek contact with a spirit which would become his own guardian spirit. There were several methods of seeking such contact: fasting on a hilltop for several days, perhaps also cutting off a finger joint as an offering, or having his back or breast pierced and a rope looped through the opening and tied to a stick round which he ran all day. Through such deprivations a vision or revelation could be sought. The giver of the revelation would then become the guardian spirit of the man, bringing him success in warfare and sometimes in marriage. This spirit might be previously unknown—a snake, a white eagle, an old couple—but the Crow belief in the diffusion of divine power throughout the universe allows it to crop up in the most unexpected places.[19]

The Shaman. In other societies where intermediaries are more important, they may be part-time or full-time specialists. The *shaman,* or curer, is one kind of intermediary, usually part-time. Under the name of witch doctor, he has been much maligned by ethnocentric Western reports. Boas gives an account of the making of a Kwakiutl (of the American Northwest Coast) shaman; Handelman recounts the history of a Washo shaman of this century.

The Kwakiutl, Quesalid, initially a skeptic who wanted to expose the tricks of the shamans, began to associate with them in order to spy on them and was taken into their group. In his first lessons, he learned

> a curious mixture of pantomime, prestidigitation, and empirical knowledge, including the art of simulating fainting and nervous fits, the learning of sacred song, the technique for inducing vomiting, rather precise notions of auscultation or listening to sounds within the body to detect disorders and obstetrics, and the use of "dreamers," that is, spies who listen to private conversations and secretly convey to the shaman bits of information concerning the origins and symptoms of the ills suffered by different people. Above all, he learned the *ars magna.* . . . The shaman hides a little tuft of down in the corner of his mouth, and he throws it up, covered with blood, at the proper moment—after having bitten his tongue or made his gums bleed—and solemnly presents it to his patient and the onlookers as the pathological foreign body extracted as a result of his sucking and manipulations.[20]

[18] Gary H. Gossen, "Temporal and Spatial Equivalents in Chamula Ritual Symbolism," in Lessa and Vogt, *Reader in Comparative Religion,* pp. 135–140.

[19] Robert H. Lowie, *The Crow Indians* (New York: Rinehart, 1956), pp. 237–255.

[20] Claude Lévi-Strauss, "The Sorcerer and His Magic," *Structural Anthropology* (New York: Basic Books, 1963), p. 169.

A Bushman shaman, in a trance (left), *puts his arms around a patient. At right, A Gururumba tribesman of New Guinea has assembled magical leaves for a curing ceremony.* (Left, Courtesy of Irven DeVore; right, Courtesy of the American Museum of Natural History.)

His suspicions were confirmed, but his first curing was a success—the patient had heard that Quesalid had joined the shamans and believed that only he would heal him. Quesalid remained with the shamans for the four-year apprenticeship during which he could take no fee, and he became increasingly aware that his methods worked. He visited other villages, competed with other shamans in curing hopeless cases and won, and finally seemed convinced that his curing system was more valid than those of other shamans; instead of denouncing the trickery of shamans, he continued to practice as a renowned shaman.[21]

In 1964, the last Washo shaman, Henry Rupert, was still practicing and still learning new techniques at the age of 70. He recalls the background to his becoming a shaman, including childhood and mystical experiences. He was never severely disciplined at home and spent much of his time either with his uncle or his sister's husband, both shamans. He had several vivid dreams, one of them prophetic, and learned from his family a great deal of Washo lore and tradition. At eight, he was taken to the harsh U.S. Army school for a ten-year stretch of "forced acculturation." He was strong enough to accept what he needed of the new culture—the lessons in academic subjects and in a trade—and to reject its regimentation and harshness, its alcohol, and its Christianity. At 17, he had his "power dream" which confirmed his call as a shaman and over the next ten years learned hypnotism, performed a few cures, and began training under an old shaman. His cures at first took four nights of ritual during which he prayed, chanted, washed the patient's face with cold water, blew smoke on the patient, sprinkled water on his paraphernalia and finally sought to attract the sickness into his own body by blowing a whistle. During the years Rupert modified his treatments as he learned new techniques, finally refusing to visit patients but having the patients come to him for a curing which he had shortened to a few hours or in some cases a few minutes. By the age of 70, he had discarded chants, whistles, smoke, and water and had added a Hawaiian spirit helper. Rupert dismissed traditional beliefs in evil spirits as the cause of illness and eventually summarized his beliefs as "we help nature, and nature does the rest."[22]

After working with witch doctors in Africa, E. Fuller Torrey, a psychiatrist and anthropologist, concludes that witch doctors are using the same mechanisms and techniques for curing patients as psychiatrists use and getting about the same results. He isolates four categories used by healers the world over:[23]

1. The naming process: If a disease has a name—"neurasthenia" or "phobia" or "possession by an ancestral spirit" will do—then it is curable; the patient realizes that the doctor understands his case.
2. The personality of the doctor: Those who demonstrate empathy, nonpossessive warmth, and genuine interest in the patient get results.
3. The patient's expectations: One way of raising the patient's expectations of being cured is the trip to the doctor; the longer the trip—to the Mayo Clinic, Menninger Clinic, Delphi, or Lourdes—the easier the cure. An impressive setting—The Medical Center—and impressive paraphernalia—the stethoscope, the couch, attendants in uniform, the rattle, the whistle, the drum, the mask—also raise the patient's expectations. The healer's training is also important: the Ute Indian has his dreams analyzed; the Blackfoot

[21] Franz Boas, *The Religion of the Kwakiutl*, Columbia University Contributions to Anthropology, Vol. 10 (New York: 1930), Pt. II, pp. 1–41, as reported in Lévi-Strauss, *Structural Anthropology*, pp. 169–173.

[22] Don Handelman, "The Development of a Washo Shaman," *Ethnology*, Vol. 6 (October 1967), pp. 444–461.

[23] E. Fuller Torrey, *The Mind Game: Witchdoctors and Psychiatrists* (New York: Emerson Hall, n.d.).

Indian has a seven-year training course; the American psychiatrist spends four years in medical school and three in hospital training and has diplomas on his wall. High fees also help to raise a patient's expectations. (The Paiute doctors always collect their fees before starting a cure; if they don't, it is believed that they will fall ill.)

4. Curing techniques: Drugs, shock treatment, conditioning techniques, and so on, have been used for some time in different parts of the world.

The Priest. Another kind of intermediary is the priest, a full-time specialist. Priests are sometimes marked by their special clothing or hair style as being different from other people. The training of a priest can be vigorous and long, including fasting and praying, physical labor, as well as learning the dogma and the ritual of his religion, or a person can set himself up as a priest of his own sect with no training. Priests in America generally complete four years of theological school and sometimes serve first as apprentices under established priests. The priest generally does not receive a fee for each of his services but is supported by donations from his parishioners or followers. Since priests often have some political power as a result of their office—the chief priest is sometimes also the head of state, or is a close councilor to the chief of state—their material well-being is a direct reflection of their position in the priestly hierarchy. It is the dependence on memorized ritual that both marks and protects the priest. If a shaman repeatedly fails to effect a cure, he will probably lose his following, for he has obviously lost the support of the spirits; however, if a priest performs his ritual perfectly, and the gods choose not to respond, the priest will usually retain his position and the ritual its assumed effectiveness—the nonresponse of the gods will be explained in terms of the people's unworthiness of supernatural favor.

Other kinds of intermediaries exist among the dead when there is a hierarchy of spirits and gods, and the chief gods must not be approached directly. Leach distinguishes the Great Gods of India as *deva* and lesser gods as *devata,* or intermediaries between men and the Great Gods. The mother goddess or Parvati, as well as other lesser deities, performs this role in Hinduism; the saints, the Virgin Mary, and Jesus act as intermediaries to God the Father in many Christian sects.[24]

Why is there more of an emphasis on intermediaries in some societies than in others? Generally it seems that societies with religious intermediaries are more complex societies in which there is greater specialization; religious specialization appears therefore to be part of this general specialization. Textor reports that societies with full-time religious specialists (i.e., priests) are likely to be dependent on food production rather than on food collecting, to have economic exchange involving the use of money, class stratification, and high levels of political integration—all features indicative of cultural complexity.[25]

Behavior Affecting the Supernatural

How to get in touch with the supernatural has proved to be a universal problem. Wallace suggests 12 types of activities used the world over in religions but not necessarily all together: prayer, music, physiological exercises, exhortation, reciting the code, simulation, mana, taboo, feasts, sacrifice, congregations, inspiration, and symbolism.[26]

[24] Edmund R. Leach, "Pulleyar and the Lord Buddha: An Aspect of Religious Syncretism in Ceylon," in Lessa and Vogt, *Reader in Comparative Religion,* pp. 302–306.

[25] Textor, *A Cross-Cultural Summary.*

[26] Wallace, *Religion: An Anthropoligical View,* pp. 52–67.

1. Prayer: Prayer, either as thanksgiving, request, or demand, generally is distinguished from ordinary use of language by a special stance, gesture, tone of voice, and perhaps by special, often archaic, speech patterns.

Prayer can be spontaneous or memorized, private or public, silent or aloud. The Lugbara do not say the words of a prayer aloud, for that would be too powerful; they simply think about the things that are bothering them. The gods know all languages.

2. Music: Musical instruments, singing, chanting, and dancing are variously used for their integrating effect upon the people as well as upon the spirits.

Needham was struck by the numerous reports of drums, rattles, sticks, bells, and gongs in religions throughout the world as devices for getting the attention of the supernatural. Further research led him to the supposition that percussion is used universally to mark the transition of man from one state to another. The tin cans tied to the car of newlyweds in America and firecrackers tied to the cart in China both mark a transition from unmarried to married. The passage from unnamed to named, from state of sin to state of grace, from life to death, from sick to well, and so on are indicated by some percussive instrument.[27]

3. Physiological experience: Drugs (peyote, the magic mushroom), sensory deprivation, mortification of the flesh (by wearing hair shirts or chains, self-flagellation, prolonged sleeplessness, piercing the flesh, chopping off a finger joint, running until exhausted), and deprivation of food or water are methods known to religions as means of producing a trance or a feeling of euphoria.

[27] Rodney Needham, "Percussion and Transition," in Lessa and Vogt, *Reader in Comparative Religion,* pp. 391–398.

4. Exhortation or preaching: The man who acts as intermediary between man and the gods acts in two directions. Since he is closer to the gods than ordinary man, he both receives messages from the gods and passes them on to men. He tells men what the gods expect and informs them what behavior is pleasing, what displeasing.
5. Reciting the code: Many religions have myths which relate the activities of the gods and describe codes of moral behavior expected by the gods. Some divine literature may be considered as dictated by the gods themselves, while some may be seen as the work of especially favored men.
6. Simulation: Voodoo employs simulation, or imitating things, in the form of dolls made in the likeness of an enemy and then maltreated in hopes that the original will also experience pain and even death.

Divination is a rather widespread form of simulation. Divination has existed in Asian, African, and European societies. Sophocles' Oedipus scorns the old seer and tells him to get back to his bird entrails, but the seer had divined correctly. Shakespeare's Julius Caesar scorns his wife's prophetic dream of death and is killed in the Senate. Many people today have their fortunes told by crystal balls, tea leaves, Ouija boards, cards, their palm or horoscope or choose a course of action by a toss of a coin or a throw of dice. All are variations of methods used in other cultures.

Lucy Mair distinguishes between three kinds of divination. One is do-it-yourself divination: an object answers questions automatically; no interpreter is needed. A Zande rubbing board gives a direct "yes" or "no" answer. A second kind of divination requires interpretation of the object or objects used. For this a diviner must depend somewhat upon his knowledge of local gossip, his ability to assess people by their gesture and tone, his intuition in grasping whether he is working toward the answer desired by the group. A third type offers the diviner as a medium who receives messages from the spirit world. The medium must sometimes go into a trance before the spirit will reveal its answer.

The ostensible purpose of divination is to learn something which only the supernatural powers know. The Yombe, who live near the mouth of the Congo River, believe that death is caused by the sorcery of an enemy or by a relative or friend who is angry. Therefore part of the funeral ritual is an attempt to discover who caused the death. They send a man out to kill a duiker (a small African antelope); if he kills a male, then the man's side of the family is responsible for the death; if he kills a female, then the woman's side is responsible. A more common means of divining uses a number of small objects—of wood or ivory—carrying symbolic designs. The diviner finds the answer in the way they fall when thrown to the ground or shaken in a bowl.

In divination, then, a person has a problem and tries to find out the cause and the solution. No matter with what degree of skepticism a person consults a diviner, the skepticism generally centers around individual diviners, not against divination as a principle. Divination remains an acceptable method of seeking information in any society which believes that the supernatural is concerned about mankind and actually gets in touch with men from time to time.

Moore has suggested that since it is quite apparent that the methods of diviners are in no way connected with the actual results—for instance, the cracks in a bone simply do not tell anyone where game is plentiful that day—societies would abandon these ineffective techniques unless there were other reasons for continuing them, some "positive latent function" in divination apart from the ostensible problem and solution. He suggests that in some cases a random strategy might be more adaptive than a strategy based on experience. For example, the Naskapi, hunters of Labrador, consult the diviner every three or four days when they have no luck in hunting. The diviner holds a caribou bone over the fire and the burns and cracks which appear indicate where the group should hunt. The device functions as a fairly sophisticated method of assuring a random way of choosing where to hunt in a society which lacks computers. Since humans are likely to develop customary patterns of action, people might be likely to look for game according to some plan. But game might learn to avoid hunters who operate according to a plan. Thus, any method of assuring against patterning or predictable plans may be an advantage to the hunting society. Divination provides such a random strategy. It also relieves any individual of the responsibility of deciding where to hunt, a decision which might arouse anger if the hunt failed. Moore suggests that divination resembles games of chance, in which problems are solved by knowing the statistical probabilities of success for competing strategies. To solve problems such as where to find game, which involve the element of chance, a society might be more often successful if the strategy employed is also a chance one. It is possible then that the Naskapi and other societies have adopted divination as a way of solving some of their recurring problems, because a chance or random strategy, as provided by divination, is the best strategy for problems involving chance.[28]

7. Mana/taboo: The idea that power can reside in things which should be touched, *mana,* and things which should be avoided, *taboo,* has already been discussed. Relics, good luck symbols, sacred stones, the Blarney stone, and the hem of Jesus'

[28] Omar Khayyam Moore, "Divination—A New Perspective," *American Anthropologist,* Vol. 59 (1965), pp. 69–74.

garment should be touched to transmit some of their power to the individual. Certain objects, foods, and people should not be touched to avoid the effects of their power.

8. Feasts: The eating of a sacred meal, for instance, Holy Communion as a simulation of the Last Supper, is found in many religions.

The Australian aborigines, forbidden to eat their totem animal, have one totem feast a year at which they eat the totem, presumably as a gesture of symbolic cannibalism. The feast is a part of marriage and funeral ceremonies, as well as a fringe benefit of the sacrifice of food to the gods.

9. Sacrifices: Some societies make sacrifices to a god in order to influence the god's action, either to divert his anger or to attract his good will.

The things sacrificed vary from society to society; a blood sacrifice is sometimes required. The Greeks' arrangement for the sacrifice served two purposes—offerings for the gods and feasts for the people. Other sorts of things may be offered as sacrifice to the god. The Nayar are vegetarians, so assume that their clan spirits are also vegetarians and make vegetarian offerings. Personal sacrifice such as abstaining from particular foods, drinks, tobacco, or sexual intercourse may be made in an effort to please one's god. Money is the usual Western sacrifice. Some societies feel that the god is obligated to act on their behalf if they make the appropriate sacrifice, that is, that they can compel the god to act. Others use the sacrifice in an attempt to persuade the god, without any guarantee that the attempt will be successful.

10. Congregation: Although anyone may perform a religious act in private, the main function of religion is social. People meet together to address the gods or to watch the shaman or the priest address the gods.
11. Inspiration: The gods pick favored people to communicate with and states of ecstasy, possession, conversion, and revelation are recognized as marking the presence of the supernatural. The state is spontaneous or self-induced.
12. Symbolism: Religious symbols can be direct representations of deities in the forms of paintings, icons, statues, masks.

The Eskimos sew small amulets containing symbols of spirits—bits of shellfish, small pebbles—onto their clothing; early Easter Islanders carved massive stone heads; West Coast Africans carved small wooden dolls as fertility symbols; Iroquois Indians made masks to represent the Great World Rim Dweller. The mandala, ⊕, and its associated forms, the cross and the swastika, appear in various religions as symbols of partition and reintegration. That the symbol sometimes is believed to contain the power of the god is apparent from the reverence with which the symbol is often treated.

Magic and Religion. All of the modes of interacting with the supernatural can be categorized in various ways. One dimension of variation is how much people in a society rely on pleading or asking or trying to persuade the supernatural being (or force) to act on their behalf, as opposed to whether they believe they can compel such behavior by certain acts. For example, prayer is asking; performing voodoo is presumably compelling. When people believe their action can compel the supernatural to act in some particular and intended way, anthropologists often refer to the belief and related practice as *magical.*

Magic may involve manipulation of the supernatural for good or evil purposes. Many societies have magical rituals to ensure good crops, the replenishment of game and the fertility of domestic animals, and the avoidance and cure

Two Gururumba tribesmen perform a magical rite to ward off an impending rainstorm. They circle the group of people assembled for food distribution, carrying a stick and calling out to the ghosts of the recently dead. They ask the ghosts to fence in the rain, just as they are fencing in the group by walking around it with the stick. (Courtesy of the American Museum of Natural History.)

of illness in humans. As we have seen, the witch doctor and the shaman often employ magic to effect a cure. But perhaps the use of magic to bring about harm has evoked the most interest.

Sorcery and Witchcraft. Sorcery and witchcraft are attempts to invoke the spirits to work harm against people. Although the words "sorcery" and "witchcraft" are often used interchangeably, they are also often distinguished. Sorcery may include the use of materials, objects, and medicines, to invoke the supernatural. In some societies, sorcery may be used by anyone; in others, there are secret part-time specialists called sorcerers, who must be enlisted to invoke supernatural malevolence. As one who knows how to invoke the supernatural, as being able to cause illness, injury, and death, the sorcerer is feared (although he might be entreated to use his knowledge for some good purpose). Since he uses materials, evidence of sorcery can actually be found, and a person can therefore be accused of sorcery because of some objects or medicines found in his house. Witchcraft, on the other hand, may be said to accomplish the same ills by means of thought and emotion alone. Evidence of witchcraft can never be found. This lack of visible evidence makes an accusation of witchcraft both harder to prove and harder to disprove.

Attributes of witches vary from society to society, but are generally disagreeable. The Madari believe that witches rub feces on articles to harm the owner, and that they dance on the graves of their victims. The Lugbara believe that witches dance naked; the Ganda believe in Basezi, people who dance naked and feast on corpses. Dinka witches have tails; Amba witches hang from their feet in trees and eat salt when they are thirsty.[29]

Two motivations for organizing witch hunts are recognized: the society wishes either to challenge and thereby frighten all witches in a village so that they will abandon their activities, or actually to accuse a person and demand either his death or his repentance. The Nupe dance ceremony could serve either function. A secret society called *ndakó gboyá* organizes a masked dance at the request of the authorities without telling the people. A dancer carrying a long pole with a basket top, the whole thing including the dancer draped in white cloth, appears in the village at dawn. All the women of the village are herded into the marketplace and the masked dancer swoops and sways over them. The dancer leaves suddenly but another appears and continues the dance. He may either leave and the village will be considered cleansed, or he will accuse one woman directly. She would be taken into the forest and made to dig into the earth with her fingernails. If blood came, she was a witch and had to make a payment to clear herself. One of the functions of the witch hunt may be to rid the village of the unpleasant or unconventional person.[30]

To the Azande, witchcraft is part of everyday living. It is not used to explain events for which the cause is known, say, carelessness or violation of taboo, but is used to explain the otherwise unexplainable. A man is gored by an elephant; he must have been bewitched because he has not been gored on the many other elephant hunts he has been on. A man goes to his beer hut at night, lights some straw and holds it aloft to look at his beer, and the thatch catches fire and burns the hut down; he has been bewitched, for huts did not catch fire on hundreds of other nights when he and others did the same thing. Some people are sitting in the cool shade under a granary and it collapses on them, injuring them; they are bewitched, for although the Azande admit that termites eating through the wooden posts caused the granary to collapse, witchcraft made it collapse at the precise moment on those particular people. Some of the pots of a skilled potter break; some of the bowls of a skilled carver crack. Witchcraft: other pots, other bowls treated exactly the same have not broken. The Azande blame many of their failures and accidents on witchcraft. Their anger—and anger is their reaction, not awe or dread—is then directed outward, never against members of their own family, often to unnamed people, sometimes directly at others. One effect of this procedure is that hostility is avoided within the extended family.[31]

The witch craze in Europe and Salem, Mass-

[29] Lucy Mair, *Witchcraft* (New York: World University Library, 1969), pp. 40–42.

[30] Mair, *Witchcraft,* pp. 65–75.

[31] E. E. Evans-Pritchard, "Witchcraft Explains Unfortunate Events," in Lessa and Vogt, *Reader in Comparative Religion,* pp. 440–444.

achusetts, reminds us that the fear of others, which the belief in witchcraft presumably represents, is not lacking in civilized societies. There had always been witchcraft beliefs in Europe, especially in rural areas, usually directed against old women and unpopular people in general. But no official action was taken against witches; in fact the early popes declared that a belief in witchcraft was un-Christian, since witches did not exist. But when feudal authorities ran into areas in Europe which resisted the establishment of feudalism and presented ideas and life styles of their own, the Church branded these intransigents heretics and the civil authorities accused them of secret meetings with the Devil and destroyed them, notably the Albigensian and the Vauclois heresies. Following the Reformation, first Protestant, then Catholic, missionaries found the method useful, though they changed the name of the heresy. The new heresy was called witchcraft, and instead of being used against *groups* that resisted the spread of the new culture, it could be used against *individuals* who were nonconformist: Protestants could kill Catholic witches; Catholics could kill Protestant witches; and they both could kill pagan witches, all under the name of heresy, or thinking unorthodox thoughts. The witch craze was led by the intellectuals, but in a time of social upheaval, it fed on widespread fear and unrest.[32]

Beatrice Whiting has suggested that sorcery or witchcraft will be found in societies that lack formal or judicial authorities to deal with crime and other offenses. The theory is that all societies need some form of social control, some way of deterring most would-be offenders and of dealing with actual offenders. In the absence of specialized judicial officials who, if present, would also deter and deal with antisocial behavior, the only thing that might tend to deter such behavior would be the fear of others who might invoke sorcery. The cross-cultural evidence seems to support this theory.[33]

RELIGION AND ADAPTATION

Anthropologists often take the view, following Malinowski, that religions are generally adaptive because they reduce anxieties and uncertainties to which all people are prey. Although we do not really know that religion is the only means of reducing anxiety and uncertainty, or even that individuals or societies *have* to reduce their anxiety and uncertainty, it seems very likely that certain religious beliefs and practices have directly adaptive consequences.

For example, the Hindu belief in the sacred cow has seemed to many to be the very opposite of a useful or adaptive custom. Their religion does not allow Hindus to slaughter cows. Why do the Hindus retain such a belief? Why do they allow all those cows to wander around freely, defecating all over the place, and not slaughter any of them? The contrast with our own use of cows could hardly be greater. However, Marvin Harris has suggested that the Hindus' use of cows may have beneficial consequences that some other use of cows would not have. In short, what may appear bizarre to us may not actually be so bizarre in other environments and may even be the best way available to handle some situation, like the keeping of cows.

Harris points out that there may be a sound economic reason for not slaughtering cattle in India. The cows (and the males they produce) provide a number of resources that could not be easily provided otherwise, and at the same time their wandering around to forage is no

[32] H. R. Trevor-Roper, "The European Witch-Craze of the Sixteenth and Seventeenth Centuries," in Lessa and Vogt, *Reader in Comparative Religion,* pp. 444–449.

[33] Beatrice B. Whiting, *Paiute Sorcery,* Viking Fund Publications in Anthropology, No. 15 (New York: Wenner-Gren Foundation, 1950), pp. 36–37; also Swanson, *The Birth of the Gods,* p. 151.

strain on the food-producing economy. The resources provided by the cows are varied. First, oxen are necessary for traction—a team of oxen and a plow are essential for the many small farms. The Indians could produce oxen with fewer cows, but to do so they would have to devote some of their food production to the feeding of those fewer cows. In the present system, they do not feed the cows, and, even though this makes them relatively infertile, males (which are castrated to make oxen) are still produced at no cost to the economy. Second, cow dung is essential as cooking fuel and fertilizer. The National Council of Applied Economic Research estimates that dung equivalent to 45,000,000 tons of coal is burned annually. Moreover, it is delivered practically to the door each day at no cost. Alternative sources of fuel, such as wood, are scarce or costly. In addition, about 340,000,000 tons of dung are used as manure, an essential in a country which is obliged to derive three harvests a year from its intensively cultivated land. Third, although Hindus do not eat beef, the cattle which die naturally or are butchered by non-Hindus are eaten by the lower castes who, without the upper-caste taboo against eating beef, might well not get this needed protein. Fourth, the hides and horns of the cattle which die are used in India's enormous leather industry. Therefore, since the sacred cows do not themselves consume resources needed by people, and since it would be impossible to provide traction, fuel, and fertilizer by other means as cheaply, the taboo against slaughtering cattle appears to be adaptive.[34]

Religious Change as Revitalization

The long history of religion includes periods of strong resistance to change as well as periods of radical change. Anthropologists have been especially interested in the founding of new religions or new sects as one of the things that may happen when cultures are disrupted by contact with dominant societies. Various classifications have been suggested for these religious movements—cargo cults, nativistic movements, messianic movements, millenarian cults. Earlier, we noted Aberle's theory, relating new religious movements to the stress arising from economic or social deprivation. But Wallace suggests that they are all examples of *revitalization movements,* efforts to save a culture by infusing it with new purpose and new life.

> Furthermore, it is attractive to speculate that all religions and religious productions, such as myths and rituals, come into existence as parts of the program or code of religious revitalization movements. Such a line of thought leads to the view that religious belief and practice always originate in situations of social and cultural stress and are, in fact, an effort on the part of the stress-laden to construct systems of dogma, myth, and ritual which are internally coherent as well as true descriptions of a world system and which thus will serve as guides to efficient action.[35]

The Seneca Indians, an Iroquois tribe, faced such a situation following the American Revolution. They had lost their lands and were confined to isolated reservations amid an alien people. They were in a state of despondency when a man named Handsome Lake received a vision from God which led him to stop drinking and to preach a new religion that would revitalize the Seneca. This was not the first such movement among the Iroquois. In the fifteenth century they were an unorganized people, warring against each other and being warred upon by other tribes. Hiawatha, living as a highwayman and a cannibal, was visited by the god Dekanawidah, and thus became God's spokesman in persuading the five tribes to give up their feuding and to unite as the

[34] Marvin Harris, "The Cultural Ecology of India's Sacred Cattle," *Current Anthropology,* Vol. 7, No. 1 (February 1966), pp. 51–63.

[35] Wallace, *Religion: An Anthropological View,* p. 30.

League of the Iroquois. The Condolence Ritual was adopted, which precluded feuding and blood revenge, and the radical new movement which had united and revitalized the Iroquois settled into a belief which conserved their integrity.[36]

Central to such movements is the link formed between the old ways and the new, a fusion of what is seen as the best of both worlds. Thus the Ghost Dance of the Paiute picked elements of Indian culture, such as games and ceremonies, as symbols of identity and unity and accepted elements of the white culture, such as weapons and tools. As another example, the Peyote Way blends traditional kinds of singing and drumming and individual religious experience with some Christian doctrines and introduces a drug/mystical experience which provides a philosophical acceptance of the harmony of existence. Melanesian cargo cults promised the arrival of boats or planes laden with abundant Western goods for the use of natives alone. The Fiji Tuka Cult of about 1885 predicted that the world would be turned upside down, which would leave the old religion and native people superior to the new religion and the alien white people, but the new order would be maintained with European efficiency and weapons. Indians in Mexico kept the ancient worship of Our Mother, Tonantzin, and united her with the Virgin Mary in the form of Our Lady of Guadalupe, a union which revitalized them and gave them the faith that they were accepted as human—i.e., were capable of salvation—by the Spanish conquerors, and the hope that they would one day be able to throw out the Spanish conquerors.

Wallace looks to the future of religion with some apprehension, aware that the discoveries of science are rapidly leading to a disbelief in things supernatural. "Belief in supernatural beings and supernatural forces that affect nature without obeying nature's laws will erode and become an interesting historical memory."[37] He sees two possible directions. One, which he fears, is that the reverence which has formerly been applied to the supernatural will be shifted to the state and its leaders. The other is a nontheistic revitalization movement with humanity as the entity to be respected and problems such as population control, technological unemployment, and intergroup conflict as the motivations for a new affirmation of the worth of living.

[36] *Ibid.*, pp. 31–34.

[37] Wallace, "Revitalization Movements," *American Anthropologist*, Vol. 58, p. 265.

SUMMARY

1. Religion is any set of attitudes, beliefs, and practices pertaining to supernatural power. Such beliefs may vary within a culture as well as among societies and may change over time.

2. Religious beliefs are evident in all known cultures and inferred from artifacts associated with *Homo sapiens* since Neandertal times.

3. Various theories have arisen about the origin of religious beliefs. Tylor suggested that religion stemmed from an intellectual curiosity about things not completely understood. Malinowski proposed that, faced with anxieties, primarily relating to death, men create rituals to affirm their social unity in the face of social disruption. In their rites, they seek to control the supernat-

ural forces they created. Freud suggested that religion reflects a neurotic Oedipal need, and Jung regarded religion as a therapeutic solution to inner conflicts. All psychological theories agree that religion serves to reduce individual anxieties. Sociological theories suggest that religion symbolizes what society considers sacred, namely, the sovereign groups within a society. Swanson believes that the spirit world man invents personifies the family and other decision-making groups in his society which have power over him. Other theories relate religion to a strain felt by people resulting from events in society.

4. There are wide variations in religious beliefs and practices. The supernatural is sometimes believed to be a disembodied force. In some cases, supernatural beings are regarded as nonhuman (gods or spirits); in others, they are believed to be of human origin (ghosts or ancestral spirits). Also, they may be invested with human personalities but imagined in the shape of animals or celestial bodies, such as the sun or the moon. Some are seen as creator gods, others as gods having special functions.

5. In some societies, all gods are equal in rank; in others, there is a hierarchy of prestige and power among gods and spirits, as among humans.

6. A monotheistic religion is one in which there is one high god and all other supernatural beings are either subordinate to or function as alternative manifestations of this god. It has been suggested that a high god is generally found in societies with a high level of political development.

7. Faced with ignorance, pain, and injustice, man frequently explains events by claiming intervention by the gods. Such intervention has also been sought by men to help them achieve their own ends.

8. Among cultures with a belief in the soul, there are many different beliefs about what happens to the soul after death.

9. A variety of methods have been used to attempt communication with the supernatural. Among them have been prayer, music, physiological exercises (drugs, fasting, mortification of the flesh), exhortation or preaching, reciting the code (divine literature), simulation (voodoo, divination), and sacrifice. In some societies, intermediaries, such as shamans or priests, communicate with the supernatural on behalf of others. Societies with religious intermediaries tend to be more complex and have greater specialization; religious specialization seems to be part of this general specialization.

10. When people believe their actions can compel the supernatural to act in a particular and intended way, anthropologists refer to the belief and related practice as "magical."

11. Sorcery and witchcraft are attempts to make the spirits work harm against people.

12. The history of religion includes periods of strong resistance to change and periods of radical change. One explanation is that religious practices always originate during periods of stress. Religious movements may also be examples of revitalization movements, efforts to save a culture by infusing it with new purpose and new life.

SUGGESTED READINGS

Banton, M. (Ed.): *Anthropological Approaches to the Study of Religion,* Association of Social Anthropologists of the Commonwealth, Monograph No. 3 (New York: Praeger, 1966).
A group of papers all with the aim of establishing explanatory principles of a general nature. Of the five papers, two are essentially critical evaluations of social anthropology. The other three are descriptive papers on African tribal social structure. Among the topics covered are religion as a cultural system and problems of explanation and description.

Lessa, W. A., and E. Z. Vogt (Eds.): *Reader in Comparative Religion: An Anthropological Approach,* 3rd ed. (New York: Harper & Row, 1971).
A collection of readings balancing the more theoretical trends and the descriptive field reports of the anthropological study of religion. The editors' general introduction gives a broad outline of the main issues, problems, and theoretical positions, as well as defining for the student the concept of "religion" from an anthropological point of view. In addition, they discuss the social functions of religion: its integrative role for individuals and groups and the maintenance of the society's values. The collected papers give the subject of religion comprehensive coverage, including such areas of study as the origin and development of religion, its social function, religious leaders and specialists, myth, and ritual. In terms of comparative study, this work is particularly valuable in that it examines religious behavior in both historically related and unrelated cultures.

Malefijt, A. deWaal: *Religion and Culture: An Introduction to Anthropology of Religion* (New York: Macmillan, 1968).
A general introduction to the study of religion. The work begins by introducing and defining the anthropological study of religion, followed by a historical survey of the study of religion from the ancient Greeks to the present and includes a discussion of the evidence for prehistoric religious practice.

Malinowski, B.: *Magic, Science and Religion and Other Essays* (Garden City, N.Y.: Doubleday, 1954).
A collection of papers representing some of Malinowski's work on ritual and religious behavior, the nature of primitive cults, magic, and faith.

Middleton, J. (Ed.): *Magic, Witchcraft and Curing,* American Museum Sourcebooks in Anthropology (Garden City, N.Y.: Natural History Press, 1967).
A sourcebook containing contributions to the study of comparative religion. The papers cover a broad selection of topics and most geographical areas in which anthropologists have studied religion.

Norbeck, E.: *Religion in Primitive Society* (New York: Harper & Row, 1961).
An introduction to the anthropological study of religion, concentrating on religious belief in primitive cultures. However, the examination of elements common to religions of all cultural types makes the book useful as a work in comparative religion. In the two main divisions of the text, Norbeck provides an overview of the types of primitive religious behavior and analyzes the social function of religion. Description is always supportive of the theoretical and analytical aspects, which generally follow the functionalist view, as in the treatment of the origins of religion and the use of magic.

Swanson, G. E.: *The Birth of the Gods: The Origin of Primitive Beliefs* (Ann Arbor: University of Michigan Press, 1960).
A cross-cultural study which explores the origins of religious beliefs and examines how various aspects of religion may be related to social and political organization. The author discusses the nature of the supernatural: the origins of belief, the conceptualization of the supernatural, the parental nature of gods, and the symbolization of that which is unknown or yet to come.

Wallace, A. F. C.: *Religion: An Anthropological View* (New York: Random House, 1966).
A systematic analysis of religious behavior which draws upon psychological theory as well as upon the structuralist-functionalist approach of anthropology. Wallace summarizes the various theoretical and methodological approaches to the study of religion, discusses the psychological and social nature of religious belief, and is also concerned with how these factors have influenced the origins and development of religion.

Whiting, B.: *Paiute Sorcery,* Viking Fund Publications in Anthropology, No. 15 (New York: Wenner-Gren Foundation, 1950).
The author's fieldwork with the Paiute Indians forms the basis of this work's theoretical premise. In the first part of the book she discusses the Paiute concept of the supernatural, the tribal theory of disease, control of aggression within the tribe, and the role of the sorcerer. From the information gained in her field study of the Paiute, Whiting suggests the hypothesis that sorcery is present most often in the absence of publicly recognized means of social control, and in the second part of the book she tests this hypothesis by means of a cross-cultural study.

20
The Arts

In virtually all cultures people experience the need to express their feelings, fears, or thoughts in what we might call an artistic medium. A Melanesian stripes his house with vertical bands; an American farmer paints a hex sign on his barn. A Hopi Indian performs a rain dance; the Plains Indians perform a sun dance. Giant stone heads are implanted in the earth on Easter Island; inch-long ivory mice are delicately carved by Chinese artists. What all of these activities have in common is that they involve a strong *emotional component.* Indeed, one could justifiably say that the expression of feeling is the central function of art, music, dance, and folklore, which is why many anthropologists and other social scientists refer to them as forms of *expressive behavior.*

Expressive activities are in part cultural activities, involving shared and learned patterns of behavior, belief, and feeling. We might question why this is so. After all, in our own society we tend to assume that a piece of art is a unique expression of the artist's personality and experience; indeed, if it is not—if it is an imitation of another's work or style—we tend to dismiss it as unoriginal. But although we require that an artist in our society be unique and innovative, the art he produces must still fall within some range of acceptable variation. He must communicate to us in a way that we can relate to, or at least learn to relate to. Often he must follow certain current styles of expression which have been set by other artists or by critics if he hopes to have his art accepted by the public. These requirements demonstrate the fact that, even allowing for the high value we place upon originality, art in our society remains in part a cultural activity.

That our values, even our artistic values, are culturally determined is best demonstrated by our changeable artistic standards. What is deemed artistic and marketable as such varies over time. Thus, Picasso, who was hardly a financial success in his early years as a painter, can now sell just about anything he produces (and at a very handsome price). The critics who ridiculed the young Picasso (and every innovator since) and the theater audiences that were shocked by actors speaking obscenities on stage—all were protesting the violation of shared values, the stretching of cultural acceptability. That is, they were expressing the cultural constraints that tend to keep the artist (particularly the successful one) within an acceptable range of variation.

The fact that our artistic activities are mainly cultural is evident not only in our changing standards but, even more obviously, when we compare what is artistic in different cultures. For example, Americans share the value of decorating the inside of their homes with pictures, either by hanging paintings or by painting directly on the wall; but we do not share the value of painting pictures on the outside walls of the house, as some cultures do. Similarly, many Americans share an appreciation of lipstick and eye shadow but do not accept the little rouge circle on the forehead which women of India may use. Earlier in this century, young German men shared the value of a fencing scar, a slash on the cheek; so valued was this scar that it was sometimes self-inflicted. Yet the fencers would have rejected decorative scarring as it is practiced in some African societies. Anthropologists seek to explain all such variations and to determine why different expressive behaviors occur in different societies.

CULTURAL VARIATIONS IN EXPRESSIVE BEHAVIOR

Some types of expressive behavior are apparently *universal*—music and decoration, for example. Yet shared values—and with them the forms and styles of artistic expression—vary from society to society. For example, while body decoration may be an art in many societies, the actual form of the decoration depends upon cultural traditions: to the fencing slash of Germany may be added the pierced ears of many societies, the pierced noses of some women in India, the elongated necks of the Mangebetu of Central Africa, the extended lips of the Ubangi of the Central African Republic, the tattooing of American males, the body painting of fashion designer, Rudy Gernreich, and the Caduveo of South America, and the varying ornaments (bracelets, necklaces, anklets, rings, feathers, belts, beads, earrings, and so on) of practically everyone.

Not only is there cultural variation in forms of expression, but there is also variation in style. Thus, while music is universally an expressive behavior, some societies produce music that is very rhythmic, and others produce music with a freer, less regular beat; in some societies music tends to repeat the same elements over and over again, while in other societies it does not. Although anthropologists and others have been collecting samples of expressive culture for many years, recently there has been an acceleration of research on what may account for variation in form and style of expressive behavior.

To illustrate the range of variation that exists in expressive behavior throughout the world, we will examine the distinctive art of two areas of the world—namely the carvings of the Indians of the northwest coast of North America and the masks and statues of some of the tribes of Africa.

Northwest Coast Indian Art

Northwest Coast Indians knew the qualities of their natural materials extremely well. Wood was the principal material used for both shelter and art. Stone and bone were also available for carving.

It is for their monumental carvings, house posts, and memorial "totem" poles that the Northwest Coast Indians are perhaps best known. House posts supported the roof beams of the houses and generally had one or two totemic figures or family crests carved into them. The houses of the rich families were further distinguished by their size, often several hundred feet long, and by a carved front post into which the door might be cut; carved posts within identified the seat of the highest-ranked man in the house. The carved poles before each house were memorials to dead members of the family. They included the family crest and representations of birds and animals which had some historical or mythical connection to the dead man. Mortuary poles contained the ashes of the body of the deceased.

Figure 1

A model of a totem pole with a human head at the top and a bear below. (Redrawn after Robert Bruce Inverarity, *Art of the Northwest Coast Indians.*)

The canoe is the other large carved structure of the Northwest Coast Indians. Hewn from a single log, the 60-foot-long canoes were carved and painted with abstract animal forms; a craft might be decorated with a killer whale, one of the fisherman's dangers, and a raven, the mythological figure who brought the sun to man.

The carvings on all of these poles and on the canoes were stylized representations in which prominent features were exaggerated to identify the animal. One encounters the large front teeth and the crisscrossed tail of the beaver, the curved beak of the eagle, the dorsal fin of the killer whale, the large mouth and round nose of the bear. One of the techniques of abstraction which makes use of this exaggeration of detail is *split representation,* in which "the animal is imagined cut in two from head to tail, so that the two halves cohere only at the tip of the nose."[1] Thus a Northwest Coast Indian blanket extends the theory of split representation by joining the two profiles of the head; beneath the head the tail is rejoined, but the other details, fins, joints, are so stylized that they are almost unrecognizable. This technique of split representation in the art of the Northwest Coast Indians resembles techniques in the art of ancient China, and of the Polynesians in what is now New Zealand.

Smaller objects, items of daily or special use, were carved with fine detail or bold lines. Dishes and spoons were carved from wood, horn, and slate. Boxes in which ceremonial paraphernalia or the shaman's tools were kept were carved with animals associated somehow with the contents of the box. Masks and headdresses symbolized the wearer's family totem or the myth of the ceremony in which it was used. Shaman's tools, woodworking tools, knives, and clubs were all stamped with a symbolic personality.

Some aspects of the Northwest Coast Indian cultures, as we know them from ethnographic reports, can be seen in their arts. For example, as all living things—humans, other animals, and plants—were believed to be receptacles in which spirits could dwell, so all man-made objects—houses, utensils, tools, canoes—were

[1] Franz Boas, *Primitive Art* (Oslo: H. Ashehoug, 1927), p. 223.

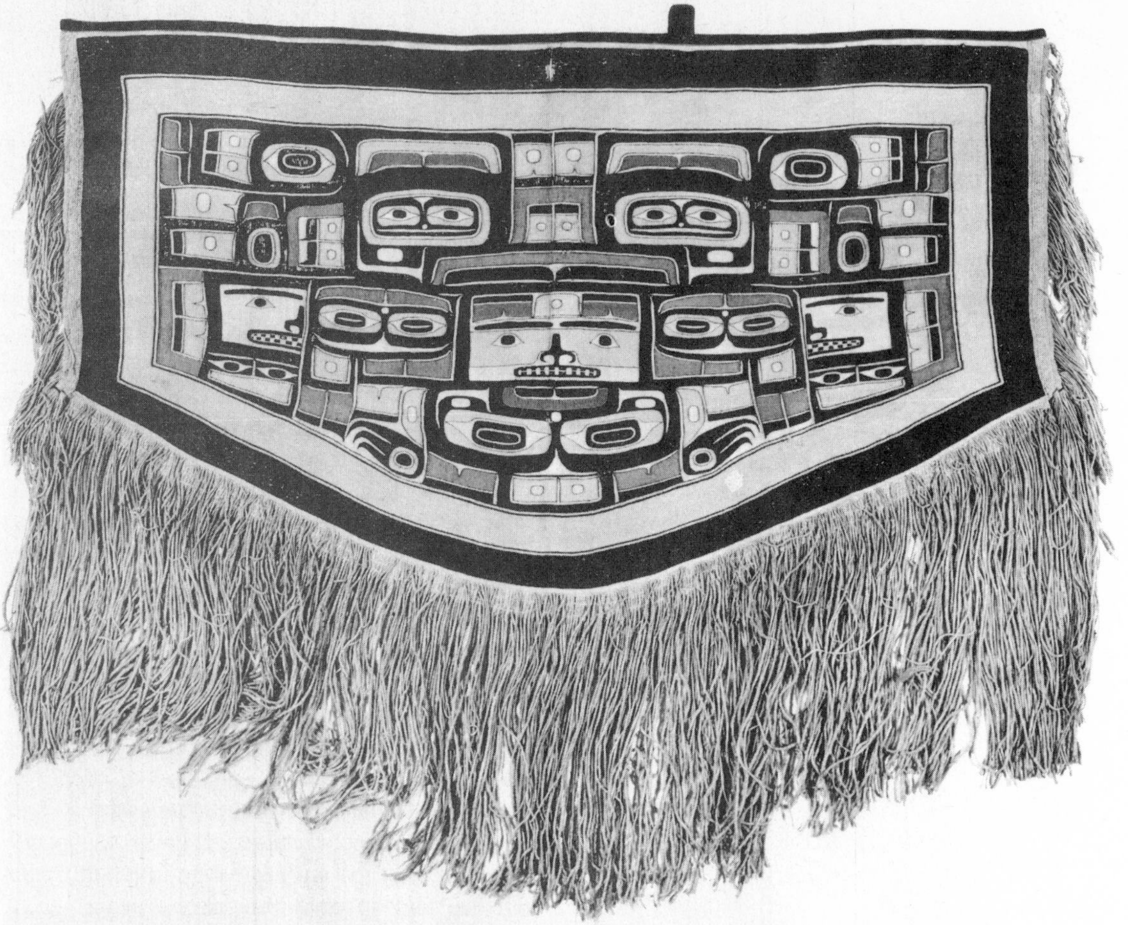

A ceremonial Chilkat blanket of the Northwest Coast Indians of Alaska, woven from the wool of mountain goats. An animal's face appears in the center, but the stylized design makes the other symbols difficult to determine. (Courtesy, American Museum of Natural History.)

thought to be inhabited by the spirit of the man, animal, bird, fish, or imaginary creature which was carved into them.

> A vase, a box, a wall, are not independent, preexisting objects which are subsequently decorated. They acquire their definitive existence only through the integration of the decoration with the utilitarian function. Thus, the chests of Northwest Coast art are not merely containers embellished with a painted or carved animal. They are the animal itself, keeping an active watch over the ceremonial ornaments which have been entrusted to its care.[2]

Art in Africa

Although the influence of African art on twentieth-century European art, particularly on the work of Modigliani and Picasso, has been noted by art historians, it is art in relation to the society that produces it that primarily interests anthropologists. Africa is a continent containing many widely divergent cultures, each with

[2] Claude Lévi-Strauss, *Structural Anthropology* (Garden City, N.Y.: Doubleday-Anchor, 1967), p. 255.

its own expressive styles. The smooth, bulbous forms of the masks and figures produced in Gabon, for example, stand in obvious contrast with the severe, angular forms of Sudanese statuettes. However, centuries of stylistic borrowing among different areas have produced many similarities as well, with the result that today it is often difficult to identify a work of art as definitely coming from one particular area.

The mask tends to dominate our view of African art, although not all African societies use masks. Among the Dan of West Africa, masks were carved for the use of a man in any of the birth/marriage/death ceremonies. If a man was particularly successful during his lifetime, the mask became the symbol of that success. At his death, his vital spirit might be said to inhabit the mask, and his personal spirit could be counted on to remain, ensuring the power of the mask in aiding his son, its new possessor. Once a mask had demonstrated its possession of power or "god spirit" (evidence was the material success of the possessor), it might be promoted to the collection of masks of the village shaman. Thus, the more ancient the mask, the more power it had collected.[3]

In northeastern Liberia, among the Mano, village elders used the mask in governing. They would retire to a secluded place, arrive at a decision concerning a particular case or a general rule, and then seek the mask's approval. They could then announce to the people that they were acting on the decision of the spirit of the mask.[4] Thus the mask functioned as the icon in which god spirit resided, and the council of elders who controlled the mask could

Northwest Coast Indian (Haida tribe) wooden dish, carved in the shape of a loon (top). *At right is a wooden comb, carved to represent a bear sitting on its haunches with a fish resting on its knees (Tlingit tribe).* (Courtesy, American Museum of Natural History.)

[3] Adrian Cerbrands, "Art as an Element of Culture in Africa," in Charlotte M. Otten, ed., *Anthropology and Art* (Garden City, N.Y.: Natural History Press, 1971), p. 366–382.

[4] Roy Seiber, "Masks as Agents of Social Control," in Yehudi A. Cohen, ed., *Man in Adaptation to the Institutional Framework* (Chicago: Aldine-Atherton, 1971).

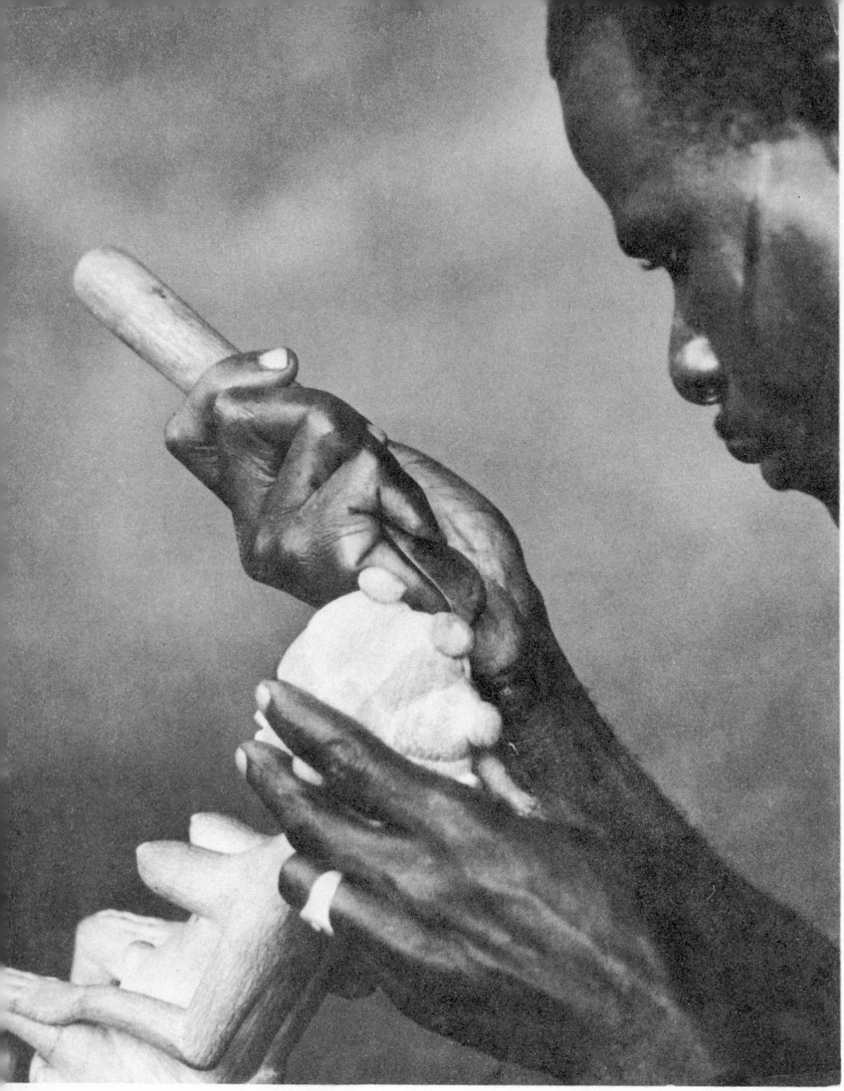

A carver works on a fetish statue for the Museum of the Ivory Coast (left). *Above is a wooden Agni (Ivory Coast) mother and child. Rings on the neck are a sign of beauty.* (Marc and Evelyne Bernheim from Woodfin Camp and Associates.)

use it to sanctify their authority. The owner of the most powerful masks among the Mano controlled the owners of lesser masks and had broad powers to keep peace, stop a war, and appoint the new priest.

Masks also symbolized power among the Igala of northern Nigeria. In a case of murder, the "chief of the masks" had the power to demand that the family or the village give over custody of the murderer and could quarantine the village until they handed him over. He could appoint a member of the victim's family to execute the murderer, and he could then purify the executioner so that neither the executed man's spirit nor his family could take revenge on him. But, since murder occurs fairly infrequently, the mask was generally concerned with lesser problems, such as arbitrating local disputes and fixing mild punishments.

Among the Bambara of the western Sudan, power was spread out, so that different masks controlled different affairs. One group, represented by its mask, was responsible for discovering and punishing thieves and unfaithful wives. Another was responsible for poisoners; another for cannibals and witches. Among the

Idoma of northern Nigeria, each mask was representative of a secret society and was used to control the behavior of the members of that society, a form of self-regulation within the segments of the society.

The association of the mask with control of social behavior is strong enough to warrant more study. Our view of African masks, however, is necessarily out of context; we cannot fully appreciate the isolated mask, for it was intended to be seen only with its full set of robes, and even then only as part of the dance movements of a full ceremony. In the same way, we cannot understand the meaning of the mask in isolation, apart from the social, judicial, religious, and political culture into which it fitted.[5] Finally, we do not yet have research to indicate why some societies use masks and others do not.

In many of the world's cultures, objects of art are associated not only with religion and government but with daily life as well. Unlike our own society, where the individual artist expects and usually gains recognition for his work, in other societies an object of art is often a communal project. For example, Paul Bohannan has described the following experience among the Tiv of central Nigeria. Bohannan had cut himself a stick to help in getting through the swamps but was told by a young man that this stick was not suitable. The young man, after a few days, returned with a staff he called suitable for a "young elder." It was a handsome staff with several carved, blackened bands around it. Within days, almost every male was making himself such a stick and anyone who put his work down might return to find that someone else had added a few designs of his own.[6] Most Westerners would probably feel offended and frustrated if their artistic at-

Art objects used in everyday life: a Baule (Ivory Coast) fly swatter, made from wood, fur, and metal (right); *a wooden bowl of the Camaroon grasslands* (below). (Courtesy of the Museum of Primitive Art, New York.)

[5] Seiber, "Masks as Agents of Social Control," pp. 434–438.

[6] Paul Bohannan, "Artist and Critic in an African Society," in Otten, *Anthropology and Art,* pp. 172–181.

tempts were given such communal treatment, but among the Tiv there is much "true folk art in which the artist is as unimportant as the composer of folk music."[7]

We do not understand very much yet about why sculpture, in the form of masks and other objects, varies as it does from society to society. It would seem that future research involving systematic comparisons, in the light of ethnographic reports, may help us to understand more about why sculpture varies in different societies.

BODY DECORATION AND ADORNMENT

The body was one of man's first objects of art, that is, an object of nature which he, by the addition of symbols, transformed into an object of culture. Many societies decorate or adorn the human body. The decorations may be either permanent—scars, tattoos, changes in the shape of a body part—or temporary—paintings and objects such as feathers, metals, skins, and in cases where it is not strictly utilitarian, clothing. Much of this decoration seems to be motivated by aesthetic considerations, which, of course, may vary from culture to culture. A missionary described the "Turkish carpet" look of the Abipone women of Paraguay and reported that the women conceived of their tattooing as making them "more beautiful than beauty itself."[8]

In addition to satisfying aesthetic needs, body decoration or adornment may be used to delineate social position, rank, sex, occupation, or religion within a society. Along with social stratification come visual means of declaring status. The symbolic halo (i.e., the crown) on the king's head, the scarlet hunting jacket of the English gentleman, the eagle feathers of the Indian chief's bonnet, the gold-embroidered jacket of the Indian rajah—each mark of high status is recognized in its own society.

A Jur woman of the southern Sudan wears a beaded headband, nose-rings, and lip-rings as ornaments. (Courtesy United Nations.)

Body decoration may also signify religious affiliation in our society: by bits of jewelry in the shape of a cross or a star of David, or by clothes which set apart the priest or nun or the member of a sect such as the Amish or Chasidic Jew. The ceremonial significance of body painting has been noted for a number

[7] *Ibid.*, p. 176.

[8] M. Dobrizhoffer, *An Account of the Abipones*, trans. from the Latin, Vol. II (London: 1822), p. 20, as quoted by Lévi-Strauss, *Structural Anthropology*, p. 251.

of societies; in each case religious content is conveyed through symbols attached to the body. The Sun Dance of the Cheyenne presents a woman, representing morning, painted red with two blue suns on her face, a blue morning star on her chest, and a blue crescent moon on her right shoulder. Various sky symbols appear on other dancers of the ceremony during which the power of the sun is sought for the men.[9] Voluntary self-flagellation is part of the Easter observance in parts of Mexico. The mystical significance of much of ancient body decoration is lost to us, but the assumption remains that much of body decoration has religious intent.

The erotic significance of body decoration is also apparent. Women draw attention to erogenous zones of the body by paintings, as on the lips, and by attaching some object: earring, a flower behind the ear, necklace, bracelet, brooch, anklet, belt. The Basuto of Basutoland in southern Africa devise a love potion for men and women by rubbing an ointment containing some of the beloved's sweat or blood or hair into open wounds. The resulting scars are evidence of love.[10] Among the Ila-speaking people of northern Rhodesia women practice scarification to heighten arousal during sexual intercourse. They repeatedly cut and reopen vertical lines on their loins and inner thighs, hidden by their skirts during the day and revealed only to their husbands.[11] Body adornment for erotic purposes is not peculiar to primitive cultures. We have only to follow the fashion trends of Europe and America in the past 300 years to trace a history of pinched waists, ballooned hips, bustled rumps, exaggerated breasts, painted faces, and exposed bosoms to realize the pertinence of body adornment for sexual provocation.

Special body decoration to mark the initiation of youth into adulthood is a form of sexual and status adornment, for it is the sexual maturity of the young person which marks him as ready for social maturity. Many societies circumcise adolescents. In the Poro initiation ceremony as practiced by the Kpelle of Liberia, the circumcised boys spend a period of seclusion in the forest with the older men. They return with scars down their backs, symbolic tooth marks indicative of their close escape from *namu,* the Great Masked Figure, which ate the child but disgorged the young adult.[12] Clitoridectomy (removal of the clitoris) marks the sexual maturity of girls in some societies.

The tendency to decorate the human body is probably universal. We have noted some of the variety of methods man has used in different societies. We are aware also of body-decoration practices which raise questions to which we have no ready answers. Perhaps vanity explains adornment of the body and such practices as scarification, bound feet, elongated ears and necks, shaped heads, pierced ears and septums, filed teeth. But what leads some members of our society to transfer body decoration to their animals: the shaped hair of the poodle, the braided manes of some horses, and various diamond collars, painted toenails, coats, hats, raincoats, and even boots for some pets? Anthropologists are only beginning to investigate such questions. Why, for example, do different societies adorn, paint, or otherwise decorate different parts of the body for sexual (or other) reasons? The intrinsically interesting quality of such questions will undoubtedly arouse more systematic research in the future.

[9] Peter V. Powell, *Sweet Medicine,* Vol. 2 (Norman, Okla.: University of Oklahoma Press, 1969), pp. 842–844.

[10] Hugh Ashton, *The Basuto,* 2nd ed. (London: Oxford University Press, 1967), p. 303.

[11] Edwin W. Smith and Andrew Murray Dale, *The Ila-speaking Peoples of Northern Rhodesia* (New Hyde Park, N.Y.: University Books, 1968; originally published in 1920 as *Ethnocentric British Colonial Attitudes*), p. 96.

[12] James L. Gibbs, Jr., "The Kpelle of Liberia," in *Peoples of Africa* (New York: Holt, Rinehart and Winston, 1965), p. 222.

Explaining Variation in Expressive Behavior

Many people would argue that expressive behavior, such as music and art, is the area of culture most free to vary. It does not seem that the particular style of art or music of a society can make any difference with respect to survival or success, and therefore it might appear that any form or style of expression could occur any time and any place. This assumption about the freedom of expression to vary may also come from our own experience in observing rapid changes in such realms as popular music and dance, films, and graphic art, in the apparent absence of equally rapid changes in the requirements of life and social conditions. However, we must realize that what looks like rapid change to us may simply be slight variation within what a foreign observer would see as a more or less constant form or style. For example, the dominant style of dancing among young people may have changed from the fox trot to rock, but we still generally see couples dancing—not individuals dancing in isolation. Furthermore, our popular music still has a beat (or combination of beats) and is still generally made by the same kinds of instruments used in the past. Thus, the fact that we think there are rapid style changes in our own expressive behaviors in the absence of other important cultural changes does not mean that these behaviors are unrelated to other aspects of culture.

Although expressive form and style may not generally *affect* how one lives, there is still the possibility that it *reflects* how one lives. Much of the recent research on variation in expressive behavior supports this possibility. Just as it is suggested that certain aspects of religion may reflect aspects of society, so it may be that expressive behavior reflects society. And just as some aspects of religion seem to be projections of feelings and conflicts, so some aspects of expressive behavior too may be ways of ventilating or vicariously expressing the conflicts and feelings of most people in society.

Perhaps the most obvious way that artistic creations reflect how we live is by mirroring the environment—the materials and technologies that are available to a society. Stone, rock walls, wood, bones, tree bark, clay, sand, charcoal, berries for staining, and a few mineral-derived ochers are rather generally available. In addition, depending on the locality, other materials become accessible: shells, horns, tusks, gold, copper, and silver. The different uses to which societies put these materials is of interest to anthropologists, who may ask, for example, why a people choose to use clay and not copper when both are available. Although we have no conclusive answers as yet, such questions have interesting ramifications, for the way in which a society views its environment is sometimes apparent in its choice and use of artistic materials. The use of certain revered metals, for example, may be reserved for ceremonial objects of special importance. Or the belief in the supernatural powers of a stone or tree may cause the sculptor to be exquisitely sensitive to that particular material.[13]

What is particularly meaningful to anthropologists is the realization that, although the materials available may to some extent limit or influence what can be done artistically, they by no means determine what is done. Why does the artist in Japanese society make sand into patterns, the artist in Navajo culture paint sand, and the artist in Roman society melt sand to form glass? Moreover, even when the material is used in the same way, the form or style of the work varies enormously from culture to culture.

A society may choose to represent objects or phenomena that are especially critical to them, and the anthropologist can learn from these representations. For example, an examination of the art of the Middle Ages tells us something

[13] James J. Sweeney, "African Negro Culture," in *African Folktales and Sculpture* (New York: Bollingen Series XXXII, Bollingen Foundation, 1952), p. 335.

The same material may be used artistically in different societies. At right, a Japanese Buddhist monk rakes sand into traditional patterns. At left, a Navajo Indian creates a sand painting to help heal a sick child. (Left: Burt Glinn, Magnum Photos; right: Courtesy, the American Museum of Natural History.)

about the medieval preoccupation with theological doctrine. In addition to revealing the primary concerns of a society, the content of its art may also reflect social stratification. Authority figures may be evidenced in rather obvious ways: in ancient Sumerian society the sovereign was represented as much larger than his followers, and the most prestigious gods were given oversized eyes. Also, differences in clothing and jewelry styles within a society usually reflect social stratification.

Certain possible relationships between the art of a society and other aspects of its culture have always been recognized by art historians. Much of this attention has been concentrated on the content of art, since European art has been representational for such a long time. But the style of the art may reflect other aspects of culture. Fischer, for example, examines the stylistic features of art; his goal is to discover "some sort of regular connection between some artistic feature and some social situation."[14] Fischer argues that all expressive behavior is a form of social fantasy, that is, in a stable society the artist will respond to those conditions in the society which bring him, and the society, security or pleasure.

Assuming that "pictorial elements in design are, on one psychological level, abstract, mainly unconscious representations of persons in the society,"[15] Fischer reasoned that egalitarian societies would tend to have different stylistic elements in their art than stratified societies. Egalitarian societies are generally composed of small, self-sufficient communities, which are structurally similar, and which have little differentiation between persons. Stratified societies, on the other hand, generally have larger and more interdependent (and different) communities, and great differences among persons in prestige, power, and access to economic resources. Fischer hypothesized, and found in a cross-cultural study, that the following elements of design were strongly related to the presence of social hierarchy.

Egalitarian Society	*Stratified Society*
Repetition of simple elements	Integration of unlike elements
Much empty or "irrelevant" space	Little empty space
Symmetrical design	Asymmetrical design
Unenclosed figures	Enclosed figures

Let us see how Fischer's findings apply to the art of some particular societies. For example, repetition of a simple design is found in the art of the Ojibwa, an egalitarian hunting-gathering people with little political organization and few authority positions. If each design element unconsciously represents individuals within a society, and the Ojibwa gain security from the essential likeness of people and the refusal to compete for a superior or outstanding position, then it seems that a connection can be postulated between the Ojibwa's social patterns and their expressive behavior. Conversely, the combining of different design elements in a complex pattern in Indian art may be seen as a reflection of the caste system of India. Each individual is well aware of the paraphernalia and the distinctive behavior which effectively separate him from every other level of society.

According to Fischer, the egalitarian society's empty space around a design is said to represent the society's relative isolation. Egalitarian societies, because they are usually small and self-sufficient, shy away from foreigners, prefering to find security within their own group. Sioux designs for the toes of moccasins present a strongly integrated, repetitious central design surrounded by empty space, suggesting a relatively egalitarian society that normally has (or tries to have) little contact with surrounding peoples.

[14] John Fischer, "Art Styles as Cultural Cognitive Maps," *American Anthropologist,* Vol. 63 (1961), p. 80.
[15] *Ibid.,* p. 81.

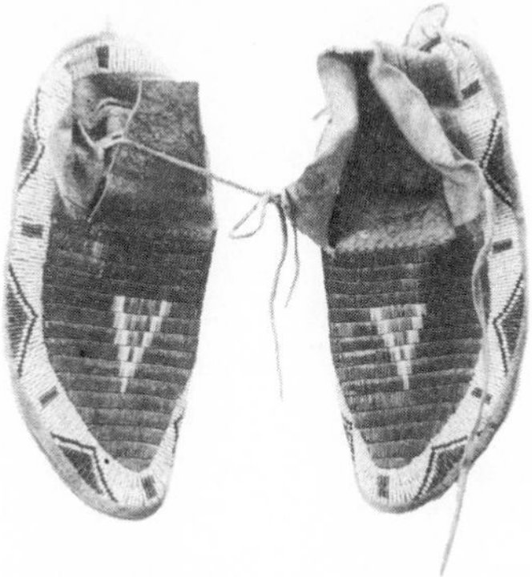

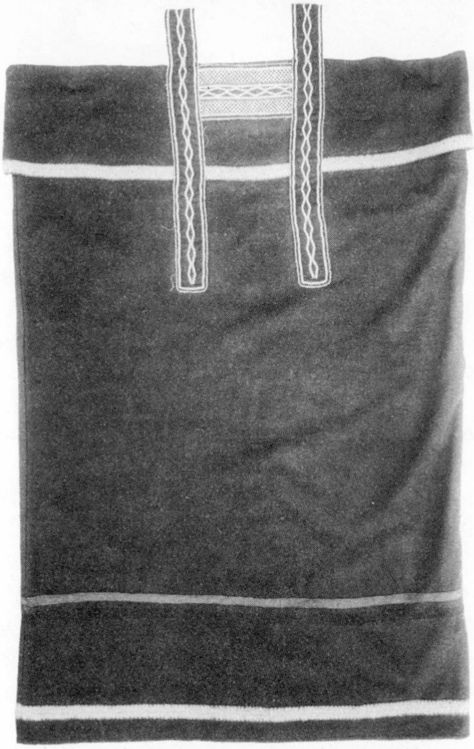

Ojibwa woolen shirt (right) *displays the repetition of a simple design; Sioux moccasins* (left) *have a repetitious central design surrounded by empty space. These designs may reflect an egalitarian social structure. The intricate textile design* (below) *may reflect the highly stratified society of India.* (Left, right: Courtesy of the American Museum of Natural History; below: Raghubir Singh, from Woodfin Camp and Associates.)

On the other hand, the art of India is generally crowded. The hierarchical society does not seek to isolate individuals or communities within the society since they must be interdependent, each level furnishing services for those above and help for those beneath. As Fischer suggests, we can, in general, discern a lack of empty space in societies where, instead of seeking security by avoiding the stranger, "security is produced by incorporating strangers into the hierarchy, through dominance or submission as the relative power indicates. In fantasy the hierarchical society seeks to encompass the universe."[16]

Symmetry, the third stylistic feature related to type of society is similar to the first. Symmetry may suggest likeness or an egalitarian society; asymmetry suggests difference and perhaps stratification. The fourth feature of interest here, the presence or absence of enclosures or boundaries, may indicate the presence or absence of hierarchically imposed rules circumscribing individual behavior. Sioux beadwork presents an unenclosed symmetrical design; elements are not separated from each other. In fact Sioux society allows free access to most property, and the fencing off of a piece of property for the use of one man only is unknown. In the art of India, the presence of boundaries is more marked. Such separations between figures in art may be seen as a reflection of the separation between persons in Indian society, which is filled with symbolic boundaries indicated by differences in dress, occupations, type of food allowed, and manners.

Studies like Fischer's offer anthropologists the possibility of new tools by which ancient societies, known only by a few pieces of pottery or a few tools or paintings, can be studied. If art reflects aspects of a culture, then the study of whatever art has been preserved may provide a way to test some of the guesses we make about a culture on the basis of more prosaic archaeological materials.

[16] Fischer, "Art Styles as Cultural Cognitive Maps," p. 83.

MUSIC

Apes have been observed having enormous musical bouts in the jungles. Apparently with no warning or any particular reason, an ape will seize a stick and begin beating the branch of a tree. Others will join in, beating rhythmically and shrieking a bit, until 50 or so apes are performing; the fest lasts about half an hour.

Not our kind of music, we say, hardly realizing that, like the expressive behavior of the

New Hebrides flute player. (Kal Muller, Woodfin Camp and Associates.)

apes, "our kind" of music has been programmed into us by our culture. We are limited to the same kinds of acceptable variations in music as in art. Even a trained musicologist, listening for the first time to music of a different culture, will not be able to hear the subtleties of tone and rhythmical structure that members of that culture hear with ease. His predicament is similar to that of the linguist who, exposed to a foreign language, cannot at first distinguish phonemes, morphemes, and other regular patterns of speech.

Music varies from society to society. Not only do instruments vary, but the music itself varies widely in style. For example, in some societies people prefer music with a regularly recurring beat; in others they prefer changes in rhythm. There are also variations in singing styles. For example, in some places it is customary to have different parts for different people; in other places people sing together. All of these and many other variations can be observed in the different music of the world societies.

Explaining Variations in Music

Is variation in music, as in the other arts, related to other aspects of culture? On the basis of a cross-cultural study of more than 3,500 folksongs from a sample of the world's societies Alan Lomax found certain relationships between cultural traits and song performance. He asserts that song styles vary with:

1. level of food production
2. degree of political development
3. degree of social stratification
4. severity of sexual mores
5. balance of dominance between males and females
6. level of social cohesiveness[17]

[17] Alan Lomax, *Folk Song Style and Culture* (Washington, D.C.: American Association for the Advancement of Science Publication No. 88, 1968), p. x.

Certain features of song style appear to be associated with cultural complexity. The societies Lomax classified as more complex tend to have higher levels of food-production technology, social stratification, and a number of levels of political jurisdiction. For example, wordiness and clearness of enunciation were found to be associated with cultural complexity: the more complex the society, the more wordy and clearly enunciated the song. The association is a reasonable one: the more a society depends upon verbal information, as in giving complex instructions for a job or in explaining different points of law, the more strongly will information passing and clear enunciation be a mark of its culture—and the more likely this will show up in the culture's expressive behavior, including song style. Thus, hunter-gatherer bands, in which people know their productive role and perform it without ever being given complex directions, are more likely than we are to base much of their singing on lines of nonwords, such as our refrain lines, "Tra-la-la-la-la." Their songs are characterized by lack of explicit information, by sounds that give pleasure in themselves, by much repetition, and by relaxed, slurred enunciation.[18]

Examples of the progression from repetition or nonwords to wordy information are found within our society. The most obvious (and universal) example of a song made entirely of repetition is the relaxed lullaby of a mother repeating a comfortable syllable to her baby, improvising her own tune.

However, this type of song is not characteristic of our own society. Although our songs sometimes have single lines of nonwords, it is rare for an entire song to be made of them. Usually, the nonwords act as respites from information:

Zippity do dah
Zippety ay
My o my
What a wonderful day

[18] Lomax, *Folk Song Style and Culture,* pp. 117–128.

or

> Deck the halls with boughs of holly
> Fa la la la la, la la la la

A song in which most of the lines contain new information but the last line of a stanza is repeated is more familiar in our culture. And, of course, the most informative songs show no repetition.

In associating variation in music with cultural complexity, Lomax also found that elaboration of song parts corresponds to the complexity of a society. Societies in which leadership is informal and ephemeral seem to symbolize their equality by an "interlocked" style of singing; each person sings independently but within the group, and no one singer is differentiated from the others. Rank societies in which there is a leader with prestige but no real power are characterized by a song style in which one "leader" may begin the song, but the others soon drown out his voice. In stratified societies, where leaders have the power of force, choral singing is generally marked by a clear-cut role for the leader and a secondary "answering" role for the others. Societies which are marked by elaborate stratification show singing parts which are differentiated and in which the soloist is deferred to by the other singers.

Lomax also found a relationship between polyphony (two or more melodies sung simultaneously) and a high degree of female participation in food getting. In those societies in which women's work is responsible for at least half of the food, songs are likely to contain more than one simultaneous melody, the higher ones usually sung by women.

> Counterpoint was once believed to be the invention of European high culture. In our sample it turns out to be most frequent among simple producers, especially gatherers, where women supply the bulk of the food. Counterpoint and perhaps even polyphony may then be very old feminine inventions. . . . Subsistence complementarity is at its maximum among gatherers, early gardeners, and horticulturists. It is in such societies that we find the highest occurrence of polyphonic singing.[19]

In societies in which women do not contribute much to production, the singing is more likely to reflect the single dominance of the male.[20]

In some societies, survival and social welfare are based on a cohesive group effort; in these societies, singing tends to be marked by cohesiveness. That is, cohesive work parties, teams of gatherers or harvesters, and kin groups who work voluntarily for the good of the family or community seem to express their interconnectedness in song by blending both tone and rhythm. For example, the !Kung Bushmen and the Mbuti Pygmies have a cohesive song style. Theirs is a culture in which production is shared by all adults—a sharing which may be seen as reflected in the cooperative blending of voices of the various work groups.

Relationships of Child-Rearing Practices to Variations in Music

We have seen that variations in music may be correlated with the degree of cultural complexity and with the division of labor within a society. Some variations may also be explained as a consequence of child-rearing practices in the society. For example, researchers are beginning to explore child-rearing practices in order to explain why some societies respond to and produce regular rhythm in their music, while others mostly produce irregular rhythm, and still others enjoy free rhythm which has no regular beat but rather approximates the rhythm of speech.

One hypothesis is that a regular beat is a simulation of the regular beat of the heart. (Speakers of English even use the word "beat" for both.) For nine months in the womb, the

[19] Lomax, *Folk Song Style and Culture*, pp. 166–167.
[20] Lomax, *Folk Song Style and Culture*, pp. 117–169.

fetus feels the mother's regular 80 or so heartbeats a minute. Moreover, mothers generally employ rhythmic tactics in quieting a crying infant—patting his back (simulating the heartbeat?), rocking him in his cradle, a rocking chair, or in the mother's arms. But the fact that children respond positively to regular rhythm does not mean that the regular heartbeat is completely responsible for their sensitivity to rhythm. In fact, if the months *in utero* were sufficient to establish a preference for rhythm, then every child would be affected in exactly the same manner by a regular beat, and every society would have the same rhythm in its music. There must be something more to cause a response to rhythmic beat in the children of some cultures and not in others.

Barbara Ayres suggests that the importance of regular rhythm in the music of a culture is related to its "acquired reward value"—that is to associations with feelings of security or relaxation. These associations are most probably forged during infancy. In a cross-cultural study exploring this possibility, Ayres found a strong correlation between a society's method of carrying infants and the type of musical rhythm it had. In some societies the mother or older sister continually carries the child, sometimes for two or three years, in a sling, pouch, or shawl, so that the child is in bodily contact with her at all times and experiences the motion of her rhythmic walking. Ayres finds that such societies tend to have a regularly recurring beat in their songs. The rhythmic movement experienced by the child in its early years which is presumably rewarding may produce a sense of rhythm that is reflected in the culture's music. Societies in which infants are carried on the hip, on the shoulder, or in mother's arms, also show a high percentage of songs with a regular beat. Those societies in which the child is put into a cradle or strapped to a cradleboard tend to have music that is based either on irregular rhythm or free rhythm. Ayres does not claim that the carrying practices necessarily give rise to a regular beat in music, but that the relationship is strong enough to warrant further study.[21]

The question of why some societies have great tonal ranges in music whereas others do not has also been researched by Ayres, who suggests that this too might be explained by certain child-rearing practices. Ayres theorized that painful stimulation of infants before weaning would result in bolder, more exploratory behavior in adulthood, which would be apparent in the musical patterns of the culture. This theory was suggested by laboratory experiments with animals in which, contrary to expectations, those animals which had been given electrical shocks or had been handled before weaning showed greater than usual physical growth and more exploratory behavior when placed in new situations as adults. Ayres equated the range of musical notes (from low to high) as comparable to the exploratory range of animals, and forcefulness of accent in music as comparable to boldness in animals. The kinds of stress she looked for in ethnographic reports were those which would be applied to all children or to all of one sex: for example, scarification; piercing of the nose, lips, or ears; binding, shaping, or stretching of feet, head, ears, or any limb; innoculation; circumcision; or cauterization. The results showed that in those societies in which infants are stressed before the age of two, music is marked by a wider tonal range than in those societies in which children are not stressed or are stressed only later. Also, in societies which stress children, a firm accent or beat is characteristic of music more often than in societies which do not stress children.[22]

[21] Barbara C. Ayres, *Effects of Infant Carrying Practices on Rhythm in Music* (Paper presented at the 68th Annual Meeting of the American Anthropological Association, November 1969, New Orleans).

[22] Barbara C. Ayres, "Effects of Infantile Stimulation on Musical Behavior," in Lomax, *Folk Song Style and Culture*, pp. 211–221.

The culture's emphasis on obedience or independence in children is another variable which may explain some aspects of musical performance. Children in some societies may be pressured to comply with traditional routines; in other societies they may be encouraged to be assertive and venturesome. In those societies in which children are generally trained for compliance, cohesive singing predominates, whereas in societies where children are encouraged to be assertive, singing is mostly individualized. Moreover, assertive training of children is associated with a raspy voice or harsh singing. A raspy voice seems to be an indication of assertiveness and is most often a male voice quality. Interestingly enough, in societies in which women's work predominates in subsistence production, the women sing with harsher voices.

Other voice characteristics may also be associated with elements of culture. For example, sexual restrictions in a society seem to be associated with voice restrictions, especially with a nasalized or narrow, squeezed tone. These voice qualities are associated with anxiety and are especially noticeable in sounds of pain, deprivation, or sorrow. Restrictive sexual practices may be a source of pain and anxiety, and the nasal tone in song may reflect such emotions.[23]

The discovery of strong correlations between a culture's social characteristics and its expressive behavior, as evidenced in these studies of musical variation, will undoubtedly provide the impetus for more such studies.

FOLKLORE

Folklore is a term so broad that it is virtually impossible to deal with it briefly. It is, as its name implies, all the lore—myths, legends, fairytales, ballads, superstitions, riddles, children's games, and so on—of all the people of a culture—ancient, modern, rural, and urban. Generally, folklore is orally transmitted, but it may also be written. Because all types of folklore cannot be covered here, we will limit our discussion to orally transmitted myths and folktales.

All societies have a repertoire of tales with which they entertain each other and teach their children. Examples of our folktales include Grimm's fairytales (which were orally transmitted prior to their being recorded) as well as many other stories from the oral traditions of England and Germany. Also included are the little tales we tell about our so-called folk heros; for example, Abe Lincoln's reading and studying by candlelight and George Washington's confessing to the execution of a cherry tree so as not to tell a lie. It seems that we tell such stories, particularly to children, to illustrate or teach certain values that we hold dear. Needless to say, not all societies tell the same stories or communicate the same meanings or values.

In an attempt to arrive at the meaning of myth—and to discover how and why myths differ from society to society—interpreters of myth have often been as fanciful as the mythmakers themselves. For example, Max Muller spent about 50 years reducing most myths to a version of the solar myth (Cinderella is the sun because she starts in the ashes of a fire but ends in a blaze of glory),[24] and Andrew Lang spent about 40 years in refuting Muller and offering his own interpretation of "savage" mythology. Such debates point up the fact that it is very easy for different people to read different meaning into the same myth or to draw different conclusions from the comparison of myths. For example, consider the myth that the Greeks tell of a golden age when only men were present on earth and during which Pandora, the first woman, spoiled everything for

[23] Lomax, *Folk Song Style and Culture,* pp. 190–197.
[24] Richard Dorson, "The Eclipse of Solar Mythology," in Alan Dundes, ed., *The Study of Folklore* (Englewood Cliffs, N.J.: Prentice-Hall, 1965), pp. 57–83.

men by releasing evil into the world. One might recall that the Hebrews told a comparable story of a paradise in which only a man was present until Eve, the first woman, arrived and ate the forbidden fruit of knowledge. One might conclude that the men in those societies had some traditional grudge against women. If the interpreter of the myth is a psychoanalyst, he might assume that the myth reflects the male's deeply hidden fears of female sexuality. A historian might believe that the myth reflects actual historical events, and that men were living in blissful ignorance until women invented agriculture (the effect of Eve's "knowledge" led to a life of digging rather than gathering). And if the interpreter is a woman, she might conclude that, as the myths were created by men, the men in those societies were probably male chauvinists.

As Lévi-Strauss states:

> Myths are still widely interpreted in conflicting ways: as collective dreams, as the outcome of a kind of esthetic play, or as the basis of ritual. Mythological figures are considered as personified abstractions, divinized heroes, or fallen gods. Whatever the hypothesis, the choice amounts to reducing mythology either to idle play or to a crude kind of philosophical speculation.[25]

Several recurrent themes in myth and folklore have been examined by Kluckhohn. He notes the recurrence of father-seekers, father-slayers, mother-slayers, and creation stories around the world. By analyzing myths from culture areas all over the world, Kluckhohn has arrived at five themes which are universal: catastrophe, generally through flood; the slaying of monsters; incest; sibling rivalry, generally between brothers; and castration, sometimes actual but more usually "symbolic castration."[26]

It may be that there was once a flood in the eastern Mediterranean area—archaeologists have recently suggested a volcanic explosion and resultant tidal wave about 4,000 years ago—but that event might not account for the presence of the flood myth in so many cultures. Fragments of the Babylonian Gilgamesh epic, in which Gilgamesh is the favorite of the god Ut-Napishtim and so is given instructions for building a boat in which he saves himself and some animals from a destructive flood, date from about 2000 B.C. The story of Noah, written later than the Gilgamesh epic, is similar enough to be seen as a case of diffusion. But diffusion cannot account for equally ancient flood myths of Asian and American origin. The theme of destruction and renewal seems to be universal, perhaps because people in many areas of the world have experienced and been terrified by floods.

The slaying of monsters is part of the general category of hero myths. Different reasons for the slaying may be given: Hercules must slay some monsters as punishment for having killed his wife and children; Bellerophon and Perseus of Greek mythology are told to slay a monster by kings who hope they will be killed in the attempt. In some African (Bantu) myths a hero slays a monster in order to restore the people (all except his father) whom the monster has killed.[27] In North America, a Cree legend relates how a man named Wee-sa-kay-jac slays a monster as revenge for the monster's having killed his younger brother, but he does not restore the brother to life (even though in related myths he seems to have that power.)[28]

The incest theme is a general one in which brother-sister incest seems to be the most popular type.[29] Thus Absalom of the Hebrew tra-

[25] Lévi-Strauss, *Structural Anthropology,* p. 204.

[26] Clyde Kluckhohn, "Recurrent Themes in Myths and Myth-making," in Dundes, *The Study of Folklore,* pp. 158–168.

[27] Kluckhohn, "Recurrent Themes in Myths and Myth-making," p. 163.

[28] James Stevens, *Sacred Legends of the Sandy Lake Cree* (Toronto, Montreal: McClelland and Stewart, 1971), pp. 22–23.

[29] Kluckhohn, "Recurrent Themes in Myths and Myth-making," p. 163.

dition kills his brother when he learns that the brother has slept with their sister; but with this success behind him he attempts next to take his father David's throne and is in turn killed for this insolence. In Greek mythology, Zeus and Hera, who are brother and sister, are also husband and wife.

Sibling rivalry is apparent in the stories of Absalom and of Wee-sa-kay-jac; it is perhaps most widely known to us in the Hebrew stories of Cain and Abel, and Jacob and Esau. Sister-sister rivalry is a theme of the Greek story of Psyche and appears as jealousy between step-sisters in the story of Cinderella. The castration theme generally appears disguised, as in the warning given to little boys: if you suck your thumb, the butcher will cut it off.

George O. Wright attempted to link the content of folktales to patterns of child rearing. Folktales were rated for aggression content as if they were reports of interpersonal behavior.[30] In a cross-cultural study of folktales from 33 societies, Wright found that more intense aggression appeared in the folktales of societies that severely punished children for aggression as compared with societies which were more tolerant of aggression. He suggests that the folktale provides a way of expressing aggression which is otherwise suppressed. He also found that the more severe the aggression training, the more aggression is seen in the folktale as coming from and directed toward strangers (those not known by the hero). The theory here is that people who are punished for aggression will have anxiety about exhibiting it and therefore, even in a story, will associate it with more peripheral and unknown characters. The Wright study suggests, then, that folklore, and perhaps other forms of expressive behavior, may reflect the anxieties and conflicts felt by most members of a society as well as the society's social and political organization.

Some anthropologists have concentrated their attention on the *form* or *structure* of folklore rather than its content alone. In these investigations, the emphasis is on how folklore may reflect cognition or styles of thinking in a society, not just social and political organization or personality patterns. Alan Dundes isolated two types of structure in the American Indian folktale. One is the movement from disequilibrium. Equilibrium is the desirable state; having too much or too little of anything is a condition which should be rectified as soon as possible. Dundes's structural model then is of a folktale which first exhibits disequilibrium, which he calls "lack," and then shows how the lack is corrected.[31] Thus the Cree version of the flood begins with disequilibrium—too much water, a decided lack of land—but by the efforts of three diving animals, Wee-sa-kay-jac obtained a bit of clay which he boiled and the overflow became land. The same structure is repeated in the creation story: there is a lack of people which Wee-sa-kay-jac corrects by molding clay figures.[32]

The structure of lack present/lack corrected is evident also in Greek and European myths and folktales. For instance, in the story of Phaëton, the dangers of disequilibrium appear by showing the sun too close to the earth (everything burns). Equilibrium is attained by getting the sun back to its proper place.

Another type of structure in myth which Dundes isolates is a sequence of interdiction, violation, consequence, and perhaps attempted escape. Thus in a Lillooet (southern British Columbia) folktale, some children are warned not to call a whale mockingly. They laugh and continue to call the whale. The whale comes and swallows them. They escape when the

[30] George O. Wright, "Projection and Displacement: A Cross-Cultural Study of Folktale Aggression," *Journal of Abnormal and Social Psychology,* Vol. 49 (1954), pp. 523–528.

[31] Alan Dundes, "Structural Typology in North American Indian Folktales," in *The Study of Folklore,* pp. 206–215.

[32] James R. Stevens, *Sacred Legends of the Sandy Lake Cree,* pp. 23–25.

people cut open the whale.[33] Two Cree legends also are examples of this pattern.

1. A woman is warned again and again not to leave her baby outside if he is crying; she ignores the warnings; the child is eaten by a wolverine;
2. An old woman sent her son for water one night but warned him not to stare at the moon; the boy stared at the beautiful moon; he was drawn up to become a part of the moon.[34]

The same sequence is familiar in the Hebrew garden of Eden tale. The couple is warned not to eat the fruit of a tree; they eat the fruit; they are cast out of their paradise. The Greek Icarus is warned not to fly too high or too low. He flies too high; the sun melts the wax that holds his feathered wings, and he falls and drowns.

The structural analysis of myths, used in conjunction with content analysis, is advocated by Lévi-Strauss as well as other anthropologists who are seeking a framework with which to approach the rich and varied folklore of the world's societies. We do not know as yet which structures in myth are universal and which may be found only in certain societies. Nor do we know much as yet about the causes of such variation. Perhaps future research will tell us.

[33] Dundes, *The Study of Folklore,* p. 209.
[34] Stevens, *Sacred Legends of the Sandy Lake Cree,* pp. 35, 81.

SUMMARY

1. In all societies people express themselves in art. Because of the arts' strong emotional content, anthropologists often refer to them as *expressive behavior.* Expressive activities are partly cultural activities, involving shared and learned patterns of behavior, belief, and feeling.

2. The body was one of man's first objects for decoration and has been adorned by different peoples in many different ways, both temporary and permanent. In addition to satisfying aesthetic needs, body decoration may be used to delineate social position, sex, or occupation. It may also have an erotic significance, for example, to draw attention to erogenous zones of the body, as in our use of lipstick. Forms of scarification such as circumcision may be used to mark the passage of a young person into adulthood.

3. The expressive behavior of different societies varies greatly in style. Studies indicate that these variations are correlated with other cultural variations. Which materials are used to produce art objects, how the materials are used, and which natural objects the artist chooses to represent all vary from society to society, revealing much about a society's relation to its environment. Other studies seem to reveal a correlation between artistic design and social structure; egalitarian societies seem to favor simple, repetitious, symmetrical designs with much unused space and few boundary lines; stratified societies lean toward integration of unlike elements, little empty space, asymmetrical design, and enclosed figures.

4. Music, like the visual arts, is subject to a remarkable amount of variation from society to society. Studies suggest that there are correlations between musical styles and other cultural patterns. Evidence suggests that cultural characteristics—such as level of food production,

degree of political development, degree of social stratification, severity of sexual mores, balance between male and female dominance, and level of social cohesiveness—are linked with such musical characteristics as wordiness and clearness of enunciation, separation or cohesiveness of vocal parts, polyphony, and synchrony. Other studies show links between child-rearing practices and a society's preference for certain rythmical patterns, tonal ranges, and voice quality.

5. Folklore, another form of expressive behavior, is a very broad category including such things as myths, legends, fairytales, ballads, superstitions, riddles, games and so on, most of which are orally transmitted. Myths, which often seem to embody a society's deepest preoccupations, are a particularly fruitful area of study. Some anthropologists have identified basic themes in myths. These include such things as catastrophe, slaying of monsters, incest, sibling rivalry, and castration. Studies have also linked content of myths to variation in child training. As well as interpreting myths on the basis of their content, anthropologists have also studied recurrent structures in myths, such as the movement from disequilibrium to equilibrium and the interdiction/violation/consequence pattern. Through such investigations, anthropologists and other researchers hope to understand the cognitive patterns which may or may not be universal in different societies.

SUGGESTED READINGS

Covarrubias, M.: *The Eagle, the Jaguar, and the Serpent* (New York: Knopf, 1954).
Presents many artistic achievements of the North American Indians. The text is extremely well illustrated with color plates and line drawings by the author and photographs of many Indian masterpieces. The art is considered in terms of the Indians' aesthetic values and in its historical context, in an effort to gain a more complete understanding of the artists and the cultural factors that shaped their development.

Covarrubias, M.: *Indian Art of Mexico and Central America* (New York: Knopf, 1957).
A profusely illustrated survey of the aboriginal arts and crafts of Mexico and Central America, classified by culture area. The arts and their cultural background are examined historically as they appear and change, from the archaic to the classic, through the historic periods.

Dockstader, F. J.: *Indian Art in South America: Pre-Columbian and Contemporary Arts and Crafts* (Greenwich, Conn.: New York Graphic Society, 1967).
An introduction to the arts of the indigenous peoples of South America. While intended primarily for laymen, the rich illustrations make the book a suitable reference for professionals as well. Accompanying each illustration is a brief commentary on the work's place of origin, its stylistic or tribal affiliation, date, and size. The author emphasizes the interconnection of widely separated peoples and art styles.

Dundes, A. (Ed.): *The Study of Folklore* (Englewood Cliffs, N.J.: Prentice-Hall, 1965).
A collection of theoretical and analytical papers dealing with folklore from a variety of perspectives: humanistic, literary, psychological, historical, and geographical. The essays explore such topics as the origins, processes, and forms of transmission of folklore.

Jacobs, M., and J. Greenway (Eds.): *The Anthropologist Looks at Myth,* American Folklore Society Bibliographical and Special Series, Vol. 17 (Austin: University of Texas Press, 1966).
A group of papers representing several varied approaches to the analysis of folklore, most of which discuss its relation to other cultural norms and goals.

Lomax, A.: *Folk Song Style and Culture* (Washington, D.C.: American Association for the Advancement of Science, Publication No. 88, 1968).
Describes a method of analyzing the stylistic elements of folksongs from societies around the world. Known as the Cantometrics Project, the data compiled were used to test hypotheses about the relationship of song style to other aspects of culture.

Merriam, A. P.: *The Anthropology of Music* (Evanston, Ill.: Northwestern University Press, 1964).
This book attempts to present music as a form of social behavior and thus subject to study using anthropological methods. It gives a detailed description of the various approaches to the study of ethnomusicology. Merriam also explores the use and function of music, which he discusses as a form of symbolic behavior, and the place of music in the study of social organization.

Munro, T.: *Evolution of the Arts and Other Theories of Culture History* (Cleveland: Cleveland Museum of Art, 1963).
Begins with a summary of the controversy over whether or not art follows an evolutionary pattern. Munro, following the evolutionary point of view as an art historian, sees art in naturalistic, empirical terms; his concern is not so much with aesthetics as with understanding art. He discusses major problems in the study of art such as the development of styles and traditions, complication and simplification in art, regressive trends and cumulative changes in art.

Wingert, P. S.: *Art of the South Pacific Islands* (New York: Beechhurst Press, 1953).
A well-illustrated catalogue of various art styles found in the South Pacific region, with both line drawings and photographs of actual objects which are identified by their present location, material, and size. In the short text of the work, Wingert discusses South Pacific art in terms of the ethnic and cultural background of the five different regions: Indonesia, Melanesia, Australia, Micronesia, and Polynesia.

Wingert, P. S.: *Primitive Art: Its Traditions and Styles* (New York: Oxford University Press, 1962).
Written as an introduction to primitive art, the author discusses the function, motivation, and meaning of art in primitive societies. Part 1 discusses the idea of art in primitive populations and the characteristic features of primitive art. Part 2, which is the longest section, surveys the major areas of primitive art and characterizes the significant forms within each area. Part 3 is devoted to comparisons of stylistic elements common to all forms of primitive art.

21
Culture and Personality

Customs and traditions vary widely from society to society, as we have seen in earlier chapters. The Nupe, for instance, developed centralized institutions of government and law; the Eskimos managed to get along without either. Some societies have a money economy in which goods and services are bought and sold; in other societies goods and services are distributed only by reciprocal gift giving. Such differences and others we have dealt with so far are by definition cultural, by which we mean that societies resemble or differ from one another with regard to their socially learned and shared patterns of behavior, beliefs, and attitudes. In this chapter we deal with another aspect of cultural variation—differences between societies with regard to common personality characteristics.

An individual's personality, the result of a complex interplay of forces, can be seen as the distinctive way he or she thinks, feels, and behaves. Each person is born unique and with certain inherited tendencies that influence his personality, but the society in which he lives may exert an even more powerful influence on his personality. The process of sharing and learning that produces other distinctive aspects of a society's culture also produces distinctive personality traits. Thus we may say that certain personality characteristics arise out of the individual's cultural conditioning; or, to put it another way, each society produces certain typical personality traits. For instance, in traditional Arab societies most women behave in a shy and withdrawn manner, whereas women in some Polynesian groups tend to be sexually bold. If such personality traits are, in fact, commonly learned, they are by definition cultural.

What accounts for personality differences in the world's societies? In this chapter, we shall discuss how personality traits are assessed by the trained observer, how a particular personality trait may become prominent in a particular society, and how typical personality traits themselves might influence other aspects of culture.

HOW PERSONALITY IS FORMED

It is generally agreed that an individual's personality is the result of an interaction between his genetic inheritance and his life experiences, although there is not much known yet about what specific factors give rise to which specific personality traits. To the extent, then, that all individuals have a unique combination of genetic traits and life experiences, we can say that in some ways no person is like any other person. But a considerable portion of one's life experiences (as well as of one's genes) are shared with others. Let us consider life experiences. Many life experiences occur within the context of family life, so much so that we often say a child's personality is shaped by the way he is brought up by his family. By virtue of this fact, the personality of members of the same family may resemble each other. But we have to consider why a particular family raises children the way it does. To some extent all families are unique; but much of the way parents rear children is influenced by their culture—by the typical patterns of family life and by shared conceptions of the "right" way to bring up children.

It is not easy to see how much members of our society share conceptions of the "right" way to bring up children, because as one looks around at various families one observes differences in upbringing. And it is these differences which often give rise to speculation about why individuals differ. It is only when we examine other societies and their patterns of child rearing that our cultural conceptions begin to become apparent. For example, we noted (in Chapter 2) that Yanomamö parents believe that children, when angry, should be aggressive to their parents—even permitting and some times encouraging them to slap their parents' faces. Although American children on occasion might slap their parents, few American parents (even in the most permissive homes) would permit such behavior, and they certainly would not encourage it.

Immediately after a child is born, the cultural conceptions of appropriate child rearing are implemented. The Marquesans of the South Pacific believe that nursing makes a child difficult to raise. Consequently, feeding is irregular and dependent on the feelings of the adult rather than the convenience of the child. In contrast, the Chenchu of India do not wean children until they are five or six.[1] In most societies, toilet training becomes intensive after the second year, but there are marked differences in the techniques used to reach the same goal. The natives of Dahomey, in West Africa, punish bed soilers by pouring a mixture of ashes and water over the head of the offender or by attaching "a live frog . . . to the child's waist, which so frightens [it] that a cure is usually effected."[2] Attitudes toward masturbation in children also vary: the Alorese of Indonesia regularly masturbate their children to pacify them; the Manus of New Guinea, however, tend to believe masturbation shameful, and our own American culture generally attempts to prevent or restrict the habit in children. Attitudes toward sex play differ, from the more restrictive approaches of the Chiricahua Apache of the American Southwest, who separate the sexes by the seventh year, to the Baiga of southern Asia, who encourage young children to engage in erotic play. The Hopi fill their young with dire warnings of the consequences of too early sexual experience, telling boys to abstain lest they become dwarfs and small girls that they will become pregnant, thereby causing all people to die and the world to come to an end.[3]

Societies also differ in their encouragement of dependency: Kwoma mothers of New Guinea keep their infants nearby at all times and respond to their every whim; the Ainu mother of northern Japan, on the other hand, places her child in a hanging cradle during the day and lets it fend for itself, which usually means

[1] John W. M. Whiting and Irvin L. Child, *Child Training and Personality* (New Haven: Yale University Press, 1953), pp. 69–71.

[2] M. J. Herskovits, *Dahomey: An Ancient West African Kingdom* (New York: Augustin, 1938), pp. 272–273, quoted in Whiting and Child, *Child Training and Personality,* p. 75.

[3] Whiting and Child, *Child Training and Personality,* pp. 80–83.

The Arts

Body decoration often has ceremonial significance. Here, a masked dancer of the Iatmul people (New Guinea) represents a clan ancestor in a pageant of the creation of the world. (Courtesy of the American Museum of Natural History.)

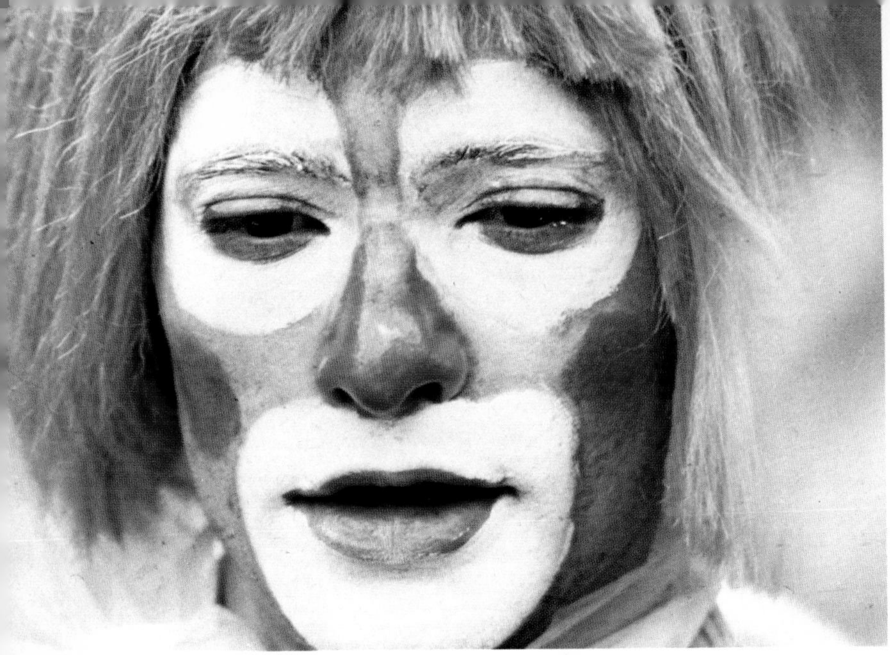

Face painting is also practiced in Western societies. This clown has decorated his face for a European carnival. (Courtesy Francisco Hidalgo, Woodfin Camp and Associates.)

A Tanna woman from the New Hebrides Islands wearing traditional red face paint and a necklace of leaves. She is decorated for a dance which celebrates the planting of yams. (Courtesy Kal Muller, Woodfin Camp and Associates.)

Body decoration may indicate status. This Indian boy's red forehead mark and jeweled clothing identify him as a prince. (Courtesy, Raghubir Singh, Woodfin Camp and Associates.)

This Siona Indian chief from Colombia decorates his face according to tribal tradition. (Courtesy Loren McIntyre, Woodfin Camp and Associates.)

This devil dancing mask from Ceylon is one of a group of masks used to drive diseased spirits from a person or an area. The mask is made of wood. (Courtesy of the American Museum of Natural History.)

A wooden mask of the Iroquois Indian False Face Society of curers. The mask is worn to ward off evil spirits. (Courtesy of the American Museum of Natural History.)

Made by a carver in the Kasai region of the Congo, this mask is used in initiation and divination ceremonies. The mask is made of wood and has a rafia beard. (Courtesy of the American Museum of Natural History.)

On the Ivory Coast, Ashanti tribe members perform a ceremony marking both the New Year and initiation rites. (Courtesy Marc and Evelyne Bernheim, Woodfin Camp and Associates.)

The Oruro of Bolivia are performing a Devil Dance, a Christian-pagan ceremony. The dance is part of the Pageant of the Seven Cardinal Sins that originated in the eighteenth century. (Courtesy Loren McIntyre, Woodfin Camp and Associates.)

"a good deal of kicking and screaming until tired of it, followed by exhaustion, repose, and resignation."[4]

As these examples suggest, societies vary in how they customarily bring up children. Differences appear not only in infancy but throughout childhood and adolescence. If we assume that the way children are reared in part determines the type of personality they will have, then it follows that different societies, with differing customs of child rearing, will tend to produce different kinds of people. Or, to put it another way, it follows that if persons in a particular society are brought up similarly, they will tend to share many personality characteristics. This is not to suggest that personalities are not unique—even though many people in a society may share certain personality traits. An individual's uniqueness is derived from his unique genetic endowment and unique life experiences—and thus one personality will always be different from another.

Inasmuch as cultural anthropologists are interested in shared patterns of behavior, belief, and feeling, they are interested in those aspects of personality which are typically shared with others, with other members of the society or with other members of some subcultural group.

Modal Personality

The typical personality in a particular society is often referred to in terms of *modal personality* characteristics, those characteristics most frequently exhibited by individuals in the society. Personality characteristics can usually be thought of as more or less of a particular attribute. For example, in describing an individual we may say that he is particularly aggressive, meaning that he is more apt than other people to exhibit physical or verbal aggression in certain situations. Aggression is not present or absent in a person but is exhibited in greater or less frequency in some people than in others. Similarly, we may say that the exhibition of a great deal of physical or verbal aggression is a modal personality trait in some societies. Such a judgment is always relative, contrasting one society with others. When we speak of a modal personality characteristic such as aggressiveness, we do not mean that all individuals in that society exhibit a great deal of physical or verbal aggression, only that most people in the society exhibit more aggressiveness than most people in some other society. For example, the Yanomamö Indians are described by Napoleon Chagnon, who did fieldwork among them, as exhibiting a great deal of aggression in their interpersonal relationships. Threats and shouting frequently characterize demands, and a man's potential for violence is often demonstrated. Chagnon suspects that this is why wives are beaten frequently, "since men can display their ferocity and show others that they are capable of violence."[5] As compared with other societies, the Yanomamö would rank high on aggressiveness as a modal personality trait.

When we deal with variation in modal personality from society to society, we are generally dealing with cultural variation. For as we have defined it, culture consists of learned and shared patterns of behavior, beliefs, and feelings. Personality too consists in part of learned ways of behaving and feeling. And inasmuch as modal personality characteristics are the most frequently exhibited personality characteristics in a society, they are shared and, hence, cultural characteristics.

Just as culture is never fixed or static, so modal personality is never static. As life ex-

[4] B. D. Howard, *Life with Trans-Siberian Savages* (London: Longmans, Green, 1893), p. 67, as quoted in Whiting and Child, *Child Training and Personality,* p. 93.

[5] Napoleon A. Chagnon, *Yanomamö, the Fierce People* (New York: Holt, Rinehart and Winston, 1968), p. 9.

periences change in a society, we would expect changes in modal personality. Individuals often alter their behavior in adaptation to changing circumstances, and when enough individuals in a society have altered their own behavior or the way they bring up their children, modal personality characteristics will presumably have also changed.

Methods of Assessing Modal Personality. A number of methods are available to the anthropologist to determine the modal personality traits in a particular society or subcultural group. Generally these methods are similar to, in fact frequently derived from, the procedures used by psychologists to assess individual personality characteristics. They include *observation,* the *collection of life histories, projective tests,* and the *analysis of cultural materials.* Whatever the method selected, the assessment of personality must be made so as to be representative of the population studied if the anthropologist is to arrive at a valid determination of modal personality characteristics. This can be done by measuring personality traits in a representative sample of individuals from a community or a society and determining the most frequent traits. Or, personality assessments may be made from certain cultural materials which presumably reflect the modal or typical personality.

Observation of Behavior. Investigators may obtain their information by closely studying the way people behave, what they say, how they perform tasks, even the postures they take and the emotions they do or do not show in their activities.

Systematic behavior observations are commonly employed in psychology to assess individual personality traits. In psychological research, behavior observations typically take place in controlled settings (such as a laboratory) or in standardized situations (such as a waiting room). The anthropological use of behavior observation, on the other hand, requires some alteration in strategy and technique, since observation more typically takes place in natural settings. In the natural setting, the observer must cope with the problem of interfering with natural reactions and routines. Not only is the observer a stranger, but he is often engaged in the fairly strange behavior of recording behavior. Since he is inevitably visible, the researcher has to make the choice of interacting with the persons he is observing or attempting to remain uninvolved and ignored.

Since behavior observation is a time-consuming and difficult process, the anthropologist has to decide whether the information may not be more easily obtained in some other way. Observation may be necessary when persons are unable to report accurately upon a particular type of behavior themselves, perhaps because the behavior patterns are unconscious and cannot be verbalized, or because behavior patterns conflict with the ideals of the society. If the researcher decides that observation is the only way to accurately assess a domain of behavior of interest to him, he must then carefully map out a plan for exactly what to observe, how to observe, and whom to observe. An observer cannot possibly record everything he sees; he must focus on particular types of behaviors taking place between certain persons or in certain situations.[6] Even if modern equipment such as a movie or videotape camera is used, the observer must still decide who and what are to be focused on.

Life Histories. These may take the form of biographies or "autobiographies" of individuals in a particular society. Life histories can be especially useful in disclosing an individual's values and attitudes and can produce significant information about childhood experiences. The effectiveness of this method greatly depends on how the anthropologist is regarded

[6] Beatrice Whiting and John Whiting, "Methods for Observing and Recording Behavior," in Raoul Naroll and Ronald Cohen, eds., *A Handbook of Methods in Cultural Anthropology* (Garden City, N.Y.: Natural History Press, 1970), pp. 282–315.

by the group and on his skills in interviewing. First, he must establish trust and respect. Sensitivity to the personality of the subject and patience are other requisites for obtaining reliable data. Themes that recur are noted, as are the underlying attitudes and values of the subject. The content of dreams, visions, and fantasies also offers clues to personality factors. Life histories representing a cross-section of the society, however, are often extremely difficult for the anthropologist to obtain. Successful members of the community are either too busy or too uninterested to cooperate. In fact, it has been suggested that life history informants may be some of the more maladjusted individuals in the society. After all, what is the motivation to spend a great deal of time talking to the anthropologist?[7] Another difficulty in collecting biographical materials is that anthropologists are often unable to attain proficiency in the native language. Cora Du Bois made conscientious efforts to acquire fluency, yet she found it necessary to continue employing an interpreter and to cross-check all her translations even after a year of studying the people of Alor.[8]

Projective Tests. Projective tests are called "projective" because they utilize stimuli that are so ambiguous that the test subject, in order to respond to those stimuli, is obliged to structure them according to his own preoccupations, needs, and conflicts—which are largely unconscious. Hence he is "projecting" his personality traits into the ambiguous test stimuli. Projective analysis takes various forms, including the interpretation of word associations and drawings. Two widely used tests are the Rorschach and the Thematic Apperception Test (TAT).

The Rorschach, invented by Hermann Rorschach, a Swiss psychiatrist, and published in 1922, consists of ten cards, each carrying an ink blot. These are always shown in the same order to each subject tested. The subject is asked to describe what he sees in the various shapes. From the kinds of images or ideas he reports, inferences can be made about his personality. For example, what one person might see as a female form, another might see as a vase. Tendencies to see the blots a certain way have also been noted in several societies. Samoans, Algerians, and Tuscarora Indians tend to see the blot whole, for example, while Zuni children tend to see it in many details.

The TAT uses a series of pictures, also shown to the subject in a given order. He is asked to tell what is going on in each illustration (which usually depicts some life situation), what happened before the scene, and how he thinks things will turn out. The narratives are then studied for insights into the subject's needs and conflicts. In an early TAT study, Henry tested 102 Hopi children using illustrations that had been redrawn by an Indian artist, so that the individuals depicted looked like Indians and the settings looked like Hopi settings. Their responses offered evidence, for example, that individual strivings are suppressed in deference to the group, and that such suppression gives rise to anxiety feelings. Their TAT stories suggested that the Hopi alleviate their anxiety with such release mechanisms as malicious gossip, sibling jealousy, and acts of stealing and destruction.[9]

One of the difficulties in the cross-cultural use of such tests as the Rorschach and the TAT is that interpretations are often culture-bound in the sense that they may be based on Western psychiatric concepts which do not necessarily pertain to individuals functioning in a very different kind of society. As Lindzey has pointed out, "it remains clear that the investigator who employs these techniques in

[7] Victor Barnouw, *Culture and Personality* (Homewood, Ill.: Dorsey Press, 1963), pp. 198–199.

[8] Cora Du Bois, *The People of Alor: A Social-Psychological Study of an East Indian Island* (Minneapolis: University of Minnesota Press, 1944).

[9] William E. Henry, *The Thematic Apperception Technique in the Study of Culture-Personality Relations,* Genetic Psychology Monograph, No. 35 (1947), p. 91.

a stereotyped manner completely consistent with that used in psychiatric diagnosis is not likely to secure information of maximum utility to the person concerned with personality in a cultural setting."[10] Care must be taken to ensure that interpretations do not simply reflect Western culture.

Analysis of Cultural Materials. Folktales, myths, and legends are a rich source of information about modal personality as well as other cultural features of a society. Such cultural materials can be seen as similar to projective materials, like the responses to the Rorschach or the TAT. Thus, it has been argued that the currency or popularity of a particular folktale in a society must be a response to certain needs and conflicts that are generally shared by the members of that society. That is, the people's attachment to the folktale is considered a projection of some of their modal personality characteristics.

McClelland, for example, measured the strength of the need to achieve in nonliterate societies through an analysis of the content of popular folktales, "on the assumption that since these stories are told and retold orally by many different people in the culture, the way in which they are told will come to reflect a kind of 'average level' of motivation among people of the tribe." The stories themselves resemble in many ways the "kinds of simple stories told by our subjects to pictures," McClelland writes, drawing a parallel between his method and the TAT.[11]

The assumption that folktales are projective of modal personality traits is supported by studies linking child-training practices in a society to measures of modal personality based on folktales. For example, Child, Storm, and Veroff found that societies with high reward for achievement in child training have a good deal of achievement motivation expressed in folktales.[12] Wright found that societies which severely punished children for aggression tend to have folktales in which aggression tended to be removed from the hero (the character usually identified with in a folktale) and more associated with strangers or individuals least like the hero. This indicates that the exhibition of aggression in folktales may indicate anxiety about aggression as perhaps felt in real life. Thus, the manifestation of aggression in a folktale may reflect typical anxieties and conflicts.[13]

The comparative study of posture and gesture may also involve a kind of projective analysis. In one such study, Gregory Bateson and Margaret Mead analyzed Balinese postures and rhythms, especially as observed in dance movements, for clues to Balinese personality. For example, they suggest that the slowness and deliberateness of many Balinese movements indicates passivity.[14] Some cultural anthropologists have extended this type of analysis to painting, music, sculpture, and other art forms. For example, Anthony Wallace has made a detailed examination of Lowland Mayan art, on the basis of which he has suggested that the Maya were introspective and "polite and formal" in social relationships.[15]

To understand why there is cultural variation

[10] Gardner Lindzey, *Projective Techniques and Cross-Cultural Research* (New York: Appleton-Century-Crofts, 1961), p. 184.

[11] David C. McClelland, *The Achieving Society* (New York: D. Van Nostrand, 1961), p. 64.

[12] I. L. Child, T. Storm, and J. Veroff, "Achievement Themes in Folktales Related to Socialization Practice," in J. W. Atkinson, ed., *Motives in Fantasy, Action and Society* (Princeton, N.J.: Van Nostrand, 1958), pp. 479–492.

[13] George O. Wright, "Projection and Displacement: A Cross-Cultural Study of Folk-Tale Aggression," *Journal of Abnormal and Social Psychology,* Vol. 49 (1954), pp. 523–528.

[14] Gregory Bateson and Margaret Mead, *Balinese Character, A Photographic Analysis* (New York: Special Publication of New York Academy of Sciences, 1942), p. 15.

[15] Anthony F. C. Wallace, "A Possible Technique for Recognizing Psychological Characteristics of the Ancient Maya from an Analysis of Their Art," *American Imago,* Vol. 7 (1950), p. 245.

in modal personality, we may pose two questions: What customs of child rearing may account for the observed differences in modal personality? And, what accounts for those differences in child rearing?

VARIATION IN MODAL PERSONALITY

Child Rearing and Modal Personality: Field Studies

Socialization or *enculturation* are terms used by both anthropologists and psychologists to describe the development, through the influence of parents and others, of patterns of behavior in children that conform to the standards deemed appropriate by the culture. Although we make the general assumption that differences in child rearing account in part for personality differences, we need to understand exactly which differences in child training make for which differences in personality. If we are to understand why the modal personality of one society differs from that of other societies we must understand first what child-rearing customs might account for the difference.

To determine cause and effect in personality, the pioneer anthropologists in the field like Margaret Mead, Ruth Benedict, and Cora Du Bois often concentrated on a single society or at most compared a few societies, seeking links between child-rearing customs and adult personality traits.

The People of Alor. Du Bois spent almost 18 months on the island of Alor, in eastern Indonesia, studying the native Alorese. She termed her study a psychocultural synthesis, and in it she used three approaches: (1) a delineation of the psychocultural environment of her subjects from infancy to adulthood; (2) the interpretation of eight biographies, each with dream material; and (3) the administration and interpretation of a broad range of projective tests—including the Rorschach, using 37 subjects; a word-association test, using 36 subjects; and interpretation of the drawings of 55 children.[16]

Du Bois broke new ground when she asked specialists in various fields to assess and interpret her projective materials independently. These authorities were given no background briefing on Alorese culture or attitudes, neither were they permitted to see Du Bois's general ethnographic notes or interpretations. Abram Kardiner was given the life histories, Emil Oberholzer the Rorschachs, and Trude Schmidl-Waehner the children's drawings. Working with only these materials, each prepared an evaluation. The effectiveness of the test procedures employed by Du Bois, and her success in eliminating her own emotional or cultural biases, were confirmed by the work of these independent authorities. To a remarkable degree, their findings concurred with hers.

A rather unfavorable modal personality for the Alorese emerges from this many-sided investigation. Alorese of both sexes are described by Du Bois and her colleagues as suspicious and antagonistic, prone to violent and emotional outbursts often of a jealous nature, as tending to be uninterested in the world around them, slovenly in workmanship and lacking an interest in goals. Kardiner drew attention to the absence of idealized parental figures in the life stories; Oberholzer noted the lack of capacity for sustained creative effort, indicated by his reading of the Rorschach scores; and Schmidl-Waehner identified a lack of imagination and a strong sense of loneliness manifested in the children's drawings.

Turning to the possible causative influences, Du Bois and her fellow researchers focused on the experiences of the Alorese during infancy and early childhood, up to the age of

[16] Du Bois, *The People of Alor.*

six or so. At the root of much of Alorese personality development, they suggested, is the division of labor in that society. Women are the major food suppliers, working daily in the family gardens, while men occupy themselves with commercial affairs, usually the trading of pigs, gongs, and kettledrums. Within about two weeks after giving birth, the mother returns to her outdoor work, leaving the infant with the father, a grandparent, or an older sibling—depriving the newborn child of the comfort of a maternal presence and of breast feeding for most of the day. In Freudian terms, the infant experiences oral frustration and the resultant anxiety. At the same time, he experiences bewildering switches in attention, from loving and petting to neglect and bad-tempered rejection.

In early childhood, the psychological pressures on the youngster increase, as Du Bois relates:

> I see it [early childhood] as the period that inflicts hunger, desertion, and discomfort, even to the point of pain, on children who have at their disposal no mechanisms of defense or mastery, either physical or mental, by which they can deal adequately with the outer world. Rebellion and protest may not be the necessary concomitants of these frustrations, but when these are linked with inconsistency of discipline and when there is no system of rewards for "being good", nothing but vigorous emotional assertion is left as the mode of expression. When the child's sense of helplessness is further reinforced by contrast with a more favorable situation in infancy . . . temper tantrums are the obvious device open to the child for achieving his ends.[17]

These tantrums, in which a child expresses its frustration by hurling itself to the ground, kicking, and screaming, are seen as the basis of future tensions in male-female relationships. The husband is seeking a nurturing mother, his wife a warm and sympathetic father, yet neither one is capable of satisfying the other's need. The modal personality Du Bois and her team have delineated for the people of Alor has generally been accepted on the basis of the corroborative data. However, the study has been criticized for the weight given to maternal neglect in infancy and early childhood. It has been suggested that the investigators should have taken into account the prevalence of debilitating diseases, especially yaws, a factor actually considered but rejected by Du Bois. Another criticism stems from a factor also conscientiously noted by Du Bois—namely, the lack of a truly representative sample in her life history section. It is felt that 8 biographies and 37 Rorschachs are insufficient as a basis for generalizations about the modal personality of a group of 600 people.

Anthropologists assume that differences in childrearing practices are to a large extent responsible for differences in adult personality. They seek to determine the variations in child training that result in specific differences in personality. Many anthropologists now believe that hypotheses about socialization processes and their effect on adult personality are more valid when supported by studies made in several cultures rather than in a single one, for a connection found in only one culture may not be found in others. For example, in the investigations of Japanese national character made separately by Gorer[18] and La Barre,[19] each suggested a link between severe anal training and deeply hidden feelings of aggressiveness. The explanation given for latent hostility was that the child resents being compelled to do something he does not understand at a time when his muscles are insufficiently developed to accomplish what is expected of him.[20] But the

[17] Du Bois, *The People of Alor,* p. 54.

[18] Geoffrey Gorer, "Themes in Japanese Culture," *Transactions of the New York Academy of Science,* Series II, Vol. 5, No. 5 (1943), pp. 106–124.

[19] Weston La Barre, "Some Observations on Character Structure in the Orient: The Japanese," *Psychiatry,* Vol. 8 (1945), pp. 35–42.

[20] Douglas G. Haring, ed., *Personal Character and Cultural Milieu, a Collection of Readings* (Syracuse: Syracuse University Press, 1949), pp. 273–290.

Russian babies, tightly swaddled. Gorer hypothesized that this cultural practice affected personality development. (Tass from Sovfoto.)

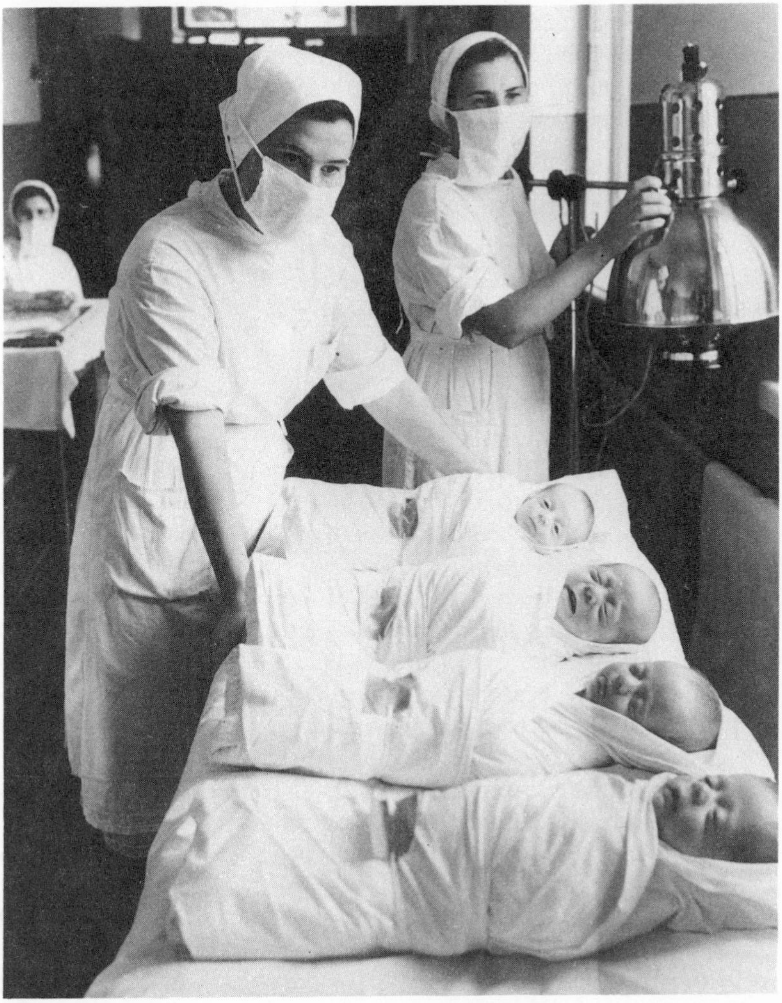

evidence for this hypothesis was not conclusive, since the data came from only one society. The suggested association may or may not be found in other societies; therefore, confirming evidence is needed from a cross-cultural study if we are to conclude that the hypothesis is probably correct.

Gorer's "swaddling hypothesis" is another case in point. In a study co-authored with Rickman in 1950,[21] Gorer suggested that the custom of child swaddling is the key to an understanding of the Great Russian character. From the day of its birth,

> The baby is tightly swaddled in long strips of material, holding its legs straight and its arms down by its sides. . . . When swaddled the baby is completely rigid; one informant said the infants were like sticks, another likened them to sausages, a third to parcels. The baby can be held in any position or by any part of it without bending.[22]

[21] Geoffrey Gorer and John Rickman, *The People of Great Russia* (New York: Chanticleer Press, 1950), p.14.

[22] Gorer and Rickman, *The People of Great Russia,* pp. 97–99.

The authors maintain that this physical restraint against a child's natural desire for movement induces manic-depressive variations of mood characteristic of the "Great Russian personality." Thus, Russians are fond of huge feasts and drinking bouts because the release of the bindings in their infancy was always accompanied by food and love; they are ready to confess even uncommitted sins, because of unconscious guilt feelings arising from rage induced by bindings. They also feel that a strong authority is necessary because they were subjected to very tight swaddling in infancy.

This hypothesis was almost immediately attacked because of the inadequacy of its sample base and because it overlooked the fact that child-training practices had undergone radical changes with the accession to power of the Bolsheviks in 1917. Today, critics would also point out that the study failed to test its central hypothesis against data from other societies. If other societies that practice swaddling or its equivalent were found to exhibit manic-depressive tendencies, the Gorer–Rickman hypothesis might receive greater acceptance.

The analysis of a single society, then, even if the descriptions are correct, is not sufficient to justify the conclusion that specific child-rearing customs are related to specific adult personality characteristics. Nevertheless, studies of single societies have a value in that they suggest possible connections for testing by comparative, or cross-cultural, studies. Also, if several single-society studies show the same relationship between a child-rearing custom and a personality trait, we can be more confident that the hypothesis linking them may be correct.

Societal Influences on Child Rearing and Personality

The cultural anthropologist seeks not only to establish connections between child-rearing customs and personality traits but to learn why those child-rearing customs differ in the first place. Some anthropologists believe that child-rearing practices are largely adaptive—that societies generally produce the kinds of personalities that are best suited to perform the activities necessary for the survival of the society. As Whiting and Child express it: "the economic, political and social organs of a society—the basic customs surrounding the nourishment, sheltering and protection of its members . . . seem a likely source of influence on child training practices."[23] The belief that child-rearing practices are generally adaptive does not mean that societies always produce the kinds of persons they need. Just as in the biological realm, where we see poor adaptations and extinctions of species and subspecies, so we may expect that societies sometimes produce modal personalities that are maladapted to the requirements of living in that society. However, we expect that most societies that survived to be recorded have produced generally adaptive modal personalities.

Economic requirements are related to child rearing practices in a study made by Barry, Child, and Bacon to determine why some societies strive to develop compliant children while others aim for self-reliance and individual initiative.[24] Based on cross-cultural evidence, the authors found that agricultural and herding societies are more likely to stress compliance, while hunting and gathering societies tend to stress individual assertion. Their theory is that agricultural and herding societies cannot afford departures from established routine since such departures might jeopardize the food supply for long periods of time, whereas departures from

[23] Whiting and Child, *Child Training and Personality,* p. 310.

[24] Herbert Barry, III, Irvin L. Child, and Margaret K. Bacon, "Relation of Child Training to Subsistence Economy," *American Anthropologist,* Vol. 61, No. 1 (February 1959), pp. 51–63.

routine in a hunter-gatherer society cannot cause much damage to a food supply that has to be collected anew almost every day. Indeed, trying out new techniques may have some advantage in hunter-gatherer societies.

Melvin Kohn has offered a parallel interpretation for the differences between working- and middle-class values about child rearing in our own society.[25] Working-class parents, Kohn writes:

> value obedience, neatness and cleanliness more highly than do middle class parents, and middle class parents in turn value curiosity, happiness, consideration, and—most importantly—self-control more highly than do working class parents; . . . working class parental values center on conformity to external proscriptions, middle class . . . on *self*-direction. To working class parents it is the overt act that matters: the child should not transgress externally imposed rules; to middle class parents it is the child's motives and feelings that matter: the child should govern himself.[26]

Kohn believes that these differences in outlook derive from differences in the working conditions of the two classes. Work done by members of the middle class generally requires initiative and self-direction, whereas those in the working class are generally expected to follow rules handed down by someone in authority. The parents' own occupational experiences, Kohn notes, "have significantly affected [their] conceptions of what is desirable behavior, on or off the job, for adults or for children."[27]

In another study, Barry, Bacon, and Child address themselves to a question of mounting interest in our own culture: why do some societies try to socialize boys and girls to be very different, while others do not stress differences so much? The difference is in degree; the general tendency is for most societies to pressure boys to be more self-reliant, independent, and achievement oriented, and girls to be more responsible and obedient. In their cross-cultural study of sex differences, using a sample of 110 cultures, the authors suggest first that there is more differentiation in cultures where physical strength of males is required. In this context, they found "large sex differences in socialization with the hunting of large animals, with grain rather than root crops, with the keeping of larger rather than smaller animals, and with nomadic rather than sedentary existence." They also suggest that the socialization of boys and girls is less different in independent nuclear families than in extended families. "The nuclear family in our society is often so isolated that husband and wife must each be prepared at times to take over or help in the household tasks normally assigned to the other."[28]

Child-rearing practices may also be affected by family form and social conditions in the household. For example, Minturn and Lambert report on the basis of data from a study of six cultures that children tend to be more strongly punished for fighting with others when the family lives in cramped quarters, and that the more people living in a house, the less apt a mother is to permit disobedience.[29] These findings are consistent with the findings of a cross-cultural study conducted by John Whiting that societies with extended-family households are more likely to severely punish aggression in children than those with nuclear families.[30]

[25] Melvin L. Kohn, "Social Class and Parent-Child Relationships: An Interpretation," *American Journal of Sociology,* Vol. 68 (1963), pp. 471–480.
[26] *Ibid.,* p. 475.
[27] *Ibid.,* p. 476.

[28] Herbert Barry, III, Margaret K. Bacon, and Irvin L. Child, "A Cross-Cultural Survey of Some Sex Differences in Socialization," *Journal of Abnormal and Social Psychology,* Vol. 55 (November 1957), pp. 327–332.
[29] Leigh Minturn and William W. Lambert, *Mothers of Six Cultures: Antecedents of Child Rearing* (New York: John Wiley and Sons, 1964), p. 289.
[30] J. W. M. Whiting, "Cultural and Sociological Influences on Development" in *Growth and Development of the Child in His Setting* (Maryland: Maryland Child Growth and Development Institute, 1959).

PERSONALITY AS INTEGRATING CULTURE

Some anthropologists as well as other students of human variation have suggested that personality or psychological processes may account for connections between two or more aspects of culture. Whiting and Child refer to this sort of connection as *personality integration of culture.* Thus if certain aspects of culture such as child-rearing customs influence the formation of certain personality traits, and these personality traits in turn give rise to other customs, then we have a case in which personality processes help us to understand the link between two aspects of culture.[31]

Kardiner, too, has suggested that cultural aspects influence personality through child rearing, and that the resulting personality in turn influences the culture. He suggests that *primary institutions,* such as family organization and subsistence techniques, are the source of early experiences that help form the basic personality. Personality, in turn, influences the growth of such *secondary institutions* as religion, folktales, and ways of thinking.[32] Presumably these secondary institutions have little connection to the adaptive requirements of society. But some of these aspects of culture like art, music, and folklore may reflect and express the motives, conflicts, and anxieties of typical members of the society. If so, then we may perhaps best understand these aspects of society by investigating the intervening personality processes which may produce them. As an example of how personality processes may integrate culture, we turn to some suggested explanations for cultural preferences for games and for the custom of male initiation ceremonies.

Cultural preferences for particular types of games have been found to be related to certain aspects of child rearing in a cross-cultural study conducted by Roberts and Sutton-Smith.[33] They suggest that these associations may be a consequence of certain conflicts generated in many people in a society by particular types of child-rearing pressures. Games of strategy, for example, are associated with child training that emphasizes obedience. Roberts and Sutton-Smith suggest that severe obedience training can create a conflict between the need to obey and the desire not to obey, arousing anxiety, and that such anxiety may or may not manifest itself against the person who instigates the anxiety. In any case, the conflict and the aggression itself can be played out on the miniature battlefields of games of strategy such as chess, or the Japanese game of Go. Similarly, games of chance may represent defiance of societal expectations of docility and responsibility. The general interpretation suggested by Roberts and Sutton-Smith is that players (and societies) initially become curious about games, learn them, and ultimately acquire high involvement in them because of particular kinds of psychological conflicts that are handled or expressed, but not necessarily finally resolved, by the games.[34]

The possible role of psychological processes in connecting different aspects of culture is also illustrated in cross-cultural work on male initiation ceremonies for boys at adolescence. In the ceremony, boys are subjected to painful tests of manhood, usually including genital operations, which indicate a boy's transition to adulthood. Burton and Whiting found that initiation ceremonies tend to occur in patrilocal societies in which infant boys initially sleep exclusively with their mothers. They suggest that initiation rites are found in such societies to break a con-

[31] Whiting and Child, *Child Training and Personality,* pp. 32–38

[32] Abram Kardiner, *The Individual and His Society* (New York: Golden Press, 1946), p. 471.

[33] John M. Roberts and Brian Sutton-Smith, "Child Training and Game Involvement," *Ethnology,* Vol. 1, No. 2 (April 1962), pp. 166–185.

[34] *Ibid.,* p. 178.

Above, Italian boys are playing LaMorra, a game of chance. Below, Japanese students playing Go, a game of strategy. (Top: David Seymour, Magnum Photos; bottom: Hiroshi Hamaya, Magnum Photos.)

flict in sex identity. The conflict is said to exist because boys in such societies would initially identify with their mothers who exercise almost complete control over them in infancy. Later, when they discover that men dominate the society, they would identify secondarily with their fathers. This sex-role conflict is assumed to be resolved by the initiation ceremony which demonstrates a boy's manhood, thus strengthening the secondary identification.[35]

The assumption that boys will need to identify with the controlling members of the society, whether male or female, has been linked to the practice of *couvade,* in which the husband in a female-dominated society attempts to participate in the birth process by closely imitating his wife in labor. A point made here is that in such societies no conflict arises between the childhood identification of boys with their mothers and their subsequent adult identification as males. Indeed, in such female-dominated societies, a man may be culturally permitted to act out his feminine identification.[36] If this theory is correct, sex-role conflict may be a psychological mechanism accounting for the relationship between initiation rites and couvade, on the one hand, and aspects of child training on the other.

CULTURE AND MENTAL ILLNESS

Throughout the chapter, we have been discussing the interaction between culture and personality, with an emphasis on modal personality traits. But cultures may also influence the development of *abnormal personalities.* It was once generally held that only the more complex, Euro-American cultures produced serious mental disorders and members of primitive societies were regarded as uncomplicated and free of neuroses. This view has recently been greatly modified. Many primitive cultures offer evidence of aberrant behavior, apparently as a result of mental illness. Among the questions raised by anthropologists have been: Is the rate of mental illness lower in technologically simple, nonliterate societies than in complex ones such as our own? Is it more difficult for individuals to adjust to some cultures than to others? What, in fact, constitutes mental "abnormality?"

This last point is crucial to the discussion, for it points to differing standards of normal behavior among the world's cultures. Many German officials, for instance, were regarded in every way as normal by their neighbors and fellow workers during the period of Nazi control, although they committed acts of inhumanity which were so vicious that to many observers in other Western societies they appeared criminally insane. The Saora of Orissa (India) provide another example of behavior normal to one culture but abnormal to another. The Saora take for granted that certain of their womenfolk regularly are courted by lovers from the supernatural world, marry them, and have children (who are never seen yet allegedly are suckled at night).[37] Behavior that is so alien to our own makes it no easy task to identify mental illness in other societies, let alone compare more complex and less complex societies for rates of mental disorder.

Whether we use absolute or culturally relative standards to define mental illness, it seems that some forms of mental illness appear in some societies and not in others. Great interest has been shown, for example, in the *Wiitiko* psychosis, a form of mental disorder found mostly among the males of some North Ameri-

[35] Roger V. Burton and John W. M. Whiting, "The Absent Father and Cross-Sex Identity," *Merrill Palmer Quarterly of Behavior and Development,* Vol. 7, No. 2 (1961), pp. 85–95.

[36] Burton and Whiting, "The Absent Father and Cross-Sex Identity," p. 91.

[37] Verrier Elwin, *The Religion of an Indian Tribe* (London: Oxford University Press, 1955), as cited in Barnouw, *Culture and Personality,* p. 364.

can Indian tribes, including the Ojibwa and Cree. The afflicted individual has the delusion that he is possessed by the spirit of a Wiitiko, a cannibal giant, and has hallucinations and cannibalistic impulses. One theory attributes the disorder to famine,[38] but critics have pointed out that not all of those afflicted with the psychosis are starving. A psychological reason has also been suggested: the subject sees the Wiitiko monster as a symbol of his mother who frustrated his dependency needs in childhood. He attempts to fight back by behaving like the monster, trying to destroy imagined persecutors by eating them.[39]

A mental disorder called *pibloktoq* occurs among some Eskimo adults of Greenland, usually women, who become oblivious to their surroundings and act in agitated, eccentric ways. They may strip themselves naked and wander across the ice and over hills until they collapse of exhaustion. Another disorder, *amok,* occurs in Malaya, Indonesia, and New Guinea. It is characterized by Honigmann as a "destructive maddened excitement . . . beginning with depression and followed by a period of brooding and withdrawal . . . [culminating in] the final mobilization of tremendous energy during which the 'wild man' runs destructively berserk."[40]

Mental disorders such as these used to be attributed to a combination of physical and psychological factors. The cold, dark, depressing aspects of arctic winters have become almost a cliché of anthropological description, as has the description of tropical regions as enervating. There is reason to suspect that such classifications stem more from the inconvenience of the stranger who makes the investigation than from the attitudes of the inhabitants, who generally have experienced no other environment. Similarly, theories that associate lack of satisfaction in childhood with later manifestations of hysteria are weakened by the fact that comparable conditions in other cultures do not always produce the disorder.

It has been suggested that certain mental illnesses like pibloktoq are not really different mental illnesses—they may merely be examples of an illness which is expressed differently in different societies. Honigmann suggests that this may be true in regard to pibloktoq. Here the hysteria ultimately subsides under the ministrations of friends and relatives. This "fits a social system like the Eskimo, where people are able freely to indulge their dependence; in a crisis it enables a distressed person dramatically to summon help and support."[41] A similar explanation has been offered for amok: "[it] discharges the individual from onerous social responsibilities without costing him social support." Amok usually occurs when a man has reached his early 30s and acquired heavy financial and social obligations which reflect his rise in power and social prestige. Once he has "run amok," an individual will be a marked man, but not in the way our society uses the term Honigmann sees amok as an "hysterical pattern of communication" and interprets its presence in the Gururumba of New Guinea in this way:

> His behavior has given evidence that he is less capable than others of withstanding pressures of social life. Hence neighbours reduce their expectations towards him, not pressing him to pay his debts promptly and not extracting from him prior commitments to provide food for feasts. He doesn't become an outcast, and he realizes he can't withdraw altogether from economic affairs, but he also knows he must limit his participation.[42]

[38] Ruth Landes, "The Abnormal among the Ojibwa," *Journal of Abnormal and Social Psychology,* Vol. 33 (1938), pp. 14–33.

[39] Seymour Parker, "The Wiitiko Psychosis in the Context of Ojibwa Personality and Culture," *American Anthropologist,* Vol. 62 (1962), p. 620.

[40] John J. Honigmann, *Personality in Culture* (New York: Harper & Row, 1967), pp. 398–406.

[41] Honigmann, *Personality in Culture,* p. 401.

[42] Honigmann, *Personality in Culture,* p. 406.

More recently, Wallace has offered a theory that biological factors such as calcium deficiency may cause hysteria, and that dietary improvement may account for its decline in the Western world since the nineteenth century.[43] By the early twentieth century, the discovery of the value of good nutrition and changes in social conditions led many people to drink milk, eat vitamin-enriched food, and spend time in the sun. These changes increased the intake of Vitamin D and helped to maintain a proper calcium level. Concurrently, cases of hysteria declined. Regarding pibloktoq, Wallace suggests that a complex set of related variables may cause the disease. The Eskimos live in an environment which supplies only a minimum amount of calcium. A low calcium diet could result in two different conditions. Rickets, as a result of low calcium, would produce physical deformities potentially fatal in the Eskimo's hunting economy. Persons whose genetic makeup made them prone to rickets would be eliminated from the population through natural selection. A low level of calcium in the blood could also cause muscular spasms known as tetany. Tetany may also result in emotional and mental disorientation similar to the symptoms of pibloktoq. Since such attacks last for only a relatively short time and are not fatal, people who develop pibloktoq would have a far greater chance of survival with a calcium-deficient diet than those who had rickets.

UNIVERSALITY OF PSYCHOLOGICAL DEVELOPMENT

This chapter has so far dealt with possible causes and consequences of cultural differences in modal personality and in abnormal personality. Investigators in the field of psychological anthropology are also concerned with the question of human similarities: To what extent do all human beings develop psychologically in the same ways, and to what extent is psychological development affected by cultural differences? This concern focuses primarily on features of human development presumed to be *pan-human,* or universal, and attempts to determine how they may be affected by cultural differences.

Most research on psychological development is done by psychologists in our own society or in other complex societies. At the present time it is still problematical whether or not the results of such research are generally valid for all societies, simple or complex. It is only by duplicating studies of psychological development or processes in a wide range of societies that we can be sure that psychological principles presumed to be universal are in fact universal.

For example, Freud assumed that young boys universally are sexual rivals of their fathers for possession of the mother (the Oedipus complex). Thus, he suggested that all boys before the age of seven or so would show hostility toward their fathers. However, Freud's suggestion might be applicable only to his own and similar societies.

Malinowski and other anthropologists who worked after him in matrilineal societies have suggested that young boys in some societies may feel hostility to the father, not as a sexual rival, but rather because of his role as the disciplinarian. This suggestion was made because it seems that, in matrilineal societies, boys feel more hostile toward the mother's brother—who is the main authority figure in the matrilineal kin group—than toward their father. This finding casts doubt on the Oedipal theory, at least as stated by Freud, as a universal principle of psychological development.

The Trobriand Islanders, Malinowski notes, trace their descent in the female line, so that the child is born into the mother's clan. The father is not seen as the sexual progenitor of

[43] Anthony F. Wallace, "Mental Illness, Biology and Culture," in F. L. K. Hsu, ed., *Psychological Anthropology,* 2nd ed. (Cambridge, Mass.: Schenkman, 1972), pp. 363–402.

children (instead, the people believe the mother is impregnated by one of her deceased female relatives). The father is neither the stern, authoritarian figure often found in European society, nor the breadwinner for the family, since he is required to support his sisters and their families with his labor, while his wife's brother and her other male relatives support her and her children.[44] Regarding the Oedipus complex, Malinowski finds no evidence in the few dreams he was able to cull from his informants (recollection of dreaming was uncommon) of repressed sexual longings for the mother, though these were occasionally evident for siblings. There are no Oedipus legends woven into the fabric of Trobriand folktales, and not a single case of mother-son incest seems to have been recorded, though a few incestuous relationships between siblings are recorded. Hostility is not generally directed to the father but rather to the maternal uncle.

On the basis of this evidence, Malinowski reached several conclusions:

1. That the Oedipus complex is not universal;
2. That every type of culture produces its own psychological complexes;
3. That fathers in many patrilineal societies may be disliked more for their authoritarianism than for their sexual power.

Clearly, then, Malinowski's critique of Freud's theory of the Oedipus complex means that it is still an open question whether or not some Oedipal rivalry (directed at a boy's father or perhaps at his mother's brother) is a crucial and universal factor in psychological development.

The controversy over the universal existence of Oedipal conflict reflects the need for a great deal of research on just how generally applicable much of our knowledge of psychological principles is. After all, much of the research is confined to fairly complex and, in many ways, similar societies. How well do these principles work in very different societies? Are they modified by different cultures or environments? If we are to attempt to arrive at universal principles of human behavior, then we must attempt to test them more universally.

[44] Bronislaw Malinowski, *Sex and Repression in Savage Society* (Cleveland: World, 1968; first published in 1927).

SUMMARY

1. The individual's personality, the distinctive way a person thinks, feels, and behaves, is the result of an interaction between his genetic inheritance and his life experiences. Different societies, with different methods of child rearing and different life experiences, will tend to produce different kinds of personalities.
2. The typical personality in a particular society is often referred to in terms of *modal personality* characteristics, those characteristics most frequently exhibited by individuals in the society. Anthropologists determine modal traits by various means: observation, life histories, projective tests, and the analysis of cultural materials.
3. Socialization or enculturation are terms used to describe the development of behavior patterns in children, through the influence of parents and others, that conform to the standards deemed appropriate by the culture. Margaret Mead, Ruth Benedict, and Cora Du Bois were among the first anthropologists to seek links between child rearing and adult personality traits. Each concentrated on a single society or compared a few societies.

4. The anthropologist seeks not only to establish connections between child-rearing customs and personality traits but to learn why these customs originated. Some anthropologists believe societies try to produce the kinds of personality that are best suited to perform the activities necessary for the survival of the society. Child-rearing practices may also be affected by family form and social and physical conditions in the household.

5. Some anthropologists have hypothesized about psychological processes as the cause of links between certain aspects of culture. This has been called *personality integration of culture.* Psychological processes may help us particularly to understand "expressive" or "projective" aspects of culture such as art, music, folklore, and games, or other aspects of culture not tied to adaptive requirements of society.

6. Anthropologists are also interested in the incidence of mental disorders in societies. The fact that different kinds of mental disorders have been observed in different societies has been attributed to variations in child rearing and other aspects of culture. There may also be biological causes of some mental illnesses.

7. Anthropologists are interested not only in variations in modal personality traits but in features and principles of human development which are presumed to be universal but which may or may not be affected by cultural differences. For example, some doubt has been cast on the theory of the formation of the Oedipus complex (at least in the form stated by Freud) on the basis of studies of matrilineal societies. It is only by duplicating studies of psychological development or processes in a wide range of societies that we can be more sure that psychological principles presumed to be universal are in fact universal.

SUGGESTED READINGS

Barnouw, V.: *Culture and Personality* (Homewood, Ill.: Dorsey Press, 1963).
An introductory text for the study of culture and personality. The first half of the book is a historical overview of the field, while the second half presents a critical evaluation of the various research strategies and techniques.

Cohen, Y. (Ed.): *Social Structure and Personality: A Casebook* (New York: Holt, Rinehart and Winston, 1961).
An introductory sourcebook and text for students, with readings drawn from the anthropological, sociological, and psychological literature. The individual articles are intended to illustrate various aspects of culture and personality theory, which are also discussed by Cohen.

Hsu, F. L. K. (Ed.): *Psychological Anthropology,* 2nd ed. (Cambridge, Mass.: Schenkman Publishing Company, 1972).
A collection of papers written especially for this book, focusing on the kinds of research conducted in different geographical regions and the different methods and techniques that have been used.

Hunt, R. (Ed.): *Personalities and Cultures: Readings in Psychological Anthropology* (Garden City, N.Y.: Natural History Press, 1967).
A sourcebook designed to expose students to actual field studies in culture and personality; thus it contains a great deal of descriptive ethnographic material. At the same time the connection of this branch of anthropological study to psychology is illustrated through readings based on Freudian theory and psychoanalytic thought. Another area of study included in this set of readings is the effect of culture change on human behavior.

Kaplan, B. (Ed.): *Studying Personality Cross-Culturally* (Evanston, Ill.: Row, Peterson, 1961).
A collection of papers on culture and personality,

the majority written expressly for this book. The editor's interdisciplinary approach is reflected in his choice of readings from the fields of sociology, psychology, psychiatry and psychoanalysis, and history, as well as anthropology. The book emphasizes both the theoretical and methodological aspects of cross-cultural studies of culture and personality.

Mead, M.: *Coming of Age in Samoa,* 3rd ed. (New York: William Morrow, 1961; originally published in 1928).
A classic field study of socialization. The author describes daily activities in a Samoan village and the process of growing up that apparently is without any sharp break and turmoil at the time of adolescence.

Mead, M.: *Sex and Temperament in Three Primitive Societies,* 3rd ed. (New York: William Morrow, 1963; originally published in 1935).
This classic study describes three New Guinea tribes which have different configurations of male and female temperaments, all of which are different from the traditional Western sexual temperaments. The book suggests that sex and temperament are culturally related.

Minturn, L., and W. W. Lambert: *Mothers of Six Cultures: Antecedents of Child Rearing* (New York: John Wiley and Sons, 1964).
The authors analyze field data on child-rearing practices in six cultures, collected according to a standard procedure by different teams of researchers, in an attempt to explain certain differences in methods of child rearing. Some of the hypotheses supported by these analyses are then tested on a sample of 76 societies from the Human Relations Area Files.

Spiro, M. E. (with the assistance of Audrey G. Spiro): *Children of the Kibbutz* (Cambridge, Mass.: Harvard University Press, 1958).
Based on fieldwork in Israel, this study is concerned with the life of children in a collective settlement whose customs were mainly designed by the members. Material is drawn from observation, interviews, tests, and questionnaires, using the children themselves, their nurses and teachers, parents, and other members of the kibbutz.

Wallace, A. F. C.: *Culture and Personality* (New York: Random House, 1961).
An introduction to questions and theories in psychological anthropology, the book deals with the connection between the evolution of culture and the development of the brain, cultural distributions of personality traits, the psychological effects of culture change, and mental health and culture types.

Whiting, J. W. M., and I. L. Child: *Child Training and Personality* (New Haven: Yale University Press, 1953).
An important contribution to the understanding of personality integration of culture. In a cross-cultural study, the authors examine the relationship between child-training practices and cultural beliefs regarding the cause and treatment of illness. They suggest that this relationship may be mediated by the psychological process of fixation. The early chapters include a general discussion of the relationship between personality and culture and descriptions of variations in child training found cross-culturally.

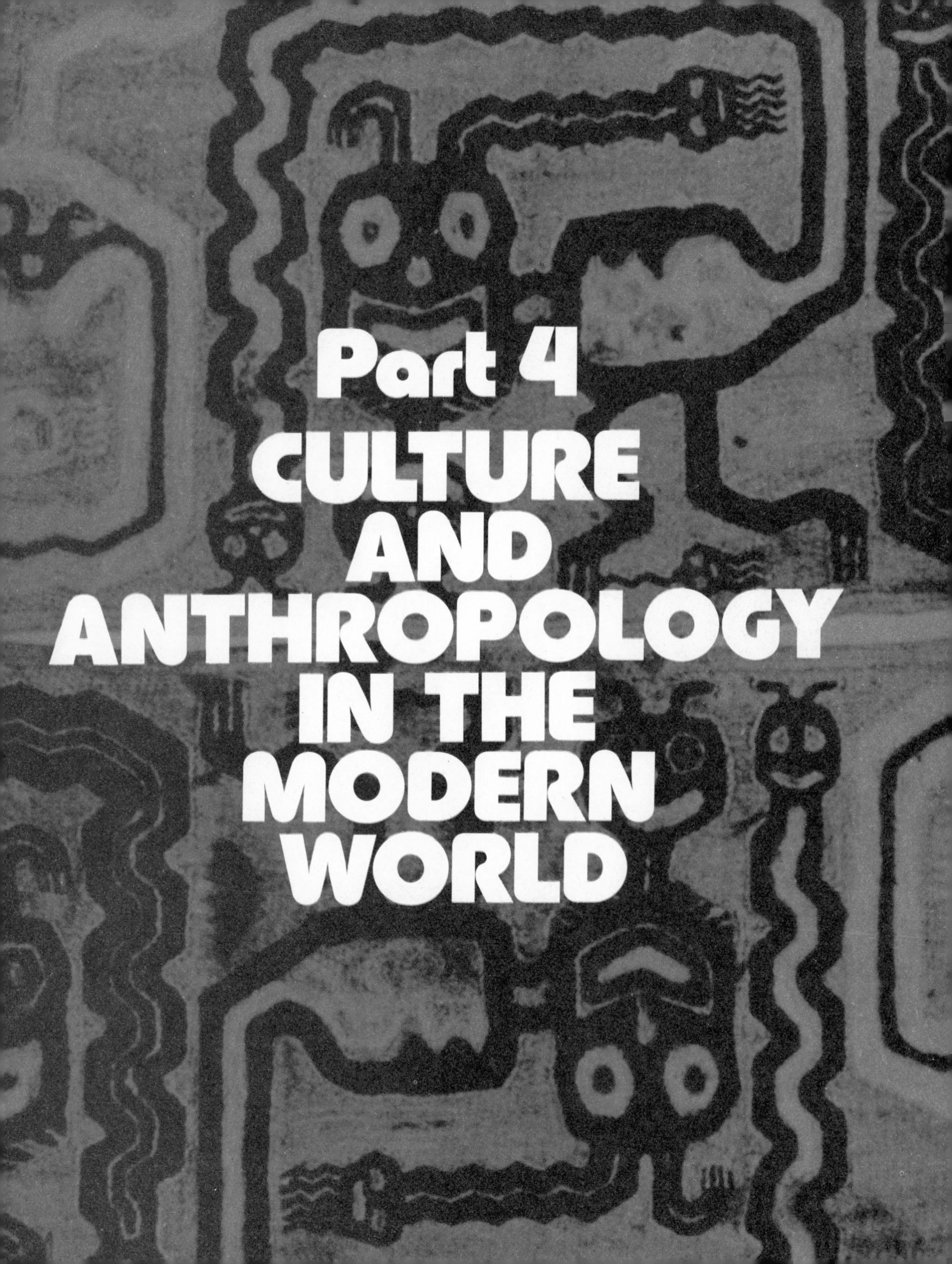

Part 4
CULTURE AND ANTHROPOLOGY IN THE MODERN WORLD

22

Culture Change

Heraclitus, a Greek philosopher of the sixth century B.C., noted, in going daily to his favorite bathing place on a river, that man can never put his foot twice in the same water—each moment he returns to the water's edge the current has flowed on. Change, he concluded, is a constant factor in man's experience.

Like all else, culture is ever changing, although at times the change is so slow as to appear static. Yet because culture consists of learned patterns of behavior and belief, cultural traits can be "unlearned" and learned anew as human needs change. Thus, no specific cultural pattern remains impervious to change; no specific item of learning is sacrosanct. In our own society in recent times members of exclusive, all-male clubs have come to learn that the admission of women does not mean the end of the world, though it does mark the end of an era. On a larger scale, the cultural patterns of twentieth-century New York are very much altered from those of seventeenth-century New Amsterdam. Most people in our society are aware that "times have changed" and with them people's attitudes and ways of life. Anthropologists wish to understand how and why "times" change—that is, how and why cultures change.

HOW CULTURES CHANGE

Discovery and Invention

Discoveries and inventions may stimulate culture change. The new element may be an object—the wheel, the plow, the computer—or it may be an idea—Christianity, Islam, Communism. According to Linton, a discovery is "any addition to knowledge."[1] The distinction between a discovery and an invention has to do with whether or not the new knowledge is used in some practical way. Thus, a person might discover that children can be persuaded to eat nourishing food by associating the food with an imaginary character who appeals to them. The discovery, however, merely adds to his personal store of knowledge. Yet, if he exploits the discovery by developing the character of Popeye, creating a series of animated cartoons in which his hero acquires miraculous strength by devouring cans of spinach in a variety of dramatic

[1] Ralph Linton, *The Study of Man* (New York: Appleton-Century-Crofts, 1936), p. 306.

Culture is constantly changing. At times the old and new cultural elements can present a sharp contrast. Here a Kikuyu tribesman takes his first ride on a double-decker bus during a visit to Nairobi. (Marc and Evelyne Bernheim from Woodfin Camp and Associates.)

situations, and thus stimulates spinach sales on a national level, he may then take credit for an invention.

"Unconscious Invention." In discussing the process of invention, it may be useful to differentiate between inventions which are the consequence of a society's setting itself specific goals, such as eliminating tuberculosis or setting a man on the moon, and those which seem to have emerged less intentionally, such as the development of the wheel or the bow and arrow. This second process of invention is often referred to as "accidental juxtaposition" or "unconscious invention." Ralph Linton has suggested that some inventions, especially those of prehistoric days, were probably the consequences of literally dozens of tiny initiatives by "unconscious" inventors, acting perhaps over many hundreds of years, without being aware of the part they were playing in bringing one invention, such as the wheel or a better form of hand ax, to completion.[2] For example, the observation of children playing on a fallen log, which rolls as they walk and balance on it, together with the need at a given moment to move a slab of granite from a cave face may suggest the use of logs as rollers and, thereby, set in motion a series of developments which culminate in the emergence of the wheel.

In reconstructing the process of invention in prehistoric times, however, we should be careful not to look back on our ancestors with a smugness born of our more highly developed technology. We have become accustomed to turning to the science sections of our magazines and newspapers and finding, almost daily, reports of miraculous new discoveries and inventions. Given this point of view, it is difficult for us to conceive of such a simple invention as the wheel taking so many centuries to come into being. One is tempted to surmise that early man was less intelligent than we are. However, since human brain capacity has been the same for perhaps 100,000 years, there is no evidence that the inventors of the wheel were less intelligent than we are. Perhaps the accelerated rate of invention today has to do with our having had more time to accumulate knowledge; and the more knowledge accumulated, the more often invention can occur.

Intentional Invention. The last 100 years or so offer a biased perspective in regard to inventors and their importance. We tend to think that societies accept inventors and their work and welcome them as full-time specialists constantly in the pursuit of social betterment. However, if intentional invention is defined as the deliberate attempt by individuals to produce new ideas or objects, then for much of recent history, the inventor has been the butt of suspicion rather than the recipient of acclaim. This was true for Galileo, who was forced by the Church to deny that the earth revolved around the sun, and for Priestley, the English chemist whose laboratory and life's work were destroyed by an angry mob, instigated by his suspicious neighbors. Even today certain developments may cause concern or dismay: consider public reactions to the idea that people should be guaranteed an annual income or that nuclear reactors should be used to supply energy.

What motivates the inventor in a complex society? In part he responds to a need, either self-perceived or publicly proclaimed. Henry Ford is an example of an inventor who perceived a future need. He believed that a market existed for a cheap, reliable automobile and invented the mass-production process required to supply it. Richard Arkwright, in late eighteenth-century England, is an example of an inventor who responded to an existing public demand. At the time, new mechanical looms were quite efficient, and textile manufacturers were clamoring for quantities of spun yarn so large that cottage laborers, working with foot-operated spinning wheels, could not meet the demand. Arkwright, realizing that prestige and financial rewards would accrue to the man who invented a water or machine-powered method of spinning, set about the task and developed the spinning jenny.

Arkwright demonstrates another motivation behind invention in advanced societies: economic reward. Specialization, the expansion of markets, and the growth of competition are just some of the factors that cause groups within society to employ, and to encourage, inventors in the hope that their efforts will increase profits; and encouragement in modern times usually means either the payment of large salaries or the offer of very large sums for the rights to an invention. Another factor motivating invention in complex societies is prestige, often obtained by winning awards such as the Nobel Prize.

Inventions, of course, do not necessarily lead to culture change. If an invention or an inventor

[2] Linton, *The Study of Man,* pp. 310–311.

is ignored, then no change results. It is only when society accepts an invention and uses it regularly that we can begin to speak of culture change. Unfortunately, we know little as yet about why inventions are accepted or rejected by a society. When we say that a culture was "ready" for a particular invention, we have not come any closer to knowing why it was "ready."

Diffusion

The source of new cultural elements may be another society. The process by which cultural elements are borrowed from another society and incorporated into the culture of the recipient group is called *diffusion.* Borrowing sometimes enables a society to bypass stages or mistakes in the development of a process or institution. For example, Germany was able to accelerate its program of industrialization in the nineteenth century—and incidentally avoid some of the errors made by its English and Belgian competitors—by taking advantage of technological borrowing, as was Japan somewhat later.

Diffusion is extremely common. Linton has set its impact at the rate of 90 percent—that is, not more than 10 percent of the traits of most cultures can be attributed to that society's own, unaided efforts. In a well-known passage, Linton conveys the far-reaching effects of diffusion by considering the first few hours in the day of an American citizen. This man

> awakens in a bed built on a pattern which originated in the Near East but which was modified in Northern Europe before it was transmitted to America. He throws back covers made from cotton, domesticated in India, or linen, domesticated in the Near East, or silk, the use of which was discovered in China. All of these materials have been spun and woven by processes invented in the Near East. . . . He takes off his pajamas, a garment invented in India, and washes with soap invented by the ancient Gauls. He then shaves, a masochistic rite which seems to have derived from either Sumer or Ancient Egypt.
>
> Before going out for breakfast he glances through the window, made of glass invented in Egypt, and if it is raining puts on overshoes made of rubber discovered by the Central American Indians and takes an umbrella, invented in southeastern Asia. . . .
>
> On his way to breakfast he stops to buy a paper, paying for it with coins, an ancient Lydian invention. . . . His plate is made of a form of pottery invented in China. His knife is of steel, an alloy first made in southern India, his fork a medieval Italian invention, and his spoon a derivative of a Roman original. . . . After his fruit [African watermelon] and first coffee [an Abyssinian plant] . . . he may have the egg of a species of bird domesticated in Indo-China, or thin strips of the flesh of an animal domesticated in Eastern Asia which have been salted and smoked by a process developed in northern Europe. . . .
>
> While smoking [an American Indian habit] he reads the news of the day, imprinted in characters invented by the ancient Semites upon a material invented in China by a process invented in Germany. As he absorbs the accounts of foreign troubles he will, if he is a good conservative citizen, thank a Hebrew deity in an Indo-European language that he is 100 per cent American.[3]

Patterns of Diffusion. *Direct Contact.* Elements of culture may be first taken up by neighboring societies and then gradually spread farther and farther afield. The spread of paper is a good example of extensive diffusion by direct contact. The invention is attributed to the Chinese Ts'ai Lun in A.D. 105. Within 50 years, paper was being made in many places in central China; by 264 it was found in Chinese Turkestan, and from then on the successive places of manufacture were: 751, Samarkand; 793, Baghdad; c. 900, Egypt; c. 1100, Morocco; 1189, France; 1276, Italy; 1391, Germany; 1494, England. Generally the pattern of accepting the borrowed trait was the same in each case. Paper was first imported as a luxury, then in ever-expanding quantities as a staple; finally, usually within one to three centuries, local manufacture commenced.

[3] Linton, *The Study of Man,* pp. 326–327.

Another example of diffusion is the spread of tobacco. From its twin European bases in England and Spain, to which it had been introduced from the New World in 1586 (by Sir Walter Raleigh) and in 1558 (by Francisco Fernandez), smoking diffused rapidly. English medical students took the custom to Holland c. 1590; English and Dutch sailors were introducing it throughout the Baltic, so that by 1634 it was considered a sufficient nuisance by the Russian authorities for laws to be enacted against its use. From Spain and Portugal a similar process spread tobacco through the Mediterranean countries and the Near East. In 1605 the Sultan of Turkey was legislating against its use; at that date too the Japanese were restricting the acreage which could be set aside for its cultivation.

Intermediate Contact. Diffusion through intermediate contact is brought about through the agency of third parties—frequently traders who carry a trait from the society originating it to another receiving it. One example of diffusion through intermediaries involves the Phoenician traders, who spread the alphabet from the other Semitic groups adjoining them to Greece. At times, soldiers also serve as intermediaries in spreading a culture trait. Greek soldiers, for example, passed on aspects of their culture to Near Eastern peoples during the Hellenistic Age; and European crusaders, like the Knights Templar and the Knights of St. John, acted as intermediaries in spreading both Christian culture to Muslim societies of North Africa and Arab culture to Europe. Today Western missionaries in all parts of the world encourage natives to wear Western clothing, with the result that in Africa, in the Pacific Islands, and elsewhere, native people can be found wearing khaki shorts, suit jackets, shirts, ties, and other typically Western articles of clothing.

Stimulus Diffusion. In stimulus diffusion, knowledge of a trait belonging to another culture stimulates the invention or development of a local equivalent. A classic example is that of the Cherokee syllabic writing system created by an Indian named Sequoya so that his people could write down their language. Sequoya received the initial idea from his contact with Europeans. Yet he did not adopt the English writing system; indeed, he did not even learn to write English. What he did was to utilize some English alphabetic symbols, alter a number of others, and invent new ones; all the symbols he used represented Cherokee syllables and in no way echoed English alphabetic usage. In other words, Sequoya took English alphabetic ideas and gave them a new Cherokee form. The stimulus originated with Europeans, the end result was peculiarly Cherokee.

The Selective Nature of Diffusion. While there is a temptation to view the dynamics of diffusion as a stone sending concentric ripples over still water, this would be an oversimplification of the way diffusion actually occurs. Not all cultural traits are as readily borrowed as the ones we have mentioned, nor do they usually expand in neat, ever-widening circles. Diffusion is, rather, a selective process. The Japanese, for instance, accepted much from Chinese culture but also rejected many traits—rhymed tonal poetry, civil service examinations, and foot-binding. The first was antipathetic to the structure of the Japanese language, the second unnecessary in view of the entrenched power of the Japanese aristocracy, the third repugnant to a people which abhorred body mutilation of any sort. Muslim societies offer another example of selective acceptance of cultural diffusion. Originally the basic test of acceptability in Muslim societies was compatibility with the Koran; hence, the failure of wine, gambling, smoking, coffee, cards, and printing—all prohibited by the Koran—to diffuse into Muslim cultures.

In addition, diffusion is selective because cultural traits differ in the extent to which they can be communicated. Elements of material culture, such as mechanical processes and techniques, and other traits such as physical sports and the like, are not especially difficult to

A society that accepts a foreign cultural item is likely to adapt it in a way that harmonizes with its own cultural traditions. This Luo tribesman has adapted Western buttons and a tin can for use as body ornaments. (Marc and Evelyne Bernheim from Woodfin Camp and Associates.)

demonstrate. Consequently, they are accepted or not on their merits. But the moment we move out of the material context, real difficulties arise. As Linton has remarked:

Although it is quite possible to describe such an element of culture as the ideal pattern for marriage . . . it is much less complete than a description of basket-making. . . . The most thorough verbalization has difficulty in conveying the series of associations and conditioned emotional responses which are attached to this pattern [marriage] and which give it meaning and vitality within our own society. . . . This is even more true of those concepts which . . . find no direct expression in behavior aside from verbalizations. There is a story of an educated Japanese who after a long discussion on the nature of the Trinity with a European friend . . . burst out with: "Oh, I see now, it is a committee."[4]

Finally, diffusion is selective because the overt form, rather than the function or meaning of a particular trait, seems frequently to determine how it will be received. For example, the enthusiasm for hair-bobbing which swept through feminine America in the 1920s never

[4] Linton, *The Study of Man,* pp. 338–339.

caught on among the Indians of northwest California. To American women, short hair was a symbolic statement of their freedom; to Indian women, who traditionally cut their hair short when in mourning, it was a reminder of death.[5]

A society accepting a foreign cultural trait is likely to adapt it in a way that effectively harmonizes the new trait with its own cultural traditions. This process of reinterpretation frequently occurs when religions diffuse. "A significant part of the success of primitive Christianity," writes Foster, "was due to its members' ability, both accidentally and consciously, to work out a formal identification of Christ's teachings with pagan customs."[6] Thus, a little church in an ancient Greek city in southern Italy has an image of Aphrodite which for centuries has been revered as the Virgin Mary; and in Haiti, Legba and Damballa, the trickster and rainbow gods derived from Dahomey in West Africa, are identified with Saint Anthony and Saint Patrick, respectively.[7]

Regarding the process of diffusion, then, we can identify a number of different diffusion patterns, we know that cultural borrowing is selective rather than automatic, and we can describe how a particular borrowed trait has been modified by the recipient culture. But we cannot specify when one or another of these outcomes will occur, under what conditions diffusion will occur, and why it occurs the way it does.

Acculturation

When a group or society is in contact with a more powerful society, the weaker group is often obliged to acquire cultural elements from the dominant group. This process of extensive borrowing in the context of superordinate-subordinate relations between societies is usually called *acculturation*. In contrast to diffusion, which involves the voluntary borrowing of culture elements, acculturation, or the wholesale borrowing of culture traits, comes about as a result of some sort of external pressure. The external pressure can take various forms. In the extreme form, under conditions of conquest, direct force is used by the dominant group to effect cultural change in the conquered group. So, for example, in the conquest of Mexico by the Spanish, the conquerors forced many of the Indian groups to accept Catholicism. Although such direct force is not always exerted in conquest situations, dominated

During colonial rule, many African societies were under pressure to adopt Western beliefs, values, and life styles. In the Lagos cemetery in Nigeria the tomb of a black man bears witness to the process of acculturation. (Marc and Evelyne Bernheim from Woodfin Camp and Associates.)

[5] George M. Foster, *Traditional Cultures and the Impact of Technological Change* (New York: Harper & Row, 1962), p. 26.
[6] Foster, *Traditional Cultures,* p. 28.
[7] Foster, *Traditional Cultures,* p. 27.

peoples often have little choice but to change. Examples of such indirectly forced change abound in the history of Indian-white relations in this country. Although the United States government made few direct attempts to force Indians to adopt American culture, it did drive many Indian groups from their lands, which forced them to give up many aspects of their traditional ways of life. In order to survive, they had no choice but to adopt many of the white man's traits. And when Indian children were required to go to American schools which taught the white man's values, the process was accelerated. Finally, a subordinate society may acculturate to a dominant society even in the absence of direct or indirect force. The dominated people may simply see "the handwriting on the wall" and elect to adopt cultural elements from the dominant society in order to survive in their changed world. Or, perceiving that members of the dominant society enjoy more secure living conditions, the dominated people may identify with the dominant culture in the hope that by doing so they may be able to share some of its benefits.

As in the case of diffusion, acculturation is a selective process. The dominated group does not adopt everything in the dominant culture. The recipient group may, for example, be very receptive to technological innovations but may be more resistant to changes in religion or social organization. But there may be an additional reason why the culture of the donor society is not completely incorporated by the recipient society. Foster suggests that the donor society itself may simplify or screen its customs, so that the cultural elements it exhibits to the subordinate society are neither all it has to offer nor exact replicas of its own cultural traits.

This screening process can either be formal or informal. Formal screening processes are those which are deliberately guided and planned by civil, military, or religious institutions. The Catholic Church of Spain, for example, intentionally reduced the Catholic ritual calendar before imposing it on Latin America. While it preserved the important ritual observances such as Epiphany, Candlemas, Lent, Holy Week, Christmas, Easter, and so forth, it eliminated most of the colorful, local celebrations which had grown up in Spain. Screening of cultural elements can also be informal, consisting of "those unplanned mechanisms whereby the personal habits of emigrants, their food preferences, superstitions, popular medicine, folklore, . . . beliefs, hopes and aspirations are selected and maintained in the new country."[8] Both these processes combine to simplify the complexity and variety of the original customs.

Rebellion and Revolt

Perhaps the most drastic and rapid way a culture can change is as a result of violent replacement of the society's rulers. Historical records, as well as our daily newspapers, indicate that there have always been revolts and rebellions. Such events primarily occur in state societies, where there is usually a distinct ruling elite, and take the form of struggles between rulers and ruled, between conquerors and conquered, or between representatives of an external colonial power and segments of the native society. However, not all peoples who are suppressed, conquered, or colonialized eventually revolt or rebel against established authority. Why this is so, and why rebellions and revolts are not always successful in bringing about culture change, are still open questions requiring further research.

A particularly interesting question is why rebellions and revolutions sometimes (perhaps even usually) fail to measure up to the high hopes of the people who initiate them. When rebellions or revolts succeed in replacing the ruling elite, the result is often the institution

[8] Foster, *Traditional Cultures,* p. 12.

of a military dictatorship even more restrictive and repressive than the government which existed before. Spain after the Civil War of 1936 is one example of such a reversal. The new ruling establishment seemed, in the eyes of many, merely to substitute one set of repressions for another, rather than bringing any real change to the society. On the other hand, some revolutions have resulted in fairly drastic overhauls of the society.

The idea of rebellion and revolt has been one of the central myths and inspirations of many societies in the past and present. The colonial empire building of countries such as England, France, and the United States, which flourished during the nineteenth and early twentieth centuries, has created a world-wide situation in which revolution has become nearly inevitable. In numerous technologically undeveloped lands, which have been exploited by more powerful countries for their natural resources and cheap labor, a deep resentment has developed against the foreign ruling classes. Where the ruling classes refuse to be responsive to these feelings, rebellion or revolution becomes the only alternative. In many areas it has emerged as a way of life.

One historian, who has closely examined four revolutions of the past—English, American, French, and Bolshevik—suggests some conditions that may give rise to rebellion and revolt:[9]

1. Loss of prestige of established authority, often as a result of the failure of foreign policy, financial difficulties, dismissals of popular ministers, or alteration of popular policies. France in the eighteenth century lost three major international conflicts, with deleterious results for her diplomatic standing and internal finances.
2. Threat to recent economic improvement. In France, as in Russia, those sections of the population (professional classes and urban workers), whose economic fortunes had only shortly before taken an upward swing, were "radicalized" by unexpected setbacks such as steeply rising food prices and unemployment.
3. Indecisiveness of government, as exemplified by lack of consistent policy, which gives the impression of being controlled by, rather than in control of, events. The frivolous arrogance of Louis XVI's regime, characterized by Marie Antoinette's "Let them eat cake," and the bungling of George III's prime minister, Lord North, with respect to the problems of the American colonies, are examples of this.
4. Loss of support of the intellectual class. Such a loss deprived the prerevolutionary governments of France and Russia of any avowed philosophical support, thus leading to their lack of popularity with the literate public.

Apart from resistance to internal authority, as in the English, French, and Russian revolutions, many revolutions in modern times have been struggles against an externally imposed authority. Such resistance usually takes the form of independence movements which wage campaigns of armed defiance against colonial powers. A brief examination of the Franco-Algerian confrontation offers a typical example.

In Algeria the conditions leading to the outbreak of the rebellion in 1954 resembled those in most colonial environments, namely, resentment of and inability to alter certain conditions: loss of land, subjection to alien laws inequitably administered, severe taxation, humiliation and degradation of the indigenous population, use of force to expropriate and punish. Two factors emerged which spurred the independence movement: the rise of a reformist Islamic movement and the growth of a large body of disadvantaged workers, mostly former sharecroppers who had been freed from bondage to the land by the new

[9] Crane Brinton, *Anatomy of a Revolution* (Englewood Cliffs, N.J.: Prentice-Hall, 1938).

French legal code and who were forced "to bear all the stigmata of a growing economic insecurity."[10]

The *Badissia,* as the Islamic movement was called, established numerous, country-wide societies, all affirming the slogan "Arabic is my language, Algeria is my country, Islam is my religion."[11] The *Badissia* received much of its support in rural areas from the middle-class peasantry, small-town merchants, businessmen, and teachers. It was especially popular for its opposition to the orthodox Muslim insistence on traditional religious feasts (expenditures for which weighed heavily on the peasantry) and for its demand that the French return all religious property.

The rural and urban workers had been forced by population growth and rural unemployment into Algerian cities and also into cities in France, where they suffered from insufficient

[10] Eric R. Wolf, *Peasant Wars of the Twentieth Century* (New York: Harper & Row, 1969), p. 231.
[11] Wolf, *Peasant Wars of the Twentieth Century,* p. 228.

Heavily armed French police search native Algerians for concealed weapons, a frequently occurring scene during the long struggle for Algerian independence from colonial rule. (United Press Photo.)

earnings, insecurity, and labor mobility. "Proletarianization" brought with it political awareness; this was especially true of Algerians who had absorbed radical socialist ideas in major French cities. In fact, most of the leaders of the independence movement were, in addition to their dedication to reformist Islam, of rural birth and educated in urban environments.

The resistance movement was accelerated by a series of events, generally typical of modern independence movements: France's failure to institute reforms; the collapse of French military resistance in 1940 and the impact of German propaganda; France's loss of Indo-China; political instability in postwar France and the weakness of successive governments in their relations with the military and French settlers. These events, then, gradually led to revolt on the part of the colonized people.

The seven-and-one-half-year conflict that followed was not so much won by the Algerians as lost by the French. The very thoroughness, brutality, and ruthlessness of the French civil and military response to the guerrillas alienated large numbers of Algerians who were not previously committed and hardened the resolve of those who were. Simultaneously, mounting costs, weariness and disillusionment (accelerated by the loss of Indo-China), and resentment at the intransigence of settlers *(colons),* all contributed to a change of attitude in France. In 1962, the French army seemed to be in a strong position—but the French people had had enough, and Algeria gained its independence.

CULTURE CHANGE IN THE MODERN WORLD

Societies all over the world are rapidly changing. Many of the changes observed have been generated, directly or indirectly, by the dominance and expansion of Western societies. Thus, much of culture change in the modern world has been externally induced. This is not to say that cultures are only changing now because of external pressures, but these externally induced changes have certainly been the most frequently studied. The study of culture change in the modern world may ultimately help us not only to understand processes of change in the present but also parallel processes of change in the past.

Commercialization

One of the principal changes resulting from the expansion of Western culture is the increasing dependence of much of the world on commercial exchange—that is, the proliferation of buying and selling in markets, accompanied by the use of money as a medium of exchange. The borrowed custom of buying and selling may at first be peripheral to traditional means of distributing goods, but as the new commercial customs take hold, the economic base of the receiving society alters. Inevitably, this alteration is accompanied by other changes, with broad social, political, and even psychological ramifications.

In examining contemporary patterns of change, however, we should bear in mind that the process of commercialization has occurred in many parts of the world in the past. The Chinese, Persians, Greeks, Romans, Arabs, Phoenicians, and Hindus are among those peoples who have maintained and spread vigorous commercial cultures. Therefore, when we examine how and why a contemporary society changes from a subsistence to a commercial economic base, what the resultant cultural changes are, and why they occur, we are probably casting some light upon how and why earlier cultures changed.

Migratory Labor. One way commercialization can occur is for members of a community to move to a place nearby that offers the

One way commercialization can occur is when members of a simple agricultural community find cash-paying jobs in a nearby industry. These Bolivian women are employed at the Milluni mine, 1,500 feet high in the Andes Mountains. (Courtesy of the United Nations.)

possibility of working for wages. This has happened in the last 30 years to Tikopia, an island near the Solomon Islands in the South Pacific. In 1929, when Raymond Firth first made a study of the island, its economy was still essentially noncommercial—simple, self-sufficient, and largely self-contained.[12] Some Western goods were known and available but, with the exception of iron and steel in limited quantities, were not sought after, their possession and use being associated solely with Europeans. This isolated situation changed dramatically with World War II, during which military forces occupied neighboring islands, and people from Tikopia migrated there to find employment. In the period following the war, several large commercial business interests extended their activities in the Solomons,

[12] Descriptive material based on Raymond Firth, *Social Change in Tikopia* (New York: Macmillan, 1959), Chs. 5, 6, 7, and 9, *passim*).

thus creating a continued demand for labor. As a result, when Firth revisited Tikopia in 1952, the economic situation was significantly altered.

Over 100 Tikopia had left the island to work for varying periods of time. The migrants wanted to earn money because they aspired to standards of living previously regarded as appropriate only to Europeans. Already living conditions were modernizing—Western-type cooking and water-carrying utensils, mosquito nets, kerosene storm lamps, and so forth, had come to be regarded as normal items in a Tikopia household.

The introduction of money into the economy of Tikopia not only altered the economic system but also affected a number of other areas of life. As compared with the situation in 1929, land in 1952 was under more intensive cultivation, manioc and sweet potato supplementing the principal taro crop. The pressures on the food supply resulting from improved living standards and an increased population seem to have weakened the ties of extended kinship. For example, the nuclear families composing the extended family (the land-holding and land-using unit in 1929) were not cooperating as much in 1952. In many cases, in fact, the land had actually been split up among the constituent nuclear families; in short, land rights had become more individualized. People were no longer willing to share with members of their extended family, particularly with respect to the money and goods acquired by working in the Solomons.

Nonagricultural Commercial Production. Commercialization can also occur when a simple, self-sufficient hunting or agricultural society comes more and more to depend on trading for its livelihood. Such a change is exemplified by the Mundurucu of the Amazon Basin who largely forsook general horticulture for commercial rubber production, and by the Montagnais of northeastern Canada who increasingly came to depend upon commercial fur trapping rather than hunting for subsistence. Murphy and Steward, who have studied the cultural changes taking place in both of these societies, suggest that "when goods manufactured by the industrialized nations with modern techniques become available through trade to aboriginal populations, the native people increasingly give up their home crafts in order to devote their efforts to producing specialized cash crops or other trade items in order to obtain more of the industrially made articles."[13] The evidence Murphy and Steward have obtained for the Mundurucu and the Montagnais indicates that the primary socioeconomic change that occurred was a shift from a condition of cooperative labor and community autonomy to one of individualized economic activity and a dependence upon an external market.

Among the Mundurucu, for example, prior to the establishment of close trading links, the native population and the Europeans had been in contact for some 80 years without the Mundurucu way of life being noticeably altered. The men did, indeed, relinquish their independently inspired warlike activities in order to perform as mercenaries for the whites, but they continued to maintain their horticultural economy. Some trading took place with whites, the chief acting as agent for the village. Barter was the method of exchange. Traders first distributed their wares, ranging from cheap cottons to iron hatchets, trinkets, and so on, then returned about three months later to collect manioc, india rubber, and beans from the Indians. At this stage (1860), however, rubber was only a secondary item of commerce.

The rapidly increasing demand for rubber which took place from the 1860s onward increased the importance of Mundurucu-trader

[13] Robert F. Murphy and Julian H. Steward, "Tappers and Trappers: Parallel Process in Acculturation," *Economic Development and Cultural Change,* Vol. 4 (July 1956), p. 353.

relationships. Traders now openly began to appoint agents, called *capitoes,* whose job it was to encourage, in every way possible, increased rubber production. As encouragement, *capitoes* were given economic privileges and, hence, power, both of which began to undercut the position of the traditional chief. In addition, the process of rubber collection itself began to alter Mundurucu social patterns, moving men away from their jungle-based communities.

Wild rubber trees are only to be found along rivers, which are often a considerable distance from the jungle habitat of the Mundurucu and can be exploited only during the dry season (late May to December). So the Mundurucu who elected to gather rubber had to separate himself from his family for about half the year. Further, rubber collection is a solitary activity: each tapper must work his territory, comprising about 150 trees, daily; and he must live close to his trees because the work lasts all day. Usually, therefore, he lives alone, or in a very small group, except during the rainy season when he returns to his village.

At this stage in the commercialization process, the Mundurucu became increasingly dependent on goods supplied by the trader. Firearms were useless without regular quantities of powder and lead; clothing required needle and thread for repairs. But these items could only be earned through increased rubber production, which in turn, led to greater dependency on the outside. Inevitably, the ability to work with traditional materials and the desire to maintain traditional crafts disappeared; metal pots took the place of clay, manufactured hammocks that of homemade ones, and so on. Gradually the village agricultural cycle ceased to be adhered to by all in the community (because rubber production would suffer), and in the same way the authority of the traditional chiefs was weakened as that of the *capitoes* was enhanced.

The point of no return was reached when significant numbers of Mundurucu abandoned the village for permanent settlement near their individual territories of trees. Such new settlements lacked the unity, the sense of community, of former village life. Property was held by nuclear families and was carefully maintained in the interest of productivity; the revenue obtained from rubber trade was used to support a raised standard of living.

Supplementary Cash Crops. A third way commercialization occurs is when those cultivating the soil produce a surplus over and above their subsistence requirements which is then sold for cash. In many cases this cash income must be used to pay rent or taxes. Under such circumstances, commercialization may be said to be associated with the formation of a peasantry. Peasants are rural people who produce food for their own subsistence, but who must also contribute or sell their surpluses to others (in towns and cities) who do not produce their own food.

Peasants first appeared with the emergence of the state and urban civilizations about 5,000–6,000 years ago and have been associated with civilization ever since.[14] To say that peasants are associated with urban societies (state societies with cities) perhaps needs some qualification, for the contemporary, highly industrialized urban society has little need for the peasant. His scale of production is insufficient, his use of land "uneconomic"—a highly industrialized society with a large population of nonfood producers requires a mechanized agriculture. As a result, the peasant has passed, or is passing, out of all but the most peripheral existence in industrial countries. It is the preindustrial city, and the social organization it represents, which generates and maintains the peasant. He cultivates land; he furnishes the required quantity of food, rent, and profit upon which the remainder of society (particularly the people in the city) depends.

[14] Eric Wolf, *Peasants* (Englewood Cliffs, N.J.: Prentice-Hall, 1966), pp. 3–4.

What changes does the development of a peasantry entail? In some respects there is little disturbance to the cultivator's (now peasant's) former way of life. He still has to produce enough food to meet family needs, to replace that which has been consumed, to cover a few ceremonial obligations as, for example, the marriage of a child, village festivals, and funerals. But, in other respects his situation is radically altered. For in addition to the traditional obligations—indeed often in conflict with them—the peasant now has to produce extra to meet the requirements of a group of "outsiders," landlords or officials of the state, for instance, who expect to be paid rent or taxes (in produce or currency), and who are able to enforce their expectations because they control the military and the police. The change from near autonomy as a local community to that of dependence on a larger society brings the peasant face to face with a situation as novel as it is unpleasant. According to Eric Wolf, he is now "forced to maintain a balance between [his local community's] . . . demands and the demands of the outsiders, and will be subject to tensions produced by this struggle to keep the balance. The outsider sees the peasant primarily as a source of labor and goods with which to increase his fund of power. But the peasant is at once both an economic agent and the head of a household. His holding is both an economic unit and a home."[15]

While no two peasant cultures are quite alike, there are similarities in form. Peasants the world over are faced with the problem of balancing the demands of an external with those of an internal society. Their response generally involves increasing production, curtailing domestic consumption, or both. In response to its dealings with the outside urban center, a peasantry tends to develop adaptive social organizations. One such social response is the development of the village council or its equivalent. The Russian *mir* (common before the revolution of 1917), for example, held title to all village land and could reapportion acreages as family size changed. It was also the clearinghouse for local grievances and could unite the village in its dealings with the outside world.

The production of supplementary crops for cash has developed in some cases more or less voluntarily. The Arusha of East Africa are an example. The Arusha came into being as a cultural group in the 1800s when some refugees settled in an enclave in Masai territory. The Arusha were largely self-sufficient cultivators, although some barter trade was carried on with the Masai, whose economy was largely pastoral. However, during 1940–1960, the Arusha began to feel the twin pressures of increasing population and decreasing availability of land for cultivation. As a result, the Arusha were obliged to abandon their "conservative attachment to traditional institutions and values, and to adopt new economic practices and attitudes."[16] The new attitudes and practices involved abandoning self-sufficient production in favor of the cultivation of cash crops such as coffee and wheat, the income from which could be utilized to purchase needed goods.

Trade by barter is therefore being replaced among the Arusha with market exchange involving currency, markets being established all over the country, not just along the border with the Masai. The possession of money is coming to be regarded as equivalent to wealth. Indeed, many Arusha are clearly prepared to spend money to achieve a higher standard of living—that is, they are becoming more profit and cash oriented, investing their incomes in goods and services formerly considered unnecessary. The Arusha, then, may have been obliged by circumstances to sell crops for cash, but, unlike the peasants, they were not externally forced by the

[15] Wolf, *Peasants,* p. 13.

[16] P. H. Gulliver, "The Arusha: Economic and Social Change," in Paul Bohannan and George Dalton, eds., *Markets in Africa* (New York: Doubleday, 1965), p. 269.

state or landlords to engage in such market transactions.

Introduction of Commercial and Industrial Agriculture. Another way in which commercialization can come about is through the introduction of commercial agriculture, in which *all* of the cultivated commodities are produced for sale rather than for personal consumption. Along with this change, the system of agriculture may be "industrialized," with some of the production processes, such as plowing, weeding, irrigation, and harvesting, being done by machine. Commercial agriculture is, in fact, often as mechanized as any manufacturing industry. Land is worked for the maximum return it will yield, labor hired and fired with impersonality equal to that which occurs in other industries.

E. J. Hobsbawm has noted some of the developments accompanying the introduction of commercial agriculture as it occurred in eighteenth-century England and in continental Europe somewhat later.[17] The close, near-familial relationship between farmer and farm laborer disappeared, as did the once personal connection between landlord and tenant. Land was regarded as a source of profit rather than a way of life, fields were amalgamated and enclosed, local grazing and similar privileges were reduced, and labor was hired at market rates and paid increasingly in wages. Eventually, machines began to replace farm laborers, as the emphasis on large-scale production for a mass market increased.

In general, the introduction of commercial agriculture brings several important social consequences. Gradually a class polarization develops: farmers and landlords become increasingly separated from laborers and tenants, just as in the town the employer becomes socially separated from his employee. Gradually, too, manufactured items of all sorts are introduced into rural areas. Laborers migrate to urban centers in search of employment, often meeting even less sympathetic conditions there than exist in the country. The trend is not entirely against the rural inhabitant. A man, no matter how small his starting point, may be able to improve his position through hard work, by making correct estimates of which crop to plant and when, and so on. He may—under such conditions of increased social mobility—be able to cross the intangible line which separates the "gentleman" from the rest of society.

[17] E. J. Hobsbawm, *Age of Revolution* (New York: Praeger, 1970).

Religious Change

The growing influence of Western societies has also led to religious change in many parts of the world. In many cases such change has been brought about intentionally through the efforts of missionaries. Frequently missionaries have been among the first Westerners to travel to interior regions and out-of-the-way places. Of course, missionaries have not met with equal success in all parts of the world. In some places, large portions of the native population have converted to the new religion with great zeal. In others, missionaries have been ignored, forced to flee, or even killed. Although we do not as yet fully understand why missionaries have been successful in some societies and not in others, the fact remains that in many parts of the world Western missionary activity has been a potent force for all kinds of cultural, and particularly religious, change.

But aside from the direct effects of missionary work, contact with Westerners has probably produced religious change in more indirect ways. In some native societies, where contact with Westerners has produced a breakdown of social structure and feelings of helplessness and spiritual demoralization, revitalization movements have arisen as apparent attempts to restore the society to its former confidence and prosperity. Such revitalization movements

The dominance and expansion of Western societies has led to religious change in many parts of the world. On the door of a Catholic church in Nigeria, a Yoruba artist uses native figures to depict biblical scenes. (Marc and Evelyne Bernheim from Woodfin Camp and Associates.)

have usually been started by a native prophet who may have visions informing him of the proper course for his people. His success in attracting a following, however, seems to be directly attributable to the amount of demoralization or deprivation brought about through Western contact.

As an example of religious conversion brought about by direct contact with missionaries, we will examine the process of conversion on the island of Tikopia. As an example of a revitalization movement, we will examine the case of the Seneca Indians of New York State, who managed, with the help of a Christian-like religion taught by a native prophet named Handsome Lake, to restore some of the tribal morale which had been lost as a result of contact with the whites.

Christianity in Tikopia. Tikopia was one of the last Polynesian societies to retain its traditional religious system into the first decades of the twentieth century. An Anglican mission was first established there in 1911, with the permanent residence of a deacon and the founding of two schools for about 200 pupils. By 1929 approximately half the population had converted, and in the early 1960s almost all of Tikopia gave at least nominal allegiance to Christianity.[18]

Traditional Tikopian belief was pantheistic, with a great number of gods and spirits of various ranks inhabiting the sky, the water, and the land. One god in particular—the original creator and shaper of the culture—was given a place of special importance, but he was in no way comparable to the all-powerful God of Christianity. Unlike Christianity, Tikopian religion made no claim to universality. The Tikopian gods did not rule over all creation, only over Tikopia; and it was thought that if one left Tikopia, one left one's gods behind.

[18] Discussion based on Raymond Firth, *Rank and Religion in Tikopia* (Boston: Beacon Press, 1970).

The people of Tikopia interacted with their gods and spirits primarily through religious leaders who were also the heads of lineages or chiefs of clans. The clan chiefs presided over rituals centering around the everyday aspects of island life, such as hut construction, fishing, planting, and harvesting. The chief was expected to intercede with the gods on the people's behalf, to persuade them to bring happiness and prosperity to the group. Indeed, when conditions were good it was assumed that the chief was doing his job well; conversely, when disaster struck, the prestige of the chief often fell in proportion. Why did the Tikopia convert to Christianity? Firth has suggested a number of contributing factors.

First, the mission offered the prospect of acquiring new tools and consumer goods. Although conversion by itself did not provide such benefits, the attachment to the mission was believed to make them more probable. Later, when it became apparent that education, particularly in reading and writing English, was helpful in getting ahead in the outside world, mission schooling became valued and provided a further incentive for adopting Christianity.

Second, conversion may have been facilitated by the ability of chiefs, as religious and political leaders, to bring over their entire kin group to Christianity. Should the chief decide to transfer his allegiance to Christianity, the members of his kin group were usually left with little alternative but to follow him, since social etiquette required that they do so. Such a situation actually did develop in 1923 when Tafua, chief of the Faea district of Tikopia, converted to the new religion, bringing with him his entire kin group—which amounted to nearly half the population of Tikopia. However, the ability of the chiefs to influence their kin groups was both an asset and a hindrance, since some chiefs steadfastly resisted conversion.

A final blow to traditional Tikopian religion appeared to come in 1955, when a severe epidemic killed at least 200 people in a population of about 1,700. According to Firth, "the epidemic was largely interpreted as a sign of divine discrimination," since three of the outstanding non-Christian religious leaders died.[19] Subsequently, the remaining non-Christian chiefs voluntarily converted to Christianity, and so did their followers. By 1966 all of Tikopia, with the exception of one rebellious old woman, had converted to the new faith.

Although many Tikopia feel that their conversion to Christianity has been a unifying, revitalizing force, the changeover from one religion to another has not been without problems. Christian missionaries on Tikopia have discouraged and, in fact, succeeded in eliminating the traditional Tikopia population control devices of abortion, infanticide, and male celibacy. It is very possible that the absence of these controls will lead in the near future to a population explosion which the island, with its limited capacity to support life, can ill afford. Firth sums up the situation which Tikopian society must now face:

> In the history of Tikopia complete conversion of the people to Christianity was formerly regarded as a solution to their problems; it is now coming to be realized that the adoption and practice of Christianity itself represents another set of problems. As the Tikopia themselves are beginning to see, to be Christian Polynesians in the modern technologically and industrially dominated world, even in the Solomon Islands, poses as many questions as it supplies answers.[20]

The Seneca and the Religion of Handsome Lake. The Seneca reservation of the Iroquois on the Allegheny River in New York State was a place of "poverty and humiliation" by 1799.[21] Demoralized by whisky and dispossessed from their traditional lands, unable to compete with white technology because of illiteracy and lack of training, the Seneca were at an impasse. In this setting, Handsome Lake, the fifty-year-old brother of a chief, had the first of a number of visions, during which he met with emissaries of the Creator who showed him heaven and hell and commissioned him to revitalize Seneca religion and society. This he set out to do for the next decade-and-a-half, using as his principal text the *Gaiwiio,* or "good word," a gospel which contains statements about the nature of religion and eternity and a code of conduct for the righteous. The *Gaiwiio* is interesting both for the influence of Quaker Christianity it clearly reveals[22] and for the way the new material has been amalgamated with traditional Iroquois religious concepts.

The first part of the "good word" has three main themes, one of which is the concept of an apocalypse. Handsome Lake offered many signs by which the faithful could recognize impending, cosmic doom. Great drops of fire would rain from the skies, a veil would be cast over the earth, false prophets would appear, witch women would openly cast spells, and poisonous creatures from the underworld would seize and kill those who have rejected the *Gaiwiio.* Second, the *Gaiwiio* emphasized sin. The great sins were disbelief in the "good way," drunkenness, witchcraft, and abortion. Sins must be confessed and repented. Finally, the *Gaiwiio* offered salvation. Salvation could be won by following a code of conduct, attending certain important traditional rites, and performing public confession.

The second part of the *Gaiwiio* sets out the code of conduct. This code seems to orient the Indian toward advantageous white practices without separating him from his culture. The code has five main sections:

[19] Firth, *Rank and Religion in Tikopia,* p. 387.
[20] Firth, *Rank and Religion in Tikopia,* p. 418.
[21] Anthony F. C. Wallace, *The Death and Rebirth of the Seneca* (New York: Alfred A. Knopf, 1970), p. 239.
[22] The Quakers, long-time neighbors and trusted advisers of the Seneca, were at pains not to interfere with Seneca religious principles and attitudes.

1. Temperance: All Seneca leaders were fully aware of the social disorders arising out of abuse of liquor. Handsome Lake went to great lengths to illustrate and explain its harmfulness.
2. Peace and social unity: Seneca leaders were to cease their futile bickering, and all Indians were to be united in their approach to whites.
3. Preservation of tribal lands: Handsome Lake, fearing the "piecemeal" alienation of Seneca lands, was far ahead of his Seneca contemporaries in demanding a halt in land sales to the whites.
4. Pro-acculturation: Though individual property and trading for profit were prohibited, the acquisition of English literacy was encouraged so that Indians would be able to read and understand treaties written by the whites and avoid being cheated.
5. Domestic morality: Sons must obey their fathers, mothers avoid interfering with daughters' marriages, husbands and wives should respect the sanctity of their marriage vows.

Handsome Lake's teaching seems to have led to a renaissance among the Seneca. Temperance was widely accepted, as were white schooling and farming methods. By 1801 corn yields had increased tenfold, new crops had been introduced (oats, potatoes, flax), and public health and hygiene had considerably improved. Handsome Lake himself acquired great power among his people and spent the remainder of his life fulfilling administrative duties, acting as a representative of the Iroquois in Washington, and preaching his gospel to neighboring tribes. By the time of Handsome Lake's death in 1815, the Seneca had clearly undergone a dramatic rebirth, attributable almost entirely to the new religion. Later in the century some of Handsome Lake's disciples founded a church in his name which, despite occasional setbacks and political disputes, survives to this day.

Unfortunately, not all native peoples have made the transition to Christianity as painlessly as the Tikopia, nor succeeded in revitalizing their culture as well as the Seneca. In fact, in most cases the record is a good deal more dismal. All too frequently missionary activity tends to destroy a society's culture and self-respect, offering nothing in return but an alien, repressive system of values which is ill-adapted to the people's real needs and aspirations. Phillip Mason, a critic of white evangelists in Africa, points out some of the psychological damage inflicted by missionary activity.[23] The missionaries' repeated stress on sin and guilt, their use of the color black to represent evil and white good, their abrasive hostility to pagan culture, and, above all, their promise that the black man, provided he adopt the white man's ways, will gain access both to the white man's heaven and to white society—all of these factors have the net effect of leaving the black native stranded between two worlds. For no matter how assiduously the black attempts to follow missionary precepts, how patiently he climbs the white socioeconomic ladder, he soon finds himself blocked from entry into white homes, clubs, and even churches and seminaries.

Commercialization and religious change are by no means the only types of changes brought about by Western expansion. Political changes have come about directly through the imposition of a foreign system of government and administration and indirectly through the changing economic structure of a society. Western influence has brought about changes in dress, music, art, and attitudes about the world. Of course, many nations (not just Western ones) have extended their influence in other parts of the globe. Hopefully, future research on the on-going processes of culture change will increase our understanding of why these changes are occurring.

[23] Phillip Mason, *Prospero's Magic* (London: Oxford University Press, 1962).

SUMMARY

1. Like all else, culture is ever changing, although at times the change is so slow as to appear static. Yet because culture consists of learned patterns of behavior and belief, cultural traits can be unlearned and learned anew as human needs change.
2. Discoveries and inventions may stimulate culture change. A discovery may be defined as any addition to knowledge, while an invention involves a practical application of knowledge. Some inventions are intentional; that is, they involve the deliberate attempt by individuals to produce new ideas or objects. Other inventions are "unconscious"; they are probably the result of dozens of tiny, perhaps accidental, initiatives over a period of many years by persons who are unaware of the part they are playing in bringing a single invention to completion.
3. The source of new cultural elements may be another society. The process by which cultural elements are borrowed from another society, and incorporated into the culture of the recipient group, is called diffusion. Several patterns of diffusion may be identified: diffusion by direct contact, in which elements of culture are first taken up by neighboring societies and then gradually spread farther and farther afield; diffusion by intermediate contact, in which third parties, frequently traders, carry the trait from the society originating it to another receiving it; and stimulus diffusion, in which knowledge of a trait belonging to another culture stimulates the invention or development of a local equivalent.
4. Not all cultural traits are as readily borrowed as others, nor do they usually expand in neat, ever-widening circles. Diffusion is, rather, a selective process. Moreover, a society accepting a foreign cultural trait is likely to adapt it in a way that effectively harmonizes the new trait with its own cultural traditions.
5. When a group or society is in contact with a more powerful society, the weaker group is often obliged to acquire cultural elements from the dominant group. This process of extensive borrowing in the context of superordinate-subordinate relations between societies is usually called acculturation. In contrast to diffusion, which involves the voluntary borrowing of culture elements, acculturation comes about as a result of some sort of external pressure which can take various forms. But like diffusion, acculturation is a selective process.
6. Perhaps the most drastic and rapid way a culture can change is as a result of violent replacement of the society's rulers. Revolts and rebellions primarily occur in state societies, where there is usually a distinct ruling elite, and take the form of struggles between rulers and ruled, between conquerors and conquered, or between representatives of an external colonial power and segments of the native society. However, not all peoples who are suppressed, conquered, or colonialized eventually revolt or rebel against established authority.
7. Many of the cultural changes observed in the modern world have been generated, directly or indirectly, by the dominance and expansion of Western societies. One of the principal changes resulting from the expansion of Western culture is the increasing dependence of much of the world on commercial exchange—that is, the proliferation of buying and selling in markets, accompanied by the use of

money as a medium of exchange. The borrowed custom of buying and selling may at first be peripheral to traditional means of distributing goods, but as the new commercial customs take hold, the economic base of the receiving society alters. Inevitably, this alteration is accompanied by other changes, with broad social, political, and even psychological ramifications.

8. One way commercialization can occur is for members of a community to become migratory workers, traveling to a place nearby that offers the possibility of working for wages. Commercialization can also occur when a simple, self-sufficient hunting or agricultural society comes more and more to depend on trading for its livelihood. A third way commercialization occurs is when those cultivating the soil produce a surplus over and above their subsistence requirements which is then sold for cash. In many cases this cash income must be used to pay rent or taxes; under such circumstances, commercialization may be said to be associated with the formation of peasantry. A fourth way in which commercialization can come about is through the introduction of commercial agriculture—in which *all* of the cultivated commodities are produced for sale rather than for personal consumption. Along with this change, the system of agriculture may be "industrialized," with some of the production processes being done by machine.

9. The growing influence of Western societies has also led to religious change in many parts of the world. In many societies such change has been brought about intentionally through the efforts of missionaries. In other societies, where contact with Westerners has produced a breakdown of social structure and feelings of helplessness and spiritual demoralization, revitalization movements have arisen as apparent attempts to restore the society to its former confidence and prosperity.

SUGGESTED READINGS

Geertz, C.: *Peddlers and Princes* (Chicago: University of Chicago Press, 1963).
An analysis of social and economic change in two Indonesian towns, one Balinese, the other Javanese, based on the author's fieldwork. The author's theoretical framework is problem oriented, focusing on economic transition as an index of social change. He sees Indonesian society as existing in a transitional stage, having lost many of its traditional customs but not yet fully developed into an industrial society. His approach is primarily historical, since he views the process of economic change as a sequence of events.

Hunter, M.: *Reaction to Conquest,* 2nd ed. (New York: Oxford University Press for the International African Institute, 1961).
A study of culture change in an African society which describes the process in both urban areas and traditional tribal territories. Hunter tends to view culture change in terms of "extending systems of relationships," an essentially process-oriented approach.

Linton, R. (Ed.): *Acculturation in Seven American Indian Tribes* (Gloucester, Mass.: Peter Smith, 1963; originally published in 1940 by D. Appleton).
Each of the papers in this collection discusses culture change in a particular community, describing its traditional culture, the nature of its contact with an outside culture, the acculturation process, and the modern situation in the community. In his conclusion, Linton presents a general discussion of acculturation going beyond the cases collected in this volume and beyond the experience of North American studies.

Little, K.: *West African Urbanization* (New York: Cambridge University Press, 1965).

This study outlines social problems in an African colony prior to independence. Little constructs a model for explaining certain aspects of social change. His study of voluntary associations suggests that such organizations appear in times of transition and upheaval of traditional social networks, binding together otherwise heterogeneous groups.

Spicer, E. H. (Ed.): *Perspectives in American Indian Culture Change* (Chicago: University of Chicago Press, 1961).
A collection of case studies of various American Indian groups, describing and analyzing culture change in each since the arrival of Europeans.

Tax, S., et al.: *Heritage of Conquest: The Ethnology of America,* 2nd ed. (New York: Cooper Square Publishers, 1968).
Concentrating mainly on rural peasants of Mexico and Central America, this work contains essays by specialists in Mesoamerican ethnology. The first part of the book contains general information on the Mesoamerican region, with a description of the general character of today's Indians. The second part approaches the various aspects of the culture, including economy and technology, community and ethnic relations, social organization, and religious and political organization. The treatment of acculturation includes an historical summary of the process as it has been going on for the past 400 years, from the arrival of the Spaniards in the sixteenth century to the present day.

Wallerstein, I. (Ed.): *Social Change: The Colonial Situation* (New York: John Wiley and Sons, 1966).
A comprehensive selection of essays with the colony as the basic unit of study. Most of the articles deal with Africa, India, or Indonesia, although other regions are represented. The 44 articles deal with various topics such as sociocultural consequences of labor migration, the role of traditional authorities in the past and present, the rise of ethnic associations and nationalist movements, the process of Westernization, and cultural revivals by the native population.

23

Applied Anthropology

All cultures are continually changing. Some of these changes happen quickly, others more slowly. Cultural change can be accidental—as when an entire group of people is uprooted because of a natural disaster, such as a volcanic eruption or a flood, and forced to move, thereby altering many of their customs. But cultural changes can also be planned. For example, the technical and health aid programs administered by such agencies as UNESCO or the Peace Corps often involve a deliberate attempt to change a culture in some particular way. Anthropologists are sometimes involved in the planning or the carrying out of such directed change; the branch of anthropology that concerns itself with planned cultural change, when it is presumably an application of anthropological knowledge, is called *applied anthropology.*

As an academic discipline, cultural anthropology is primarily concerned with recording and analyzing the cultures of other peoples. An anthropologist might enter the field to live with and write about the culture of a particular society, but he would try to interfere in that culture as little as possible, and under no circumstances would he consciously attempt to change it. On the other hand, in applied anthropology, the purpose of fieldwork is to introduce a particular change into a society's way of life—generally a new kind of diet, sanitation system, health care program, or agricultural process. Applied anthropology, therefore, is to anthropology what engineering is to physical science. Just as engineering depends for its effectiveness on physical scientists' understanding of the laws of nature, so applied anthropology depends for its effectiveness on anthropologists' understanding of the laws of cultural variation and change.

THE ACCEPTANCE OF APPLIED ANTHROPOLOGY

At the present time, relatively few anthropologists are doing applied work. In 1969, there were fewer anthropologists employed in American technical aid programs than there had been at any time during the previous 15 years. And the same was true of the major international agencies concerned with the sorts of development programs which would normally utilize anthropologists. Perhaps one reason is that international and government agencies who plan cultural changes and who have the money to implement them have not often felt the need to consult or employ anthropologists. Traditionally, anthropologists and administrators have not worked well together: generally, the administrators feel that the anthropologists are working too slowly, submit reports too technical to be useful, and are too sympathetic to the problems of the people under study. Similarly, the anthropologists tend to see administrators as unconcerned bureaucrats, who want to implement change too quickly, expect unreasonable results, and are insensitive to the problems of the people to be affected.[1] Many anthropologists interested in applied anthropology think that some of the difficulties and confusion so often encountered by persons attempting to introduce change into a culture different from their own—whether these "agents of change" are religious missionaries, private businessmen, or governmental officials—would be greatly reduced through the employment of competent anthropologists familiar with the area being studied.

Another reason for the limited amount of applied anthropological work under way today is the reluctance of many anthropologists to participate in planned change. Some anthropologists would say that anthropological knowledge about particular areas and peoples is not yet sufficient to justify its application. In addition, many anthropologists refuse to engage in applied work because they feel it is not right for anthropologists or other well-intentioned individuals to interfere in the lives of other people. Realistically, of course, everyone's life is interfered with to some extent. The typical American is "interfered with" by a lengthy succession of people, including his parents, his teachers, his government, and so forth, all of whom are seeking to introduce some form of change into his life. But according to some, it is quite a different matter for an anthropologist to interfere with the life of a group of people whose culture differs from his own, and on whom the effects of such interference can only be guessed.

[1] George M. Foster, *Applied Anthropology* (Boston: Little, Brown, 1969), p. 155.

The Ethics of Applied Anthropology

The ethics of applied anthropology are a complicated and much debated issue. The question of ethics seldom arises in normal anthropological fieldwork, since there is generally no reason to suspect that merely living with people, and observing how they live, will change or harm them in any significant way. But specifically planning and implementing change introduces the ethical question: Will the change benefit the target population? In the early days of the discipline, anthropologists adhered to an unwritten, informally established ethical code. But soon the field expanded, technology advanced, and the negative as well as the positive potential of fieldwork became apparent. So in May, 1946, the Society for Applied Anthropology set up a committee on ethics, to draw up a specific code by which professional applied anthropologists could work. After many meetings and revisions, the final version of their code was adopted by the Society in 1948.

This code of ethics serves essentially the same purpose for applied anthropologists as the Hippocratic oath does for doctors or as the oaths of office do for public officials. That is, it is to be used as a guide, in addition to the anthropologist's own personal code of ethics, so that the scientist will take appropriate precautions in his work. This is extremely important, because "it is clear that an applied anthropologist could create a great deal of harm if his investigative efforts . . . endangered the people among whom he worked."[2] The code specifies the responsibilities of the applied anthropologist toward various people involved in his work. It stresses in particular that he must always be careful to keep the names of his informants secret; in some societies, the use of an informant's real name, particularly in a publication, can cause him real harm. It further states that the applied anthropologist must agree to conduct his investigations scientifically, and to

[2] *Human Organization,* Vol. 10 (Summer 1951), p. 4.

inform his scientific colleagues of his findings. In addition, he is pledged to uphold the dignity and general well-being of the people among whom he works, whose safety must not be intentionally jeopardized. Finally, he "must take responsibility for the effects of his recommendations, never maintaining that he is merely a technician unconcerned with the ends toward which his applied scientific skills are directed."[3] Thus, the applied anthropologist is held directly responsible for everything he does and is considered indirectly responsible for the way in which his employer eventually uses his findings.

A major ethical consideration is whether or not a project of planned change will actually benefit the target population. This is a problem that bureaucratic agencies sometimes ignore, but one which is of great concern to anthropologists, who, after all, are pledged to the principle of cultural relativity and the respect for other cultures which that principle fosters. Often governmental agencies only wish to employ anthropologists in order to help "sell" the intended changes to the target population. Furthermore, when they work with governmental agencies, the anthropologists may be hampered in their work, or in the final reports of their results, by political sensitivities; obviously, no governmental agency is going to be happy about paying a scientist for doing research which yields results that are critical of that agency.

On the other hand, there are some anthropologists who believe that applied anthropology is justifiable—and even required—by the problems of the modern world. They would argue that, although they may not know enough yet, anthropologists know more about cultural variation and culture change than those not trained in anthropology, and the problems of the modern world demand as much expert attention as possible. Clearly, even if an applied anthropologist refuses to participate in a particular project, the agency or company in charge of the project would undoubtedly go ahead with it anyway, using another, considerably less "expert," consultant.

There is also the further argument made by proponents of applied anthropology that it is unethical *not* to participate in or comment on programs of directed culture change, for they exist and are part of the human condition studied by anthropologists. Particularly in areas such as preventive medicine, it is difficult ethically to justify *not* providing vaccine against smallpox or other such diseases to societies prone to those diseases who do not have adequate medical treatment.

The Development of Applied Anthropology

According to George Foster, "applied anthropology enjoys less prestige than does theoretically oriented anthropology."[4] The two most important reasons Foster gives for the lower status currently enjoyed by applied anthropology are the questions of cultural relativity and of individual freedom.[5] Many anthropologists feel that it is extremely important in all aspects of anthropology to retain one's sense of cultural relativity, to avoid making value judgments about another people's culture or acting in terms of such judgments. Obviously, when an anthropologist participates in an applied program, it is nearly impossible to follow this requirement completely. Secondly, the anthropologist is likely to value highly his freedom as an individual scientific worker. As a university professor, an anthropologist has a kind of academic, personal, and professional freedom that is generally denied him in applied work, where he must always be careful to act in accordance with the wishes and demands of whatever agency employs him. The debate over when

[3] *Human Organization,* p. 4.

[4] Foster, *Applied Anthropology,* p. ix.

[5] Foster, *Applied Anthropology,* pp. 131–137.

or if anthropologists should participate in planned social change will undoubtedly continue for many years.

The early history of the use of applied anthropology also has something to do with its present status. Applied anthropology was first used by officials from some of the larger countries of Europe in their colonial administrations. Such officials were generally not anthropologists, but their work required them to gain at least a basic understanding of the primitive people whose lives they had come to administer. Unfortunately, this knowledge, once gained, was so frequently used to undermine the needs and wishes of the people themselves that applied anthropology began its career with a questionable reputation.

Today, however, new techniques are often introduced at the request of the host country—for example, when a nation requests aid in industrialization or birth control. Of course, such requests almost always come from the country's ruling elite, who may or may not be as exploitative as their former colonial masters. As a result, applied anthropologists are often compelled to deal with resistance or antagonism in the segment of the population to which the program of directed change is addressed. "When a change that is to be applied to the common man, usually a village peasant, has been agreed upon by a member of the ruling elite and the overseas specialist, the problem is how to convince this common man to accept the new ideas without using force."[6]

Applied anthropologists in the United States were particularly called upon for advice during the second World War, when confused and perplexed American military men wanted to understand why their Japanese enemies refused to behave like "normal" people. One of the things that most distressed American military leaders was the tendency of Japanese soldiers captured in battle to try to kill themselves, rather than allow themselves to be taken prisoner by the Americans. Certainly, American prisoners of war did not behave in this manner. Eventually, the military hired a number of anthropologists as consultants to the Foreign Morale Analysis Division of the War Office's Information Department to help them understand the Japanese code of honor, which was obviously different from the American one. After working with the anthropologists, the American military men were surprised to find that a major reason for the strange behavior of the Japanese prisoners was the Japanese belief that to surrender in a wartime situation, even to greatly superior odds, or even to be taken prisoner when injured and unconscious and therefore unable to avoid it, was a grave disgrace. The Japanese further believed that the American soldiers killed all prisoners. Thus, given the fact that the Japanese prisoners felt so disgraced that they could never reenter their normal lives, and the fact that they fully expected to be unceremoniously executed by their captors in any case, it is hardly surprising that so many captured Japanese soldiers preferred honorable death by their own hands. Once the Americans learned what the Japanese thought, they made efforts to explain to the Japanese that they would not be executed if captured, with the result that far more Japanese surrendered. Some prisoners even helped give military information to the Americans—not in order to act against their own country, but rather to try and establish new lives for themselves, since the disgrace of being captured prevented them from resuming their old ones.

Since World War II, applied anthropologists have concentrated on more traditional types of projects—introducing health care and housing improvements, teaching Peace Corps trainees about the area they are to work in, and so forth. But even these apparently simple projects are far more complex than they seem.

[6] Conrad M. Arensberg and Arthur H. Niehoff, *Introducing Social Change: A Manual for Americans Overseas* (Chicago: Aldine, 1964), p. 66.

All over the modern world, cultures are rapidly changing. Many of these changes have been caused, directly or indirectly, by the expansion of Western societies. Often the new cultural patterns present a sharp contrast to the traditional. For example, the life style of many Japanese young people closely parallels youth culture in the United States. In contrast, a Buddhist priest presents a mood of silent meditation. (Photos by Burt Glinn © 1968 Magnum Photos.)

Culture Change

Guides at the Tokyo Exposition offer a sharp contrast to the traditional dress and demeanor of Japanese women. (Photo of Expo guides by Rene Burri, © 1970 Magnum Photos; photo of women in traditional dress by Dennis Stock, © 1969 Magnum Photos.)

The influence of Western societies can be seen in many different parts of the world. This New Guinea girl has made decorative use of the light bulb, which serves a very different function in industrialized societies. (Courtesy of the American Museum of Natural History.)

Since the late nineteenth century, "cargo cults" have periodically arisen among the islands of Melanesia. Such cults are based upon the belief that Western ships and planes, laden with large cargoes of Western goods for the native populations, will someday arrive. On the island of Tanna in the New Hebrides, a cult cherishes the articles—dog tags, money, army pants —left behind by an Americqn G.I. during World War II. (Photo by Kal Muller, Woodfin Camp and Associates.)

In some societies, culture change has been planned and directed by Westerners. Here Western missionaries teach child care and hygiene to a group of Turkana women in northern Kenya. Such planned change often has far-reaching consequences in many aspects of traditional life. (Photo by Marc and Evelyn Bernheim, Woodfin Camp and Associates.)

One of the principal cultural changes resulting from the expansion of Western societies is the increasing dependence of much of the world on commercial exchange. In India, billboards encourage farmers to increase rice production through the use of chemical fertilizers. The surplus yield, over and above subsistence requirements, is then taken to market and sold for cash. (Photo by Tony Howarth, Woodfin Camp and Associates.)

The advanced technology of industrialized societies has also spread to many parts of the world. An Ivory Coast computer technician, in traditional dress, works with American IBM equipment. (Photo by Marc and Evelyne Bernheim, Woodfin Camp and Associates.)

Although Western societies have had a strong influence in many parts of the world, elements of other cultures have also had an impact on the West. In the United States today, for example, many blacks have adopted traditional African dress and hair styles. (Photo by Mary Ellen Mark, Woodfin Camp and Associates.)

Similarly, the recent establishment of communes in many parts of the United States reflects a desire to adopt the cultural patterns of less complex societies. (Photo by Eve Arnold, © 1969 Magnum Photos.)

DETERMINING THE OVERALL BENEFITS OF PLANNED CHANGE

The first problem that applied anthropology faces in approaching a new project is how to decide whether or not some proposed change would be beneficial to the target population. And, surprisingly, this decision is not always easy to make. One would think that in certain cases, where improved medical care is involved, for example, the benefits offered to the target group would be unquestioned. We all feel sure that health is better than illness, but even this may not always be true. Consider a public health innovation such as inoculation. Although it would undoubtedly have a beneficial effect on the survival rates in a population, there might be unforeseen consequences of a reduction in the mortality rate that might in turn produce new problems. If, once the inoculation program were begun, the number of children

In a medical clinic in the Congo, thousands of people are vaccinated against smallpox. Even such clearly humanitarian programs, however, may at times have unforeseen, negative consequences in the long run. (Courtesy of the United Nations.)

surviving increased, but the rate of food production could not be proportionately increased given the level of technology, capital, and land resources possessed by the target population, then the death rate might climb back up to its previous level and perhaps might even exceed it. In such a case, the inoculation program would merely be changing the causes of death, at least in the long run. The point of this example is that, even if a program of planned change has beneficial consequences in the short run, a great deal of thought and investigation has to be given to its effects in the long run. One of the most important, and most difficult, problems for applied anthropology is the need to anticipate all the effects that are likely to be produced as a result of the single cultural change that is proposed.

An example of how a population's health can actually be harmed when foreign health care is introduced into the culture without also introducing other related customs, can be seen in a program that was attempted in a West African rural community. In that community, the women traditionally continued to work in the fields during pregnancy. Then, in an attempt to improve prenatal care, pregnant women were kept from their work. However, because the people who effected this change neglected to encourage the West Africans to adopt, in addition to work stoppage, a program of physical activity and other exercise such as a pregnant European woman would engage in, the West African women actually suffered *increased* chances of ill health and infant mortality.[7]

In some cases where the long-range consequences of a proposed cultural change are obviously detrimental, the anthropologists may determine that the change is not worth the cost to the community even if they desire it and accordingly advise that the program be dropped. In the Gezira part of the Sudan, for example, agricultural production had always been extremely low, because of a lack of sufficient water. Consequently, an extensive program of crop irrigation was proposed in order to increase the yield. The program was started, and the crops did improve greatly. However, the increased quantities of water near areas where the natives lived, and the increase in the local population's contact with this water, created a major health hazard. A parasitic disease called *bilharziasis,* which is seldom fatal but which greatly weakens its victims, occurred only occasionally in the Sudan before the irrigation canals were built. Afterwards, about 80 percent of the local children were found to have the disease. The increased amounts of water in the area had increased the breeding opportunities for the organism that carries *bilharziasis,* and the larger proportion of the population working near this water likewise increased the disease's toll. It was decided that, until the cycle of the disease could be broken—by eliminating the snail which is the carrier of the parasite—the crop irrigation program would have to be halted.[8]

In determining the overall benefits of planned change, it is important to understand some of the basic aspects of a society's culture which are likely to be influenced by such programs. Cities are likely to show results first, since the upper classes of a target population are frequently the first to adopt new techniques and ideas. Changes then appear in family organization, as the economic basis of earning one's livelihood changes through the introduction of new technical processes. Generally, in places where the emphasis has traditionally been on the extended family, kin-group ties tend to weaken. As cash crops are introduced into a technologically primitive society, and as money becomes more important in the people's lives, their traditional rural cooperative work patterns are also altered. For example, in Haiti and in parts of West Africa, field work was tradition-

[7] Arensberg and Niehoff, *Introducing Social Change,* pp. 80–81.

[8] Foster, *Applied Anthropology,* pp. 79–80.

ally performed by large numbers of workers, who were entertained as they worked by groups of singers and drummers—the music both helped increase the worker's productivity and provided an extremely important social outlet. However, once money was introduced, and the landowners had to pay for each person out in the fields, the musicians were eliminated, thus ending a long-standing work tradition.

Dietary deterioration is yet another unfortunate but common side effect of planned cultural change. Once people have been convinced that certain foreign foodstuffs are more desirable than local products, because of nutritional value, prestige, or flavor, they may often find that they cannot afford ample quantities of them. Also, rapid acculturation is often accompanied by an increase in village factionalism and divisiveness. In many developing countries, the rural residents are quick to resent the acquisition by one of their neighbors of a new latrine or article of clothing, because their traditional rules of sharing and reciprocity lead them to think that no one person can prosper without taking something away from his neighbors.[9]

THE DIFFICULTIES OF INSTITUTING PLANNED CHANGE

Before any attempts can be made at cultural innovation, the innovators must determine whether or not the target population is aware of the benefits of the proposed change. In many situations where significant sanitary or other health problems exist, target populations are not always aware of these problems. And this lack of awareness can become a major barrier to solving those problems. For example, there are many cases in which health workers have had difficulty in convincing scientifically unsophisticated people that they were becoming ill because something was wrong with their water supply since the concept of water pollution is unknown in many areas of the world. According to many people's understanding of the nature of disease, it could not possibly be transmitted through such an agent as water. In other cases, like that of certain Taiwanese women who were introduced to family planning methods in the 1960s, the target population is perfectly well aware of the problem. The Taiwanese women knew they were having more children than they wanted or could easily afford, and they wanted to control their birth rate. There was no resistance involved—they merely had to be given the proper devices and instructions—and the birth rate fell quite quickly to a more desirable, and manageable, level.[10]

Resistance to Planned Change among the Target Population

Yet even when a target population is aware of the possible benefits of a proposed change, it is not always a simple task to get the local people to accept an innovation, or to change their behavior. And an innovation, if rejected by the target population, is thereby rendered useless. For this reason, the future success or failure of a project of planned change is often difficult to ascertain.

> Directed culture change goals are dual, almost always involving changes both in the physical environment and in the behavior of people. . . . Environmental modification, which means design and construction, is often looked upon as the heart of national development and modernization, and the achievement of physical goals symbolizes the successful completion of each project. Yet if the appropriate changes in behavior do not accompany environmental modification, a project is of dubious merit.[11]

[9] G. M. Foster, *Traditional Cultures* (New York: Harper & Row, 1962), pp. 29–43.

[10] Arthur H. Niehoff, *A Casebook of Social Change* (Chicago: Aldine, 1966), pp. 255–267.

[11] Foster, *Applied Anthropology,* p. 5.

In other words, where the aim of a project is to install some kind of new facilities, the mere physical installation of those facilities is not sufficient to call the project successful. In order to be completely successful, those new facilities must be actually used by the people for whom they were intended. Similarly, when a project aims to introduce an agricultural innovation—such as a higher-yield crop—local residents, after becoming acquainted with the new crop, must also continue to grow it if the project is to be considered a success. For example, after a few years of growing an improved breed of hybrid corn introduced by an extension agent, a group of Spanish-American farmers in Arizona suddenly rejected it, returning to the old variety. After questioning the farmers, the innovator found that the project had ultimately failed because the farmers' wives felt the new corn was too hard to grind into tortillas, and because they preferred the taste of the older type of corn.[12]

A society's resistance to planned cultural change is often based on factors that the planners would seldom anticipate—for example, a lack of understanding of the various symbols used to describe the innovation. Even the symbols that seem totally unambiguous to us can be interpreted in many different ways by different peoples.

In many U.S. foreign aid programs, for instance, the symbol of a pair of hands clasped in friendship is displayed on trucks, walls, and other highly visible areas, in order to demonstrate that our intentions in these various local projects are entirely honorable, even friendly. It apparently never occurred to the designers of that symbol that it could be interpreted differently. But in certain areas, it has been pointed to as proof that the Americans are only interested in going to other countries in order to pull the native peoples into slavery (hence, the two hands, coming from opposite directions). To local people in Thailand, the symbol suggests the spirit world, clearly because disembodied hands do not appear in the real world. Another case of mistaken symbol identification took place in Rhodesia, where European health officials, wishing to emphasize to local villagers the great dangers inherent in tuberculosis, a disease that was becoming prevalent in the area, distributed posters in which tuberculosis was personified as a dangerous crocodile. The linking of tuberculosis (which was not even recognized as a disease by the natives) to the crocodile (long recognized as the natives' chief deadly enemy) did not work out as planned. Instead of learning to fear and therefore to do something about tuberculosis by participating in the European-run health programs, the natives assumed that crocodiles *caused* tuberculosis, thus giving them yet another reason to fear the reptiles, but in no way encouraging them to attend health clinics.[13]

Problems associated with differential perception of symbols are hardly confined to technologically underdeveloped regions, where the language and customs differ greatly from those of the authorities initiating programs of planned change. A similar difficulty was reported some years ago by an English company that wanted to advertise that one of its food products was used by upper-class as well as working people. (Apparently, it was felt that if this impression could be conveyed to the working-class people in England, they would be more eager to buy the product, in an attempt to emulate their class superiors.) So, to indicate that the product was used by upper-class families, the company ran an ad showing a table set with the product, on which rested some lighted candles, presumed to be symbolic of gracious dining. However, to people in the working class of northwestern England, this ad gave exactly the opposite impression: they interpreted the can-

[12] Arensberg and Niehoff, *Introducing Social Change*, p. 80.

[13] Foster, *Applied Anthropology*, pp. 10–11.

dles as being required by the family using the product, obviously working class people like themselves whose gas had been cut off for nonpayment of the bill, an all-too-common occurrence among them.[14]

Even in cases where the possibility of misinterpreting a particular symbol is not crucial, there are other factors which may act as barriers to planned cultural change. Such factors can be roughly divided into three categories: *cultural* barriers, *social* barriers, and *psychological* barriers. These categories, however, may sometimes appear to overlap.

Cultural barriers have to do with shared behaviors, attitudes, and beliefs that tend to impede the acceptance of an innovation. For example, members of different societies may view gift giving in different ways. In some societies, particularly commercialized societies, things received for nothing are often believed to be worthless. When the Colombian government instituted a program of giving seedling orchard trees to farmers in order to increase their fruit production, there was virtually no interest in the seedlings, many of which died as a result of neglect. However, when it was realized that the experiment had apparently failed, the government began to charge each farmer a nominal fee for the seedlings. Soon the seedlings became immensely popular, and fruit production increased.[15] The farmers' demand for the seedlings may have increased because they were charged a fee and therefore came to value them; or perhaps the increased demand was a response to other new conditions of which we have no knowledge, such as an increase in the market demand for fruit.

Religious beliefs and practices may also hinder the acceptance of a planned change. Thus, in 1940, health workers encountered religious barriers while trying to help contain an epidemic of pulmonary tuberculosis among the Zulu tribesmen of South Africa. The natives there had already become more susceptible to the disease, because of widespread malnutrition and bad health conditions in general. Treatment was difficult because despite the many changes which had already occurred in the Zulu family structure, clothing style, and so forth, as a result of contact with Western cultures, they had retained their belief that "all natural phenomena, including crop failures, lightning and storms, as well as sickness, are caused by witchcraft and sorcery." When the foreign doctors suggested having an infected girl hospitalized, her father refused, since if he allowed this to be done, he would be admitting that his daughter could spread disease and was therefore a witch.[16]

Social barriers to planned change may arise when traditional patterns of interpersonal relations or traditional social institutions conflict with the innovation being introduced. The structure of authority within the family, for example, is sometimes a factor hindering the acceptance of a planned program of change. In many places, including parts of Korea, Mexico, and among the Navajo Indians, a person cannot be hospitalized or receive extended medical help simply on his own request. His entire family, which often includes a great many people, must consent, even in emergency cases. Obviously, this process frequently requires a great deal of time and sometimes results in the death of a patient whose physical condition cannot accommodate so much delay.[17]

When planned change is introduced into a society, acceptance may also depend on psychological factors—that is, how the individual perceives the innovation. A psychological barrier caused rural Venezuelan mothers to reject the innovation of powdered milk for their in-

[14] Foster, *Applied Anthropology*, p. 111.

[15] Foster, *Applied Anthropology*, pp. 122–123.

[16] Benjamin D. Paul, *Health, Culture, and Community: Case Studies of Public Reactions to Health Programs* (New York: Russell Sage Foundation, 1955), p. 18.

[17] Paul, *Health, Culture, and Community*, pp. 106–107.

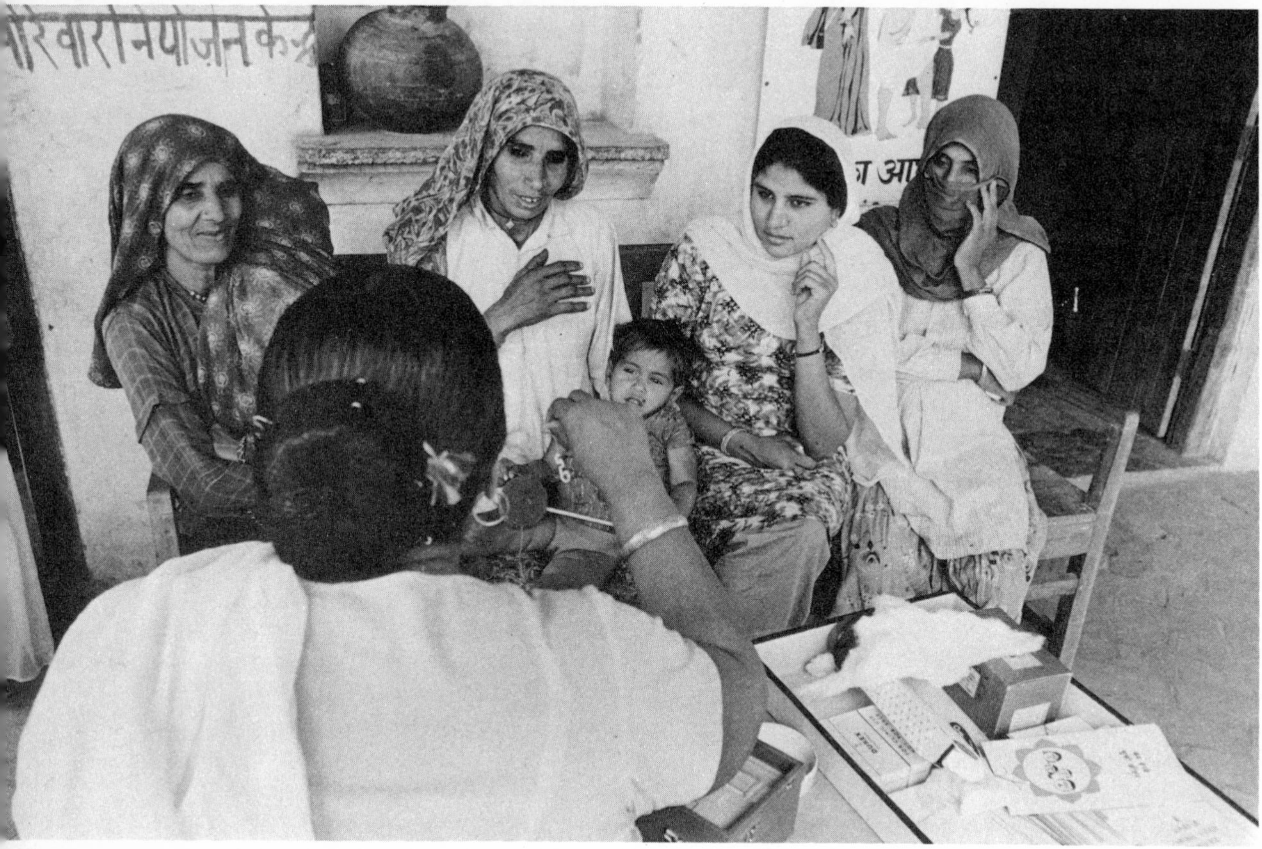

In the village of Deoli near New Delhi, India, a family-planning fieldworker discusses the use of contraceptive devices with village women. In such cases, the fieldworker must be careful to convey the information clearly, or the program might fail because of faulty communication. (Courtesy of the United Nations.)

fants. Although government officials were distributing the milk without cost at rural clinics, surveys showed that many mothers refused to give it to their children. A psychological barrier to accepting the powdered milk was involved in that the women perceived the new milk as a threat to their own role as mothers. Many viewed the program as a deliberate attempt to say that mothers' milk was no longer good enough for infants.[18]

[18] Foster, *Applied Anthropology,* pp. 8–9.

An individual's psychological reaction to an innovation is of course affected by the way in which it is communicated to him. In some situations the planner cannot be sure that the people with whom he is working completely understand the nature or purpose of the change he is trying to introduce. Some common examples of cases in which the agent of change may think he has effectively communicated to his subjects the details of a process, when this is not really the case, are in the fields of birth control and medical instructions. Typically, a public health nurse or other type of field-worker will explain to the mother of a sick infant, for example, that she must give him medicine every three hours. The mother may appear to understand, but later the worker may discover that she gave the child the medicine on each of three consecutive hours or at irregular intervals because she had no clock and did not live by a concept of time that included ideas such as "every three hours." Of course, this problem of faulty communication may be merely due to the public health nurse not realizing that she and the mother speak different languages or dialects and thus have to make a special effort in translating from one language to the other.

The Problems Facing the Innovator

As we have seen, there are many factors within the target population that cause it to reject cultural changes which have been planned and introduced by outsiders. But the procedures followed by the outsider, or agent of change, also have an impact on the success or failure of a program. Often such agents must make a self-conscious effort to overcome certain of their own natural tendencies which would otherwise prevent a program from being successful.

The Importance of Effective Follow-Through Programs. One important problem facing the cultural innovator is the necessity for an effective follow-through program for whatever projects he introduces. That is, he must take into consideration the fact that the native population does not already possess the skills necessary to maintain a project requiring relatively advanced technical knowledge. Of course, they can easily learn these skills, but the innovator, or his agents, must specifically and carefully teach such skills to them, before leaving them to their own devices. For example, it makes little sense for a group of technical experts to introduce a system of wells to obtain safe water supplies more easily, if they do not make sure to teach members of the target population how to maintain these wells. Otherwise, in a few days, weeks, or years—however long it takes for all the wells in the area to break down, with no adequately trained mechanics available to fix them—the project will have disappeared, as though wells had never been built, and the people will return to their old ways of drawing and storing water.

The Problem of Ethnocentrism. Agents of planned change must also attempt to guard against problems created by their own ethnocentrism. Because many of these agents have been trained in America, according to American rules, beliefs, and values, they often try to insure the success of their projects by transplanting American-style behavior to whatever country they are working in, whether or not that style applies there. An example of this type of insensitivity to cultural variations is the "technical expert" who designed a series of shower baths to improve the health conditions for a group of people in Iran, without bothering to discover that Iranian men in that area did not like to be seen naked by other people, even other males. Because he did not know this, the innovator based his shower baths on the design of a typical American men's gymnasium shower, without partitions between the stalls. Needless to say, this design was not popular with the Iranian men, who simply ignored the showers.[19]

This same American ethnocentrism has shown up in several programs meant to help improve nutrition in various technologically underdeveloped regions. It has been found that the diets of many technologically primitive peoples are, in fact, rather good from a nutritional standpoint. Many people substitute, for

[19] Foster, *Traditional Cultures,* pp. 179–180.

Government officials in the Congo, with the assistance of United Nations agencies, introduce a program designed to raise agricultural production as well as the standard of living of farmers. Here farmers are taught how to incorporate organic matter into the soil. Such a project requires an effective follow-through program if the desired goals are to be achieved. (Courtesy of the *United Nations.)*

our traditional selections from the "five food groups," such things as wild berries, roots, nuts, animal fat or hide, and many other perfectly good sources of vitamins, minerals, and proteins. Even Vitamin C can be derived from sources other than citrus fruits. But many change agents, rather than studying the beneficial aspects of a people's traditional diet and attempting to find a way to supplement its nutritional value by using locally available materials, spend their time and energy trying to get people from other cultures to consume such typically American foodstuffs as orange juice, eggs, and bacon—which are nutritionally unnecessary in most cases, unavailable in almost all cases, and often repulsive to the target people.

The Danger of "Pseudoimprovements." One further pitfall which the cultural innovator must guard against is the introduction of "pseudoimprovements"—that is, new techniques or processes which appear to help raise the quality of life among a group of people, but which in reality do not. For example, early American-style, wood-burning stoves were introduced to some parts of northern Rhodesia in recent years, as one type of housing improvement. Traditionally, local women had cooked outdoors on raised clay hearths. Once the "improved" stoves were built, it was found that the Rhodesian women did not like them. Although the new stoves looked more modern and therefore seemed to be more efficient, in reality they were not. The old-style hearths made it easier to regulate the heat, and wood of any size could be used. The new version, on the other hand, required that the wood be broken up into pieces of a certain size, it was harder to regulate and required the cook to remain indoors, alone—keeping her away from one of her primary forms of social contact, around the outdoor cooking fires. Clearly, these new stoves were not really an improvement at all, and, needless to say, their life expectancy was not high.[20]

[20] Foster, *Applied Anthropology,* pp. 7–8.

Medical teams have initiated child-care clinics in hundreds of rural villages in India. A European doctor, however, must guard against imposing his own attitudes and values on the Indian mothers. (Courtesy of the United Nations.)

Recognizing the need to use local channels of influence, a government health worker asks permission of the witch doctor in a Ghana village before spraying the huts with DDT to help fight malaria. (Marc and Evelyne Bernheim from Woodfin Camp and Associates.)

Discovering and Utilizing Local Channels of Influence. In planning a project involving cultural change, the administrator of the project should also be certain to find out what the normal channels of influence are in his target population. In most communities, there are preestablished networks for communication as well as persons of high prestige or influence who are looked to for everyday guidance and direction. An understanding of such channels of influence is extremely valuable in deciding how to introduce a program of planned change into an area. In addition, it is useful to know at what times and in what sorts of situations one channel is likely to be more effective in spreading information and approval than another.

An example of the effective use of local channels of influence occurred when an epidemic of smallpox broke out in the Kalahandi district of Orissa state in India some years ago. The efforts of health workers to vaccinate villagers against the disease were consistently resisted. Villagers, naturally suspicious and fearful of these strange men with their equally strange medical equipment, were unwilling to offer themselves, and particularly their babies, to whatever peculiar experiments they wished to perform. Afraid of the epidemic, the villagers appealed for help to their local priest, whose opinions on such matters were trusted. The priest went into a trance, explaining that the illness was the result of the goddess Thalerani's anger with the people. She could only be appeased, he continued, by massive feasts, offerings, and other demonstrations of the villagers' worship of her. Realizing that the priest was the village's major opinion leader, at least in medical matters, the frustrated health workers attempted to get the priest to convince his people to undergo vaccination. At first, the priest refused to cooperate with the strange men; but when his favorite nephew fell ill, he decided in desperation to try every possibility available to cure the boy. Thus, the priest went into another trance, telling the villagers that the goddess also wished all her worshippers to be vaccinated. Fortunately, the people agreed, and the epidemic was largely controlled.[21] Agents of change, then, are well advised to identify and work through the existing channels of influence in their target populations.

Considering the powerful barriers to change which may exist in many societies, as well as the many difficulties that agents of change may make for themselves, how do cultures ever come to accept planned innovations? In some situations most of the members of the target population may simply and consciously *want* to change. In such cases, the natives' own desire to adopt the innovations being offered is the most powerful "stimulant" to cultural change. In other situations, however, there may be certain cultural, social, or psychological factors that favor change even though the target population does not actively seek it. But at the present time, not much is known about why some societies or segments of societies seem to be more generally predisposed to change than others.

[21] Niehoff, *A Casebook of Social Change*, pp. 219–224.

SUMMARY

1. All cultures are continually changing—either quickly or slowly, and either accidentally (because of natural disasters or other uncontrollable factors) or as part of a program of planned cultural change, directed by a governmental agency, a missionary group, or a private business. Applied anthropologists enter the field, not merely to observe a culture as it is, but to help introduce a specifically planned innovation, such as health care programs or housing improvements.

2. There are relatively few applied anthropologists, partly because the agencies which plan and finance cultural change do not generally seek the advice of anthropologists, and partly because many anthropologists themselves do not choose to do applied work. Some anthropologists feel their knowledge of other cultures is insufficient to apply effectively; others believe they have no right to interfere in the lives of others. Still others, however, feel obligated to share whatever knowl-

edge they have. The ethics of applied anthropology are a complicated and highly debated issue.

3. Applied anthropology has a lower status than its theoretical counterpart, because many anthropologists feel they cannot retain their sense of cultural relativity or their individual freedom in applied fieldwork. Because applied anthropology was first used in the exploitative colonial administrations of the European nations, its initial reputation was questionable.
4. The first problem to be faced in approaching a new applied project is whether or not the proposed change will benefit the target population. The effect of this change on the entire culture of that population, both in the short and the long run, must be considered.
5. Even if a planned change will prove beneficial to its target population, they may not accept it. And, if the proposed innovation is not utilized by the intended target, the project cannot be considered a success. Target populations may reject a proposed innovation for various reasons: because they are unaware of the need for the change; because they prefer their traditional way of living; because they misinterpret the symbols used to explain the change or fail to understand its real purpose; because their customs and institutions conflict with the change; or because they are afraid of it.
6. The innovator must overcome certain difficulties in order for his projects to succeed. He must institute an effective follow-through program; he must guard against his own ethnocentrism and the lure of "pseudoimprovements"; and he must discover and use the traditional local channels of influence for introducing his project to the target population.

SUGGESTED READINGS

Arensberg, C. M., and A. H. Niehoff: *Introducing Social Change: A Manual for Americans Overseas* (Chicago: Aldine, 1964).
A manual written for American "change agents" but also useful for the beginning student. It is intended to improve understanding of cultural patterns, problems, and change and to increase the change agent's ability to interact in other cultures. The authors begin with a definition of culture and a description of unplanned and planned changes. They then analyze the culture patterns common to most developing nations and evaluate American cultural patterns that may affect those working in such areas.

Foster, G. M.: *Applied Anthropology* (Boston: Little, Brown, 1969).
Historical and contemporary discussion of the relationship between theoretical and applied anthropology in terms of the involvement of applied anthropology in social and cultural change. Applied anthropology is defined and illustrated with case studies of planned change. Emphasis is on the problems related to this area of anthropology and the reasons for its importance.

Foster, G. M.: *Traditional Cultures: And the Impact of Technological Change* (New York: Harper & Row, 1962). Examination of the effect of technology on cultures throughout the world and of the way that an understanding of past effects will help solve current problems. Based on the author's experiences in Latin America, Asia, and North America, this book is an analysis of the factors that hinder and help to create culture changes.

Niehoff, A. H. (Ed.): *A Casebook of Social Change* (Chicago: Aldine, 1966).
A collection of papers on attempts to bring about cul-

tural change in the major underdeveloped areas of the world. The editor critically analyzes each case in terms of its social, economic, and technological success. He believes that the key to faster culture change in these areas is an understanding of the process of change and the reasons for the different rates of change, as well as the sociocultural elements which may impede change.

Paul, B. D. (Ed.): *Health, Culture, and Community: Case Studies of Public Reactions to Health Programs* (New York: Russell Sage Foundation, 1955). A collection of papers that deal with health problems throughout the world, the reactions to them, and their possible solutions. In each study, the author begins by describing the living conditions and cultural traditions of the people and goes on to discuss his experiences in treating and dealing with them. Topics include diphtheria control in a Thai community, nutrition programs in Guatemala, and a comprehensive health program among the South African Zulu.

24

Anthropology in the Modern World

For many centuries the idea of traveling to the moon was only a dream, yet in 1969 it became a reality when an American Air Force officer gingerly planted his space boot in the moon dust. As the moon shot demonstrates, we know a great deal about the laws of nature in the physical world; if we did not understand so much, the technological achievements we are so proud of would not be possible.

In comparison, we know much less about people, how and why they behave as they do. Given the great number of social problems facing mankind, the importance and relevance of continuing research in cultural anthropology and the other social sciences becomes evident. For it is only on the basis of efforts to understand human behavior that we can have any hope of doing something about our problems. Good intentions are not enough. We need knowledge as accurate and reliable as that which enabled scientists to put men on the moon. Since social problems such as violence in the streets and wars between nations are products of human activity, we need to find out what conditions produce those problems. Once we gain such understanding, it may then be possible to change the conditions and so solve the problems.

This is not to say that social scientists should concern themselves exclusively with practical problems. Often, the most useful insights in science occur to researchers who have no other object than the pursuit of knowledge for its own sake. This is true of virtually all of the older sciences—physics, biology, and so on—and it seems reasonable to assume that it is true of the social sciences too. It seems that many of the most creative achievements in science were products of minds that were not constrained in any way, neither by the limits of understanding at the time nor by practical concerns. The experiments of Gregor Mendel, an obscure monk fascinated by inherited characteristics in pea plants, contributed to the science of genetics, which has practical implications for such things as the fight against inherited diseases. Einstein's theories, born in the realm of pure thought, pointed the way to the harnessing of atomic energy. In the social sciences, too, it may be that our best chance of achieving solutions to practical problems is to engage in research of all kinds, limited only by the intellectual curiosity of the scientist, not by practical concerns.

We might ask why we know so little as yet about man. To be sure, the fields of anthropology, sociology, and psychology are newer than the physical and biological sciences and therefore cannot be expected to be as well developed. Yet the fact that anthropology and other sciences dealing with man began to develop only relatively recently is not by itself an explanation of why we know so little. Why, in the quest for knowledge of all kinds, did man wait so long to study himself? Leslie White has pointed out that in the history of science it seems that those phenomena most remote from man and the least significant as determinants of human behavior were the first to be studied. He suggests that this has been so because man has thought of himself as an impregnable citadel of free will, subject to no laws of nature. Hence there is no need to see man as an object to be explained.[1] Even today the unwillingness to accept the notion that human behavior is objectively explainable is reflected in the popularity of astrology as an explanation of human behavior. That the stars could account for human behavior, when there are no known mechanisms by which they could influence people, is highly improbable. Yet, as long as such far-removed and improbable "causes" can pass for explanations of human behavior, no other more probable explanations will be sought.

The belief that it is impossible to explain human behavior scientifically, either because our actions and beliefs are too individualistic and complex; or because we are explainable only in other-worldly terms, is a self-fulfilling idea. We shall not be able to discover laws explaining human behavior if we neither believe there are such laws nor bother to look for them. The result is assured from the beginning—those who do not believe in laws of human nature will be reinforced by their finding none. If we are to increase our understanding of man, we have to want to, and we have to believe that it is possible.

Anthropology's Contribution to the Modern World

Even if one is not involved in anthropological research, or in attempts to solve social problems, the study of anthropology encourages attitudes that may be useful in the modern world. Knowledge of man's past may bestow both a feeling of humility and one of accomplishment. If we are to attempt to deal with the problems of our world, we have to be aware of our vulnerability, so that we do not think that the problems will solve themselves; and we have to think enough of man's accomplishments to believe that it is possible for us to achieve solutions to our problems.

Perhaps much of the trouble man gets himself into is a result of his exaggerated feeling of self-importance and invulnerability—in short, his lack of humility. Knowing something about our evolutionary past may help us to understand and accept our place in the biological world. After all, man is an animal, related to other vertebrates, other mammals, and, most particularly, to other primates. We and the other living primates share a common ancestor and not surprisingly we are discovering that we share a good many behavioral patterns as well. And, like any other organism, we are subject to natural selection. There is no guarantee that any particular human population, or even the entire human species, will perpetuate itself indefinitely. The earth changes, the environment changes, and man himself changes, so that what is adaptive at the present may not be so in the future.

The forces of natural selection affect man's culture just as they affect his biological makeup. True, there is the important difference that, unlike biological evolution, cultural evolution involves adaptations produced, often deliberately, by humans. But both types of evolution involve the same high stakes—survival. And, as in the case of biological evolution, no particular culture trait or combination of culture traits has a guaranteed future. Societies must adapt to changing circumstances, and if they do not, they

[1] Leslie A. White, "The Expansion of the Scope of Science," in Morton H. Fried (ed.), *Readings in Anthropology,* 2nd ed., Vol. 1 (New York: Thomas Y. Crowell, 1968), pp. 15–24.

James Irwin with the lunar roving vehicle on the surface of the moon (Mount Hadley in the background). The Apollo 15, which carried astronauts Irwin, Scott, and Worden to the moon was launched July 26, 1971, two years after man first landed there. (Courtesy NASA.)

may lose some of their advantages. Thus, no particular people is intrinsically more advanced than any other. Rather, at any one point in time, a given geographical area may be more advantaged than others only, at some later point in time, to be surpassed. What seems like a pinnacle of civilization to the members of a society may in fact be only a dead end. We who face possible extinction through overpopulation, pollution, or atomic war ought to be especially aware of this sobering fact.

Yet our vulnerability should not make us feel powerless. There are many reasons to feel confident about the future. Consider what man has accomplished so far. By means of tools and weapons fashioned from sticks and stones, early man was able to hunt animals larger and more powerful than himself. He discovered how to make and use fire, to keep himself warm and augment his food supply by cooking. He domesticated plants and animals, which enabled him to increase his control over his food supply and settle down more permanently. He mined and smelted ores to fashion more durable tools. He built cities and irrigation systems, monuments and ships. He made it possible to travel from one continent to another in a single day. He has prolonged human life. In short, man and his culture have changed considerably over the course of his history; it seems then that at least some human populations, different ones at different times, have been able to adapt to changing circumstances, and, hopefully, will continue to be able to find the necessary adaptations to meet the challenges that now face us.

One of the problems that threatens the survival of our species is conflict within and between societies. At least part of that conflict may stem from the tendency of people to think of their own culture as an absolute standard by which all other cultures are to be judged. We refer to this attitude as "ethnocentrism." Probably, this attitude has always existed. In many cultures—the Cheyenne, for example—the name of the tribe means, essentially, "The People," while others are designated as "Non-People" or "enemies."[2] But, as Roger Brown points out, this attitude is far more problematic today than in the past:

> In earlier centuries unlike cultures were seldom in contact and the peoples having such cultures had no great need to cooperate. Orientals could think of us as ugly barbarian "white devils" and we could think of them as wily, superstitious "heathen." Today when Africans, Orientals, Europeans, and Americans must often meet and must somehow avoid conflict, it is recognized that ethnocentrism is an inadequate and dangerous world-view.[3]

The study of anthropology may contribute to increased tolerance of other peoples. If we increase our understanding of how and why other people are different from ourselves, then we may have less reason to condemn them for behavior which may appear strange to us, to make fun of how other people look, and to feel patronizingly superior. If we understand that many differences among people may be physical and cultural adaptations to different environments, then we should have no reason to feel superior just because our environment and social circumstances are different.

For example, someone not very knowledgeable about the !Kung Bushmen of the Kalahari Desert of South Africa might decide that they are "inferior savages," since they wear little clothing, have few possessions, live in meagre shelters, and exhibit none of our technological niceties. But it is important to reflect on how well a typical American community might fare if it woke to find itself in a similar environment. They would undoubtedly find that the absence of arable and pasture land made both agriculture and husbandry impossible, and so they would have to adopt a nomadic existence. They might then discard many of their material possessions so that they could travel easily to take advantage of changing water and wild food supplies. Because of the extreme heat and the lack of extra water for doing laundry, they might find it more practical to be naked than to wear clothes. They would undoubtedly find it impossible to build elaborate homes, and for social security, they might start to share the food that was brought into the group. Thus, if they survived at all, it is very likely that they would end up looking and acting far more like "ignorant savages" than like typical, middle-class Americans.

Physical differences too may be seen as adaptations to the environment. For example, in our society we admire people who are tall and slim.

[2] E. Adamson Hoebel, *The Cheyenne: Indians of the Great Plains* (New York: Holt, Rinehart and Winston, 1960), p. 1.

[3] Roger Brown, *Social Psychology* (New York: Free Press, 1965), p. 183.

However, if these same individuals were forced to live above the Arctic Circle, they might wish that they could trade their tall bodies for short, compact ones, since stocky physiques appear to conserve body heat more effectively and may therefore be more adaptive in cold climates.

Keeping in mind the principle of "cultural relativism" might help to alleviate some of the misunderstandings that arise between people of different cultural groups. Some of these misunderstandings may result from very subtle causes which operate below the level of consciousness. For example, different cultures have different conceptions of what gestures and interpersonal distances are appropriate under various circumstances. Arabs consider it proper to stand close enough to another person to smell him.[4] Americans, judging from the popularity of deodorants in our culture, seem to prefer to keep the olfactory dimension out of interpersonal relations. Thus, when someone comes "too close," we may feel that he is being too intimate; we may be offended and decide to avoid him and all other members of his culture. However, if we remember that this person may only be acting according to his culturally conditioned conception of what is proper in a given situation, we might be more willing to forgive his breaking of our cultural rules, which he is unaware of, and not be so inclined to view his behavior as intrusive.

If intolerance for others results in part from a lack of understanding of why peoples vary, the knowledge accumulated by anthropologists about other peoples may help lessen intolerance. The more we know and understand about others, the less apt we are to misinterpret how they behave. The knowledge gained by anthropologists can help us see the rationale for the behavior patterns and characteristics of other people and make us better able to appreciate their special adaptations to environmental and social conditions.

[4] Edward T. Hall, *The Hidden Dimension* (Garden City, N.Y.: Doubleday, 1966), pp. 144–153.

The Effect of the Modern World on Anthropology

In many respects, the world of today is a shrinking one. Not, of course, physically shrinking, but shrinking in the sense that it takes a shorter time to travel around it and even a shorter time to communicate around it—witness the worldwide network of TV satellites. Today it is possible to fly halfway around the globe in the time it took preindustrial man to visit a nearby town. Newspapers, radio, TV, and movies have done much to make different cultures more familiar and accessible to one another.

The world is shrinking culturally too, in the sense that more and more people are drawn each year into the world market economy, buying and selling similar things, and, as a consequence, altering the patterns of their lives. Perhaps the most obvious illustration of what is happening to the world culturally is the appearance of Coca-Cola, razor blades, steel tools, and even drive-in movies in places that not too long ago lacked such things. But the diffusion of these items is only a small part of the picture. More important than the spread of material goods has been the introduction of selling and buying and wage labor—conditions of life that make it possible for peoples all over the world to acquire the technological "goodies" they now see and hear about. The diffusion of market exchange all over the world reflects the expansion of certain nations' spheres of influence over the last century. In some places as a result of colonization or conquest, in others as a result of economic and military aid programs, and in still others because of a desire to emulate the dominant cultures (American, British, Chinese, and so on), the hundreds of different cultures that survive in the world have become more similar over the last 100 years.

Aside from whether or not these changes are desirable, from our point of view or from the point of view of the peoples experiencing them, we might ask how the shrinking cultural world affects the field of anthropology, particularly, of course, cultural anthropology.

Some cultural anthropologists have worried about the possible demise of their discipline because of the virtual disappearance of the primitive or noncommercial world, which in the past "provided the discipline with most of its data as well as the major inspiration for its key concepts and theoretical ideas."[5] Some of the societies known to ethnography have completely disappeared because of depopulation produced by the introduction of foreign infectious diseases; others have been so altered by contact with dominant societies that their cultures now retain few of the characteristics that made them unique. To be sure, there are still some cultures in the world (in the interior of New Guinea and a few other large Melanesian islands, and in the back areas of Brazil, Peru, and Venezuela) that have not yet drastically changed. But most of these have changed somewhat, largely under the impact of commercialization, and they will probably continue to change.

Some of those who are worried about the future of cultural anthropology foresee the disappearance of their discipline because it has traditionally focused on cultural variation, and that variation is diminishing. Cultural anthropology, for these people, is synonymous with the ethnographic study of exotic, out-of-the-way cultures not previously described. Nowadays it is difficult to find cultures which have been preserved in such an undescribed and unaltered state. Thus, it is said, we are running out of subject matter because we are running out of new cultures to describe, in part because many have already been described, in part because many have disappeared, and in part because many have so drastically altered as to be indistinguishable from others. Thus, some of the more pessimistic cultural anthropologists envision a time when the last ethnography has been written and the last native has been handed a bottle of Coca-Cola, and the death knell rings upon cultural anthropology as a discipline. Evidence suggests, however, that such a view may be mistaken.

There is no reason to believe that cultural variation, of at least some sorts, will ever disappear. The development of commonly held ideas,

[5] David Kaplan and Robert A. Manners, "Anthropology: Some Old Themes and New Directions," *Southwest Journal of Anthropology,* Vol. 27 (Spring 1971), p. 71.

Cultural variations will probably continue to exist as adaptations to different physical and social environments. At right, two women on a modern street in Stanleyville, The Congo, wear traditional dress. The Masai tribesman (below) *is visiting a dam construction site in Tanzania.* (Courtesy, United Nations.)

beliefs, and behaviors—in other words, culture—depends upon the existence of groups of people relatively separate from one another. After all, most people in their daily lives are isolated from individuals at the opposite ends of the earth, or even down the road, and inasmuch as this continues to be so, they will invariably develop some cultural differences. While it may be that modern techniques of transportation and communication facilitate the spread of cultural characteristics to all parts of the globe with great rapidity, thus diminishing cultural variability, it is unlikely that all parts will become alike. Thus, while a native of Melanesia and a native of the United States may hear the same song on the same transistor radio, this does not mean that their cultures will not retain some of their original characteristics or will not develop some distinctive adaptations. People in different parts of the world are confronted with different physical and social environments (different climates, soil conditions, natural resources, contacts, and opportunities), and, hence, the chances are that some aspects of their cultures will always be different, assuming that cultures generally consist of common responses that are adapted to particular environmental requirements.

Although cultural variability has undoubtedly decreased recently, it may also be true that much of what we see in the way of cultural variation depends upon what groups we choose to look at and when we look at them. If we move our perspective back in time, we may find (and justifiably, it seems, on the basis of present evidence) that there was less cultural variability in the Lower Paleolithic, when man was solely dependent upon hunting and gathering, than in the beginning of the Neolithic. In some areas of the world 10,000 years ago, man was dependent upon agriculture and domesticated animals; in other areas he was dependent upon sedentary food-collection; and in still other areas he was still dependent upon nomadic hunting and gathering. With the spread of agriculture, cultural variability may have again decreased as hunting and gathering began to disappear.

We might expect, then, that whenever a generally adaptive cultural pattern develops and spreads over the globe, cultural variability decreases, at least for a time. Hence, with the recent spread of commercial exchange, and even more significant, with the on-going diffusion of industrial culture, we may be witnessing a temporary diminution of cultural variability, as mankind experiences another great cultural change. But there is no reason to believe that further and differential cultural change, stemming from varying physical and social environmental requirements, will not occur in different parts of the world.

In short, it does not seem likely that cultural anthropology, the study of cultural variation, will soon run out of variability to study. The same thing can be said for physical anthropology, archaeology, and linguistics. With respect to physical anthropology, there is no reason to expect variation in biological characteristics between human populations to disappear in the future, as long as physical and social environments continue to vary. It will be a long time before the whole of mankind lives under identical environmental conditions, in one great "greenhouse." Moreover, there will always be that great depository of human variability to explore and study—the fossil and more recent human paleontological records; similarly, we shall always have the remains of past cultures to study and explain. And, with respect to linguistics, even if all linguistic variation disappears from the earth, we shall always have the descriptive data on past languages to study, with all the variability in those records still to be explained.

Yet, a larger question remains. Why should we study primitive cultures at all, either those that exist today or have existed in the past? What conceivable bearing could such studies have on the problems that beset modern technological man as he enters the closing decades of the twentieth century? To answer this question we must remind ourselves that man, whichever culture he may belong to, is still man, and, as a species, shares certain significant needs and characteristics in common. If we are to discover laws that account for human behavior, then, all cultures past and present are equally important. As Claude Lévi-Strauss has recently said:

> The thousands of societies that exist today, or once existed on the surface of the earth, constitute so many experiments, the only ones we can make use of to formulate and test our hypotheses, since we can't very well construct or repeat them in the laboratory as physical and natural scientists do. These experiments, represented by societies unlike our own, described and analyzed by anthropologists, provide one of the surest ways to understand what happens in the human mind and how it operates. That's what anthropology is good for in the most general way and what we can expect from it in the long run.[6]

New Directions in Cultural Anthropology

As we have seen, cultural anthropologists have, in the past, focused mainly on the cultures of the primitive or noncommerical world. Now

[6] Claude Lévi-Strauss, *New York Times* (January 21, 1972), p. 41; reprinted from *Diacritics*, Cornell University.

that most of these cultures have disappeared or have drastically changed, many anthropologists are turning their attention to societies that are more in the mainstream of technological and economic development. Such societies (the advanced nations of Europe and Asia or the developing countries of the Third World) have in former times been studied by other disciplines such as economics and political science. Now anthropologists have begun to use some of the techniques developed in the study of primitive cultures to study more complex societies. Urban anthropology, for example, a branch of cultural anthropology which is very much a part of this trend, offers possibilities for new research and has begun to attract many younger students who feel that the study of man in cities may lead to valuable insights into current problems.

In addition to the new interest in complex societies, cultural anthropologists have become interested in aspects of culture which ethnographers have previously neglected. For example, many anthropologists have begun to study unconscious cultural patterns—all those mental and physical habits which are shared by members of a culture but which manifest themselves below the level of conscious awareness. How people position themselves in various situations, how they sit, what they do with their arms and legs, whether they avoid or seek eye contact while speaking—all are aspects of this emerging field of study. The new interest in unconscious cultural patterns also involves an interest in the different ways in which people perceive and order the world around them. Most of these new investigations of unconscious cultural patterning are still essentially descriptive in orientation. Their intent is to find out how unconscious patterns vary, not so much yet why they vary. However, even the relatively few studies that have been done so far reveal fascinating similarities and differences in human behavior which, though not yet explainable in terms of tested and validated theory, are nonetheless extremely suggestive and promise much interesting work to come.

Finally, more and more comparative studies are being conducted which make use of descriptive data collected by other anthropologists in an effort to discover possible causal explanations of variable cultural characteristics. Just as we have the fossil and archaeological records, we have an enormous body of ethnographic data on different peoples, which will never disappear. There are many questions to be asked—and possibly many answers that can be gained—from the data we already have. The challenge of uncovering more definitive answers to how and why populations vary—in the past, present, and future—will always be with us.

SUMMARY

1. Man's understanding of his behavior has lagged behind his understanding of the physical world. This imbalance must be corrected if man is to solve the pressing human problems that now confront him. Perhaps the best way of achieving solutions to these problems is to exploit man's ingenuity by encouraging "pure" research of all types.

2. If man is to solve his problems he must abandon outmoded explanations of his behavior which portray him either as an impregnable citadel of free will or as an

automaton in the grip of external forces. If we are to understand human behavior we must want to, and we must believe that it is possible.

3. Anthropology is valuable in that it teaches us that no culture is intrinsically superior to any other; rather, human beings everywhere exercise roughly equal amounts of intelligence, ingenuity, and imagination in dealing with the conditions in which they find themselves. Anthropology can also teach us humility by showing us that man is an animal, related both physically and behaviorally to other animals, and subject as they are to the perils of natural selection—that he must adapt or die out. Yet, anthropology can also give us confidence by reminding us of man's adaptational ability in the past. If man has survived as well as he has in the past, perhaps there is reason to believe that he will be able to do so in the future.

4. Anthropology may help to destroy prejudice by breaking down ethnocentrism. Ethnographic studies can show us why other peoples are the way they are, both culturally and physically, as well as explaining how the behavior of peoples of other cultures which may strike us as improper or offensive is really just as proper as our own behavior within its particular cultural context.

5. The world is becoming smaller both physically and culturally; there are few unknowns left on the anthropological map. Although some see the growing cultural homogeneity of the world as an unfavorable omen for anthropological research, this is not really the case. Different environmental conditions still produce variability in culture, despite superficial resemblances imposed by the spread of commercial, industrial society. Moreover, if things *are* becoming more similar, historical evidence tells us this is probably only temporary. We need to continue studying human societies, both past and contemporary, because each represents a valuable experiment in adjusting to the conditions of life.

6. Given recent changes in the world, anthropologists have taken new directions in research. Anthropologists now study advanced as well as primitive cultures, including life patterns in the urban environment. Other new fields include the study of variability in "unconscious patterning" as it is revealed in candid films and tape recordings of daily life in various cultures, and comparative or cross-cultural research, which draws universal inferences from ethnographic data already collected. All evidence seems to show that there is still much for man to learn about himself.

Glossary
Bibliography
Index

GLOSSARY

N.B. **Boldface** indicates that a word in a definition is also defined.

Abbevillian tradition: early Acheulean tool tradition associated with *Homo erectus* (same as **Chellean**).

acculturation: the process that occurs when a group of people is brought into prolonged contact with a more powerful society. The weaker group tends to acquire cultural elements of the dominant group.

Acheulean: tool-making tradition of *Homo erectus* producing percussion-flaked hand axes.

achieved qualities: those the individual acquires by doing something.

affinal: related by marriage.

age-grade: a category of persons who happen to fall within a particular, culturally distinguished, age range.

age-set: a group of persons of similar age and sex who move through some or all of life's stages together.

allele: one member of pair of **genes** which determine a trait.

ambilineal descent: affiliates an individual with kinsmen related to him or her through men *or* women (also called **cognatic descent**).

animatism: a belief in supernatural forces.

animism: a term used by Edward Tylor to describe the belief in a dual existence for all things—a physical, visible body and a psychic, invisible soul.

anthropoids: man's closest living primate relatives classified as three separate superfamilies—New World monkeys **(Ceboidea)**, Old World monkeys **(Cercopithecoidea)**, and apes and man **(Hominoidea)**—about 150 arboreal and terrestrial species.

applied anthropology: the planning or the carrying out of directed culture change through an application of anthropological knowledge.

archaeology: the study of the cultures of prehistoric and historic peoples through the analysis of material remains.

artifact: a material object made by man.

association: organizations which have membership based on commonly shared characteristics or interests.

atlatl: Aztec word for spear thrower.

Aurignacian: an Upper Paleolithic culture dating from 35,000 to 22,000 B.C. **Burins,** used mainly for carving wood, bone, and ivory, were widely used.

Australopithecus africanus: bipedal hominid living during the late Pliocene through the early Pleistocene; had rounded brain case and cranial capacity between 428 and 485 cc.

Australopithecus robustus: bipedal hominid larger than *A. africanus,* possibly an open-country vegetarian.

avunculocal residence: whereby a married couple goes to live with or near the husband's mother's brother.

balanced reciprocity: giving with the expectation of a more or less immediate and equivalent return.

band: fairly small, usually nomadic, self-sufficient, autonomous group of people.

bifacial tool: a tool flaked or worked on two sides.

bilateral descent: affiliates an individual more or less equally with his or her mother's and father's relatives of all types.

bilocal residence: whereby a married couple lives with or near the husband's parents or the wife's parents.

bipedalism: locomotion on two legs.
B.P.: abbreviation for "before present."
brachiation: locomotion through the trees by swinging arm over arm.
bride price: money or goods given to the bride's kin by the groom or his kin before or upon marriage (also called bride wealth).
bride service: work performed by a prospective groom for his bride's family of short or long duration. It can be done before or after the marriage is finalized; in some cases bride service may supplement, or even be substituted for, the bride price.
burin: chisel-like stone tools used for carving.

carbon^{14}: a radioactive isotope of carbon used to date organic material.
caste system: a closed hierarchical system of groups with differential access to prestige and economic resources whose membership is completely ascribed by birth.
catarrhine: flat nosed; i.e., Old World monkeys.
Ceboidea: Anthropoid superfamily, New World monkeys.
Cercopithecoidea: Anthropoid superfamily, Old World monkeys.
Chellean tradition: early **Acheulean** tool tradition associated with *Homo erectus* (same as *Abbevillian*).
chiefdom: a group with a formal authority structure integrating a multicommunity political unit.
chromosome: a structure in the nucleus of a cell containing **genes** that transmit traits from one generation to the next.
civilization: urban society, from the Latin word for "city-state."
Clactonian: Middle Paleolithic flake tool tradition.
clan: a set of kin whose members believe themselves descendants of a common ancestor or ancestress, but the links back to that ancestor cannot be specified (also called a **sib**); often designated by an animal or plant name.
class: a category of persons who have about the same chance to obtain economic resources and prestige.
class/caste society: society having structured unequal access to both economic resources and prestige.
cognate: words or **morphemes** of similar sound and meaning.
cognatic descent: affiliates an individual with kinsmen related to him or her through men *or* women (also called **ambilineal descent**).
commercialization: buying and selling in markets, accompanied by the use of money as a medium of exchange.
communal ownership: every member of a group having equal access to a resource.
coprolites: fossilized excrement of animals.
corvée: a system of required labor.
couvade: the practice in which a husband attempts to participate in the birth process by closely imitating his wife in labor.
Cro-Magnon man: earliest known specimen of modern man *(Homo sapiens sapiens)*, emerged about 50,000–30,000 years ago.
cross-cousins: children of siblings of the opposite sex.
cultural relativity: the attitude that a society's customs should be viewed in the context of that society's culture and environment.
culture: the set of learned beliefs, values, and behaviors generally shared by the members of a society.
culture trait, culture element: a unit of learned behavior, value, or belief, or its product.
cuneiform: wedge-shaped writing invented by the Sumerians in the fourth millennium B.C.
cusp: point on the chewing surface of a tooth.

dendrochronology: tree-ring dating method.
descriptive linguistics: that branch of anthropology which is concerned with variations in the structure and meaning of languages.
diastema: a space between the teeth to accommodate the canine.
diffusion: a process by which culture traits or elements are borrowed from another culture as the result of nonviolent contact, for example, through trade.
divination: the process of trying to contact the supernatural, generally to find an answer to some question regarding the future, by any one of several means: drawing straws, reading palms or bones or entrails, rubbing-boards, trance states, and so on.
DNA: deoxyribonucleic acid; a long, two-stranded molecule in helical form holding the chemical code of the **gene.**
dominant: the **allele** of a gene pair that is always expressed in the **phenotype.**
double descent: affiliates an individual for some purposes with a group of **matrilineal** kinsmen, and for other purposes with a group of **patrilineal** kinsmen.
dowry: a substantial transfer of goods or money from

the bride's family to the married couple or to the groom's family.
Dryopithecus: Miocene fossil having **Y-5 trait** characteristic of hominoid molars.

ecology: the study of the interrelationships between organisms and their environment.
econiche: ecological niche; different parts of the same habitat that provide different resources and opportunities for adaptation.
economic system: customs regulating the access to natural resources, customs for transforming those resources through labor into necessities and other desired items, and customs for distributing (and perhaps exchanging) goods and services.
egalitarian society: a society in which all persons of a given age-sex category have equal access to economic resources and to prestige.
Ego: in kinship, the central reference point; the focal member.
embryology: the study of the formation and development of embryos.
enculturation: the development, through the influence of parents with reinforcement by others in society, of patterns of behavior in children that conform to the standards deemed appropriate by the culture (also called **socialization**).
endogamy: a rule specifying marriage to a person within one's own culturally defined group or community.
Eocene: geologic epoch 54 to 35 million years B.P.; tropical and subtropical forest belts, increased sophistication of arboreal primates, lemurs and tarsiers (stereoscopic vision, reduced snout, grasping thumbs and big toes).
ethnocentrism: the attitude that another society's customs and ideas can be judged in the context of one's own culture.
ethnography: a detailed description of a society's customary behaviors, beliefs, and attitudes.
ethnology: the study of how and why cultures differ.
ethnoscience: an approach attempting to derive rules of thought from the logical analysis of ethnographic data.
evolution: development of one form from a previous form.
exogamy: a rule specifying marriage to a person outside one's own group or community.
expressive behavior: activities such as art, music, dance, and folklore, which presumably express thoughts and feelings.
extended family: a family consisting of two or more monogamous, polygynous, or polyandrous families linked by a blood tie.
extensive (shifting) cultivation: farming method in which the land is worked for short periods, then left to regenerate some years before being used again.

family: a social unit consisting minimally of a married couple and the children that couple may have.
family of orientation: the family one is born into.
family of procreation: the family one forms by marriage.
fetish: an object which is believed to contain supernatural power and is worshipped because of it.
feuding: a state of recurring hostilities between families or groups of kinsmen, usually motivated by a desire to avenge an offense against a member of the group.
fluted point: lance-like point that has had a flake removed down the center of the point to the base; unique to the New World.
foramen magnum: the hole in the base of the skull through which the nerves of the spinal cord pass.
fossil: the preserved remains of plants and animals that lived in the past.
functionalism: a theoretical orientation which assumes that all culture traits are useful parts of the society in which they occur.

gene flow: process by which **genes** move from one **gene pool** to another through intergroup mating.
gene pool: the total number and variety of **genes** possessed by the members of a given population.
generalized reciprocity: gift giving without any immediate return or conscious thought of one.
general-purpose money: serves as a medium of exchange, a standard of value, and a store of wealth which is nonperishable, transportable, and divisible.
genes: chemical units of heredity located on chromosomes.
genetic drift: the process whereby descendants of a small band of migrants come to have different frequencies of certain genetic traits as compared with the frequencies in the ancestral population, merely because the migrants initially and accidentally had different frequencies of those traits.
genitor: one's biological father.

genotype: the hereditary potential of a gene or set of genes; an individual's genetic make-up.
geographical race: a set of populations (at least formerly neighboring) which has certain distinctive trait frequencies.
ghosts: supernatural beings who were once human; the souls of dead people.
Gigantopithecus: the largest known fossil primate having ape-like molars.
gods: supernatural beings of nonhuman origin, they are named personalities and often anthropomorphic.
Gravettian: Upper Paleolithic culture centered primarily in eastern and central Europe from about 22,000–18,000 B.C.

half-life: the time it takes a given amount of radioactive material to lose one-half of its radioactivity.
heterozygous: having differing **genes** or **alleles** in corresponding locations on a pair of **chromosomes.**
historical linguistics: the study of how languages change over time and how languages may be related.
holistic: describing a phenomenon as a whole, rather than as a sum of parts.
hominid: man-like to the exclusion of apes; refers to those creatures who diverged from the ape-like **hominoids** to form the human evolutionary line.
hominoid: man-like, but refers to apes as well as man; primates distinct from monkeys.
Hominoidea: anthropoid superfamily, apes and man.
Homo erectus: fossil species of man from the Pleistocene exemplified by Peking man; had a cranial capacity of 1,000 cc and may have been able to speak.
Homo habilis: designation for the skeletal remains of several **hominids** found at Olduvai Gorge (Tanzania), which date from about 1.8 million years ago; may have been a tool maker.
Homo sapiens: species of animal to which modern man belongs. Technically, modern man today is known as *Homo sapiens sapiens.*
Homo sapiens sapiens: modern man.
homozygous: having identical **genes** or **alleles** in corresponding locations on a pair of **chromosomes.**
horticulture: plant cultivation carried out with relatively primitive tools and methods.
hunter-gatherers: peoples who subsist on the collection of naturally occurring plants and animals.

ideal culture: patterns which most members of the society say they ought to follow in particular situations.
incest taboo: the prohibition of sexual intercourse or marriage between mother and son, father and daughter, and brother and sister.
initiation ceremony: a ceremony symbolizing changed status, usually the passage from childhood to adulthood.
intensive agriculture: food production characterized by use of the plow, draft animals, fertilizers, irrigation, water-storage techniques, and other improved techniques.

joint family: an **extended family** in which the constituent families are linked through a sibling tie.

kindred: a group composed of an individual's close **bilateral** relatives.
Kula ring: a ceremonial exchange of valued shell ornaments in the Trobriand Islands in which white shell armbands are traded in a counterclockwise direction around the islands while red shell necklaces travel in a clockwise direction.

law: rules stipulating what is permissible and what is not; codified law is written law.
lemur: nocturnal, arboreal **prosimian** having stereoscopic vision. Several species; found only on the island of Madagascar.
Levalloisian: flake-tool tradition which developed during the **Acheulean** period whereby tools of a predetermined size could be produced by chiseling off flakes from a shaped core with a prepared striking platform.
levirate: custom whereby a man marries his brother's widow.
lexicon: the vocabulary of a language.
lineage: a set of kin whose members trace descent from a common ancestor through known links.
local race: a breeding population, or local group, whose members usually interbreed with each other.

Magdalenian: the last tradition of the Upper Paleolithic of Western Europe dating from 15,000–8,000 B.C. The use of microliths increased and cave art reached a peak during this period.
magic: the practice of certain rituals which are believed to compel the supernatural powers to act in a particular way.
mana: a supernatural force inhabiting certain objects and people, which confers success and/or strength.

manioc: cassava; a tropical plant with large starchy tubers.
market exchange: distribution of goods and services by means of commercial or monetary exchange.
marriage: a socially approved sexual and economic union between individuals which is presumed, both by those involved and by others, to be more or less permanent, and which subsumes reciprocal rights and obligations between spouses.
matriclan: a clan tracing descent through the female line.
matrilineage: a kin group whose members trace descent through known links in the female line from a common ancestress.
matrilineal descent: affiliates an individual with kinsmen related to him or her through women only.
matrilocal residence: whereby a married couple lives with or near the wife's parents.
megaliths: huge monuments made of stone, generally used to mark burial sites, erected in parts of the Middle East and throughout Europe.
Meganthropus: fossil jaw fragments of large **hominid** found in Asia; may be *A. robustus.*
meiosis: the process by which the reproductive cells are formed. In this kind of division, the number of chromosomes in the new-formed cells is reduced by half, so that when fertilization occurs, the resulting zygote (the product of the egg and the sperm) will have the normal number of chromosomes appropriate to its species, rather than double that number.
melanin: dark brown or black pigment in plants and animals.
Mesolithic: Middle Stone Age during which preagricultural villages were founded, beginning about 12,000 B.C.
microlith: a very small stone artifact.
Miocene: geologic epoch 25 million to 13 million years B.P.; warm temperate and cool temperate climates, increasing savannas, apes flourished and the **hominids** began to develop.
mitosis: cellular reproduction involving duplication of each pair of chromosomes.
modal personality: a composite of those personality characteristics that are exhibited most frequently by individuals in a society.
modal personality characteristics: those characteristics most frequently exhibited by individuals in a society.
mode: a statistical term referring to the most frequent occurrence in a given series.
moiety: a **unilineal descent** group, when the society is divided into two such groups.
monogamy: marriage between only one man and only one woman at a time.
monotheistic religions: those in which there is a single, powerful god to whom all other supernatural beings are subordinate (or are alternative manifestations of the supreme being).
morph: the smallest unit of a language that has meaning.
morpheme: one or more **morphs** with the same meaning.
morphology: the ways in which **morphemes** are combined to form words.
Mousterian: Neandertal tool-making tradition using prepared core and percussion flaking, the flakes retouched to make specialized tools.
mutation: a change in the molecular structure, or **DNA** code, of a gene.

natural selection: the process by which those members of a particular species which are better adapted to their environment live longer and produce more offspring than those which are not so well adapted. In this way, a better-adapted species, one which is likely to continue to survive, eventually evolves.
Neandertal man: evolved from early *Homo sapiens* about 80,000 years ago; looked like *Homo erectus* but had a larger brain.
negative reciprocity: an attempt to take advantage of another for one's own self-interest.
Neolithic: New Stone Age beginning in the Near East. 11,000–10,000 years ago; characterized by plant and animal domestication.
neolocal residence: whereby a married couple lives apart from the relatives of either spouse.
norm: a culturally shared statement of how people ought to behave in particular situations.
nuclear family: a family consisting of a married couple and any children they may have.

oath: the act of calling upon a deity to bear witness to the truth of what one says.
Oligocene: geologic epoch 35 to 25 million years B.P.; subtropical climates with cooling trend, forests and expanding grasslands; new primates include the ancestors of later monkeys and apes.
Oligopithecus: primate genus represented by a jaw found in the Fayum Depression (Egypt) and dating from the **Oligocene** epoch.

ordeal: a means used to determine guilt or innocence by submitting the accused to dangerous or painful tests believed to be under supernatural control.
Oreopithecus: fossil dated to the late Miocene or early Pliocene; possibly ancestral to the living apes or to humans or possibly to neither.

Paleocene: geologic epoch 65 to 54 million years B.P.; tropical and subtropical climates, uplift and drainage of land, emergence of arboreal primates.
Paleolithic: The Old Stone Age, dating from about 500,000 to 80,000 years ago; characterized by the use of stone hand axes.
paleontology: study of past life through fossil remains; study of past life forms relevant to man is called *human paleontology.*
Paleozoic: geologic era beginning about 500 million years ago and lasting until about 200 million years ago.
parallel-cousins: children of siblings of the same sex.
Parapithecus: Oligocene fossil from Fayum (Egypt), related to **prosimians** or **anthropoids.**
pastoralism: a type of food production based largely upon the maintenance of large herds of animals.
pater: one's sociological father.
patriclan: a clan tracing descent through the male line.
patrilineage: a kin group whose members trace descent through known links in the male line from a common ancestor.
patrilineal descent: affiliates an individual with kinsmen of both sexes related to him or her through men only.
patrilocal residence: whereby a married couple lives with or near the husband's parents.
peasants: rural people who produce food for their own subsistence, but who must also contribute or sell their surpluses to others (in towns and cities) who do not produce their own food.
percussion flaking: a tool-making technique where one stone is struck with another stone to remove a flake.
personality: the distinctive way an individual thinks, feels, and behaves.
personality integration of culture: the theory that personality or psychological processes may account for connections between certain aspects of culture.
phenotype: the observable physical appearance of an organism, which often does not reflect his complete genetic constitution, or **genotype.** (For example, a person who has brown eyes may also carry a **recessive** gene for blue eyes.)
phone: a speech sound in a language.
phoneme: a class of slightly varying sounds which do not make any difference in meaning to the speakers of a language.
phratry: a **unilineal descent** group composed of a number of supposedly related **clans** or **sibs.**
physical anthropology: the study of man as a physical organism; deals with the emergence and evolution of man and contemporary biological variation among human populations.
Pithecanthropus erectus: Java man; now known as *Homo erectus.*
platyrrhine: broad nosed, that is, nostrils which are wide apart; i.e., New World monkeys.
Pleistocene: the geologic epoch during which man became the dominant life form, dating from about 2.5 million to 10,000 years ago.
Pliocene: geologic epoch of warm climates during which early hominids diverged from apes, dating from 6 to 2.5 million years ago.
Pliopithecus: Miocene fossil having five-cusped molars, probably an ancestor of the gibbon.
polyandry: marriage of one woman to two or more men at a time.
polygamy: marriage to more than one spouse simultaneously.
polygyny: marriage of one man to two or more women at a time.
polytheistic religions: those in which there are a number of powerful gods.
Poro: a secret society with membership open to all males, contingent upon passing a series of grueling physical tests; existing among the Kpelle, Mende, and Temne of West Africa.
postpartum: the period following the birth of a baby.
potassium-argon dating: method of absolute dating using the rate of decay for radioactive potassium.
potlatch: a feast in which large quantities of food are consumed and great numbers of other objects given away to gain prestige.
pressure flaking: tool-production technique whereby small flakes are struck off by pressing against the core with a bone, wood, or antler tool.
priest: a full-time religious intermediary between gods and men.
Primate: mammalian order divided into the sub-

orders **prosimians** and **anthropoids;** over 200 living species including man.

private property: the exclusive right of an individual to use and dispose of a resource.

Proconsul: Dryopithecus-like, early Miocene fossil; an early **hominoid** of which three species are known to have existed.

projective tests: tests (such as the **Rorschach** ink blot and the **Thematic Apperception** tests) which utilize ambiguous stimuli; the test subject must project his own personality traits in order to structure the ambiguous stimuli.

Propliopithecus: Oligocene fossil from Fayum (Egypt) believed to be **hominoid** at or near the beginning of the line from which man and the living apes were to emerge; had five-cusped molars.

prosimian: the oldest suborder of primates; includes tree shrews, lemurs, and tarsiers.

quipu: a memory device utilizing strings and knots used by the pre-Columbian Incas.

radiocarbon dating: a widely used method for dating organic remains up to 60,000–50,000 years old using the rate of decay for radioactive **carbon**^{14}.

raid: a short-term use of force, usually carefully preplanned and organized, to realize a limited objective.

Ramapithecus: the earliest known **hominid** fossil consisting of an upper jaw with a few teeth attached; estimated to be about 14 to 12 million years old.

random sample: a sample of a population, chosen so that every individual in that population has an equal chance to be chosen.

rank society: society having no structured unequal access to economic resources, but having structured unequal access to status positions and prestige.

recessive: a **gene** or **allele** which is only expressed in the **homozygous** condition.

reciprocity: giving and taking without the use of money.

redistribution: the accumulation of goods by a particular person or in a particular place for the purpose of subsequent administered distribution.

religion: any set of attitudes, beliefs, and practices pertaining to supernatural forces or beings.

Rorschach test: ink-blot **projective test** using an ordered set of ten cards.

secret society: associations characterized principally by limited membership and secret rituals.

segmentary lineage system: a hierarchy of more and more inclusive lineages, which usually functions only in conflict situations.

shaman: a religious intermediary whose primary function is to cure people, by using sacred songs, pantomime, and other means.

sib: a set of kin whose members believe themselves descendants of a common ancestor or ancestress, but the links back to that ancestor cannot be specified (also called a **clan**); often designated by an animal or plant name.

sister-exchange: the custom whereby a sister or other female relative of the groom is exchanged for the bride.

slavery: a system in which a class of persons do not own their own labor or the fruits thereof.

socialization: the development, through the influence of parents and others, of patterns of behavior in children that conform to the standards deemed appropriate by the culture (also called **enculturation**).

social stratification: structured unequal access to advantages (both prestige and economic resources).

society: a group of people occupying a particular territory and speaking a common language which is not generally intelligible to neighboring peoples.

sociolinguistics: the study of how people customarily use language in different social contexts.

Solutrean: Upper Paleolithic culture in France and Spain which dates between 18,000 and 15,000 B.C.; known for fine stone tools, particularly laurel leaf blades.

sorcery: the use of certain materials to harm people through the manipulation of supernatural powers.

sororate: custom whereby a woman marries her deceased sister's husband.

special-purpose money: objects of value for which only some goods and services can be exchanged.

speciation: the development of a new species.

spirits: unnamed supernatural beings of nonhuman origin, who may be either helpful or malicious toward men.

status: prestige position in a society.

stimulus diffusion: a pattern of diffusion in which knowledge of a trait belonging to another culture stimulates the invention or development of a local equivalent.

structural-functionalism: a theoretical orientation which assumes that various aspects of social behavior exist to maintain a society's social structure.

syntax: the ways in which words are arranged to form phrases and sentences.

taboo: a supernatural force inhabiting certain objects and people, which can cause harm to anyone coming into contact with them.

tarsier: nocturnal, arboreal **prosimian** found on the islands of southeastern Asia, named because of elongated tarsal, or ankle bone; three living species.

Thematic Apperception Test (TAT): projective test using an ordered set of illustrations which usually depict some life situation.

totem: a plant or animal name given to a **clan** or **sib** which provides for group identification and may have other special significance for the group.

tree shrew: insect-eating, arboreal, clawed **prosimian.**

tribe: egalitarian group with associations that can potentially integrate more than one local group into a large whole.

unifacial tool: a tool flaked or worked on one side.

unilineal descent: affiliation with a group of kinsmen through descent links of one sex only.

unisex associations: an association restricting membership to one sex.

universally ascribed qualities: those one is born with and thus acquires automatically (such as age and sex).

variably ascribed qualities: those acquired at birth but not found in all persons of a given age-sex category.

Voodoo: a form of religion practiced by some natives of the Caribbean, combining aspects of Catholicism and various African religions.

witchcraft: the practice of attempting to harm people by supernatural means, but through the emotions and thought processes alone, not using any tangible objects.

Y-5 trait: five cusps on a molar arranged in a Y shape.

Zinjanthropus boisei: skull fragment found in a rock slide at Olduvai Gorge (Tanzania) by Mary Leakey, later classified as an australopithecine.

BIBLIOGRAPHY

Aberle, D. F.: "A Note on Relative Deprivation Theory as Applied to Millenarian and Other Cult Movements," W. A. Lessa and E. Z. Vogt (Eds.), *Reader in Comparative Religion,* 3rd ed. (New York: Harper & Row, 1971), pp. 528–531.

Aberle, D. F., et al.: "The Incest Taboo and the Mating Patterns of Animals" (*American Anthropologist,* Vol. 65 [1963]), pp. 253–265.

Adams, F. T.: *The Way to Modern Man: An Introduction to Human Evolution,* ed. S. T. Kimball (New York: Columbia University Press, 1968).

Adams, R. M.: *The Evolution of Urban Society* (Chicago: Aldine, 1966).

———: "The Origin of Cities" (*Scientific American,* Vol. 203 [1960]), pp. 153–168.

Alland, A., Jr.: *Evolution and Human Behavior* (Garden City, N.Y.: Natural History Press, 1967).

Arensberg, C. M., and A. H. Niehoff: *Introducing Social Change: A Manual for Americans Overseas* (Chicago: Aldine, 1964).

Armstrong, W. E.: "Rossel Island Money: A Unique Monetary System" (*The Economic Journal,* Vol. 34 [September 1924]), pp. 423–429.

Asch, S. E.: "Studies of Independence and Conformity: A Minority of One against a Unanimous Majority" (*Psychological Monographs,* Vol. 70 [1965]), pp. 1–70.

Ashton, H.: *The Basuto,* 2nd ed. (London: Oxford University Press, 1967).

Ayres, B. C.: "Effects of Infant Carrying Practices on Rhythm in Music" (Paper presented at the 68th Annual Meeting of the American Anthropological Association, November 1969, New Orleans).

———: "Effects of Infantile Stimulation on Musical Behavior," in A. Lomax, *Folk Song Style and Culture* (Washington, D.C.: American Association for the Advancement of Science Publication No. 88, 1968), pp. 211–221.

Balandier, G.: *Political Anthropology,* trans. from the French by A. M. Sheridan Smith (New York: Random House, Pantheon Books, 1970).

Banton, M. (Ed.): *Anthropological Approaches to the Study of Religion,* Association of Social Anthropologists of the Commonwealth, Monograph No. 3 (New York: Praeger, 1966).

———: *Political Systems and the Distribution of Power,* Association of Social Anthropologists of the Commonwealth, Monograph No. 2 (New York: Praeger, 1965).

Barnouw, V.: *Culture and Personality* (Homewood, Ill.: Dorsey Press, 1963).

Barry, H., III, M. K. Bacon, and I. L. Child: "A Cross-Cultural Survey of Some Sex Differences in Socialization" (*Journal of Abnormal and Social Psychology,* Vol. 55 [November 1957]), pp. 327–332.

Barry, H., III, I. L. Child, and M. K Bacon: "Relation of Child Training to Subsistence Economy" (*American Anthropologist,* Vol. 61, No. 1 [February 1959]), pp. 51–63.

Barth, F.: "Nomadism in the Mountain and Plateau Areas of South West Asia," in *The Problems of the Arid Zone* (Paris: UNESCO, 1960).

——: *Nomads of South Persia* (Oslo: Universitetets-forlaget, 1964; New York: Humanities Press).

Bartram, W.: *The Travels of William Bartram* (New Haven: Yale University Press, 1958).

Bateson, G., and M. Mead: *Balinese Character: A Photographic Analysis* (New York: Special Publication of New York Academy of Sciences, 1942).

Belshaw, C. S.: *Traditional Exchange and Modern Markets* (Englewood Cliffs, N.J.: Prentice-Hall, 1965).

Benedict, R.: *The Chrysanthemum and the Sword* (Boston: Houghton Mifflin, 1946).

Berlin, B.: "A Universalist-Evolutionary Approach in Ethnographic Semantics" (*Current Directions in Anthropology,* Vol. 3 [September 1970]), pp. 3–18.

Bernardi, B.: "The Age System of the Nilo-Hamitic Peoples" (*Africa,* Vol. 22 [October 1952]), pp. 316–332.

Binford, L. R.: "Post-Pleistocene Adaptations," in S. R. Binford and L. R. Binford (Eds.), *New Perspectives in Archeology* (Chicago: Aldine, 1968), Ch. 16.

Birdsell, J.: *Human Evolution* (New York: Macmillan, 1972).

Boas, F.: *Geographical Names of the Kwakiutl Indians* (New York: Columbia University Press, 1934).

——: *Primitive Art* (Oslo: H. Ashehous, 1927).

——: *The Religion of the Kwakiutl.* 2 vols. (New York: Columbia University Contributions to Anthropology, 1930), Pt. II, pp. 1–41.

Bohannan, P.: "The Migration and Expansion of the Tiv" (*Africa,* Vol. 24 [1954]), pp. 2–16.

Bohannan, P. (Ed.): *Law and Warfare: Studies in the Anthropology of Conflict,* American Museum Sourcebooks in Anthropology (Garden City, N.Y.: Natural History Press, 1967).

Bohannan, P., and G. Dalton (Eds.): *Markets in Africa* (Evanston, Ill.: Northwestern University Press, 1962).

Bolinger, D.: *Aspects of Language* (New York: Harcourt Brace Jovanovich, 1968).

Bordaz, J.: *Tools of the Old and New Stone Age* (Garden City, N.Y.: Natural History Press, 1970).

Bordes, F. H.: *The Old Stone Age,* trans. J. E. Anderson (New York: World University Library, 1968).

Boserup, E.: *The Conditions of Agricultural Growth: The Economics of Agrarian Change under Population Pressures* (Chicago: Aldine, 1965).

Brace, C. L., and A. Montagu: *Man's Evolution: An Introduction to Physical Anthropology* (New York: Macmillan, 1965).

Braidwood, R. J.: "The Agricultural Revolution" (*Scientific American,* Vol. 203 [1960]).

Braidwood, R. J., and G. Willey.: "Conclusions and Afterthoughts," in *Courses toward Urban Life* (Chicago: Aldine, 1962).

Briggs, L. C.: *The Tribes of the Sahara* (Cambridge, Mass.: Harvard University Press, 1960).

Brinton, C.: *Anatomy of a Revolution* (Englewood Cliffs, N.J.: Prentice-Hall, 1938).

Brown, R., and M. Ford: "Address in American English" (*Journal of Abnormal and Social Psychology,* Vol. 62 [1961]), pp. 375–385.

Brues, A.: "The Spearman and the Archer," in Y. Cohen (Ed.), *Man in Adaptation: The Biosocial Background* (Chicago: Aldine, 1968).

Buettner-Janusch, J. : *Origins of Man: Physical Anthropology* (New York: Wiley, 1966).

Bunzel, R.: "The Nature of Katcinas," in W. A. Lessa and E. Z. Vogt (Eds.), *Reader in Comparative Religion,* 3rd ed. (New York: Harper & Row, 1971), pp. 493–495.

Burling, R.: *Man's Many Voices: Language in Its Cultural Context* (New York: Holt, Rinehart and Winston, 1970).

Burton, R. V., and J. W. M. Whiting, "The Absent Father and Cross-Sex Identity" (*Merrill-Palmer Quarterly of Behavior and Development,* Vol. 7, No. 2 [1961]), pp. 85–95.

Butterworth, D. S., "A Study of the Urbanization Process among Mixtec Migrants from Tilantongo to Mexico City," in W. Mangin (Ed.), *Peasants in Cities: Readings in the Anthropology of Urbanization* (Boston: Houghton Mifflin, 1970).

Butzer, K. W.: *Environment and Archeology: An Ecological Approach to Prehistory,* 2nd ed. (New York and Chicago: Aldine Atherton, 1971).

Campbell, B. G.: *Human Evolution: An Introduction to Man's Adaptations* (Chicago: Aldine, 1966).

Carneiro, R. L.: "Slash-and-Burn Cultivation among the Kuikuru and Its Implications for Cultural Development in the Amazon Basin" (*Antropologica,* Supplement No. 2 [September 1961]).

———: "A Theory of the Origin of the State" (*Science,* Vol. 169 [August 21, 1970]), pp. 733–738.

Carpenter, C. R.: "A Field Study in Siam of the Behavior and Social Relations of the Gibbons, Hylobateslar" (*Comparative Psychological Monographs,* Vol. 16, No. 15 [1940]), pp. 1–212.

Carroll, J. B. (Ed.): *Language, Thought, and Reality: Selected Writings of Benjamin Lee Whorf* (New York: Wiley, 1956), pp. 65–86.

Casagrande, J. B.: "Comanche Baby Talk" (*International Journal of American Linguistics,* Vol. 14 [1948]), pp. 11–14.

Casagrande, J. B. (Ed.): *In the Company of Man: Twenty Portraits by Anthropologists* (New York: Harper & Row, 1960).

Chagnon, N. A.: *Yanomamö, the Fierce People* (New York: Holt, Rinehart and Winston, 1968).

Chard, C. S.: *Man in Prehistory* (New York: McGraw-Hill, 1969).

Childe, V. G.: *Man Makes Himself* (New York: Mentor Books, New American Library, 1951).

Clark, G.: *World Prehistory: A New Outline* (New York: Cambridge University Press, 1969).

Clark, G., and S. Piggott: *Prehistoric Societies* (New York: Alfred A. Knopf, 1965).

Clark, J. D.: *The Prehistory of Africa* (New York: Praeger, 1970).

Clark, J. G. D.: *Prehistoric Europe: The Economic Basis* (Stanford: Stanford University Press, 1962).

Clark, W. E. Le G.: *The Antecedents of Man: An Introduction to the Evolution of the Primates* (New York: Harper Torchbook, 1963).

———: *History of the Primates: An Introduction to the Study of Fossil Man* (Chicago: University of Chicago Press, 1949, 1965).

Coe, M. D.: *The Maya* (New York: Praeger, 1966).

Cohen, R., and J. Middleton (Eds.): *Comparative Political Systems,* American Museum Sourcebooks in Anthropology (Garden City, N.Y.: Natural History Press, 1967).

Cohen, Y.: *Social Structure and Personality: A Casebook* (New York: Holt, Rinehart and Winston, 1961).

Coles, J. M., and E. S. Higgs: *The Archaeology of Early Man* (London: Faber and Faber, 1970).

Coon, C. S.: *The Origin of Races* (New York: Alfred A. Knopf, 1962).

Coult, A. D., and R. W. Habenstein: *Cross Tabulations of Murdock's* World Ethnographic Sample (Columbia, Mo.: University of Missouri Press, 1965).

Covarrubias, M.: *The Eagle, the Jaguar, and the Serpent* (New York: Alfred A. Knopf, 1954).

———: *Indian Art of Mexico and Central America* (New York: Alfred A. Knopf, 1957).

Crabtree, D. E., and B. R. Butler: "Notes on Experiment in Flint Knapping: 1 Heat Treatment of Silicia Materials" (*Tebiwa,* Vol. 7, No. 1), p. 1.

Curtis, G.: "A Clock for the Ages: Potassium-Argon" (*National Geographic* [October 1961]).

Dalton, G.: "Primitive Money" (*American Anthropologist,* Vol. 67 [1965]), pp. 44–65.

Dalton, G. (Ed.): *Tribal and Peasant Economies: Readings in Economic Anthropology* (Garden City, N.Y.: Natural History Press, 1967).

Dart, R.: *Adventures with the Missing Link* (New York: Harper & Row, 1959).

———: "*Australopithecus africanus:* The Man-Ape of South Africa" (*Nature,* Vol. 115 [1925]), pp. 195–199.

Davenport, W.: "Non-Unilineal Descent and Descent Groups" (*American Anthropologist,* Vol. 61 [1959]), pp. 557–572.

———: "Sexual Patterns and Their Regulation in a Society of the Southwest Pacific," in F. A. Beach (Ed.), *Sex and Behavior* (New York: Wiley, 1965), pp. 164–174.

Davis, K., and W. Moore: "Some Principles of Stratification," in C. Heller (Ed.), *Structured Social Inequality: A Reader in Social Stratification* (New York: Macmillan, 1969).

de Lumley, H.: "A Paleolithic Camp at Nice" (*Scientific American,* Vol. 220 [1969]), pp. 42–50.

DeVore, I. (Ed.): *Primate Behavior: Field Studies of Monkeys and Apes* (New York: Holt, Rinehart and Winston, 1965).

Dobzhansky, T.: "Evolution—Organic and Superorganic" (*The Rockefeller Institute Review,* Vol. 1, No. 2 [1963]), pp. 1–2.

——: *Genetics and Evolutionary Process* (New York: Columbia University Press, 1971).

——: *Mankind Evolving: The Evolution of the Human Species* (New Haven: Yale University Press, 1962).

Dockstader, F. J.: *Indian Art in South America: Pre-Columbian and Contemporary Arts and Crafts* (Greenwich, Conn.: New York Graphic Society, 1967).

Dorson, R.: "The Eclipse of Solar Mythology," in A. Dundes (Ed.), *The Study of Folklore* (Englewood Cliffs, N.J.: Prentice-Hall, 1965).

Drucker, P.: *Cultures of the North Pacific Coast* (San Francisco: Chandler, 1965).

Du Bois, C.: *The People of Alor: A Social-Psychological Study of an East Indian Island* (Minneapolis: University of Minnesota Press, 1944).

Dundes, A. (Ed.): *The Study of Folklore* (Englewood Cliffs, N.J.: Prentice-Hall, 1965).

Dunn, L. C.: *Heredity and Evolution in Human Populations* (Cambridge, Mass.: Harvard University Press, 1959).

Durkheim, E.: "The Elementary Forms of the Religious Life," in W. A. Lessa and E. Z. Vogt (Eds.), *Reader in Comparative Religion,* 3rd ed. (New York: Harper & Row, 1971), pp. 28–36.

——: *The Rules of Sociological Method,* 8th ed. Trans. S. A. Solovay and J. H. Mueller, ed. G. E. E. Catlin (New York: Free Press, 1936).

Dyson-Hudson, N.: *Karimojong Politics* (Oxford: Clarendon Press, 1966).

Eimerl, S. and I. DeVore, *The Primates* (New York: Time-Life, 1965).

Eiseley, L. C.: *Darwin's Century: Evolution and the Men Who Discovered It* (Garden City, N.Y.: Doubleday, 1958).

——: *The Firmament of Time* (New York: Atheneum, 1965).

Eisenstadt, S. N.: "African Age Groups" (*Africa,* Vol. 5 [1954]), p. 102.

——: *From Generation to Generation: Age Groups and Social Structure* (Glencoe, Ill.: Free Press, 1956).

Ember, C. R.: "Warfare and Unilineal Descent" (Paper presented at the Annual Meeting of the American Anthropological Association, 1971, New York City).

Ember, M.: "The Emergence of Neolocal Residence" (*Transactions of the New York Academy of Sciences,* Vol. 30 [December 1967]), pp. 291–302.

——: "The Relationship between Economic and Political Development in Nonindustrialized Societies" (*Ethnology,* Vol. 2 [April 1963]).

——: "Warfare, Sex-Ratio, and Polygyny" (Paper presented at Annual Meeting of the American Anthropological Association, November 1972, Toronto, Canada).

Ember, M., and C. R. Ember: "The Conditions Favoring Matrilocal versus Patrilocal Residence" (*American Anthropologist,* Vol. 73 [June 1971]), pp. 571–594.

Evans-Pritchard, E. E.: "The Nuer of the Southern Sudan," in M. Fortes and E. E. Evans-Pritchard (Eds.), *African Political Systems* (New York: Oxford University Press, reprint of 1940 edition).

——: "Witchcraft Explains Unfortunate Events," in W. A. Lessa and E. Z. Vogt (Eds.), *Reader in Comparative Religion,* 3rd ed. (New York: Harper & Row, 1971), pp. 440–444.

Firth, R.: *Rank and Religion in Tikopia* (Boston: Beacon Press, 1970).

——: *Social Change in Tikopia* (New York: Macmillan, 1959).

Firth, R. (Ed.): *Themes in Economic Anthropology* (New York: Tavistock, 1967).

Fischer, J.: "Art Styles as Cultural Cognitive Maps" (*American Anthropologist,* Vol. 63 [1961]), p. 80.

Fischer, J. L.: "Social Influences on the Choice of a Linguistic Variant" (*Word,* Vol. 14 [1958]), pp. 47–56.

Flannery, K. V.: "The Ecology of Early Food Production in Mesopotamia" (*Science,* Vol. 147 [March 12, 1965]), pp. 1247–1255.

——: "Origins and Ecological Effects of Early Domestication in Iran and the Near East," in S. Struever (Ed.), *Prehistoric Agriculture* (Garden City, N.Y.: Natural History Press, 1971), pp. 50–79.

Ford, C. S.: *Smoke from Their Fires* (New Haven: Yale University Press, 1941).

Ford, C. S., and F. A. Beach, *Patterns of Sexual Behavior* (New York: Harper & Row, 1951).

Fortes, M., and E. E. Evans-Pritchard (Eds.): *African Political Systems* (New York, London: Oxford

University Press for the International African Institute, 1940).

Foster, G. M.: *Applied Anthropology* (Boston: Little, Brown, 1969).

———: *Traditional Cultures: And the Impact of Technological Change* (New York: Harper & Row, 1962).

Fox, R.: *Kinship and Marriage: An Anthropological Perspective* (Baltimore: Penguin, 1967).

Frake, C. O.: "The Eastern Subanun of Mindanao," in G. P. Murdock (Ed.), *Social Structure in Southeast Asia* (*Viking Fund Publications in Anthropology*, No. 29 [1960]).

Freilich, M. (Ed.): *Marginal Natives: Anthropologists at Work* (New York: Harper & Row, 1970).

Fried, M. H.: *The Evolution of Political Society: An Essay in Political Anthropology* (New York: Random House, 1967).

Fried, M. H., M. Harris, and R. Murphy (Eds.): *War: The Anthropology of Armed Conflict and Aggression* (Garden City, N.Y.: Natural History Press, 1968).

Friedl, E.: *Vasilika: A Village in Modern Greece* (New York: Holt, Rinehart and Winston, 1962).

Frisch, K., von: "Dialects in the Language of the Bees" (*Scientific American* [August 1962]), p. 3.

Garn, S. M.: *Human Races*, 3rd ed. (Springfield, Ill.: Charles C. Thomas, 1971).

Geertz, C.: *The Religion of Java* (Glencoe, Ill.: Free Press, 1960).

Genovese, E. D.: *The Political Economy of Slavery* (New York: Pantheon, 1965).

Gibbs, J. L., Jr.: "The Kpelle of Liberia," in *Peoples of Africa* (New York: Holt, Rinehart and Winston, 1965).

Giglioni, P. P.: *Language and Social Context* (London: Nicholls, 1972).

Gillin, J. P.: *For a Science of Social Man* (New York: Macmillan, 1954).

Gleason, H. A.: *Introduction to Descriptive Linguistics* (New York: Henry Holt, 1955).

Golde, P. (Ed.): *Women in the Field: Anthropological Experiences* (Chicago: Aldine, 1970).

Goldstein, M. C.: "Stratification, Polyandry, and Family Structure in Central Tibet" (*Southwestern Journal of Anthropology*, Vol. 27, No. 1 [Spring 1971]), pp. 64–74.

Goodall, J. van L.: *In the Shadow of Man* (Boston: Houghton Mifflin, 1971).

———: "My Life among the Chimpanzees" (*National Geographic* [August 1963]).

Goode, W. J.: *The Family* (Englewood Cliffs, N.J.: Prentice-Hall, 1964).

———: *World Revolution and Family Patterns* (New York: Free Press, 1970).

Goodenough, W. H.: *Explorations in Cultural Anthropology: Essays in Honor of George Peter Murdock* (New York: McGraw-Hill, 1964).

———: *Property, Kin and Community on Truk* (New Haven: Yale University Press, 1951).

Goodman, M.: "Immunochemistry of the Primates and Primate Evolution" (*Annals of the New York Academy of Sciences* [December 28, 1962]).

Goodrich, L. C.: *A Short History of the Chinese People* (New York: Harper & Row, 1959).

Gorer, G.: "Themes in Japanese Culture" (*Transactions of the New York Academy of Sciences*, Ser. 2, Vol. 5, No. 5 [1943]), pp. 106–124.

Gorer, G., and J. Rickman: *The People of Great Russia: A Psychological Study* (New York: Chanticleer, 1950).

Gough, E. K.: "The Nayars and the Definition of Marriage" (*Journal of the Royal Anthropological Institute*, Vol. 89 [1959]), pp. 23–34.

Gould, R. A.: "Chipping Stones in the Outback" (*Natural History* [February 1968]).

———: *Yiwara: Foragers of the Australian Desert* (New York: Scribner's, 1969).

Greenberg, J. H.: *Anthropological Linguistics: An Introduction* (New York: Random House, 1968).

Gubser, N. J.: *The Nunamiut Eskimos: Hunters of Caribou* (New Haven: Yale University Press, 1965).

Gulliver, P. H.: "The Arusha: Economic and Social Change," in P. Bohannan and G. Dalton (Eds.), *Markets in Africa* (Garden City, N.Y.: Doubleday, 1965).

Gumperz, J. J.: "Speech Variation and the Study of Indian Civilization" (*American Anthropologist*, Vol. 63 [1961]), pp. 976–988.

Gunders, S., and J. W. M. Whiting: "Mother-Infant Separation and Physical Growth" (*Ethnology*, Vol. 7, No. 2 [April 1968]), pp. 196–206.

Hahn, E.: "Chimpanzees and Language" (*New Yorker* [April 24, 1971]), p. 54.

Hall, E. T.: *The Silent Language* (Greenwich, Conn.: Fawcett, 1959).

Haller, M. H.: "Social Science and Genetics: A Historical Perspective," in David C. Glass (Ed.), *Genetics* (New York: The Rockefeller University Press and Russell Sage Foundation, 1968), pp. 215–225.

Harlan, J. R., and D. Zohary: "Distribution of Wheats and Barley" (*Science,* Vol. 153 [September 2, 1966]), pp. 1077–1079.

Harner, M. J.: "Population Pressure and the Social Evolution of Agriculturalists" (*Southwestern Journal of Anthropology,* Vol. 26 [1970]), pp. 67–86.

Harris, M.: "The Cultural Ecology of India's Sacred Cattle" (*Current Anthropology,* Vol. 7 [February 1966]), pp. 51–66.

———: *The Rise of Anthropological Theory* (New York: Thomas Y. Crowell, 1968).

Harrison, G. A., L. S. Weiner, L. M. Tanner, and W. A. Barnicot: *Human Biology: An Introduction to Human Evolution, Variation and Growth* (New York: Oxford University Press, 1964).

Heider, K.: *The Dugum Dani* (Chicago: Aldine, 1970).

Heller, C. (Ed.): *Structured Social Inequality: A Reader in Social Stratification* (New York: Macmillan, 1969).

Henry, W. E.: "The Thematic Apperception Technique in the Study of Culture-Personality Relations" (*Genetic Psychology Monograph,* No. 35 [1947]), p. 91.

Heyer, V.: "Relations between Men and Women in Chinese Stories," in M. Mead and R. Metraux (Eds.), *The Study of Culture at a Distance* (Chicago: University of Chicago Press, 1953), pp. 221–234.

Hiatt, L. R.: "Ownership and Use of Land among the Australian Aborigines," in R. B. Lee and I. DeVore (Eds.), *Man the Hunter* (Chicago: Aldine, 1968), pp. 99–102.

Hickey, G. C.: *Village in Vietnam* (New Haven: Yale University Press, 1964).

Hockett, C. F.: *A Course in Modern Linguistics* (New York: Macmillan, 1958).

Hockett, C. F., and R. Ascher: "The Human Revolution" (*Current Anthropology,* Vol. 5 [1963]), pp. 135–168.

Hoebel, E. A.: *The Cheyenne: Indians of the Great Plains* (New York: Holt, Rinehart and Winston, 1960).

———: *The Law of Primitive Man* (Cambridge, Mass.: Harvard University Press, 1954; 4th reprint, 1967).

Hoijer, H.: "Cultural Implications of Some Navaho Linguistic Categories" (*Language,* Vol. 27 [1951]), pp. 111–120.

Hoijer, H. (Ed.): *Language History from* Language *by Leonard Bloomfield* (New York: Holt, Rinehart and Winston, 1965).

Hole, F., and R. F. Heizer: *An Introduction to Prehistoric Archeology,* 2nd ed. (New York: Holt, Rinehart and Winston, 1969).

Hollis, A. C.: *The Nandi: Their Language and Folklore* (Oxford: Clarenden Press, 1909).

Honigmann, J. J.: *Personality in Culture* (New York: Harper & Row, 1967).

Howell, F. C.: *Early Man* (New York: Time-Life, 1970).

———: "Remains of Hominidae from Pliocene/Pleistocene Formation in the Lower Omo Basin, Ethiopia" (*Nature,* Vol. 223 [1970]), pp. 1234–1239.

Howell, F. C., and F. Bourlieve (Eds.): *African Ecology and Human Evolution* (Chicago: Aldine, 1963).

Hsu, F. L. K. (Ed.): *Psychological Anthropology* (Cambridge, Mass.: Schenkman, 1972).

Hunt, R. (Ed.): *Personalities and Cultures: Readings in Psychological Anthropology* (Garden City, N.Y.: Natural History Press, 1967).

Hunter, M.: *Reaction to Conquest: Effects of Contact with Europeans on the Pondo of South Africa,* 2nd ed. (London: Oxford University Press, 1961).

Huntingford, G. W. B.: *The Nandi of Kenya: Tribal Control in a Pastoral Society* (London: Routledge and Kegan Paul, 1953).

Hutton, J. H.: *Caste in India: Its Nature, Function and Origins,* 4th ed. (London: Oxford University Press, 1963).

Huxley, J.: *Evolution in Action* (New York: Mentor Books, 1957).

Huxley, T. H.: *Man's Place in Nature* (Ann Arbor: University of Michigan Press, 1959; reprint of original 1863 edition).

Hymes, D. (Ed.): *Language in Culture and Society: A*

Reader in Linguistics and Anthropology (New York: Harper & Row, 1964).

Itani, J.: "The Society of Japanese Monkeys" (*Japan Quarterly,* Vol. 8 [1961]), pp. 421–430.

Itkonen, T. I.: "The Lapps of Finland" (*Southwestern Journal of Anthropology,* Vol. 7 [Spring 1951]).

Ito, Y.: "Groups and Family Bonds in Animals in Relation to Their Habitat," in L. R. Aronson et al. (Eds.), *Development and Evolution of Behavior* (San Francisco: W. A. Freeman, 1970).

Jacobs, M., and J. Greenway (Eds.): *The Anthropologist Looks at Myth.* American Folklore Society Bibliographical and Special Series, Vol. 17 (Austin: University of Texas Press, 1966).

James, P. E.: *A Geography of Man* (Waltham, Mass.: Blaisdell, 1966).

Jay, P.: "The Common Langur of North India," in I. DeVore (Ed.), *Primate Behavior* (New York: Holt, Rinehart and Winston, 1965).

Jay, P. (Ed.): *Primates: Studies in Adaptation and Variability* (New York: Holt, Rinehart and Winston, 1968).

Jenness, D.: *The People of the Twilight* (Chicago: University of Chicago Press, 1959).

Jennings, L.: *Prehistory of North America* (New York: McGraw-Hill, 1968).

Jensen, A.: "How Much Can We Boost I.Q. and Scholastic Achievement?" (*Harvard Educational Review,* Vol. 29), pp. 1–123.

Jolly, C. J.: "The Seed Eaters: A New Model of Hominid Differentiation Based on a Baboon Analogy" (*Man,* Vol. 5, No. 1), pp. 5–24.

Kaplan, B. (Ed.): *Studying Personality Cross-Culturally* (Evanston, Ill.: Row, Peterson, 1961).

Kaplan, D.: "The Mexican Marketplace Then and Now," in June Helm (Ed.), *Essays in Economic Anthropology,* Proceedings of the 1965 Annual Spring Meeting of the American Ethnography Society, pp. 86–92.

Kardiner, A.: *The Individual and His Society* (New York: Golden Press, 1946).

Keller, H.: *The Story of My Life* (New York: Dell; reprint of original 1902 edition).

Klein, R. G.: *Man and Culture in the Late Pleistocene* (San Francisco: Chandler, 1969).

Klineberg, O.: *Negro Intelligence and Selective Migration* (New York: Columbia University Press, 1935).

Kluckhohn, C.: "As an Anthropologist Views It," in A. Deutsch (Ed.), *Sex Habits of American Men* (Englewood Cliffs, N.J.: Prentice-Hall, 1948), p. 101.

Kohn, M. L.: "Social Class and Parent-Child Relationships: An Interpretation" (*American Journal of Sociology,* Vol. 68 [1963]), pp. 471–480.

Kramer, S. N.: *The Sumerians: Their History, Culture and Character* (Chicago: University of Chicago Press, 1963).

Kroeber, A. L.: *The Nature of Culture* (Chicago: University of Chicago Press, 1952).

Kummer, H.: *Primate Societies, Group Techniques on Ecological Adaptation* (Chicago: Aldine-Atherton, 1971).

Kuper, H.: *A South African Kingdom: The Swazi* (New York: Holt, Rinehart and Winston, 1963).

———: "The Swazi of Swaziland," in James L. Gibbs, Jr. (Ed.), *Peoples of Africa* (New York: Holt, Rinehart and Winston, 1966).

La Barre, W.: "Some Observations of Character Structure in the Orient: The Japanese" (*Psychiatry,* Vol. 8 [1945]).

Lambert, W. W., L. M. Triandis, and M. Wolf: "Some Correlates of Beliefs in the Malevolence and Benevolence of Supernatural Beings: A Cross-Societal Study" (*Journal of Abnormal and Social Psychology,* Vol. 58 [1959]), pp. 162–169.

Landauer, T. K., and J. W. M. Whiting: "Infantile Stimulation and Adult Stature of Human Males" (*American Anthropologist,* Vol. 66 [1964]), p. 10,008.

Landes, R.: "The Abnormal among the Ojibwa" (*Journal of Abnormal and Social Psychology,* Vol. 33 [1938]), pp. 14–33.

Langer, S.: *Philosophy in a New Key* (New York: New American Library, Mentor Books, 1942).

Laughlin, W. S., and R. H. Osborne (Eds.): *Human Variation and Origins: An Introduction to Human Biology and Evolution* (San Francisco: W. A. Freeman, 1967).

Leach, C. R. (Ed.): *Aspects of Caste in South India, Ceylon, and Northwest Pakistan* (Cambridge: Cambridge University Press, 1960).

Leach, E.: *Claude Levi-Strauss* (New York: Viking Press, 1970).

Leach, E. R.: "Pulleyar and the Lord Buddha: An Aspect of Religious Syncretism in Ceylon," in W. A. Lessa and E. Z. Vogt (Eds.), *Reader in Comparative Religion,* 3rd ed. (New York: Harper & Row, 1971).

Leakey, L. S. B.: "Finding the World's Earliest Man" (*National Geographic* [September 1960]), p. 424.

Leakey, M. D.: "A Review of the Oldowan Culture from Olduvai Gorge, Tanzania" (*Nature* [April 30, 1966]), pp. 462–466.

Leakey, R. E. F.: "Hominid Remains and Early Artifacts from Northern Kenya" (*Nature,* Vol. 226 [April 1970]), pp. 223–230.

LeClair, E. E., Jr., and H. D. Schneider (Eds.): *Economic Anthropology: Readings in Theory and Analysis* (New York: Holt, Rinehart and Winston, 1968).

Lee, R. B.: "Population Growth and the Beginnings of Sedentary Life among the !Kung Bushmen," in B. Spooner (Ed.), *Population Growth: Anthropological Implications* (Cambridge, Mass.: MIT Press, 1972).

Lee, R. B.: "What Hunters Do for a Living or How to Make Out on Scarce Resources," in R. B. Lee and I. DeVore (Eds.), *Man the Hunter* (Chicago: Aldine, 1968).

Lee, R. B., and I. DeVore (Eds.): *Man the Hunter* (Chicago: Aldine, 1968).

Leeds, A., and A. P. Vayda (Eds.): *Man, Culture and Animals: The Role of Animals in Human Ecological Adjustments.* Publication No. 78 of the American Association for the Advancement of Science (Washington, D.C.: American Association for the Advancement of Science, 1965).

Lehmann, W. P.: *Historical Linguistics: An Introduction* (New York: Holt, Rinehart and Winston, 1962).

Leroi-Gourhan, A.: "The Evolution of Paleolithic Art" (*Scientific American* [February 1968]).

Lenski, G.: *Power and Privilege* (New York: McGraw-Hill 1966).

Lessa, W. A., and E. Z. Vogt (Eds.): *Reader in Comparative Religion: An Anthropological Approach,* 3rd ed. (New York: Harper & Row, 1971).

LeVine, R. A., and B. B. LeVine: "Nyansongo: A Gusii Community in Kenya," in B. B. Whiting (Ed.), *Six Cultures* (New York: Wiley, 1963).

LeVine, R. A., and W. H. Sangree: "The Diffusion of Age-Group Organizations in East Africa" (*Africa,* Vol. 32 [April 1962]), p. 38.

Lévi-Strauss, C.: *Structural Anthropology* (New York: Basic, 1963).

———: *Totemism* (Boston: Beacon Press, 1962).

Lewis, I. M.: *A Pastoral Democracy* (New York: Oxford University Press, 1961).

Lewis, O.: *Life in a Mexican Village: Tepoztlan Revisited* (Urbana: University of Illinois Press, 1951).

Lewis, O. (with the assistance of V. Barnouw): *Village Life in Northern India* (Urbana: University of Illinois Press, 1958).

Linton, R.: *The Cultural Background of Personality* (New York: D. Appleton, 1945).

———: *The Study of Man* (New York: D. Appleton, 1936).

Little, K.: "The Political Function of the Poro" (*Africa,* Vol. 35 [October 1965]), pp. 349–365; (Vol. 36 [January 1966]), pp. 62–71.

———: "The Role of Voluntary Associations in West African Urbanization" (*American Anthropologist,* Vol. 59 [1957]), pp. 582, 586–587, 593.

———: *West African Urbanization* (New York: Cambridge University Press, 1965).

Lindzey, G.: *Projective Techniques and Cross-Cultural Research* (New York: Appleton-Century-Crofts, 1961).

Lomax, A.: *Folk Song Style and Culture* (Washington, D.C.: American Association for the Advancement of Science Publication No. 88, 1968).

Loomis, W. F.: "Skin-Pigment Regulation of Vitamin-D Biosynthesis in Man" (*Science,* Vol. 157 [August 9, 1967]), pp. 501–506.

Lowie, R. H.: *The Crow Indians* (New York: Rinehart, 1956).

———: *Primitive Society* (New York: Boni and Liveright, 1920).

Lyons, J.: *Introduction to Theoretical Linguistics* (New York: Cambridge University Press, 1968).

Lynd, R. S., and H. M. Lynd: *Middletown* (New York: Harcourt, Brace, 1929).

———: *Middletown in Transition* (New York: Harcourt, Brace, 1937).

McClelland, D. C.: *The Achieving Society* (New York: Free Press, 1967).

McGregor, J. C.: *Southwest Archeology* (Urbana: University of Illinois Press, 1965).

MacNeish, R. S.: "The Origin of New World Civilization" (*Scientific American,* Vol. 211 [1964]).

Mair, L.: *Witchcraft* (New York: World University Library, 1969).

Malefijt, A. de W.: *Religion and Culture: An Introduction to Anthropology of Religion* (New York: Macmillan, 1968).

Malinowski, B.: "The Group and the Individual in Functional Analysis" (*American Journal of Sociology,* Vol. 44 [May 1939]), pp. 938–964.

———: "*Kula:* The Circulating Exchange of Valuables in the Archipelagoes of Eastern New Guinea" (*Man,* Vol. 2 [1920]), pp. 97–105.

———: "The Life of Culture," in G. E. Smith et al. (Eds.), *The Diffusion Controversy* (New York: Norton, 1927).

———: *Magic, Science and Religion and Other Essays* (Garden City, N.Y.: Doubleday, 1954).

———: *Sex and Repression in Savage Society* (Cleveland: World, 1968, first published in 1927).

———: *The Sexual Life of Savages in North-Western Melanesia* (New York: Halcyon House, 1932).

Mangin, W. P.: "The Role of Regional Associations in the Adaptation of Rural Migrants to Cities in Peru," in D. B. Heath and R. N. Adams (Eds.), *Contemporary Cultures and Societies in Latin America* (New York: Random House, 1965).

———: "Urbanization Case History in Peru," in *Peasants in Cities: Readings in the Anthropology of Urbanization* (Boston: Houghton Mifflin, 1970).

Manners, R. A., and D. Kaplan (Eds.): *Theory in Anthropology: A Sourcebook* (Chicago: Aldine, 1968).

Marshall, L.: "!Kung Bushmen Bands," in R. Cohen and J. Middleton (Eds.), *Comparative Political Systems* (Garden City, N.Y.: Natural History Press, 1967), p. 41.

———: "Sharing, Talking and Giving" (*Africa,* Vol. 31 [1961]), pp. 239–241.

Mayr, E.: *Animal Species and Evolution* (Cambridge, Mass.: Harvard University Press, 1963).

———: *Systematics and the Origin of Species: From the Viewpoint of a Zoologist* (New York: Dover, 1964).

Mead, M.: *Coming of Age in Samoa,* 3rd ed. (New York: William Morrow, 1961, originally published in 1928).

———: *Growing Up in New Guinea, a Comparative Study of Primitive Education* (New York: William Morrow, 1930).

———: *Sex and Temperament in Three Primitive Societies,* 3rd ed. (New York: William Morrow, 1963).

Medawar, P. B.: *The Future of Man: The BBC Reith Lectures* (New York: Basic, 1960).

Meggers, B.: "Environmental Limitations on the Development of Culture" (*American Anthropologist,* Vol. 56 [1959]), pp. 801–824.

Meggitt, M. J.: "Male-Female Relationships in the Highlands of Australian New Guinea" (*American Anthropologist* [Special Issue, 1964]).

Meillassoux, C.: *Urbanization of an African Community* (Seattle: University of Washington Press, 1968).

Mellaart, J.: *Earliest Civilization of the Near East* (New York: McGraw-Hill, 1966).

———: "A Neolithic City in Turkey" (*Scientific American,* Vol. 210 [1964]).

Merriam, A. P.: *The Anthropology of Music* (Evanston, Ill.: Northwestern University Press, 1964).

Middleton, J. (Ed.): *Magic, Witchcraft and Curing,* American Museum Sourcebooks in Anthropology (Garden City, N.Y.: Natural History Press, 1967).

Middleton, J. M.: "The Cult of the Dead; Ancestors and Ghosts," in W. A. Lessa and E. Z. Vogt (Eds.), *Reader in Comparative Religion,* 3rd ed. (New York: Harper & Row, 1971), pp. 488–492.

Middleton, R.: "Brother-Sister and Father-Daughter Marriage in Ancient Egypt" (*American Sociological Review,* Vol. 27, No. 5 [October 1962]), p. 606.

Miner, H.: "Body Rituals among the Nacirema" (*American Anthropologist,* Vol. 58 [1956]).

Minturn, L., and J. T. Hitchcock: *The Rājpūts of Khalapur, India* (New York: Wiley, 1966).

Minturn, L., and W. W. Lambert: *Mothers of Six*

Cultures: Antecedents of Child Rearing (New York: Wiley, 1964).

Montagu, M. F. A.: *Touching: The Human Significance of the Skin* (New York: Columbia University Press, 1971).

Montagu, M. F. A. (Ed.): *Culture: Man's Adaptive Dimension* (New York: Oxford University Press, 1968).

Moore, O. K.: "Divination—A New Perspective" (*American Anthropologist,* Vol. 59 [1965]), pp. 69–74.

Morgan, L. H.: *Ancient Society* (Cambridge, Mass.: Belknap Press, 1964).

Morris, L. N.: *Human Populations, Genetic Variation and Evolution* (San Francisco: Chandler, 1971).

Motulsky, A.: "Metabolic Polymorphisms and the Role of Infectious Diseases in Human Evolution," in L. N. Morris, *Human Populations, Genetic Variation and Evolution* (San Francisco: Chandler, 1971), p. 223.

Munro, T.: *Evolution of the Arts and Other Theories of Culture History* (Cleveland: Cleveland Museum of Art, 1963).

Murdock, G. P.: "The Common Denominator of Cultures," in *The Science of Man in the World Crisis* (New York: Columbia University Press, 1945).

———: "Comparative Data on the Division of Labor by Sex" (*Social Forces,* Vol. 15, No. 4 [1937]), pp. 551–553.

———: "Kinship and Social Behavior among the Haida" (*American Anthropologist,* Vol. 36 [1934]).

———: "The Science of Culture" (*American Anthropologist,* Vol. 34 [1932]), pp. 200–215.

———: *Social Structure* (New York: Macmillan, 1949).

Murphy, R. F., and J. H. Steward: "Tappers and Trappers: Parallel Process in Acculturation" (*Economic Development and Cultural Change,* Vol. 4 [July 1956]).

Musil, A.: *The Manners and Customs of Rwala Bedouins* (New York: The American Geographical Society, Oriental Exploration Studies, No. 6, 1928).

Nadel, S. F.: *A Black Byzantium: The Kingdom of Nupe in Nigeria* (London: Oxford University Press, 1942).

———: "Nupe State and Community" (*Africa,* Vol. 8 [1935]), pp. 257–303.

Nader, L. (Ed.): "The Ethnography of Law" (*American Anthropologist,* Special Publication, Vol. 67, No. 6, Pt. 2 [December 1965]).

Napier, J. R.: *The Roots of Mankind* (Washington, D.C.: Smithsonian Institute Press, 1970).

Naroll, R., and R. Cohen (Eds.): *A Handbook of Method in Cultural Anthropology* (Garden City, N.Y.: Natural History Press, 1970).

Nash, M.: *Primitive and Peasant Economic Systems* (San Francisco: Chandler, 1966).

Needham, R.: "Percussion and Transition," in W. A. Lessa and E. Z. Vogt (Eds.), *Reader in Comparative Religion,* 3rd ed. (New York: Harper & Row, 1971), pp. 391–398.

Nieboer, H. J.: *Slavery as an Industrial System* (The Hague: Martinus Nyhoff, 1900).

Niehoff, Arthur H.: *A Casebook of Social Change* (Chicago: Aldine, 1966).

Nimkoff, M. F. and R. Middleton: "Types of Family and Types of Economy" (*The American Journal of Sociology,* Vol. 66, No. 3 [November 1, 1960]), pp. 215–225.

Norbeck, E.: "Continuities in Japanese Social Stratification," in L. Plotnicov and A. Tuden (Eds.), *Essays in Comparative Social Stratification* (Pittsburgh: University of Pittsburgh Press, 1970).

Norbeck, E.: *Religion in Primitive Society* (New York: Harper & Row, 1961).

Oakley, K. P.: *Man the Tool-Maker* (Chicago: University of Chicago Press, 1967).

———: "On Man's Use of Fire, with Comments on Tool-Making and Hunting," in S. L. Washburn (Ed.), *Social Life of Early Man* (Chicago: Aldine, 1964).

Oliver, D.: *A Solomon Island Society* (Cambridge, Mass.: Harvard University Press, 1955).

Otten, C. M. (Ed.): *Anthropology and Art* (Garden City, N.Y.: Natural History Press, 1971).

Otterbein, K. F.: *The Evolution of War: A Cross-Cultural Study* (New Haven: HRAF Press, 1970).

Parker, S.: "The *Wiitiko* Psychosis in the Context of Ojibwa Personality and Culture" (*American Anthropologist,* Vol. 62 [1962]), p. 620.

Paul, B. D.: *Health, Culture and Community: Case Studies of Public Reactions to Health Programs* (New York: Russell Sage Foundation, 1969).

Pelto, P. J.: *Anthropological Research: The Structure of Inquiry* (New York: Harper & Row, 1970).

Pfeiffer, J. E.: *The Emergence of Man* (New York: Harper & Row, 1969).

Piggott, S.: *Ancient Europe from the Beginnings of Agriculture to Classical Antiquity: A Survey* (Chicago: Aldine, 1965).

———: *Prehistoric Europe* (Chicago: Aldine, 1965).

Pilbeam, D.: *The Ascent of Man* (New York: Macmillan, 1972).

Pospisil, L.: *The Kapauku Papuans* (New York: Holt, Rinehart and Winston, 1963).

Powell, P. V.: *Sweet Medicine,* Vol. 2 (Norman, Okla.: University of Oklahoma Press, 1969).

Prins, A. H. J.: *East African Age Class Systems* (Gronigen, Djakarta: J. B. Walters, 1953).

Pyle, T.: *The Origins and Development of the English Language* (New York: Harcourt Brace Jovanovich, 1964).

Radcliffe-Brown, A. R.: *The Andaman Islanders* (Cambridge: Cambridge University Press, 1933).

———: *Structure and Function in Primitive Society* (London: Cohen and West, 1952).

Radcliffe-Brown, A. R., and D. Forde (Eds): *African Systems of Kinship and Marriage* (New York: Oxford University Press, 1950).

Rappaport, R. A.: "Ritual Regulation of Environmental Relations among a New Guinea People" (*Ethnology,* Vol. 6 [1967]).

Renfew, C.: "Trade and Culture Process in European History" (*Current Anthropology,* Vol. 10 [April–June 1969]).

Roberts, D. F.: "Body Weight, Race and Climate" (*American Journal of Physical Anthropology,* n.s. 2 [1953]), pp. 533–558.

Roberts, J. M.: "Oaths, Autonomic Ordeals, and Power," in C. S. Ford (Ed.), *Cross-Cultural Approaches: Readings in Comparative Research* (New Haven: HRAF Press, 1967), p. 169.

Roberts, J. M., M. J. Arth, and R. R. Bush: "Games in Culture" (*American Anthropologist,* Vol. 61 [1959]), pp. 597–605.

Roberts, J. M., and B. Sutton-Smith: "Child Training and Game Involvement" (*Ethnology,* Vol. 1, No. 2 [April 1962]).

Robinson, J. T.: "The Australopithecines and Their Bearing on the Origin of Man and of Stone Tool-Making," in W. Howells (Ed.), *Ideas on Human Evolution: Selected Essays 1949–1961* (Cambridge, Mass.: Harvard University Press, 1962), pp. 279–294.

Ruskin, J.: "Of King's Treasuries," in J. D. Rosenberg (Ed.), *The Genius of John Ruskin: Selections from His Writings* (New York: George Braziller, 1963), pp. 296–316.

Sahlins, M. D.: *Moala: Culture and Nature on a Fijian Island* (Ann Arbor: University of Michigan Press, 1962).

———: "On the Sociology of Primitive Exchange," in M. Banton (Ed.), *The Relevance of Models for Social Anthropology* (New York: Praeger, 1965).

———: "The Segmentary Lineage: An Organization of Predatory Expansion" (*American Anthropologist,* Vol. 63 [1962]), p. 338.

———: *Social Stratification in Polynesia* (Seattle: University of Washington Press, 1958).

———: *Tribesmen* (Englewood Cliffs, N.J.: Prentice-Hall, 1968).

Sahlins, M. D., and E. R. Service: *Evolution and Culture* (Ann Arbor: University of Michigan Press, 1960).

Sanders, W. T., and J. Marino: *New World Prehistory: Archeology of the American Indian* (Englewood Cliffs, N.J.: Prentice-Hall, 1970).

Sanders, W. T., and B. J. Price: *Mesoamerica: The Evolution of a Civilization* (New York: Random House, 1968).

Sapir, E.: "Conceptual Categories in Primitive Languages" (*Science,* Vol. 74 [1931]), p. 578.

Schaller, G.: *The Mountain Gorilla* (Chicago: University of Chicago Press, 1963).

Schapera, I.: *Government and Politics in Tribal Societies* (London: C. A. Watts, 1956).

Schneider, D. M.: *American Kinship: A Cultural Account* (Englewood Cliffs, N.J.: Prentice-Hall, 1968).

———: "The Distinctive Feature of Matrilineal Descent Groups," in D. M. Schneider and K. Gough (Eds.), *Matrilineal Kinship* (Berkeley: University of California Press, 1961).

———: "Truk," in D. M. Schneider and K. Gough

(Eds.), *Matrilineal Kinship* (Berkeley: University of California Press, 1961), pp. 202–233.

Schneider, D. M., and K. Gough (Eds.): *Matrilineal Kinship* (Berkeley: University of California Press, 1961).

Schultz, A.: "Postembryonic Age Changes" (*Primatologia,* Vol. 1), pp. 887–964.

Schusky, E. L.: *Manual for Kinship Analysis* (New York: Holt, Rinehart and Winston, 1965).

Schwartz, R. D.: "Social Factors in the Development of Legal Control: A Case Study of Two Israeli Settlements" (*Yale Law Journal,* Vol. 63 [February 1954]), p. 475.

Seiber, R.: "Masks as Agents of Social Control," in Y. A. Cohen (Ed.), *Man in Adaptation to the Institutional Framework* (Chicago: Aldine, 1971).

Semenov, S. A.: *Prehistoric Technology,* trans. M. A. Thompson (Bath, Eng.: Adams and Dart, 1970).

Service, E. R.: *The Hunters* (Englewood Cliffs, N.J.: Prentice-Hall, Foundations of Modern Anthropology Series, 1966).

———: *Primitive Social Organization: An Evolutionary Perspective* (New York: Random House, Random House Studies in Anthropology, 1962).

———: *Profiles in Ethnology,* rev. ed. (New York: Harper & Row, 1963).

Sharon, S., and T. W. McKern: *Tracking Fossil Man* (New York: Praeger, 1970).

Simmons, L. W.: *Sun Chief* (New Haven: Yale University Press, 1942).

Simons, E. L.: "The Early Relatives of Man" (*Scientific American* [July 1964]), p. 60.

Simpson, G. G.: *The Meaning of Evolution: A Study of the History of Life and of Its Significance for Man* (New Haven: Yale University Press, 1967, originally published in 1949).

Smith, E. W., and A. M. Dale: *The Ila-speaking Peoples of Northern Rhodesia* (New Hyde Park, N.Y.: University Books, 1968, originally published in 1920 as *Ethnocentric British Colonial Attitudes*).

Smith, M. G.: "Pre-Industrial Stratification Systems," in N. J. Smelser and S. M. Lipset (Eds.), *Social Structure and Mobility in Economic Development* (Chicago: Aldine, 1966), p. 152.

Solecki, R. S.: "Shanidar Cave" (*Scientific American* [November 1957]), pp. 63–64.

Southwick, C. H.: *Genetic and Environmental Variables Influencing Animal Aggression: Selected Readings* (New York: Van Nostrand-Reinhold, 1970).

Spencer, B., and F. J. Gillen: *The Arunta: A Study of a Stone Age People,* Vol. 1 (London: Macmillan, 1927).

Spencer, R. F.: "Spouse-Exchange among the North Alaskan Eskimo," in P. Bohannan and J. Middleton (Eds.), *Marriage, Family, and Residence* (Garden City, N.Y.: Natural History Press, 1962), p. 187.

Spindler, G. D. (Ed.): *Being an Anthropologist: Fieldwork in Eleven Cultures* (New York: Holt, Rinehart and Winston, 1970).

Spiro, M. E. (with the assistance of A. G. Spiro): *Children of the Kibbutz* (Cambridge, Mass.: Harvard University Press, 1958).

Spiro, M. E., and R. G. D'Andrade, "A Cross-Cultural Study of Some Supernatural Beliefs" (*American Anthropologist,* Vol. 60 [1958]), pp. 456–466.

Stephens, W. N.: *The Family in Cross-Cultural Perspective* (New York: Holt, Rinehart and Winston, 1963).

Stevens, J.: *Sacred Legends of the Sandy Lake Cree* (Toronto, Montreal: McClelland and Stewart, 1971).

Steward, J. H.: *Theory of Culture Change* (Urbana: University of Illinois Press, 1955).

Steward, J. H., and L. C. Faron: *Native Peoples of South America* (New York: McGraw-Hill, 1959).

Struever, S. (Ed.): *Prehistoric Agriculture* (Garden City, N.Y.: Natural History Press, 1971).

Sturtevant, W. C.: "The Fields of Anthropology," in M. H. Fried (Ed.), *Readings in Anthropology* (New York: Thomas Y. Crowell, 1968).

Sussman, R.: "Child Transport, Family Size, and the Increase in Human Population Size during the Neolithic" (*Current Anthropology,* Vol. 13 [1972]).

Suttles, W.: "Coping with Abundance: Subsistence on the Northwest Coast," in R. B. Lee and I. DeVore (Eds.), *Man the Hunter* (Chicago: Aldine, 1968), pp. 64–67.

Swanson, G. E.: *The Birth of the Gods* (Ann Arbor: University of Michigan Press, 1969).

Swartz, M. J. (Ed.): *Local-Level Politics: Social and Cultural Perspectives* (Chicago: Aldine, 1968).

Swartz, M. J., V. W. Turner, and A. Tuden (Eds.): *Political Anthropology* (Chicago: Aldine, 1966).

Sweeney, J.: "African Negro Culture," in *Folktales and Sculpture* (New York: Bollingen Foundation, 1952).

Talmon, Y.: "Mate Selection in Collective Settlements" (*American Sociological Review,* Vol. 29 [August 1964]), pp. 491–508.

Textor, R. B. (Comp.): *A Cross-Cultural Summary* (New Haven: HRAF Press, 1967).

Thieme, P.: "A Comparative Method for Reconstruction in Linguistics," in D. Hymes (Ed.), *Language in Culture and Society* (New York: Harper & Row, 1964).

Thomas, E. M.: *The Harmless People* (New York: Alfred A. Knopf, 1959).

Thompson, E. B.: *Africa, Past and Present* (Boston: Houghton Mifflin, 1966).

Thurnwald, R. C.: "Pigs and Currency in Buin: Observations about Primitive Standards of Value and Economics" (*Oceania,* Vol. 5 [1934]), pp. 119–141.

Trevor-Roper, H. R.: "The European Witch-Craze of the Sixteenth and Seventeenth Centuries," in W. A. Lessa and E. Z. Vogt (Eds.), *Reader in Comparative Religion,* 3rd ed. (New York: Harper & Row, 1971), pp. 444–449.

Tuden, A., and Plotnicov, L. (Eds.): *Social Stratification in Africa* (New York: Free Press, 1970).

Turnbull, C.: *Forest People* (New York: Simon and Schuster, 1961).

Tylor, E. B.: "Animism," in W. A. Lessa and E. Z. Vogt (Eds.), *Reader in Comparative Religion,* 3rd ed. (New York: Harper & Row, 1971).

———: *Primitive Culture* (New York: Harper Torchbooks, 1958).

Ucko, P. J., and G. W. Dimbleby (Eds.): *The Domestication and Exploitation of Plants and Animals* (Chicago: Aldine, 1969).

Ucko, P. J., and A. Rosenfeld: *Paleolithic Cave Art* (New York: McGraw-Hill, 1967).

Vayda, A. P.: "Pomo Trade Feasts," in G. Dalton (Ed.), *Tribal and Peasant Economies* (Garden City, N.Y.: Doubleday, 1967), pp. 494–500.

Vayda, A. P., and Rappaport, R. A.: "Ecology: Cultural and Noncultural," in J. H. Clifton (Ed.), *Introduction to Cultural Anthropology* (Boston: Houghton Mifflin, 1968).

Verrier, E.: *The Religion of an Indian Tribe* (London: Oxford University Press, 1955).

Wagner, G.: "The Political Organization of the Bantu Kavirondo," in M. Fortes and E. E. Evans-Pritchard, (Eds.), *African Political Systems* (New York: Oxford University Press, 1940), pp. 197–236.

Wallace, A.: *Culture and Personality* (New York: Random House, 1961).

———: *The Death and Rebirth of the Seneca* (New York: Alfred A. Knopf, 1970).

———: "Mental Illness, Biology and Culture," in F. L. K. Hsu (Ed.), *Psychological Anthropology* (Cambridge, Mass.: Schenkman, 1972), pp. 363–402.

———: "A Possible Technique for Recognizing Psychological Characteristics of the Ancient Maya from an Analysis of Their Art" (*American Imago,* Vol. 7 [1950]).

———: *Religion: An Anthropological View* (New York: Random House, 1966).

———: "Revitalization Movements" (*American Anthropologist,* Vol. 58), pp. 264–281.

Wardhaugh, R.: *Introduction to Linguistics* (New York: McGraw-Hill, 1972).

Warner, L., and J. C. Abegglin: *Occupational Mobility in American Business* (Minneapolis: University of Minnesota Press, 1955).

Warner, W. L.: *A Black Civilization* (New York: Harper & Row, 1937).

Warner, W. L., and P. S. Lant: *The Social Life of a Modern Community* (New Haven: Yale University Press, 1941).

Washburn, S. L.: "The Analysis of Primate Evolution with Particular Reference to the Origin of Man," in W. Howells (Ed.), *Ideas on Human Evolution* (Cambridge, Mass.: Harvard University Press, 1962).

———: "Australopithecus: The Hunters or the Hunted?" (*American Anthropologist,* Vol. 59 [1957]), pp. 612–614.

——: "Tools and Human Behavior" (*Scientific American,* Vol. 203 [September 1960]), p. 69.

Washburn, S. L., and V. Avis: "Evolution of Human Behavior," in A. Roe and G. G. Simpson (Eds.), *Behavior and Evolution* (New Haven: Yale University Press, 1958), pp. 421–436.

Washburn, S. L., and D. A. Hamburg: "The Study of Primate Behavior," in I. DeVore (Ed.), *Primate Behavior: Field Studies of Monkeys and Apes* (New York: Holt, Rinehart and Winston, 1965).

Watanabe, H.: "Subsistence and Ecology of Northern Food Gatherers with Special Reference to the Ainu," in R. B. Lee and I. DeVore (Eds.), *Man the Hunter* (Chicago: Aldine, 1968), pp. 69–79.

Weber, M.: *The Theory of Social and Economic Organization,* trans. A. M. Henderson and T. Parsons (New York: Oxford University Press, 1947).

Whitaker, I.: *Social Relations in a Nomadic Lappish Community* (Oslo: Utgitt av Norsk Folksmuseum, 1955).

White, L. A.: *The Science of Culture: A Study of Man and Civilization* (Garden City, N.Y.: Doubleday, 1969).

Whiting, B. B.: *Paiute Sorcery* (New York: The Viking Fund Publications in Anthropology, No. 15, 1950).

Whiting, J. W. M.: *Becoming a Kwoma* (New Haven: Yale University Press, 1941).

——: "Cultural and Sociological Influences on Development," in *Growth and Development of the Child in His Setting* (Maryland: Maryland Child Growth and Development Institute, 1959).

——: "Effects of Climate on Certain Cultural Practices," in W. H. Goodenough (Ed.), *Explorations in Cultural Anthropology* (New York: McGraw-Hill, 1969).

Whiting, J. W. M., and I. L. Child: *Child Training and Personality: A Cross-Cultural Study* (New Haven: Yale University Press, 1953).

Whiting, J. W. M., R. Kluckhohn, and A. Anthony: "The Function of Male Initiation Ceremonies at Puberty," in E. Maccoby, T. M. Newcomb, and E. L. Hartley (Eds.), *Readings in Social Psychology* (New York: Holt, Rinehart and Winston, 1958).

Williams, T. R.: *Field Methods in the Study of Culture* (New York: Holt, Rinehart and Winston, 1967).

Wilson, M.: *Good Company: A Study of Nyakyusa Age-Villages* (Boston: Beacon Press, 1963).

Wingert, P. S.: Art of the South Pacific Islands (New York: Beechhurst Press, 1953).

——: *Primitive Art: Its Traditions and Styles* (New York: Oxford University Press, 1962).

Wittfogel, K.: *Oriental Despotism: A Comparative Study of Total Power* (New Haven: Yale University Press, 1957).

Wolf, A.: "Adopt a Daughter-in-Law, Marry a Sister: A Chinese Solution to the Problem of the Incest Taboo" (*American Anthropologist,* Vol. 70 [1970]), pp. 864–874.

Wolf, E. R.: *Anthropology* (Englewood Cliffs, N.J.: Prentice-Hall, 1964).

——: *Peasants* (Englewood Cliffs, N.J.: Prentice-Hall, 1966).

——: *Peasant Wars of the Twentieth Century* (New York: Harper & Row, 1969).

Woodburn, J.: "An Introduction to Hadza Ecology," in R. B. Lee and I. DeVore, (Eds.), *Man the Hunter* (Chicago: Aldine, 1968), pp. 49–55.

Woolley, C. L.: *Ur of the Chaldees* (New York: Norton, 1965).

Wright, G. A.: "Origins of Food Production in Southwestern Asia: A Survey of Ideas" (*Current Anthropology,* Vol. 12, Nos. 4–5 [October–December 1, 1971]), pp. 447–477.

Wright, G. O.: "Projection and Displacement: A Cross-Cultural Study of Folk-Tale Aggression" (*Journal of Abnormal Social Psychology,* Vol. 49 [1954]), pp. 523–528.

Young, F.: *Initiation Ceremonies: A Cross-Cultural Study of Status Dramatization* (New York: Bobbs-Merrill, 1965).

Zeuner, F. E.: *A History of Domesticated Animals* (New York: Harper & Row, 1963).

INDEX